The HUTCHINSON CHRONOLOGY OF WORLD HISTORY

COMPACT EDITION

Other titles of interest

Chronology of the Ancient World
Chronology of the Medieval World
Chronology of the Expanding World
Chronology of the Modern World

The HUTCHINSON CHRONOLOGY OF WORLD HISTORY

COMPACT EDITION

H E L Mellersh

R L Storey

Neville Williams

Philip Waller

Helicon

First published in hardcover 1995
First published in paperback 1996
Reissued and updated paperback edition published 1998

Helicon Publishing Limited
42 Hythe Bridge Street
Oxford OX1 2EP
e-mail: admin@helicon.co.uk
Web Site: http://www.helicon.co.uk

Typeset by Mendip Communications Ltd, Frome, Somerset

Printed in Great Britain by The Bath Press Ltd, Bath

ISBN 1–85986–250–0

British Library Cataloguing in Publication Data

A catalogue record for this book is available from the British Library

Contents

Introduction

Welcome to the *Chronology of World History – Compact Edition*, a new single-volume edition of the original four-volume work. The book has been carefully reworked and material selected to retain the breadth of the original work, in a shorter, more easily accessible edition.

Material within the *Chronology* is organized primarily by year. Within each year, the material is split into events followed by themes, such as Sport, Statistics, or Science, Technology, and Discovery. The entries in the events section are arranged by month and day, where known. For some events, particularly in the earlier years, it is impossible to assign a specific month to an event – these entries are placed at the start of each year.

Themed Headings

Politics, Government, Law, and Economy
Society, Education, and Religion
Science, Technology, and Discovery
Humanities and Scholarship
Art, Sculpture, Fine Arts, and Architecture
Music
Literature (includes Drama)
Everyday Life
Sport and Recreation
Media (includes Film, Radio, and Television)
Statistics

The *Chronology* is an invaluable work for students, researchers, or simply as part of the family library, providing the reader with instant access to the most important landmarks of history since the dawn of civilization. All too often, historical events are considered in isolation, divorced from the context which often gave rise to them and without which no understanding can be complete. The *Chronology*'s organization of material into events and themes allows the reader not just to find out when an event occurred but to fully appreciate the political, social, and cultural milieu of the period. Finally, a comprehensive index of all the entries allows the reader to access material by subject matter as well as by date.

The Earliest Human Societies

10,000–3000 BC

10,000 In northern Europe the Mesolithic or Middle Stone Age begins.

Science, Technology, and Discovery

(–7000 BC) The mesolithic (Middle Stone Age) way of life produces some important inventions: the barbed fish-hook and harpoon; the bow and arrow, with its 'microlith' flint tip; the flint socketed-axe; the woven basket; the cooking pot of baked clay; and the comb.

8000 In the Middle East – where the Mesolithic Age is barely established – the Neolithic Age begins.

Everyday Life

The Neolithic Age brings in a new way of life which depends on two fundamental inventions: the domestication of animals and the cultivation of crops. (The domestication of sheep may have occurred nearer 9000 than 8000 BC).

7500 The ice covering much of the earth has by now melted to roughly modern levels. This destroys many land bridges, for instance across the Mediterranean. The separation of the British Isles from the European mainland occurs about this time.

Everyday Life

The dog is domesticated.

7000 **Science, Technology, and Discovery**

(–5000 BC) Progress is rapid in the neolithic age compared with palaeolithic times. Cultivation of crops probably occurs first in temperate climes which are more conducive to the natural process. Pottery is improved; spinning and weaving are used for flax and wool; corn is ground by pestle and mortar and the art of cooking improved; fermentation is recognized, allowing the production of leavened bread, wine, and beer. New flint tools are also produced to fit the new way of life: the sickle, the hoe, and a better-made axe.

6800 **Society, Education, and Religion**

The earliest known township of Jericho possesses a protective wall, a sign that organized raiding and warfare has appeared.

5000 **Society, Education, and Religion**

The neolithic way of life strengthens religious feeling, particularly the belief in the magical connection between the cycle of seed-time and harvest and the cycle of human life. Human sacrifice is practised, particularly of the great, so that their death and rebirth in their successor may have beneficial influence. The Urban Revolution also increases the importance of religion; most towns are ruled by a priest-king.

Everyday Life

Towns and villages, previously isolated and exceptional, now proliferate. This 'Urban Revolution' brings a change of life style.

4500 The fourth of the great neolithic river-valley civilizations is formed on China's Hwang-ho or Yellow River, the other three being the Nile, the Tigris–Euphrates, and the Indus Valley. The oldest culture is known as Tang-shao, economically based on millet, the pig, the goat, and the dog.

4400 **Art, Sculpture, Fine Arts, and Architecture**

The Halafians make distinctive polychrome pottery, clay figurines, the first known seals, and amulets (in the form of the double axe which will later be the great Minoan symbol).

4200 The Sumerian civilization begins, though the Sumerian language may have come with later influxes. The first move is made to occupy the marshland of the twin rivers Tigris–Euphrates, probably from the Iranian plateau to the east. Townships begin to be formed, of which the first is traditionally Eridu.

Settlements begin to appear on the banks of the Nile. The earliest cultures, probably lasting for the rest of this millennium and perhaps beyond, are known as the Tasian and Badarian.

4100 The Chalcolithic age begins at the end of this millennium and continues for the first half of the next, affecting most of the 'Fertile Crescent', from the Nile valley through Palestine and Syria to the Tigris–Euphrates valley. Tools as well as ornaments are now made of copper and copper tools exist alongside stone ones.

4000 The Amer-Indians develop three distinct ways of life adapted to their environment. In the north there is a hunting and fishing culture, similar to the European mesolithic. In the eastern plains, there is a bison-hunting culture although as yet without the aid of the horse, similar to the European palaeolithic. To the west of the continent's mountain backbone the population is sparse and exists in harsher conditions; they develop their own 'neolithic revolution', learning to harvest the gourd and the potato and more importantly maize.

The neolithic way of life develops in Northern Europe, including Britain, in this millennium.

The 'Windmill Hill People', named after their best known site near Avebury in Wiltshire, appear in Britain.

3500 In Egypt, towns are developing in two distinct groups: the Upper, or Delta; and the Lower, along the most fertile strip of the Nile.

Science, Technology, and Discovery

The first wheels capable of being used for transport appear in Sumeria and with them the first war chariot.

Art, Sculpture, Fine Arts, and Architecture

A Thracian copper age produces gold harness decorations at Varna, the oldest gold artifacts in Europe.

3300 The Jemdet-Nasr period begins in Sumeria, a temporary domination of peoples from the Iranian hills. Cities in the south multiply and in Egypt there are signs of Sumerian influence.

3200 **Politics, Government, Law, and Economy**

The Bronze Age begins in the Middle East and lasts for about two millennia. It begins later in the rest of the world, mostly in the next thousand years but in some areas, e.g. Australia, not at all.

Science, Technology, and Discovery

(–3000 BC) The art of writing is invented in both Sumeria and Egypt, the Sumerian cuneiform developing slightly ahead of the Egyptian hieroglyphic. Neither method of writing reaches the alphabetical stage.

3100 In Egypt, King Menes (apparently called Namer in the hieroglyphics), advances from his southern capital of Thinis (Abydos) and overcomes the Lord of the Delta Land. He creates the so-called First Dynasty of the combined Old and New Kingdoms of Egypt.

The First Civilizations

3000–800 BC

3000 **Science, Technology, and Discovery**
Bronze is produced in Egypt – an alloy of copper and tin.
During their early dynasties both Egypt and Sumeria develop systems of numbering (decimal and sexuagesimal respectively), and also some practical geometry acquired in the measurement and parcelling out of land.

2900 The most likely date for the Deluge or Flood commemorated in Sumerian and Biblical legend. Archaeological evidence suggests more than one flood.
The Indus Valley civilization (known as the Harappan) is formed. Considerable Sumerian influence is apparent.

Art, Sculpture, Fine Arts, and Architecture
Work starts on building the Sumerian temple-tower or Ziggurat. It is continued by Chaldean Babylon: hence the Biblical Tower of Babel.

2800 **Society, Education, and Religion**
The first pre-megalithic Stonehenge: a neolithic monument comprising a circular earthwork 320 ft. in diameter with 56 small pits around the circumference (later known as the Aubrey holes).

2750 Likely date for the founding of the first city of Troy, the small but strongly walled fortress of a petty chieftain.

2700 The Sumerian city of Ur first comes to prominence, under King Meskalam-dug and the Queen Shub-ad.

2686 Egypt's 3rd Dynasty is formed, the start of Egypt's 'Old Kingdom'. Zoser, either its first or second pharaoh, builds the first, step-sided, pyramid, at Saqqara.

2675 **Politics, Government, Law, and Economy**
Trade and prospecting flourish and are considered heroic occupations. Egypt imports cedar wood from Lebanon, and so too apparently does Sumeria.

Literature
King Gilgamesh becomes a legendary hero and has an epic written about him.

2650 **Science, Technology, and Discovery**
Imhotep, the great artist-inventor of Egypt, flourishes (cf. Daedalus in Crete). He is credited with designing the pyramids, and with being a great physician.

2600 The bronze age begins in Crete – although some authorities set the date three centuries earlier – with the so-called Early Minoan period, also called its Pre-Palace period.

Society, Education, and Religion
The royal graves of Ur: Queen Shub-ad is buried with great wealth, but also no less than 74 human beings – drivers, musicians, ladies in waiting etc. – who take poison before they pass into the next world to serve their queen.

2575 **Art, Sculpture, Fine Arts, and Architecture**
Pharaoh Khufu (Cheops) builds the great pyramid at Giza.

2550 **Art, Sculpture, Fine Arts, and Architecture**
The Pharaoh Chephren sets up the Sphinx.

2520 The city of Ur rises again, under the king Mes-anni-pad-da.

2500 This is the time of China's legendary – and most benign and exemplary – kings, culminating in the Hsia Dynasty (2205 BC).

Science, Technology, and Discovery

The Mesopotamians develop a positional numbering (place-value) system in which the value of a digit depends upon its position in a number.

Art, Sculpture, Fine Arts, and Architecture

In Crete, the Minoan civilization, still in its Early Period (about 2600–2000 BC), is beginning to display great skill and exuberance in art, particularly pottery.

2400 A more considerable and prosperous city than previously ('Troy II') is founded at the site of Troy.

Politics, Government, Law, and Economy

Troy begins to take advantage of its strategic position to grow rich. The city commands a strip of coast where sea currents probably make it necessary to carry cargoes overland by porters for any ship trading with the Euxine or Black Sea.

Humanities and Scholarship

At the time of Egypt's 5th Dynasty, Ptah-hotep, governor of Memphis, writes his *Instructions* to his son – the first known book of philosophy.

2350 **Politics, Government, Law, and Economy**

The Harappan civilization exhibits skill in building, town-planning, and drainage. The city's great central store-houses, its lines of workmen's dwellings, and its communal bath house all indicate a paternal government and a regimented way of life. Its script has not been deciphered and no details of its history are known.

2331 Sargon, a man of humble origin, usurps the throne at Kish, sweeps south, and makes himself master of all Sumeria. He conquers Elamite Susa and may even have conquered Cyprus.

2296 **Science, Technology, and Discovery**

The Chinese record the sighting of a comet, the earliest mention of the phenomenon.

2270 Pepi II comes to the Egyptian throne as a child and is said to rule for over 90 years. During his reign, the Old Kingdom lapses into a period of near-anarchy and revolution (known as Egypt's First Intermediate Period).

2250 **Society, Education, and Religion**

The Egyptian scarab beetle, used as an amulet, begins to appear.

Art, Sculpture, Fine Arts, and Architecture

Naram-sin, Sargon's third son, boasts of his conquests and shows himself trampling upon his enemies in his *Stele of Victory*.

2205 Traditional date for the beginning of the civilization of China with the Hsia Dynasty, founded by Yü the Great, although another source gives the date as 1989 BC.

2190 The empire of Sargon is swept away by barbarians from the north, whom the Sumerians call the Guti or 'the Vipers from the Hills'.

2150 **Literature**

The Dream of Gudea and other religious poems are inscribed on clay cylinders found at Lagash.

2145 Silbury Hill, the great man-made hill near Avebury, Wiltshire, is built about this time.

2113 Sumeria revives for the last time under the Third and most famous of Ur's dynasties founded by Ur-nammu.

2060 Mentuhotep II of the 11th Dynasty achieves the reunion of Egypt, establishing the 'Middle Kingdom'.

2050 Troy II is destroyed and the inhabitants hide caches of valuables and jewellery (one of which is discovered by Heinrich Schliemann in 1871 and greeted erroneously as 'the Treasure of Priam').

2000 At the beginning of this Second Millennium BC, disturbances force Aryan-speaking Indo-Europeans southward into Asia Minor, N Greece, and N Italy.

At about the same time 'the Beaker People', named after their distinctive drinking vessel, the bell beaker, migrate from Spain. They reach areas in modern S Germany, Czechoslovakia, and England.

Sumeria is invaded from the north by the Amorites, led by the king of Mari, and from the east by the Elamites. The city of Ur is invested and its great Third Dynasty comes to an end.

Politics, Government, Law, and Economy

A feudal age is created in Egypt by the 12th Dynasty, the Pharaoh ruling with enhanced economic and religious sanction but through the local nobles, or *nomarchs*.

Society, Education, and Religion

The building of megalithic monuments, probably by the spread of an idea rather than of a people, begins along the coasts of northwest Europe.

Art, Sculpture, Fine Arts, and Architecture

Crete, in its Middle Minoan Period I and II, becomes famous for its ceramics, creating the delicate *Kamares* ware.

Palaces are first built on Crete, at Knossos, Phaestos, Mallia, and Zakro.

1991 Amenemhat I, first pharaoh of the great 12th Dynasty, comes to the throne and completes the reunification of Egypt begun by the 11th Dynasty.

1950 **Society, Education, and Religion**

The autobiography of Sinuhe shows that the Pharaoh is by now considered virtually a god.

Literature

The adventure story first appears in Egypt, for example, the nautical fantasy of *The Shipwrecked Sailor* and the more factual *Biography of Sinuhe.*

1900 From the ashes of the unimportant villages known to archaeologists as Troy III, IV, and V, Troy VI rises with its walls and palace.

1850 **Science, Technology, and Discovery**

In Egypt, Senusret III's engineers cut a channel 260 ft long and 34 ft wide through the cliffs of the Nile's First Cataract so that his war galleys may pass.

1842 Amenemhat III, the greatest monarch of the Middle Kingdom, comes to the throne and reigns for 45 years.

1820 **Science, Technology, and Discovery**

Amenemhat III's engineers create the artificial lake of Moeris in the Fayum (or improve upon an earlier effort), to help control the Nile flood.

1800 Abraham leaves the city of Ur.

Neolithic farming reaches the Orkneys in the shape of a settlement of well-built stone huts skilfully protected from the elements at Skara-Brae.

In NW Europe the typical barrow or tumulus becomes the round barrow rather than the neolithic or megalithic long or chambered barrow. The use of round barrows continues into the Iron Age.

1792 Hammurabi the Great creates the first Babylonian Empire and a golden age of peace, prosperity, and law and order. He extends his empire west to the Mediterranean, east to Elam, and north to the land of the as-yet unimportant Assyrians.

1790 **Politics, Government, Law, and Economy**

Hammurabi establishes a great bureaucracy to run his empire and personally attends to details such as correcting the calendar. His *Code of Laws*, although harsh, attempts to fit punishments to crimes: it protects the rights of women and recognizes an upper class, imposing harsher penalties for upper-class transgressors.

1750 **Science, Technology, and Discovery**

The Babylonians under Hammurabi extend Sumerian mathematical and astronomical knowledge. They compile tables of square and cube roots, are aware of the Pythagorean property of the right-angled triangle, and closely observe the risings of Venus for purposes of divination.

1715 Under Shamsi-Adad II Assyria begins to show military prowess, pressing westwards toward Syria. Nineveh is built.

1700 Egypt's Second Intermediate Period begins. The Hyksos ('The Shepherd Kings' or more correctly 'The Hill People'), Bedouin tribesmen, infiltrate into Egypt and gradually take over.

Society, Education, and Religion

An Aryan-speaking people of the Ukraine and N Turkey begins to spread westward at about this time. They are called 'the battle-axe people' from their choice of weapon. They finally reach

Scandinavia where, in a curious reversal of usual practice, the bronze axe of their original culture is imitated in more primitive stone copies.

Everyday Life

The horse has made a significant impact by this time. It is brought to Babylonia with the Kassites and to Egypt with the Hyksos. It is also enthusiastically taken up by the Mitanni and Hittites in Asia Minor and revolutionizes both transport and – with the chariot – war.

1680 King Labarnas unites the hardy people of the Anatolian plateau (whose proper name is unknown) to form the powerful empire of the Hittites.

1600 In the Aegean, Greek-speaking invaders have penetrated into the Peloponnese, where they begin to prosper and grow rich. They evolve the Mycenaean culture, named after its chief stronghold, Mycenae.

Politics, Government, Law, and Economy

The Minoans' favourable position on trade routes across the eastern Mediterranean, extends their influence throughout the Aegean. Their new palaces develop into political, economic, administrative, and religious centres, also containing storehouses and craftsmen's workshops. Their rulers go down in Greek legend as great law-makers.

The Mycenean 'shaft graves', discovered by Heinrich Schliemann in 1876 at Mycenae, contain great wealth and fine art and weaponry, indicating the Mycenaean princes are rapidly accumulating wealth.

Society, Education, and Religion

The Minoans change from a largely pictographic hieroglyphic script to 'Linear A'.

The 'snake goddess' and other artefacts found at Knossos and elsewhere in Crete indicate a Minoan worship of a 'Mother-Earth' goddess. The 'bull-leap' fresco at Knossos and similar works demonstrate a great Minoan preoccupation with the bull, perhaps symbolizing the power of the earthquake. There is also evidence of both human and animal sacrifice on Crete around this time.

Stonehenge probably reaches its final form about the end of this century.

Art, Sculpture, Fine Arts, and Architecture

The four great palaces of Crete are built or rebuilt in this century with an architectural and artistic skill and sophistication that causes surprise when they are later discovered. The palaces are at Knossos, Phaistos (with its 'summer residence' at nearby Hagia Triada), Mallia, and Zakro.

1590 Sekenre III, established in folklore as the liberator of Egypt from the Hyksos is killed in battle. The Hittite king Mursilis I is murdered and a period of anarchy sets in, with insurrections internally and loss of territory externally.

1575 **Society, Education, and Religion**

The Book of the Dead increasingly appears in the tombs of the great in Egypt from the time of the 18th Dynasty. It contains the spells and incantations necessary for passage to the other world.

1557 The last ruler of China's Hsia Dynasty, the tyrant Chieh, is deposed by the victorious T'ang, who founds the Shang Dynasty.

1550 **Science, Technology, and Discovery**

Egyptian medicine makes further advances. Papyri list clinical cases in great detail and the brain's central control function is realised for the first time.

1528 Tuthmosis I succeeds Amenophis I; the 18th Dynasty is now well established, and experiences a century and a half of greatness at its capital, Thebes.

1500 The Urnfield cultures flourish in this and the following century in England (Wessex), S Germany, and Denmark. The Urnfield people are pastoral rather than agricultural, use bronze extensively, and are ruled by a warrior class of aristocracy. They cremate chiefs and their families and place the remains in urns which are then interred in cemeteries – hence the name 'Urnfield'. The culture continues into the Iron Age.

In America, neolithic skills similar to those in Europe – weaving, basket-making, pottery-making, the building of houses, and the formation of villages – develop, as well as a priest class. However, the use of iron, of the wheel, of the plough, and of money do not develop in America until the coming of European colonialists.

The Mitanni, a people whose own records have not been discovered, dominate the scene in Asia Minor and Syria.

An explosion of the volcanic island of Thera (modern Santorin) covers the town of Thera with pumice.

Politics, Government, Law, and Economy

Hittite law codes from this period put less accent on 'fitting' and harsh punishment than Hammurabi. The only offences incurring capital penalties are rape, unnatural sexual intercourse, defiance of the authority of the State, and disobedience by a slave. Slaves are otherwise generally fairly well provided for.

Society, Education, and Religion

In India, the period of Vedic hymns and religious rituals begins.

1488 Queen Hashepsowe has probably established herself as Pharaoh by this time. She assumes the double crown of Egypt, dresses as a man, and even wears the Pharaoh's ritual wooden beard.

1469 **Politics, Government, Law, and Economy**

Tuthmosis III enlists the help of the Theban priesthood in asserting his power in Egypt; the priesthood's power grows, culminating in the usurpation of the Pharaoh by Hrihor. From this time onward, decisions of state are increasingly made by means of oracles directed by priests.

1468 Egyptian pharaoh Tuthmosis III advances north to defeat the petty Palestine princes under the Prince of Kadesh at Megiddo. This battle should not be confused with either of the Biblical battles of Megiddo (1125 BC, 609 BC).

1460 A new dynasty appears in the land of the Hittites under King Tudhaliyas II. The 'Hittite Empire' dates from his accession, but for the rest of this century Tudhaliyas and his two successors do little more than struggle against their surrounding enemies under the tutelage of the Mitanni.

1450 **Society, Education, and Religion**

(–1400 BC) At Knossos, the Linear B script supercedes Linear A. It is an early form of Greek.

Science, Technology, and Discovery

Glass begins to be used in Egypt for ornamental use but not for windows.

1405 Amenophis III becomes Pharaoh. Egypt, through trade, conquest, and the exploitation of Nubian gold, has become fabulously rich and the new Pharaoh does little campaigning but is content to rest on his gilded laurels.

1380 Both the Babylonian and the Mitanni kings are allied by royal marriage to Egypt.

Suppiluliumas, the Hittites' greatest king, comes to the throne. He begins by strengthening his capital city and prepares for his main task, which is to destroy the power of the Mitanni.

During Suppiluliumas' reign, the first Hittite reference to people of consequence called the Ahhiyawa, generally thought to have been the Homeric *Achaioi* or Achaeans, i.e., the Mycenaean Greeks, occurs.

1370 **Politics, Government, Law, and Economy**

(–1350 BC) The 'El-Amarna' correspondence takes place between the rulers of the Fertile Crescent civilizations – Egypt, Babylon, the Hittites, the Mitanni, Assyria, and Syria. It is written in Babylonian cuneiform, the diplomatic language of the age, on tablets found in 1887 at Tell el-Amarna. They are written in polite language as from one brother potentate to another, but show the naivety and crudity of the diplomatic exchanges of the great powers of the day. They also show that Egypt has, or is believed to have, accumulated great wealth.

1363 Amenophis IV changes his name to Akhneten, builds a new capital, Akheteten ('The Horizon of Aten'), for himself halfway between Thebes and Memphis, and institutes a religious and cultural revolution.

Politics, Government, Law, and Economy

Akhneten's religious revolution has its political aspect, a struggle against the established domination of the priesthood.

Society, Education, and Religion

Akhneten institutes his religious revolution by changing the worship of Amun-Re to that of the Aten, a monotheistic religion embodying no great moral teaching.

Music

Some time after changing his name, Akhneten composes his 'Hymn to the Sun'. This famous hymn, which Psalm 114 strikingly resembles, proclaims the beneficient power of the 'beginner of life'.

1350 The king of the Mitanni, Tushratta, having sought alliance with Egypt and been let down, is deposed and assassinated by a faction who have sought help from Assyria. Mitanni power is waning, while Assyria is rising.

1347 Another boy king, Tutankhaten, ascends the Egyptian throne. He changes his name to Tutankhamen and returns to Thebes – the 'religious revolution' is over and the new capital is left to crumble.

1340 Suppiluliumas defeats and ends the power of the Mitanni, capturing Carchemish and making Syria his dependency. However, the Assyrians absorb the Mitanni's lands.

1339 **Art, Sculpture, Fine Arts, and Architecture**

Tutankhamen's tomb contains great wealth including iron daggers; a chariot; a wooden chest, depicting the Pharaoh in battle behind his prancing chariot horses; the throne-panel showing Ankhesnamun endearingly touching her husband; and the scene on an ivory chest of the young Ankhesnamun and Tutankhamen picking flowers.

1309 Egypt's 'Keeper of the Horse' founds its 19th Dynasty, calling himself Rameses I.

1300 The great city of the Shang Dynasty – An Yang on the Huan river, north of the Hwang-ho – is founded about now, although the date could be up to 100 years earlier. The traditional founder is the tribal chief Pan-Keng.

Politics, Government, Law, and Economy

(–1250 BC) Mycenaean maritime trade is extensive, extending into Syria in the east and probably as far as the British Isles in the west.

Society, Education, and Religion

'Linear B' tablets found at Mycenaean Thebes and at Tiryns are thought to date from about this time, thus bridging the gap between those at Knossos and Pylos.

1291 **Art, Sculpture, Fine Arts, and Architecture**

The Hypostyle Hall at Karnak (started by Haremheb 1320 BC but now completed by Rameses II) shows the Pharaoh magnificent in his chariot behind prancing steeds and Seti I with a couple of prisoners under each arm as well as an avenue of ram-headed sphinxes.

1285 The inconclusive battle of Kadesh on the Orontes is fought between Egypt under Rameses the Great and the Hittites under Muwatallis.

1276 With the accession of Shalmaneser I, Assyria emerges into the first of its three periods of power. Shalmaneser strikes north and west, taking Carshemish but leaving Babylon to his successor.

1250 (–1240 BC) Most likely date for the war of the Mycenaeans against the Trojans (the war of Homer's *Iliad*). At this time there is another Hittite reference to the Ahhiyawa, their king being described as of equal rank to the Hittite king.

Egypt's struggles, from now into the ensuing century, against the 'Peoples of the Sea' show a general increase of turmoil and movement and unrest in the Mediterranean area. The Peoples of the Sea seem to have been essentially displaced persons seeking new homes.

Literature

The legend of Jason and the golden fleece may emanate from a Mycenaean sea-venture into the Black Sea of about the same time as their greater venture to Troy. The practice of catching river-gold in a sheep's fleece may indicate a real search for gold behind the legend.

1235 Most likely date for the 'Exodus' of the Israelites from Egypt: almost certainly in the reign of Rameses II, though possibly earlier.

Politics, Government, Law, and Economy

The Laws of Moses (including the Ten Commandments) show some similarity to Hammurabi's, for example, in their harsh insistence of appropriate punishments – 'an eye for an eye'.

Society, Education, and Religion

The Commandments of Moses are said, like Hammurabi's, to be god-given, but also show a deeper conception of deity. Although Jahweh is a tribal god, it is held that even the Egyptians will have to submit to his rule.

1200 Probable date for the first arrival of the Dorian Greeks, or at least a new group of Greek speakers, in the Peloponnese. Their arrival was followed during the remainder of the century by the destruction of the Mycenaean palaces.

This century sees the end of the Bronze Age in the Middle East and the Aegean and the beginning of a Dark Age, at least in the latter area. The turmoil caused by the People of the Sea may have been caused by renewed pressure, from the north, of Indo-European tribes; as the century progresses these tribes, in particular the Phrygians and Dorian Greeks, penetrate into Asia Minor and Greece.

Society, Education, and Religion

In China, *The Book of Changes*, or *I Ching*, a dissertation on divination, probably appears in this century.

Humanities and Scholarship

At Pylos in the Peloponnese (legendary home of the Homeric Nestor) the Linear B tablets expand from their traditional function of ration indents and so forth to record a series of military and naval dispositions – perhaps made in an effort to stay the invasion of the Dorian Greeks.

1195 Probable date of the death of Moses and the entrance of the Israelites into Palestine under their military leader Joshua. They cross the Jordan and capture Jericho.

1183 Traditional date for the end of the Trojan War (but 1250–40 BC is more likely).

1177 Egypt's 20th Dynasty's only pharaoh of note, Rameses III, beats off a renewed attack by the Libyans and spectacularly defeats the People of the Sea.

1174 **Politics, Government, Law, and Economy**

The twelve tribes of Israel, struggling to establish themselves in Palestine against both the Canaanites and later the Philistines, meet at the sanctuary of Shiloh to develop unity. They are ruled by their 'Judges', national heroes who also help to keep them on the straight course of their monotheistic religion.

1173 Kassite Babylon finally ends, after spending nearly a century intermittently at war with Assyria, although it is the Elamites who deliver the *coup de grace*.

1150 Probable date at which the Biblical Samson flourishes.

1125 The second great battle of Megiddo is fought, in which the Israelites, called to arms by their 'Judge', the prophetess Deborah, defeat the Canaanites under their general, Sisera.

1122 Traditional date (although possibly 75 years too early) for the end of China's Shang Dynasty and the beginning of her Chou Dynasty, said to have been founded by Kings Wén and Wu. This dynasty made China, for at least three centuries, stable and prosperous. For the first time China is knit, though loosely, into one feudal kingdom.

1115 Tiglath-Pileser I comes to the Assyrian throne and consolidates Assyrian power.

1100 The Dorians spread to Crete. The Minoans finally reach the end of their distinctive civilization after three centuries of Mycenaean domination during which they have still retained their identity. The dispossessed Mycenaeans flee, partly to Arcadia, but largely to Attica and Athens itself. They also begin the so-called Ionian migration into the Aegean coastline of Asia Minor.

Politics, Government, Law, and Economy

In the last third of the century there is a struggle among the Israelites, between those who want to continue as a theocracy and those who want to be like other nations with a king. The latter win.

1095 In the reign of Rameses XI, the priesthood, in the person of Hrihor, finally takes over the power of the pharaohs, creating a theocracy at Thebes. After his death Egypt falls apart into a new form of double kingdom. The 21st Dynasty begins with Smerdes ruling from Tanis in the north, while Hrihor and his descendants rule, more or less undisturbed, at Thebes in the south.

1075 **Society, Education, and Religion**

The Syrio-Palestinian Semitic peoples are developing a true alphabetical script.

Gideon persuades the Israelites away from the temptations of the worship of Baal, a less austere faith than that of Jahweh.

1050 The Israelites reach the nadir of their struggle with the Philistines as the Ark of the Covenant is captured.

1030 Samuel, last of the Judges, achieves a temporary victory over the Philistines.

1025 Saul is made King of Israel, and saves his country from the Amalekites (in the Negeb).

1020 **Science, Technology, and Discovery**

Goliath, the Philistine, has bronze armour (Biblical brass) but is armed with iron.

1003 David, having defeated the faction of Saul, becomes king of a united Israel and Judah; he defeats the Jebusites and from their city creates his new capital, Jerusalem, the city of David.

1000 Egypt suffers two centuries of confusion and rebellion during its 21st, 22nd, and 23rd Dynasties, with occasional upsurges of interference in the Near East, where its reputation, though lessened, is still considerable.

Primitive settlements exist on the site of Rome.

A bronze-age Celtic settlement is established at Halstatt (30 m SW of Salzburg): the presence of salt is the primary attraction.

(–970 BC) David comes to the combined throne of Israel and Judah, probably in 1003. His reign is undisturbed by any outside power but faces some internal dissent. The chief events of his reign (to which exact dates cannot be given) are: – David brings the Ark of the Covenant to his new city, Jerusalem. He becomes prosperous and subdues his enemies, including the Edomites, whom he all but exterminates. During the Ammonite war David has Uriah the Hittite 'put in the forefront of the battle' so that he can take his wife Bathsheba for his own. She bears David two children of whom the second is the future king Solomon. Internal troubles begin. Absalom murders his half-brother for the incestuous rape of his sister and flees the court. He is forgiven by David, but then revolts against him. David in turn has to flee Jerusalem. Absalom is defeated, slain, and ultimately lamented. Further revolts and wars bring David's reign to a close. The end of his reign is also marked by pestilence, seen as divine retribution for his effrontery in seeing how many fighting men he can muster.

Society, Education, and Religion

By this century the Phoenicians (among other Semitic peoples) have acquired their alphabet.

Art, Sculpture, Fine Arts, and Architecture

Pottery in Greece in this period is, as in Crete, of the angular-patterned, 'Geometric' style.

Literature

Both the 'Homeric' poems of Greece and the *Vedas* of India are being recited and verbally transmitted from one generation to another throughout this period.

970 **Politics, Government, Law, and Economy**

Solomon, having been blessed by God with an understanding heart, judges between two harlots, each of whom claims that of two babies (one of which has died and one which is still alive) she is the mother of the living child (I Kings 3).

Literature

King David leaves behind him a reputation as a great poet, 73 of the Psalms being credited to him.

959 Solomon's Temple at Jerusalem is completed and he proceeds to build palaces for himself and his wife.

931 **Literature**

King Solomon leaves behind a great literary reputation, centring on his 'wisdom'. The Biblical Proverbs, Ecclesiastes, the Song of Solomon, and Psalms 72 and 127 are all ascribed to him.

925 (–914 BC) Rehoboam, Solomon's son, is faced with discontent from his people as well as many external enemies. This dual pressure results in the split into a double kingdom: Israel (or the Ten Tribes) in the north under Jeroboam, with its capital at Samaria; and Judah (hence 'the Jews') in the south, with its capital at Jerusalem.

900 The Etruscans begin to infiltrate into N Italy in this century, probably coming from the East.

The Phrygians reach the height of their prosperity during this century, under their Midas dynasty of kings.

Society, Education, and Religion

The orgiastic religious system of the Phrygians leaves an impression on Greece and, later, Rome; their mother-goddess is Cybele and the male attendant-god Atys.

The Phoenician alphabet reaches India and the Greeks, who copy it and evolve their own.

Music

The music of the Phrygians is sufficiently famous to make an impact upon classical Greece. This is seen both in the great use of the flute in Greek music and in the legend of Midas judging a musical contest between Pan and Apollo.

889 Assur-nasir-pal II, one of Assyria's great conquerors, comes to the throne.

876 **Science, Technology, and Discovery**

In India, a symbol for zero is first used.

870 **Politics, Government, Law, and Economy**

(–840 BC) The political influence of Elijah and Elisha is considerable, including (as with Samuel) the power of king-making. Both denounce Ahab for his marriage to Jezebel, a follower of Baal, and Elisha backs Jehu as his successor. They have enormous moral as well as political power, making it clear to the kings of Israel and Judah that rectitude and obedience to the one God is more important than economic prosperity.

842 (–836 BC) Jehu, the prophet Elisha's chosen successor to Ahab, massacres the royal families of both Israel and Judah (including Jezebel), though King David's line survives in Judah in the person of Jehoash. Jehu reigns in Israel until 814 BC and pays tribute to Assyria.

841 The oppressive Chinese King, 'Li' is dethroned in favour of the Kung Ho or Public Harmony regency. Authentic chronology in Chinese history begins henceforth; a feudal age follows, until the arrival of the Han dynasty.

The Classical World

800 BC–499 AD

800 The Greeks begin colonization and foundation of new cities along the mid-Mediterranean and Aegean coasts. This movement is caused by increased prosperity and the pressure of expanding populations.

Society, Education, and Religion
In India, the metaphysical prose-works known as the *Upanishads* begin to be produced. The imported religion of the Indo-Europeans, which later becomes Hinduism, has become well established.

776 **Sport and Recreation**
Traditional date for the first recorded victor in the pan-Hellenic games, the Olympiad. The games, on which the modern Olympics are based, are held every four years and have political, economic, and social significance on top of the genuinely athletic and competitive element.

771 The original Chou Dynasty of China ends with the deposing of its king Yu and the shifting of the capital city.

765 **Society, Education, and Religion**
During the next 30 years Amos and Hosea flourish. They are the first to write down their prophecies and denounce the public immorality and social injustice of Judah.

763 **Science, Technology, and Discovery**
The Assyrian archives record an eclipse of the sun, the earliest mention of an eclipse.

754 **Politics, Government, Law, and Economy**
In Sparta, the *Ephoi* list, a board of five overseers or rulers, is established.

753 Traditional date for the founding of Rome by Romulus: this is the year from which the Romans date all subsequent events (e.g., 100 AUC; '*ab urbe condita*').

750 **Politics, Government, Law, and Economy**
In Greece the city-state, or *polis*, is on the rise; it is distinguished by common gods and common law administered from a fixed place. With the political change comes different military needs and the *hoplite* formation, heavily armed infantrymen in close order behind a wall of shields, is developed.

Literature
Homer, a Greek from Asia Minor, is born at about this time. His birthplace is most probably Smyrna or the island of Chios. Most scholars accept that he is the author of both the *Iliad* and the *Odyssey*.

745 Greek colonization continues: the colonies at Cumae in Italy, at Poseideion on the Orontes, and at Syracuse and Naxos in Sicily are traditionally said to be founded during the next decade and Sybaris in S Italy 720 BC.

733 (–722 BC) Israel and Syria, with some backing from Van and the Neo-Hittites, form a confederacy against Assyria, which King Ahaz of Judah refuses to join. Tiglath-Pileser III comes to the support of Ahaz and invades Syria and northern Israel. He extinguishes the Syrian monarchy, sets up a puppet king, Hosea, in Israel, and deports the leading citizens of Galilee.

Society, Education, and Religion
The prophets Micah and Isaiah announce their warnings and denunciations for action to avoid disaster. Both regard Assyria as the necessary instrument of God's displeasure if the people will not mend their ways.

730 **Music**
A Greek myth credits a Phrygian musician called Olympus with inventing the enharmonic scale of quarter tones.

728 Tiglath-Pileser III establishes full sovereignty over Babylon and declares himself its king.

722 Samaria falls after a three-year siege and 27,290 Israelites are deported wholesale into Mesopotamia. This marks the end of Israel as a nation and the start of the so-called Captivity of the Ten Tribes. Judah is left alone.

715 Traditional date for the accession of Rome's first king after Romulus and Remus, Numa Pompilius.
Society, Education, and Religion
Numa Pompilius, Rome's first king, is also traditionally the founder of their religious observances.

714 Sargon II of Assyria defeats the Vannic army and seizes its king's treasure.

709 The Neo-Hittite kingdom comes to an end following defeat by Assyria.

705 **Literature**
Hesiod, the Boeotian poet and farmer, writes his *Works and Days*, a compilation of practical and ethical advice, and his *Theogony*, giving an account of the origin of the world and the birth of the Greek gods. He and Homer are said to have 'given the Greeks their gods'.

700 The rulers of the old civilizations, Egypt, Babylon, and Assyria, spend much of this period warring amongst themselves and so fail to appreciate the threat presented by new powers of different races, such as the Cimmerians, Scythians, Phrygians, Medes, Lydians, and Ionian Greeks.
Sennacherib, continues his campaign in Palestine and besieges Jerusalem. Hezekiah, King of Judah, with Isaiah's moral support, defies the Assyrian general, who retires.

683 **Politics, Government, Law, and Economy**
In Athens, the office of *archon* (lit. 'ruler') is restricted to annual terms.

671 Assyria renews its attack on Egypt. The Pharaoh Taharka is defeated but escapes to Ethiopia. Esarhaddon appoints local rulers, including Necho of Sais, and then retires to deal with home affairs.

670 Gyges ('Gugu' in Assyrian) comes to the Lydian throne and begins to build up the country's power and wealth.
Society, Education, and Religion
Delphi's reputation as an oracle for seeking the inspiration and advice of the gods is already well-established.

668 Assur-bani-pal succeeds to the throne, the last great Assyrian king. He concludes a treaty with Tyre and the Phoenician coastal cities acknowledge Assyrian sovereignty.
Science, Technology, and Discovery
(–631 BC) The library accumulated by Assur-bani-pal at Nineveh shows the extent of Assyrian scientific achievement.
Literature
Assur-bani-pal collects ancient texts going back to Sumerian times in his library, including the story of Gilgamesh and Sumerian grammars.

663 In his final Egyptian campaign Assur-bani-pal claims to have penetrated to Thebes and to have carried away vast booty. However, the Egyptians also claim a victory. Both the Pharaoh and the Assyrians retire.

660 The first recorded Greek naval battle takes place between Corinth, at this time probably the most powerful city-state on the Greek mainland, and her colony Corcyra (Corfu).
The traditional date for Japan's first emperor, Jimmu. A Mongolian people begin to enter Japan, probably coming through Korea and oust the indigenous Ainus.

655 The aristocratic Bacchiadae, rulers of Corinth, are expelled.

652 The Cimmerians return to attack Lydia once more and capture its capital, Sardis, and kill King Gyges.

651 Assyria retreats from Egypt for the last time, in order to deal with trouble nearer home.

650 The Halstatt people learn to make use of iron and blossom forth as the great Iron Age Celtic culture of northern Europe.

Politics, Government, Law, and Economy

Stamped coinage (as opposed to a mere standard weight of metal) is introduced by Lydia during this period amongst the trading states and cities of the Asia Minor coast.

648 Babylon capitulates to Assyria and is once more devastated, but Assur-bani-pal orders that the city be rebuilt once more.

Literature

Archilochus of Paros, one of the earliest of the Greek lyric poets, is writing about this time.

632 In Athens, Cylon, after his victory in the Olympic games, seizes the Acropolis with the intention of making himself Tyrant. He is besieged and takes refuge at the altar of Athena, but is lured away and put to death.

630 **Politics, Government, Law, and Economy**

The revolt and second subjugation of the Messenians around this time may well have led to the unique system of government at Sparta. Particularly noted for its peculiar harsh laws and customs, it created a dedicated military aristocracy perennially suppressing a subjugated serf class of Messenians known as the *helots*. The Spartans themselves credit their laws and constitution to a semi-mythical figure, Lycurgus.

626 The Assyrians endeavour to oust their own administrator, Nabopolasser, from Babylon following his rebellion. They fail and he becomes acknowledged as king of Babylon, founding his Chaldean dynasty and the city's final but most splendid period of greatness.

Society, Education, and Religion

Jeremiah warns his countrymen of the disaster that is about to befall them in the shape of the Captivity in an invective full of phrases that have become part of the legacy of European literature. The Biblical Lamentations and Book of Jeremiah are attributed to him. This is also the time of the prophets Zephaniah, Nahum, and Habakkuk.

625 Periander becomes Tyrant of Corinth; he has a reputation as a philosopher.

Music

A poet and musician, Arion, is said to have converted the Dionysiac *dithyramb* into a trained chorus. The Greek system of *modes*, or eight-note scales, probably dates from this time.

Literature

Alcman, the Spartan lyric poet, writes his 'Parthenion', or choir-song for maidens, part of which survives.

623 (–616 BC) There is a prolonged and inconclusive war between Assyria and Babylon, with a small Egyptian force either helping Assyria or seeking to defend its country's own interests in Syria.

621 **Politics, Government, Law, and Economy**

Traditional date for Athens' Draconian Laws – said to be written in blood, not ink, because death was the punishment for nearly all crimes.

616 Traditional date for Tarquinius Priscus becoming king of Rome, marking the start of the reign of the Etruscan Tarquins, the last line of kings before Rome becomes a Republic.

612 The Medes persuade the Scythians to join with them and the Babylonians. They besiege Nineveh which falls after three months and the Assyrian king perishes in the burning capital. An Assyrian general, Assuruballit, assumes the kingship and takes up a new stand at Harran.

608 The Assyrians under Assuruballit fail to recapture Harran from the Babylonians and Medes and fade out of the records. The victorious Medes turn upon the Scythians, their temporary allies, who retire to their own lands.

Pharaoh Necho II, seeing the chance to fill the vacuum left by Assyria, and to reassert Egypt's traditional sway over Syria, sends his full army north. King Josiah of Judah, who still considers himself Assyria's vassal, meets the Egyptians single-handed at Megiddo and is slain. It is this battle of Megiddo that so penetrates the Jewish consciousness that it gave its name to the prophetic world-battle of Revelations: 'Har' (the Mountain of) 'Megiddo', Armageddon.

604 The people and towns of the old Assyrian empire acknowledge Nebuchadnezzar, the Chaldean king of Babylon, as their new master.

600 In Greece, the future great rivals Sparta and Athens settle into what are to become their defining characteristics: Sparta, the closed military power of the Peloponnese; Athens, the politically free (but no less aggressive) trading and maritime city-state.

In northern India, history begins to emerge with some certainty. Tribes are settling down into either monarchies (primarily in the Ganges plain) or republics (mainly based in the foothills of the Himalayas and the Punjab). The monarchy of Magadha, NW of modern Calcutta, is gradually coming to the fore.

Science, Technology, and Discovery

Chaldean (or Neo-Babylonian) science has progressed considerably. In medicine, though there is a large element of priestly incantation, surgeons not only perform operations but have some idea of the prognosis of a disease. Chaldean astronomers divide the sky into zones, and invent the signs of the Zodiac, as well as the names of many constellations, many of which are still in use today. Similarly, the seven-day week and 24-hour day are invented in this period. Chaldean mathematicians use a system which is based partly on decimals and partly on sexagesimal numbers.

The Greeks probably invent the trireme, their famous warship with three banks of oars, during this period.

Literature

The lyric poets Sappho and Alcaeus, from Mytilene on the island of Lesbos, are active during this period.

597 King Jehoiakim of Judah allies himself with Egypt but is replaced by Nebuchadnezzar with Jehoiachin. Nebuchadnezzar lays siege to Jerusalem in January and finally captures it in March. A puppet king, Zedekiah, is installed, while Jehoiachin and the leading men and artisans of the city are deported into Babylonia.

596 Sparta, by now the most powerful Greek city, arbitrates on the long dispute and war between Athens and Megara over the island of Salamis and finds for Athens.

595 **Politics, Government, Law, and Economy**

The Amphictyonic League of Anthela, near Thermopylae, intervenes in the Sacred War to protect pilgrims to the shrine of Apollo. The League is one of the earliest authenticated examples of cooperation among the Greek city states. Members agree not to destroy each other's cities or cut off their water supply.

Art, Sculpture, Fine Arts, and Architecture

During this period, Nebuchadnezzar rebuilds Babylon. He gives it its famous terraced or 'hanging' gardens, chariots can pass each other along the walls, and its towers are of bronze.

594 Solon is called upon to mediate between contending factions in Athens and is appointed archon with unlimited powers. He uses them with great effect, in effect providing Athens with a set of laws and a constitution. He then leaves Athens to travel abroad the following year.

Politics, Government, Law, and Economy

In Athens, Solon's laws end the practice of selling bad debtors into slavery and make a compulsory reduction in all debts. The reforms also include: opening the Assembly to the lowest classes – a first step to the democracy which later characterized Athens; the codification of the law; democratic reforms in the law courts; and a system of appointment to office by the drawing of lots amongst all citizens.

590 Tarquinius Priscus, who traditionally reigns from 616 to 578 BC, has his greatest successes in this decade. He does much to establish Rome as powerful and prosperous, quelling the Sabines and other Latin tribes.

Society, Education, and Religion

Zoroaster reforms rather than invents the Persian religion, converting a form of polytheism, not unlike the Indian Vedic system, to the worship of a single god, the 'Wise Lord' or Ahura Mazda.

Science, Technology, and Discovery

According to the Greek historian Herodotus, iron-welding is invented about this time and the king of Lydia (father of Croesus) presents a welded salver to Delphi.

589 Athens has no archon for two years – i.e. technically Athens is in 'anarchy', although the state continues to function.

586 The siege of Jerusalem is renewed, and the city falls – this time it is completely destroyed. This is the end of Judah as a nation, 136 years after the end of Israel.

585 **Science, Technology, and Discovery**

(28th May) Thales of Miletus, pioneer of Greek rational thinking, is said to have correctly predicted the eclipse of this year.

582 **Society, Education, and Religion**
The Delphic Oracle grows in importance and security now that it is being managed by the Amphictyonic League. The Pythian Games, held every four years, are inaugurated at Delphi.

580 Greek colonists found the city of Acragas (Agrigentum) in Sicily..
Little is known of the last twenty years of Nebuchadnezzar's reign. The Bible is alone in saying that he goes mad, but his own inscriptions refer to a four-year suspension of interest in public affairs.

578 Servius Tullius becomes king of Rome.

Politics, Government, Law, and Economy
Servius Tullius, who reigns for 43 years, organizes Rome as a soldier-state, dividing all citizens into 'classes' according to their material worth. Taxation is based on these classes as is a citizen's role in the Army. For example, the *equites* ('knights') are deemed sufficiently wealthy to equip themselves for service in the cavalry.

572 **Sport and Recreation**
Control of the Olympian festival passes to the Elians. The games and festival are assuming great importance in the Greek world.

570 Pharaoh Apries tries to help the Libyans to destroy the Greek city of Cyrene but fails and loses his throne. After a short civil war Amasis comes to the throne.
Athens finally succeeds in winning the island of Salamis from Megara. The young Pisistratus makes his name on the expedition.

Politics, Government, Law, and Economy
First Greek coinage is minted at Aegina by about this time.

Science, Technology, and Discovery
Anaximander is credited with having produced the first map.

Humanities and Scholarship
Anaximander continues Thales' speculation on ultimate reality, speaking of the four elements (earth, air, fire, and water) emanating from a single more fundamental source.

Literature
Aesop, a freed slave of Samos, gains a reputation as a teller of fables.

566 **Society, Education, and Religion**
The festival of the Panathenaea (as depicted on the Parthenon frieze) is established at Athens.

561 In Athens, Pisistratus earns himself a reputation. He wounds himself and then shows the wounds in the Agora, saying he has been attacked. The people are taken in and grant him a bodyguard for his protection, which he later uses as a personal force in his bid for power.

560 Pisistratus becomes Tyrant of Athens.
Croesus becomes king of Lydia and embarks upon a policy of expansion, extending his power along the whole coast of Asia Minor as far as the mouth of the River Halys.

Politics, Government, Law, and Economy
Croesus, King of Lydia, reigns for 14 years, and becomes a byword for great wealth as Lydia is well situated for trade between East and West. The Greek cities on the coast of Asia Minor also benefit from this trade and so, despite their precarious situation, find it worthwhile to pay tribute to Croesus.

556 Neriglissar's son is deposed after only three months on the throne of Babylon by the last of the Chaldean or Neo-Babylonian kings, Nabonidus, a Syrian.
Pisistratus, tyrant of Athens, is ousted and forced into exile.

553 Cyrus, king of Anshan, begins his three-year struggle against Astyages, King of the Medes.

550 Cyrus wins the Median throne and spends the next two years consolidating his position as king of the Medes and Persians combined.
Celts begin to arrive in the British Isles, mainly in Ireland, but also in Scotland and England to a small extent.

Politics, Government, Law, and Economy
Rome's second Etruscan king, Servius Tullius (by tradition 578–534) achieves his greatest political successes in this decade. He begins an alliance with his neighbours in the shape of a Latin League, while at home he is reputed to have given a modicum of power to the Assembly of the Plebs, set up in addition to the existing Senate of elders which advised the king.

Science, Technology, and Discovery

The Greek mathematician Pythagorus formulates his theorem relating the lengths of the sides of a right-angled triangle.

Humanities and Scholarship

Anaximenes, philosopher of Miletus, is active during this period.

Art, Sculpture, Fine Arts, and Architecture

The Halstatt skill in weapons and distinctive mode of decoration (reminiscent of the Scythian) spreads through NW Europe.

546 Croesus retires to his capital, Sardis, for the winter and sends for help from Egypt, Sparta, and Babylon. However, Cyrus follows up rapidly, and Sardis falls.

545 The Ionian Greek cities of Asia Minor are forced to accept Persian suzerainty, although they retain their freedom to trade so long as they pay tribute.

540 King Bimbisara rises to power in the Ganges kingdom of Magadha, controlling trade with the delta ports and building roads.

Pisistratus returns to Athens once more and remains Tyrant until his death in 527 BC.

Polycrates becomes tyrant of Samos, defying Persia, allying himself with Egypt, and building up a fleet of 100 ships.

Politics, Government, Law, and Economy

Pisistratus' tyranny in Athens is remarkable for his respect for law and constitutional procedure, and his encouragement of agriculture and trade.

Humanities and Scholarship

Xenophanes, a Greek Eleatic philosopher of Asia Minor, opposes anthropomorphism and polytheism – 'Men have made God in their own image.'

Art, Sculpture, Fine Arts, and Architecture

Polycrates of Samos has a temple to Hera built on his island. In Athens, Pisistratus builds a new temple to Dionysus at the foot of the Acropolis. He also begins the temple of Olympian Zeus (completed by Hadrian), and restores the temple of Athena *Polis* on the Acropolis.

Literature

Pisistratus has Homer's *Iliad* and *Odyssey* written down. He also helps to lay the foundation of Greek tragic drama by founding the new festival of 'the Great Dionysia'.

539 Rebellion has broken out in Babylon, and the city is in no state to withstand a siege.

Oct: **29th**, Cyrus triumphantly enters Babylon. The Persian Empire takes over from the short-lived Babylonian Empire and absorbs the kingdom of the Medes.

538 Cyrus occupies Jerusalem and allows all the Jews in Babylon who wish to do so to return to their native land.

534 Traditional date for the accession of the last of Rome's kings, Tarquinius Superbus ('the Proud' or 'Arrogant') who reigns for 24 years.

530 **Society, Education, and Religion**

Gautama, at the age of 30, cuts loose from his princely life and becomes an ascetic.

Science, Technology, and Discovery

Besides announcing his theorem about a right-angled triangle, Pythagoras of Samos develops a whole doctrine of numbers and preaches immortality and transmigration of souls.

Art, Sculpture, Fine Arts, and Architecture

The golden age of Athenian vase pottery begins in this period. It is distinguished by red figures, left in the natural colour of the clay, on black. Euphronius and Euthymides are two artists of the time known to us.

529 Cyrus' son Cambyses succeeds him. The Persian Empire has now been firmly established, and this is considered to be its foundation date.

527 Hippias and Hipparchus, sons of Pisistratus, continue his Tyranny in Athens.

525 Cambyses invades Egypt, wins the stubbornly fought battle of Pelusium, and besieges and invests Memphis. Egypt passes into the Persian Empire under Persian kings (the 27th Dynasty).

524 **Society, Education, and Religion**

Gautama abandons the life of strict asceticism when he sits under the famous Bo tree at Benares and has a vision of what he must teach. He becomes the Buddha and he and his disciples spend the next 40 years or so teaching by word of mouth.

521 After dynastic trouble, Darius I becomes King of Persia. There are revolts in Babylon and other parts of the Persian Empire.

520 Tarquinius Superbus makes Rome undisputed head of the Latin League.

Society, Education, and Religion

In Rome, Tarquinius Superbus initially refuses to buy the Sibylline Books of Oracles for 300 pieces of gold. After the Sibyl has burnt most of them he realises their worth and pays the money. They remain in Roman possession until AD 405 and supposedly play a vital role in state decisions.

Art, Sculpture, Fine Arts, and Architecture

The tomb of the princess of Vix (on the Seine) contains great riches, which include cups and wine-mixing bowls from Greece.

In Rome, Tarquinius Superbus begins building the famous Capitol with the spoils of war.

517 **Humanities and Scholarship**

The Chinese philosophers, Confucius and Lao Tzu, are believed to have met around this time. Lao Tzu writes *Tao Te Ching/The Book of the World Law and its Power.*

514 In Athens, there is a conspiracy against the tyrants led by Harmodius and Aristogeiton. It fails, although Hipparchus is killed, and the tyranny becomes even harsher.

512 To protect his empire from potential enemies beyond the Bosphorus, Darius invades Thrace with the help of conscripts from the Greek cities of Asia Minor. Thrace and Macedonia acknowledge Persian overlordship.

510 King Cleomenes of Sparta helps the Athenians oust the sons of Pisistratus and the period of 'tyranny' in Athens ends. In return, Athens is forced to join Sparta's Peloponnesian League.

Tarquinius Superbus is banished from Rome and with his expulsion the monarchy ends; Rome becomes a full-fledged republic during this decade. The experiences of this time make Romans determined never again to have a king. In exile, he allies himself with the Veii and then with Lars Porsena.

Society, Education, and Religion

In the Ganges area, Mahavira, aged about 30, takes up the ascetic life and founds the religious sect of the Jainites.

Everyday Life

Under Darius, the Persians develop a system of roads, the first empire-builders to pay proper attention to this necessity. In particular, they construct the great Royal Road running from Sardis in Asia Minor to Susa north of the Persian Gulf, a distance of over 1500 miles and considered a journey of three months for a man on foot.

509 **Politics, Government, Law, and Economy**

After the expulsion of King Tarquinius Superbus the Romans draw up a republican constitution. The system of twin consulate is established along with the twin office of quaestors as financial and legal officers.

507 Cleisthenes (a member of the noble Alcmaeonid family and grandson of Cleisthenes of Sicyon) rises to power in Athens as a champion of Solon's ideas. Cleomenes of Sparta attempts to interfere but is forced off.

Politics, Government, Law, and Economy

In Athens, Cleisthenes' legal and constitutional reforms firmly establish her particular form of democracy. The four ancient tribes are abolished and replaced by 10 new ones, and all citizens are enfranchized with a personal vote in the popular Assembly.

500 Darius the Great, King of Persia, is enraged by mainland Greek intervention in Asia Minor in this decade. He demands earth and water, the symbols of submission, from the Greek city states. Some, including Aegina, submit but Athens and Sparta disdainfully reject his demand – the Spartans push the Persian herald into a well. Darius will not tolerate this defiance of his supremacy and the Persian Wars begin.

In this century, the Amer-Indians in central America are starting their 'formative' period which lasts for some eight centuries and develops into the distinctive culture of the Mayas, particularly noted for its astronomical skills.

Science, Technology, and Discovery

Alcmaeon of Creton carries out the first formal studies of the structure and behaviour of animals.

Sushruta, a professor of medicine at Benares, writes a system of diagnosis and surgery in Sanskrit.

Humanities and Scholarship

Heraclitus of Ephesus centres his philosophy on the proposition 'Everything flows'.

Literature

In India the epic poem, the *Mahahharata*, and the popular collection of cosmic stories, the *Puranas* are first composed. Both gradually grow, over the best part of the next thousand years.

499 Aristagoras, governor of Miletus induces the Ionian cities of Asia Minor to revolt against Persia. The Spartans fail to respond to a request for help but Athens and Eretria (in Euboea) send troops.

498 **Literature**

The first Pindaric ode is composed.

497 **Society, Education, and Religion**

Confucius sets out on his travels as a wandering teacher, moving from court to court amongst the many rulers in a now divided China.

496 The exiled Roman king Tarquinius Superbus and his ally Lars Porsena are finally defeated at the battle of Lake Regillus, near Clusium.

494 The Ionian revolt against Persia ends with the Persian capture of Miletus and the defeat of the Greek fleet at the battle of Lade.

Politics, Government, Law, and Economy

At the end of a military campaign, the plebeian element in the Roman army retires to the Sacred Mount outside Rome – the so-called 'Secession of the Plebs' – and threatens to found a new city. The Senate grants concessions, including establishing the Tribunate, an office charged with the protection of plebeian interests.

493 In the Ganges kingdom of Magadha, King Bimbisara is murdered by his son Ajatashatru, who takes the throne, fortifies his capital city, and expands his kingdom by force of arms.

Politics, Government, Law, and Economy

Rome and the Latin League recognize commercial contracts binding throughout their cities. Rome abandons her claim to hegemony over the League.

492 The Persian general Mardonius subdues Thrace and Macedonia.

490 In late summer, the Greeks, under the skilful generalship of Miltiades (see 496 BC), defeat the Persians without Spartan help at the battle of Marathon.

Darius launches his expedition across the Aegean. The city of Eretria is destroyed and Athens is also in great danger.

Science, Technology, and Discovery

Hanno, the Carthaginian navigator, makes his famous voyage, as set out in *Periplus*, about this time. He sets out with 60 ships and 30,000 people intending to found colonies. The armada sails through the 'Pillars of Hercules' (the Straits of Gibraltar) and round the coast of Africa, probably reaching beyond Cape Verde and to within 12 degrees of the Equator, coming across 'troglodytes' and gorillas.

487 **Politics, Government, Law, and Economy**

In Athens, archons are to be appointed by lot from all citizens.

486 Encouraged by the news of Marathon, the Egyptians revolt against Persian rule.

Literature

Comedy becomes part of the City Dionysia (religious dramatic festival) at Athens.

484 **Literature**

Aeschylus wins the Athenian Tragedy prize for the first time.

483 Darius' son, Xerxes, having crushed the Egyptian revolt, prepares for his great expedition to crush the Greeks. Over the next few years he assembles an enormous force; Egypt alone contributes 481 ships.

Humanities and Scholarship

Confucius returns from his wanderings and devotes himself to the compilation of his *Dialogues*. He also writes appendices to the *Book of Changes*.

482 **Politics, Government, Law, and Economy**

In Athens, ostracism (i.e., expulsion by majority vote) is frequently used by political leaders against their rivals as a means of securing power. Themistocles establishes himself as the leading politician at Athens by securing the ostracism of his opponents, including Aristides 'the Just'.

481 In China central control becomes weaker still: the 'period of the Warring States' begins and lasts until 221 BC.

480 Celts of the Halstatt culture begin to arrive in Britain in substantial numbers. This is the main period of Celtic immigration, greatly augmenting and changing the balance of Britain's population and is known as Britain's 'Iron Age' culture.

Aug: —, A small force under the Spartan king Leonidas, primarily of Peloponnesians, holds the Persian land force at the pass of Thermopylae. They are wiped out but their bravery becomes almost legendary.

Sept: —, The Persians are checked but Athens is invested and burnt. The Athenians abandon the city for their fleet and win a naval battle in the Bay of Salamis under Themistocles and Aristides.

Society, Education, and Religion

In India, at the death of Gautama Buddha, there are many more monks and nuns wandering, preaching, and seeking alms. Their teaching supplements considerably the education provided by the brahmans.

479 Xerxes leaves the conduct of the war to his general, Mardonius, and the Persians are defeated at the battle of Plataea. At sea the Persians are defeated at the battle of Mycale, off the coast of Asia Minor.

478 The Confederacy of Delos, an alliance of Greek states around the Aegean, is formed to continue the fight against the Persians.

Politics, Government, Law, and Economy

Athens is refortified as well as rebuilt after the Persian destruction, in spite of Spartan opposition.

477 Pausanias captures Byzantium. He begins to foster autocratic ambitions and appears to want to become tyrant of all Greece, with Persian help.

476 Cimon ousts Pausanias and the Spartans from the area of the Bosphorus. The Spartans, hearing that Pausanias is intriguing with the Persians, recall him.

475 **Science, Technology, and Discovery**

The Greek philosopher Parmenides says the world is a sphere.

Humanities and Scholarship

The Greek philosopher Parmenides (of Elea in Italy) stresses the idea of immutability in opposition to the philosophy of Heraclitus.

474 **Humanities and Scholarship**

The *Histories* of Herodotus end their narration with this year.

Literature

The Greek poets Pindar and Bacchylides both visit the rich court of Hieron, tyrant of Syracuse, around this time and sing his praises for his victories in the Olympic Games, although Pindar also celebrates many other Olympic winners.

472 **Literature**

The earliest extant play of Aeschylus, the *Persae*, dealing with the Persians at the battle of Salamis, wins the Athenian Tragedy prize.

471 Themistocles is ostracized by the often fickle Athenians who suspect him of corruption.

470 **Humanities and Scholarship**

The disciples of Confucius collect and write down his teachings.

469 The island of Naxos tries to secede from the Delian Confederacy but is blockaded by the Athenian-dominated fleet, a high-handed action resented by the rest of Greece and widely seen as an early attempt by the Athenians to treat the confederacy as their own personal empire.

468 **Literature**

In Athens, Sophocles (aged 27) defeats Aeschylus in the prize for Tragedy at the Dionysia.

467 (–466 BC) Cimon carries the war against Persia into Asia Minor and wins the battle of the river Eurymedon – the decisive defeat of Persia, though it continues to be an enemy of the Greeks.

Literature

Aeschylus' *Seven Against Thebes* written.

465 (–463 BC) Athens attacks and defeats the island of Thasos in a naval battle after trade disputes over gold mining rights in the area – an obviously imperialist move.

(–462 BC) Sparta is unable to help the Thasians fight off the Athenians, despite her increasing concern at Athens' rise as an imperial power, as she is suffering at home from a severe earthquake and the ensuing revolt of the helots (serfs) in Messenia.

463 **Politics, Government, Law, and Economy**

(–461 BC) Ephialtes, with the support of Pericles, introduces a package of radical democratic reforms. They reduce the powers of Athens' Council of the Areopagus, which is composed of former archons *ex officio* and hence seen as a stronghold of aristocratic oligarchs. The powers lost by the Areopagites are transferred to 'democratic', popular institutions – the Council of Five Hundred, the Assembly, and the popular law courts. The office of Judge becomes paid (so that it is no longer the exclusive preserve of the wealthy) and is recruited by lot from a list open to any citizen.

462 Cimon sends troops to Sparta to help them suppress the helots revolt but suffers a severe setback when Spartan mistrust leads them to tell him that his help is not wanted and the following year he is ostracized.

461 In Athens, Ephialtes and Pericles push through a series of radical reforms (see 463 BC) and Ephialtes is assassinated.

460 Athens' foreign policy, now under the control of the nationalistic Pericles, becomes very aggressive and imperialist. Athens moves closer to Argos rather than Sparta.

459 Athens launches an expedition to help Inaros revolt against the Persians in Egypt.

458 The Romans escape disaster at the hands of the Volscians by calling Cincinnatus from his farm to command their army and take on the office of Dictator.

After a great effort Athens is victorious over her Peloponnesian enemies and Aegina is forced to join the Delian Confederacy. A Spartan force, going to the help of Boeotia in a local dispute, is nearly cut off by the Athenians on its return, and Boeotia becomes a member of the Confederacy.

Society, Education, and Religion

Ezra is sent by Artaxerxes to Jerusalem to enforce the Jews' own laws (it is possible this may have happened sixty years later).

Literature

Aeschylus' trilogy, the *Oresteia*, is performed.

457 **Politics, Government, Law, and Economy**

On the Spartans' return from their Boeotian expedition they are drawn into fighting with the Athenians and at the ensuing battle of Tanagra, Cimon's friends fight so well that he is allowed to return from exile.

456 (–454 BC) The Athenian-led expedition to Egypt ends in disaster with the fleet defeated with heavy losses and the army retreating in disarray.

455 **Literature**

Euripides' first play, *The Daughters of Pelias*, appears.

452 (–451 BC) The warring Greek city-states are temporarily exhausted, and a 5 year truce is arranged between Athens and the Peloponnese.

451 **Politics, Government, Law, and Economy**

The Roman plebeian class, suffering from economic and financial ills, force the patricians into reform. A Board of ten, the *Decemviri*, is established to reform and codify the laws, followed by a second board of which half the members are plebeian. They produce the twelve Tables of the Law but refuse to disband themselves and threaten to take dictatorial powers. The attempt collapses after the plebeians in the army strike, but the twelve tables are adopted 449 BC.

450 At La Tène the lake of Neuchatel becomes a site for Celtic votive offerings. These mark definite progress in Celtic art and have given their name to the iron-age culture of northwestern Europe of this time.

Society, Education, and Religion

The growth of democracy in many of the Greek city-states during this period, especially in Athens, has created a demand for education, particularly in the art of rhetoric.

449 The Greek city-states finally make peace with Persia, the so-called Peace of Callias; there is peace between Greeks and Persians for most of the next century.

Politics, Government, Law, and Economy

Pericles' building programme is as much aimed at relieving unemployment as glorifying Athens. It includes the refortification of Athens' port, the Piraeus, and the long walls which connect it to Athens.

Statistics
The total population of Attica has reached as many as a quarter of a million, very large for a *polis*, but nearly half of these may have been slaves.

448 **Art, Sculpture, Fine Arts, and Architecture**
Under supervision of Phidias, a friend of Pericles, work starts on the great temple of Athena, the Parthenon; it is completed 10 years later.

Literature
Cratinus, one of the famous writers of Athenian comedies, wages literary war against Pericles.

446 Pericles rounds off a difficult period in foreign affairs by negotiating a somewhat humiliating peace treaty with Sparta and her Peloponnesian allies, extending the 5 years truce for another 30 years. Achaea regains her independence. Euboea revolts from Athens.

445 Nehemiah, the Jewish cup-bearer to Artaxerxes at Susa, returns to Jerusalem as governor. He inspires the people of Jerusalem with great enthusiasm and the city's walls are rebuilt in spite of active gentile opposition.

Society, Education, and Religion
In Rome the *Lex Canuleia* removes the ban on inter-marriage between the orders, i.e. plebeian with patrician.

Science, Technology, and Discovery
Greek philosopher and scientist Empedocles distinguishes the 'four elements' – earth, fire, water, and air – which he claims all substances are made of and explains the development of the universe by the forces of attraction and repulsion.

443 **Politics, Government, Law, and Economy**
The Roman consul's task is lightened by the creation of two Censors; one of their jobs is to oversee the morals of senators.

442 Thucydides (not the historian) continues his opposition to Pericles' abuse of the Delian funds to rebuild Athens and is ostracized by the people with whom Pericles' policy is very popular, both for glorifying Athens and providing employment. Pericles is now unopposed and governs Athens for a further 15 years.

441 **Literature**
Sophocles' *Antigone* is written.

439 **Politics, Government, Law, and Economy**
The distribution of cheap corn is tried for the first time to alleviate famine in Rome.

438 **Literature**
Euripides' *Alcestis*.

437 **Art, Sculpture, Fine Arts, and Architecture**
Phidias' chryselaphantine statue of Athena which stands some 36 ft high is set up and the Parthenon is dedicated.

435 Corinth attacks her recalcitrant colony Corcyra in a dispute concerning the latter's colony Epidamnus. This is one of the first incidents in the build-up to the Peloponnesian War.

433 Athenian ships are deployed at the battle of Sybota, enraging the Corinthians. The quarrel spreads to Potidaea, a member of the Athenian Empire but originally a Corinthian colony, which now revolts in sympathy.

432 The Athenians invest the city of Potidaea; Corinth appeals to Sparta. At an inter-city assembly at Sparta Athens is accused of breaking the Thirty Year Peace treaty.

Society, Education, and Religion
Thucydides, the historian, in describing the Assemblies held to decide on the Athenian-Corinthian dispute, draws a series of contrasts between the Athenian and Spartan (i.e., Ionian and Dorian) characters.

431 The Peloponnesian war is precipitated by an incident at Plataea, the only pro-Athenian city in Boeotia. A Theban raid on the city is a failure and the Plataeans take 180 prisoners and put them to death. Athens supports Plataea and Sparta aligns herself on the other side. Sparta enlists the help of the Greek cities of Italy and Sicily, and both sides appeal unsuccessfully to Persia.

May: —, The Spartans invade Attica. The Athenian army is outclassed by the Spartans and Athens' power lies in her navy so Pericles withdraws the population of the country districts within the city of Athens while pursuing an active naval war.

Art, Sculpture, Fine Arts, and Architecture

Phidias moves to Olympia and carves his statue of Zeus.

Literature

Euripides' *Medea.*

430 The Peloponnesian war, essentially a struggle between a land power and a sea power, is initially dominated by the sea power, Athens, but after 424 BC, largely thanks to their more daring general Brasidas, Sparta begins to gain the upper hand.

The Spartans make the second of their five invasions of Attica. The Athenians have some successes in sea raids on their enemies and Potidaea is taken. In Athens itself, full to bursting point with refugees, plague breaks out..

Humanities and Scholarship

In Athens, Socrates – having given up his trade as a sculptor, and between his bouts of military service – begins to establish himself as a teacher and general instigator of thought.

Herodotus, who has been living at Thurii, publishes the last part of his *History.*

429 Pericles dies. Cleon, the tanner, a more radical opponent and popular demagogue, takes over his premier position in Athenian politics.

Literature

Sophocles' *Oedipus Rex.*

428 **Literature**

Euripides' *Hippolytus.*

427 Plataea surrenders to Sparta, and Mytilene to Athens. The Athenians are more merciful in victory than the Spartans.

Politics, Government, Law, and Economy

In Rome the quaestorship is opened to the plebs.

Literature

Euripides, in his *Andromache*, attacks Spartan cruelty and duplicity.

425 Demosthenes lands at Pylos with an Athenian fleet and fortifies it and the neighbouring island of Sphacteria. Sparta breaks off the invasion of Attica to send troops to Pylos. Cleon takes command and wins a victory for Athens. Sparta makes peace overtures which Cleon persuades Athens to reject.

424 The Athenians spread the war into Boeotia, but are defeated at the battle of Delium. They suffer worse defeats in Thrace at the hands of the Spartan general Brasidas who captures the city of Amphipolis.

Humanities and Scholarship

Following his banishment, Thucydides travels widely and begins to write his *History of the Peloponnesian War.*

Literature

Aristophanes' *The Knights.*

423 A year's truce in the Peloponnesian war is agreed.

Literature

Aristophanes' *The Clouds.*

422 Cleon ends the truce in the Peloponnesian War and resolves on the rescue of Amphipolis. In a battle outside the city both Cleon and Brasidas are killed, but the victory goes to the Spartans.

Literature

Aristophanes' *The Wasps.*

421 Nicias, leader of the aristocratic pro-peace faction in Athens, arranges a peace treaty with Sparta and her Peloponnesian allies. Some of the allies, most notably the Corinthians, consider the terms unjust and break with Sparta, making an alliance with Argos.

420 Athens enters into alliance with Argos, and the young and popular Alcibiades is elected *Strategos* (one of a board of ten generals).

Rome continues to increase its dominance in Italy during this period, defeating the Aequii and clearing the coastal plain of the Volscians.

In India a new dynasty, the Shishunaga, reigns successfully at Magadha for about half a century.

Science, Technology, and Discovery
The Gauls invent the claymore or 'great sword', a double-edged and double-handled weapon.

Art, Sculpture, Fine Arts, and Architecture
The Corinthian column is introduced to Greek architecture about now.

418 Sparta invades Argos, and Athens, breaking the peace, comes to the aid of the Argives.
The Argives are defeated at the Battle of Mantinea and go over from Athens to Sparta, as do their allies. Athens is becoming increasingly isolated.

415 **Society, Education, and Religion**
Alcibiades is ordered to return from Sicily to face charges of blasphemy.

Literature
Euripides' *Troades.*

414 Nicias lays siege to Syracuse and initially gains the upper hand but is soon outflanked and finds himself under siege.

Literature
Aristophanes' *The Birds.*

413 The Spartans advance almost to the gates of Athens. The Athenians send a second fleet to Sicily, under the command of Demosthenes.

Sept: —, The Athenian Sicilian expedition is heavily defeated in a joint land and sea battle near Syracuse.

Literature
Euripides' *Electra.*

412 The Spartans sign a treaty of mutual aid with the Persian satrap of Lower Asia, Tissaphernes. Alcibiades deserts the Spartans in turn, and goes to the court of Tissaphernes whom he then dissuades from helping Sparta.

411 In Athens, after an unsuccessful oligarchic revolution, the democrats under Thrasybulus takes control. He wins a naval battle over the Spartans at Cynossema in the Hellespont.

Politics, Government, Law, and Economy
In Athens, an oligarchic Council of 400 seizes power in an effort to exert more efficient control in the conduct of the war. The oligarchs are ousted in Sept and the old democratic Council of 500 re-established; the Assembly resumes its old form of a committee of all citizens.

Humanities and Scholarship
Thucydides' *History* ends in this year and Xenophon continues where he leaves off.

Literature
Aristophanes' *Lysistrata* in which the women seek to force their menfolk to make peace, thus voicing the war-weariness of Athens.

410 Celtic tribes (soon to become known to the Romans as the Gauls – see 390 BC) migrate south across the Alps during this period.

409 Hannibal, grandson of Hamilcar, invades Sicily with a strong force and defeats the Sicilian Greeks at a second battle of Himera.

Art, Sculpture, Fine Arts, and Architecture
The Athenian Erechtheion is completed.

Literature
Sophocles' *Philoctetes.*

408 **Literature**
Euripides' *Orestes* is produced.

407 King Darius II of Persia sends his second son Cyrus as satrap to Sardis with instructions to increase Persian support for Sparta.

406 Athens wins her last naval battle at Arginusae, near Lesbos.
The Carthaginians again invade Sicily. Plague kills Hannibal and Himilco assumes command, and invests Acragas.

405 In Sicily, the tyrant Dionysius the Elder rises to power. He makes peace with Carthage, and fortifies Syracuse.
Athenian naval supremacy is finally shattered by the defeat at the battle of Aegospotami. Shortly after, the Peloponnesians lay siege to Athens itself.

Literature
Aristophanes' *Frogs*.

404 Athens, over-full of refugees herded into the city by Lysander, falls to the Spartans. The Peloponnesian War is over. The long walls are pulled down and a puppet oligarchic government, the Council of Thirty, is set up; it rules by a bloody reign of terror.

403 In Athens, Thrasybulus deposes the oligarchic Council of Thirty and restores democracy.

Politics, Government, Law, and Economy
Lysias, Athenian orator, writes speeches against the Thirty in the campaign to oust them.

Humanities and Scholarship
Thucydides the historian returns to Athens and dies shortly after. His *History of the Peloponnesian War* is published posthumously.

401 Cyrus sets out from Sardis with his army in an attempt to win the Persian throne but is defeated at the battle of Cunaxa (north of Babylon).

400 Sparta turns on Persia and wars against her in Asia Minor.
Artaxerxes II, the Persian king, appoints Tissaphernes to take over all the districts in Asia Minor over which Cyrus has been governor.

Politics, Government, Law, and Economy
Athens is still important as a trade centre, and the Piraeus increases in size and importance. Commercial banks spring up, taking over depositing and lending money from the temples and priests.

Society, Education, and Religion
In the Troad a satrap's widow, Mania, strikes an early blow for women's rights, persuading Pharnabazus to let her govern in place of her deceased husband.

Science, Technology, and Discovery
Hippocrates, of Cos, recognizes that disease has natual causes. The corpus of the Hippocratic medical treatises is probably laid down about this time.

Art, Sculpture, Fine Arts, and Architecture
A Scythian king is buried with treasure of Greek craftsmanship (the 'Tolstoi' burial north of the Crimea).

399 **Humanities and Scholarship**
Socrates is convicted of charges of corrupting the young and not believing in the gods and is condemned to drink hemlock.
The death of Socrates is described in Plato's *Phaedo*. Socrates' last discourse is largely taken up with his attempt to prove that there is a life after death.

397 To avenge Dionysius' massacre of Carthaginians, Himilco is sent to Sicily from Carthage with a fresh army, puts Dionysius on the defensive, and besieges Syracuse. He is defeated and flees back to Carthage

396 Camillus is made Dictator by the Romans and finally destroys the Etruscan town of Veii.
Agesilaus, King of Sparta, campaigns with some success in Asia Minor against the Persian satraps Pharnabazus and Tissaphernes.

Politics, Government, Law, and Economy
During the siege of Veii Roman citizen-soldiers are paid for the first time.

395 The 'Corinthian War' begins, with Corinth, Thebes, and Argos, soon joined by Athens, all allied against Sparta.

394 Conon, an Athenian general, and Pharnabazus win a naval victory over the Spartans at Cnidus.

392 Dionysius of Syracuse, is now attacked by a second Carthaginian expedition, and allies himself with the Sicels (indigenous Sicilians). The Carthaginians are defeated, make peace, and leave.

390 **June: —**, A wandering tribe of Celts (whom the Romans call Gauls) defeat the Romans, deserted by their allies, at the battle of Allia and Rome is besieged for six months until only the Capitol is unconquered. The Gauls are probably bought off with gold, though the legend grows that Camillus is recalled from exile and defeats them.

Humanities and Scholarship
Antisthenes, pupil of Socrates and founder of the Cynics, is active in this period.

Literature
Aristophanes' *Plutus*, his last extant play, is written during this period.

388 **Humanities and Scholarship**
Plato travels to Syracuse at the invitation of Dion, the Tyrant's brother-in-law. He exercises the right of free speech too freely and is deported by Dionysius.

387 Sparta is unsuccessful in the war against Persia and the attempt at empire and so concludes 'the King's Peace' (sometimes known as the Peace of Antalcidas, after the Spartan envoy) which hands back the Greek cities of Asia Minor (once saved by Marathon and Thermopylae) to Persian rule.

Science, Technology, and Discovery
Iphicrates introduces the *peltastae* or targeteers into the Athenian army. They are equipped with a lighter target or shield, lighter armour, and a longer sword and spear.

386 (–381 BC) Persia, freed from Spartan attacks, turns to quietening Cyprus and Egypt and is occupied there for the rest of the decade.

385 **Humanities and Scholarship**
Back in Athens, Plato writes his *Symposium*, a disquisition on homosexual love, and founds his Academy, teaching mathematics, astronomy, and other sciences as well as philosophy.

383 Sparta sends an expedition northwards to disrupt the Chalcidian League of petty kings with whom King Amyntas, grandfather of Alexander of Macedon, has formed a temporary alliance. On their way north, they gain control of the Theban citadel helped by a pro-Spartan party of Thebans.

Humanities and Scholarship
Xenophon writes his *Hellenica*, beginning in the year 411 when Thucydides' history ends.

380 Egypt's 30th Dynasty, the last according to Manetho, begins with the Pharaoh Nectanebes (or sometimes Nectabeno).

Literature
Isocrates' *Panegryic.*

379 Epaminondas comes to power in Thebes after an Athenian-backed coup.
In Sicily, Dionysius suffers a severe defeat and has to make a disadvantageous peace, surrendering some western towns to the Carthaginians.

378 (–377 BC) Athens allies herself with Thebes and forms a second Athenian Confederacy; most of the other Boeotian cities and some of the Ionian islands join the pact. War breaks out between the Thebans and Spartans in Boeotia
The Thebans form their Sacred Band of 150 pairs of friends and lovers. All are dedicated and highly trained warriors and their ferocity and loyalty in battle, heightened by their loyalty to each other, becomes renowned.

377 **Politics, Government, Law, and Economy**
Athenian taxation is reorganized: the richer citizens are responsible for collection of the taxes from the less well-off.

376 **Politics, Government, Law, and Economy**
In Rome, Licinius is Tribune and strives to end the traditional class enmity between patricians and plebs with liberalizing laws.

375 **Humanities and Scholarship**
Plato publishes his *Phaedrus* and is working on his *Republic.*

373 Artaxerxes II invades Egypt in an attempt to bring it back under Persian rule. The expedition, led by Pharnabazus, has some initial successes but is then forced to retreat.

371 Sparta and Athens make peace, another 'Peace of Callias'.

July: —, At the battle of Leuctra, the Theban general Epaminondas wins a decisive victory over the Spartans. The Arcadians decide to re-assert their independence and form an Arcadian League.

Science, Technology, and Discovery
At the battle of Leuctra the accepted science of hoplite warfare is changed by Epaminondas, who does not draw out a long even line of soldiers but forms a heavy wedge, 50 men deep, on one wing, including the Theban 'Sacred Band'.

370 The Spartans invade Arcadia which, having appealed in vain to the Athenians, turns to the Thebans. Epaminondas arrives with an army, finds the Spartans gone home, and follows them, ravaging all in his path.

The short-lived low-caste Nanda dynasty is founded in the Magadha kingdom of India.

369 Epaminondas frees Messenia from Spartan rule. Not wishing to disturb the balance of power, Athens allies herself with Sparta, her traditional enemy.

368 **Humanities and Scholarship**

Plato's *Republic* is completed.

367 **Politics, Government, Law, and Economy**

The Licinian laws are promulgated in Rome. One of the two consuls must be a plebeian and the offices of Praetor (magisterial) and of aedile (a civil office, equivalent to Mayors of Rome) are greatly enlarged in scope and the number of aediles is doubled from two to four.

Humanities and Scholarship

Plato is again invited to Syracuse by Dion. For a while Dionysius II is eager to learn, but reaction and intrigue soon set in – Dion is exiled and Plato returns once more to Athens.

366 Thebes makes peace with Sparta and turns against its other rival, Athens.

365 **Art, Sculpture, Fine Arts, and Architecture**

Antiphanes, writer of Athenian comedies, is active around this time.

364 **Art, Sculpture, Fine Arts, and Architecture**

About this time, Praxiteles of Athens makes his *Hermes* and his *Aphrodite* of Cnidus.

362 Arcadia is drifting into an alliance with Sparta. The Thebans invade and win the battle of Mantinea, but Epaminondas is killed. His dying wish, for *Koine Eirene* (a general peace), is met and the brief supremacy of Thebes comes to an end.

361 The Persian empire is weakening, despite the failure of a joint Egyptian-Spartan expedition to the Phoenician coast, and many satraps revolt, including Straton I at Sidon.

Politics, Government, Law, and Economy

The Nanda dynasty of Magadha taxes efficiently, creates a large army, and builds canals.

360 **Humanities and Scholarship**

Plato probably writes the *Timaeus* and the *Critias* and finishes his *Laws* in this decade.

359 The Macedonian king Perdiccas is succeeded by his infant son, Amyntas; his uncle, Philip, assumes the regency.

Science, Technology, and Discovery

Philip of Macedon improves on the strength-in-depths principle of Epaminondos and invents the more open and freer-moving *phalanx*.

356 Philip of Macedon assumes the full title of King and takes Potidaea and other Athenian strongholds in Thessaly and Chalcidice.

The internecine quarrels of the Greek world continue. Caria, Chios, Cos, and Rhodes rebel against Athens and another 'Sacred War' breaks out following the seizure of Delphi by the Phocians.

354 Rome allies with the Samnites and defeats the Etruscans at Caere.

353 **Art, Sculpture, Fine Arts, and Architecture**

A royal tomb with a colossal statue is built at Halicarnassus for the dead king of Caria, Mausolus – hence the name 'mausoleum'.

352 After two initial defeats, Philip drives the Phocians south. Athens and Sparta support the Phocians and Philip is checked at Thermopylae but then moves against Thrace. Athens votes for increased armaments but is saved by Philip falling ill.

Science, Technology, and Discovery

In China, the earliest known record of a supernova.

351 **Politics, Government, Law, and Economy**

Demosthenes delivers his first Philippic against Philip of Macedon.

350 By the beginning of this decade the Romans have finally recovered from the set-back caused by the sack of their city in 390 and have re-asserted their ascendancy in Italy. The Gauls, once more threatening Rome, are decisively beaten.

Sidon, the centre of the revolt against Persia, is taken and punished with great cruelty by Artaxerxes III.

Politics, Government, Law, and Economy

In Rome a plebeian is elected as Censor for the first time.

Coinage is introduced in China, along with the use of the horse as a cavalry charger rather than for drawing chariots.

Art, Sculpture, Fine Arts, and Architecture

Greek sculpture begins to show facial expression which enables individual portraiture.

349 Philip cements his control over the remaining Greek cities in Macedonia, in particular taking the city of Olynthus.

347 (–346 BC) Athens sends embassies to Philip, and the peace of Philocrates establishes a *status-quo ante*. Greece and Macedonia spend much of the rest of the decade preparing for war in an interval of uneasy peace.

Politics, Government, Law, and Economy

In Rome coinage is introduced for the first time, leading to much borrowing and a financial crisis.

346 **Society, Education, and Religion**

Philip of Macedon punishes the Phocians for starting the Sacred War and is elected president of the Pythian games and a member of the Greek religious body, the Amphictyonic League.

344 **Politics, Government, Law, and Economy**

Isocrates' *Letter to Philip*. Demosthenes' second *Philippic* and, three years later, his third appeals for a Hellenic League against Macedonia.

343 The Samnites successfully appeal to Rome to settle their internal quarrels and to save their city, Capua, from destruction.

Dionysius II surrenders to Timoleon, who has been sent from Corinth at the request of the Syracusans. In the next few years, Timoleon attacks other tyrannies throughout Sicily and prepares against an anticipated Carthaginian invasion.

Artaxerxes III invades Egypt and Pharaoh Nectanebos, the last native pharaoh, flees to Ethiopia. Artaxerxes and his favourite general Bagoas retire loaded with spoil.

Politics, Government, Law, and Economy

Timoleon repopulates Syracuse and revives the democratic constitution that had existed before the Carthaginian defeat of 409 BC.

Humanities and Scholarship

Aristotle goes to Macedon as tutor to Alexander.

Literature

Middle Comedy, more naturalistic than previous forms, flourishes in Athens, Antiphanes and Alexis being its best-known exponents.

342 (–341 BC) Philip conquers Thrace; this is regarded by Athens as a further threat to her safety.

340 The Romans defeat the Latin League at a battle on the Campanian coast, near Mt. Vesuvius according to Livy.

Politics, Government, Law, and Economy

Rome gives remarkably liberal peace terms to the cities of the defeated Latin League.

339 Timoleon defeats a much larger force of Carthaginians at the battle of Crimisus (in western Sicily).

338 Timoleon makes advantageous peace terms with Carthage, deposes two more tyrants in Sicily, and gives the island a peace that lasts for the next 20 years.

At Chaeronea, west of Thebes, Philip wins the battle for the supremacy of the Greek world. He advances into the Peloponnese, subdues Sparta, and summons a pan-Hellenic congress at Corinth where he announces that the Greeks will set about re-liberating the Greek cities of Asia Minor from Persian rule.

336 Philip is murdered at a wedding feast and his son, Prince Alexander, becomes King of Macedonia, aged 20. He puts down rebellion at home and subdues Thebes. He is elected by the Greeks assembled at Corinth as their commander against Persia.

Bagoas murders the Persian king, Arses, and is himself murdered. Darius III succeeds to the throne.

335 **Humanities and Scholarship**

Aristotle returns to Athens and founds his 'peripatetic' school in the old gymnasium called the Lyceum.

334 Alexander of Macedon sets out on his conquest of the Persian Empire. He defeats a Persian army commanded by the Greek mercenary, Memnon, at Granicus and subdues Miletus and Halicarnassus.

Science, Technology, and Discovery

At Granicus, Alexander adds a considerable force of cavalry on his wings to his father's *phalanx*.

333 **Oct:** —, Alexander defeats King Darius III at the River Issus. He is now master of Syria.

332 **Humanities and Scholarship**

The Chinese philosopher Mencius begins travelling from court to court as Confucius had done: his is also an ethical rather than a religious teaching.

331 **Oct:** —, Alexander advances against Darius and finally defeats him at the battle of Gaugamela (sometimes called the battle of Arbela, Darius' HQ). He is now master of the Persian Empire.

Society, Education, and Religion

Alexander takes the first major step in his hellenizing process by founding the greatest of the cities he names after himself, Alexandria, in the Nile Delta. Many Greeks emigrate to these new cities.

330 Darius is made prisoner by his satrap of Bactria, Bessus, and is assassinated in July, just as Alexander catches up with the Persians who cease all resistance.

Politics, Government, Law, and Economy

(–328 BC) Alexander, regards himself as the new king of Persia. He begins to wear Persian dress and to observe Persian customs and court ritual.

Humanities and Scholarship

(–323 BC) Aristotle composes his *History of Animals*, *Rhetoric*, *Physics*, *Metaphysics*, *Ethics*, *Logic*, *Poetics*, and *Politics* during this period and the preceding five years.

327 Alexander marries Roxana, the captured princess of a Bactrian chief. He invades India and defeats the Indian king Porus in a well-contested battle on the river Hydaspes.

326 Roman intervention in the dispute over Naples causes the Samnites to declare war on Rome – the Second Samnite War.

Alexander reaches his farthest point east, the River Hyphasis where his Macedonian troops refuse to go any farther.

325 **Science, Technology, and Discovery**

Aristotle refers to the Greek water clock; it is much improved from the Egyptian version and approaching perfection.

324 **Society, Education, and Religion**

In another effort to bring East and West together, Alexander establishes military schools in conquered territory: by this date he is said to have 30,000 hellenized barbarians at his disposition for military service.

323 Alexander reaches Babylon, which he intends to develop as the capital of his empire, and plans the conquest of Arabia.

June: **13th**, Alexander develops a fever and dies in the palace of Nebuchadnezzar.

322 In Babylon the struggle to succeed Alexander develops. A compromise is reached whereby Roxana's son, Alexander Aegus, and the dead king's young dim-witted half-brother, Arrhidaeus, are to be considered rulers. Perdiccas, Alexander's head general to whom he had given his signet ring, tries to keep effective control.

Humanities and Scholarship

Aristotle is accused of impiety by the Athenians, but escapes to Chalcis in Euboea, where he dies later in the year.

321 Perdiccas invades Egypt but is murdered by his own mutinous army, led by Seleucus. A truce is arranged, leaving Ptolemy in power in Egypt and Seleucus in Babylon.

In India the young adventurer Chandragupta Maurya defeats the Nandas and begins to create the Mauryan empire by gaining control of the Ganges valley.

A Roman army is caught by the Samnites at a mountain pass, the Caudine Forks, and forced to capitulate. It suffers the indignity of 'passing under the yoke'.

320 Following the death of Alexander, his empire disintegrates and there is a major power struggle between his former generals, the *Diadochoi*.

Judaea and Syria are annexed by Ptolemy and remain part of the Egyptian domains of the Ptolemies until the beginning of the 2nd century BC.

Society, Education, and Religion

The *Diadochoi* deliberately diffuse Hellenic culture, partly by founding new cities. Conversely, the religions of the East begin to affect Greek thought and rulers find themselves deified but do not object.

Science, Technology, and Discovery

Pytheas, the navigator of Marseilles, writes his *Ocean* and *Periplus*, only fragments of which remain.
Euclid begins his work in Alexandria.

316

Agathocles becomes tyrant of Syracuse, and extends his rule over most of Sicily.
Eumenes is defeated by Antigonus and executed.
Cassander has Philip's widow, Olympias, murdered and Alexander's widow and son imprisoned. He puts them to death five years later.
The Romans try to seize Luceria and are badly beaten; the Samnites reach to within 20 miles of Rome.

Literature

Athens' so-called New Comedy: the chief exponents are Philemon and Menander whose *Dyscolus* wins first prize at the Lenaea.

315

Antigonus is recognized as the common enemy by the other *Diadochoi.*

Science, Technology, and Discovery

The Romans abandon the *phalanx* in favour of the *maniple* or 'handful' of men, 120 strong, armed with javelin and short sword, a less cumbersome formation.

314

The Romans inflict a crushing defeat on the Samnites at the battle of Tarracina.

313

Cassander largely loses his grip on central Greece and Antigonus declares the 'freedom' of Greek cities.

312

The Syracusans ask the Carthaginians for help against their tyrant Agathocles. After a victory on the Himeras River, the Carthaginian general Hamilcar besieges Agathocles in Syracuse.

Politics, Government, Law, and Economy

Appius Claudius, Roman Censor, asserts the right of freed slaves to hold office. The great southern road named after him, the Via Appia, is begun.

311

Antigonus makes a truce with his rivals, except Seleucus who now holds Babylon.

310

Agathocles escapes from captivity in Syracuse and over the next three years nearly succeeds in conquering Carthage which is in the throes of a civil war against its would-be tyrant Bomilcar. He is eventually paid off.

Politics, Government, Law, and Economy

During the 4th century BC, the Hellenic world is stricken by rampant inflation. Prices rise disproportionately to wages and the drachma loses half its value.

Society, Education, and Religion

Euhemerus writes his *Sacred History*, ascribing a historical basis to all myths.

307

Society, Education, and Religion

Ptolemy I begins the foundation of Alexandria's famous library and museum.

306

Science, Technology, and Discovery

In physics, the Greek philosopher Epicurus (see 306 BC) supports the atomic theory of Democritus.

Humanities and Scholarship

Epicurus of Samos takes up permanent residence in Athens and establishes his Epicurean school. He follows Plato's Academy in allowing women pupils.

305

Seleucus consolidates his Asian empire as far as India where he is checked by Chandragupta who gains control of the Indus valley as well as the Ganges valley, laying the foundations of the Mauryan empire.

304

The Second Samnite war ends with a peace under which Rome gains no territory but the Samnites renounce their hegemony over Campania.

303

Cassander and Lysimachus persuade Seleucus and Ptolemy to join them in trying to destroy Antigonus.

301 Lysimachus joins up with Seleucus, and Antigonus is defeated at the 'Battle of the Kings' at Ipsus in Phrygia.

300 **Politics, Government, Law, and Economy**

Seleucus I founds the city of Antioch, some 20 miles up the river Orontes, naming it after his father. At his capital city of Seleucia he establishes an absolute monarchy.

The early Ptolemies set up an efficient bureaucracy in Egypt, run mostly by Greeks. Trade, mainly conducted by Jews, prospers in the region.

Science, Technology, and Discovery

Greek science reaches its height in this Hellenistic age, chiefly at Alexandria.

Euclid lays out the laws of gemoetry in his *Elements*; it remains a standard text for 2,000 years.

Humanities and Scholarship

Zeno of Cyprus opens his school of philosophy in Athens at the *Stoa Poikile*; his disciples become known as the Stoics.

Ptolemy I, in the last 15 years of his reign, writes a history of the wars of Alexander the Great.

299 The Samnites start the Third Samnite War aided by Gaulish marauders and Etruscan allies.

297 In India Chandragupta abdicates in favour of his son Bindusara who extends the Mauryan empire as far south as Mysore.

Society, Education, and Religion

Chandragupta is said to have gently starved himself to death as prescribed by Jainism.

296 **Literature**

Even so late in the disintegrating Chou dynasty, China's literary output is still immense: the books found buried in a king's tomb of this date are said to have filled 10 wagons.

295 Pyrrhus regains his Epirot throne with forces supplied by Ptolemy.

293 Rome suffers from the Plague.

291 The Third Samnite War ends, with the Samnites subdued but recognized by the Romans as autonomous allies.

290 **Art, Sculpture, Fine Arts, and Architecture**

A school of sculpture develops in Rhodes during this period.

289 **Politics, Government, Law, and Economy**

In Rome the *Lex Hortensia* gives much greater power to the plebeian Assembly in its relations with the Senate.

Humanities and Scholarship

After the death of Mencius his disciples publish his teachings as the *Book of Meng-tzu*.

287 Demetrius Poliorcetes is deserted by his troops, who proclaim Pyrrhus king of Macedonia.

286 Pyrrhus is driven out by Lysimachus, who for a while becomes king of Macedon.

285 **Science, Technology, and Discovery**

Herophilus, an anatomist working at Alexandria, dissects the human eye and brain and establishes the latter as the seat of thought.

283 At a battle near Lake Vadimo Rome finally quells the allied Etruscans and Gauls, becoming undisputed master of northern and central Italy.

Science, Technology, and Discovery

Sostratus of Cnidus builds the great Alexandrine lighthouse on the island of Pharos.

282 Pergamum gets rid of Lysimachus and begins its years of greatness.

281 Seleucus I invades Macedonia and kills Lysimachus in battle, leaving Seleucus the only surviving *Diadochos*.

280 Pyrrhus responds to Tarentum's appeal for help against Roman interference. He defeats the Romans at Heraclea but his losses are nearly as great as theirs, giving rise to the phrase 'Pyrrhic victory'.

Politics, Government, Law, and Economy

Under the Seleucids the cities of Asia Minor regain commercial prosperity and even achieve some specialization, Miletus becoming a textile centre. There is some slave-based mass production.

Society, Education, and Religion
Ptolemy II develops Alexandria as a centre of art, science, philosophy, and literature.

Science, Technology, and Discovery
Aristarchus of Samos, astronomer, is active in this period and for the next 20 years. He writes *On the Size and Distances of the Sun and the Moon.*

Art, Sculpture, Fine Arts, and Architecture
The *Colossus of Rhodes*, the greatest of many new statues in this now flourishing city, is finally set up. It is 105 ft high and holds a torch aloft.

Everyday Life
Ptolemy II introduces the camel and with it a camel-post to Egypt.

279 **Politics, Government, Law, and Economy**
The Aetolian League, north of the Corinthian Gulf, and the Achaean League to the south are refounded. They adopt a common coinage and foreign policy, and pool their armed forces.

278 A band of Gauls, having swept through Greece, cross to Asia Minor where they eventually settle down to become the 'Galatians'.
(–276 BC) The Carthaginians besiege Syracuse which appeals to Pyrrhus. He again wins battles and even thinks of attacking Carthage. But after two years the Greeks of Sicily ask him to leave, which he does, leaving, as he says, a 'fair wrestling ring' for Carthage and Rome.

275 Celts of the La Tène culture (known in Britain as the Iron Age B culture) settle in England, particularly in the Yorkshire Wolds.

274 Antiochus I, successor to Seleucus' empire, defends his possessions in the First Syrian War.

272 Asoka succeeds Bindusara on the Mauryan throne and continues his predecessor's policy of war and expansion.

267 The Athenians turn out their Macedonian garrison.

266 **Science, Technology, and Discovery**
Eudoxus of Cnidus builds an observatory and is said to be the first to teach the Greeks the motions of the planets.

265 The Romans and Carthaginians are drawn into a conflict between the Mamertines and Hieron: the first Punic war has begun.

263 **Humanities and Scholarship**
Cleanthes succeeds Zeno in his Stoic school at Athens.

262 The Carthaginians are defeated by the Romans at Agrigentum.

261 Antigonus II recaptures Athens.

260 The Mauryan emperor Asoka completes the conquest of virtually the whole of the Indian sub-continent by the bloody defeat of Kalinga.
The Romans win a resounding naval victory over the Carthaginians off Mylae.
(–253 BC) The Seleucids and Ptolemies are at war again in the 2nd Syrian War.

Humanities and Scholarship
Callimachus of Cyrene, poet and grammarian, catalogues the library at Alexandria.

258 **Society, Education, and Religion**
Asoka is repelled by his conquests and becomes a Buddhist and a pacifist, spreading the original teachings of Gautama Buddha.

Art, Sculpture, Fine Arts, and Architecture
The great Buddhist *stupa* at Sanchi (in the Madhya Pradesh, India) is probably founded about this time, under the direction of Asoka.

256 The state of Ch'in makes war upon the last of the Chou emperors, who abdicates.

255 Regulus, sent to capture Carthage, is defeated and taken prisoner.

252 **Statistics**
A census gives the number of Roman citizens as 297,797 although the reliability of the figures is doubtful.

250 **Society, Education, and Religion**

Ptolemy II encourages the Jews in Alexandria to have their Bible translated into Greek. By tradition there were 70 translators: hence the name of this Bible, the Septuagint.

Science, Technology, and Discovery

Hero of Alexandria discovers the formula for the area of a triangle in the terms of its sides. He also invents many ingenious machines, including automatically opening doors and a steam engine working on the jet-reaction principle. No practical use is made of these inventions with the exception of the water clock.

249 Regulus is sent to Rome with Carthaginian peace terms. They are refused on his advice, but he still honourably returns to captivity and is tortured to death.

247 Arsaces, chief of the Parsii, murders the Seleucid governor of Persia and establishes the kingdom of the Parthians.

246 The short-lived Ch'in Dynasty is set up in China with the accession of Shih-Huang-ti.

Ptolemy III sets out on a career of conquest in the Seleucid empire, now under Seleucus II: the Third Syrian War.

245 (–241 BC) Ptolemy III temporarily defeats and permanently weakens most of the Seleucid empire. However, he is forced to return to Egypt to meet internal trouble and the Seleucid rulers resume control.

Art, Sculpture, Fine Arts, and Architecture

In Greece and Egypt the art of the mosaic, with cube tesserae, comes into use.

242 **Politics, Government, Law, and Economy**

In Rome, a second praetor is appointed to deal with law suits involving non-citizens; this official's yearly edict becomes the basis of Rome's code of law for foreigners, the *Jus Gentium*.

241 The Romans win a resounding victory off Lilybaeum with their new fleet and the Carthaginians accept severe peace terms.

240 (–237 BC) Carthage's rulers refuse to pay the troops returning from Sicily, provoking a ruthless civil war. Hamilcar Barca finally puts down the rebellion.

Politics, Government, Law, and Economy

The emperor Shih Huang-ti attempts to change China's feudal system into a totalitarian one, with communal land-holding and a standardization of all weights, measures, and tools throughout the land.

Science, Technology, and Discovery

Eratosthenes writes on most current branches of knowledge. His systematic treatise on geography is later to be of great use to Strabo.

The Chinese record the earliest mention of a sighting of Halley's comet.

Literature

Livius Andronicus, the first known Roman poet and playwright, has his first tragedy produced in Rome. He translates the *Odyssey* into Latin.

237 Over the last three decades Carthage's hold on Spain has weakened and Hamilcar Barca is sent to re-establish it.

235 Rome closes the gates of the Temple of Janus as a sign that it is at peace.

Attalus I, Pergamum's greatest king, begins to build up the city's power and importance.

230 Rome becomes embroiled for the first time with the affairs of Greece by taking retaliatory action for the murder of Italian merchants and Roman envoys in Illyria. The Greeks congratulate Rome on quelling the Illyrian pirates but the Macedonians are antagonised.

Science, Technology, and Discovery

Eratosthenes develops a method of finding all prime numbers.

Art, Sculpture, Fine Arts, and Architecture

The defeat of the Gauls by the city of Pergamum is celebrated by statuary, including the *Dying Gaul*, (Byron's 'Dying Gladiator').

228 **Society, Education, and Religion**

After Rome's success over the Illyrians, Romans are offered initiation into the Eleusinian mysteries by Athens.

225 At the battle of Telamon, the Romans decisively defeat Gauls who have been threatening Rome.
The Emperor Shih Huang-ti begins building China's Great Wall against the encroachment of the Huns, incorporating some early fortifications, and stretching in all over 2000 miles. It is said to have taken 12 years to build.

223 **Politics, Government, Law, and Economy**
The Emperor of China, Shih Huang-ti, and his premier Li Ssu, order 'the burning of the books' and discourage ancient learning as being too conservative and reactionary, although a copy of Confucius' works is officially retained.

221 Hasdrubal, still campaigning to increase the Carthaginian hold over Spain, is murdered and succeeded by Hannibal, Hamilcar Barca's young son.
Shih Huang-ti, having defeated all his enemies, is now undisputed Emperor of China.

220 (–217 BC) There is a period of internal wars in Greece known as the Social War.
Science, Technology, and Discovery
The Via Flaminia is built.
Literature
Apollonius Rhodius works as chief librarian at Alexandria. His *Argonautica* is still extant.

219 The two post-Alexandrian empires, of the Ptolemies and the Seleucids, go to war over the ownership of Phoenicia and Palestine – the 4th Syrian War.
Hannibal begins the Second Punic War by attacking Rome's Spanish city, Saguntum.

218 In Spring, Hannibal sets out from New Carthage (Cartagena) to march round the Mediterranean coast, over the Rhone and the Alps, to invade Italy, reputedly with nearly 100,000 men and 50 elephants.
Dec: —, Publius Scipio is wounded in a minor engagement with the Carthaginians at Ticinus. The less skilful general, Sempronius, is defeated at the battle of the River Trebia.

217 Quintus Fabius is elected Dictator and earns the cognomen *Cunctator* by avoiding a set battle and creating a 'scorched earth' area around Hannibal's army to deprive the Carthaginians of supplies.
Antiochus the Great is defeated in his war with the Ptolemies at the battle of Raphia.

216 Quintus Fabius *Cunctator* is relieved of his command by an impatient Senate. The Romans suffer a devastating defeat at Cannae; Q. Fabius is reinstated. Capua sides with Hannibal, and the Carthaginian army winters there.
Philip V of Macedon, resenting Rome's interference in Illyria, seizes his opportunity and invades Illyria: the First Macedonian War begins.
Sport and Recreation
At the funeral of one of the Lepidus family a spectacle of 22 combats is staged – the Greek funeral games are turning into the Roman gladiatorial combats.

215 (–212 BC) The Carthaginians fail to recapture Sardinia. Hannibal captures Tarentum but is denied any reinforcements from Spain by the activities of Publius Scipio senior and his brother Cnaeus. Syracuse revolts against Rome and holds out for four years.

213 **Science, Technology, and Discovery**
Archimedes' inventions help Syracuse to withstand the Roman siege: he is killed when it is taken while intent upon a mathematical problem.

211 The Romans besiege Capua and Hannibal, as a diversion, makes an unsuccessful attempt on Rome. Capua falls, and is punished for its treachery.

210 **Art, Sculpture, Fine Arts, and Architecture**
A magnificent tomb is built for the dead Chinese emperor Shih Huang-ti. To avoid any possibility of theft or deceit, the workmen are said to have been buried alive in it.

209 In Spain, Scipio the younger (Africanus) besieges and captures New Carthage. He recruits the young Numidian chief, Masinissa.

207 **Politics, Government, Law, and Economy**
Nabis, a Syrian slave, comes to power in Sparta and brings about a social revolution. He frees the helots, redistributes land, cancels debts, and destroys the ruling oligarchy.

206 Scipio, having successfully driven the Carthaginians out of Spain, is elected consul. He prepares to carry the war into the enemy's country but is hampered by a jealous Senate.

205 Philip V of Macedon makes a temporary peace with Rome.

203 The Numidian chief Syphax joins the Carthaginian general, Gisco. Scipio defeats the joint force and Hannibal is persuaded to return home from Italy.

202 **Oct: —**, The Carthaginians are defeated at the battle of Zama; the last battle of the Punic Wars. The peace terms, agreed the following year, are harsh: Carthage has to surrender all but 10 ships of its great fleet, pay an indemnity of 10,000 talents, allow Masinissa independence as King of Numidia, renounce all claims to foreign possessions, and subordinate its foreign policy to Rome.

200 Following appeals from the Aetolian League and many other Greek cities, the Romans declare war on Philip V of Macdeon: the Second Macedonian War.

The Han Dynasty , which is to last for four centuries, begins its consolidation of China during this period. It gradually increases its trade with the West, institutes a settled bureaucracy with recruitment by examination basis, and expands its population, even beyond the Great Wall.

Society, Education, and Religion

The Biblical book of Ecclesiastes may have been written about this time.

197 Flamininus defeats the Macedonians at Cynoscephalae and dictates peace terms.

196 **Politics, Government, Law, and Economy**

Hannibal, who has been struggling to rehabilitate Carthage, is elected Magistrate. He restores democratic elections and reorganizes public finance and taxation only to go into exile the following year when the Romans demand his surrender.

Society, Education, and Religion

The Rosetta stone (written in both Greek and ancient Coptic and hence helping greatly the decipherment of Egyptian hieroglyphics) describes the coronation of Ptolemy V.

Science, Technology, and Discovery

The foundation of a library at Pergamum leads to the invention of parchment.

195 **Humanities and Scholarship**

Aristophanes of Byzantium introduces accents in the writing of Greek and the use of punctuation in the ancient writings generally.

193 Nabis is defeated by the general of the Achaean League, Philopemon, and is later assassinated. The Aetolian League asks for help from Antiochus the Great in revolting against Rome.

Art, Sculpture, Fine Arts, and Architecture

The *Venus de Milo* is made some time during this century.

192 Antiochus is defeated at Thermopylae and only just manages to escape.

190 Scipio Africanus, with his brother Lucius, finally defeats Antiochus III at the set battle of Magnesia in Caria. Hannibal is forced to flee from Carthage and seeks refuge first in Crete and then with the king of Bithynia.

189 The Romans force the Galatians into subjection to Pergamum. In mainland Greece, the Aetolian League is punished and made a subject-ally.

Politics, Government, Law, and Economy

Booty and indemnity settlements from her various recent wars bring Rome great wealth on such a great scale that it encourages extravagance and financial speculation. At Flamininus' triumph, besides marble and bronze statues, 18,000 lbs of silver and 3,714 lbs of gold are paraded.

188 (–181 BC) The Greek cities and leagues continue to quarrel amongst themselves and the conviction grows in Rome that there will be no peace in that land until she takes full control.

183 **Art, Sculpture, Fine Arts, and Architecture**

A lifelike bust is made of Scipio Africanus, one of the earliest examples of Roman skill in this form of sculpture.

Literature

During this period Ennius, 'the father of Roman poetry', along with Plautus, the writer of comedies, introduce the Roman citizen to the art of drama. Ennius writes his *Annals*, a history of Rome, and is accorded Roman citizenship.

182 When the Romans demand Hannibal's extradition from Bithynia, he commits suicide.

180 The descendants of Arsaces are making Parthia a powerful kingdom, which is partly hellenized.

In the Ganges area, the warlike Shungas follow the Mauryan kings and exist as a dynasty for about 100 years. Brahmanism returns and Buddhism decays. The western part of the Mauryan empire is largely taken over by the line of kings known as the Indo-Greeks during this period.

Society, Education, and Religion

The *Wisdom* of Joshua ben-Sira (known as the Apocryphal book of *Ecclesiasticus*) is written at about this time.

Literature

Aristarchus of Samothrace, librarian at Alexandria, publishes an edition of Homer. It is the basis of the modern text, dividing the *Iliad* and *Odyssey* into 24 'books' each.

177 T. Gracchus senior subdues Sardinia, enslaving some of the population.

175 **Society, Education, and Religion**

Antiochus IV imposes hellenization, including the worship of Zeus, on the Jews. Swine are sacrificed in the temple, a terrible blasphemy against the Jewish religion, and a Greek gymnasium is opened in Jerusalem.

172 Rome declares war on Perseus of Macedon who is as anti-Roman as his father was: the short Third Macedonian War. The Romans initially suffer several defeats due to bad leadership. Epirus joins Macedonia, but the Greek leagues hold back.

171 **Politics, Government, Law, and Economy**

Under the benevolent government of Tiberius Gracchus, Spanish claims for redress against official extortion are heard in Rome.

170 (–168 BC) The Ptolemies and Seleucids continue to make war upon one another until ordered to cease by the Roman ambassador to the Seleucids.

Society, Education, and Religion

Cato probably writes his book on agriculture, *De Re Rustica*, during this decade.

168 (–167 BC) Aemilius Paullus takes charge in Thessaly. At the battle of Pydna, he defeats and captures Perseus who adorns his subsequent triumphal parade.

Literature

(–166 BC) Terence, a freed slave from Carthage, has his play *Andria* produced after impressing an established playwright.

167 Mattathias refuses to sacrifice to Zeus and slays the enforcing official and the Jews who attempt to obey. He leads a rebellion but dies the following year and is succeeded by his son Judas, the Maccabee.

Politics, Government, Law, and Economy

Under the terms of peace imposed on Macedon by Aemilius Paullus, the monarchy is suppressed; the country is divided into four administrative areas; and an elaborate democratic constitution is invented which lasts for no more than 20 years.

165 **Society, Education, and Religion**

The book of Daniel, the hero of the time of the Jewish captivity in Babylon, is written about this time, in an effort to boost Jewish morale.

164 **Dec: —**, Judas Maccabaeus defeats the Seleucid forces by guerrilla tactics and gains control of Jerusalem. He cleanses and rededicates the Temple.

161 Judas Maccabaeus strengthens himself by an alliance with Rome, but is slain in battle, leaving his brother Jonathan to continue the struggle.

159 **Statistics**

In the space of a century the number of Roman citizens has grown by about an eighth to 338,314.

157 Jonathan Maccabaeus is recognized by the Seleucids as a minor king within the Syrian dominions.

155 Menander (or Milinda) the most famous of the Indo-Greek kings, rules for about 25 years and extends his kingdom north and east.

153 The Carthaginians appeal to Rome against the depredations of Masinissa of Numidia. Rome sends out a commission, of which Cato is a member, and he is so alarmed by the prosperity that he witnesses that he begins his campaign for the final destruction of Rome's old enemy.

149 The Third Punic War begins. The oligarchic government of Carthage capitulates unconditionally. However, the Roman terms are so harsh the people put their leaders to death and install new ones – two Hasdrubals and a Himilco.

148 (–146 BC) Carthage endures a prolonged and terrible siege and is finally taken by Scipio Aemilianus. The city is levelled and the province of 'Africa' is established.

(–146 BC) In Macedonia popular discontent breaks out into a revolt which is crushed by the praetor Metellus. Macedonia's period of self-government under the Romans ends and it becomes a Roman province.

Humanities and Scholarship

(–146 BC) Polybius begins to accumulate information for his great *History* of Rome (spanning from 221 to 144 BC, of which only part is still extant).

147 A Roman delegation, arriving in Corinth to resolve the Spartan–Achaean League dispute, is snubbed and insulted and the League declares war on Sparta. Metellus hurries south from Macedon and defeats a Greek force but is recalled at the end of his term of office.

146 Metellus is replaced by Mummius, by no means a Hellenophile. Corinth is destroyed, its treasures shipped to Rome, and its population sold into slavery.

140 China's greatest Han emperor, Wu Ti, comes to the throne and accelerates the expansion of China.

Politics, Government, Law, and Economy

Wu Ti makes great social reforms, curbing speculators and middlemen, creating state monopolies and socialized industries, and regulating prices and incomes. He also enlarges the currency, issuing coins of silver alloyed with tin.

134 **Society, Education, and Religion**

The conflict over the interpretation of the Jewish Law, the Pentateuchal texts, comes to a head, resulting in the formation of the rival sects of the Pharisees and the Sadducees.

133 Tiberius, the elder of the two Gracchi brothers, is elected Tribune of the Plebs. He institutes drastic and highly controversial agrarian reforms and embarks on a radical programme.

Attalus III of Pergamum dies and bequeaths his treasure and his kingdom to the Romans. Tiberius Gracchus attempts to control the legacy, an unprecedented interference in foreign policy which has always been dictated by the Senate. After much political strife, he is killed in a riot before his term of office has ended.

Politics, Government, Law, and Economy

Tiberius Gracchus, in an effort to create a middle class of agriculturalists, enforces the Licinian laws, restricting the amount of land any individual may own, and appoints a Land Commission to direct the redistribution. He demonstrates the latent power of the tribunate against both the Senate and the *imperium* of the magistracy (i.e., the consuls and praetors). When his term of office is running out, he takes the unprecedented course of seeking immediate re-election, an action that raises fears that he is aiming for dictatorship. All this is too much for the conservative Senate and aristocracy and there is a riot on the Capitol, during which Tiberius Gracchus himself and many of his followers are killed.

131 As a result of Tiberius Gracchus' legislation, more than 80,000 Roman citizens are resettled on the land.

129 Scipio Aemilianus, a conservative opponent of the Gracchi, is found dead, apparently murdered by the followers of the Gracchi.

128 The Shakas (Scythians), ousted from China by the Yüeh-Chi, infiltrate into Bactria and Parthia.

125 Fulvius Flaccus, a follower of the Gracchi, fails in an attempt to obtain Roman enfranchisement for the Italians; the town of Fregellae revolts and is destroyed.

123 Gaius, the younger of the Gracchi brothers, having served a term as quaestor in Sardinia, is elected Tribune.

Politics, Government, Law, and Economy

(–122 BC) Gaius Gracchus attacks the power of the Senate by seeking to enhance the powers of the 'Equites' (the business class), transferring control of the jury panels examining cases of praetorial extortion to the Equites. He also extends the 'corn dole' to the Roman populace, under which they receive bread at a cheap rate. When he tries to obtain Roman citizenship for the Italians the people turn against him because of the dole: an increase in citizenship may mean less corn to go round.

122 Gaius Gracchus is re-elected Tribune and leaves Rome to visit his colonies at Carthage. In his absence his popularity wanes, particularly since the Senate support a tribunician colleague of his, Livius Drusus.

Science, Technology, and Discovery

Aquae Sextiae is founded by the Romans in Narbonese Gaul; its medicinal waters are widely valued.

121 Gaius Gracchus fails to get elected Tribune for a third time. He appears in the Forum to protest against the repeal of some of his enactments and a riot ensues. Gaius is induced to flee, but, on the point of capture, prevails on his slave to kill him; about 3,000 of his followers are killed in the subsequent blood-letting.

120 **Literature**

The Roman poet Lucilius pioneers the literary genre of satire – later developed by Horace and Juvenal – with scenes and commentaries of social life, known as *satura* ('mixture' or 'hotchpotch').

118 The two grandsons of Masinissa are bequeathed the Numidian throne but have to share it with their cousin Jugurtha. Jugurtha kills one grandson and forces the other out, then appeals to Rome to confirm him as king.

115 **Statistics**

The number of Roman citizens registered in the Census has gone up to 394,336, although the reliability of this and earlier Census figures is not known (see also 252 BC and 159 BC).

113 A Roman army is defeated by the Cimbri, a group of Celtic tribes threatening northern Italy.

Politics, Government, Law, and Economy

In China, all existing coins are declared of no value, and all minting is placed under central control.

111 The Roman Senate finally take action against Jugurtha by sending one of the consuls, Bestia, to subjugate him. However, Bestia achieves little and makes peace.

The Chinese Emperor Wu Ti conquers and annexes the kingdom of Nan Yüeh (modern S China and N Vietnam).

110 The Romans hold an enquiry into Jugurtha, but while in Rome he murders a rival and is sent home in disgrace. War is declared against him once more. The Roman army, under the consul Albinus, pursues Jugurtha into the desert but is trapped and made to pass under the yoke. Both Bestia and Albinus are exiled and the command passes to the consul Metellus.

108 With the Jugurthan war threatening to relapse into stalemate, Marius presses Metellus to let him return to Rome to seek election as consul, and at the end of a whirlwind demagogic campaign gets himself elected to both the consulship and the African command.

105 Sulla persuades King Bocchus to turn against Jugurtha who is lured to a conference, and kidnapped.

The Cimbri inflict a more serious defeat on the Romans, at Arausio (modern Orange) on the Rhone – now the Province of Transalpine Gaul seems at their mercy and Rome itself threatened.

104 Marius is elected consul again and reforms the army to meet the threat of the Cimbri. There is another Servile War, as imported slaves in Sicily revolt, which is only subdued after three years at the cost of 100,000 lives.

Politics, Government, Law, and Economy

Marius' army reforms make the Roman army both more democratic and more professional. He increases the Legion from about 5,000 to 6,000; creates a closer and more flexible formation by changing the 120-strong maniple to the 600-strong cohort; changes the heavy *hasta* for the lighter *pilum*; and lightens the soldier's pack. He abolishes dependence upon class for recruitment to various ranks of the army and converts the cavalry to an auxiliary arm. He gives the legions names and numbers and introduces the Eagle as a standard for each.

102 The Cimbri, with Teutonic allies, return to mount a determined and concerted attack on Rome. Marius defeats the Teutons utterly at Aquae Sextiae and the following year massacres the Cimbri at Vercellae. He returns to Rome a hero to face his great political opportunity.

100 (–98 BC) Marius, a better soldier than politician, becomes involved with two unscrupulous demagogues during his successful campaign to be re-elected consul for the sixth time. He has to oust his erstwhile backers who have created widespread civil disorder and seized the Capitol and then leaves Rome in disgust.

Celts, probably of the Iron Age B culture of England, build their most remarkable stone forts in Scotland during this period. The forts, known as *broches*, are dry-stone towers surrounding a circular internal area of about 28 ft diameter with walls as thick as 13 ft, in which rooms and staircases are sometimes inset.

Politics, Government, Law, and Economy
Q. Mucius Scaevola becomes Pontifex Maximus, and institutes a scientific study of the Law. He is considered the founder of Roman jurisprudence.

Science, Technology, and Discovery
Chinese mathematicians begin using negative numbers.

92 Mithridates of Pontus has forced the king of Cappadocia off the throne, and Sulla is sent to restore the *status quo* which he successfully does.

91 M. Livius Drusus becomes Tribune of the Plebs and proposes enfranchising the increasingly discontent Italians (sometimes known as Confederates or *Socii*). The Senate vote his reforms down with a procedural technicality and he forms a conspiracy but is then murdered. The Italians revolt: the Social War begins.

Art, Sculpture, Fine Arts, and Architecture
The Celts bring their distinctive curvilinear type of decorative art of the so-called La Tène culture into Britain during this period.

90 (–89 BC) During the Social War, Rome is seriously threatened by the Italians, who even establish a federal capital at Corfinium, east of Rome. The Senate, with an apprehensive eye on the threat of Mithridates, compromises. While giving command in Campania to Sulla – who achieves a resounding victory – it offers the Italians, with only few provisos, what they are fighting for: Roman citizenship.

88 Mithridates invades the Roman province of Asia. He captures the city of Pergamum and massacres unpopular Roman and Italian merchants and officials.
Sulla is elected Consul and given the much-prized command against Mithridates. Marius, however, gets a law pushed through giving himself the command. Sulla enters Rome with his army and after bitter street fighting, Marius flees and is declared an outlaw.

87 Sulla defeats Mithridates' general Archelaus at a battle near Chaeronea in Boeotia. In Rome Cinna, the consul left behind by Sulla, a patrician turned democrat, stirs up trouble and after a riot is forced to leave Rome. He joins forces with an ageing and vindictive Marius. The two return to Rome, name themselves consuls and institute a massacre of patricians, a five-day reign of terror. After only 18 days of his last consulship Marius dies of pleurisy.

Science, Technology, and Discovery
The Chinese record a comet, probably Halley's, which appears about every 75 years.

84 At a meeting near Troy, Sulla and Mithridates agree peace terms. Sulla hurries back to Rome where Cinna is ruling as a tyrant.

82 Sulla enters Rome as victor, and institutes his 'Proscription' lists – lists of enemies who are to be murdered and have their property confiscated.

81 **Politics, Government, Law, and Economy**
Cicero acting as an advocate in the Forum makes his first extant speech, *Pro Quinctio*.

80 The second wave of Belgae arrives in Britain during this period. They settle mostly in the southeast and for the first time in Britain the less well drained and still forested land is tackled and farmed with a plough that can turn the sod. They are probably responsible for the white horse on the Downs at Uffington.
The Shakas, having streamed through Parthia, enter the Indus valley through the Bolan Pass and found a dynasty in Gandhara.
Sertorius, sent to Spain by Cinna, is driven into Africa by Sulla's troops. He returns on the invitation of the Lusitanians and sets up an anti-Sullan regime with the enthusiastic support of the natives.

Politics, Government, Law, and Economy
In an effort to restore the Senate's authority, Sulla curbs the power of the tribunes and restricts the Assembly to the discussion only of what the Senate allows; he also regulates overseas commands with the *Lex Annalis*.

78 The consul Lepidus quarrels with his co-consul to the point of bloodshed. He collects a scratchy army, advances on Rome, is beaten and flees the country. The task of rounding up the rebels is entrusted to Pompey, although some escape to join Sertorius in Spain.

76 Pompey obtains the Spanish command but finds it difficult to come to grips with Sertorius and his men.

75 **Art, Sculpture, Fine Arts, and Architecture**
The *Laocoon* group, later to reach Nero's Palace, is sculptured in Rhodes about this time.

73 Spartacus, a gladiatoral trainer, takes up the cause of the badly treated agricultural slaves, and sets up bandit headquarters on the slopes of Vesuvius. Crassus, another of Sulla's former officers, is given six legions to suppress the revolt.

72 Sertorius is murdered by his lieutenant Perpenna and his regime crumbles.

Politics, Government, Law, and Economy
Crassus, a notoriously rich man, has made his money by clever speculation in the Roman property market, buying up the slum tenements or *insulae* at opportune moments.

71 Crassus drives the Spartacists into the tip of the peninsula, defeats them, and has 6,000 of them crucified along the Appian Way. Pompey defeats some remnants and the two argue over who has stamped out the rebellion. They are persuaded to settle their differences and stand for the consulate.

Pompey defeats some remnants of the Spartacists and falls out with Crassus over who has stamped out the rebellion. They are persuaded to settle their differences and stand for the consulate.

70 Pompey and Crassus become consuls and repeal Sulla's laws.

Politics, Government, Law, and Economy
Cicero makes his name by his prosecution of Caius Verres for misgovernment of Sicily, but reaches the height of his career in 63/62 BC with his exposure and denunciation of the Catiline conspiracy.

68 **Literature**
The extant correspondence of Cicero begins.

67 Pompey clears the Mediterranean of pirates, who have again become a menace, rapidly and efficiently. Crete is taken over by Rome.

66 A bill is passed, with the support of Cicero and Caesar, giving Pompey pro-consular command in the East, with powers of declaring war. Pompey sets out on a 4-year career of conquest and settlement in the East.

65 Tigranes and Mithridates are defeated by Pompey who spends some time working out his 'Eastern settlement' to thoroughly pacify the area.

64 Pompey arrives at Antioch and dictates terms: Antiochus XIII is deposed and the Seleucid dynasty ends.

63 In Rome, while Cicero is consul he exposes the Catiline conspiracy to obtain power by a *coup d'état*. Catiline, who was disqualified from becoming consul in 66 BC after being convicted of bribery, flees Rome but is defeated in battle in January the following year.

Society, Education, and Religion
Julius Caesar is elected Pontifex Maximus or High Priest of Rome. The post carries little political benefit, but some financial benefit and, certainly with the people, some religious kudos. During his term of office, Clodius (or Claudius) Pulcher, a profligate nobleman, sneaks into the mystic female rites of Bona Dea dressed as a woman. This ceremony is conducted by Caesar's second wife Pompeia and he is forced to divorce her.

61 Pompey, having returned from the East and laid down his army, is snubbed by the Senate, who refuse to ratify his political settlements in the East or his land settlements in favour of his disbanded soldiers.

60 Caesar returns from a successful campaign in Spain but is refused a Triumph by the Senate. Caesar, Pompey, and Crassus form the First Triumvirate, a political alliance to acquire and divide power by mutual cooperation.

Society, Education, and Religion
Druidism is flourishing in Britain and Gaul during this period and Mithraism is beginning to permeate the Roman legions, spreading from Persia via Asia Minor.
The Jewish sect of the Essenes probably begins to flourish in this decade.

Literature
Catullus' *Love Poems to Lesbia*.

59 Caesar's year as consul, on behalf of the triumvirate. He passes various legal reforms and in return for forcing the Senate to sanction Pompey's eastern settlement receives help from Pompey in getting his coveted command in Gaul.

Politics, Government, Law, and Economy

Caesar, as Consul, introduces his Agrarian Laws, which would resettle Pompey's veterans at the expense of aristocratic land-owners, and has them ratified by the popular Assembly. His *Leges Juliae* clamp down on bribery, corruption, and immorality generally.

58 Caesar begins his campaign to subdue the Celtic tribes of Gaul. Ariovistus, with a Teutonic army said to be 120,000 strong and stationed between the Vosges and the Rhine, is defeated in a battle near modern Colmar.

Clodius has Cicero banished, although he is reprieved and recalled in the following year.

Humanities and Scholarship

Lucretius publishes *De Rerum Natura*, on the doctrines of Epicurus.

55 Caesar defeats the Teutons on the Meuse with a terrific massacre, for which he is criticized in the Senate.

Caesar sails for Britain with two legions. He is content to do no more than show his superiority in arms, but is received with popular acclaim in Rome.

54 Cassivellaunus, Chieftain of the Catuvellauni, crosses the Thames to meet Caesar and is repulsed. He is defeated again in his stronghold near modern Wheathampstead and sues for peace. Caesar, having shown his strength, returns to Gaul.

53 **June: —**, Crassus rashly penetrates into the Mesopotamian desert. He is killed and his army utterly defeated at the battle of Carrhae by the Parthians under their Arsacian king Orodes.

52 The Gauls unite in revolt under Vercingetorix but are defeated at the battle and siege of Alesia, Caesar's greatest military success in Gaul.

In a rapidly deteriorating situation of mob warfare in Rome, Clodius is killed by the tribune Milo, leading a rival gang, and Pompey is made sole Consul in an effort to restore order.

Humanities and Scholarship

Caesar's *De Bella Gallico* is probably written about this time.

50 Caesar is declared an enemy of the people by the Senate after arguments over the consulship he was promised at the end of his Gallic command (without which he faces prosecution) and the demand that he should disband his army.

The Kalingas throw up a militant king Kharavela, who lays claim on land from the Deccau to Burma. Indian culture also penetrates into Cambodia about this time.

Science, Technology, and Discovery

The water mill, a mill-wheel driven by water-power, seems to have been invented about this time.

Humanities and Scholarship

(–44 BC) Caesar's only other extant publication, *The Civil War*, is written during this period.

49 Caesar pacifies Italy with clemency, gains control of Sicily, and defeats Pompey's forces in Spain.

Jan: —, Caesar, accompanied by Mark Antony, crosses the River Rubicon and hence onto Roman soil without giving up his army – an act of war. The civil war has begun.

48 Caesar is elected Consul again. He follows Pompey to Greece, loses the battle of Dyrrhacium but defeats Pompey at Pharsalus in August. Brutus and Cassius are pardoned, as is also Cicero, despite having fought on Pompey's side. Pompey flees to Egypt where he is assassinated.

Humanities and Scholarship

(–44 BC) Cicero writes De Natura Deorum and De Divinatione which include unfavourable criticism of astrology. He perishes in the triumvirate's proscriptions of 43 BC after criticizing Mark Antony.

47 Caesar settles affairs in Egypt, restoring Cleopatra to her throne, and defeating her brother, Ptolemy XII. He then marches rapidly through Syria and Asia Minor and defeats Pharnaces, King of Pontus, at the battle of Zela where he famously boasts 'Veni, vidi, vici!'.

46 Caesar overwhelmingly defeats the Pompeian forces at the battle of Thapsus in Carthaginia.

Caesar returns to Rome and is made Dictator and Consul for 10 years, as well as Censor. He declares an amnesty for those who have borne arms against him.

Everyday Life

Caesar introduces the Julian Calendar; the year is made into one of 365 days with an extra day every fourth year and the months are lengthened to fit.

44 Octavian, Caesar's grand-nephew, (born 63 BC) returns to Rome from Illyria, learns of his adoption into the *Gens Julia*, and claims the right to succeed his adoptive father, Caesar. Rivalry over the succession breaks out between him and Mark Antony, as well as other minor contenders. There is frantic jostling for power by anyone with a power-base and troops to command.

March: 15th, A conspiracy of 60 senators, led by Cassius and Marcus Brutus, reaches fruition and Julius Caesar is assassinated.

43 Mark Antony is besieged in Mutina and defeated by Octavius. A reconciliation is achieved and the Second Triumvirate is formed by Lepidus, Octavian, and Mark Antony to divide power between them. Octavian becomes consul.

42 At the battle of Philippi, Octavian and Mark Antony defeat Cassius and Brutus, who both kill themselves.

Humanities and Scholarship
Sallust writes the *Jugurthan War* and the *Catalinarian War*. Cicero leaves behind many famous writings, including *De Oratore*, *De Republica*, *De Legibus*, *De Officiis*, *De Senectute*, *De Amicitia*, *De Finibus* (an enquiry into the chief good), and *Tusculan Disputations*; his other works include his *Orations* and his *Letters*, covering some 26 years, to Atticus, his family, and others.

41 The Triumvirate divide the Roman world between them: Africa goes to Lepidus; the East to Mark Antony; and the West (including the vital home front) to Octavian. War breaks out sporadically in Italy between Octavian and Mark Antony's forces.

40 **Oct: —**, The Pact of Brundisium is arranged by Octavian's friend Maecenas, reconciling the Triumvirate and slightly rearranging their territories and command of troops.

Literature
Virgil's *Eclogues*.

39 The Treaty of Misenum is signed between Mark Antony, Octavian, and Sextus Pompeius, Pompey's surviving son, who has held possession of Sicily with a powerful fleet since Caesar's death and has constantly interrupted Rome's vital corn supply.

36 **Politics, Government, Law, and Economy**
Octavian cements his power: in 36 BC he is granted the traditional tribunician rights of sacrosanctity; in 32 BC he makes his adherents and troops swear and oath of personal loyalty; in 31 BC he is granted the first of nine successive consulships.

34 **Society, Education, and Religion**
(–33 BC) Octavian, endeavouring to rekindle pride in the old Roman religion, repairs many of Rome's ancient temples and creates new patrician families to recruit to the priesthood.

33 Mark Antony lapses into the life of an eastern potentate with Cleopatra, his wife since 37 BC. They claim that Cleopatra's son Caesarion is also Caesar's and so the rightful heir to the Roman Empire.

32 The two consuls and some senators defect to Mark Antony, and Octavian formally declares war on him.

31 **Oct: —**, Octavian's fleet, under Agrippa, defeats Antony and Cleopatra at the battle of Actium; they flee back to Alexandria.

Literature
Virgil's *Georgics* completed.

30 Mark Antony and Cleopatra commit suicide.

Literature
During this period, what has been regarded as the 'Golden Age' of Latin literature takes hold. Maecenas is patron of many Roman writers, in particular Horace and Virgil, and the elegiac poet Propertius. Livy is writing his *History of Rome* and Dionysius of Halicarnassus begins his *Roman Antiquities*.
Tibullus' *Elegies*.

29 Octavian returns to Rome and begins his political reformation. He receives a triple triumph and is hailed by the Senate and people as their saviour.

28 **Politics, Government, Law, and Economy**
Octavian purges the Senate, brings its numbers back to 600, and in theory though not in practice restores it to its republican power.

27 Octavian is given the title *Augustus*. He visits Gaul and then Spain, leaving his right hand man Agrippa in charge at Rome.

Politics, Government, Law, and Economy

The Senate, in gratitude, bestow on Octavian the name of *Augustus*. Augustus remains *Imperator* (later to become our term 'Emperor'), that is to say head of the Army, and invents for himself the new title of *Princeps* ('leader'). He prefers to use his *auctoritas* as an elder statesman and ex-consul rather than any formal power of office, although this authority gradually hardens into imperial power. The Senate also give him the powers of a tribune, probably by a *Lex de Imperio*, and provincial *imperium* for 10 years. Octavian begins to create a civil service for both domestic and foreign affairs and to regularize the taxation of the provinces, each new province being subjected to a census to assess its tax potential.

Art, Sculpture, Fine Arts, and Architecture

Agrippa builds the first Pantheon in Rome. Augustus' beautification of Rome, by the building of temples, theatres, public baths, monuments, etc. gathers pace.

Literature

At the instigation of Augustus, who wishes the Romans to become more conscious of their noble heritage, Virgil begins his *Aeneid*.

25 The doors of the temple of Janus are closed for the first time since 235 BC, signifying that peace reigns.

23 Augustus falls ill. He meets discontent by attempting to make concessions to republican sentiment but thanks to senatorial sycophancy ends up with enhanced powers. In the following year, he refuses dictatorial powers and the consulship for life.

Society, Education, and Religion

The later deification of emperors is foreshadowed by the cult reluctantly permitted by Augustus of *Augustus et Roma*.

Literature

First three books of Horace's *Odes* are published.

20 Augustus recovers from the Parthians the Roman standards lost at the battle of Carrhae and those prisoners still alive – a diplomatic triumph.

18 **Politics, Government, Law, and Economy**

A *Lex Julia* encourages procreation within the family, in an attempt to reinvigorate the aristocracy which has been thinning out.

17 A second son, Lucius, is born to Julia and Agrippa, three years after Gaius; Augustus, with an eye on the succession, adopts his two grandsons, giving them the title Caesar.

Society, Education, and Religion

The Secular Games are celebrated in Rome to mark the inception of a new and better age. The Sibylline books are re-copied and all the old religious customs are observed.

Music

Horace's 'Carmen Saeculare' is sung at the Secular Games by a choir of traditional size, 27 boys and 27 girls.

16 Tiberius is made praetor and Drusus quaestor, and their period of responsible and successful military command begins. Augustus leaves Rome again to quell trouble on the northern frontiers.

13 **Literature**

Book IV of Horace's *Odes*, celebrating the military fame of Tiberius and Drusus, is completed.

12 Tiberius successfully continues the Danubian war after Agrippa's death, while Drusus, warring against the German tribes, advances to the Elbe.

Science, Technology, and Discovery

The comet later to be called Halley's probably appears about this time.

9 Drusus successfully draws his German campaigns towards completion but in the same year dies from a fall from his horse. He and his brother Tiberius are at last allowed the military title of *Imperator* by Augustus.

8 **Politics, Government, Law, and Economy**

Augustus' *imperium* is renewed and another census taken.

Art, Sculpture, Fine Arts, and Architecture
The aqueduct at Nemausus (Nímes) built.

6 Tiberius, having successfully completed Drusus' German campaign and held the consulship the previous year, is finally made a colleague of the ageing Augustus with the grant of tribunician powers. However, he feels that Gaius and Lucius Caesar are being favoured over him and retires to Rhodes for seven years.

Science, Technology, and Discovery
First draft of Strabo's *Geography* is completed.

4 Most probable date for the birth of Jesus Christ.
Herod massacres Pharisees who have attempted to pull down the Roman eagle from the Temple and may also have instituted the Biblical 'massacre of the innocents'. He dies in March.

2 Augustus is made *Pater Patriae*; he forms the Praetorian Guard, the imperial bodyguard within the city of Rome. Minimum service is for 12 years.
Augustus' daughter Julia, left behind by Tiberius soon after his enforced marriage to her and his retirement to Rhodes, is accused of misconduct with many men (including Mark Antony's son), and is banished.

1 **Literature**
Ovid's *Ars Amatoria.*

AD:

1 Beginning of the Christian Era (AD 1, *anno domini* – a system first used by Dionysius Exiguus in AD 527).
Phraates V and the young Gaius Caesar meet on an island in the Euphrates and Rome recognizes Parthia as a power of some standing while Parthia renounces the right to interfere in Armenia.

Literature
Ovid's *Metamorphoses.*

3 Tiberius, out of favour for absenting himself to Rhodes, is allowed to return to Rome.

4 Gaius Caesar dies of his wounds in February. Augustus, with all his hoped-for successors dead except Tiberius, officially adopts Tiberius as his heir, and makes him do the same for Germanicus, son of his dead brother Drusus.

5 **Politics, Government, Law, and Economy**
The legionary's term of service is lengthened from 16 to 20 years and that of a praetorian guardsman from 12 to 16. A legionary receives 10 *asses* (5/8ths of a denarius) a day and a gratuity of 3000 denarii; a praetorian guard receives 2 denarii a day and a gratuity of 5000 denarii.

8 **Society, Education, and Religion**
Probable date of the visit of Mary and Joseph to Jerusalem, and of the young Jesus to the temple.

Everyday Life
The Julian calendar settles down to accuracy.

9 In a bad year all round for Augustus he is forced to banish his grand-daughter, Julia, for immorality.
During the summer the German petty leader Arminius (Hermann) massacres three Roman legions (17th, 18th, and 19th).

13 **Art, Sculpture, Fine Arts, and Architecture**
The Portland vase (probably made in Greece for a Roman) dates from about this decade.

14 Augustus dies aged 75 and is succeeded by the 55-year old Tiberius.
Germanicus campaigns in Germany, with doubtful success. He visits the scene of Varus' disaster but fails to subdue Arminius.

Society, Education, and Religion
After his death, Augustus is deified and granted a temple and priests.

17 **Science, Technology, and Discovery**
The physicians of Rome found a meeting place in Rome, a *Schola medicorum.*

Everyday Life
There is an earthquake in Asia Minor and Ephesus suffers particularly.

18 Germanicus is given special powers over all the governors of the eastern provinces and installs Artaxias on the throne of Armenia. Peace reigns there until his death in AD 34. Tiberius appoints Cn. Piso Governor of Syria as a counterbalance to Germanicus.

19 Germanicus falls foul of Piso, whom he apparently orders home. At Antioch he dies of some kind of fever, convinced that Piso has had him poisoned. Piso is investigated by the Senate the following year but commits suicide before a verdict is reached: Tiberius is suspected of some form of cover-up.

21 Tiberius begins to groom his son Drusus junior for office, making him joint consul and granting him tribunician powers the following year.

23 Drusus junior is poisoned – almost certainly by Sejanus, commander of the Praetorian guard.

24 China, under the Han Dynasty, suffers a recession around this time. Wang Mang usurps the throne but is assassinated. As well as a joint drought and famine, there is an invasion of Mongolian barbarians from the north. The capital city is shifted east and the less successful second (Eastern) Han Dynasty begins.

27 John the Baptist is imprisoned and executed by Herod Antipas, Tetrarch of Galilee (son of Herod the Great), afraid of rebellion. Jesus Christ begins his mission.

Tiberius retires to Capri where Sejanus saves his life from a rockfall. More popular than ever with the Emperor, Sejanus governs Rome with a reign of terror.

30 **April: —**, Most probable date for the death of Jesus Christ.

Society, Education, and Religion

(3rd April) On the 14th day of the Jewish month of Nisan, almost certainly in this year, Christ eats the Passover supper with his disciples in Jerusalem where he is betrayed by Judas Iscariot and taken to the house of Caiaphas, the High Priest. The next day he is taken before Pontius Pilate and is crucified.

Science, Technology, and Discovery

Aurelius Celsus' *De Artibus*, covers agriculture, war, oratory, law, philosophy, and medicine. Only the treatise on medicine is still extant: it shows very considerable medical and surgical knowledge.

Art, Sculpture, Fine Arts, and Architecture

The art of glass blowing comes to Rome from Sidon or Alexandria and reaches great artistic heights.

33 **Society, Education, and Religion**

Saul of Tarsus, on his way to Damascus to persecute the followers of Christ, is converted to Christianity and is later known as St. Paul.

In Jerusalem, Stephen is brought before the Sanhedrin, convicted of blasphemy and subversive teaching and stoned to death – he is the first Christian martyr.

36 The Samaritans complain of Pontius Pilate's severity and he is replaced and ordered to return to Rome. He is believed to have been banished and to have ended his days at Vienne on the Rhone.

37 Tiberius dies and is succeeded as emperor by Caius Caesar, son of Germanicus and Agrippina – known as Caligula (or 'Little Boot'), his pet name with his father's soldiers as a child. He is 25.

39 Caligula advances with an army to the Rhine, diverts it to the coast to invade Britain, but then cancels his orders.

40 Tiberius is finally convinced of the treasonable intentions of Sejanus and has him executed. He returns to Rome briefly and then retires to Capri.

Politics, Government, Law, and Economy

Caligula exhausts the Roman treasury by his extravagance.

Society, Education, and Religion

Philo Judaeus of Alexandria's writings, seeking to reconcile the Jewish Scriptures and Platonic philosophy, are to have a great influence on the Christian Church. The conception of the *Logos* (the 'word'), or the wisdom of the power of God, is owed to him.

41 **Jan: —**, Caligula is murdered by soldiers of the Praetorian Guard and his uncle Claudius (nephew of Tiberius and brother of Germanicus) is made emperor in his place.

43 The Romans invade Britain with four legions under Aulus Plautius. They land unopposed and defeat Caractacus and his army decisively on the Medway. Claudius visits briefly, receives the submission of many tribes at Colchester, and returns to Rome. Plautius spends the next four years consolidating the Roman grip on the South and East.

44 **Society, Education, and Religion**

Herod Agrippa has James the Apostle killed and Peter put in prison. Herod dies in the same year, 'eaten by worms' according to the Bible (Acts 12).

45 **Society, Education, and Religion**
(–AD 47) Paul sets out on the first of his missionary journeys.

48 Claudius has his third wife, the nymphomaniac Messalina, put to death for infidelity and plotting against him. He marries Caligula's sister Agrippina who persuades him to adopt her son Nero and set aside his own son Britannicus.

49 **Politics, Government, Law, and Economy**
The Romans begin to exploit the Mendip lead mines.

Humanities and Scholarship
Seneca returns to Rome to become the tutor of the young Nero.

50 **Politics, Government, Law, and Economy**
The town of Colonia Agrippinensis (later Cologne) is founded to help control the Rhine frontier.

51 **Society, Education, and Religion**
(–60) Paul travels extensively again, preaching and writing to fledgling Christian communities across the Middle East. He is arrested by the Romans, as much to save him from irate Jews as for any crime, and is kept under house arrest for two years. He appears before Festus and Agrippa and his request to be sent to Rome for trial is granted.

Humanities and Scholarship
During this decade Seneca writes his series of books *De Beneficiis* (*On Clemency*, *On Anger*, etc.).

54 Agrippina has her husband Claudius poisoned and her son Nero made emperor in his stead.

57 A Japanese chieftain sends an envoy to the Chinese court.

Politics, Government, Law, and Economy
Rome's central administration appears to remain efficient while Nero commits his excesses: the governors of both Cilicia and Asia are recalled on the grounds of misgovernment.

60 Suetonius Paulinus, the new governor of Britain, begins his campaign in Wales. The king of the Iceni leaves his kingdom jointly to his widow Boudicca and Rome. The Romans interpret this will very much in their own favour, sparking rebellion.

Politics, Government, Law, and Economy
Roman trade with both North and South India is extensive by this time, not only native goods such as muslin but also goods from farther East, such as turquoise from Afghanistan, silk along the Silk Route, spices from the East Indies, etc.

61 Suetonius Paulinus reaches the Menai Straits, crosses them, and massacres the druid hordes on the shores of Anglesey. Meanwhile, Boudicca and the Iceni revolt: there are massacres of Romans and Romano-Britons at Colchester, Verulamium, and London. Paulinus returns and defeats the rebels at a battle somewhere in the Midlands.

Society, Education, and Religion
The Roman conquest of Anglesey brings an end to Druidism in Britain. On crossing the Menai Straits the legionaries are faced with women in ceremonial dress mingled with the warriors and druid priests standing by the fires of human sacrifice.

64 Rome suffers a great fire, which Nero is said to have watched, reciting lines on the destruction of Troy. There is no evidence that he caused it but he is suspected, and he blames the Christians. He does much to relieve the suffering of those who have lost homes or loved ones in the devastation.

Society, Education, and Religion
Nero blames the great outbreak of fire in Rome on the Christians and has many tortured and killed, including Peter, first Bishop of Rome.

65 **Society, Education, and Religion**
(–AD 67) The Chinese emperor sends envoys to India to study Buddhism; Buddhist missionaries begin to visit China.

Art, Sculpture, Fine Arts, and Architecture
After the great fire, Nero starts to build a less congested, nobler, and more handsome Rome. He also starts to build his vast and extravagant Golden House.

Literature
The young poet Lucan is implicated in a plot against Nero and is forced to commit suicide, as is his uncle, Seneca. Lucan leaves an epic poem, *De Bello Civili*, sometimes known as the *Pharsalia*. Seneca leaves his *Letters*, ten tragedies, and many works on philosophy and ethics.

66 Revolt breaks out in Judaea against Florus, probably the worst of the procurators since Pontius Pilate. The following year Vespasian is despatched to restore order.

67 The experienced soldier Vespasian (who has been touring Greece with Nero) is sent to bring order to Judaea.

Humanities and Scholarship

(–AD 70) Josephus in his *Jewish War* tells of the horrors and degradations, on both sides, of the sieges of Jotapata and Jerusalem.

68 (–AD 69) 'The Year of the Four Emperors'. Following Nero's assassination, there is anarchy in Rome, with four emperors claiming the throne in thirteen months. Vespasian finally establishes himself as emperor and leaves the Jewish war to his son Titus. He is the first of the Flavian dynasty of emperors – the *Flavia Gens*.

June: —, A revolt by the legions in Gaul and Spain is followed by one on the part of the Praetorian Guard in the city itself. Nero flees from Rome, but on being surrounded commits suicide.

Politics, Government, Law, and Economy

(–AD 69) Galba, backed by the legions in Spain and Gaul, wins the throne but becomes unpopular because of his austerity and anti-bribery measures. He is assassinated by the Praetorian Guards who then set up their own puppet Otho. The armies of the frontiers then intervene, and the race for power is between Vitellius of the armies of the Rhine and Vespasian of the armies of the East. Vitellius makes a spectacular crossing of the Alps and establishes himself as emperor for a few months. In July 69 Vespasian is declared Emperor at Alexandria and then goes to Rome where he defeats Vitellius and firmly establishes himself as the first of the Flavian emperors.

70 After a siege lasting 139 days, Jerusalem is taken but largely destroyed.

Society, Education, and Religion

The Jewish dispersal or *diaspora* begins with the sack of Jerusalem. The oral laws of Moses are added to the Pentateuch to form the *Torah* which will in future bind Jews together.

Probable date for the writing of *The Revelations of St. John the Divine* (almost certainly not John the Apostle).

71 **Society, Education, and Religion**

The Gospel according to St Luke is probably written in this decade. It is thought that both Luke and Matthew draw on Mark, and that all four gospels are written between AD 65 and 100.

73 **April:** —, The Herodian fortress of Masada, occupied by the Jewish Zealots, is finally taken by the Romans under Titus after a two year siege – the last of the garrison commit suicide

Society, Education, and Religion

The Romans destroy the community at Qumran near the Dead Sea; the inhabitants leave behind the so-called *Dead Sea Scrolls* hidden in nearby caves.

75 **Art, Sculpture, Fine Arts, and Architecture**

The magnificent Romano-British palace at Fishbourne near Chichester is being built at about this time: it must have been for the Romanized Briton King Cogidubnus.

77 In NW India, Kanishka (either of Yueh-Chi or Shaka origin) founds the Kushan kingdom of Kashmir. He favours Buddhist missionary efforts.

Humanities and Scholarship

The *Historia Naturalis* of Pliny the Elder appears.

79 Vespasian dies and is succeeded as Emperor by his son Titus.

Aug: —, Vesuvius erupts and Herculaneum, Pompeii, and Stabiae are overwhelmed; there is also a fire in Rome. Titus does what he can to repair the damage.

Literature

The Mime or *Pantomime*, besides the chariot race and the gladiatorial show, has supplanted the drama in Rome.

80 **Art, Sculpture, Fine Arts, and Architecture**

The Colosseum, begun by Vespasian, is finished by Titus. It seats 87,000 spectators.

Literature

Martial grows to fame under Titus and continues so under Domitian. He is read, he claims, even by the Goths.

81 Emperor Titus dies: his brother Domitian succeeds him and is suspected of hastening his end.

82 **Art, Sculpture, Fine Arts, and Architecture**
(–AD 90) After its fires Rome has its temple of Jupiter, Juno, and Minerva restored at great expense, along with the Pantheon and the public libraries.

83 Agricola wins the set battle of Mons Graupius and considers that he has conquered Scotland.

86 The Dacians, possibly an Aryan people from Thrace, now living between the Danube and the Carpathians, cross the Danube under their king Decebalus.

88 The Roman governor of Upper Germany, A. Saturninus, persuades two legions at Mainz to declare him emperor, but the revolt is suppressed.

89 **Humanities and Scholarship**
Domitian has astrologers and philosophers expelled from Rome.

91 **Society, Education, and Religion**
The Epistles of the apostle John are written about this time.

Science, Technology, and Discovery
At about this time the Chinese invent a rudimentary compass.

96 The Senate have all statues of Domitian destroyed and appoint one of their own members as Emperor, M. Cocceius Nerva.

98 Nerva dies and is succeeded as Emperor by Trajan.

Humanities and Scholarship
Tacitus' *Germania* and his *Life of Agricola* are written about this time.

100 **Humanities and Scholarship**
About this time Plutarch returns to his native Chaeronea, where he holds various magisterial offices and concentrates on writing his parallel *Lives* of Greeks and Romans.

101 King Decebalus has revived and is implacably anti-Roman. Trajan invades Dacia and, after a difficult campaign, forces Decebalus to surrender.

Politics, Government, Law, and Economy
Trajan proves himself a careful and hardworking administrator. Agriculture is encouraged throughout Italy, 5% state mortgages being given for buying farming land. Family allowances are instituted and in Rome poor children receive the corn dole as well as their parents.

Art, Sculpture, Fine Arts, and Architecture
Christians begin to bury their dead in the catacombs outside Rome: the frescoes on the walls mark the beginning of distinctive Christian art.

104 (–106) Decebalus revolts again, and Trajan invades Dacia again, with 10 legions. After a difficult and hard-fought campaign, Decebalus and his chiefs commit mass suicide.

105 **Science, Technology, and Discovery**
Ts'ai Lun invents a better and lighter writing material than silk and bamboo; it is made of rags and fish-net, bark and hemp – the first paper.

108 **Society, Education, and Religion**
Ignatius, Bishop of Antioch since AD 69, is summoned to Rome and martyred for refusing to abjure his faith.

109 **Literature**
Juvenal's *Satires*, written about this time, still serve as a devastating indictment of the worse side of Roman society.
The *Library* of Greek mythology, attributed to Apollodorus of Athens of the 2nd century BC, is probably actually written during this century.

112 **Art, Sculpture, Fine Arts, and Architecture**
Trajan gives Rome another larger and more magnificent forum. Trajan's column inside the forum shows the Emperor's victorious campaigns.

114 (–116) Trajan mounts a campaign of spectacular conquest. He takes Ctesiphon, the Parthian capital and reaches the Persian Gulf.

116 **Science, Technology, and Discovery**

Soranus, a physician of Ephesus practising at Alexandria, publishes his work on gynaecology. He suggests methods of contraception and recommends abortion where delivery would endanger the mother's life.

117 Revolt breaks out behind Trajan in many parts of the Empire – even the newly subdued King Chrosroes revolts. There is also trouble along the African coast, and in northern Britain.

The revolts are suppressed but Trajan suffers a stroke and dies on the way back to Rome. Hadrian succeeds to the throne.

118 Hadrian reaches Rome. He halts his predecessor's expansionist policy: like Augustus he accepts the Euphrates as the Roman frontier. This policy is not popular with his generals, nor does he achieve popularity at home, in spite of liberal gestures.

(–120) There are serious revolts in Britain, with the 9th (Hispana) Legion, stationed at Lincoln, totally disappearing from the records.

Humanities and Scholarship

Suetonius becomes private secretary to Hadrian, but loses his job due to the hostility of Hadrian's wife, Sabina, and retires to write his *Histories of the Caesars*.

Quintilian dies – his chief work is a system of rhetoric, *Institutiones Oratoriae*.

120 **Humanities and Scholarship**

Tacitus dies, leaving behind his chief works – the *Historiae*, covering the period AD 68 to 96; and his *Annales*, covering the period from the death of Augustus to the death of Nero.

121 Hadrian, having improved government administration at home, spends the decade in a series of businesslike and beneficial tours of the Roman Empire. He improves the lot, and the discipline, of the legionaries.

Politics, Government, Law, and Economy

Before setting out on his travels, Hadrian builds a more efficient machine of government, with a *concilium* of business men, jurists, and senators to consider policy, and a better bureaucracy to put policy into practice.

125 The Chinese general Pan Yong, son of Pan Chao, temporarily reconquers the Tarim basin from the Huns.

127 **Politics, Government, Law, and Economy**

Hadrian's Wall is virtually completed in Britain. It is 73 miles long and interspersed with forts: if well-manned it will be almost impregnable.

128 **Politics, Government, Law, and Economy**

Hadrian orders a codification of the laws of Athens.

Art, Sculpture, Fine Arts, and Architecture

Hadrian builds a library, a gymnasium, an aqueduct, and temples to Hera and Zeus in Athens and completes the *Olympieum* (temple to Zeus) started by Pisistratus.

131 **Politics, Government, Law, and Economy**

Hadrian orders a codification of the Roman law which has grown enormously over-complicated, with a vast amount of judgement law added to the original Twelve Tables of the ancient city.

132 (–135) Simeon Bar-Cochba, who has declared himself Messiah, leads the Jews in revolt. They have some success initially, but are finally destroyed after holding out for two years. This is the final destruction of the Jews as a nation in Judaea: they are even forbidden to enter Jerusalem, renamed Aelia Capitolina.

Science, Technology, and Discovery

In China, Zhang Heng develops the first seismograph for indicating the position of an earthquake centre.

138 Hadrian adopts Titus Aurelius Antoninus (aged 52) as his son and heir, and at the same time instructs Antoninus to adopt two young men, Marcus Aurelius and Lucius Verus. He dies in July and Antoninus succeeds him.

139 **Science, Technology, and Discovery**

Claudius Ptolemaeus (Ptolemy), born in Egypt, is making astronomical observations in Alexandria and does so for at least another 12 years. His greatest works are the *Syntaxis* (known to the medieval world as the *Almagest*) and his *Geographia*.

140 **Humanities and Scholarship**
Appian writes his *Histories* of Rome and its wars.

141 **Society, Education, and Religion**
Probable date for the *Apologies* of Justin of Samaria, who, having come to Rome, addresses these tracts to the Emperor in defence of the Christians as good citizens.

148 900th anniversary of the founding of Rome.

149 **Literature**
Lucius Apuleius is believed to be in Rome in this year, lecturing on philosophy. His fame rests on his fantastic 'novel', *The Golden Ass*.

152 (–153) The Egyptian peasants revolt but are put down. Rome's corn supply is cut and widespread unrest breaks out. Antoninus makes a distribution from his own funds – as he does on eight other occasions during his reign.

154 The Brigantes in the north of England revolt. Reinforcements have to be brought from Germany to quell the uprising.

156 **Society, Education, and Religion**
In Phrygia, Montanus denounces the worldliness of the Christian Church and pronounces himself to be the *Paraclete* bringing the promised Kingdom of Heaven upon Earth.

160 **Politics, Government, Law, and Economy**
Antoninus has established an outstandingly humanitarian rule, both at home and in the provinces. He punishes the harsh masters of slaves and instructs his governors and client kings similarly to punish any resort to violence.

161 **March: —**, Marcus Aurelius succeeds Antoninus and has Lucius Verus made his full colleague. This sets a precedent for later divisions of the imperial *maiestas*.

162 Rome cannot easily remain at peace with barbarians on the Empire's borders: the Britons and the German Chatti revolt, while the Parthian king, Vologeses III, declares war and invades Armenia.

Society, Education, and Religion
The Christians develop their *agapē* or Feast of Love, a forerunner of the Mass. At the same time the Mithraic mysteries increase in popularity both in Rome and among the legionaries, including those stationed in London and on Hadrian's Wall.

Science, Technology, and Discovery
(–164) Galen is at Rome during these years and attends both emperors as physician.

Humanities and Scholarship
Although he models himself as a philosopher-king, Aurelius is a conservative one: he tells himself 'never to hope to realize Plato's Republic'.

165 **Literature**
Lucian, satirist and wit, settles in Athens and writes his *Dialogues*.

167 (–170) Plague – probably bubonic – is brought back by Roman troops from the East. Asia Minor, Greece, Gaul, and Egypt are affected as well as Italy.
The second wave of the northern barbarians rises in the shape of the Marcomanni, the Quadi, and the Vandals. They pose a serious threat and Aurelius has to recruit from all classes of the population and bring in help from other barbarian tribes.

173 China suffers from the plague as has Rome earlier: it lasts for eleven years.

Humanities and Scholarship
Pausanias, probably a Lydian, writes his famous guide book of Greece, *Periegesis*.

174 Aurelius comes back to Rome from fighting the third Marcomannian war but then returns to the war front. He is successfully subduing the barbarians and extending the Empire's boundaries to the Carpathians.

Humanities and Scholarship
While campaigning, Marcus Aurelius composes his philosophical and disillusioned work, *Meditations*.

175 Cassius suppresses a rebellion in Egypt and declares himself emperor. Aurelius, asserting that he will gladly yield to Cassius if the soldiers wish it, advances eastwards to meet him but Cassius is killed by one of his own centurions. Aurelius is forced to abandon any plan of absorbing the German tribes and makes peace.

178 (–180) Aurelius, believing that Rome will only be safe with her frontiers extended to the Carpathians, renews the Third Marcomannian War.

180 Having reached as far as Vindobona (Vienna), Marcus Aurelius dies; his son Commodus ends the war.

181 In this decade of Commodus' reign there is virtually no trouble from the barbarians of the north whom Aurelius had fought. Commodus is more interested in dissipation than running the Empire.

183 Lucilla, sister of the Emperor, plots his assassination, She is executed, along with most of the important men of the day. Informers reappear in Rome.

184 Ulpius Marcellus is sent to Britain to drive the Highland tribes back over the Antonine wall and restore discipline in the army. However he is recalled by Commodus, possibly because his discipline is too harsh.

The Han dynasty, continuously weakened by the misrule of eunuch ministers, suffers from a popular rising known as the rebellion of the Yellow Turbans. China is now sinking into division and anarchy.

185 Helvius Pertinax is sent to restore order among the legionaries in Britain; they cease to be mutinous but hint Pertinax should usurp Commodus. The Antonine wall is dismantled.

189 **Society, Education, and Religion**

Rabbi Jehuda writes down the old laws of Moses which are known as the *Mishna.*

190 Hsien-Ti, the last of the Han emperors, ascends the Chinese throne though still a young boy – he is little more than a puppet.

192 In China a usurper assumes power, imprisoning the boy-emperor. The court eunuchs are destroyed and the 400-year rule of the Han Dynasty is now virtually at an end.

Commodus is poisoned by one of his concubines and the head of the Praetorian Guard.

193 Pertinax returns to Rome from Britain at the start of the year and is chosen Emperor. However, he earns the displeasure of the soldiers for instituting much-needed economies and reforms and is murdered. The Praetorian Guard put the throne up to the highest bidder. The rich Didius Julianus wins but lasts only two months.

Septimius Severus, in command in Pannonia, arrives in Rome and is declared Emperor. One of his first acts is to reorganize and tame the Praetorian Guard.

Art, Sculpture, Fine Arts, and Architecture

The Column of Marcus Aurelius is completed. Sometimes called the Antonine column, it stands in Rome's Piazza Colonna and is now topped by a statue of St Paul.

197 **Society, Education, and Religion**

Tertullian writes his *Apology*, assuring the Romans that Christians are good citizens.

198 Caracalla is made Augustus and Severus' other son Geta is made Caesar.

200 The Japanese warrior empress, Jingu, invades and subdues part of Korea.

201 By the time of the reign of Septimius Severus, the Goths have founded an empire on the northern shores of the Black Sea and around the Danube Delta.

Politics, Government, Law, and Economy

Severus raises the Roman Army to a position of paramount importance, at the expense of the Senate, the aristocracy, and civilians generally. From this time, urban life throughout the empire decays as the centre of gravity has been transferred from the town to the camp. There is a general economic decline during this century, with trade falling off, high taxation, and the currency being debased after Septimius increases the alloy in the denarius to 50%.

203 Plautianus, head of the Praetorian Guard, is made one of the consuls for the year. He has great influence over the Emperor.

Society, Education, and Religion

Among the Christian martyrs at Carthage is Perpetua, who in her *Passion* gives an account of her last days in prison.

Art, Sculpture, Fine Arts, and Architecture

The arch of Septimius Severus, overlooking the Forum of Rome and commemorating his victories in the East, is dedicated.

205 Caracalla and Geta, Severus' sons, are made consuls for the year. Caracalla accuses Plautianus of a plot against the Emperor and he is murdered by a court attendant.

208 (–210) Severus campaigns in northern Britain. Hadrian's Wall has now been repaired, and he plans to subdue the land to the north of it, ravaging it so severely that a second wall will not be necessary.

211 **Feb: —**, Septimius Severus dies at York. His sons, bequeathed the Empire jointly, end the war forthwith and return to Rome.

Politics, Government, Law, and Economy

Severus' final advice to his sons – 'Enrich the Army!' – embodies his philosophy of rule, that the need for a strong army is paramount.

212 Caracalla inherits the oriental cruelty of his father but none of his statesmanship and has his brother Geta and many of his supporters murdered.

Art, Sculpture, Fine Arts, and Architecture

In Rome the magnificent baths of Caracalla are begun. They are completed four years later.

213 (–214 BC) Caracalla expels some German marauders from Gaul, and gives himself the title of Germanicus. He then claims a victory over the *Alemanni* ('All Men').

217 While campaigning in Parthia, Caracalla is assassinated by his legionaries. Macrinus, head of the Praetorian Guard, declares himself Emperor. Peace is made with Parthia.

218 The fate of Rome continues to be decided in the East. Julia Maesa, sister of Julia Domna, declares her grandson Elagabalus emperor. Macrinus advances westwards to meet Julia Maesa, who fights in person, defeats him, and has him executed.

Society, Education, and Religion

Calixtus, the 16th Pope (217–222) is declared unfit by a priest called Hippolytus, who sets up a rival Church.

221 Julia Maesa is unable to control Elagabalus' excesses and so begins training her other grandson Alexander Severus to become emperor. He is declared Caesar and Elagabalus and his mother try to enlist the Praetorian Guard against him but are themselves killed by the Praetorians early next year.

The puppet Chinese Emperor Hsien Ti is finally deposed. This is the end of the Han Dynasty and it is followed by a 45-year period of treachery and violence known as the period of the Three Kingdoms.

222 Alexander Severus becomes Emperor, having responded to a philosophic and severe training as successfully as had Marcus Aurelius.

Politics, Government, Law, and Economy

Alexander Severus curbs the power of the Army and endeavours to restore the power of the Senate and the aristocracy. He reduces taxes, lends money at 4%, encourages traders' and workers' associations, and censors public morals. He is advised by the jurist Ulpian.

Society, Education, and Religion

During the reign of Alexander Severus all persecution of Christians ceases.

224 The kingdom of Parthia comes to an end. Ardashir, King of Persis, defeats Artabanus IV, the last of the Parthian Arsacid Dynasty.

226 Ardashir has himself crowned 'King of Kings' and founds a new Persian dynasty, the Sassanid.

Society, Education, and Religion

Ardashir forms a strong national Church and produces a new edition of the *Avesta*, the Holy Writ of the god Mazda.

229 **Humanities and Scholarship**

Dio Cassius is made consul and then retires to finish his great *History of Rome*.

233 (–235) Severus' troops mutiny while he deals with incursions from the Alemanni and Marcomanni and declare their Thracian commander Maximinus as Emperor. Rome enters another anarchic period during which power rests with the legionaries and no less than 37 men are declared Emperor within 35 years.

235 **Society, Education, and Religion**

Hippolytus, the first 'Antipope', is excommunicated.

238 Gordian accepts the Emperorship jointly with his son. They are defeated by Maximinus who is killed by his soldiers. The Praetorian Guard make a third Gordian, son of Gordian II and grandson of Gordian I, their emperor.

239 **Humanities and Scholarship**
Philostratus of Lemnos writes his *Lives of the Sophists.*

240 The worst danger that Rome has so far experienced: enemies active on several fronts at the same time. Africa revolts, and tribes in NW Germany, under the name of the Franks, combine into a warlike federation.

241 Shapur I ascends the Persian throne and continues his father's policy of expansion.

Society, Education, and Religion
At the coronation of Shapur I of Persia, a young mystic of Ctesiphon, Mani, proclaims himself a messiah. His teaching, known as Manichaeism, borrows from Zoroastrianism, Judaism, Mithraism, and Gnosticism and divides the world into the rival realms of Light and Darkness.

244 While campaigning in Persia, Gordian III is murdered and replaced by his army commander Philip who makes peace with Persia and returns to Rome as its first Arab Emperor.

Humanities and Scholarship
Plotinus arrives in Rome and for the next 10 years teaches his neo-Platonist philosophy of hunger for reabsorption into the One. He leads a saintly and abstemious life.

247 Rome celebrates the thousandth year of its existence. From this time until the death of the Emperor Gallienus in 269 a time of confusion reigns which historians have found difficult to record accurately.

248 **Society, Education, and Religion**
Origen answers Celsus' *True Word* with his *Contra Celsum.*

249 Discontented at having an Arab as Emperor, the legionaries in several provinces revolt. Philip's general, Decius, sent to pacify the legionaries, turns on Philip and becomes Emperor.

250 **Society, Education, and Religion**
Decius begins persecuting the Christians anew as scapegoats for all public ills and suffering. The motive is more political than religious, an attempt to achieve national unity and divert attention from public ills.

Science, Technology, and Discovery
Diophantus of Alexandria writes his *Arithmetica*, a treatise on algebra which owes something to Chaldean mathematics.

Literature
Heliodorus of Emesa writes his *Aethiopica* or *Egyptian Tales*, the first novel of romantic adventure.

251 Decius is defeated and killed by the Goths in a battle in Moesia (north of Thrace). Trebonianus Gallus is elected emperor by the troops.

Science, Technology, and Discovery
In China, mica is first used for windows in this period.

252 **Society, Education, and Religion**
Cyprian holds a council of bishops at Carthage, which urges stricter control over the Church and the universal acceptance of Rome as the head of the Church. He writes his plea for Church unity: *De Catholicae Ecclesia Unitate.*

253 Aemilianus supplants Gallus and is then himself replaced by Valerian of the Rhine legions.

254 The empire is threatened simultaneously by the Franks, Alemanni, and Marcomanni, by the Persians, and by the Goths. Valerian makes his son Gallienus ruler of the West and himself of the East of the empire.

258 In Gaul the Roman general Postumus assumes the titles of ruler of Gaul and of Emperor. He declines a personal duel with Gallienus and holds his title for a decade – even if it is only recognized by his soldiers, who eventually kill him in 268.

Politics, Government, Law, and Economy
Gallienus makes the Roman army more flexible and mobile. In particular he improves and increases the cavalry arm, which has so far always been weak. He also improves the catapult and ballista.

260 Valerian is captured while campaigning against Shapur I of Persia and ends his days a captive: he is said to have suffered the indignity of being used by the Persian king as his mounting block. Gallienus becomes Emperor.

261 (–263) King Shapur of Persia is unexpectedly halted and driven back by Odenathus, Rome's vassal king of Palmyra. Odenathus declares himself king of the area west of the Euphrates and in 263 is declared 'Dux Orientalis' by Rome.

(–263) Revolts break out throughout the Empire, and Gallienus has difficulty retaining his throne.

Politics, Government, Law, and Economy

Archaeological evidence indicates Britain's towns are suffering economic decline in the last half of the 3rd century.

263 **Society, Education, and Religion**

Longinus, who has taught Porphyrius at Athens, goes to Palmyra where he becomes the adviser and teacher of Queen Zenobia, widow of Odenathus.

265 For the next 50 years China's northern kingdom of Wei exerts some suzerainty over the other kingdoms as the Tsin Dynasty.

Science, Technology, and Discovery

Pei Hsin, geographer, produces a large map of China in 18 sections.

268 (–270) Gallienus is killed by his soldiers. Claudius II, an Illyrian of obscure origin, becomes emperor and saves the Empire from the Goths; his major victory is a battle at Naissus.

270 Claudius succumbs to plague and Aurelian, another Illyrian, becomes Emperor. He wins a further battle over the Goths and then makes peace with them. Aurelian relinquishes Dacia to the Goths and transferrs the name to a province south of the Danube.

271 Zenobia declares herself Queen of the East and sends her eldest son to invade Egypt.

Politics, Government, Law, and Economy

(–275) Aurelian persuades the Senate to finance the building of new walls round Rome. Fortifying walls are being built around cities throughout the Empire during this period, reflecting the upheavals of the time.

Aurelian moves toward a regimented State, beginning the regulation of the trade corporations and the direction of labour. He also acts to stabilize the currency which is suffering from inflation.

272 Aurelian sends his commander, Probus, to restore Roman rule in Egypt, and himself advances on Queen Zenobia's capital, Palmyra which he takes after a difficult campaign.

274 Postumus has been succeeded as 'Emperor of Gaul' by Tetricus who Aurelian easily defeats. Rome greets Aurelian as 'Restitutor Orbis' and accords him a magnificent Triumph.

275 **Society, Education, and Religion**

St Antony (born in upper Egypt) retires to a solitary life in the desert and is thus considered to have inaugurated monasticism.

St Denis converts Paris to Christianity.

276 Tacitus becomes emperor after Aurelian is murdered by his officers. He dies after only six months and is succeeded by Probus.

277 (–279) Probus continues Aurelian's forcible pacification of the Empire, expelling Franks, Goths, and Vandals and quelling trouble in Britain, Egypt, and Illyria.

282 The Army grows more and more discontented with Probus as a result of his crackdown on discipline. His soldiers mutiny and kill him. Carus, said to be a scholar as well as a soldier, is elected emperor.

283 (–285) Carus dies in mysterious circumstances near Ctesiphon. One of his sons, Numerianus, is murdered in the East and the other, Carinus, fights for the throne with Diocletian, the army's choice, who defeats and kills him.

285 **Politics, Government, Law, and Economy**

Diocletian transfers his capital from Rome to Nicomedia near Byzantium, as a more strategic base from which to defend the empire. Similarly, Maximian chooses Milan.

286 Diocletian makes Maximian his joint ruler with responsibility for the West, reviving the practice of splitting command of the Empire between East and West.

290 Carausius, a self-proclaimed emperor who has established himself in Britain, is acknowledged by Maximian and Diocletian as a third Augustus.

291 **Humanities and Scholarship**

The *Historia Augusta* is probably begun about this time, and continues to be written until some time in the reign of Constantine. It covers the reigns of the emperors from Hadrian to Carus and is reputedly written by six different authors.

293 The empire is to be ruled jointly by two Augusti (for the East and West respectively), each of whom is to have a Caesar to help him. The Caesar chosen by Diocletian is Galerius and Maximian chooses Constantius Chlorus.

Politics, Government, Law, and Economy

The 'Quattuor Principes Mundi' have genuine power: all laws and edicts are to be issued in the names of all four rulers and are to be equally valid; no sanction from the Senate is required. Diocletian introduces economic reforms. A vast bureaucracy and a system of what is essentially state socialism and managed economy is set up. The coinage is successfully tied to gold, most production is nationalized, and the freedom of the individual to change his job is further restricted.

296 Constantius invades Britain, defeats and slays Allectus, and is greeted at the gates of London with the title *Redditor Lucis Aeternae*. He rebuilds at York, London, and Verulamium, fortifies the 'Saxon Shore' (the Wash to the Isle of Wight), and does much to restore prosperity to Britain.

In Persia the first strong king since Shapur I comes to the throne, Narses.

Society, Education, and Religion

Marcellinus becomes the 29th Bishop of Rome or Pope.

298 Galerius redeems his humiliation of the previous year by winning a complete victory over King Narses of Persia, who cedes Mesopotamia and five provinces beyond the Tigris to Rome.

301 **Politics, Government, Law, and Economy**

Diocletian finances law schools and has post-Trajanic legislation codified in the *Codex Gregorianus*.

Everyday Life

In southern China the habit of tea drinking begins, probably learnt from Tibet.

303 **Society, Education, and Religion**

(Feb) The four rulers meet and agree to a decree that the Christians' churches shall be destroyed, their books burnt, their property confiscated, and their congregations dissolved.

304 In north China the Huns under the Chinese-educated Liu Yüan decide to connect themselves with China's past and form a 'Hun Han' dynasty.

305 Diocletian abdicates and forces Maximian to do the same. They are succeeded as Augusti by Constantius and Galerius.

Art, Sculpture, Fine Arts, and Architecture

Tetrach statues are carved, e.g., the group built into the corner of San Marco, Venice.

306 **Art, Sculpture, Fine Arts, and Architecture**

Maxentius starts to build an immense *basilica* in Rome; it marks the climax of classical architecture in the West.

309 Shapur II, sometimes called the Great and grandson of Shapur I, ascends the Sassanid throne as an infant following internal wars.

310 Maximian is captured by Constantine and commits suicide. Galerius begins to suffer from a fatal illness.

312 Constantine defeats Maxentius at the battle of the Milvian (or Mulvian) Bridge; this may be called Rome's first battle of the Christian religion.

Politics, Government, Law, and Economy

The Roman gold coinage is further stabilized; the *solidus* is set at a value of 72 to a pound of gold.

Society, Education, and Religion

Before the battle of the Milvian Bridge, Constantine is said to have seen a vision in the sky of the Christian cross.

313 Constantine meets Licinius in Milan. They issue a joint edict and agree to cooperate.

Constantine defeats Licinius in Pannonia and exacts surrender of all Roman Europe except Thrace.

Society, Education, and Religion

The Edict of Milan confirms the official toleration of Christianity announced by the dying Galerius, and extends it to all religions. Helena, mother of Constantine, becomes a Christian about this time or possibly earlier.

316 The Tsin Dynasty abandons all northern China to the competing Hunnish kings.

320 In the Magadha area of India (the Ganges plain) the first of the Gupta dynasty, Chandra Gupta, establishes a powerful kingdom.

323 In two battles, near Adrianople and Chrysopolis (Scutari), Constantine defeats Licinius.

325 **Society, Education, and Religion**

Constantine, afraid that Christianity is losing its central unity, summons a univeral or ecumenical council at Nicea in Bithynia to consider the Arian heresy. Athanasius opposes the heresy, insisting on the consubstantiality of Christ with God. Finally the Nicean Creed is formulated stating that Christ is 'of one substance' with the Father. Only Arius and two other bishops refuse to sign: they are anathematized and exiled by Constantine.

Science, Technology, and Discovery

The Mayans seem obsessed with the significance of time and its calculation; their arithmetic is based on a duodecimal system and involves the relatively advanced concept of zero.

328 **Literature**

A Mayan stela at Uaxactun makes it seem likely that Mayan hieroglyphics have already existed for some time. The characters are ideograms rather than pictograms and most, though not all, can now be read.

330 The culture of the Amer-Indian Mayas ends its 'Formative' and to have begun its 'Classic' Period which lasts about 600 years.

Constantine makes Nova Roma, or Constantinople, his new, Christian, capital. This effectively brings the long history of Rome as the centre of the world to an end.

Society, Education, and Religion

St Nicholas, Bishop of Myra in Lycia (and patron saint of Russia) is active around this time.

335 Constantine, hoping to effect a peaceful transition of power at his death, apportions responsibilities among his sons and nephews: there are six young Caesars.

In India Samudra Gupta, the second and greatest of his dynasty, comes to the throne.

336 **Society, Education, and Religion**

Arius is readmitted into the Church but dies later in the same year. Arianism spreads in the East.

Art, Sculpture, Fine Arts, and Architecture

Constantine patronizes the arts in his last peaceful years. He endows the schools of Athens and encourages his governors to establish provincial schools of architecture. The first churches of St. Peter and of St. Paul Without the Walls are built.

337 (–338) The Army rejects the authority of all the dead emperor's intended heirs except his sons.

May: —, In the thirtieth year of his reign, having at last been baptized as a Christian, Constantine dies.

Humanities and Scholarship

Eusebius writes a *Life* of Constantine.

338 The three surviving sons – Constantine, Constantius, and Constans – meet in Pannonia and try to compose their differences.

341 During this decade Samudra Gupta extends his kingdom or his influence over most of India.

Society, Education, and Religion

Athanasius, deposed from the bishopric of Alexandria, comes to Rome and introduces the monastic system into Europe.

Literature

Ulfilas translates the Bible into Gothic (which is not a literary language) and composes an alphabet based on Greek for the purpose. This is the only extant example of this Gothic language.

342 The Picts and Scots combine for the first time and pose a threat to Wales and western England. Constans crosses the Channel and makes peace with them, probably allowing them to settle in Roman Britain.

346 **Society, Education, and Religion**
A meeting of bishops at Milan declares its adherence to the Nicean creed: the split between the Eastern and Western churches is beginning to develop.

348 War is renewed between Constantius and Shapur.

349 (–350) Constans is extremely unpopular; a Gaul Magnus Magnentius usurps the throne and Constans flees to Spain where he is assassinated.
(–350) Constantius has to abandon dealing with Shapur II to sort out the trouble in the West.

350 **Humanities and Scholarship**
Julian is sent by a jealous Constantius to Nicomedia, where he studies under pagan philosophers.

351 Gallus (see 345) is made a Caesar and Governor at Antioch, while his younger brother Julian is allowed to wander in search of teachers of philosophy.
In this quarter-century the Roman empire of the West is saved by a series of efficient emperors from repeated attacks of Germanic 'barbarians' who are no longer really barbarous. However, pressure, as yet unfelt by the Romans themselves, is growing from the Huns.

Art, Sculpture, Fine Arts, and Architecture
During the reign of the Gupta kings in India, Buddhist art reaches a high standard, as in the frescoes of the Ajanta caves of Hyderabad.

352 (–353) Constantius, at the battle of Mursa, overthrows the pretender to the empire in the West, Magnentius, and becomes undisputed sole emperor.

355 The Huns begin their great drive westward with an advance into Russia. They overcome and absorb the Alans.
Julian is given Constantius' sister in marriage and made Caesar and governor of Gaul.

360 In Paris Julian's troops declare him Emperor and refuse to go East to the aid of Constantius struggling against Shapur II.

361 On the way to confront Julian, Constantius dies. Julian takes over the combined emperorship of East and West and rules from Constantinople. He declares himself a pagan and makes a final attempt at hellenizing the Empire.

Literature
Julian, both as Caesar and as Emperor, collects books and himself writes many books and pamphlets.

363 Julian invades Persia and is mortally wounded in a skirmish. Jovian, Captain of the Guard, succeeds him but only lives for seven months.

364 The soldier Valentinian is elected Emperor. He retains the West and makes his younger brother Valens emperor of the East.

369 The Japanese invade Korea and establish a small colony and base.

372 The Huns, under Balamir, cross the Volga and defeat the Ostrogoths in the Ukraine.

375 Valentinian dies suddenly, while negotiating with the Quadi. His son Gratian succeeds him as Emperor of the West.

376 (–379) The Visigoths north of the Danube, defeated by the Huns, are allowed to settle in Roman territory but revolt and overrun Thrace. Valens, Emperor of the East, meets them near Hadrianople, and is defeated and killed, leaving Constantinople itself in danger from the Goths.
Theodosius succeeds as Emperor of the East in response to an appeal from Gratian.

379 **Society, Education, and Religion**
Buddhism is declared the state religion of China.

382 **Society, Education, and Religion**
Jerome begins his translation of the Old Testament into Latin, the *Vulgate* version.

383 Gratian has relapsed into a weak and inefficient ruler and Magnus Maximus, the Spanish commander left behind by Theodosius the elder in Britain, claims the throne of the Western empire. He defeats Gratian near Paris and becomes master of Gaul and Spain – in Britain Hadrian's Wall is overrun and falls into ruin. Valentinian II succeeds his half-brother Gratian as Emperor of the West.

387 Magnus Maximus invades Italy. Valentinian II flees with his mother and sister to Thessalonica where Theodosius meets him and marries the sister.

388 Maximus is defeated and killed by Theodosius.
Chandra Gupta II begins a war against the Shakas, which finally gives him control of NW India. He calls himself *Vikramaditya* ('Sun of Prowess').

390 **Society, Education, and Religion**
Ambrose, bishop of Milan, demonstrates the power of the Church by refusing to administer Mass to the Emperor until he enters the cathedral as a penitent. Theodosius, after hesitation, complies.

Music
Ambrose inaugurates a custom of singing hymns and psalms 'in the oriental manner': i.e., antiphonal singing.

Sport and Recreation
After a popular charioteer is imprisoned for gross immorality in Thessalonica the mob tear the governor to pieces; Theodosius massacres 7,000 of the population in revenge.

392 Valentinian II is assassinated while advancing into Gaul against a Frankish usurper, Arbogast who appoints a weakling, Eugenius, as Emperor of the West.
Theodosius defeats Arbogast and Eugenius near Aquileia, at the battle of the river Frigidus and becomes sole Emperor of both East and West for the next three years.

Society, Education, and Religion
St Augustine becomes bishop of Hippo and holds this office, while writing and teaching, until his death.

395 Shortly before his death, Theodosius appoints his 11-year-old son Honorius Emperor of the West and his 18-year-old son Arcadius Emperor of the East.

396 Stilicho, a Vandal-born Roman, controls Honorius and becomes virtual ruler of the West. The Goths under Alaric sweep through Greece. Stilicho advances, makes peace with the Goths, and allows them to settle in Epirus.

400 **Science, Technology, and Discovery**
Zosymus of Panopolis describes semi-mystical experiments which show that some genuine chemical enquiry is being made. The first use of the still (Greek *ambix*, Arabic *alembic*) probably occurs about this time, although it is only fully developed by the Arabs some 500 years later.

Literature
Sanskrit is becoming established as the literary language of India and the Hindu epics are written down in it.

401 By the beginning of this century the Slavs are moving south and begin to appear in Western history.
Alaric invades Italy in a wave of destruction which sends flights of refugees before him.

Society, Education, and Religion
Augustine writes his autobiography, *Confessions*.

402 Honorius bribes Alaric to leave Italy.

403 Honorius deserts Milan for Ravenna, which he makes the Western capital.

405 A barbarian called Radagaisus collects an army of Ostragoths, Vandals, and others with which he invades Italy. Stilicho saves Florence from his horde and brings him in chains to Honorius.

Politics, Government, Law, and Economy
The Chinese traveller Fa-Hsien reports on the prosperity and social liberty that India is enjoying under the Guptas.

406 Vandals and other barbarians overrun much of Gaul, almost reaching the Channel.

409 The Vandals and their allies pour into Spain and plunder her rich cities.

410 Alaric takes Rome after besieging the city intermittently throughout 409. He continues south to conquer Sicily, but dies of a fever on the way.

411 Honorius tells the Britons that they must look to their own defences, finally abandoning the Romans' claims to the island.

Society, Education, and Religion
The Donatists, always prone to violence and fanatical self-immolation, form a sect called the *Circumcelliones* ('Prowlers'), essentially a robber band. Honorius convenes a council to curb the Donatists.

412 (–414) Alaric's brother-in-law Ataulf (Adolphus) marries Honorius' half-sister Placidia and sets up a Visigoth kingdom in Gaul, theoretically subject to the Empire.

413 **Society, Education, and Religion**
(–426) Augustine writes his *City of God*; he seeks to show that the fall of Rome is not due to the Christians.

415 Ataulf is assassinated and Wallia becomes king of the Visigoths.

423 Honorius, Emperor of the West, dies, and there is a struggle for the throne.

425 The usurper John is defeated and the young Valentinian III becomes Emperor of the West.

Society, Education, and Religion
A university is founded at Constantinople, concentrating on Latin and Greek rhetoric.

Science, Technology, and Discovery
Flavius Vegetius, a pioneer of veterinary science, writes a book on the medical treatment of mules.

426 The Franks are spreading throughout the Netherlands in this period. King Chlodio is succeeded (date uncertain) by Merovech ('Son of the Sea') who gives rise to many legends and gives his name to the Merovingian Dynasty.

428 **Society, Education, and Religion**
Nestorius argues with Cyril of Alexandria over the nature of Christ and the Mother of God.

430 The Vandals are helped by the local Moors and the Donatists in their successful invasion of Africa. They besiege and take Hippo, Augustine dying during the siege.

431 **Society, Education, and Religion**
Nestorius is excommunicated by the Council of Ephesus.

Science, Technology, and Discovery
Persecuted Nestorians are welcomed in Persia for their medical and astronomical knowledge: they build an observatory with royal encouragement.

432 **Society, Education, and Religion**
St Patrick is made a bishop at Auxerre, and then goes to convert the Irish to Christianity.

433 For the first years of his reign Attila consolidates his power in his Hungarian capital, probably on the site of Buda. Both Emperors, Theodosius II in the East and Valentinian III in the West, bribe him to keep the peace.

438 **Politics, Government, Law, and Economy**
The *Codex Theodosianus* divides the Eastern and Western Empires administratively and provides the barbarian inheritors of Rome with a code of laws.

439 (–450) Genseric breaks the peace with the Romans and seizes Carthage, which he despoils with much cruelty but then builds it up to prosperity again.

446 The Britons, suffering attacks from the Picts, Scots, and Saxons, send an appeal for help to Aëtius. The Saxons begin to arrive in numbers to settle.

447 The Huns enter Thrace, Thessaly, and Scythia, sacking towns with great cruelty as they go, but are bought off and they turn to the Western Empire.

449 King Vortigern invites the Saxons under their leaders Hengist and Horsa to settle in Kent in order to help him against the Picts and Scots.

Society, Education, and Religion
Another council at Ephesus finds in favour of the 'Monophysite' heresy, which states that Christ's human and divine natures are one but this decision is overturned two years later at the Council of Chalcedon.

450 Theodosius II is succeeded as Emperor of the East by Marcian who refuses to continue the tribute to Attila. Valentinian III of the West follows his example.

Art, Sculpture, Fine Arts, and Architecture

A Romano-Briton buries a treasure of plate at Mildenhall in Suffolk, including a dish decorated in classical style with gods and nymphs.

Literature

Musaeus writes his poem *Hero and Leander.*

451 Attila makes his grand attack on the Empire of the West. His army is reputedly half a million strong, including the Franks and Visigoths led by Wallia. He is defeated at the battle of the Catalaunian Fields (or Chalons, sometimes called the battle of Troyes) by Aëtius, and Wallia is killed.

During this period, Britain is falling apart into a patchwork of warring local chiefs, sometimes fighting each other, sometimes the Saxons.

In India, the Gupta kingdom falls to the White Huns at some time during this period: the last certain date for a Gupta king is 467.

Society, Education, and Religion

Persecuted Monophysites translate major Greek philosophical works into Syrian and greatly stimulate cultural and scientific advance in Persia.

At the Council of Chalcedon a long struggle for ecclesiastical supremacy between Constantinople and Alexandria ends in defeat for Alexandria.

452 Attila advances into Italy. Valentinian III flees from Ravenna to Rome and sends Pope Leo I to persuade Attila to return to his capital.

453 After a wedding feast, Attila is found dead in bed with a burst blood vessel. His empire is divided between his sons and the Hunnish threat to the West is ended.

455 Valentinian III is murdered and a puppet, Avitus, is put on the Western throne. Genseric the Vandal, seeing an opportunity, attacks and loots Rome.

Politics, Government, Law, and Economy

Much of northern Italy is devastated by this time: towns are walled, farms are abandoned, and the population has shrunk; it is estimated Rome has shrunk from about a million and a half citizens to a third of a million.

Society, Education, and Religion

(–461) St Patrick writes his *Confessions*, telling of his perils and difficulties in Ireland.

456 (–457) Rome goes through a period of chaos and changing rulers, with the Visigoth Ricimer the power behind the throne. Similarly, in the East Leo I is installed by Aspar the Alan.

468 **Society, Education, and Religion**

Sidonius, now in Rome as prefect of the city, describes its society life in cultured prose.

472 Ricimer captures Rome but dies soon after.

475 Theodoric the Great succeeds to the throne of the Ostrogoths.

476 More Germanic tribes invade Italy, and in Rome Romulus Augustulus resigns his throne to their general, Odoacer. Odoacer agrees to become King of Italy whilst Zeno of Constantinople becomes Emperor of the re-combined Roman empires of East and West. The last Emperor of Rome has fallen.

481 Clovis becomes king of the Franks at the age of 15.

482 **Society, Education, and Religion**

The Emperor Zeno causes a schism between the Churches of Rome and Constantinople with his *Henoticon* ('Union Scheme').

486 Clovis defeats a Roman army at Soissons and begins to extend his Frankish kingdom.

488 Theodoric the Great, with the Emperor Zeno's blessing, advances over the Alps to win back Italy from Odoacer.

489 Theodoric defeats Odoacer and takes Milan.

493 Theodoric invites Odoacer and his son to a peace treaty and feast at Ravenna, and assassinates them. He extends his realm to the western Balkans and to Sicily and settles down as a king with nominal subordination to Constantinople.

Politics, Government, Law, and Economy

Theodoric the Great observes Roman laws and institutions and is respectful to the Senate at Rome. He allots two-thirds of the land to the Romans and one-third to the Goths.

Society, Education, and Religion
Clovis, married to a Christian, is baptized.

499 **Society, Education, and Religion**
The Babylonian version of the Jewish *Talmud* is completed. The Palestinian version was probably completed a hundred years or more earlier.

The Dark Ages

500–999

500 At about this time 'Arturus, Dux Bellorum', the legendary King Arthur, takes up the struggle against the Saxons. In 12 battles he subdues the Saxons, the last battle being at Mons Badonicus (site unknown).

By the end of the 5th century AD, the Japanese have coalesced into one nation and culture.

Humanities and Scholarship

Böethius studies the Greek classics in Athens prior to making Latin translations of them.

501 **Politics, Government, Law, and Economy**

At the beginning of the 5th century Constantinople is using Egypt as a granary to the extent of some 175,000 tons of wheat a year.

During this period the Salic laws of the Franks are formulated, written according to tradition by 'four venerable chieftains'.

Sport and Recreation

There is widespread violence in Constantinople, caused by the enmity of the circus factions, the 'Greens' and the 'Blues', each backing their favourite chariot drivers. On this occasion 3,000 are said to have died.

502 (–506) The Emperor at Constantinople, Anastasius, having met trouble in both Egypt and Thrace, is at war again in Armenia with a revived Persia; after an inconclusive struggle a seven-year peace is signed.

507 (–510) Clovis defeats the Visigoth Alaric II at the battle of Vouglé, near Poitiers. He is made a Roman consul and patrician. Clovis ends the division between the Riparian and Salic Franks and moves his capital to Paris: Gaul has now become France.

511 Clovis dies and leaves his kingdom to his four sons who expand it.

516 **Science, Technology, and Discovery**

The Indian astronomer and mathematician, Aryabhata, writes in verse on eclipses, quadratic equations, and the value of π.

523 Theodoric, ageing and suspicious, hears of a senatorial conspiracy to depose him. Boethius is among three suspected ringleaders and is imprisoned and executed the next year.

Humanities and Scholarship

Boethius writes his *De Consolatione Philosophae* and the shorter *De Musica*.

526 In Constantinople, Justin gives Belisarius his first task – combatting the renewed aggression of Persia.

Society, Education, and Religion

Priscian, a professor at Constantinople University, compiles a Latin and Greek Grammar.

527 **Society, Education, and Religion**

The use of the chronological notation 'AD' is introduced by the monk Dionysius Exiguus.

528 The White Hun king Mihirakula (sometimes called the Atilla of India) is deposed and the Hunnish invasion of India, which never produces a kingdom, begins to lose its force.

Politics, Government, Law, and Economy

Justinian appoints a panel of ten jurists to systematize, reform, and clarify the law.

529 **Politics, Government, Law, and Economy**

The first *Codex Constitutionum* is issued.

Society, Education, and Religion

St Benedict ends his career as an anchorite, owing to the jealousy of local priests, and founds his monastery of Monte Cassino.

Humanities and Scholarship

Justinian finally closes the great Platonic Academy of Athens.

531 The greatest of the Sassanid kings, Chosroes or Khosru I, comes to the Persian throne; Belisarius is recalled.

Art, Sculpture, Fine Arts, and Architecture

(–537) The great church of St Sophia is rebuilt in Constantinople. A dome has by now become a favourite architectural feature.

533 (–534) Belisarius sets sail to win back Vandal Africa to the Empire. He takes Carthage but North Africa remains Byzantine until the Muslims come.

Politics, Government, Law, and Economy

The *Digesta* or *Pandecta* (of Case Law) is issued along with a handbook or guide to the Codex, the *Institutionis*.

535 Justinian, making himself safe from the Franks by an alliance, sets out to recover Italy from the Goths. Belisarius captures Sicily.

536 (–540) Belisarius captures Naples and enters Rome unopposed.

539 King Chosroes of Persia declares war on Justinian.

(–543) Chosroes raids Asia: Justinian buys him off and negotiates a five years' peace, extended for another five years.

540 **Humanities and Scholarship**

Cassiodorus writes a *History of the Goths*, which is extant only in the shape of an epitome.

543 (–546) Another Gothic king, Totila captures Rome but moves to Ravenna and Belisarius retakes Rome.

548 (–549) Belisarius is recalled and Totila recaptures most of Italy.

550 **Art, Sculpture, Fine Arts, and Architecture**

The Mayan 'classic' culture produces magnificent buildings at Tikal, some 190 miles north of Guatemala City.

551 Narses, the successor to Belisarius, defeats Totila and expels the Goths from Italy.

Literature

In the latter part of the 6th century the pre-Muslim Arabs, proud of their language, hold contests for their poets at the yearly Ukaz fair.

552 **Society, Education, and Religion**

Buddhism is introduced into Japan and gradually becomes the official religion.

553 **Politics, Government, Law, and Economy**

By the end of the Gothic war Italy is economically ruined. Rome's population has dwindled to about 40,000, with its aristocracy so depleted that the Senate peters out.

559 The Bulgars cross the Danube into modern Bulgaria and advance toward Constantinople. The city is saved by the aged Belisarius.

561 Chlotar I has amassed a large Frankish kingdom, which includes Burgundy, Provence, and Swabia. He divides it into Austrasia (the Rhineland), Neustria (western France), and Burgundy, and bequeaths a part to each of his three sons.

562 Chosroes and Justinian at last sign a 50-year peace agreement.

563 **Society, Education, and Religion**

St Columba flees from Ireland and founds a monastery on the Hebridean island of Iona.

565 **Science, Technology, and Discovery**

Alexander of Tralles, a physician, writes a medical textbook that is later translated into Latin and Arabic and has a lasting influence.

568 Up to 130,000 Lombards, pressed from behind by Avars, cross the Alps into the plains of the River Po and overrun northern Italy. Refugees flee, to join the earlier refugees from Aquileia and the city of Venice is founded.

Humanities and Scholarship
The statesman and historian Cassiodorus dies, leaving his history of the Goths, *De Rebus Geticis*.

570 **Society, Education, and Religion**
Mohammed is born in Mecca, a member of the Hashemite faction of the ruling merchant family, the Quraish.

576 **Science, Technology, and Discovery**
Toward the end of this century, Hindu mathematicians begin to use a number system with place notations and the symbol zero.

577 The Saxons win the battle of Deorham and become virtual masters of England. During this period, they form a heptarchy of kingdoms in South and East England: the Jutes in Kent; the Angles in Mercia, Northumbria, and East Anglia; and the Saxons in Essex, Sussex, and Wessex.

584 Chilperic, the Frankish king of Neustria, is murdered. Brunhilda, Sigebert's widow, is still in power in Austrasia.

589 China approaches unity again under the warlike Yang Chien of the short-lived Sui dynasty.

590 Bahram seizes the Persian throne, forcing the young Chosroes to flee to Syria where he seeks Roman protection. The Emperor Maurice establishes him firmly on the throne as Chosroes II and makes a favourable peace with him.

592 Shotoku (or Kotoku) becomes ruler of Buddhist Japan.
(–593) The Emperor Maurice turns against the Avars who are spreading over the Balkans under their king Baian. They are driven back across the Danube and the war continues for the rest of the century.

Politics, Government, Law, and Economy
Shotoku (sometimes called the Asoka of Japan) gives his country a written constitution and decrees based on Buddhist ethics.

594 **Humanities and Scholarship**
St Gregory of Tours dies, leaving behind his *History of the Franks*, the chief source of knowledge of the Merovingian kings.

597 **Society, Education, and Religion**
St Augustine is sent to Kent by Pope Gregory and becomes first bishop of Canterbury.

598 **Society, Education, and Religion**
Canterbury's first school is believed to have been founded about this time.

602 Maurice is forced to flee Constantinople after widespread unrest, appealing for aid from the young Persian king, Chosroes II. Phocas, a leader of the unrest, moves rapidly however and Maurice is murdered. Chosroes declares war.

604 **Art, Sculpture, Fine Arts, and Architecture**
Ethelbert builds the first church of St Paul in London.

Music
Pope Gregory systematizes and improves the Church's 'plainsong', which becomes known as the 'Gregorian Chant'.

Literature
Pope Gregory leaves behind 14 books of *Epistles* which are later known to Bede and Boniface.

606 In N India a king of the old Gupta line, Harsha, brings prosperity back during his reign of 40 years.

609 The Byzantines appeal for deliverance from Phocas to the military governor of Roman Africa, Heraclius. The governor sends his son, another Heraclius, who deposes Phocas the following year.

610 **Society, Education, and Religion**
Mohammed receives a vision in which Gabriel tells him he is the messenger of Allah.

614 Chosroes II declares holy war on the Christians and sacks Jerusalem, capturing the True Cross.
The Frankish Queen Mother, Brunhilda, is murdered and the young Chlotar II reigns over a reunited (Merovingian) Frankish kingdom.

616 (–619) Chosroes II conquers Egypt and Asia Minor, despoiling as he goes, weakening these lands before the imminent Arab invasions.

618 The Avars march up to the gates of Constantinople and take many prisoners as slaves; Heraclius is on the verge of transferring his capital to Carthage.
China, newly fertilized by Hunnish blood and Buddhist ideas, begins a new era of greatness under its T'ang Dynasty at the capital city of Ch'ang-an.

620 Heraclius makes peace with the Avars.

622 Mohammed's flight from Mecca to Medina precipitates a war between the two cities and the start of his career as a military leader.
(–625) Heraclius sets out on a brilliant campaign against the Persians, penetrating as far as Ispahan.

Society, Education, and Religion
Mohammed flees to Medina (by invitation) from Mecca – the *Hegira* – and establishes himself there as a religious and political leader. His faith becomes known as *Islam*, the 'surrender' to Allah, and his followers *Muslimin*, 'surrendering ones' or Muslims.

624 **Society, Education, and Religion**
Heraclius avenges the Persians' sack of Jerusalem by destroying the birthplace of Zoroaster.

626 Medina is unsuccessfully besieged by the Meccans and a truce is arranged.
In central India, the Pallava kings achieve temporary supremacy. Both here and in the north, after the demise of King Harsha, India is lapsing into a Dark Age in which the warlike princes of Rajputana will slowly rise to power.

628 Chosroes II is murdered by his son, and Heraclius makes an advantageous peace with the Persians. This is the end of the greatness of the Sassanid dynasty.
The Merovingian king Chlotar II dies and is succeeded by Dagobert. Power is passing into the hands of the Mayor of the Palace, Pepin the Elder, the first of the Pepins who are later to found the Carolingian dynasty.

Politics, Government, Law, and Economy
(–635) The Chinese Emperor T'ai Tsung codifies the law, reintroduces the examination system and reissues the Chinese classics, and greatly increases his country's trade and prosperity.

Society, Education, and Religion
In leading his exiled followers back to Mecca, Mohammed incorporates the ancient worship of the symbolic black stone, housed in the Kaaba, into his religion and makes Mecca into a holy city which no unbeliever may enter.

629 During this decade, the warrior Srong-tsan establishes himself in Tibet, annexes Nepal, and builds himself a capital at Lhasa. He reigns until about 650 and establishes the golden age of Tibet.

630 Mohammed breaks the truce with Mecca; he enters the city without opposition and makes it his capital.

632 Mohammed dies and his companion and disciple, Abu Bekr, is elected *Caliph* or 'Representative'. He responds to a request from the Arabs in Syria for help against Byzantine persecution and begins the era of Muslim conquest.

633 Edwin, who has called himself Bretwalda, or Overlord, of Britain, is defeated and killed at Hatfield Chase near Doncaster by the pagan king of Mercia, Penda, in alliance with the Welsh king, Cadwallon.

Society, Education, and Religion
Abu Bekr has Mohammed's revelations made into the *Koran*.

634 Abu Bekr's general Khalid defeats Heraclius at a decisive engagement on the Yarmuk River near Damascus. The Byzantine name for the Moslems, the 'Saracens', now comes into use.

638 Jerusalem is captured by the Moslems, now ruled by Omar.

639 **Society, Education, and Religion**
Srong-tsan, founding Lhasa, invites Buddhist monks from India and is said to have retired from government for 4 years in order to learn to read and write. Lhasa becomes the great stronghold of Buddhism, and the building of monasteries begins in Tibet.

640 The Saracens invade Egypt at the invitation of the Monophysite Copts.
Slav tribes enter Pannonia and Illyria to become the Serbs and Croats.

642 The Christian King Oswald of Northumbria is defeated and killed by the pagan king Penda of Mercia at the battle of Mansfield.

645 In Japan a palace revolution leads to the 'great reform'. Japan becomes a more closely knit state, with an autocratic monarchical government.
King Penda of Mercia conquers Wessex.

647 **Society, Education, and Religion**
With Syria, Palestine, and Egypt (all strongholds of various heresies) lost to the Byzantine Empire, the Eastern Church is free to become 'Orthodox' and the heretics free from persecution.

648 **Society, Education, and Religion**
The first church at Westminster is built.

650 By the end of the period, the conquering Saracen generals, under the Caliphate of Othman, have reached east to Kabul and north to the Black Sea.

Science, Technology, and Discovery
The Chinese probably invent the horse collar about this time, enabling the animal to pull from the shoulders without restricting its wind-pipe.

Literature
The Anglo-Saxon epic poem about the dragon-slaying hero Beowulf is written, presumably in England.

655 Penda of Mercia is defeated and killed at the battle of the river Winwaed, the final decline of paganism in England.

656 Egyptian fanatics penetrate to Othman's palace and murder him. Ali becomes Caliph.
Muawiya of the Umayyad clan revolts and Ali temporarily defeats him at the Battle of the Camels at Khoraiba in South Iraq.

660 **Art, Sculpture, Fine Arts, and Architecture**
The Sutton Hoo ship burial comprises much fine jewellery, mostly of Saxon origin and including a sceptre in the shape of a whetstone, but also a purse filled with gold coins coming from various mints in France, and a silver dish from Constantinople.

661 A fanatical sect, the *Khariji* or 'Seceders', breaks away from Ali, and finally murders him. Muawiya becomes Caliph, forming the Umayyad dynasty and making Damascus his capital.

Society, Education, and Religion
The Moslem *Shia* sect is formed on the death of Ali.

663 Constans II visits Rome, the first emperor to be in the capital for 190 years.

664 **Society, Education, and Religion**
King Oswy of Northumbria calls the Synod of Whitby which asserts the supremacy of the Roman Church in Britain.

669 **Literature**
The Northumbrian Benedict Biscop collects books from Rome and sets up a library at his monastery at Wearmouth and later at Jarrow.

673 The Saracens renew their naval attacks on Constantinople, which they make annually for five years.

Science, Technology, and Discovery
'Greek Fire', a mixture of naphtha, quicklime, sulphur, and pitch is used to great effect in the defence of Constantinople against the naval attacks of the Saracens.

676 **Music**
By the end of this century the Moslems are writing *mensurable* music; i.e. the notes show duration as well as pitch.

680 The Caliph Muawiya dies and a war of succession breaks out among the Saracens again.

Society, Education, and Religion
The Shia Moslems build a shrine at Kerbela where Husein has fallen.

683 On the death of Kao Tsung the Empress Wu openly assumes sovereignty in China.

687 Pepin le Gros defeats his rivals at the battle of Testry and becomes virtual ruler of all the Frankish empire (except Aquitaine).

688 (–690) The Emperor Justinian II takes Armenia from the Saracens and then makes another advantageous peace with them.

690 **Politics, Government, Law, and Economy**
Anglo-Saxon laws are still primitive, for example, in regarding murder a personal matter and deserving only of a fine: 'If one man slay another, 100 shillings wergeld.'

691 (–693) Justinian loses the battle of Sebastopol against the Saracens, partly owing to the defection of the Slavs, on whom he takes vengeance in a massacre.

Art, Sculpture, Fine Arts, and Architecture
Caliph Abd-el-Malik builds in Jerusalem: the 'Farther' Mosque and the Dome of the Rock (known later as the Mosque of Omar).

703 **Humanities and Scholarship**
Bede intensifies his great effort toward scholarship in his long, quiet career at Jarrow monastery as a writer and historian.

705 Walid I succeeds his father Abd-el-Malik as Caliph, continuing his efficient rule and extending the Saracen empire.

706 **Science, Technology, and Discovery**
A hospital, the Bimaristan, is founded in Damascus and it also becomes a medical school.

Art, Sculpture, Fine Arts, and Architecture
(–714) Under the Caliph Walid, the great mosque of Damascus is built.

711 **July: —**, The Moors invade Spain and at the battle of Lake Janda decisively defeat Roderick, the last Visigoth king of Spain.

712 Liutprand comes to the throne of Lombardy and begins to consolidate the loose-knit kingdom.

Humanities and Scholarship
The *Kojiki* or 'Record of Ancient Things', more legend than history, is published in Japan.

713 Hsuan Tsung comes to the T'ang throne of China.

Art, Sculpture, Fine Arts, and Architecture
Hsuan Tsung inaugurates a 'second blossoming' of T'ang culture. He encourages poets, artists, and scholars and establishes a college of music.

714 Pepin II dies, and in the next three years his illegitimate son Charles Martel makes himself undisputed ruler of the Frankish kingdom, uniting Neustria and Austrasia.

716 Ethelbald becomes king of Mercia. He increases its power and reigns for 41 years.

717 The Saracens make their last and greatest effort to take Constantinople. The city's walls and defenders both hold out through a winter's siege and the Saracens retire.

718 **Society, Education, and Religion**
After an initial unsuccessful attempt to evangelize the Germans and then a blessing from Pope Gregory II, St Boniface returns to try again.

720 **Humanities and Scholarship**
A more accurate history of Japan, the *Nihongi/Record of Nippon*, is published.

724 Hisham becomes Caliph. His reign sees the decline of the Umayyad dynasty and of Saracen aggression.

725 Charles Martel is busy holding back an attack from the Allemanni and Saxons. The Saracens take Autun, but Duke Eudo stops their further advance.

726 The Emperor Leo III issues his iconoclastic decree. It arouses much opposition and a rival emperor is even proclaimed in Greece but he, and his fleet, are defeated while attempting to capture Constantinople.

Society, Education, and Religion
Leo's iconoclastic decree requires the complete removal of icons from churches and church murals are to be covered, while all representations of Christ and the Virgin are forbidden. Pope Gregory II summons the Western bishops and anathematizes the Iconoclasts.

728 (–729) King Liutprand of the Lombards approaches too near to Rome in the extension of his kingdom, and is rebuked and checked by the Pope.

731 **Humanities and Scholarship**
Bede's *Ecclesiastical History* is completed.

732 The fanatical Saracen general Abd-er-Rahman is defeated by Eudo and Charles Martel at the battle of Tours (sometimes called the battle of Poitiers). The advance of the Saracens into Europe is halted.

737 Charles Martel takes Avignon from the Saracens.

738 The German barbarians feel the power of Charles Martel, who campaigns against them and exacts tribute.

740 **Literature**

Chinese poetry, shaking off all formalism, reaches its heights under the patronage of Hsuan Tsung: Li Po and Tu Fu are its great exponents.

741 Pepin the Short and Carloman succeed, in combination, to Charles Martel; Zacharias succeeds Gregory III as Pope; Walid II succeeds Hisham as Caliph; and Constantine V succeeds Leo III as Emperor.

742 **Science, Technology, and Discovery**

The most famous alchemist of the period, Gebir, also practises as a physician at Kufa.

743 **Art, Sculpture, Fine Arts, and Architecture**

Caliph Walid II builds a winter palace at Mshatta in the Syrian desert, providing fine examples of sculpture in the Muslim tradition, which forbids the making of 'idolatrous' statues.

744 Walid II is assassinated. The Umayyad caliphate is now sliding to its end.
Liutprand dies: Lombardy has reached its apogee.

748 **Media**

First printed newspaper appears, in China.

750 Abu-al-Abbas besieges and invests Damascus, massacres his opponents and becomes the founder of the dynasty of Abbasid caliphs.

Literature

The *Manyoshu*, an anthology of four centuries of Japanese poetry, is published.

751 Pepin the Short has himself made king of the Franks, in name as he has already been virtually since 750. The Pope appeals for help against the encroachment of King Aistulf of Lombardy.

Society, Education, and Religion

Java is taken over by a Buddhist dynasty of Sumatran origin and Buddhism becomes the official religion.

754 (–756) Pepin takes Ravenna from the Lombards and gives it – the so-called 'donation' – to the Pope. Pepin puts a client-king, Desiderius, on the Lombard throne: the independent Lombard kingdom is at an end.

757 Offa succeeds Ethelbald as king of Mercia, reigning for 39 years and bringing about the height of Mercian power. He is addressed by Popes as King of England without qualification.

762 The Caliph Mansur founds a new capital for himself at Baghdad. The effect of the foundation of Baghdad is profound: the Saracens change from military conquerors to liberal administrators.

763 **Humanities and Scholarship**

The *Life* of Mohammed (revised and enlarged from that of Ibu Ishaq) is issued by Ibu Hisham.

768 Pepin dies and divides his kingdom between his two sons, Charles (known to history as Charlemagne) and a second Carloman.

Society, Education, and Religion

Under Offa's patronage Alcuin teaches theology at York.

769 Charlemagne and Carloman quarrel. Constantine V's son, another Leo, marries Irene, later to become Empress and Regent.

771 Carloman dies, leaving Charlemagne, aged 29, sole king of the Frankish dominions.

773 (–774) The Lombard king Desiderius invades the Roman states and Pope Hadrian (or Adrian) I appeals to the Franks for help. Charlemagne besieges Desiderius in Pavia and banishes him to a monastery. Charlemagne takes the crown of Lombardy himself.

775 Caliph Mansur dies on a pilgrimage to Mecca and is succeeded by his more open-handed son, al Mahdi.

776 Charlemagne is successful against the Saxons, who, when defeated, face baptizm or death.

778 **Literature**
The story of the paladin Roland and of how he unavailingly blew his great horn is attributed to the contemporary Archbishop of Rheims, Turpin.

781 The Byzantine regent Irene abandons all claim to sovereignty over the Papal state.

782 (–784) Al Mahdi's son Prince Haroun defeats a Byzantine invasion of Asia Minor and gains the title *al Rashid* ('the Upright').

785 Charlemagne finally subdues the Saxons.
Science, Technology, and Discovery
King Offa builds his dyke, between the rivers Severn and Dee, to keep out the Welsh.

786 Al Hadi dies and is succeeded as Caliph by Haroun al-Rashid.
Literature
Haroun al Rashid records stories in his state archives – thus giving rise to the legend of Scheherezade and the *Thousand and One Nights* which is founded on an earlier Persian collection of tales.

787 The first recorded Viking raid on England occurs, somewhere on the Wessex coasts.

788 (–791) Charlemagne successfully campaigns against the Slavs and Avars.

790 **Science, Technology, and Discovery**
Haroun and the Barmakid family increase their patronage of the sciences, particularly medicine, astronomy, and chemistry, but also astrology and alchemy.
Literature
Cynewulf the Northumbrian writes his chief poem *Elene*, telling of Helena's discovery of the true cross.

792 Offa annexes East Anglia to his kingdom.

796 **Politics, Government, Law, and Economy**
A commercial treaty is signed between Offa and Charlemagne.

799 Pope Leo III is imprisoned in a monastery but escapes to Charlemagne who returns Leo to Rome under escort and demands that both Leo and his accusers shall appear before him in Rome in the following year. This sets in train the events that lead to the crowning of Charlemagne in the following year as 'Augustus', head of the Holy Roman Empire.
At the end of this century Japan's new 'Capital of Peace' the city of Kyoto, is founded and will remain for the next four centuries which are sometimes known as Japan's golden age.
The Khmers of Cambodia begin their rise to prosperity about this time, leading to the building of their great Hindu temples at the end of the 9th century.
The Mayan civilization begins an inexplicable exodus from its cities (in modern Guatemala and Honduras) at about the end of this century, its place being partly taken by the more warlike civilization of the Toltecs from Mexico (predecessors of the Aztecs).
The great migration by canoe and raft into the Polynesian islands of the Pacific probably starts at this time: certainly from the Indonesian peninsula and possibly also from Peru. The dates of the various Peruvian cultures prior to the Incas are too uncertain to be usefully given.
Politics, Government, Law, and Economy
Charlemagne sees to the administration of his empire. He arranges military service on a feudal basis and appoints a 'Seneschal' or Head of his Administration, a 'Count Palatine' or Chief Justice, and 'Palgraves' or Judges. He issues capitularies, or chapters, of legislation. He institutes biennial assemblies of nobles, bishops etc. to consider and approve his edicts and to report on the state of affairs in their particular regions.
Society, Education, and Religion
At about this time the great illuminated Four Gospels, the *Book of Kells*, is being produced, the last great work of the monastery of Iona.
Humanities and Scholarship
Shankara, the Brahman philosopher, is active around this time.

800 Ibrāhim ibn-al-Aghlab, Emir of Mzab (Algeria), establishes Aghlabid dynasty of Kairāwan (–909), ruling north-west Africa in only nominal subjection to the Caliph of Baghdād.

Dec: 25th, revival of title of Emperor in Western Europe by Pope Leo III's coronation of Charlemagne (–814).

Society, Education, and Religion

The Athanasian Creed.

The Cha'an (or Meditation) Sect now becoming the strongest movement in Chinese Buddhism (better known by the Japanese name of Zen Buddhism).

Science, Technology, and Discovery

Al-Fazāri, the first astronomer in Islam.

Al-Batrīq produces translations into Arabic of the major medical works of Galen and Hippocrates.

Humanities and Scholarship

Alcuin, *Works [Lives] of the Saints*; some poems; other Latin writings on Ethics, Rhetoric and Grammar; together with some hundreds of letters, many to Charlemagne).

Art, Sculpture, Fine Arts, and Architecture

Abbey gateway at Lorsch.

801 **Humanities and Scholarship**

T'ung tien/Comprehensive Compendium; the first Chinese historical encyclopedia.

802 Irene, the Greek Empress, deposed by her minister of finance who succeeds as Nicephorus I (–811); thus end her (alleged) negotiations with Charlemagne for their betrothal.

The monastery of Iona sacked by Vikings.

Politics, Government, Law, and Economy

An assembly of nobles and other subjects at Aachen accepts Charlemagne's codification of laws (Capitularies); his system of annual *missi* (itinerant surveyors of justice, royal rights, etc.) is now fully developed.

Society, Education, and Religion

Alfonso II of Oviedo establishes an archbishopric at his capital, Oviedo.

803 Hārūn-ar-Rashīd, Caliph of Baghdād, destroys the Barmakids, the Persian dynasty responsible for the administration of his (the 'Abbasīd) Empire.

Politics, Government, Law, and Economy

Codes of laws of Saxons, Frisians and Thuringians.

804 Charlemagne depopulates much of northern Saxony and Nordalbingia in one of his last measures for the subjection and conversion of the Saxons; with the end of this war, Germany to the River Elbe is incorporated into the Frankish dominions.

Society, Education, and Religion

Fridugis becomes Abbot of St. Martin's, Tours; its *scriptorium* flourishes under his rule.

805 Charlemagne conquers Venetia, Dalmatia and Corsica.

Society, Education, and Religion

Saichō, returning to Japan from an embassy to China, introduces the Tendai Sect of Buddhism; its monastic centre was founded on Mount Hiei.

806 Charlemagne's son defeats the Sorbs (Slavs of the Elbe-Saale area), enforcing their submission.

Hārūn-ar-Rashid takes Heraclea and other places in Cappadocia in a campaign which forces Nicephorus to resume his payment of tribute.

Death of Kammu, Emperor of Japan, who had founded his capital at Heian (i.e., Kyōto).

Art, Sculpture, Fine Arts, and Architecture

Oratory (extant but restored) of the palace built by Theodulf, Bishop of Orléans, at Germigny-des-Prés.

807 **Science, Technology, and Discovery**

Hārūn-ar-Rashid presents a water-clock to Charlemagne.

809 **March: 24th**, the Caliph Hārūn-ar-Rashid dies after suppressing a revolt in Samarqand; his empire now divided between his sons al-Ma'mūn (–833) and al-Amīn (–813).

Society, Education, and Religion

Hārūn-ar-Rashīd founds the first hospital in Baghdād. He is credited with establishing the postal service in his empire and is said to have contemplated making a canal through the Suez Isthmus.

810 **July:** **8th**, death of Pepin, King of Italy, after failing to take Venice. The Venetians resume nominal recognition of Byzantine authority and begin their city on the Rialto. Bernard succeeds as King of Italy (–818).

Politics, Government, Law, and Economy

Establishment in Japan of the Bureau of Archives to draft imperial decrees and transmit petitions to the Emperor.

Humanities and Scholarship

Georgios Syncellos, *Chronicle* (from the Creation to 284).

Literature

Abū Nuwās, court poet of Hārūn-ar-Rashīd.

811 Formation of the Spanish March completed with the surrender of Tortosa to Louis, son of Charlemagne.

A Frankish army sent into Pannonia in (probably) the last campaign against the Avars; they are now finally subjected to Charlemagne and converted to Christianity.

July: **26th**, Nicephorus I, after taking Pliska, killed in the destruction of his army by the Bulgars; succeeded by Michael I Rangabe (–813).

813 **June:** **22nd**, Michael defeated by the Bulgars at Versinicia (near Adrianople). He was consequently deposed in favour of Leo V the Armenian (–820), while the Bulgars took Adrianople and attacked Constantinople.

Sept: **11th**, in an assembly of magnates at Aachen, Charlemagne gives the imperial crown to Louis, his only surviving son.

25th, al-Ma'mūn reunites the 'Abbasīd Empire by the capture of Baghdād and murder of his brother, al-Amīn.

Society, Education, and Religion

The tomb of St. James the Greater identified at Santiago de Compostela; it attracts pilgrimages from western Europe.

814 **Jan:** **28th**, Charlemagne dies; succeeded by Louis the Pious (–840).

April: **14th**, Krum, Khan of the Bulgars, dies; succeeded by Omortag (–831), who made peace with Leo V.

815 **Society, Education, and Religion**

Ma'rūf al-Karkhi of Baghdād, the first Sūfi (mystic) saint.

(March) Leo V deposes the Patriarch Nicephorus and holds a synod of the Greek Church which reaffirms the iconoclastic decrees of the council of 754.

Science, Technology, and Discovery

Māshā'allāh wrote on astrology, the astrolobe and meteorology; his book on prices is the oldest extant scientific book in Arabic.

816 **Society, Education, and Religion**

Kūkai founds the monastic headquarters of the Shingon sect on Mount Koya, Japan.

817 **July:** —, *Divisio imperii*: in a council at Aachen, Lothar created Emperor as the colleague of his father, Louis (–831), whose other sons, Pepin (–838) and Louis the German (–876) respectively receive Aquitaine and Bavaria as sovereign yet dependent kingdoms.

Society, Education, and Religion

Louis the Pious orders all monasteries of his empire to observe the Rule of St. Benedict of Nursia.

Humanities and Scholarship

Theophanes Confessor, continuation of Syncellos' *Chronicle* (Theophanes' *Chronicle* was continued to 961).

Art, Sculpture, Fine Arts, and Architecture

Mosaics in the apses of Sta. Maria in Dominica, Sta. Prassede and Sta. Cecilia, Rome (–824).

Literature

Li Ho, *Poems* (regarded as one of the greatest poets of the T'ang Dynasty).

818 **Society, Education, and Religion**

Louis establishes the bishopric of Hildesheim.

Theodulf of Orléans was one of the first bishops to attempt to set up schools in his diocese; he also tried to produce a critical version of the Bible.

819 **Art, Sculpture, Fine Arts, and Architecture**
Consecration of (the second) abbey-church of Fulda, a building which greatly influenced the development of architecture in western Europe.

820 Tāhir appointed as the Caliph's governor of Khurāsān (eastern Persia); he founded the Tāhirid dynasty (–872).

Dec: 25th, murder of the Greek Emperor, Leo V; succeeded by Michael II, founder of the Amorian dynasty (–867).

Politics, Government, Law, and Economy
Institution in Japan of the Examiners of Misdeeds, who soon developed into a police force (as the Police Commissioners).

Society, Education, and Religion
Al-Shāfi'i, founder of the Shāfi'ite rite of Islam.

Art, Sculpture, Fine Arts, and Architecture
Manuscript plan for a monastery, at St. Gall.

821 Conquest of Tibet by the Chinese.

822 **Society, Education, and Religion**
Louis orders the reform of schools.

823 **Humanities and Scholarship**
Al-Wāqidi, *Kitāb al-Maghāzi/History of the Wars*, (of Muhammad); *Kitāb al Tabaqāt al-Kabīr/The Great Book of the Classes*; biographies of the Prophet and his associates.

824 **Births and Deaths**
Han Yü, Chinese poet and philosophical essayist, dies around this time.

825 Egbert of Wessex, after defeating the Mercians at 'Ellendun' (now Neither Wroughton), conquers Kent, Sussex and Essex.
Hamsavati (now Pegu) founded as the capital of the Mon kingdom of south Burma.

Science, Technology, and Discovery
Lock-gates in canals first mentioned in China.

827 **June:** —, Ziyādat Allāh I of Kairāwan, exploiting a Christian revolt against Greek rule, begins the Muslim conquest of Sicily.

828 **Literature**
Abu-al-'Atāhiyah, 'the father of Arabic sacred poetry'.

830 **April:** —, Pepin and Louis the German lead a considerable Frankish revolt against their father, Louis the Pious. In the autumn, a reaction in Louis the Pious' favour enables him to regain command.

Humanities and Scholarship
Einhard begins his *Vita Karoli Magni/Life of Charlemagne.*

Art, Sculpture, Fine Arts, and Architecture
Great Mosque of al-Qayrawān (Kairāwan; –*c.* 890).

831 **Society, Education, and Religion**
Foundation of the bishopric of Hamburg in newly converted lands.
Paschasius Radbertus, *De sacramento Corporis et Sanguinis Domini nostri* (asserting the transubstantiation of bread and wine in the Eucharist).

832 **Art, Sculpture, Fine Arts, and Architecture**
Utrecht Psalter.

833 Death of Junna, Emperor of Japan; his (Heian) dynasty continued but effective power exercised by the Fujiwara family.
The Chinese Emperor Wen-tsung's attempt to regain power from the eunuchs fails with the massacre of his ministers in 'the Sweet Dew incident'.

June: 24th, at 'The Field of Lies' (near Colmar), following Pope Gregory's attempt to mediate between Louis the Pious and his again rebellious sons, Lothar, Louis, and Pepin, Louis senior is deserted by his followers and surrenders. He is deposed.

Aug: 7th, death of the Caliph al-Ma'mūn while preparing an expedition to Constantinople;

succeeded by his brother, al-Mu'tasim (–842). The almost all Turkish army which al-Ma'mūn had created now in control of the Caliphate.

Science, Technology, and Discovery

The Caliph al-Ma'mūn founds an observatory at Baghdād and encourages geographical exploration.

834 Vikings ravage Frisia and thereafter make almost annual descents on the Channel coast of France.

March: 1st, Louis the Pious restored as emperor in consequence of a breach between Lothar and his brothers Louis and Pepin.

835 **Science, Technology, and Discovery**

First reference to a printed book in China.

836 Al-Mu'tasim transfers his capital from Baghdād to Sāmarra; here he and his successors as Caliph were virtually prisoners of their Turkish bodyguard.

839 **May: 30th**, by a new division of the Frankish Empire made at Worms, Louis the Pious assigns lands west of the Meuse, Moselle and western Alps to Charles the Bald, and to the east to Lothar, excepting Bavaria (which remains to Louis the German). Although Charles is invested as King of Aquitaine, he is opposed by Pepin II, son of Pepin I, who was proclaimed King there.

840 Saracens from Sicily take Taranto and Bari, then plunder the Adriatic coast to Venice.

The Uighurs driven from their empire on the Orkhan River by the Khirgiz and settle in the Tarim basin (Turfan).

June: 20th, death of Louis the Pious on his return from an expedition against Louis the German; succeeded as emperor by his son, Lothar (–855).

Science, Technology, and Discovery

The gold altar of Sant'Ambrogio, Milan, has the earliest pictorial representation of a stirrup.

841 **June: 25th**, the Emperor Lothar, supported by Pepin II of Aquitaine, defeated at Fontenoy by his brothers, Louis the German and Charles the Bald, who oppose his claims to authority under the *Constitutio* of 817.

842 Langdarma, King of Tibet, attempting to suppress Buddhism, murdered by a lama; the collapse of his empire followed.

June: 15th, Lothar, deserted by his followers, makes peace with Louis and Charles.

Society, Education, and Religion

The oaths of Strasbourg provide the first distinction between the French and German languages.

843 Scotland first united when Kenneth MacAlpin, King of the Scots, becomes King of the Picts (–858).

Aug: —, Treaty of Verdun partitioning the Carolingian Empire; Lothar retains the title (only) of Emperor and receives 'the Middle Kingdom' (of Italy, lands between the Rhine and Rhóne-Saóne-Scheldt, and Frisia), while Louis (–876) receives Germany and Charles the Bald (–877) France and the Spanish March.

Society, Education, and Religion

(March) A synod of the Greek Church repeals the iconoclastic decrees and re-establishes Orthodoxy; end of the Iconoclast Controversy.

845 **Society, Education, and Religion**

Alien religions prohibited in China; Buddhist property confiscated.

Literature

Abū-Tammām, *Dīwān* (collection of Arabic poetry); *Dīwān al-Hamāsah* (poems celebrating valour in battle).

846 Vijayālaya captures Tanjore, in the Pāndya kingdom of South India; this event marks the birth of the Chola Empire (–1279).

Aug: 26th, the basilica of St. Peter and other places outside the walls of Rome plundered by Saracens.

847 **Art, Sculpture, Fine Arts, and Architecture**

Mosque at Sāmarra (the oldest surviving ruin of the 'Abbasīd period; –861).

848 Traditional date for the fortification of Pagan (on R. Irrawaddy), the capital of an emerging Burmese kingdom (–1287).

849 **Society, Education, and Religion**

Gottschalk condemned as a heretic because of the predestinarian views of his *Confessio Prolixior*; this was refuted by Hincmar, in *De prædestinacione Dei*, and by Erigena.

850 Vikings now operating from camps on the Rhine, Scheldt, Somme, Seine, Loire and Garonne.

(–860) Kiev taken from the Khazars by Askold and Dir, Vikings; this was the beginning of the Varangian empire of the Ros (the Swedish name for seamen, whence 'Russia').

April: —, Louis II, son of Lothar, crowned in Rome as Emperor and King of Italy (–875).

Science, Technology, and Discovery

The Persian mathematician Al-Khwārizmī writes *Hisāb al-Jahr w-al Muqābalah*/*The Calculation of Integration and Equation* – whence 'algebra' possibly originates; *Sūrat al-Ard*/*Image of the World*, with a map of the world and heavens); astronomical tables.

Earliest Chinese reference to gunpowder.

851 **Society, Education, and Religion**

Johannes Scotus Erigena, *De divina proedestinatione* (refuting Gottschalk's work of 849).

Literature

Silsilat al-Tawārikh (anon. Arabic account of journeys by Sulaymān the merchant from the Persian Gulf to India and China; a source of the stories of Sindbād the Sailor).

853 (or later?) Mufarrij-ibn-Sālim establishes an independent Saracen dynasty at Bari; it becomes a base for plundering central Italy.

855 **Sept:** **28th**, death in retirement, of the Emperor Lothar; he had partitioned his lands among his three sons, the Emperor Louis II (Italy), Lothar II (from Frisia to the Alps, called *Lotharii regnum* i.e., Lorraine) and Charles (the kingdom of Provence).

Society, Education, and Religion

Ahmad ibn-Hanbal, founder of the Hanbalite sect of Islam, *Musnad* (collection of 30,000 traditions).

856 **Aug:** —, Vikings, led by Sidroe, establish a camp on the Seine, at Pitres, and ravage as far as the Loire; Paris burnt in December.

Society, Education, and Religion

Rabanus Maurus, *De institutione clericorum* (treatise on education); Biblical encyclopedia.

857 Garcia Ximenez establishes the kingdom of Navarre (–880).

Politics, Government, Law, and Economy

Foundation of the perpetual regency of the Fujiwara family, which continued even when the Japanese emperors were of age (–1867).

Science, Technology, and Discovery

Yuhannā ibn-Māsawayh writes *Daghal al-'Ain*/*Disorder of the Eye*; oldest extant, systematic treatise on ophthalmology in Arabic).

859 Conquest of Sicily by the Saracens completed.

860 **June:** **1st**, Charles the Bald and Louis the German make peace at Coblenz.

Science, Technology, and Discovery

Muhammad, Ahmad and Hasan, sons of Mūsā ibn-Shakīr write the *Book of Artifices* (the earliest extant treatise on mechanics).

862 Charles the Bald, by the new method of fortifying bridges, begins to hamper Danish raiders.

Riurick of Jutland (–873) founds the first dynasty of Princes of Russia at Novgorod.

May: **29th**, al-Musta'īn succeeds his brother, al-Muntassir, as Caliph (–866).

Society, Education, and Religion

At the request of Rostislav of Moravia, the Emperor Michael sends the brothers Constantine (later called Cyril) and Methodius to convert Slovakia; Cyril devised a Slavonic script ('Glagolitic', i.e., Cyrillic script) and translated the Bible and liturgical texts into Slavonic.

863 **Sept:** —, (and Oct) victories of Michael III over the Arabs of Armenia which mark a turning point in the wars between Byzantium and the Muslims.

Society, Education, and Religion

Caesar Bardas founds a secular university in Constantinople under Leo the Mathematician.

864 Michael III compels Boris I, Khan of the Bulgars, to receive baptizm as a Christian.

865 **Society, Education, and Religion**

St. Anskar, Bishop of Hamburg (from 826), the 'apostle of the north', has established Christianity in Denmark and Sweden by this time.

Humanities and Scholarship

Johannes Scotus Erigena, *De Divisione Naturæ* (a dialogue, condemned as pantheistic and later placed on the Index; it was 'the one purely philosophical argument of the middle ages' – W. P. Ker).

866 **Jan: 24th**, the Caliph al-Musta'in deposed by his Turkish guard and succeeded by his brother, al-Mu'tazz (–869).

May: 17th, death of Ordoño I, King of Oviedo; succeeded by his son, Alfonso III, the Great (–910).

Nov: 1st, the 'Great Army' of the Danes, who had established a base in East Anglia, takes York.

867 Ya'qūb ibn-al-Layth al-Sāffar, governor of Sijistān, establishes the Saffārid dynasty (–908).

Sept: 24th, the Greek Emperor, Michael III, murdered and succeeded by Basil I (–886), founder of the Macedonian dynasty (–963).

868 By raising the siege of Ragusa by Muslim forces, the Greek Empire completes its control over the Balkans.

Ahmad-ibn-Tūlūn, the Turkish governor of Egypt, makes himself independent of the Caliph; he founded the Tulunid dynasty (–905).

Science, Technology, and Discovery

(11th May) Printed roll, dated 11 May 868, of Chinese translation of the Buddhist Diamond Sutra (the earliest surviving work in print).

869 **June: 16th**, the Caliph al-Mu'tazz deposed by his Turkish guard and succeeded by his brother, al-Muhtadi (–870).

870 **Feb: —**, Boris, Khan of the Bulgars, accepts the ecclesiastical authority of the Patriarch of Constantinople.

Nov: 20th, St. Edmund, King of East Anglia, killed by Danes.

Society, Education, and Religion

Al-Bukhārī, *al-Sahīh* (*The Genuine Collection*; a system of Muslim theology and law).

871 London occupied by the Danes.

April: —, death of Ethelred, King of Wessex; succeeded by his brother, Alfred (–899).

872 Al-Saffār destroys the Tāhirid dynasty of Khurāsān.

Science, Technology, and Discovery

Ibn-Tūlūn founds the first hospital in Cairo; hospitals are now common in the Muslim countries.

873 **Births and Deaths**

Al-Kindī, Arab Neo-Platonic philosopher, alchemist, astrologer, optician and musical theorist, dies around this time.

874 Burgred, the last King of Mercia, expelled by the Danes.

Alfonso III of Oviedo defeats the Moors of Toledo at the Orbedo.

Nasr ibn-Ahmad founds the Sāmānid dynasty of Transoxiana (–999); its capital at Bukhāra becomes the centre for a Persian cultural revival.

A peasant rising led by Wang Hsien-chih and Huang Ch'ao takes control of eastern China.

Society, Education, and Religion

A Greek archbishop is sent as a missionary to Russia following a treaty between the Emperor and the Swedes of Kiev.

875 (or 876) Halfdan founds the Danish kingdom of York (–954); Danes now settling here.

Bořivoj I, Prince of Bohemia, baptized by Methodius.

Dec: 25th, Charles the Bald crowned as Emperor by Pope John VIII in Rome (–877).

876 **Aug: 28th**, death of Louis the German; his lands divided by his sons Carloman (Bavaria and the East March; –880), Louis the Younger (Saxony and Franconia; –882), and Charles the Fat (Alemannia; –888).

Art, Sculpture, Fine Arts, and Architecture
Ibn-Tūlūn Mosque, Cairo, begun.

877 Ibn-Tūlūn of Egypt seizes Syria.

Oct: 6th, death of Charles the Bald after his return from Italy, where the French nobles deserted him.

Politics, Government, Law, and Economy
(14th June) a capitulary of Charles the Bald issued in an assembly at Quierz seemingly recognizes the hereditability of fiefs though it was designed to order government in his absence; while it may not be regarded as a charter for 'the feudal system', feudalism had effectively come into being in Charles' time by his grants to vassals, e.g., the practical establishment of Richard the Justiciar as the first Duke of Burgundy.

Science, Technology, and Discovery
Al-Battāni begins his astronomical observations in al-Raqqah (–918).

878 **May: —**, Alfred of Wessex defeats the Danes at Edington; by the peace of Wedmore, their leader, Guthrum, baptized as a Christian.

Society, Education, and Religion
Disappearance of Muhammad al-Muntazar, twelfth Imām of the Ismā'ite sect of the Shī'ites (al-Mahdī, the 'Hidden Imām', whose followers still await his return).

879 Chinese rebels led by Huang Ch'ao sack Canton.

Politics, Government, Law, and Economy
120,000 'foreigners' said to have been killed in Canton (despite its exaggeration, this figure indicates the size of foreign, viz. Arab, Persian, etc., trading communities who at this time dominate China's export trade, particularly with Korea and Japan).

880 Death of Rhodri the Great, King of Gwynedd, Powys and Seisyllwg; his kingdom now disintegrates.

The Chinese peasant leader, Wang Hsien-chih, defeated and executed by the Sha-t'o, the Turkish allies of the emperor.

March: —, Treaty of Ribemont: partition of France between Louis III (Francia and Neustria) and Carloman (Burgundy and Aquitaine).

881 **Feb: 12th**, Charles the Fat of Alemannia crowned as Emperor by John VIII (–888).

Aug: 3rd, Louis III of France defeats Vikings at Saucourt (on the Somme).

Music
The *Ludwigslied* (in praise of Louis of Bavaria and his victory in 881; the first historical ballad in German literature).

882 **Jan: 20th**, death of Louis of Saxony and Bavaria; succeeded by Charles the Fat (–888), who thus reunites Germany.

884 Diego de Porcelos founds Burgos, which becomes the capital of Castile.

The usurping emperor, Huang Ch'ao, defeated and killed by the Turkish Sha-t'o; their leader Li K'o-yung now disputes control of North China with Chu Wen, Huang's lieutenant.

June: —, Carloman pays the Viking army to leave France; the main part goes to England, the rest into Lorraine.

Dec: 12th, death of Carloman; succeeded, on the invitation of the French nobles, by Charles the Fat (–888), who thus reunites the empire of Charlemagne.

885 **Nov: 24th**, the Viking army under King Sigefrid lays siege to Paris, where the defence is led by Odo, son of Robert the Strong, Marquess of Neustria. Charles the Fat pays the Vikings to leave, for Burgundy.

Literature
'La Vie de Sainte Eulalie' (anon.; the first extant French poem – a fragment).

886 Alfred expels the Danes from London and, in a treaty with Guthrum, defines the frontier of the Danelaw.

Aug: 29th, death of Greek Emperor, Basil I the Macedonian; succeeded by his son, Leo VI (–912).

Politics, Government, Law, and Economy
Basilica (a new Greek version of Roman Law of Justinian) in sixty volumes, prepared by order of Basil I, and published by his son, Leo VI.

Art, Sculpture, Fine Arts, and Architecture
Apse mosaics in Sancta Sophia, Salonika.

887 **Politics, Government, Law, and Economy**
Rikkokushi/Six National Histories; official court histories written in Chinese on the model of Chinese court records covering Japanese affairs 791–887).

888 **Jan: 13th**, death of Charles the Fat, followed by dismemberment of his empire; German vassals declare his successor to be Arnulf of Carinthia, illegitimate son of Carloman of Bavaria (–899); in Italy, Berengar, Marquess of Friuli, and Guy, Duke of Spoleto, contend for the crown; Boso's son, Louis, held Provence; Rudolph of Auxerre, Duke of Jurane Burgundy, establishes a kingdom of Burgundy (–911); while in France, surviving royal authority disintegrates.

889 Last periodic *stelae* in Mayan cities of South Yucatán; end of the Old Empire, with migration to the north, where the New Empire emerges.

Art, Sculpture, Fine Arts, and Architecture
Indravarman I of Cambodia built Bakong Temple (the first terraced stone pyramid), Angkor; his successor, Yasovarman I, builds the first city there.

890 Death of Mihira Bhoja I, founder of an empire in northern India centred on Kanauj.

Literature
Taketori Monogatari (*The Story of the Bamboo Gatherer*; the earliest Japanese prose narrative).

891 **Oct: —**, King Arnulf defeats the Danes on the Dyle, in Brabant; but they subsequently defeat Odo of France in Vermandois.

Literature
Photius compiles *Myriobiblon/Library*; an enormous collection of note-books on works read, with learned commentaries and judgements on style, quotations and citations from Greek authors whose writings would otherwise have disappeared).

892 **Oct: 15th**, death of the Caliph, al-Mu'tamid; succeeded by his son, al-Mu'tadid (–902), who restores the capital to Baghdād.

Humanities and Scholarship
Alfred the Great (–899) translates St. Gregory, *Cura Pastoralis*; Orosius, *Historia adversus Paganos* (a universal history of 410 with geographical information); Bede *Historia Ecclesiastica*; Boethius, *De Consolatione Philosophiæ*; St. Augustine, *Soliloquies*.

893 Alfonso III of Oviedo defeats and kills Ahmād ibn-Mu'āwiya, who claimed to be the Mahdi, at Zamora.

894 **Dec: —**, death of the Emperor, Guy; succeeded by his son and co-emperor, Lambert of Spoleto (–898).

895 Spytihněv, son of Bořivoj I, regains Bohemia's independence from Moravia and accepts the supremacy of Arnulf of Germany.

Leo VI prompts the Magyars (settled between the Dnieper and the Danube) to attack Bulgaria. The Khan, Symeon, retaliates by inciting the Pechenegs, recent arrivals on the Dnieper, to invade Magyar territory. Consequently the Magyars, after their expulsion from Bulgaria, are forced to seek lands elsewhere and settle in central Europe, on the Theiss.

Society, Education, and Religion
Consequent to Spytihněv's settlement with Arnulf, Bohemia accepts the Latin liturgy and the ecclesiastical jurisdiction of a German bishop.

896 **Feb: —**, after forcing his way into Rome, King Arnulf crowned as Emperor by Pope Formosus, who had invoked his aid against the Romans. When Arnulf is subsequently forced to leave Italy, Lambert of Spoleto retrieves ground as its king.

897 Āditya I defeats and kills Aparājita, the last Pallava King, whose lands are now annexed by the Cholas.

899 **Sept: 24th**, After being routed by King Berengar on the Brenta, Magyar raiders defeat Italian forces and ravage Lombardy.

Oct: 26th, death of King Alfred the Great of Wessex; succeeded by his son, Edward the Elder (–924).

Nov: —, (or Dec) death of King Arnulf of Germany; succeeded by his son, Louis the Child (–911).

900 The Samanid ruler, Ismā'il, seizes Khurāsān from the Saffārids; Transoxiana now under Muslim rule.

Harold Fairhair completes the unification of Norway by his victory in Hafrsfjord.

Art, Sculpture, Fine Arts, and Architecture

The Nea (New Church) built for Basil I in Constantinople.

901 **Feb:** —, Louis (III), King of Italy and Provence, crowned as Emperor by Pope Benedict IV (–905).

902 **March:** **6th**, death of the Caliph, al-Mu'tadid; his successors were, generally, ephemeral puppets.

904 **Jan:** **29th**, following Christopher's expulsion, Sergius III crowned as Pope; this is the beginning of the period in Papal history known as 'the Pornocracy' (–963).

905 With the extinction of the Tulunid dynasty, the Caliph recovers control of Syria and Egypt.

July: **21st**, Berengar of Friuli captures the Emperor, Louis III, at Verona, blinds him, and expels him from Italy to his kingdom of Provence.

Literature

Ki no Tsurayuki, Ōshikōchi no Mitsune, Mibu no Tadamine and Ki no Tomonori, *Kokinshū* (an anthology of about 1,100 Japanese and Chinese poems; completed 922).

906 After defeating a German and Slav army at Pressburg, the Magyars overrun Moravia and destroy its empire; they also raid Saxony.

907 The Russian ruler, Oleg, sacks the suburbs of Constantinople.

The imperial Chinese dynasty of the T'ang extinguished with the murder of its last emperor by the peasant leader, Chu Wen (–923), who declared himself to be Emperor; thus begins the 'Period of the Five Dynasties and the Ten Kingdoms' (–960), with the empire disintegrating. Yeh-lü A-pao-chi declares himself Emperor of the Khitan (semi-nomadic Mongol tribes of north China, also known as 'Kitai', whence 'Cathay').

908 The Magyars defeat the Bavarians, killing the Margrave Liutpold, and raid Saxony and Thuringia.

The Sāmānids finally extinguish the Saffārids of Sijistān.

Origin of tribal dukes in Germany: the Bavarians elect Arnulf as their Duke (–937) to organize defence against the Magyars; almost simultaneously, Burchard is elected in Swabia (–926), Conrad in Franconia (–918), and Reginar (grandson of Lothar I) in Lorraine.

909 **Dec:** **7th**, following his destruction of the Aghlabid dynasty of Kairāwan, Sa'īd ibn-Husayn proclaimed as 'Ubaydullāh al-Mahdī in Tunis and so founds the Fātimid dynasty.

Society, Education, and Religion

(11th Sept) Abbey of Cluny founded, with the monks installed in a Gallo-Roman villa.

911 Charles the Simple receives the homage of Rollo, the Norse leader established on the Seine, at St. Clair-sur-Epte; Rollo (–931) baptized as a Christian and granted Rouen, Lisieux, Evreux, etc. Thus begins the duchy of Normandy, while Viking raids on north France come to an end.

Treaty of peace concluded between the Greek Empire and the Russians at Kiev.

Jan: **21st**, death of King Louis the Child, the last Carolingian ruler of Germany.

Nov: —, Duke Conrad of Franconia elected King of the Germans (–918). Charles the Simple of France accepted as King of Lorraine.

912 **Oct:** **15th**, death of 'Abdallāh, Emir of Spain; succeeded by his grandson, 'Abd-ar-Rahmān III (–961), whose state, as a result of rebellion, is almost confined to Cordova (–932).

Music

Notker Balbulus, a musician, develops the sequence in Church poetry, writing *The Sequentia*.

913 **Aug:** —, an invasion by Symeon, Khan of the Bulgars, reaches the walls of Constantinople.

914 Death of Garcia I; succeeded by Ordoño II (–923), who transfers the capital from Oviedo to Leon, whence the kingdom now takes its name.

Oct: —, Edward the Elder begins the conquest of the Danelaw.

915 On the initiative of John X, the Saracen base on the Garigliano destroyed by Byzantine and Italian forces, thus ending the Saracen presence in central Italy and reducing their devastations.

Humanities and Scholarship
Regino of Prüm, *World Chronicle* (from AD 1 to 908).

916 King Indra III of Rāshtrakūta takes Kanauj; its King, Mahīpala, recovers possession, but his empire is now in decline.

917 Edward the Elder destroys the Danish kingdom of East Anglia.
'Ubaydullāh conquers Sicily.

Aug: **20th**, the Khan Symeon, demanding that he should be recognized as Greek Emperor, defeats the imperial forces near Anchialus, on the Achelous; he next invades Thrace and makes himself master of the Balkans.

918 **June:** **—**, Edward the Elder takes control of Mercia. He also conquers the Danish midlands.

Dec: **23rd**, death of King Conrad I of Germany.

919 **May:** **—**, Henry the Fowler, Duke of Saxony, crowned as King (Henry I) of the Germans (–936).

920 'Abd-ar-Rahmān defeats Ordoño II of Leon and Sancho of Navarre at Val de Junqueras.

Science, Technology, and Discovery
Earliest European reference to a collar in the harness of horses (which would permit the drawing of heavy loads and ploughs).

923 Murder of Chu Wen, Emperor of China; succeeded by Li K'o-yung, leader of the Shat-t'o, who founded the [Later] T'ang dynasty.

Sept: **—**, death of Ordoño II of Leon; succeeded by his brother, Froila II (–924); outbreak of civil war.

924 The Magyars resume their raids: in Italy, they burn Pavia, but King Rodolph and Hugh of Arles, the effective ruler of Provence, drive them off into south France; they also invade Germany, where King Henry obtains a truce for Saxony which he uses to strengthen his duchy by building fortified towns.
'Abd-ar-Rahmān sacks Pampeluna, the capital of Navarre.
Symeon's final attempt to take Constantinople fails.

July: **17th**, death of Edward the Elder, King of England; succeeded by his son, Athelstan (–939).

925 The viscounts of Anjou now being known as counts to mark their independence from the suzerainty of the dukes of Normandy; this is an illustration of the disintegration of authority in the French duchies.

927 **May:** **27th**, death of Symeon, Khan of the Bulgars and self-styled emperor; succeeded by his son, Peter, who makes peace with the Greek Emperor.

July: **12th**, in a meeting near Penrith, Cumberland, the Kings of Scotland and Strathclyde recognize Athelstan as their overlord.

928 Ziyarid dynasty established in Jurjan (Persia; –1043).

929 **Jan:** **16th**, 'Abd-ar-Rahmān III, Emir of Spain, begins to style himself Caliph, thus consummating his independence of Baghdād.

Sept: **28th**, (St.) Wenceslas of Bohemia murdered and succeeded by his brother, Boleslav I (–967), who asserts his independence of the German king.

Oct: **7th**, death of Charles the Simple, still the prisoner of Herbert of Vermandois.

930 Qarmatians sack Mecca and remove the Black Stone (restored 951).
On the death of the Emperor Daigo of Japan, the Fujiwara family acquire full powers as regents.

Politics, Government, Law, and Economy
The Althing (general court) established in Iceland; it is now the oldest national assembly in the world.

932 With the capture of Toledo, 'Abd-ar-Rahmān completes his reunification of Muslim Spain (begun in 912).

Science, Technology, and Discovery
Féng Tao, Prime Minister of China, orders the printing of Confucian, Buddhist and Taoist canons. This was done with wooden blocks (–1019).

933 **March:** **15th**, Henry I defeats the Magyars at 'Riade', near Merseburg.

934 Henry I forces King Gorm the Old of Denmark to make peace and establishes the march of Schleswig; he also completes his subjection of the Wends of the Lower Oder.

935 Wang Chien establishes himself as Emperor of China, founding the Later Chin Dynasty (–947).
Wang Kon reunites Korea on the extinction of the Silla dynasty; he founds the Koryō dynasty (whence 'Korea'), with the capital at Kaesōng.

Feb: —, Muhammad al-Ikhshīd founds the Ikshīdid dynasty of Egypt.

Humanities and Scholarship
Ki no Tsurayuki, *Tosa nikki* (the earliest extant diary of travels in Japanese, with poems by the author).
Al-Ash'arī of Baghdād, founder of Muslim scholastic philosophy.

936 The Khitan settle in northern China, making Peking their southern capital.

July: **2nd**, death of King Henry I of Germany; succeeded by his son, Otto I (–973).

Art, Sculpture, Fine Arts, and Architecture
'Abd-ar-Rahmān begins the palace of al-Zahrā, Cordova.

937 Athelstan wins a defensive victory against a coalition of Scots, Strathclyde Welsh, and Norsemen at 'Brunanburgh'.

938 Otto I seizes King Conrad of Burgundy and his kingdom, enforces recognition of his authority in Bavaria, and repulses a Magyar force in Saxony.

939 Ngo Quyen defeats the Chinese and founds the kingdom of Dai-co-viet (North Vietnam), with his capital at Co-loa.
Otto I suppresses a rebellion in Saxony and Thuringia.

July: **22nd**, Ramiro II of Leon defeats 'Abd-ar-Rahmān at Simancas.

Sept: —, Otto repels an invasion by Louis IV, who is supporting a German rebellion; this collapses after the deaths of Dukes Everard of Franconia and Gilbert of Lorraine in a skirmish at Andernach; Otto takes possession of Franconia.

Literature
Ise, *Monogatari* (the Japanese *Tales of Ise*).

940 **Politics, Government, Law, and Economy**
Louis IV grants the county of Reims to its Archbishop (an illustration of the continuing disintegration of the larger territorial units in France; in such cases of grants to ecclesiastical lords, however, the crown benefited when it could influence the election of bishops).

Society, Education, and Religion
Dunstan appointed Abbot of Glastonbury; he initiates reforms which influence the English Church.

942 **Literature**
Al-Jahshiyari, first version of *Alf Laylah wa-Laylah*/*A Thousand and One Nights – The Arabian Nights*; his heroines include Shahrazād – 'Sheherazade').

944 **Oct:** —, Sayf ad-Dawla establishes himself in Aleppo and extends his authority over northern Syria (–967), founding the Hamdānid dynasty (–1003).

946 **Jan:** **17th**, 'Adud ad-Dawla, the Shī'ite ruler of western Persia, expels the Turks from Baghdād; his dynasty, the Buwayhids, now rules the Caliphate from their capital at Shīrāz and has the title of Sultan.

May: **26th**, murder of King Edmund of England; succeeded by his brother, Edred (–955).

Humanities and Scholarship
Liu Hsü, *Chiu T'ang shu* (official history of the T'ang Dynasty, 618–907).

947 The Khitan destroy the Later Chin dynasty and claim the Chinese throne, founding the Liao dynasty of North China (–1125).

948 The Caliph of Kairāwan appoints Hasan ibn-Ali as governor of Sicily; the office continues in his family (the Kalbite dynasty) and it establishes an ordered state in Sicily.

Politics, Government, Law, and Economy
Qudāma ibn-Ja'far, *Kitāb al-Kharāj* (account of the land-tax of the Muslim Empire, with description of its postal service).

949 (or 950) Death of Hywel the Good, King of Deheubarth, Gwynedd, Powys and Seisyllwg; this empire now disintegrates.

Politics, Government, Law, and Economy

Hywel Dda, *Leges Walliae* (earliest code of Welsh laws).

950 **Society, Education, and Religion**

Gyula, the Magyar 'leader', baptized in Constantinople and returns with the first Hungarian bishop as a missionary.

Literature

Anthologia Palatina (the *Greek Anthology* collected by Constantine Cephalas; ms. found in the library of the Elector Palatine, Heidelberg. It consists of poems and brief inscriptions by some 300 writers from the fifth century BC to the sixth century AD).

951 Hou-Chou dynasty of China (–960).

Sept: —, Otto enters Pavia and assumes the Italian crown; he marries Adelaide, widow of Lothar II of Italy.

953 Sayf ad-Dawla defeats a Byzantine army under Bardas Phocas near Germanicea (Mar'-ash).

954 Eric Bloodaxe, the last Scandinavian King of York, killed by rebels; Edred takes possession of the kingdom and so holds all England.

955 **Aug: 10th**, Otto defeats the Magyars on the Lechfeld, near Augsburg; their raids on western Europe now cease and they begin a settled life in Hungary.

Oct: 16th, Otto defeats the Wends in Mecklenburg.

956 Arrival of the Ghuzz (or Oghuz) Turks, led by Seljuq, from Turkestan, in Transoxiana (–1037).

Humanities and Scholarship

al-Mas'ūdi ('The Herodotus of the Arabs') writes *Murūj al-Dhahab wa-M'ādin al Jawhar/Meadows of Gold and Mines of Gems*; a historico-geographical encyclopedia, it gives the earliest known description of windmills (in Sijistan, Persia) and mentions horse-racing and (?) tennis.

958 The Byzantine general, John Tzimisces, takes Somosata and defeats Sayf ad-Dawla at Ra'bān (Syria).

Humanities and Scholarship

Liutprand of Cremona, *Antapodosis* (record of events 886–950; continued in *De Rebus Gestis Ottonis (I)* for 960–64).

959 **Oct: 1st**, death of King Edwy of England; succeeded by Edgar (–975), who recalled Dunstan from exile.

Politics, Government, Law, and Economy

Constantine VII, *De administrando imperio, De cerimoniis aulæ Byzantinæ* and *De thematibus* (all about Byzantine government, the first being a handbook for his son); he also writes a *Life of Basil I* and encourages the production of encyclopedias.

960 'Abd-ar-Rahmān, exploiting the civil war in Leon, takes Oviedo, and, with Garcia of Navarre, restores Sancho I as King of Leon (–967).

The Karakhanids of central Asia become the first Turkish tribe to be converted *en masse* to Islam.

Chao K'uang-yin (as T'ai-Tsu; –976) founds the Northern Sung dynasty of Chinese Emperors (–1279).

961 Death of 'Abd-ar-Rahmān III, Caliph of Spain.

March: —, Nicephorus Phocas recovers Crete from the Saracens.

Sept: —, Otto and his son, Otto, acknowledged as Kings of Italy on their capture of Pavia.

Politics, Government, Law, and Economy

T'ang hui yao/Assembled Essentials of the T'ang; encyclopedic collection of materials on Chinese government and economics under the T'ang, 618–907.

Society, Education, and Religion

St. Athanasius the Athonite establishes the first notable foundation on Mount Athos, the Great Laura.

'Abd-ar-Rahmān founds the University of Cordova.

962 Alptigīn founds the Turkish dynasty of the Ghaznavids (–1186) with the seizure of Ghaznī.

Feb: 2nd, coronation of Otto as Holy Roman Emperor (–973) by Pope John XII, who becomes his subject; the imperial title was thus restored in western Europe.

963 **Aug: 16th**, Nicephorus II Phocas crowned as Greek Emperor (–969).

965 Svjatoslav of Kiev destroys the power of the Khazars.

Aug: —, Nicephorus II regains Cyprus from the Saracens.
16th, he takes Tarsus in the conquest of Cilicia.

Society, Education, and Religion
Baptism of Harold Bluetooth; he officially establishes Christianity in Denmark.

966 Mieszko I of Poland converted to Christianity, following his marriage to Dobrava, daughter of Boleslav I of Bohemia; the first (Roman) missionary bishop comes to Poland.
Nicephorus Phocas campaigns on the middle Euphrates.

967 **Feb: —**, death of Sayf ad-Dawla, Emir of Aleppo.

Dec: 22nd, Otto, son of Otto, crowned as Emperor by John XIII (–983).

Society, Education, and Religion
Foundation of Magdeburg Cathedral.

Literature
Al-Isfahānī, *Kitāb al-Aghāni* (*Great Book of Songs*; an anthology of quotations from Arabic poetry, with biographies of the poets and of the composers who set the words to melodies).

968 **Society, Education, and Religion**
Creation of the Archbishopric of Magdeburg which John XIII limited to the land between the Elbe and the Oder so that the conversion of the Slavs should not be made under Otto's influence; Adalbert is the first Archbishop.

Science, Technology, and Discovery
Discovery of silver-bearing ore at Goslav; the production of copper, zinc and lead was also developed here later.

969 **July: 6th**, the fourth Fātimid Caliph, al-Mu'izz, already ruling Tunis and Morocco, conquers Egypt and extinguishes the Ilkshidid dynasty; he builds his capital at Cairo, which becomes the centre of a Shī'ite empire.

Oct: 28th, Antioch taken by Byzantine forces; Aleppo also taken in this campaign of reconquest which Nicephorus regarded as a crusade.

Dec: 10th, murder of the Greek Emperor, Nicephorus II Phocas; succeeded by John Tzimisces (–976).

970 Svjatoslv of Kiev invades Thrace and is defeated at Arcadiopolis by the Greek general, Bardas Sclerus.

Literature
Beowulf (probably first written down *c.* 700; ms. of this epic, the oldest complete poem of length in any modern language, written in a West Saxon dialect of Old English).

971 **April: 23rd**, John Tzimisces defeats Svjatoslav at Silistra (Dorystolum).

July: 21st, Tzimisces again defeats Svjatoslav and compels him to evacuate Bulgaria and the Crimea.

972 **(Spring):** Svjatoslav of Kiev killed in his defeat on the cataracts of the Dneiper by the Pechenegs under Kurya.
The Bulgarian Tsar, Boris II, abdicates, and Bulgaria is annexed by the Greek Empire.

April: 14th, an alliance of the Greek and Western Empires made by the marriage of Otto's son, Otto, to Theophano, a niece of John Tzimisces.

Society, Education, and Religion
Foundation of the Azhar Mosque, Cairo; it includes a university.
Edgar holds a council of the English church to organize monastic reform; it approves of Ethelwold's *Regularis Concordia.*

973 **May: 7th**, death of the Emperor Otto I the Great; succeeded as German King by his son, Otto II (–983).
11th, Edgar crowned at Bath as King of all England; he then went to Chester, where eight Scottish and Welsh kings rowed him on the Dee.

Society, Education, and Religion
Essen Minster (–1002); the west choir and a tower survive.

974 Otto defeats Harold Bluetooth of Denmark.
In his second Mesopotamian campaign, John Tzimisces, supported by Ashot III of Armenia, enters Nisibis and (possibly) comes near to Baghdād before withdrawing.

975 **April: 29th**, John Tzimisces enters Baalbek (Heliopolis) in the course of his third campaign (or crusade), when he conquers northern Palestine, taking Caesarea.

July: 8th, death of Edgar, King of England.

Society, Education, and Religion
Foundation of the bishoprics of Prague and Olomuc, for Bohemia and Moravia.
The Great Mosque, Cordova (begun 786), extended.

976 **Jan: 10th**, death of the Greek Emperor, John Tzimisces; succeeded by Basil II (–1025) and Constantine VIII (–1028), the sons of Romanus II. The Bulgarian war of independence follows, led by Samuel (–1014).

Nov: 14th, death of Chao K'uang-yin (T'ai-Tsu), the first Sung emperor, who had almost reunited China.

Society, Education, and Religion
Al-Hakam enlarges Cordova University, now preeminent in Europe and the Muslim world; he also founds free schools in the city.

Statistics
The Chinese (Sung) regular army totals 378,000 men.

978 **March: 18th**, Edward the Martyr, King of England, murdered by servants of his stepbrother, Ethelred II, who succeeds (–1016).

Society, Education, and Religion
Mainz Cathedral begun.

Science, Technology, and Discovery
Completion of 'Adud ad-Dawla's teaching hospital, al-Bimāristān al-'Adudi, Baghdād; its 24 physicians form a medical faculty.

980 Vikings renew their raids on England (–1016).
Le Dai Hanh (–1005) usurps the imperial throne of Dai-co-Viet.

Nov: —, Otto II begins his expedition to Italy.

981 Almanzor, Regent of Cordova, takes Zamora and subjugates Leon.

982 Le Dai Hanh destroys Indrapura, capital of the Champa kingdom (South Vietnam).

July: 13th, Otto II defeated at Basientello, in Apulia, by Saracens and Greeks.

Science, Technology, and Discovery
Eric the Red begins the Viking colonization of Greenland.
Yasuyori Tamba, *Ishinō* (oldest extant Japanese treatise on medicine).

983 Death of Ahmad ibn-Buwayh 'Adud ad-Dawla, ruler of the Caliphate, who had consolidated his control in Persia and assumed the title Shāhanshah (King of Kings).
The Caliph of Egypt now ruling over Palestine and southern Syria.

Dec: 7th, death of the Emperor, Otto II; succeeded by his son, Otto III (–1002), under the guardianship of his mother, Theophano (–991).

984
Science, Technology, and Discovery
Ahmad and Mahmud, sons of Ibrāhim the astrolabist, of Isfahan, make the earliest dated astrolabe (now at Oxford).

985 Basil II defeats a palace conspiracy and begins his personal rule as Greek Emperor (or 986).
Mieszko of Poland does homage to John XV.

July: 1st, Almanzor sacks Barcelona.

986 **Aug: 17th**, Basil II routed by the Bulgarians in 'Trajan's Gate'.

Science, Technology, and Discovery
Abbo of Fleury, *De numero mensura et pondere* (mathematical commentary).

987 In Yucatán, Hunac Ceel expels the ruling Mayan dynasty from Chichén-Itzá and establishes the new Mayan Empire, under the Cocom dynasty, with its capital at Mayapán (–*c.* 1441).

May: 21st, (or possibly 22nd) death of Louis V *le Fainéant*, the last Carolingian King of France, without issue.

July: 3rd, Hugh Capet, Duke of the Franks, the effective ruler of France, having been elected to succeed Louis, crowned as King of France (–996), so founding the Capetian dynasty (–1328).

Dec: 30th, Hugh Capet has his son, Robert, crowned as co-King of France and his heir. (This method of associating the heir with his father, the King, was the Capetian practice until Philip II abandoned it.)

988 **Summer** : The rebel Bardas Phocas defeated at Chrysopolis by imperial forces assisted by Vladimir of Kiev. (This was the origin of the Greek Emperors' Varangian Guard, of Viking stock.)

Almanzor razes the city of Leon and makes its king tributary to Cordova.

989 **Oct: 11th**, Bardas Phocas surrenders to Basil II and renounces his imperial pretensions; he dies soon afterwards (by poison ?).

Society, Education, and Religion

A local Synod at Charroux announces a Truce of God. This example is followed by other French ecclesiastical assemblies in order to reduce anarchy.

990 **Society, Education, and Religion**

Foundation of the Orthodox Church in Russia.

Art, Sculpture, Fine Arts, and Architecture

Mosque of al-Hākim, Cairo (–1012).

991 Basil subjugates Albania and begins his pacification of Bulgaria (–995).

June: 15th, death of the Empress Theophano, who had been ruling as 'Emperor' for Otto III; Adelaide, Otto I's widow, takes her place (–995).

992 The independence of Venice recognized in treaties with the Greek and Western Empires.

993 (or 994) Delhi founded by Ānangapāla, chief of the Tomara tribe.

Society, Education, and Religion

John XV canonizes Ulric, Bishop of Augsburg; this was the first canonization by a Pope.

994 Fulk of Anjou builds one of the earliest known castles, at Langeais, as a means of strengthening his authority; yet, as in other cases, it becomes the stronghold of semi-independent vassals.

Science, Technology, and Discovery

'Ali ibn-al-'Abbas (Haly Abbas), *Kāmil al-Sinā 'ah al-Tibbīyah/The Whole Medical Art*; Persian encyclopedia of medicine, known in Latin as *Liber Regius*.

995 **April: —**, Basil raises the siege of Aleppo by the Egyptians and campaigns as far south as Tripoli.

996 **May: 21st**, Otto III crowned as Holy Roman Emperor by Pope Gregory (–1002).

997 The Īlek Khāns extinguish the Sāmānid dynasty of Transoxiana.

Death of the Emperor T'ai Tsung; he had subdued the remaining Chinese provinces save for the northern area ruled by the Khitan.

(or 998) the Bulgarian leader, Samuel, proclaims himself Tsar; he aspires to create a Balkan empire.

Society, Education, and Religion

(23rd April) Adalbert martyred on a mission to convert the Prussians.

998 In order to thwart Samuel, Basil grants the protectorate of Dalmatia to Venice.

Politics, Government, Law, and Economy

Otto III unites his chanceries for Germany and Italy, thus restoring the Carolingian system of a single secretariat.

999 Quetzalcóatl, founder of the Mexican Toltec empire (–1168), expelled from its capital, Tollán; he stays (? rules) in Mayapán until his return to Mexico.

April: 3rd, (or 4th) election of Gerbert of Aurillac as Pope Silvester II; he was the first French Pope (–1003).

The Divided World

1000–1492

1000 Svein of Denmark (–1014) defeats and kills Olaf I at 'Svold', and thus conquers Norway.
Otto III makes his permanent residence in Rome.
Sweden now united as a kingdom under Olaf the Tax-king, who established Christianity.

March: 31st, Boleslav crowned as King of Poland by Otto III. The Archbishopric of Gniezno is created for Poland, with Silesia and Pomerania subject to it; thus Poland is recognized as independent both politically and ecclesiastically.

Aug: 15th, Stephen crowned as King of Hungary (–1038); he had put the country under the protection of the Pope, from whom he received the crown and the establishment of a Hungarian ecclesiastical hierarchy, under the Archbishopric of Gran.

Society, Education, and Religion

Development of cathedral schools at Tours, Orleans, Utrecht, Reims, Chartres, Liège and Paris; they are to eclipse the monastic schools and universities arise from some.

Literature

Sei Shōnagon, *Makura no Sōshi (The Pillow Book*; a Japanese court lady's common place book of reflections, odd facts and anecdotes, with short poems).

1002 **Jan: 23rd**, death of Otto III, the Holy Roman Emperor; he was unmarried.

June: 7th, Henry of Bavaria crowned as King of the Germans (–1024).

Aug: 10th, death of Almanzor, regent of Cordova, after his defeat at Calatañazor by the Kings of Leon and Navarre; succeeded by his son, al-Muzaffar (–1008).

1003 **Spring** : Basil II defeats Samuel, the Bulgarian Tsar, near Skopje.
Brian Bórumha now High King of Ireland (–1014).

Science, Technology, and Discovery

Voyage of Leif Ericsson to North America, where he discovers 'Wineland' (Nova Scotia).
Gerbert of Aurillac (Pope Silvester II); various mathematical works attributed, including treatises on the abacus, the astrolabe and Spanish-Arabic numerals.

1004 **May: 14th**, Henry II crowned as King of Italy (–1024).

1005 **March: 28th**, Henry II makes an alliance with the Wends against Boleslav of Poland, who had seized territory between the Oder and the Elbe. He later invades Poland as far as Poznan and is defeated by Boleslav.

Politics, Government, Law, and Economy

Wang Ch'in-jo (principal editor), *T'sé-fu yūan-kuei* (encyclopedia of Chinese government; completed 1013 in 1,000 books).

Society, Education, and Religion

Al-Hākim founds the Dār al-Hikmah ('Hall of Wisdom', a college of theology), Cairo.

1007 Kakuyid dynasty of Hamadan and Isfahan founded (–1050).

Nov: 1st, Henry founds the Bishopric of Bamberg for the conversion of the Wends, but also in furthering the policy (followed by Otto I) of founding royal authority on the Church as a counter to feudal particularism.

Society, Education, and Religion

First known use of the word 'burgess' or 'bourgeois' (*burgensis*) in charter of Fulk Nerra of Anjou establishing the 'Free borough' of Beaulieu.

Art, Sculpture, Fine Arts, and Architecture
Bamberg Cathedral (–1012).

Literature
Al-Hamadhāni, *Maqāmāt* (Arabic prose fiction).

1008 Al-Muzaffar, regent of Cordova, poisoned and succeeded by his brother, 'Abd-ar-Rahmān; the latter is soon afterwards killed by the populace, and the military now effectively rule in Cordova.

1009 Mahmūd of Ghaznī conquers the principality of Ghūr. Muslims now settling in northwest India.

Sept: **27th**, the church of the Holy Sepulchre at Jerusalem destroyed by order of the Caliph al-Hākim.

Art, Sculpture, Fine Arts, and Architecture
Paderborn Cathedral begun.
Completion of the Siva Temple at Tanjore (the largest and most mature work of South Indian architecture in the Chola period).

1010 Ly Thai-to (–1029) usurps the imperial throne of Dai-co-viet, and founds a new capital at Thang-long; he founds the Ly dynasty (–1225).

Politics, Government, Law, and Economy
King Robert proclaims a Peace of God in France.

Literature
Murasaki Shikibu ('Lady Murasaki'), *Genji Monogatari/Tale of Genji*; the first psychological novel in literature).

1012 **Everyday Life**
Rice is introduced into China from Champa, and becomes the staple diet.

1013 Svein of Denmark, having been accepted as king in Northumbria and the Danelaw, conquers Wessex; Ethelred II flees to Normandy.

May: **24th**, by the Peace of Merseberg, Boleslav of Poland does homage to Henry II and is permitted to retain all his conquests with the exception of Bohemia; he is now able to make war in Russia.

1014 **Jan:** **—**, Henry II holds a synod at Ravenna which makes decrees for ecclesiastical reform.

Feb: **3rd**, death of Svein Forkbeard, King of Denmark, Norway and England; succeeded by his sons, Harold, in Denmark (–1019), and Cnut, in England, but Ethelred restored by the English and Cnut leaves the country.
14th, Henry crowned as Holy Roman Emperor by Pope Benedict VIII (–1024).

April: **18th**, in the battle of Clontarf, Brian Bórumha, High King of Ireland, killed while victorious over a great Viking confederation; Irish unity collapses but the Vikings in Ireland are thereafter peaceful and subject to Irish rulers.

July: **29th**, Basil II captures and blinds a Bulgarian army in the Pass of Kleidion.

Oct: **6th**, death of Samuel, the Bulgarian Tsar.

1015 Death of St. Vladimir I, Great Prince of Russia (Kiev); succeeded by his son(?), Sviatopolk I, after he has restored unity by murdering his brothers, Boris and Gleb; another brother, Jaroslav, holds Novgorod against him.

1016 The first Normans arrive in southern Italy as military adventurers.
Mahmūd of Ghaznī captures Samarqand.
Death of Rājarāja the Great, King of the Cholas, who had made himself supreme in southern India and Ceylon.
Cnut and Edmund make a treaty partitioning England after Cnut's victory at Ashingdon, Essex.

April: **23rd**, death of Ethelred II the Redeless, King of England; succeeded by his son, Edmund Ironside.

Nov: **30th**, death of Edmund Ironside; Cnut now accepted as sole King of England (–1035).

1018 **Oct:** **—**, Byzantine army defeats south Italian rebels at Cannae.

Dec: **20th**, Mahmūd of Ghaznī takes Kanauj, the capital of the kingdom of Pañchāla.

Society, Education, and Religion
In a council at Pavia, Benedict VIII promulgates decrees against clerical marriage and concubinage.
Thietmar, Bishop of Merseburg, *Chronicon* (908–1018; argues that Poland is under German imperial and ecclesiastical authority).

1019 Cnut of England takes possession of the Danish throne in succession to his brother, Harold (–1035).

Basil II completes his conquest of Bulgaria and its former empire in the Balkans; his western frontier now extends to the Adriatic and in the north along the Danube.

1020 **Literature**

Firdausī, *Shāh-Nāma/The Book of Kings*; Persia's national epic.

1021 **Dec:** —, Henry begins his third expedition to Italy in response to further Byzantine successes in Benevento which are endangering Rome.

1022 Henry's Italian expedition checks the Byzantine advance; he takes Capua and Troia before sickness compels the German army to retire.

Society, Education, and Religion

The Emperor promotes Church reform.

1023 Aleppo lost to the Greeks with the establishment there of the independent Mirdāsid emirate (–1079).

1024 **July:** **13th**, death of the Holy Roman Emperor, (St.) Henry II, without issue; he was the last of the Saxon line of emperors.

Sept: **4th**, Conrad (II) of Franconia, the first of the Salian line, elected King of the Germans (–1039).

Politics, Government, Law, and Economy

The Sung government takes over the banks of Chengtu, in Szechwan, and their certificates of deposit then become official and thus the first paper currency in the world.

Art, Sculpture, Fine Arts, and Architecture

Abbey-church of Mont-St.-Michel (–1084).

1025 **Jan:** —, Mahmūd of Ghaznī sacks Somnāth (now Dwārka), the great centre of Hinduism.

June: **17th**, death of Boleslav the Brave, King of Poland, whose kingdom bounded by the Elbe, Baltic, Dneiper, Danube and Theiss now collapses.

Dec: **15th**, death of the Greek Emperor, Basil II the Bulgarslayer.

1026 Cnut defeated in the sea battle of the Holy River by Kings Anund of Sweden and Olaf of Norway and Ulf, his own regent of Denmark.

Conrad crowned as King of Italy (–1039).

Mahmūd of Ghaznī conquers Gujarāt.

1027 **March:** **26th**, Conrad II crowned as Holy Roman Emperor by Pope John XIX (–1039).

1028 Cnut expels Olaf, King of Norway, from his kingdom, which he had united.

Sancho II of Navarre unites Castile to his kingdom.

Society, Education, and Religion

Fulbert dies; he had promoted the great cathedral school, under Hildegaire, at Chartres.

1029 Vikramabāhu I expels the Cholas from Ceylon and becomes King (–1041).

1030 **April:** **21st**, death of Mahmūd, Emir of Ghaznī, founder of the Muslim empire in north-west India; succeeded by his son, Mas'ūd I (–1040).

July: **29th**, (St.) Olaf killed in the battle of Stiklestad while attempting to recover his kingdom of Norway from the Danes.

Art, Sculpture, Fine Arts, and Architecture

Tower of Victory built by Mahmūd at Ghazni.

Cathedral of Speyer (completed 1137).

1031 **Nov:** **30th**, the Spanish Caliphate abolished by the Cordovans with the deposition of Hishām III, the last Umayyad; a score of independent Moorish kingdoms arose in Andalusia.

1033 Sancho III of Navarre creates the kingdom of Castile for his son, Ferdinand I (–1065).

1034 **March:** **15th**, death of Mieszko of Poland; succeeded by his son Casimir I, a minor. The immediately subsequent history of Poland is obscure: there is a resurgence of paganism in which the Church establishment is destroyed.

1035 Death of Sancho III, King of Spain; succeeded in Navarre by his son, Garcia III (–1054); while another son, Ramiro I (–1065), had been established in the newly created kingdom of Aragon.

Death of Rājendra-Choladeva I, King of the Cholas; he had conquered the Pegu kingdom in Burma and the Nīcobar and Andaman Islands, and built a new capital at Gangaikonda-Cholapuram, in Trichinopoly.

July: 2nd, death of Robert I the Devil (or 'the Magnificent'), Duke of Normandy; succeeded by his illegitimate son, William I (– 1087).

Nov: 12th, death of Cnut, King of England, Denmark and (nominally) Norway; succeeded by his son, Harthacnut, in Denmark (–1042), with Harold Harefoot, another son, his regent in England (–1037). In Norway, Magnus I (–1047), the son of St. Olaf, had been established as King in a revolt against Cnut.

Society, Education, and Religion

A collection of approximately 10,000 religious paintings, books and manuscripts in Chinese, Tibetan, Uighur and other languages, walled up for safety at Tun-huang in the Hsi Hsia Kingdom (discovered in 1900).

1037 The Seljuq Turks, who had emigrated from central Asia late in the tenth century, are now, by conquest, established in Khurāsān.

March: —, Conrad holds a diet at Pavia to determine Lombard disputes and arrests Archbishop Aribert of Milan; the latter's escape leads to Conrad's abortive siege of Milan.

Science, Technology, and Discovery

Ibn Sīna (Avicenna) writes *al-Qānūn fi al-Tibb/The Canon of Medicine*, an encyclopedia codifying Greco-Arabic medical learning which dominates medical teaching until the 17th century.

Art, Sculpture, Fine Arts, and Architecture

Kiev Cathedral, with mosaics (–1100).

1038 Conrad takes Capua then returns to Germany.

Li Hüang-hao declares himself Emperor of the Tanguts of Hsi Hsia (Tibetan tribes in western China) and ceases paying tribute to the Sung.

Aug: 15th, death of St. Stephen I, King of Hungary; Peter the German elected as his successor (–1042).

1039 **June: 4th**, death of the Holy Roman Emperor, Conrad II; succeeded by his son, King Henry III (–1056).

1040 Melfi, in Apulia, seized from the Greeks by the six sons of Tancred d'Hauteville and becomes the centre of their (Norman) principality.

Feb: —, Mas'ūd I of Ghaznī deposed following his defeat at Tāliqān by Turks led by the Seljuqs, Tughril Bey and Chagi Bey, who conquer the Ghaznavid territories in Persia.

Literature

Vie de Saint Alexis (anon. poem of 125 strophes each of 5 lines, considered to be the beginning of French literature).

1041 **May: —**, after a second, and successful, campaign in Bohemia, Henry III compels Břatislav to acknowledge his supremacy and surrender his Polish conquests except Silesia.

Statistics

The Chinese army totals 1,259,000 during a war against Tibetan tribes.

1042 **June: 8th**, death of Harthacnut, King of England and Denmark; succeeded in England by his adopted heir, Edward the Confessor, son of Ethelred II (–1066); and in Denmark by Magnus, King of Norway (–1047).

1043 Henry forces Obo of Hungary to cede various territories, thereby establishing the Austro-Hungarian frontier (until 1919).

Aug: —, On a 'Day of Indulgence', Henry III announces his pardon of all his enemies and urges all his subjects to forget their private enmities.

1044 The Sung Emperor undertakes to pay tribute to the Hsi Hsia, after defeating their attempt to conquer China.

Aniruddha becomes (the first historical) King of Pagan (in Burma; –1077).

Ly Thai-tong of Dai-co-viet defeats and kills Jaya Simhavarman II, King of Champa, and sacks Vijaya, his capital.

Society, Education, and Religion

Archbishop Aaron, monk of Brauweiler, begins the reconversion of Poland, establishing a see at Cracow (instead of Gniezno).

1045 **May: 1st**, Benedict IX resigns, selling the Papacy to John Gratian, who is elected as Gregory VI (–1046).

Society, Education, and Religion
Constantine IX re-founds the University of Constantinople, establishing faculties of law and philosophy; the notable jurist, John Xiphilin, was first head of the new law school.

Science, Technology, and Discovery
Earliest dated use in China of (earthenware) movable type for printing, invented by Pi Shéng.

Art, Sculpture, Fine Arts, and Architecture
Novgorod Cathedral burnt; rebuilt in stone.

1046 **May: 8th**, Guillaume d'Hauteville, Count of Apulia, defeats Greek forces at Trani.

Oct: 25th, in a council held by Henry at Pavia, the corrupt ecclesiastical practice of simony is denounced.

Dec: 20th, in the Synod of Sutri held by Henry, Benedict IX and Gregory VI are deposed from the Papacy.
25th, Pope Clement II crowns Henry as Holy Roman Emperor (–1056).

1047 William assumes personal rule of his Duchy of Normandy and, assisted by King Henry, defeats Norman rebels at Val-ès-Dunes, near Caen.

Politics, Government, Law, and Economy
Établissements de Saint-Quentin (drawn up in 1151 but dating from 1047–80 and thus the earliest known code of laws and customs in a French town).

1048 The Pechenegs begin their continuous ravages in the Balkans.

Dec: —, Bruno of Egisheim, Bishop of Toul, elected as Pope Leo IX (–1054).

Science, Technology, and Discovery
Al-Bīrunī ('the master'), *Ta'rikh al-Hind* (*Description of India*); an astronomical encyclopedia; a summary of mathematics, astronomy and astrology.

1049 **Society, Education, and Religion**
(Oct) reforming decrees (against simony, etc.) enacted in church councils held by Leo IX at Reims and Mainz.

Art, Sculpture, Fine Arts, and Architecture
Abbey-church of St. Remi, Reims, dedicated.

1050 Tughril Bey (–1063), the Seljuq leader, takes Isfahan, which becomes the capital of his empire in Persia and Khurāsān; end of the Kakuyid dynasty.

Society, Education, and Religion
Berengar of Tours, author of *De Caena Domini*, condemned for heresy by the council of Vercelli.

Humanities and Scholarship
Raoul Glaber, *Historiae sui temporis* (mainly French history, 900–1044).

Art, Sculpture, Fine Arts, and Architecture
Mosaics in church of Nea Moni, Chios.

Music
Guido d'Arezzo, *Micrologus de Disciplina Artis Musicæ* (his innovations include changing two-line stave into five-line stave, the system of hexachords, new notations and the ut-re-mi-fa-so-la names for notes).

Literature
Konjaku Monigatari (collection of hundreds of stories in Japanese classic literature).
Digenes Akritas (Greek epic).

1052 Henry III makes his last expedition into Hungary, where he suppresses a rebellion.

1053 **June: 18th**, in the battle of Civitate, the Normans led by Humphrey d'Hauteville, Count of Apulia, capture Pope Leo IX, who had proclaimed a 'holy war' against them; he renounces it to obtain his release.

1054 **Feb: —**, King Henry of France, now as the ally of Geoffrey Martel, invades Normandy and is defeated by Duke William at Mortemer.

March: —, Henry III begins an expedition into Italy.

April: 19th, death of Pope Leo IX.

Sept: 3rd, Ferdinand I of Castile defeats and kills his brother, Garcia III of Navarre, at Atapuerca, near Burgos; Garcia's son, Sancho IV, succeeds as King of Navarre (–1076).

Society, Education, and Religion

Cerularius, Patriarch of Constantinople, refuses to meet Cardinal Humbert and other legates (sent by Leo IX, now dead) who excommunicate him; this was the final breach between the Roman and Greek Churches.

1055 Henry III makes his second expedition to Italy.

Feb: **7th**, death of Jaroslav I, Great Prince of Russia. By his will, Jaroslav divides his lands among five sons; civil war follows, and the 'Golden Age of Kiev' thus ends.

Dec: **18th**, Baghdād surrenders to the Seljuq Turks, who thus end Buwayhid rule. Tughril Bey, proclaimed as Sultan, so asserts his supremacy over the Islamic lands, centring on Persia, which the Seljuqs had conquered. (The Caliph remains the spiritual ruler of Islam.)

1056 **Oct:** **5th**, death of the Holy Roman Emperor, Henry III; succeeded by his son, Henry IV (–1105), with his widow, Agnes, as regent (–1062).

1057 Aniruddha of Pagan defeats Makuta, King of the Mons of Thaton, and annexes the Irrawaddy Delta.

Aug: **—**, Robert Guiscard succeeds as Count of Apulia.

1058 **Nov:** **28th**, death of Casimir the Restorer, Duke of Poland, who had restored the unity of the Polish tribes, recovered lost territories and had the Church reconstructed.

Humanities and Scholarship

Solomon ben Gabīrōl (Avicebron), *Yanbū'al-Hayah/Fountain of Life*; Neo-Platonic Muslim philosophy.

1059 **Aug:** **—**, by the treaty of Melfi, Pope Nicholas II invests Robert Guiscard as Duke of Apulia and Calabria and Count of Sicily, and his vassal (–1085).

Art, Sculpture, Fine Arts, and Architecture

The Nan Paya and the Manuha Temples, Pagan, Burma.

1060 Bhoja, King of Mālwā, defeated and killed by the Kings of Gujarāt and Chedi.

1061 **Summer:** Roger Guiscard begins the Norman conquest of Sicily with the capture of Messina; he had been invited into the island by Ibn ath-Thimna, one of the Saracen leaders in a civil war.

Society, Education, and Religion

Cardinal Humbert, *Liber adversus Symoniacos*.

1063 **Art, Sculpture, Fine Arts, and Architecture**

Pisa Cathedral and campanile ('Leaning Tower'; –1271).

S. Marco, Venice, with mosaics (–1095).

1064 Alp Arslan conquers Ani (central Armenia) and the kingdom of Kars.

Politics, Government, Law, and Economy

(or 1069) Raymond-Berengar of Catalonia publishes the *Usatges* (the earliest feudal code).

1065 Alp Arslan makes conquests in Transoxiana; other Seljuq Turks invade Syria.

May: **8th**, Ramiro I of Aragon killed attacking the Moors in Graus; succeeded by his son, Sancho Ramirez (–1094). His death attracts assistance from western Europe for the crusade against the Moors.

Society, Education, and Religion

Foundation of the Nizāmīyah (theological college; the Nizāmī University), Baghdād; others soon followed at Neyshabur, Damascus, Jerusalem, Cairo and Alexandria.

1066 **Jan:** **—**, Henry IV begins his personal government in Germany after dismissing Archbishop Adalbert.

5th, death of Edward the Confessor, King of England.

6th, Harold of Wessex elected as his successor.

Sept: **25th**, Harold Hardrada, King of Norway, and Tostig defeated and killed by Harold of England at Stamford Bridge.

Oct: **14th**, Harold defeated and killed by William of Normandy at Hastings.

Dec: **25th**, William crowned as King of England (–1087).

1068 Yūsuf-ibn-Tāshfīn, a founder of the Murābit (or Almoravid, Berber) Empire, founds Marrakesh (Morocco) as his capital.

The Cumans defeat the Russian princes near Pereyslavl.

Ly Thanh-tong of Dai-co-viet (which he renames Dai Viet) defeats and captures Rudravarman III of Champa, and annexes his northern provinces.

Politics, Government, Law, and Economy

In Japan there begins the 'Camera system' of rule by the retired emperors (the father and/or grandfather or the reigning emperor, usually a minor), in competition with the Fujiwara regents.

1070 Vijayabāhu completes the destruction of Chola power in Ceylon.

Aug: —, Henry IV deprives Otto of Nordheim, because of his treason, of his estates in Saxony and of the Duchy of Bavaria.

15th, William I deposes Stigand and appoints Lanfranc as Archbishop of Canterbury.

Society, Education, and Religion

Canterbury Cathedral and abbey-church of Bury St. Edmunds begun.

1071 Henry IV suppresses a Saxon revolt in favour of Otto of Nordheim.

April: —, with the capture of Bari, Robert Guiscard completes the expulsion of the Greeks from Italy.

Aug: 19th, Alp Arslan destroys a Greek army at Manzikert, in Armenia, and captures Romanus IV, whom he frees for a ransom and the payment of tribute; the Seljuq Turks now complete their conquest of Armenia and overrun most of Asia Minor. In this year, they also conquer Syria and Atsiz ibn-Abaq takes Jerusalem (from the Egyptians).

Society, Education, and Religion

The new abbey-church of Montecassino dedicated.

1072 **Jan: 10th**, Robert Guiscard captures Palermo.

Dec: 15th, the Seljuq Sultan, Alp Arslan, murdered while campaigning in Transoxiana; succeeded by his son, Malik Shah (–1092).

Politics, Government, Law, and Economy

Ou-yang Hsiu developed the first censorship rules, in China.

Pravda (Compilation of Russian laws by Jaroslav's sons).

1073 Sulaymān ibn-Qutlamish, a Seljuq, begins the systematic conquest of Asia Minor.

April: 22nd, Hildebrand elected as Pope Gregory VII (–1085).

Aug: —, Henry IV expelled from Saxony in a new rising under Otto of Nordheim.

1074 **Society, Education, and Religion**

Gregory sends legates to France to reform the Church there; he announces the excommunication of married priests.

Science, Technology, and Discovery

Malik Shah builds a new observatory (at Ray or Neyshabur), where 'Umar al-Khayyām is engaged to reform the old Persian calendar.

1075 **June: 9th**, Henry defeats the Saxons at Homburg-on-Unstrut.

Society, Education, and Religion

Gregory VII, *Dictatus Papae* (detailing his vision of papal powers).

Cathedral of Santiago de Compostela (–1211); French masons recruited.

1076 The Berbers destroy Ghana, capital of the (Mandingo) Negro Empire of Ghana (Western Sudan).

Jan: 24th, Henry responds to a letter from Gregory threatening excommunication by holding, at Worms, a council where the German bishops renounce their allegiance to Gregory; the Pope (in Lent) then excommunicates Henry.

Dec: 25th, Boleslav crowned as King of Poland with a crown sent by Gregory to reward his zeal in restoring the Church in Poland, under the direction of papal legates, and for supporting the Pope against Henry.

Politics, Government, Law, and Economy

Dismissal of Wang An-Shih, Chief Councillor of the Sung Empire (from 1069), due to opposition to his extensive reforms of government.

Society, Education, and Religion

A national university established in Dai Viet.

1077 Robert Guiscard occupies the Lombard principality of Salerno.

Sulaymān ibn-Qutlamish (–1086) establishes the Seljuq sultanate of Rūm (–1307), with his capital at Nicaea.

Death of Aniruddha, first King of united Burma and founder of its Pagan dynasty.

Jan: —, Henry submits to Gregory at Canossa and is absolved from excommunication.

March: 13th, in a diet at Forchheim, Henry's German enemies affirm that the German crown is elective and choose Rudolf, Duke of Swabia, as King.

Humanities and Scholarship
Lambert of Hersfeld, *Annales* (from the Creation to 1077).

1078 **Aug:** **7th**, Rudolf of Swabia obliged to withdraw after an otherwise indecisive battle with Henry at Mellrichstadt.

Nov: **—**, Gregory publishes a decree condemning lay investiture into spiritual offices.

Society, Education, and Religion
Legates sent by Gregory reorganize the English Church.
Gregory orders all bishops to found cathedral-schools.

Humanities and Scholarship
Michael Psellus, *The Chronography, 976–1078* (historical narrative of events in Constantinople and the Empire; personal commentary for the period of the writer's life).

1079 **Science, Technology, and Discovery**
(15th March) the Jalālī Era computed by 'Umar al-Khayyām in his *Astronomical Calendar* adopted in Persia.

1080 **Jan:** **27th**, Henry defeated at Flarchheim and compelled to abandon Saxony.

March: **7th**, Gregory pronounces in favour of Rudolf of Swabia and declares Henry to be deposed.

June: **25th**, Henry holds a council of bishops at Brixen which declares Gregory to be deposed and elects Guibert, Archbishop of Ravenna, as Pope Clement III (–1100).
29th, by the treaty of Ceprano, Gregory makes an alliance with Robert Guiscard and recognizes his conquests.

Oct: **15th**, in a battle near Hohen-Mölsen, Henry is defeated but Rudolf is mortally wounded.

Society, Education, and Religion
Gniezno and Cracow Cathedrals.
Abbey of St. Sernin, Toulouse, founded.

Art, Sculpture, Fine Arts, and Architecture
Bayeux Tapestry (a pictorial record of the Norman Conquest of England).
Rebuilding of S. Ambrogio, Milan, begun.

1081 Alfonso VI of Castile exiles Rodrigo (or Ruy) Diaz de Vivar ('The Cid').

March: **—**, the Greek Emperor, Nicephorus III, deposed in favour of Alexius I Comnenus (–1118).

April: **—**, a rebellion in Poland forces Boleslav into exile; succeeded by his brother, Vladislav I Hermann (–1102), under whom the Polish territories disintegrate in civil war and its crown falls into abeyance.

June: **—**, the conquests east of the Dracon by Sulaymān, Sultan of Rūm, are recognized in a treaty with Alexius.
17th, Robert Guiscard, invading the Greek Empire, begins his siege of Durazzo; he occupies Corfù.

Oct: **18th**, Guiscard defeats Alexius near Durazzo.

1082 Alexius grants Venice extensive rights to trade in the Greek Empire.

1083 **June:** **3rd**, Henry captures St. Peter's Rome; his negotiations with Gregory collapse.

1084 **March:** **21st**, Henry enters Rome.
24th, Clement III crowned as Pope.
31st, Clement crowns Henry as Holy Roman Emperor.

May: **—**, Guiscard expels the Germans from Rome and his Normans sack the city.

Society, Education, and Religion
St. Bruno founds his hermitage at Chartreuse (origin of the Carthusian Order).

1085 **May:** **25th**, death of Pope Gregory VII the Great at Salerno.
25th, Alfonso of Castile and Leon takes Toledo, then subjects the Muslim Kings of Valencia.

July: **17th**, death of Robert Guiscard; succeeded, as Duke of Apulia, by his son, Roger Borsa (–1111), who withdraws the Normans from Greece. Robert's brother, Roger, succeeds in Sicily and Calabria (–1101).

Dec: **25th**, William orders the survey of England subsequently recorded in *Domesday Book*, possibly because of the threat from Cnut.

Politics, Government, Law, and Economy
Henry IV extends the 'Peace of God' over the whole Empire.

Literature
Somadeva, *Ocean of the Streams of Story* (as translated from the collection of Sanskrit folk stories).

1086 Sulaymān, Sultan of Rūm, defeated and killed by Tutush while attempting to take Aleppo; succeeded by his son, Kilij Arslan I (–1107).

Oct: **23rd**, Yūsuf ibn-Tāshfin, the Berber ruler, who had been called into Spain by al-Mu'tamid of Seville, defeats Alfonso of Castile and Leon at Azagal (or Zalaca, near Badajoz).

Humanities and Scholarship
Sšu-ma Kuang, *Tžu chih t'ung chien/Universal Mirror to Assist Government*; comprehensive history of China, 403 BC–AD 959, in 294 chapters.

1087 The Pechenegs attempt to storm Constantinople.

Sept: **9th**, death of William I the Conqueror, King of England.

Politics, Government, Law, and Economy
Nizām-al-Mulk regularizes the system of military fiefs in the Seljuq Empire; these become hereditary and assist its disintegration.

Science, Technology, and Discovery
Constantine the African produces the first translation of Arab medical works into Latin.

Statistics
Domesday Book records 5,624 water-mills for corn south of the Trent and Severn – roughly one mill for every 400 people, some stamping-mills for crushing iron-ore, and hammer-mills.

1088 **Art, Sculpture, Fine Arts, and Architecture**
Cluny 'III' (the largest of all abbey-churches; –1130).
Tower of London ('The White Tower').

1089 The Fātamids recover Ascalon, Tyre and Acre from the Seljuqs.

1090 **April:** **29th**, Alexius defeats the Pechenegs, who are settling in Bulgaria, at Mount Levunium.

Nov: —, Yūsuf ibn-Tāshfin, returning to Spain from Africa, takes Granada; he founds the Almoravid dynasty in Spain (–1147).

Science, Technology, and Discovery
First dated Chinese reference to a flyer in silk-working machinery.

1091 Yūsuf destroys, and unites, the Muslim kingdoms of Andalusia.
Roger Guiscard takes Butera, so completing the conquest of Sicily from the Saracens.
Malik Shah makes Baghdād the Seljuq capital.

April: **11th**, Henry takes Mantua and, subsequently, defeats the forces of Matilda of Tuscany at Tricontai.

Science, Technology, and Discovery
(or 1042) Walcher of Malvern observes an eclipse of the moon (one of the earliest west European observations).

1092 Kilij Arslan seizes Nicaea and Smyrna from independent Turkish rulers.

Nov: —, Death of Malik Shah, Sultan of Persia; succeeded by his son, Mahmūd I (–1094), who fights his brothers, while the Seljuq Empire disintegrates with the emergence of independent rulers.

Politics, Government, Law, and Economy
Nizām-al-Mulk, *Siyāsat-nāmah* (treatise on the art of government).

1093 Alfonso of Castile and Leon takes Santarem, Lisbon and Cintra.

Science, Technology, and Discovery
Shén Kua writes *Méng-ch'i* (*Essays from the Torrent of Dreams*; sections on mathematics, music, archaeology and other sciences, with earliest literary mention of a magnetic needle and description of printing with movable type).

Art, Sculpture, Fine Arts, and Architecture
Durham Cathedral (–1133); here ribs first appeared in the vaulting (as decoration).

1094 The Cid captures Valencia and holds it against the Moors (–1099).

Urban II regains possession of the Lateran Palace, so completing his recovery of Rome from adherents of the anti-pope, Clement III; Henry's cause in Italy is now ruined, although he is unable to leave; the Empress Adelaide deserts him.

Dec: 29th, death of al-Munstansir, Caliph of Egypt; his north African empire now rapidly declines and the caliphate is held by a succession of powerless nonentities, several of whom are murdered.

Society, Education, and Religion

Anselm, *Cur Deus Homo/Why did God become man?*.

1095 Death of the Seljuq prince, Tutush; his dominions disintegrate, as his sons, Ridwān and Duqāq, ruling Aleppo and Damascus respectively, cannot prevent other Turkish leaders from establishing themselves in Jerusalem, etc.

Feb: 25th, in a council at Rockingham, Archbishop Anselm of Canterbury quarrels with William II over the issue of episcopal obedience to the King and/or Pope.

Nov: 18th, –28th Urban holds a council at Clermont and (on the 27th) proclaims the First Crusade, granting an indulgence to participants. The Crusade's aim is to liberate Jerusalem.

Science, Technology, and Discovery

(–1123) At St. Bertin, water-power applied to water-lifting and irrigation wheels.

Literature

Eiga Monogatari (*A Tale of Glory*; a romanticized chronicle of the Fujiwara family 889–1092; thus the earliest known Japanese historical novel).

La Chanson de Roland earliest extant example of a *chanson de geste*; 'eleventh century: certainly not later than 1095' – Saintsbury.

1096 Pedro of Aragon defeats the Moors at Alcaraz and takes Huesca.

Aug: 1st, Crusaders led by Peter the Hermit arrive in Constantinople.

Oct: 21st, Kilij Arslan destroys the army of 'the People's Crusade' at Civetot.

Art, Sculpture, Fine Arts, and Architecture

Abbey-church of Ste. Madeleine, Vézelay (–1104).

1097 The Russian princes descended from Jaroslav meet at Liubech (near Kiev) and agree to unite against the Cumans who are now in occupation of the southern Russian steppes, to the Dneiper.

Aug: —, the Crusaders take Iconium (now Konya), Kilij Arslan's capital.

Oct: —, Archbishop Anselm begins his first exile from England.

1098 **June: 3rd**, the Crusaders take Antioch.

Society, Education, and Religion

(21st March) Robert of Molesme founds Cîteaux Abbey (and the Cistercian Order).

1099 Death of the Cid; the Moors then recover Valencia.

Jan: 5th, Henry, son of Henry IV, elected as King of the Romans; Henry IV had now made peace with his enemies in Germany.

July: 15th, the Crusaders take Jerusalem.

22nd, Godfrey of Bouillon elected as Defender of the Holy Sepulchre; thus, in effect, is the Latin Kingdom of Jerusalem founded.

Society, Education, and Religion

Foundation of the Order of Knights of St. John of Jerusalem.

1100 **Aug: 2nd**, William II Rufus, King of England, killed.

5th, coronation of William Rufus' brother, Henry I, as king (–1135); he issues a 'charter of liberties' and recalls Anselm.

Politics, Government, Law, and Economy

Irnerius establishes the glossatorial method in the rising law-school at Bologna. His successors were 'the Four Doctors', viz. Bulgarus, (–1166), Martinus, Jacobus and Hugo.

Science, Technology, and Discovery

'Theophilus' writes *Diversarum artium schedula*, an encyclopedia of arts and crafts; it gives the earliest European account of bell-founding and describes processes in metallurgy).

Humanities and Scholarship

Adelard of Bath translates Euclid into Latin from Arabic.

1102 Matilda, Countess of Tuscany, grants 'the Patrimony of St. Peter' to the Papacy.

Science, Technology, and Discovery
A public medical service is organized in China.

1103 **April:** **27th**, Anselm begins his second exile after quarrelling with Henry I.

1104 **May:** **—**, Baldwin of Jerusalem takes Acre.

Dec: **12th**, Henry revolts against his father, the Emperor Henry IV.

Society, Education, and Religion
Saewulf, monk of Malmesbury, account (Latin) of his early pilgrimage to Jerusalem, 1102–03 (the earliest extant pilgrim-narratives).

1105 **Aug:** **27th**, Baldwin defeats the Egyptians in the third battle of Ramleh, ending their attempts to reconquer Palestine.

Dec: **—**, Henry IV captured by his son, Henry, and forced to abdicate; he escapes early in 1106. Henry V thus succeeds as King of the Germans (–1125).

1107 **July:** **—**, Kilij Arslan I, Sultan of Rūm, killed near Mosul, which he had recently taken, in battle with other Turks; succeeded by his brother, Malik Shah (–1117).

Aug: **—**, Henry I and Anselm settle their disagreement over the investiture of bishops.

Art, Sculpture, Fine Arts, and Architecture
Mi Fei, an outstanding Chinese painter and calligrapher.

1108 **Sept:** **—**, by the Treaty of Devol, Bohemond, who had surrendered to Alexius, becomes the Emperor's vassal as Prince of Antioch.

Society, Education, and Religion
William of Champeaux founds a theological school in the Abbey of St. Victor, Paris.

1109 **June:** **30th**, death of Alfonso I of Castile and VI of Leon; succeeded by his daughter Urracca (–1126), married to Alfonso I of Aragon, who styles himself Emperor of the Spains.

July: **12th**, Tripoli surrenders to Baldwin of Jerusalem.

1110 **Aug:** **—**, Henry V begins his first expedition to Italy.

Society, Education, and Religion
Basil, leader of the Bulgarian heretics (Bogomils), burnt by order of Alexius.

Humanities and Scholarship
Nestor of Kiev, *The Ancient Chronicle* (the first Russian chronicle, from the Deluge to 1110).

Art, Sculpture, Fine Arts, and Architecture
Temple of Anantapanna (or Ananda), Pagan (the greatest work of Burmese architecture).

1111 Russian princes win a decisive victory over the Cumans on the Salnitsa.

Feb: **4th**, by the Treaty of Sutri, Henry V compels Paschal II to agree to his terms for the settlement of the investiture controversy; the agreement is withdrawn in the following years.

April: **13th**, Henry V crowned as Holy Roman Emperor (–1125).

Science, Technology, and Discovery
Al-Ghazzāli (Algazel), the Persian theologian and mystic (Sūfi), inspires Muslim intolerance to science and its study now declines in Islamic lands.

Humanities and Scholarship
Guibert of Nogent, *Gesta Dei per Francos* (history of the First Crusade, 1095–1101).

1112 **Sept:** **—**, Henry V excommunicated in the Synod of Vienne.

1113 A Saxon rebellion against Henry V defeated at the battle of Warmstadt.

Society, Education, and Religion
Peter Abelard opens a school for rhetoric, philosophy and theology in Paris.

1114 **Art, Sculpture, Fine Arts, and Architecture**
Tower of Victory built by Mas'ūd III at Ghaznī.

Everyday Life
Earliest record of the great international fairs of Champagne, at Bar-sur-Aube and Troyes.

1115 The Christian conquest of the Balearic Islands completed; Raymond-Berengar of Barcelona takes possession of Majorca and Iviza.

A-ku-ta, leader of the Jürched (Ju-chen; Tungusic tribes in Manchuria) in rebellion against the Liao, declares himself Emperor, with the Chinese dynastic name of 'Chin'.

July: 24th, death of Matilda, Countess of Tuscany; she bequeaths her lands to Henry V, setting aside a previous bequest to the Papacy.

Society, Education, and Religion

Ivo of Chartres, *Panormia Decretum; Tripartite Collection* (canon law).

Art, Sculpture, Fine Arts, and Architecture

The tympanum of the portal of Moissac priory-church, portraying Christ in majesty, signals the revival of sculpture in western Europe.

1117 **March: —**, Pope Paschal II flees from Rome as Henry V approaches, and enters, returning to Germany in the following years.

Science, Technology, and Discovery

Earliest Chinese reference to a compass for navigation at sea, in Chu Yü's *Pingchow Table Talk*.

1118 Sanjar of Khurāsān becomes supreme Seljuq Sultan on the death of Muhammad I (–1157).

Jan: 24th, John of Gaeta elected as Pope Gelasius II (–1118).

March: 8th, Henry V has Maurice Bourdin, Archbishop of Braga, elected as Pope Gregory VIII and installs him in Rome (–1121).

Aug: 15th, death of the Greek Emperor, Alexius I Comnenus; succeeded by his son, John II (–1143).

Dec: 19th, Alfonso of Aragon captures Saragossa from its Muslim ruler.

Politics, Government, Law, and Economy

Alexius had established a form of feudalism in the Greek Empire by a grant of estates conditional upon military service (*pronoia*).

1119 **Jan: 29th**, Pope Gelasius II dies at Cluny.

Feb: 2nd, Guy, Archbishop of Vienne, elected as Pope Calixtus II (–1124).

June: 28th, on 'the Field of Blood', the Frankish army of Antioch is destroyed by Ghāzi, the Danishmend ruler.

Aug: 20th, Henry I of England defeats Louis VI of France at Brémule.

Society, Education, and Religion

Ballāl Sen, King of East Sengal, is said to have reorganized the Indian caste system.

The Order of Knights Templars founded in Jerusalem.

(23rd Dec) Calixtus II confirms the Cistercian rule (*Carta Caritatis*).

Art, Sculpture, Fine Arts, and Architecture

Autun Cathedral; Gislebert's sculpture (–1130).

1120 Alfonso of Aragon defeats the Muslims at Cutanda and Daroca. The Sung ally with the Jürched against the Liao.

Nov: 25th, William, the son and heir of Henry I, drowned with 'The White Ship'.

Art, Sculpture, Fine Arts, and Architecture

Abbey-church of Ste. Madeleine, Vézelay, burnt; rebuilt (–1132).

1121 **Sept: 29th**, in a diet at Würzburg, Henry V makes peace with his German enemies.

Nov: 27th, Muhammad ibn-Tūmart (–1129), leader of the Almohads of the Atlas mountains, hailed as Mahdī by his followers and begins his conquest of the Almoravid territories in north west Africa.

Society, Education, and Religion

Abelard condemned for erroneous theological opinions at the council of Soissons.

William of Champeaux, a founder of Realist philosophy, the first famous master of the Cathedral School, Paris.

1122 The Greeks exterminate the Pechenegs.

The Liao Empire collapses and A-ku-ta establishes the Chin dynasty in its place (–1234).

Sept: 23rd, the Investiture Contest ends with the Concordat at Worms between Calixtus II and Henry V.

Society, Education, and Religion
Peter Abelard, *Sic et Non*? (logical discussion of certain writings of the Christian Fathers).

Literature
Al-Harīri, *Maqāmāt* (Arabic *belles-lettres*; 50 picaresque stories).

1123 John II defeats the Serbians.

April: 18th, Baldwin II of Jerusalem captured and his army destroyed in a surprise attack on his camp near Gargar, on the Euphrates, by Balak of Khanzit.

May: 29th, an invading Egyptian army flees before the Franks at Ibelin; the Venetians destroy their fleet off Ascalon.

Society, Education, and Religion
(18 March) (–April 5th) Calixtus II holds the first general council of the Church in west Europe (the First Lateran Council); its condemns simony and the marriage of priests. He also sends a legate to complete the organization of the Polish Church; three new bishoprics founded, including one for Pomerania.

Literature
'Umar al-Khayyām, *Rubaiyat* (Persian quatrains).

1124 John II defeats the Hungarians.
(–1125) Lothar, Duke of Saxony, penetrates the lands of the pagan Slavs as far as the lower Oder and destroys their great temple at Retra.

Aug: —, Henry V attempts to invade France as the ally of Henry I, but retires as the French vassals respond to Louis' summons to military service.

1125 The Jürched take Peking and destroy the Liao, the ruling dynasty of the Khitan; they next advance against their former ally, the Emperor Hui Tsung, who abdicates.

May: 23rd, death of Henry V, the last Salian Emperor, without issue.

Aug: 30th, Lothar of Supplinburg, Duke of Saxony, elected as King of the Romans (i.e., Germany; –1137).

Humanities and Scholarship
(–1149) Raymond, Archbishop of Toledo, organizes the translation into Latin of Arabic texts of Aristotle's works.

1126 The Jürched take Kaifeng, the Sung capital; they expand to the east and west, Korea and Hsi Hsia becoming vassals, and south to the River Huai.

Society, Education, and Religion
Bernard of Clairvaux, *On the Love of God*.

Science, Technology, and Discovery
Earliest European notice of an artesian well (in *Artois*).

1127 'Imad ad-Din Zangi (–1146) appointed *atabeg* (governor) of Mosul in succession to il-Bursuqi; he becomes the Muslim champion against the Franks and founds the Zangid dynasty (–1262).
Kao Tsung, son of Hui Tsung, establishes the southern Sung dynasty, with his capital in Hangchow (–1279).

1128 **June: 17th**, Henry I's daughter, Matilda, widow of Henry V, marries Geoffrey Plantagenet of Anjou; she is recognized in England as her father's heir.

Society, Education, and Religion
Al-Shahrastānī, *Kitāb al-Milal w-al-Nihal (Book of Religions and Sects*; comprehensive history of religions).

1129 **May: —**, Fulk V, Count of Anjou, joins Baldwin of Jerusalem and marries his daughter, Melisande; Fulk's son, Geoffrey, succeeds as Count of Anjou (–1151).

1130 Yeh-lü Ta-shih, a surviving member of the Liao, founds the Kara-Khitai (or Western Liao) Empire in East Turkestan (–1211).

Feb: 13th, death of Pope Honorius II; on the same day, both Gregory Papareschi (as Innocent II; –1143) and Peter Pierleoni (as Anacletus II; –1138) elected as Pope; Innocent is forced to leave Rome.

Sept: 27th, Roger undertakes to recognize Anacletus as Pope in return for his creation as King of Sicily and Apulia.

Politics, Government, Law, and Economy
Pipe roll of the English Exchequer for 1129–30 (the earliest surviving example of an administrative record kept annually).

Science, Technology, and Discovery
Earliest European reference to breast-strap harness for horses (allowing drawing of heavier loads, ploughs, etc.).

Art, Sculpture, Fine Arts, and Architecture
(25th Oct) Conques abbey-church completed.

1131 **Humanities and Scholarship**
'Ain al-Qudāt al-Hamadhānī, *Apologia* (written when this great Sūfī mystic philosopher was in prison awaiting execution).

1133 **June:** **4th**, Lothar III crowned as Holy Roman Emperor (–1137), by Innocent II, in Rome.

1135 **May:** **26th**, Alfonso of Castile and Leon acclaimed as Emperor of Spain.

Dec: **1st**, death of Henry I, King of England.
26th, Stephen of Blois, nephew of William I, crowned as King of England (–1154).

Science, Technology, and Discovery
Al-Jurjāni, *Dhakhīra al-Khwārizmshāhī*, (*The Treasure of the King of Khwārizm*; immense medical encyclopedia, in Persian).

Art, Sculpture, Fine Arts, and Architecture
Hui Tsung, former Emperor of China, a painter and great patron of the arts; the catalogue of his collection shows he possessed 6,192 paintings.

1136 (–1137) Lothar overruns Apulia and Calabria, meeting little opposition because the inhabitants simultaneously revolt against Roger of Sicily.

Aug: **15th**, when assembling his army for his Italian expedition, Lothar (probably now) invests Henry of Bavaria as Duke of Saxony, making him the most powerful prince in Germany (–Jul 1138).

Science, Technology, and Discovery
Discovery of silver-bearing ore at Freiburg, Saxony; a 'silver-rush' follows, and Freiburg becomes a centre for metallurgy.

1137 **July:** **4th**, by the treaty of Tuy, Alfonso Henriques of Portugal recognizes the suzerainty of Alfonso, Emperor of Spain.

Aug: **29th**, John II Comnenus conquers Lesser Armenia (Cilicia).

Dec: **4th**, death of the Holy Roman Emperor, Lothar III.

Science, Technology, and Discovery
Oldest extant Chinese maps, engraved on a stone slab.

Humanities and Scholarship
Geoffrey of Monmouth, *Historia Regum Britanniae* (*History of the Kings of Britain* – the apocryphal 'British history' with the story of Arthur as a heroic king-figure introducing Merlin & Co.; it is the source of the stories about King Lear, Cymbeline, Gorboduc, etc.).

1138 Boleslav III of Poland defeated while invading Russia, and dies; thus ends a period of Polish expansion. His lands are partitioned by his sons and civil war follows.

Jan: **25th**, death of the anti-pope, Anacletus II.

March: **3rd**, Conrad of Hohenstaufen elected as King of the Romans. He is opposed by Henry the Proud.

May: **—**, Robert, Earl of Gloucester, begins a civil war in England by declaring himself against Stephen.

1139 Death of Jaropolk II of Kiev; Vsévolod II seizes the city (–1146). The surviving political unity of the Russian federation now finally collapses with the rivalry of princes for leadership and the provincial separatism of their subjects.

July: **22nd**, Pope Innocent II defeated and captured by Roger of Sicily on the Garigliano; by the treaty of Mignano (25th July), he gains his liberty by recognizing Roger as King.

Sept: **30th**, Matilda comes to England to lead her partisans against Stephen.

Oct: **20th**, death of Henry the Proud, former Duke of Bavaria and Saxony; his son, Henry the

Lion, claims to succeed but Conrad had granted Bavaria to Leopold of Austria and Saxony to Albert the Bear of Brandenburg.

Society, Education, and Religion

(–1141) Gratian of Bologna, *Concordia discordantium canonum* (better known as the *Decretum*; it founded the codification of canon law).

1140 **Dec:** —, Conrad defeats Welf (VI), Henry the Lion's uncle, who was leading opposition to the grant of Bavaria to Leopold; in the battle, at Weinsberg, there seemingly originate the appellations of 'Welf' (Guelf) and 'Weibling' (Ghibelline).

Politics, Government, Law, and Economy

The St. Gothard Pass now open as a commercial route; a bridge had been made over the Schollenen gorges.

Society, Education, and Religion

Peter Abelard condemned at the council of Sens at the instance of St. Bernard.

Judah ha-Levi, *Zion ha-lo tish'ali* (*Ode to Zion*; Hebrew poem); *Kitāb al-Khazarī* (dialogue in Arabic defending revealed religion from philosophy).

Art, Sculpture, Fine Arts, and Architecture

The new west front of St. Denis', Paris, now completed with a façade, which in design and sculpture marks the beginning of Gothic architecture; Abbot Suger now begins a new east end, with 'Gothic' vaulting and stained glass windows.

Literature

Cantore di mio Cid (*Poema del Cid Campeador: The Song of the Cid*; Spanish epic poem about the deeds of Rodrigo or Ruy Diaz de Vivar, d. 1099).

1141 **Feb:** **2nd**, Robert of Gloucester defeats and captures Stephen at Lincoln.

March: **3rd**, Matilda proclaimed as Queen of England in Winchester.

Sept: **9th**, Sanjar, the Seljuq Sultan, defeated on the Qatwān Steppe, at Samarqand, by the Kara-Khitai, who are establishing an empire stretching from China to the Oxus.

Dec: —, death of the Danishmend Malik ('King'), Muhammad ibn Ghāzī; his territories in Anatolia disintegrate.

Humanities and Scholarship

Hugh of St. Victor, *De sacramentis Christiane Fidei; Didascalicon de studio legendi* (encyclopedia of knowledge); *De arca Noë* (treatise on Noah's ark).

1142 **May:** —, the civil war in Germany terminated in a diet at Frankfurt; Conrad grants Saxony to Henry the Lion (–Jan 1180) and Bavaria to Henry Jasomirgott, brother of Leopold of Austria (now dead).

Sept: **25th**, John Comnenus reaches Baghras, after campaigning against the Turks in Anatolia, and sends Raymond orders to surrender Antioch to him; on Raymond's refusal, John withdraws into Cilicia and dies the following year.

Humanities and Scholarship

William of Malmesbury, *Historia Regum Anglorum* and *Historia Novella* (history of England to 1142); *Gesta Pontificum Anglorum* (the English Church to 1120).

Literature

Peter Abelard, *Letters* (to Héloise; including the celebrated autobiographical *Historia Calamitatum Mearum*).

1143 **Politics, Government, Law, and Economy**

Venice begins the formation of its communal institutions with the establishment of the *Consilium sapientium*.

Henry the Lion founds Lübeck as an outpost against the Slavs.

Society, Education, and Religion

Robert of Chester and Hermann the Dalmatian, first Latin translation of the Koran.

1144 **Dec:** **25th**, Zangī takes Edessa, massacring the Franks.

1145 Suryavarman II of Cambodia conquers Champa (–1149).

Society, Education, and Religion

'The Friday Mosque', Isfahan.

Art, Sculpture, Fine Arts, and Architecture

The Portail Royal, Chartres Cathedral, begun.

1146 **March:** **1st**, Eugenius III proclaims the Second Crusade on God's behalf.

Sept: **14th**, Zangī of Mosul murdered; one son, Sayf ad-Din Ghazī, succeeds in Mosul, while a second, Nūr ad-Din Mahmūd (–1174) , takes control of Aleppo.

Society, Education, and Religion

Otto, Bishop of Freising, *Chronica sive Historia de duabus civitatibus* (philosophical history of the spiritual and material worlds, to 1146; gives the first reference to 'Prester John').

1147 **April:** **—**, 'Abd-al-Mu'min completes his conquest of the Almoravid kingdom of Morocco with the capture of Marrakesh; he then crosses into Spain, where the Almoravid kingdom had disintegrated into several kingdoms established in Cordova, Valencia, Murcia, etc.

June: **26th**, the Wends sack Lübeck, and, the following month, defeat the Danes.

Oct: **25th**, Conrad III's crusading army destroyed by the Turks on the Bathys, near Dorylaeum.

1148 **Jan:** **1st**, Louis VII and his crusaders force their way through the Turks to cross the bridge to Antioch.

July: **24th**, the crusaders camp outside Damascus.
28th, the crusaders retreat from Damascus: so ends the Second Crusade.

Society, Education, and Religion

The Council of Reims condemns protectors of heresy in Gascony and Provence.

Humanities and Scholarship

Anna Comnena, *Alexiad* (a rhetorical life of her father, Alexius I, and chronicle of his reign, 1081–1118, begun by her husband, Nicephorus Bryennius).

Literature

Kalhana, *Rājatarangini* (*Stream of Kings*; verse history of all the Kings of Kashmir; one of the few extant Hindu chronicles).

1149 'Abd-al-Mu'min completes his conquest of the Muslim kingdoms in Spain.
Jaya Harivarman of Champa recaptures Vijaya, his capital, from Suryavarman of Cambodia.

June: **29th**, Raymond of Antioch defeated and killed by Nūr ad-Dīn.

Art, Sculpture, Fine Arts, and Architecture

(15th July) Church of the Holy Sepulchre, Jerusalem, dedicated.

1150 **Society, Education, and Religion**

Peter the Lombard, *Sententiarum libri IV* (popular theological text-book).

Art, Sculpture, Fine Arts, and Architecture

Temple of Angkor Vat, the mausoleum of King Suryavarman II.

Literature

Le Jeu d'Adam (the most ancient '*jeu*' – religious drama – in French literature; it is an Anglo-Norman dramatic piece on the Fall, Cain and Abel, in rhyming couplets).

1151 Manuel Comnenus makes his first attack on Hungary in a war which lasts, intermittently, until 1167.
'Alā' ad-Dīn Husayn, Sultan of Ghūr (Afghanistan), earns his title 'the World-Burner' by his destruction of Ghaznī.

1152 **Feb:** **15th**, death of Conrad III, King of the Romans.

March: **4th**, Frederick I Barbarossa of Hohenstaufen, his nephew, elected King of the Romans (–1190).

May: **16th**, Henry (II), Count of Anjou and Maine, marries Eleanor of Aquitaine.

1153 Roger of Sicily takes Bona, in north Africa; his empire there now extends from Tripoli to Tunis.
The Jürched (Chin Emperors) move their capital from Manchuria to Peking.

Jan: **—**, Henry (II) lands in England and begins his campaign of conquest.

May: **24th**, death of David I, King of Scotland, who had established an administration on Anglo-Norman lines and created feudal tenures; succeeded by his grandson, Malcolm IV (–1165).

Nov: **7th**, in the treaty of Wallingford, Henry recognizes Stephen as King while Stephen accepts Henry as his heir.

Society, Education, and Religion

There are now 343 houses of the Cistercian Order.
St. Bernard, Latin hymns and treatises, especially *De Diligendo Deo* and *De Gradibus Humilitatis* (on God, mankind and divine love).

1154 **April:** **25th**, Nūr ad-Dīn takes Damascus, thus completing his mastery of Muslim Syria.

Oct: —, Frederick begins his first expedition to Italy.
25th, death of Stephen, King of England.

Dec: **19th**, Henry II crowned as King of England (–1189).

Humanities and Scholarship
Al-Edrisi produces a planisphere and writes *al-Kitāb al-Rujarī* (*Roger's Book*; description of the world, the most elaborate in medieval times, with maps. Both for Roger II of Sicily, d. 1154).

1155 Pope Adrian IV grants Ireland to Henry II.
'The Wars of Pretenders' begin in Norway and Sweden; they last until about 1230.

April: **17th**, Frederick crowned as King of Lombardy in Pavia.

June: **18th**, Frederick is crowned as Holy Roman Emperor by the Pope.

Society, Education, and Religion
The Carmelite Order (of friars) originates in the establishment of a community of hermits on Mount Carmel.

1156 Death of Vikrāmanka, King of Rāshtrakūta (in the Deccan); his kingdom, which had been the most powerful in India for three centuries, now collapses.

June: —, by the Treaty of Benevento, Adrian recognizes William as King of Sicily and receives his homage.

Sept: **17th**, in a diet at Regensburg, Frederick creates the Duchy of Austria for Henry Jasomirgott and settles the Duchy of Bavaria on Henry the Lion of Saxony (–Sep 1180).

1157 After invading Poland, Frederick compels Boleslav IV to admit, in the Peace of Krzyszkowo, the imperial overlordship of Poland (for the last time).
Death of Sanjar, the Seljuq Sultan; the disintegration of his empire, centred on Persia, now accelerates.

Politics, Government, Law, and Economy
Henry the Lion founds Munich.

Society, Education, and Religion
The Council of Reims condemns Cathars.

1158 Adrian arranges a peace between William of Sicily and Manuel Comnenus, who ends his military intervention in Italy.

April: —, Baldwin of Jerusalem defeats Nūr ad-Din at Butaiha.

July: —, Frederick begins his second Italian expedition with the capture of Brescia and, in September, takes Milan.

Nov: **11th**, in a diet at Roncaglia, Frederick promulgates his peace constitution for the Empire.

Society, Education, and Religion
Frederick I grants his charter, 'The Authentic', to Bologna University.

1159 **July:** —, Frederick begins the siege of Crema. Several Lombard cities, Genoa the first, are revolting against his authority. William of Sicily engineers a league of the Papacy, Brescia, Milan and Piacenza against Frederick.

Sept: **7th**, Roland Bandinelli elected as Pope Alexander III (–1181) by a majority of the cardinals, but a party favouring Frederick elects Cardinal Octavian as Pope Victor IV (–1164); neither is able to control Rome.

Politics, Government, Law, and Economy
John of Salisbury, *Policraticus* (*Statesman's Book*).

1160 **Summer:** Henry the Lion begins the systematic conquest of Wendish territory east of the Elbe.
Taira Kiyomori (–1185), leader of a Japanese 'feudal' confederacy, wins control of the imperial government after defeating his rivals.

Jan: —, the fall of Mahdīyah completes the loss, by insurrection, of all the conquests by the King of Sicily in north Africa.

Politics, Government, Law, and Economy
Andrew, Duke of Vladimir, builds Moscow.

1161 **April:** **16th**, William crushes a rebellion in Sicily and then turns to subdue Apulia and Calabria.

Sept: —, Frederick begins the siege of Milan and, the following March, sacks it.

Everyday Life

Kilij Arslan II builds two baths at Kavza; the Seljuqs developed spas and also created a hospital service.

1162 **June:** **3rd**, Thomas Becket consecrated as Archbishop of Canterbury.

July: **6th**, the Germans and Danes crusading against the Wends defeat them at Demmin; Henry the Lion's campaign ends soon afterwards with their surrender.

1163 **Oct:** —, Frederick withdraws from Lombardy.

1st, Archbishop Becket refuses Henry's demand for the punishment of clergy in secular courts.

Art, Sculpture, Fine Arts, and Architecture

Nôtre Dame Cathedral, Paris, planned and begun (–1220).

1164 **Jan:** —, in the Constitutions of Clarendon, Henry II defines the relations of Church and State in England.

Oct: **8th**, Becket condemned for his contempt of the King by the Council of Northampton.

Nov: **2nd**, Becket begins his exile in France.

Literature

Chrétien de Troyes, *Erec et Énide* (poetic romance in the Arthurian cycle).

1165 **Nov:** **23rd**, Alexander, returning from exile in France, enters Rome, and is established in the Lateran by Sicilian forces.

Science, Technology, and Discovery

Ibn-Daud (Avendeath) makes translations into Latin from Arabic of scientific and philosophical works, introducing 'arabic numbers'; includes the most popular version of *Secretum secretorum*, falsely attributed to Aristotle.

1166 Frederick begins his fourth expedition to Italy.

Politics, Government, Law, and Economy

Henry II, in the Assize of Clarendon, formulates measures for prosecution of criminals, originating (grand) juries to present the accused.

1167 **April:** **27th**, the Lombard League, formed to oppose Frederick, initiates the reconstruction of Milan.

June: **24th**, Frederick camps outside Rome, subsequently forcing an entry; the papal forces surrender, Alexander flees to Benevento and the anti-pope Paschal III is installed.

Aug: —, Frederick's army destroyed by fever, so he hastily returns to Germany.

Society, Education, and Religion

A council of Cathari (heretics) meets near Toulouse.

1168 The Toltec Empire destroyed by barbarous tribes from northern Mexico (including Aztecs).

1169 **March:** **8th**, Andrew of Suzdal (–1174) seizes and sacks Kiev; now the most powerful Russian prince, he assumes the title of Great Prince and establishes his capital at Vladimir.

May: —, 'The First Conquerors' land in Ireland; they are Normans from Wales enlisted by Dermot MacMurrough to recover his kingdom of Leinster.

1170 The Korean palace guards massacre civil officials and enthrone a new king; a period of civil war follows (–1196).

Dec: **29th**, murder of St. Thomas Becket in Canterbury Cathedral.

Science, Technology, and Discovery

Roger of Salerno writes *Practica chirurgiae*, the earliest European textbook on surgery.

Literature

Thomas of Brittany, an Anglo-Norman poet, a narrative poem on the legend of Tristan and Iseult (the extant fragment – 3,144 lines – being the earliest text on this theme).

1171 **Sept:** **13th**, death of the last Fātimid Caliph of Egypt, al-'Ādid; Egypt is now nominally subject to the Caliph of Baghdād, and actually ruled by Saladin (–1193).

1173 Vladislav II, King of Bohemia, abdicates in favour of his son, Frederick; there follows a period of civil war, with ten changes of ruler in twenty-four years, in which royal officials become established as feudal magnates; there is a simultaneous increase in German influence, and settlement, in Bohemia (–1197).

Science, Technology, and Discovery
Benjamin ben Jonah of Tudela, *Masse'oth Rabbi Binyamin* (narrative, in Hebrew, of his journey from Castile to the Middle East, 1160–73; published in Constantinople, 1453).

Literature
Chrétien de Troyes, *Le Chevalier au Lion* (poetic romance in the Arthurian cycle); *Percevale le Gallois* or *Le Conte du Graal* (this Arthurian romance contains the earliest reference to the Holy Grail).

1174 Kilij Arslan of Rūm completes his conquest of the Danishmends (of eastern Anatolia).

Oct: 29th, in his fifth Italian expedition, Frederick begins the siege of Alessandria; he buys Tuscany and Spoleto from Welf VI.

Nov: 26th, Saladin, aspiring to take over Nūr ad-Dīn's empire, enters Damascus and takes possession.

Art, Sculpture, Fine Arts, and Architecture
The choir of Canterbury Cathedral destroyed by fire; the French mason, William of Sens, has charge of its rebuilding (–1179). Beginnings of English Gothic.

1175 **April: 16th**, Frederick makes the Treaty of Montebello with the Lombard League.

May: —, the Caliph of Baghdād recognizes Saladin as Sultan of Egypt and Syria.

Society, Education, and Religion
Genkū (Hōnen Shōnin) founds the Pure Land Sect (Jodo) of Japanese Buddhism.

1176 **May: 29th**, the Lombard League defeats Frederick at Legnano.

Sept: 17th, Manuel, attempting to conquer the Danishmend lands, is trapped and his army destroyed by Kilij Arslan, at Myriocephalum.

Oct: —, by the Treaty of Anagni, Frederick makes peace with Pope Alexander III, recognizing him as Pope and so ending the schism.

Politics, Government, Law, and Economy
In the Assize of Northampton, Henry II establishes common rules for criminal justice in England.

1177 Jaya Indravarman IV of Champa sacks Angkor, Cambodia; Tribhuvanadityavarman, who had usurped the throne, is killed, and Jayavarman, son of Dharanindravarman II, assumes leadership of Cambodian resistance.

July: 23rd, in the Treaty of Venice, Frederick makes a truce with the Lombard League and Sicily.

1179 Alfonso VIII of Castile and Alfonso II of Aragon conclude a treaty defining the boundary between their future conquests from the Muslims.

March: 5th, (–19th) the Third Lateran Council, held by Alexander, condemns heretics, their protectors and defenders; it also refuses Christian burial to men killed in tournaments.

1180 Minamoto Yoritomo begins his revolt against the Taira rulers of Japan (–Apr 1185).

Sept: 16th, in a diet at Altenburg, Frederick partitions the Duchy of Bavaria.

Politics, Government, Law, and Economy
Ranulf Glanville (but more probably Hubert Walter?) *Legibus et Consuetudinibus Regni Angliæ* (the first reasoned account of legal procedure).
Bruges now the principal international mart of north Europe.

Society, Education, and Religion
Josce of London founds the first college in the emerging University of Paris, the Collège des Dix-huit.

Science, Technology, and Discovery
Earliest European reference to a stern-post rudder (instead of an oar for steering).
First mention of a windmill in western Europe, at St. Sauvère de Vicomte, Normandy.

1181 Frederick, supported by Waldemar of Denmark, completes his dispossession of Henry the Lion when Lübeck surrenders; Henry submits and is banished (to England) for three years, retaining only Brunswick.
Jayavarman VII crowned as King of Cambodia (–*c.* 1218) following his expulsion of the Chams.

1182 **Sept: —**, Andronicus I Comnenus (–1185), nephew of John II, usurps the Greek Empire, murdering Alexius II, his mother and her advisers.

Art, Sculpture, Fine Arts, and Architecture
Mosaics in Monreale Cathedral.

1183 **June:** **18th**, Saladin takes Aleppo and in August makes Damascus his capital.
25th, by the Treaty of Constance, Frederick makes peace with the Lombard League, freeing its members from his government.

1184 **Society, Education, and Religion**
The Council of Verona held by Pope Lucius and Frederick organizes proceedings against heretics.
William of Tyre, *Historia rerum in partibus transmarinis gestarum* (history of the Crusades, 1095–1184).

1185 Philip II suppresses the office of chancellor to avoid the danger of influential offices being held by magnates.
April: **25th**, the naval battle of Dan-no-ura finally destroys the Taira and establishes Minamoto Yoritomo as the effective ruler in Japan, with the title Sei-i-tai Shogun ('barbarian-suppressing generalissimo'). Feudal government is now effectively established in Japan, with its capital at Kamakura (near Tokyo).
July: **—**, by the Treaty of Boves with Philip of Flanders, Philip II acquires Amiens and other lands and titles in north-east France, thus doubling the extent of the royal domain.
Society, Education, and Religion
Oxford University apparently now established.
Literature
Slovo o polku Igorevé (*The Campaign of Igor*; prose poem in epic form about the campaign of Igor of Novgorod-Séveresk against the Cumans in 1185; the beginning of Russian literature).

1186 **Autumn:** the brothers Theodore and Asen liberate Bulgaria while their allies, the Cumans, ravage Thrace.
Muhammad of Ghūr destroys the Ghaznavid kingdom of the Punjab and takes Lahore.
Jan: **27th**, Henry (VI), son of Frederick I, marries Constance, the presumptive heiress to the kingdom of Sicily; he is crowned as King of Burgundy, Germany and Italy, and entitled *Caesar*.

1187 Isaac II Comnenus makes a truce with Theodore and Asen, recognizing Bulgarian independence *de facto*; Theodore (now named Peter) crowned as Tsar (–1197), although Asen actually rules.
July: **3rd**, the army of the kingdom of Jerusalem, advancing to raise the siege of Tiberias, trapped and destroyed by Saladin at the Horns of Hattin; Guy captured and Reynald of Châtillon beheaded. Saladin now rapidly takes possession of Palestine, including Jerusalem.
Dec: **17th**, death of Pope Gregory VIII who had just proclaimed the Third Crusade to liberate Jerusalem.
Science, Technology, and Discovery
Gerard of Cremona produces translations into Latin from Arabic of nearly 100 Greek and Arab works on philosophy, mathematics, astronomy, physics, medicine, alchemy and astrology, including *The Book of the Seventy*, attributed to Jābir, al-Rāzi's *Book of Secrets*, Avicenna's *Canon of Medicine*, and al-Khwārizmī's *The Calculation of Integration and Equation* (this became the principal textbook on mathematics in western Europe until the sixteenth century).

1188 **Jan:** **—**, Henry II and Philip, meeting at Gisors to discuss a truce, are persuaded to make peace and go on Crusade; they impose Saladin tithes to finance their expeditions.
March: **27th**, Frederick takes the Cross; by his order, Henry the Lion goes into exile.
Politics, Government, Law, and Economy
Alfonso IX holds the first Cortes of Leon known to have been attended by representatives of towns as well as prelates and nobles.
Saladin sends Chinese porcelain to Damascus (known in China from the ninth century but the first notice in the Middle East).
Art, Sculpture, Fine Arts, and Architecture
Mosque at Rabat, intended to be the largest in the Muslim world.
Literature
Ilyās ibn-Yūsuf Nizāmī, *Laylā and Majnūn* (Persian romance).

1189 Yoritomo destroys the Fujiwara of Kiraizumi and so completes his subjection of Japan.
July: **6th**, death of Henry II, King of England.
Aug: **28th**, Guy of Jerusalem begins the siege of Acre.
Sept: **3rd**, Richard I crowned as King of England (–1199); this date becomes the limit of legal memory (from 1290).

Oct: —, Henry the Lion returns to Germany and recovers much of Saxony and Holstein.

Nov: **18th**, death of William II, King of Sicily, without issue; his bastard cousin, Tancred (–1194), Count of Lecce, seizes the throne.

Literature

Heinrich von Veldeke, *Eneit* (beginnings of the *roman d'antiquité* in Germany).

1190 Foundation of the Knights of the Cross (later known as the Teutonic Knights).

Ballāla II, the Hoysala King, completes the destruction of the Chalukya Empire in southern India.

Feb: —, by the treaty of Adrianople, Isaac II permits Frederick and his Crusaders to pass into Asia Minor.

May: **18th**, Frederick fights his way into Konya, the capital of Rūm. .

June: **10th**, Frederick is drowned in the Saleph (now Göksu), in Cilicia; succeeded by his son, Henry VI (–1197).

July: **4th**, Philip II and Richard I meet at Vézelay and set off on the Crusade.

Science, Technology, and Discovery

(–1230) notices of coal-mining for iron forges at Liège; coal was apparently first mined for this purpose, also in France.

Literature

Friedrich von Hausen, poems and lyrics (in Middle High German, in praise of idealized love; earliest extant lyrics of the twelfth–thirteenth century *Minnesingers*).

1191 **April:** **15th**, Pope Celestine III crowns Henry VI as Holy Roman Emperor; Henry then begins his conquest of his wife's kingdom of Naples.

July: **12th**, the Crusaders take Acre; it becomes the capital of the Kingdom of Jerusalem.

Sept: **7th**, Richard leads the Crusaders to victory over Saladin at Arsūf.

Society, Education, and Religion

Eisai introduces the Rinzai sect of Zen Buddhism into Japan from China.

Everyday Life

Eisai introduces tea into Japan and writes *Kissa-yōjō-ki* (on its merits).

1192 Prithvī Rāj (or Raī Pithōra), the ruler of Ajmēr Delhi, defeated and killed at Tarāorī by Muhammad, Sultan of Ghūr, who thus conquered northern India.

Sept: **2nd**, Richard and Saladin conclude a treaty for a truce for three years; so ends the Third Crusade.

Literature

Chand Bardāī, *Chand Raīsā* (epic poem in Hindi about Prithvī Rāj, the last Hindu ruler of Delhi, d. 1192).

1193 **Jan:** —, Delhi taken by Aybak, Muhammad's viceroy, and becomes the Muslim capital in India.

March: **3rd**, death of Saladin; his dominions now disintegrate; one son, al-'Azīz, succeeds in Cairo (–1196).

Art, Sculpture, Fine Arts, and Architecture

Jami' or Quwwat al-Islām mosque, Delhi (–1199); the first great Indian mosque.

(10th June) Chartres Cathedral burnt, save for the west front; its rebuilding initiates 'High Gothic' architecture.

1194 Tekish of Khwārizm defeats Tughril, the Seljuq Sultan of Persian Iraq, and establishes himself as Sultan (–1200).

Muhammad of Ghūr conquers the kingdom of Kanauj.

July: **4th**, Richard I of England routs Philip II of France at Fréteval.

Nov: **20th**, having subdued southern Italy, Henry VI enters Palermo, completing his conquest of Sicily.

1195 **Aug:** **6th**, death of Henry the Lion.

Literature

Bernart de Ventadour, *Chansons d'amour* (love lyrics of a Provençal troubadour).

1196 Ch'oe Ch'ung-hon, a Korean general, massacres his rivals, takes control of the kingdom and restores its unity; his family, the Ch'oe, retain power until 1258.

Jan: —, Richard and Philip make peace by the Treaty of Louviers.

July: **18th**, Berber forces sent by Ya'qūb inflict a crushing defeat on Alfonso VIII of Castile at Alarcos (west of Ciudad Real); Ya'qūb now assumes the title Al-Mansūr (Spanish, Almanzor, 'the Victorious').

Society, Education, and Religion
Ephraim of Bonn, *Emek habacha* (account of persecution of Jews in Germany, France and England, 1146–96).

1197 **Sept: 10th**, death of Henry of Champagne, King of Jerusalem.

1198 Ottokar I crowned as King of Bohemia, at Mainz, in return for his support of Philip of Swabia; with the establishment of the Kingdom of Bohemia, its succession ceases to be a regular cause of dispute and civil war.

July: —, the Welf, Otto IV, son of Henry the Lion, after capturing Cologne, crowned as King of the Romans (–1215); thus there is civil war in Germany between him and the Hohenstaufen party of Philip of Swabia.

Aug: 15th, Innocent III proclaims the Fourth Crusade to recover Jerusalem and offers an indulgence to those who fight the Albigensians in southern France.

Society, Education, and Religion
The series of Papal Registers, recording the Pope's correspondence, dates from 1198.

Humanities and Scholarship
Ibn-Rushd (Averroës), commentaries on Aristotle.

1199 Death of Minamoto Yoritomo, first Shogun of Japan; his followers retain control of government but fight for supremacy (–1216).

Society, Education, and Religion
Innocent III taxes the universal church for the proposed Fourth Crusade, the first direct papal taxation of the church.

Literature
(*c.* 1200) Kamban, *Rāmāyanam* (or *Rāmāvatāram*; outstanding epic poem in Tamil literature, which had its golden age under the Chola Empire of south India, *c.* 850–*c.* 1200).

1200 Beginning of the domination of the Incas in the Cuzco Valley, Peru (–1438).

Society, Education, and Religion
Philip II's charter to Paris University provides the first documentary recognition of its corporate existence.

Humanities and Scholarship
Chu Hsi, a leading influence in the establishment of Neo-Confucian orthodoxy, known as Chu Hsi-ism, which because of its rigidity led to scholasticism instead of speculative philosophy; he has consequently often been compared with St. Thomas Aquinas (*c.* 1274).

Literature
Das Nibelunggenlied (folk epic in Old High German).

1201 **June: 8th**, by the Diploma of Neuss, Otto IV cedes imperial authority in Italy to the Pope. Innocent recognizes Otto as King of the Romans.

1202 With the fall of Kālinjar, Muhammad of Ghūr completes his conquest of Upper India; other Muslims, under Ikhtiyār ad-Dīn, seize Bengal.

April: 30th, Philip declares that John of England has forfeited his French lands because he failed to appear in Philip's court to answer the barons of Poitou, John's vassals in revolt against him.

Nov: 15th, the Crusaders take Zara from the King of Hungary, for Venice; here they agree to take Constantinople on behalf of Alexius Angelus, son of Isaac II.

Science, Technology, and Discovery
Leonardo Fibonacci of Pisa writes *Liber Abaci*, the earliest Latin account of Arabic (i.e., Hindu) numerals, including a study of the sequence of numbers (1, 1, 2, 3, 5, 8, 13, 21, ...) in which each number is the sum of the two preceding ones.

1203 Jayavarman VII of Cambodia conquers and annexes Champa (–1220).

1204 The Crusaders defeat Michael Ducas at Koundoura in Messenia; this was a decisive victory in their conquest of the Morea.

April: 12th, the Crusaders force their way into Constantinople and sack it for three days.

May: —, Alexius Comnenus, grandson of Andronicus I, seizes Trebizond and establishes a new Greek empire there (–Sept 1461).

16th, Baldwin, Count of Flanders, crowned as Latin Emperor of Constantinople (–1206).

June: 24th, with the fall of Rouen, Philip's conquest of Normandy is complete; in France, only Gascony and the Channel Islands remain in English hands.

Oct: —, Baldwin, the Venetians and Crusaders partition the Greek Empire by treaty.

Society, Education, and Religion

Moses ben Maimōn, *Dalālat al-Hā'irīn* (*The Guide to the Perplexed*; philosophical treatise to reconcile Jewish theology and Muslim Aristotelianism).

1205

Jan: **6th**, Philip of Swabia crowned as King of the Romans (–1208).

Society, Education, and Religion

Diego of Osma, assisted by Dominic, begins his mission to the Albigensians (or Cathari) of southern France.

The Çifte Medrese (College), Kayseri, founded; first Seljuq hospital in Anatolia.

1206

Spring: the Mongol prince, Temujin, who had united Mongolia and taken the title of Ghengiz Khan, recognized as Khan (–1227) in an assembly of Mongols; the Mongol Empire thus founded.

March: **15th**, Muhammad of Ghūr murdered by Aybak, his viceroy in India, who assumes the title of Sultan, founding the dynasty of Slave Kings of Delhi (–Jun 1290).

Politics, Government, Law, and Economy

Ghengiz Khan promulgates the Great Yasa (imperial law-code) for the Mongols.

1207

Han T'o-chou, the Southern Sung Emperor, killed by the Chin when attempting to reconquer northern China.

Jan: **—**, Philip of Swabia takes Cologne, so completing his dominance in Germany.

1208

Al-Nasir destroys the last Almoravid strongholds in North Africa.

June: **21st**, Philip of Swabia, whom Innocent had just recognized as King of the Romans, murdered by Otto of Wittelsbach.

Nov: **11th**, Otto IV elected, unanimously, as King of the Romans.

17th, Innocent III appeals to the nobility in northern France to intervene against the Albigensians.

1209

Aug: **15th**, Carcassone is taken by the Albigensian crusaders; Simon de Montfort is then elected leader and expropriates land, becoming lord of Béziers and Carcassone.

Oct: **4th**, Innocent crowns Otto IV as Holy Roman Emperor.

1210

Nov: **—**, Otto opens his campaign to conquer Apulia and is therefore excommunicated by Innocent, who frees Otto's subjects from obedience, thus starting a rebellion in Germany.

Politics, Government, Law, and Economy

Most ancient Burmese law code dates from reign of Jayasura II (d. 1210).

Society, Education, and Religion

Innocent III verbally sanctions St. Francis' Order (the Friars Minor).

Humanities and Scholarship

Latin translation of Aristotle's *Metaphysics*.

Art, Sculpture, Fine Arts, and Architecture

Reims Cathedral begun.

Literature

Gottfried von Strassburg, *Tristan und Isolde* (Middle High German narrative poem in couplets).

1211

Ghengiz Khan destroys the Kara-Khitai Empire in east Turkestan and invades China.

Sept: **—**, in a diet at Nuremburg, German princes in revolt against Otto offer the crown to Frederick II of Hohenstaufen.

1212

July: **16th**, on a crusade, Alfonso VIII of Castile, Sancho VII of Navarre and Pedro II of Aragon win a resounding victory over the Muslims at Las Navas de Tolosa.

Dec: **9th**, Frederick crowned as King of the Romans.

Society, Education, and Religion

The Children's Crusade: the French contingent wrecked off Sardinia and its survivors captured by Saracens.

Literature

Wolfram von Eschenbach, *Parzival* (Middle High German epic on the Grail theme, introducing Lohengrin; continued in *Titurel* and *Willehalm*).

Kamo Chōmei, *Hōjō-ki* (*Annals of ten-feet square*; on his eremetical bliss, with historical events of his time; a Japanese classic).

1213 Alfonso of Castile defeats an invasion by the Almohads at Febragaen.
Kālinga Vijaya-Bāhu conquers Ceylon and founds a dynasty.

April: **19th**, (–29th) Innocent III proclaims the Fifth Crusade and removes the indulgences for the Fourth (Albigensian) Crusade.

July: **12th**, by the Golden Bull of Eger, Frederick recognizes the Papacy's territorial claims in Italy and renounces imperial control over the Church in Germany.

Sept: **12th**, Simon de Montfort and his crusaders defeat Raymond of Toulouse and kill his ally, Pedro II of Aragon, at Muret.

Politics, Government, Law, and Economy
(15th Nov) knights representing shires are called, for the first known time, to a council held at Oxford by King John.

Literature
Geoffroi de Villehardouin, *De la Conquête de Constantinople* (*c.* 1198–1207, the crusader-historian taking part: 'the first great French prose book' – Saintsbury).

1214 'Alā' ad-Dīn Muhammad, the Khwārizm Shah, takes Ghaznī; he had now conquered most of Persia and Transoxiana.

July: **27th**, Philip defeats John's allies, among them Otto IV, at Bouvines; by capturing the Counts of Flanders and Boulogne, he establishes French control there. As Otto's defeat also assists Frederick's cause in Germany, the battle is considered one of the most important in European history.

1215 Ghengiz Khan takes Peking; the Chin then make Kaifeng their capital.

June: **19th**, John and his opponents agree on terms for peace, published (from the 24th) in Magna Carta, whereby the King agrees to various curtailments of his powers and concedes 'liberties' to different classes of his subjects.

Nov: **11th**, (–30th) Innocent III legislates at the Fourth Lateran Council for the organization of the Fifth Crusade, especially concerning taxation; Simon de Montfort is confirmed in his lands in southern France.

Society, Education, and Religion
(11th Nov) (–30th) the Fourth Lateran Council provides for the reform of diocesan organization and of the Benedictine and Augustinian Orders; it imposes the first papal tithe on the clergy; and orders that Jews should wear distinctive dress.

1216 Māravarman Sundara, the Pāndya ruler, drives Kulottunga III, the Chola Emperor, into (temporary) exile; the second Pāndya Empire is now founded.

Oct: **19th**, King John dies at Newark, after losing his baggage when crossing the Wash.
28th, John's son, Henry III, a minor, crowned at Gloucester (–1272).

Society, Education, and Religion
(22nd Dec) Honorius III recognizes St. Dominic's Order of Friars Preachers (or Dominicans).

1217 **May:** **20th**, William the Marshal, leading the loyalists for Henry III, defeats Louis (VIII) and the rebels at Lincoln. Louis is paid to leave England

Sept: **25th**, Alfonso of Portugal defeats the Muslims at Alcazar do Sal.

Society, Education, and Religion
St. Francis holds a chapter of his order which makes its first constitution.

1218 **June:** **25th**, Simon de Montfort killed at the siege of Toulouse, where Duke Raymond VI had been restored by a revolt.

Art, Sculpture, Fine Arts, and Architecture
Jayavarman VII of Cambodia rebuilds and walls the city of Angkor Thom; the temple of Bayon is his greatest building.

1219 Ghengiz Khan invades the Khwarismian Empire (Transoxiana and Persia).
Murder of Minamoto Sanetomo, Shogun of Japan, the only surviving member of Yoritomo's family; Hōjō Yoshitoki, leader of the triumphant faction, assumes power as regent of the Shogunate and defeats a bid for power by the retired Emperor, Go-Toba, in the Shōkyū War. The Hōjō family retains this power until 1333.

Nov: **5th**, the Fifth Crusade takes Damietta.

Society, Education, and Religion
(Aug) St. Francis preaches in Egypt, to both the Sultan and the Crusaders; missions of his friars sent to France, Germany, Hungary and Spain.

1220 Jaya Parameshvaravarman II becomes King of Champa on the withdrawal of the Khmers (of Cambodia).

Feb: —, Ghengiz Khan takes Bukhāra; it is depopulated and destroyed.

Sept: 8th, the crusaders evacuate Damietta; end of the Fifth Crusade.

Nov: 22nd, Honorius crowns Frederick II as Holy Roman Emperor (–1250).

Dec: —, 'Alā' ad-Dīn dies in flight from Ghengiz Khan who has conquered Transoxiana; succeeded by his son, Jalāl ad-Dīn (–1231).

Society, Education, and Religion
(22nd May) the first general chapter of the Dominican Order rejects its ownership of property and makes a constitution; this embodies the principle of representation of the Order's provinces in general chapters.

Art, Sculpture, Fine Arts, and Architecture
Amiens Cathedral begun.

1221 **Nov: 24th**, Ghengiz Khan defeats Jalāl ad-Dīn and destroys his army in Afghanistan; the Mongols next invade India.

Science, Technology, and Discovery
Chiu Ch'ang-ch'un, journey from Peking to Persia (–1224); described by Li Chih-ch'ang, *Hsi yu chi*.

1222 **May: 31st**, a Mongol army defeats the Russians and Cumans on the Kalka, near the Sea of Azov.

June: —, Ghengiz Khan takes Herat and massacres its population; he had now conquered Afghanistan.

Politics, Government, Law, and Economy
Andrew of Hungary grants his Golden Bull, a charter of liberties.

Literature
Snorri Sturlason, *The Edda* (the prose, i.e., 'The Younger' *Edda*: Icelandic myths, from an earlier poetic version, written by Snorri).

1224 Death of the Almohad Emperor, Yūsuf II; the disintegration of his empire in Morocco and Spain accelerates.
Ghengiz Khan destroys the state of Hsi Hsia, in north China.

Feb: —, Amauri de Montfort cedes the conquests by the Albigensian Crusade in Toulouse to Louis VIII.

May: 5th, Louis declares war on Henry III; he then overruns Poitou and most of Gascony north of the Garonne.

Society, Education, and Religion
(5th June) Frederick II founds Naples University.

1225 Ferdinand III of Castile takes Andujar in his first campaign against the Muslims.
Jalāl ad-Dīn liberates Persia from the Mongols; after defeating the Georgians at Garnhi, he sacks Tiflis.
Tran Thai-tong becomes sole Emperor of Dai Viet (–1258), founding the Tran dynasty (–1400).

Nov: 9th, Frederick marries Queen Yolande, the daughter of John of Brienne, who had abdicated; he thus assumes the Kingdom of Jerusalem (–1250).

Politics, Government, Law, and Economy
Eike von Repkow, *Sachsenspiegel* (Latin treatise on Saxon customs; the oldest German legal writing).

Literature
Francis of Assisi, *Il Cantico di Frate Sole* (*Canticle of Brother Sun*; earliest masterpiece of Italian poetry).

1226 **Jan: 30th**, Louis VIII assumes direction of the crusade against Raymond of Toulouse.

March: 6th, a second Lombard League, against Frederick II, formed by Milan, Bologna, Brescia, Mantua, Bergamo, Turin, Vicenza, Padua, and others.

Nov: **8th**, death of Louis VIII; succeeded by his son, Louis IX (–1270), with his widow, Blanche of Castile, acting as regent (–1236).

1227 **Aug:** **24th**, death of Ghengiz Khan; succeeded as Great Khan by his son, Ogodai (–1241). Ghengiz's empire is divided: Ogodai rules eastern Asia from the capital at Karakorum; Chaghadai, his brother, Turkestan; Tuluy, another brother, in Mongolia; and Batu (–1255), grandson of Ghengiz, Kazakhstan and European Russia, the origin of 'The Golden Horde' .

Statistics

The Mongol army numbered about 129,000 at the death of Ghengiz Khan.

1228 **June:** **28th**, Frederick II sails for Palestine on the Sixth Crusade.

Art, Sculpture, Fine Arts, and Architecture

Church and convent of S. Francesco, Assisi (–1239).

1229 Ferdinand of Castile sends an army to Africa which restores his ally al-Ma'mūn as Emperor of the Almohads; the latter permits Castilians to settle at Marrakesh.

The invading Shān tribe of Āhōm founds the Kingdom of Assam.

Feb: **8th**, Iltutmish, who had subjected the Muslim conquests, recognized as Sultan of India by the Caliph of Baghdād.

18th, Frederick makes a treaty of peace with al-Kāmil, whereby Jerusalem is partitioned; the Holy Places thus come under Christian control and the Sixth Crusade so ends without any fighting.

March: **18th**, Frederick crowns himself as King of Jerusalem, in Jerusalem.

April: **11th**, the Treaty of Paris ends the Albigensian Crusade; Raymond VII submits to Louis IX, ceding the Duchy of Narbonne and the reversion to Toulouse, which he was to hold for his life.

June: **—**, al-Ashraf takes Damascus; as he recognizes the supremacy of his brother, al-Kāmil, the Ayyūbid (Saladin's) Empire is now reunited.

Society, Education, and Religion

(Nov) the Inquisition established in Toulouse.

1230 Muhammad ibn-Yūsuf (–1273) seizes Granada, founding the Nasrid dynasty (–1492).

Herman von Salza, the Grand Master, takes possession of Chelmno; the Knights now begin their conquest of Prussia.

Bang Klang T'ao (assuming the title Indrapatindraditya) becomes King of Sukhodaya, the first Thai (Siamese) state to free itself from Cambodia (–1376).

April: **—**, John Asen of Bulgaria defeats and captures Theodore Ducas of Epirus at Klokotinitza; the Bulgarian Empire now extends from the Black Sea to the Danube, Adriatic and Thessaly.

July: **23rd**, by the Treaty of San Germano, Frederick makes peace with Pope Gregory IX.

Sept: **23rd**, death of Alfonso IX of Leon; succeeded by his son, Ferdinand III of Castile (–1252), who thus finally unites the two kingdoms.

Art, Sculpture, Fine Arts, and Architecture

Siena Cathedral begun.

Literature

Approximate end of a long era of Minnesingers – German court poets and singers who wrote love lyrics of a formal style and aristocratic beauty. Among the most eminent names was Wolfram von Eschenbach (–1220) and Walter von der Vogelweide who may have died in this year.

1231 The Mongols begin their campaigns to conquer Korea (–1258).

May: **—**, Henry, King of the Romans, concedes the 'Constitution in favour of the princes', granting them territorial sovereignty.

Politics, Government, Law, and Economy

Frederick II promulgates his *Liber* (or *Lex Augustalis*) for the Kingdom of Sicily (the first medieval code of laws based on Roman jurisprudence).

Frederick initiates the *augustales* (the first gold coinage in western Europe).

Society, Education, and Religion

Frederick orders that medical teachers and practitioners should be examined by the University of Salerno.

Pope Gregory IX appoints inquisitors against heresy in Germany.

1232 **July:** **29th**, Henry III dismisses the justiciar, Hubert de Burgh, Earl of Essex, and begins the centralization of royal finances under Peter des Rivaux.

Oct: **16th**, death of the Almohad Emperor, al-Ma'mūn; succeeded by his son, 'Abd-al-Wāhid, but Muhammad ibn-Yūsuf of Granada proclaims himself King in Spain (–1273).

Politics, Government, Law, and Economy

Jōei shikimoku (codification of the Minamoto family law regulating the Japanese warrior class, drawn up by the Administrative Board, the central organ of the Shogun's feudal government).

Outbreak of disorder in Abbeville; there were similar disturbances, due to conflict between artisans and richer citizens, in other west European towns in the thirteenth century.

1233 **Society, Education, and Religion**

Penitentiary movement, 'The Great Hallelujah', in north Italy.

Gregory IX confirms the establishment of the University of Toulouse and grants the scholars privileges.

(April) Gregory IX organizes the Holy Office (Inquisition).

Humanities and Scholarship

Ibn-al-Athir, *Kitāb al-Kāmil fi-al-Ta'rīkh*/*The Complete Book of Chronicles*; abridges al-Tabari's work (923) and continues Arab history to 1231.

1234 The Mongols take Kaifeng and destroy the Chin dynasty.

Society, Education, and Religion

The Caliph al-Mustansir founds al-Mustansīryah University, Baghdād (–1395).

1235 **July:** **—**, in a diet at Worms, Henry deposed as King of the Romans following his revolt against Frederick, his father.

Humanities and Scholarship

Michael Scot, translations of Aristotle from Arabic and Hebrew.

Literature

Ibn-al-Farīd, Egyptian mystic poet.

1236 A Mongol army led by Batu, grandson of Ghengiz Khan, conquers the Volga Bulgars.

June: **29th**, Ferdinand of Castile and Leon takes Cordova, the capital of a Muslim kingdom.

July: **—**, in a diet at Piacenza, Frederick announces his intention of recovering Italy for the Empire; Gregory replies by claiming the supreme temporal dominion of the Papacy under the 'Donation of Constantine'.

Art, Sculpture, Fine Arts, and Architecture

Byzantine frescoes in Mileševo church.

1237 James of Aragon conquers Murcia.

Kayqubād of Rūm murdered and succeeded by his son. Kaykushraw II (–1246); the Sultanate, which had achieved its greatest prosperity in his reign, now declines.

Nov: **27th**, Frederick defeats the Lombard League at Cortenuova; by insisting on unconditional surrender, however, he stimulates further resistance.

Dec: **21st**, Batu's Mongol army destroys the city and principality of Riazan, Russia.

Literature

Guillaume de Lorris, *Le Roman de la Rose* (the most famous of all narrative and – in part – allegorical poems of the Middle Ages, with some satirical sections in the later continuation).

1238 **Feb:** **8th**, Batu takes Vladimir, and then destroys Moscow and other central Russian cities, massacring their inhabitants.

March: **4th**, Batu defeats the princes of northern Russia on the Sita, near Yaroslavl, but fails to take Novgorod.

Sept: **—**, James of Aragon takes Valencia.

Society, Education, and Religion

Some Carmelite Friars migrate from Palestine to Sicily and south France; the Order then spreads over Europe.

1239 Jaroslav of Vladimir begins the payment of tribute to the Mongols in Russia (the 'Golden Horde').

March: **20th**, Gregory excommunicates Frederick.

June: **—**, Frederick invades the Romagna and Tuscany.

1240 Sundiata, leader of a Mandingo-Negro confederation in Kangaba, defeats Sumanguru, the dominant ruler in the former Empire of Ghana; Sundiata thus founds the Empire of Mali.

Feb: **22nd**, Frederick reaches the outskirts of Rome, but withdraws to Sicily when Gregory rouses the Romans to resist. Gregory, ineffectively, orders a crusade against Frederick in Germany.

July: **15th**, Alexander Nevski of Novgorod defeats the Swedes on the Neva.

Dec: **6th**, Batu takes and sacks Kiev, then ravages Galicia.
20th, Frederick recognizes the inhabitants of the three Swiss Forest Cantons of Schwyz, Uri and Unterwalden as freemen immediately subject to the Empire.

Society, Education, and Religion

The Mongol empire, by permitting safe travel through Asia, allows the first European contact with China (– *c.* 1340). There is also contact with western Asia and China receives the influence of Persian culture and Muslim religion, while Chinese civilization influences central and western Asia.

Ibn-'Arabī, *al-Fūtūhāt al-Makkīyah; Fusūs al-Hikam* (treatises giving Sūfi pantheism its philosophical framework).

1241 **April:** **9th**, a Mongol army led by Khaidu, after sacking Cracow, defeats the Poles, Silesians and Teutonic Knights at Leignitz; Duke Henry II the Pious killed. The Mongols ravage Silesia; repulsed by the Bohemians, they go through Moravia into Hungary.
11th, the main Mongol army, under Batu, defeats the Hungarians on the Sajo, at Mohi; they ravage the Danube plain, but are repulsed at Grobnok by the Croatians. A crusade proclaimed against them in Germany.

Dec: **11th**, death of Ogodai, Great Khan of the Mongols.
22nd, Lahore taken and destroyed by the Mongols.
25th, Batu takes Buda[pest].

Politics, Government, Law, and Economy

Hamburg and Lübeck form a peace-keeping league (which has been regarded as the origin of the Hanseatic League).

Louis IX founds Aigues-Mortes (one of the last 'new' French towns in the Middle Ages and the first French royal port on the Mediterranean; the walls – still standing – built, 1280–80).

1242 **Spring:** the Mongols evacuate central Europe, where they were harrying Austria and Dalmatia, in order to return to their capital, Karakorum, to elect Ogodai's successor (–1246). Batu (–1255) now organizes his empire in Russia (the Khanate of Kypchak, or 'The Golden Horde') as an autonomous Mongol state.

April: **5th**, Alexander Nevski, Prince of Novgorod, defeats the Teutonic Knights on Lake Peipus.

July: **21st**, Louis IX defeats Henry III of England at Taillebourg; after an engagement at Saintes, Henry withdraws from France.

1243 **June:** **26th**, the Mongols defeat Kaykhusraw II of Rūm and his Greek allies at Köse Dagh, near Erzinjan; he becomes their tributary, as does Queen Rusadan of Georgia.

Society, Education, and Religion

The Jews of Belitz, near Berlin, all burnt in the earliest known case of a massacre due to an alleged desecration of the Host.

(Dec) the Order of Friars Hermit of the Order of St. Augustine (Austin Friars) originates in the appointment by Innocent IV of a protector for some Tuscan eremetical communities.

Art, Sculpture, Fine Arts, and Architecture

Sainte Chapelle, Paris (–1248).

1244 **Aug:** **23rd**, the Christians finally expelled from Jerusalem, and the city sacked, by the Khwarismian exiles employed by Ayyūb of Egypt in his war against Damascus.

Oct: **17th**, the Egyptians defeat the Christian army of Outremer and its Muslim allies of Damascus at Harbiyāh (or La Forbie), near Gaza.

Society, Education, and Religion

Montségur, last refuge of heretics in southern France, falls to the Catholics.

1245 Daniel of Halich, the dominant prince in eastern central Europe, does homage to Batu.
The Mongols take Multān, in the Punjab.

July: **17th**, in the General Council at Lyons, Pope Innocent IV formally declares Frederick deposed from the Empire.

Society, Education, and Religion

Innocent IV's declaration permitting the Friars Minor to hold property, which leads to the division of the Order into its 'Conventual' and 'Spiritual' branches.

Innocent sends John de Plano Carpinis, a friar minor, to the court of the Great Khan, at Karakorum; this embassy leads to the establishment of Christian missions in China until *c.* 1368.

Art, Sculpture, Fine Arts, and Architecture

Westminster Abbey church begun.

1247 Guyuk, the Great Khan, appoints Alexander Nevski as Prince of Kiev and his brother Andrew as Grand Duke of Vladimir (–1252).

Politics, Government, Law, and Economy

Louis initiates the *enquêteurs* (itinerant commissioners to receive complaints of maladministration).

1248 **Aug: 26th**, Louis IX sails from France on Crusade (–1254).

Dec: 22nd, Seville surrenders to Ferdinand of Castille and Leon.

Humanities and Scholarship

Al-Qiftī, *Ikhbār al'Ulamā' bi-Akhbar al-Hūkamā'/History of Philosophers*; biographies of 414 Greek, Syrian and Islamic physicians, astronomers and philosophers.

1249 **June: 5th**, Louis lands in Egypt, from Cyprus and enters Damietta, without opposition.

1250 **Feb: 8th**, Louis defeats the Egyptians at Mansūrah but is subsequently defeated and captured.

May: 2nd, Tūrān Shāh, the last Ayyūbid Sultan of Egypt, murdered by his Mamlūk (i.e., slave) guards, who elect their commander 'Izz ad-Dīn Aybāk as regent while Shajar ad-Durr, Ayyūb's widow, is nominal ruler. After 80 days, Aybāk marries her and assumes the Sultanate (–1257), founding the Mamlūk dynasty.

6th, Louis surrenders Damietta as part of the price for his release; he leaves for Acre, where he is accepted as ruler of Outremer.

Dec: 13th, death of the Holy Roman Emperor, Frederick II, 'Stupor mundi'; his son, Conrad IV, King of the Romans, succeeds as King of Sicily and (nominal) King of Jerusalem (–1254).

Society, Education, and Religion

The Dominicans found the first school of oriental studies at Toledo.

Science, Technology, and Discovery

Illustration of a wheel-barrow (a medieval invention in Europe, although known in China in AD 231).

Art, Sculpture, Fine Arts, and Architecture

Towers of Bamberg Cathedral, choirs of Coutances and Naumberg Cathedrals, and north tower and trancepts (architect: Jean de Chelle) of Nôtre Dame, Paris.

Byzantine frescoes in Sopočani church.

Sculptures in Mainz, Naumberg and Meissen Cathedrals, by 'the Master of Naumberg'.

Sport and Recreation

Frederick II, *De arte venandi cum avibus/The Art of Falconry.*

1251 **Jan: 7th**, Florence admits the exiled Guelfs (anti-imperialists).

Feb: 2nd, Aybāk defeats an-Nāsir, invading Egypt, at Abbasa.

March: —, risings against Conrad in the Kingdom of Sicily.

July: —, the Ghibellines (imperialists) exiled from Florence.

1252 **May: 30th**, death of St. Ferdinand III, King of Castile and Leon; succeeded by his son, Alfonso X (–1284).

31st, Simon de Montfort defends himself and quarrels with Henry III of England when answering charges arising from his government of Gascony.

Society, Education, and Religion

Innocent IV's bull *ad extirpanda* orders the use of torture in the examination of heretics.

1253 Louis IX sends the friars, William of Rubruck and Bartholomew of Cremona, to the court of the Great Khan at Karakorum to seek his alliance against the Muslims of Syria and Egypt.

Hūlāgū, a grandson of Ghengiz Khan, begins his conquest of the Islamic Empire (–1258).

Kublai Khan conquers the Kingdom of Nanchao (in Yunnan); its Thai people migrate to Siam. He also attacks Dai Viet.

April: —, an-Nāsir cedes Palestine to Aybāk of Egypt in a treaty of peace.

Oct: **10th**, Conrad completes his suppression of a Sicilian rebellion with the recovery of Naples.

Society, Education, and Religion
Robert Grosseteste establishes philosophical studies at Oxford and writes his commentaries on Aristotle.

Science, Technology, and Discovery
William of Rubruck travels in Central Asia on his embassy to Karakorum for Louis IX (–1255).

1254 The Teutonic Knights found Königsberg.

May: **21st**, death of Conrad IV, King of the Romans, Sicily and Jerusalem, when on his way to recover control in Germany; succeeded in Sicily by his son, Conrad II (Conradin; –1268).

July: **11th**, Louis IX returns to France.

Oct: **11th**, Innocent enters the Kingdom of Sicily to receive recognition as its sovereign.

Nov: **2nd**, Manfred, illegitimate son of Frederick II, begins an anti-papal revolt in the Regno with the seizure of Lucera and subsequently defeats the papal army near Foggia.

Politics, Government, Law, and Economy
An ordinance of Louis IX regulates the conduct of baillis and seneschals (his regional governors).
Registers of the Parlements (of Paris) date from 1254.

1255 **Art, Sculpture, Fine Arts, and Architecture**
Leon Cathedral.

1256 **Dec:** —, a Mongol army under Hūlāgū (–1265), recently appointed Ilkhan of Persia, besieges the Assassins' stronghold at Alamūt; their Grand Master, Rukn ad-Dīn Kūrshāh, surrenders and is put to death. The Mongols now annihilate the Assassins in Persia.

1257 Alfonso of Castile and Muhammad of Granada expel the last Almohads from Spain.
The Mongols sack Hanoi but Tran Thai-tong forces them to leave Dai Viet.

Jan: **13th**, Richard, Earl of Cornwall, (–1272) elected King of the Romans by a majority of the College of Seven Electors (now mentioned for the first time).

Humanities and Scholarship
Ibn-al-Jawzi, *Mir'āt al-Zamān fi Ta'tīkh al-Ayyam* (universal Arab history from Creation to 1256).

1258 Kublai Khan invades China.
Following the murder of the last Ch'oe dictator, Korean resistance to the Mongols ends; the Koryō kings remain as vassals.

Jan: **11th**, the Mongols defeat the Caliph at Anbar.

Feb: **10th**, they take and destroy Baghdād.
20th, the last 'Abbāsid Caliph, al-Musta'sim, and his family are put to death by Hūlāgū's orders.

June: **11th**, by the Provisions of Oxford, baronial control over Henry III's government is established.

Aug: **10th**, Manfred assumes the crown of Sicily (–1266).

Politics, Government, Law, and Economy
Louis IX forbids private warfare.

Society, Education, and Religion
Robert de Sorbon begins to establish a college for theologians of the University of Paris (the first foundation for mature, i.e., graduate, scholars).
Following the sack of Baghdād, the al-Azhar Mosque, Cairo, becomes the chief university for Islam (in theology and law).

1259 **May:** —, Siena accepts Manfred as its overlord to have his protection against Florence.

Sept: **11th**, the Mongols invade Syria.

Dec: **4th**, Louis and Henry make peace in the Treaty of Paris: Henry renounces Normandy, Maine, Anjou and other lost Angevin territories and does homage for Gascony to Louis, who cedes lands on its eastern borders which cannot be precisely defined.

Politics, Government, Law, and Economy
Louis IX abolishes the judicial duel.
(13th Oct) The Provisions of Westminster, a plan for legal reforms, enacted in a baronial council at the instance of the 'bachelry' (knights?) of England.

Humanities and Scholarship
Matthew Paris, *Chronica Majora* (chronicle of the world from the Creation, but more particularly of England in the author's lifetime).

1260 **March: 1st**, Damascus surrenders to the Mongols, who now occupy all Syria, extinguishing the Ayyūbid Sultanate; Hūlāgū is soon forced to withdraw most of his forces because of a succession dispute: about now, Kublai and Ariqboga, brothers of Mongka, are both separately elected Great Khan of the Mongols (–1261).

Sept: 3rd, the Egyptians, led by Baybars, destroy the remaining Mongol army at 'Ayn Jālūt, in Palestine, and then occupy Syria.
4th, Manfred's forces defeat the Florentines at Montaperto.

Politics, Government, Law, and Economy
Accursius (Francisco Accorso), the last great glossator-jurist of Bologna, *Glossa ordinaria* (or *Accursiana*; standard work on civil law).

Society, Education, and Religion
Kublai Khan, as ruler of China (–1294), upholds the cult of Confucius, although the Mongols' toleration of all religions antagonizes the Chinese; Islam and Christianity thus enter, and Buddhism and Taoism revive, while the Mongols themselves prefer Lamaism (the debased Tibetan form of Buddhism).
Flagellants tour Italian cities.

Art, Sculpture, Fine Arts, and Architecture
Nicolò Pisano, Pulpit in the Baptistery, Pisa (sculpture).

1261 Kublai establishes his supremacy as Great Khan (–1294); he continues the conquest of China, where Peking is rebuilt as his winter capital.

March: 13th, in the Treaty of Nymphaeum, the Genoese undertake to assist Michael VIII to recover Constantinople in return for trading concessions hitherto enjoyed by the Venetians.

June: 12th, Henry III publishes Pope Alexander IV's bull absolving him from his oath to observe the Provisions and dismisses the baronial officials.

July: 4th, Baybars assumes the Sultanate of Egypt (–1277).
25th, Michael VIII recovers Constantinople and is crowned there, deposing John IV; end of the Latin Empire of 'Romania'.

Humanities and Scholarship
Thomas Aquinas and William of Moerbeke begin translation of Aristotle's works (–1269).

1262 **June: —**, Pedro, son and heir of James of Aragon, marries Constance, daughter and heir of Manfred of Sicily.

Politics, Government, Law, and Economy
Baybars establishes the first of a series of puppet Caliphs of the 'Abbāsid dynasty in Cairo (–1517).

Society, Education, and Religion
Shinran, a follower of Hōnen; founds the Shinsū (True) Sect of Japanese Buddhism.

Art, Sculpture, Fine Arts, and Architecture
The choir of St. Urbain, Troyes, begun by Johannes Anglicus.

1263 **April: —**, Simon de Montfort returns to England to lead a new baronial movement against Henry.

1264 **Jan: 23rd**, in the Mise of Amiens, Louis, as arbitrator, pronounces in favour of Henry against the barons.

May: 14th, Simon de Montfort defeats and captures Henry at Lewes.

Humanities and Scholarship
Vincent of Beauvais, *Speculum maius* (encyclopedia of universal knowledge and history).

1265 Baybars takes Caesarea and Arsūf.

Feb: 8th, death of Hūlāgū, the Mongol Ilkhan of Persia; succeeded by his son, Abāqa (–1282).

April: —, Pope Clement IV grants the Kingdom of Sicily to Charles of Anjou.

June: 28th, he invests Charles as King and appoints him to lead the crusade against Manfred.

Aug: 4th, Henry III and Edward defeat and kill Simon de Montfort at Evesham.

Politics, Government, Law, and Economy
(20th Jan) the Parliament held under Simon de Montfort is the first attended by elected shire-knights and burgesses.

Society, Education, and Religion

Jacobus de Voragine, *Legenda Aurea/The Golden Legend* (Lives and legends of the Saints).

1266 Alfonso of Castile, aided by James of Aragon, conquers Murcia.

Jan: **6th**, Charles of Anjou crowned as King of Sicily (–1285).

Feb: **6th**, Charles defeats and kills Manfred at Benevento.

Oct: **31st**, in the Dictum of Kenilworth Henry grants terms to de Montfort's adherents.

Humanities and Scholarship

Roger Bacon, *Opus Maius* (on metaphysics).

1267 Alfonso of Castile and Alfonso of Portugal define their frontier in the Convention of Badajóz; Algarve now annexed to Portugal.

1268 **April:** **17th**, Clement appoints Charles of Anjou as imperial vicar in Tuscany; he also cedes him the office of Senator of Rome.

May: **21st**, Baybars takes Antioch and destroys the city with unprecedented slaughter.

Aug: **23rd**, Conradin, invading to recover his father Conrad IV's Kingdom of Sicily, defeated by Charles at Tagliacozzo.

Oct: **29th**, Charles has Conradin executed, extinguishing the house of Hohenstaufen.

1269 Ya'qūb III takes Marrakesh and finally destroys the Almohads; he founds the Marīnid dynasty (–1465).

Death of Jatāvarman Sundara, the Pāndya ruler, who had made himself supreme in south India and Ceylon; succeeded by Māravarman Kulasékhara (–1308/9).

The Mongols invading Sung China lay siege to the twin cities of Hsiang-yang (–1273).

Art, Sculpture, Fine Arts, and Architecture

Mosque of Baybars I, Cairo.

1270 **July:** **1st**, Louis sails from France on Crusade.

Aug: **25th**, death of St. Louis IX, King of France; succeeded by his son, Philip III (–1285).

Nov: **1st**, Charles of Anjou, now leader of the Crusade, makes a treaty of peace with the Emir of Tunis, intending to direct the fleet against Constantinople.

23rd, the crusaders' fleet destroyed by storm at Trapani, preventing Charles from directing it against Constantinople.

Politics, Government, Law, and Economy

Hemādri, minister of the Yādava kingdom (south India), *Caturvargacintāmani* (encyclopedic Sanskrit digest of Hindu law).

Science, Technology, and Discovery

Earliest notice of a map being used in navigation (in St. Louis' Crusade).

Humanities and Scholarship

Phagspa devises a new Mongol alphabet for Kublai Khan.

Statistics

Population of Hangchow (the Sung capital) estimated to be 391,000 households.

1271 Kublai Khan adopts the Chinese dynastic name of Yüan (–1367).

April: **8th**, Baybars takes the Knights Hospitallers' fortress of Krak des Chevaliers.

May: **9th**, Edward (I) Plantagenet arrives at Acre on crusade.

Aug: **21st**, death of Alfonse of Poitiers; his nephew, Philip III of France, thus inherits the counties of Poitou and Toulouse, which are absorbed into the royal domain.

Politics, Government, Law, and Economy

Durandus, *Speculum judiciale* (synthesis of civil and canon law; first printed 1474).

Science, Technology, and Discovery

Villard de Honnecourt, architectural sketch-book (includes plans of water-driven machinery, viz. saw-mills, and a screw-jack for lifting – a recent invention?).

Art, Sculpture, Fine Arts, and Architecture

Foundation of the Gök Madrasa (college), Sivas.

1272 **May:** **22nd**, Baybars makes a treaty of peace for ten years with the Kingdom of Acre.

Nov: **16th**, death of Henry III of England.

20th, his son, Edward, proclaimed as King by hereditary right (–1307).

Science, Technology, and Discovery
Manufacture of paper introduced to Italy (from Muslim sources in Sicily or Spain?).

Humanities and Scholarship
Hermann the German, translations of Averroës' commentaries.

1273 The Mongols take Hsiang-yang.

Oct: **1st**, Rudolf, Count of Habsburg, elected as King of the Romans (–1291) at the instigation of the enemies of Ottokar of Bohemia, who is excluded from the election.

Society, Education, and Religion
Raymond Lull begins his missions to Muslims.
Al-Rūmi's followers establish the Dervish Order of the Mevlevīye.

Art, Sculpture, Fine Arts, and Architecture
Muhammad al-Ghālib founds the Alhambra Palace, Granada.

Literature
Al-Rūmī, *Masnavī-i ma'navī* (Sūfī mystical poem in six books, explaining by means of fables and anecdotes the mystic Sūfi doctrine); *Divan-i Shams-i Tabriz* (lyrical odes by the greatest Persian mystic poet).

1274 A fleet sent by Kublai Khan to conquer Japan repulsed at Hakata Bay and subsequently destroyed by a storm.

July: **6th**, Michael VIII's ambassadors at the General Council of Lyons take an oath accepting the Pope's supremacy; Gregory then causes Charles to make a truce with Michael.

Sept: **26th**, Pope Gregory X recognizes Rudolf as King of the Romans.

Society, Education, and Religion
Thomas Aquinas, *Summa Theologiae*.
(7th May) Gregory X opens the General Council of Lyons, held to end the schism with the Greek Church. The Council recognizes the Dominican, Franciscan, Carmelite and Austin Friars, and orders the suppression of all smaller mendicant orders.

1275 **Oct:** **—**, Gregory obtains German support in north Italy by an agreement with Rudolf; Charles of Sicily's influence there now wanes.

Politics, Government, Law, and Economy
Edward holds his first Parliament attended by lords and elected knights and burgesses. The first Statute of Westminster, *inter alia*, corrects abuses in local government; one of several important statutes in this reign.

Art, Sculpture, Fine Arts, and Architecture
Nave of Strasbourg Cathedral completed. The west facade begun 1278.

1276 Kublai Khan takes Hangchow, the Sung capital.

Nov: **25th**, following Rudolf's siege of Vienna and a revolt in Bohemia, Ottokar, by the Treaty of Vienna, surrenders Austria, Styria, Carinthia, and all his other lands except Bohemia and Moravia, for which he does homage to Rudolf. Rudolf then makes Vienna the capital of his (Habsburg) lands.

Art, Sculpture, Fine Arts, and Architecture
Döner Kümbet (mausoleum), Kayseri.

1277 **April:** **—**, Baybars invades Anatolia and defeats the Mongols at Elbistan: he withdraws on the approach of an army sent by the Ilkhan Abāqa, which restores Mongol control over the Sultanate of Rūm.

June: **24th**, Edward begins his first Welsh campaign following Llewelyn's refusal to do homage. In November, Llewelyn submits to Edward in the Treaty of Conway.

July: **1st**, death of Baybars, Sultan of Egypt and Syria.

1278 **Jan:** **—**, Charles of Sicily crowned as King of Jerusalem.

Aug: **28th**, Přemysl Ottokar II of Bohemia defeated and killed by Rudolf and Ladislas of Hungary at Dürnkrut, on the Danube near Stillfried; succeeded by his son, Wenceslas II (–1305), in Bohemia only, where civil war breaks out.

1279 Florence, Lucca, Siena, and others form a Tuscan Guelf League, with a customs union, and jointly employing an army.
Māravarman Kulasékhara of Pāndya defeats Rājendra III, the last Chola ruler.
Kublai Khan completes the Mongol conquest of China with a naval victory, near Macao; the southern Sung dynasty extinguished.

Feb: **14th**, Rudolf recognizes the superior authority of the Papacy over the Empire and cedes all claims to sovereignty over the Papal States and southern Italy.

Aug: **—**, Baraka, Sultan of Egypt and Syria, forced to abdicate in favour of his brother Salāmish; Qalāwun, the leader of the coup, soon afterwards assumes the Sultanate (–1290).

1280 Death of Mangu-Temir, Khan of 'the Golden Horde'; his brother, Tuda-Mangu, succeeds (–1287), but Nogay assumes joint rule in Russia as Khan of the Nogay Horde, ruling between the Dnieper and Danube (–1299).

Oct: **20th**, the Mongols sack Aleppo.

Society, Education, and Religion

Albertus Magnus, *Summa theologica*; also numerous scientific works.

Science, Technology, and Discovery

Notice of the spinning-wheel in Drapers' Statutes, Speyer.

1281 **April:** **10th**, Pope Martin IV excommunicates the Greeks and renounces the union of 1274.

July: **3rd**, in the Treaty of Orvieto, the Venetians undertake to assist Charles of Sicily to restore the Latin Empire in Constantinople; Pope Martin IV declares Michael VIII deposed.

Aug: **15th**, (and 16th) a second fleet sent by Kublai Khan to conquer Japan destroyed by a typhoon in Hakata Bay.

Oct: **30th**, Qalāwūn of Egypt defeats the Mongols, Armenians and Knights Hospitallers at Homs.

1282 **March:** **21st**, David, Llewelyn's brother, begins a widespread Welsh revolt against Edward.
30th, the French garrison in Palermo massacred in the 'Sicilian Vespers'; the revolt spreads, leading to Charles' loss of the island of Sicily, whose people offer the crown to Pedro of Aragon, as Manfred's heir.

April: **1st**, death of Abāqa, Ilkhan of Persia (with his capital at Tabriz); succeeded by his brother Tekuder, who announces his conversion to Islam, taking the style 'Sultan Ahmad' (–1284).
25th, the Welsh revolt against Edward collapses with the surrender of Harlech castle.

Aug: **—**, Edward begins his second Welsh campaign.
30th, Pedro of Aragon lands in Sicily, soon taking possession as King Peter I (–1285).

Nov: **18th**, Martin declares Pedro deprived of the crown of Aragon and proclaims a crusade against him.

Society, Education, and Religion

Nichiren founds the Nichiren (or Lotus) Sect of Japanese Buddhism (a popular, nationalistic movement; cf. friars).

1283 Skurdo, the last Prussian leader, flees to Lithuania; the Teutonic Knights have now exterminated or subjugated the Prussians, whose lands are colonized by Germans and Poles.
Indravarman V successfully resists a seaborne Mongol invasion of Champa (–1284).

Science, Technology, and Discovery

Compass now known by Islamic, French, and Italian seamen.

1284 **Feb:** **—**, Philip of France accepts Martin's offer of the crown of Aragon; it was granted by Martin to Philip's second son, Charles of Valois.

April: **4th**, death of Alfonso X the Wise, King of Castile and Leon; a civil war follows.

June: **5th**, the Genoese, Roger Loria, defeats the Angevin navy in the Bay of Naples and captures Charles' heir, Charles, who is delivered to Peter of Aragon.

Aug: **6th**, Pisa ruined by the destruction of its fleet by the Genoese off the island of Meloria.
16th, Philip (IV), son of Philip III, marries Joanna I, Queen of Navarre and Countess of Champagne.

Literature

Alfonso X, King of Castile (*El Sabio* – The Wise or Learned), *Cantigas de Santa María* (poems in Galician); *Grande y general historia* (the first general history of Spain in Spanish, to 1252); *Septennario* (encyclopedia). A treatise written for him gives the first description of the game of chess in a European language. He also has translations made of Arab works on astronomy, astrology, clocks, etc.

1285 The Teutonic Knights found Strassburg, on the Drewenz; thus begins their occupation, colonization and conversion of Lithuania.

June: **27th**, Philip III of France invades Aragon on his 'crusade' and begins the siege of Gerona, but later withdraws.

Oct: **5th**, death of Philip III the Bold, King of France; succeeded by his son, Philip IV the Fair (–1314).

Nov: 2nd, death of Pedro III the Great; succeeded by his sons, Alfonso III in Aragon and James in (the island of) Sicily (–1291).

1286 Kublai Khan's army invading Dai Viet defeated; he therefore abandons his preparations for the conquest of Japan.

Society, Education, and Religion

Durandus, *Rationale divinorum officiorum* (on liturgy; first printed 1459).

Humanities and Scholarship

William of Moerbeke translates from Greek Aristotle's *Politics* and *Nicomachean Ethics*, etc.

1287 Kublai Khan's army invading Dai Viet repelled but then invades Burma and destroys the Kingdom of Pagan.

June: 23rd, James repulses an Angevin invasion of Sicily and Roger Loria defeats the Angevin fleet off Castellammare.

1288 **Feb: —**, Jerome of Ascoli elected as Pope Nicholas IV (–1292); he soon receives an ambassador from the Illkhan Arghūn of Persia who had been visiting the European kings to organize a joint crusade against Egypt.

Art, Sculpture, Fine Arts, and Architecture

Palazzo Communale, Siena (–1309).

1289 **June: 2nd**, Florence defeats Arezzo at Campaldino and so establishes her supremacy in Tuscany.

Society, Education, and Religion

John of Monte Corvino sent by the Pope to the Ilkhan of Persia (until 1290) and the Great Khan (until 1295).

Science, Technology, and Discovery

Completion of extension of the Chinese Grand Canal (of c. AD 605) to link Peking, with the Yellow River.

1290 **June: 13th**, Kaiqubād, the last Slave King of Delhi, murdered; succeeded by Fīrūz II (–1295), founder of the Khaljī dynasty (–1320).

July: 18th, by the Treaty of Brigham, the guardians of Scotland agree to the marriage of Margaret to Edward (II), son of Edward I but she dies in September.

Nov: 10th, death of Qalāwūn, Sultan of Egypt; succeeded by his son, al-Ashraf Khalīl (–1293).

Society, Education, and Religion

Edward expels the Jews from England.

1291 **May: 10th**, Edward holds an assembly of Scottish lords at Norham which accepts his claim for recognition as overlord before he determines the succession to the Scottish throne.
18th, al-Ashraf takes and destroys Acre.

June: 18th, death of Alfonso III of Aragon; he bequeaths the kingdom to his brother, James II (–1327), provided that the latter cedes Sicily to their brother, Frederick; James, in fact, retains Sicily.

July: 31st, with the fall of Beirūt to the Egyptians, the Latin presence in Palestine and Syria (Outremer) liquidated.

Art, Sculpture, Fine Arts, and Architecture

Charing Cross, London, and nine other stone crosses raised to mark the stops of Queen Eleanor's funeral cortege; their ogee arches mark the beginning of the 'curvilinear' style of English Gothic.

1292 Albert of Habsburg defeats the Swiss Confederation but fails to take Zurich.
Kublai Khan sends a fleet to conquer Java.

May: 10th, Adolf, Count of Nassau, elected as King of the Romans (–1298).

Nov: 17th, Edward awards the Scottish crown to John Balliol (–1296).

Politics, Government, Law, and Economy

Edward I orders the judges to provide training for the English legal profession (origin of education for the bar by the Inns of Court).

1293 **Art, Sculpture, Fine Arts, and Architecture**

The Mongol Scroll (a pictorial record of the repulse by the Japanese of the Mongol invasions of 1274 and 1281).

1294 Death of Kublai Khan, Great Khan and Mongol (Yüan) Emperor of China; succeeded by his grandson, Temür (–1307).

Jan: —, Edward, by proxy, answers his summons to the Parlement of Paris to answer for attacks by Gascons on French seamen, and agrees to surrender castles in Gascony during an enquiry; the consequent French seizure of Gascony leads to war.

Art, Sculpture, Fine Arts, and Architecture

Florence Cathedral begun (architect: Arnolfo di Cambio).

1295 Death of Sancho IV of Castile and Leon; succeeded by his son, Ferdinand IV (–1312), and a civil war.

Ghazan, Ilkhan of Persia, adopts Islam as the state religion and, styling himself Sultan, declares his independence of the Great Khan.

Rama Khamheng, (second) King of Sukhodaya, conquers the Mekong and Menam valleys (in Cambodia) and the Malay Peninsula.

June: —, Boniface arranges a treaty of peace, at Anagni, between Philip of France, Charles of Sicily and James of Aragon, who cedes Sicily to Charles.

1296 Mangrai, a Thai leader, founds Chiang Mai (now in Siam), the capital of the new kingdom of Lan Na (–1775).

Jan: **15th**, the Sicilians elect Frederick II of Aragon as their King (–1337).

Feb: **29th**, Boniface, in his bull *Clericis Laicos*, forbids kings to tax the clergy.

March: **30th**, Edward takes Berwick as he begins his campaign to subdue Scotland.

April: **27th**, Edward defeats the Scots at Dunbar.

Aug: —, Edward returns from Scotland, bringing 'the Stone of Destiny' from Scone.

Art, Sculpture, Fine Arts, and Architecture

Master Honoré decorates a breviary, possibly for Philip IV (in the Bibliothèque Nationale; he is one of the first identified French miniaturists).

1297 Boniface organizes a crusade by Charles of Naples, James of Aragon, and the Genoese, against Frederick of Sicily.

'Alā' ad-Dīn conquers the Hindu kingdom of Gujarāt.

Sultan Malik al-Saleh is the first Muslim ruler of Samudra, in north Sumatra.

July: **31st**, under pressure from Philip IV, Boniface renounces his claims in *Clericis Laicos* in the bull *Etsi de statu*.

Aug: **24th**, Edward sails to Flanders to lead his allies of the Low Countries against France.

Oct: **10th**, Edward's regent reissues Magna Carta and the Charter of the Forest, with supplementary articles, in a parliament, to allay protests against Edward's administration by the magnates and London.

Politics, Government, Law, and Economy

The Shogunate cancels all debts of its retainers in order to relieve their growing impoverishment – the consequence of high living standards and partible inheritances; the Japanese 'feudal' structure is collapsing under these strains.

1298 **July:** **2nd**, in a battle near Göllheim (near Worms), Adolf of Nassau is defeated and killed by Albert of Habsburg.

22nd, Edward defeats the Scots at Falkirk but is unable to subdue Scotland.

27th, Albert elected King of the Romans (–1308).

Society, Education, and Religion

Marco Polo writes *Travels to Tartary and China* (thought to have been dictated in French from travel notes, and taken down by a fellow-prisoner, one Rusticiano of Pisa, at Genoa, after the battle of Curzola; the first European account of the geography, economy, civilization and government of China).

1299 Tokhta defeats and kills Nogay on the Kagamlyk; the Mongols in eastern Europe are thus reunited.

'Alā' ad-Dīn repulses a Mongol army outside Delhi.

May: —, Matteo Visconti negotiates a peace between Genoa and Venice, ending their war (since 1261) to control trade with the Greek Empire.

Nov: **23rd**, Ghazan of Persia defeats the Egyptians at Salamia, near Homs.

1300 Wenceslas II of Bohemia takes possession of Greater Poland and Pomerania, deposing Vladislav; having thus reunited most of Poland, he was crowned as its King (Václav).

A new wave of Turks ('Ottoman'), driven westward by the Mongols, are in occupation of western Anatolia, where the Greek Empire holds only Nicaea, Heraclea, Symrna, etc.

The Aztecs paramount in Mexico.

Jan: —, Damascus surrenders to Ghazan, Ilkhan of Persia.

Science, Technology, and Discovery

'Marc the Greek' writes *Liber Ignium* which gives the first western recipe for gunpowder.

Art, Sculpture, Fine Arts, and Architecture

Giotto(?), Frescoes in S. Francesco, Assisi.

Literature

Dante Alighieri completes *Vita Nuova* (begun *c.* 1294; consists of 25 sonnets, 4 canzoni and a ballata, with linking prose: the story of the poet's love for Beatrice from their first meeting in 1274).

Kuan Han-ch'ing, Chinese plays (comedies and tragedies; drama – and the novel – flourish in China in the Mongol period).

Everyday Life

Boniface VIII announces the Jubilee Year.

1301 **Jan:** **14th**, death of Andrew III of Hungary, the last of the Árpád dynasty; Wenceslas II of Bohemia declines the crown, but his son Wenceslas is elected and crowned, taking the Hungarian name of Ladislas (–1304); Boniface supports the candidature of Charles Robert of Anjou.

July: **27th**, Ghāzi 'Osmān, founder of the Ottoman dynasty, defeats Greek forces at Baphaeum (?Koyunhisār), near Nicaea.

Dec: —, Boniface, in his bulls *Salvator Mundi* and *Ausculta Fili*, rebukes Philip of France for misgovernment and announces his trial, thus responding to Philip's proceedings against Bernard Saiset, Bishop of Pamiers, for treason.

Art, Sculpture, Fine Arts, and Architecture

Al-Kāshāni, treatise on Persian pottery; includes description of the Chinese technique of glazing earthenware (faïence).

1302 **April:** **10th**, Philip holds the first known meeting of the Estates General in Paris to rally national opinion against Boniface.

July: **11th**, the Flemish craftsmen defeat Philip at Courtrai.

Sept: **24th**, following the destruction of Charles of Valois' army by malaria, a truce is made, by the Treaty of Caltabellotta, between Charles of Naples and Frederick of Sicily, whose kingdom is named Trinacria; thus ends the War of the Sicilian Vespers.

Nov: **18th**, in the bull *Unam Sanctam*, Boniface asserts the superiority of the Pope's spiritual authority over secular princes.

Science, Technology, and Discovery

Bartolomeo de Varignana of Bologna conducts the first *post mortem* examination.

1303 The Egyptians defeat the Mongols of Persia at Marj as-Saffar and recover Damascus for an-Nāsir.

May: **20th**, Philip and Edward make peace in the Treaty of Paris; Gascony restored to Edward.

Sept: **7th**, an Italian force, led by Philip's agent, Guillaume de Nogaret, arrests Boniface at Anagni. He is subsequently freed but then dies in October.

24th, Boniface, in *Super Petri solio*, releases the French from their allegiance to Philip.

1304 Mongols raiding India defeated.

Society, Education, and Religion

John of Monte Corvino baptizes 6,000 converts in China.

Art, Sculpture, Fine Arts, and Architecture

The Cloth Hall, Ypres (destroyed in World War I).

Everyday Life

Hopped beer reported to have been common in the Low Countries for 30–40 years.

1305 **Aug:** **4th**, Wenceslas II of Bohemia murdered; end of the Přemvslid dynasty.

Society, Education, and Religion

Moses de Leon, the *Zohar* (the classic compilation on cabalistic literature, first studied in Jewish circles).

Literature
Jean de Meun (Jean Clopinel), *Le Roman de la Rose* (continued from the poem by Guillaume de Lorris); *Le Testament maistre Jehan de Meung.*

1306 A Mongol invasion of India defeated on the Indus.

March: 25th, Robert Bruce crowned as King of Scotland (–1329).

Art, Sculpture, Fine Arts, and Architecture
Giotto, frescoes in the Arena Chapel, Padua (–1309).

Literature
Jacopone da Todi, *Laudi spirituali; Stabat Mater* (religious verse, hymns and early dramatic poetry).

1307 The Mongols annex Rūm, extinguishing the Seljuq sultanate.
Death of Temür, the Great Khan; Mongol rule in China now declines into dissension and civil war (–1333).

July: 7th, death of Edward I, King of England, leading an army to Scotland; succeeded by his son, Edward II (–1327). Edward II campaigns in Scotland, briefly; on his withdrawal, Bruce establishes himself.

Aug: —, Edward II campaigns in Scotland, briefly; on his withdrawal, Bruce establishes himself.

1308 The Ilkhan Uljāytū invades Syria and reaches Jerusalem.

Jan: 25th, Edward II marries Isabella, daughter of Philip of France.

Aug: 15th, the city of Rhodes surrenders to the Hospitallers; it becomes their headquarters.

Nov: 27th, Henry (VII), Count of Luxemburg, elected as King of the Romans (–1313).

Society, Education, and Religion
Duns Scotus, *Quaestiones super IV libros sententiarum* (of Peter the Lombard), etc.

Art, Sculpture, Fine Arts, and Architecture
Duccio, *Maestà* for Siena Cathedral (–1311; painting).

1309 The Teutonic Knights complete their seizure of East Pomerania; their Grand Master moves his headquarters from Venice to Marienburg.

May: 8th, death of Charles II of Naples; succeeded by his son, Robert (–1343).

June: 3rd, Henry VII recognizes the Swiss Confederation.

Society, Education, and Religion
Clement V begins his (and the Papacy's) residence at Avignon (–1376).

Humanities and Scholarship
Jean, Sire de Joinville, *Mémoires; ou Histoire de Chronique du très chrétien roi Saint Louis* (eye-witness record, including an account of the private life of Louis IX and his deeds on crusade).

1310 'Ala' ad-Dīn sends an army to plunder southernmost India and compels the Kings of Dvāravatīpura and Madura to pay tribute.

May: 16th, the English magnates compel Edward to appoint a commission of reform (the Lords Ordainers).

Aug: 30th, Elizabeth, daughter of Wenceslas II of Bohemia, marries John, son of Henry VII, who invests him as King of Bohemia.

Art, Sculpture, Fine Arts, and Architecture
Mosaics in the monastery of Chora (now the Kahrieh Djami), Constantinople (–1320).
The Doges' Palace, Venice.

1311 On leaving north Italy for Rome, Henry appoints Matteo Visconti as imperial vicar of Milan, and Can Grande della Scala as vicar of Verona, thus legitimizing their despotisms. Florence appoints Robert of Naples as its lord to defend it against Henry.

Jan: 6th, Henry crowned as King of Lombardy in Milan.

Society, Education, and Religion
(16th Oct) assembly of the General Council of Vienne: at the instance of Raymond Lull, it decrees the creation of chairs in Arabic and Tartar at Paris, Louvain and Salamanca; it also suppresses the Béguins and Beghards.

Science, Technology, and Discovery
Pietro Vesconte makes the earliest dated *portolano* (navigational map, of the Mediterranean and Black Sea); he also made atlases (–1327).

Art, Sculpture, Fine Arts, and Architecture
'A'lā'i-Darwāza gateway to the Quwwat al-Islām, Old Delhi.

1312 Death of Tokhta, Khan of 'the Golden Horde'; succeeded by Uzbeg (–1341), a Muslim who completed the conversion of the horde to Islam.

April: —, Pope Clement V declares the suppression of the Order of Knights Templars.

June: 29th, Henry VII crowned as Holy Roman Emperor in Rome, in the Lateran because St. Peter's is held by hostile Romans supported by Robert of Naples.

Politics, Government, Law, and Economy

John II of Brabant saves himself from bankruptcy by conceding to his towns (Brussels, etc.) for their aid, the establishment of an elected council to preserve communal privileges.

1313 Tran Anh-tong, Emperor of Dai Viet, occupies Champa and establishes Che Nang, of the Cham royal dynasty, as puppet ruler (–1318).

Aug: 24th, death of Henry VII, while leading an army against Naples.

Science, Technology, and Discovery

Alessandro della Spina, associated, with Salvino degl'Armati, with the invention of spectacles.

1314 The Egyptians establish a Muslim as King of Dongola (north Sudan), ending a Monophysite Christian monarchy dating from 543; from this time Arabs fleeing Mamlūk rule begin to settle in the Sudan.

June: 24th, Robert Bruce defeats Edward II at Bannockburn and so completes his expulsion of the English from Scotland.

Oct: 19th, Frederick of Austria elected as King of the Romans (–1325); the following day Lewis of Bavaria is also elected (–1347) – civil war ensues.

Nov: 30th, death of Philip IV of France; succeeded by his son, Louis X (–1316).

Politics, Government, Law, and Economy

Philip IV holds the fourth Estates-General in Paris and, for the first time, seeks its consent to taxation.

Humanities and Scholarship

Rashid al-Dīn, *Jāmi'altāwarikh/Collection of Histories*; universal history based on Arabic, Persian, Mongol and Chinese source-material. The dated manuscript is the first of the great Persian illustrated books.

Literature

Dante Alighieri, *Divina Commedia* begun: the *Inferno* in 34 cantos, *Purgatorio* in 33 cantos and *Paradiso* in 33 cantos (the greatest poetic work of the Middle Ages; with it Dante is regarded as the maker of the Italian language; first printed edition 1472).

1315 **Aug: 29th**, Uguccione of Pisa routs the forces of Florence and Naples at Montecatini.

Art, Sculpture, Fine Arts, and Architecture

Simone Martini, *Maestà* (fresco) in Siena Town Hall.

1316 **May: 2nd**, Edward Bruce crowned as King of Ireland.

Society, Education, and Religion

Famine in western Europe causes heavy mortality, presumably arresting population growth.

1317 Robert of Naples promotes a general peace in Tuscany.

March: 31st, John XXII claims imperial rights in Italy for the Papacy.

Art, Sculpture, Fine Arts, and Architecture

Simone Martini, *St. Louis of Toulouse* painted for Robert of Naples.

1318 Tran Minh-tong, Emperor of Dai Viet, deposes Che Nang of Champa and appoints Che A-nan as military governor (–1326).

Aug: 9th, in the Treaty of Leake, Edward confirms the Ordinances; at the instances of Aymer de Valence, Earl of Pembroke, and other magnates, Thomas of Lancaster loses his position of influence.

Oct: 14th, Edward Bruce, King of Ireland, defeated and killed by English forces at Faughard, near Dundalk.

Society, Education, and Religion

John XXII creates ten suffragans for the Archbishop of Sultāniyah (Persia); he delimits the Asian mission fields, assigning Greater Armenia, Persia and India to the Dominicans and northern Asia, including China, to the Franciscans.

Art, Sculpture, Fine Arts, and Architecture
Mosque of al-Nasir, Cairo (–1335).

1319 **Politics, Government, Law, and Economy**
The death of Eric of Denmark ends his attempts to suppress the trading operations of the Hanse. It forms a settlement at Bergen and expels the English and Scots, so gaining a monopoly of trade with Norway.

1320 John of Bohemia abandons the government of the country to Henry of Lipa and other nobles so that he can pursue a career of knight-errantry.

Politics, Government, Law, and Economy
Modus tenendi parliamentum (propaganda treatise by a political partisan on how the English parliament *should* function).

Art, Sculpture, Fine Arts, and Architecture
Church of the Holy Cross, Schwäbisch Gmünd, begun (architect: Heinrich Parler. It initiates German 'late Gothic').

1321 **Aug:** **19th**, Edward II of England compelled in Parliament to banish Hugh Despenser and his son, Hugh.

1322 **March:** **16th**, Edward II defeats Thomas of Lancaster at Boroughbridge.
22nd, Lancaster executed for treason.

Sept: **28th**, Lewis the Bavarian, aided by John of Bohemia, defeats and captures Frederick of Austria on the Inn, at Mühldorf.

Art, Sculpture, Fine Arts, and Architecture
Choir of Cologne Cathedral completed (begun 1248).

1323 Michael Šišman of Vidin founds the last Bulgarian dynasty (–1330).
Tughluq of Delhi annexes the Hindu kingdom of Telingāna; its capital, Warangal, is renamed Sultāpur. A Mongol invasion of India repulsed.

Feb: **—**, Bertrand du Poujet, a papal legate, opens his campaign against the Lombard 'Ghibellines' with the capture of Tortona and Monza. In June, he lays siege to Milan.

July: **28th**, Milan reinforced by troops sent by Lewis and the siege abandoned.

Oct: **8th**, in consequence of Lewis claiming imperial authority in north Italy, John XII asserts his right to confirm imperial elections and requires Lewis to surrender the kingship of the Romans.

Politics, Government, Law, and Economy
The Cowick Ordinances and the Westminster Ordinances of 1324 and 1326 order the reorganization of the Exchequer records, in the reforms of Walter Stapeldon, Bishop of Exeter, the Treasurer.

Society, Education, and Religion
John XXII condemns the doctrine of apostolic poverty in his bull *Cum inter nonnullos*, causing a revolt by the Spiritual Franciscans.

Science, Technology, and Discovery
Notice of water-driven bellows for an iron-forge at Briey, France.

Music
Foundation of academy for troubadours at Toulouse, with prizes for music competitions (now called Académie des Jeux Floraux).

1324 **March:** **22nd**, in the Appeal of Sachsenhausen Lewis denounces John and denies his claim to temporal authority in Germany.
23rd, John excommunicates Lewis for his refusal to surrender the Kingship of the Romans.

Politics, Government, Law, and Economy
Marsilio of Padua, *Defensor Pacis* (treatise on government famous for its subordination of the Church to princely authority).

Science, Technology, and Discovery
Earliest European notice of cannon being made, of forged iron, at Metz.

1325 The Cortes of Castile declares that Alfonso XI is of age; the anarchy prevailing since 1312 soon ends.
In China, there is the first popular rising against the Mongol dynasty.
The Aztecs finally settle on an island in Lake Texcoco; this is the origin of Tenochtitlan (Mexico City).

Politics, Government, Law, and Economy
Muhammad of Delhi initiates the compilation of registers of the revenues and expenditure of his provincial governors.

1326 **April:** **6th**, Ghāzi Orkhān, succeeding his father 'Osmān I as ruler of the Ottoman Turks (–1359), takes Brusa (Bursa) and makes it his capital.

Sept: **24th**, Isabella, estranged wife of Edward II, and Roger Mortimer land at Orwell, Essex, and soon attract a considerable following.

Society, Education, and Religion
St. Peter, the Russian Metropolitan (1308–26), makes his residence in Moscow.

1327 After suppressing a Hindu revolt in the Deccan, Muhammad transfers his capital from Delhi to Deogīr (renamed Daulatābād).

Jan: **7th**, a Parliament demands that Edward II be deposed.
20th, Edward abdicates in favour of Edward III (–1377).

Sept: **21st**, Edward II murdered.

Society, Education, and Religion
Master Eckhart, German mystic.

Art, Sculpture, Fine Arts, and Architecture
Jean Pucelle, important manuscript illuminator, decoration of a Bible (in the Bibliothèque Nationale).

Literature
The *Chester Cycle* (of Miracle Plays).

1328 The Karaman Turks take Konya, the former capital of Rūm, and extend their control here as the Ilkhanate of Persia disintegrates.

Jan: **7th**, Lewis enters Rome; he is crowned as Emperor by the Four Syndics of the Roman People. Pope John declares a crusade against him and Lewis declares John deposed.

Feb: **1st**, death of Charles IV, the last Capetian King of France; Philip of Valois becomes regent while Charles' widow is pregnant.

March: **17th**, in the Treaty of Edinburgh, Edward makes peace with Scotland, recognizing Bruce as King. It is ratified at Northampton (4th May).

Science, Technology, and Discovery
The manufacture of mirrors and silk now begun at Venice.

1329 Joanna II crowned as Queen of Navarre (–1349); this kingdom was thus separated from France. (She was the daughter of Joanna I and Louis X of France, and the wife of Philip of Évreux.)

June: **7th**, death of Robert I Bruce, King of Scotland.

Dec: **—**, Lewis returns to Germany; so ends the last attempt to restore imperial authority in Italy.

Humanities and Scholarship
Levi ben Gerson, *Milhamot Adonai* (*The Wars of the Lord*; discussion of Aristotelian philosophy in relation to the Jewish faith).

Literature
Albertino Mussato, 'the initiator of humanism', collected mss. of classical authors; *Historia Augusta* and *De Gestis Italicorum* (Italian history, 1310–21); *Eccerinis* (tragedy in Latin verse about Ezzelin da Romano, 1194–1259).

1330 **June:** **28th**, Stephen Uroš III, King of Serbia, defeats and kills Michael Šišman, the Bulgarian Tsar, near Velbužd, and so establishes Serbian dominance in Macedonia; Michael succeeded by John Alexander (1331–61).

Aug: **4th**, by the Treaty of Hagenau, the Habsburgs recognize Lewis as King.

Art, Sculpture, Fine Arts, and Architecture
Andrea Pisano, southern (bronze) doors of the Baptistery, Florence (–1336).

1331 Go-Daigo, Emperor of Japan, who had refused to abdicate (according to custom) but attempted to rule, defeated and deposed by the Hōjō Regency (for the Shogun).

March: **2nd**, Orkhān takes Nicaea.

Politics, Government, Law, and Economy
Ching-shih ta-tien/The Great Standard of Administration; Chinese official encyclopedia, mainly of Mongol institutions, with maps).

Art, Sculpture, Fine Arts, and Architecture
'Perpendicular' work begun in Gloucester Abbey (now Cathedral).

1332 Death of Alexander III, Grand Duke of Vladimir; succeeded by Ivan I Kalitá ('the Pouch') of Moscow (–1341). With the Metropolitan, Peter (–1342), also preferring to reside, Moscow as now the civil and ecclesiastical capital of Christian Russia.

Sept: —, the League of Ferrara formed by Italian rulers against John of Bohemia and the papal legate, Bertrand du Poujet.

Society, Education, and Religion
The Black Death apparently originates in India.

Everyday Life
Introduction to France from Italy of techniques for distilling liqueurs.

1333 Go-Daigo, assisted by Ashikaga Takauji, a great feudatory, defeats the Hōjō Regency and establishes himself as Emperor of Japan; the Hōjōs extinguished and the effective capital restored to Kyōto from Kamakura.

July: 19th, Edward III defeats the Scots at Halidon Hill.

Politics, Government, Law, and Economy
A series of famines (–1347) and flooding of the Yellow River ruin the Chinese economy and further weaken the Yüan (Mongol) dynasty.

Art, Sculpture, Fine Arts, and Architecture
(–1335) Charles IV begins to build a new palace in Prague.

1334 **Art, Sculpture, Fine Arts, and Architecture**
The Palace of the Popes, Avignon (–1352).

1335 Death of Abū Sa'īd, Sultan of Persia; the Mongol Ilkhanate of south-west Asia now disintegrates.

Nov: —, Kings John of Bohemia, Charles of Hungary and Casimir of Poland meet in congress at Vyšehrad, near Buda; the first two award that the Teutonic Knights should restore Kuyavia and Dobrzyń to Poland but retain Pomerania as Casimir's vassals; Casimir recognizes Bohemian overlordship over Silesia, while John renounces his title to the Polish crown.

Literature
Illustrated copy of the Persian epic, the Demotte *Shāh-nāma*, made at Tabriz ('probably Persia's greatest book').

1336 Go-Daigo's attempt to restore imperial authority in Japan collapses; Ashikaga Takauji takes Kyōto and enthrones a new Emperor, but Go-Daigo escapes and sets up court at Yoshino, in south Yamoto.

April: 18th, Harihara I, who had led a Hindu revolt against Muslim rule, crowned in his newly built capital, Vijayanagar; foundation of the Sangama dynasty (–1486) of the Vijayanagar Empire of south India (–1649).

1337 Death of Mansa Musa, under whom the Empire of Mali had reached its greatest extent (it included Gao and Timbuktu; Niani, its capital, has disappeared).

May: 24th, Philip announces the confiscation of Gascony because of Edward's 'rebellion'; its seizure began 'The Hundred Years War' (–1453).

Oct: 7th, Edward claims the French crown through his mother, Isabella, daughter of Philip IV.

Art, Sculpture, Fine Arts, and Architecture
Ambrogio Lorenzetti, frescoes in Siena Town Hall.

1338 Ashikaga Takauji restores the Shogunate; it remained in his family until 1573, but its control of Japan was never complete and 'feudal' anarchy prevailed.

Politics, Government, Law, and Economy
Ashikaga Takauji, Shogun of Japan (from 1338) issues the *Kemmu Code*, organizing his government, with its capital at Kyōto.

1339 Venice makes her first conquest on the Italian mainland with the seizure of Treviso.

Society, Education, and Religion
Andronicus III sends an embassy to Benedict to negotiate the reunion of the Churches.

1340 Death of al-Nāsir, Sultan of Egypt; he is followed by a succession of 12 puppets, ruled (and removed) by their emirs (–1382).

Jan: 25th, in Ghent, Edward assumes the title of King of France and is so recognized by the Flemings.

June: **24th**, the English win a naval victory over the French at Sluys.

Sept: **24th**, Edward and Philip make a truce, at Esplechin.

Politics, Government, Law, and Economy

Francesco Balducci Pegolotti, *Practica della mercatura* (handbook for international commerce, giving routes, tables of tariffs, dates, measures, etc.; including China).

Science, Technology, and Discovery

Iron blast-furnaces known in the Liège district; at Namur, water-power is used to operate a tilt-hammer.

First European papermill at Fabriano, Italy.

Art, Sculpture, Fine Arts, and Architecture

Mosque of al-Māridāni, Cairo.

1341 Death of Gedymin, Grand Prince of Lithuania, who had extended his hold over western Russia and established his capital at Vilna; succeeded by his son, Olgierd (–1377).

Oct: **26th**, John Cantacuzenus, Grand Domestic of the Greek Empire, proclaims himself its Emperor; so begins civil war, with the nobility supporting John Cantacuzenus while the populace defended John V.

Politics, Government, Law, and Economy

Musō Kokushi, a Zen monk, has the Tenryūji monastery, Kyōto, built from profits of a trading expedition to China; other monasteries follow suit, so participating in the contemporary growth of Japanese overseas trade; this is accompanied by increasing piracy.

Art, Sculpture, Fine Arts, and Architecture

Francesco Petrarch, *Le Rime* (sequence of love poems). He is crowned as poet laureate on the Capitol, Rome.

1342 **March:** **31st**, with the capture of Roxburgh, the Scots complete their expulsion of the English.

1343 **July:** **8th**, the Treaty of Kalisz ends the war between the Teutonic Knights and Casimir of Poland, who cedes Pomerania.

Society, Education, and Religion

The first European commission of public health established in Venice.

1344 Casimir of Poland defeats the Mongols on the Vistula.

Lewis I of Hungary expels Mongols from Transylvania.

Society, Education, and Religion

Clement VI erects the bishopric of Prague into an archbishopric, thus detaching Bohemia from the province of Mainz.

Art, Sculpture, Fine Arts, and Architecture

Prague Cathedral (–1385).

1345 **Nov:** **18th**, Andrew of Hungary, King of Naples, murdered, supposedly at the instigation of his wife, Joanna; his brother, Lewis of Hungary, consequently makes war on Naples.

1346 The Teutonic Knights annex the Danish provinces of Viro and Harju, in Estonia, by purchase from Waldemar IV.

April: **—**, by abandoning imperial claims in Italy, Charles of Bohemia receives the consent of Clement to his election as King of the Romans; Clement then orders the German electors to choose a King in place of Lewis.

July: **11th**, Charles IV elected as King of the Romans (–1378).

Aug: **26th**, Edward III defeats the French at Crécy; among those killed on the French side are John of Bohemia (succeeded by Charles; –1378), and Louis of Nevers, Count of Flanders.

Oct: **17th**, David of Scotland, invading England, defeated and captured at Neville's Cross, outside Durham.

Society, Education, and Religion

The Black Death in Georgia, and 'the Golden Horde'.

Bridget of Sweden founds the Brigittine Order of monks and nuns.

Art, Sculpture, Fine Arts, and Architecture

Bernardo Daddi, *Madonna* in Or San Michele, Florence.

1347 Ramadhipati, ruler of the (Thai) principality of U Thong, founds a new capital at Ayudhya (on an island in the Menam).

Feb: **3rd**, John VI Cantacuzenus enters Constantinople; end of the civil war (–Nov 1354).

Aug: **3rd**, Hasan, the leader of the Muslim rebels in the Deccan, acclaimed as Bāhman Shāh (–1358); he founds the Bāhmanī dynasty of Kulbarga (–1527).

Oct: **11th**, death of Lewis IV the Bavarian, King of the Romans; Charles IV had already been crowned and now receives general recognition.

Society, Education, and Religion

The Black Death in Constantinople, Naples, Genoa and south France.

1348 Edward founds the Order of the Garter.

Jan: **15th**, Joanna of Naples sells Avignon to the Papacy.

Politics, Government, Law, and Economy

Charles founds the 'New Town' of Prague.

Society, Education, and Religion

The Black Death in Italy, Spain, central and northern France, and southern England.
Charles founds Prague University.

1349 Casimir of Poland conquers Galicia.

Society, Education, and Religion

The Black Death in northern England, Ireland and Scandinavia; and in Germany and Switzerland, where Jews are massacred for their supposed responsibility for the pestilence. Flagellants, inspired by the plague, condemned as heretics by Clement VI.

Humanities and Scholarship

William of Ockham's numerous philosophical works, attacking universals, establish the Nominalist tradition (–1390); as a polemicist, he also wrote anti-papal tracts for Lewis the Bavarian.

1350 Louis of Taranto, King of Naples, flees to Provence when Lewis of Hungary invades; Lewis withdraws after conquering Naples, but his rule is ineffective.

Politics, Government, Law, and Economy

Ramadhipati I (–1359), Siamese legal codes.

Humanities and Scholarship

Beginning of first Cambodian chronicles.

Literature

Simhabhūpala of Rājakonda, *Rasārnavasudhākara* (major treatise on Hindu drama).

1351 The Chinese government provokes great revolts by impressing labour to rebuild dykes along the Yellow River, and loses control of much of central China.

March: **20th**, death of Muhammad Tughluq of Delhi, whose kingdom had disintegrated; succeeded by his cousin, Fīrūz (–1388).

Politics, Government, Law, and Economy

The Statute of Labourers regulates wages in England; they are rising as a consequence of the Black Death.

Society, Education, and Religion

A Byzantine Church Council endorses the mystical theology of Gregory Palamas, an ascete of Athos ('Palamism').
The first Statute of Provisors forbids papal appointments to ecclesiastical benefices in England.

Science, Technology, and Discovery

Iron wire manufactured with water-power at Augsburg.

1352 **Jan:** **14th**, Lewis of Hungary makes peace with Joanna of Naples.

March: **2nd**, the Ottoman Turks take Gallipoli; although they came as allies of John VI in his new war with John V, they remain, making this their base for conquests in Europe.

Art, Sculpture, Fine Arts, and Architecture

Peter Parler of Gmünd succeeds as architect of Prague Cathedral.

1353 Fa Ngum, a Thai prince who had conquered the Upper Mekong Valley, proclaimed at Luang Prabang as Ch'ieng Dong Ch'ieng Tong, King of Lan Ch'ang ('the country of a million elephants', i.e., Laos).

June: **30th**, Innocent appoints Cardinal Gil Albornoz as legate in the Papal States.

Literature

Giovanni Boccaccio, *Decameron*.

1354 **June:** **5th**, by the Treaty of Montefiascone, Albornoz receives the submission of Giovanni di Vico, Prefect of Rome, who had built a state in the Papal States, including Viterbo and Orvieto.

Nov: **—**, John VI Cantacuzenus forced to abdicate, leaving John V as the sole Greek Emperor (–1391).

Science, Technology, and Discovery
Ibn-Battūtah, *Tuhfat al-Nuzzār ...* (*Gift to Observers dealing with the Curiosities of Cities and Wonders of Journeys*; account of his travels in the Middle and Far East and the interior of Africa, 1325–54).

1355 Death of Stephen Dušan when advancing to take Constantinople; his Serbian Empire now collapses.

April: **5th**, Charles IV crowned in Rome as Holy Roman Emperor; he immediately returns to Germany.

1356 Che Yüan-chang, leader of the Chinese peasants in revolt, takes Nanking.

Sept: **19th**, the Black Prince, raiding central France from Gascony, defeats and captures John at Maupertuis, near Poitiers.

Politics, Government, Law, and Economy
(Dec) in a diet at Metz, Charles IV publishes his Golden Bull regulating procedure for the election of Kings of the Romans by a college of seven Electors, who are conceded regalian rights in their territories, which are to be indivisible.

Art, Sculpture, Fine Arts, and Architecture
Madrasa of Sultan Hasan, Cairo (–1368).

1357 **Politics, Government, Law, and Economy**
(10th March) the Dauphin Charles, under pressure from the Estates-General, concedes *La Grande Ordannance* for the reform of French government.

1358 Casimir of Poland finally suppresses the separatist confederation of the nobles of Great (western) Poland.
Death of Thinhkaba, who had founded a new kingdom in south Burma.

Feb: —, death of Bāhman Shāh of Kulbarga; his kingdom now bestrides central India.
23rd, a Parisian mob led by Étienne Marcel compels the Dauphin Charles to confirm *La Grande Ordonnance*.

May: **28th**, the Jacquerie, a peasant revolt, breaks out in the Beauvaisis.

June: **24th**, The Jacquerie revolt is savagely suppressed.

1359 Death of Orkhān, the Ottoman ruler, now styled Sultan, who had founded an organized state in control of western Anatolia and Thrace; succeeded by his son, Murād I (–1389).

Humanities and Scholarship
Isāmy, *Futuh-us-salatin* (the only extant contemporary history of the Bāhmanī kingdom of Kulbarga, south India; also of the Sultanate of Delhi, from 1302; in verse, modelled on Firdausī's *Shāh-Nāma*).

1360 Timur begins his conquest of Transoxiana with the seizure of Kesh.

April: **17th**, Albornoz takes possession of Bologna.

May: **8th**, at Brétigny, Edward III concludes the preliminary terms of a treaty of peace with France, later confirmed in the Treaty of Calais.

Aug: **31st**, the Hanse, Norway, Sweden and the Teutonic Knights make an alliance against Denmark.

Politics, Government, Law, and Economy
Richard FitzRalph, *De Pauperie Salvatoris* (a tract against the mendicants, important for its theory on political authority).
Giovanni da Legnano, *Tractatus de bello/Treatise on war*, including its legal aspects; important as an early contribution to international law).

Art, Sculpture, Fine Arts, and Architecture
Alcazar Palace, Seville (–1402).

Everyday Life
Regulations against 'Schapsteufel' ('Schnaps fiend', viz. brandy, now common in Germany).

1361 Nevruz, Khan of 'the Golden Horde', murdered and succeeded by Khidyr; the horde is now disintegrating, with its court involved in succession disputes.
Che Bong Nga (–1390) succeeds as King of Champa and begins his attacks on Dai Viet.

Society, Education, and Religion
Second outbreak of the Black Death in western Europe (–1362).

Music
Philippe de Vitri, *Ars Nova* and *Ars contrapunctus* (theoretical treatises on the 'new style' of music, with shorter notes).

1362 Lewis of Hungary defeats and captures Strascimir of Bulgaria; he conquers northern Bulgaria, extending his control over the Balkans.

July: —, Waldemar defeats the Hanse off Helsingborg; he detaches its allies, Norway and Sweden, with the marriage of Margaret, his daughter, to Haakon, their heir.

Politics, Government, Law, and Economy
The English wool-staple established at Calais.

1363 Olgierd of Lithuania defeats the Mongols near the mouth of the Bug and reaches the Black Sea.

Sept: 6th, John of France grants the Duchy of Burgundy to his son, Philip the Bold (–1404).

Humanities and Scholarship
Al-Safadi, *Kitāb al-Wāfibi-wafayāt* (the largest compilation of Muslim biographies).

1364 **Feb: 10th**, by the Treaty of Brno, Charles IV grants Tyrol to Rudolf of Austria; both concede that, should the issue of either fail, the other and his heirs would inherit.

April: 8th, death of John II of France; succeeded by his son, Charles V (–1380).

May: 16th, Bertrand du Guesclin defeats the Captal de Buch, leading the army of Charles of Navarre in rebellion against Charles V, at Cocherel, on the Eure.

Sept: —, in the Congress of Cracow, Casimir of Poland mediates between Charles IV and Lewis of Hungary; together with Kings Waldemar of Denmark and Peter of Cyprus they also consider a proposal to crusade against the Turks.

Society, Education, and Religion
Casimir III founds Cracow University.

Music
Guillaume de Machaut, mass for the coronation of Charles V (polyphony, for four voices).

1365 **March: 6th**, Charles V makes peace with Charles of Navarre.

Oct: 10th, a Crusade led by Peter I of Cyprus takes Alexandria; it departs after sacking the town and massacring its population.

Society, Education, and Religion
Rudolf IV, Duke of Austria, founds Vienna University.

1366 **March: 5th**, having expelled Pedro the Cruel, Henry of Trastamare crowned as King of Castile (–1379).

Aug: 23rd, Amadeus of Savoy, crusading against the Turks, takes Gallipoli; he then rescues John V from Bulgaria by attacking Varna.

1367 Chu Yüan-chang, having defeated rival rebel leaders, takes Peking and expels Toghan Temur, the last Yüan (Mongol) Emperor; he becomes, as Hung-wu, founder of the Ming Dynasty (–1644), with his capital at Nanking.

Timur becomes effective ruler of the Asiatic Mongols, as Great Emir to puppet Great Khans.

April: 3rd, the Black Prince, invading Castile on behalf of Pedro the Cruel, defeats Henry and captures du Guesclin, at Nájera; illness then forces him to withdraw and new rebellions against Pedro follow.

Oct: 16th, Urban restores the Papacy to Rome.

Society, Education, and Religion
With the accession of Timur, Islam spread through the Mongol lands and Christian missions to central Asia ceased.

Art, Sculpture, Fine Arts, and Architecture
The Kremlin, Moscow.

1368 **Literature**
Hāfiz (i.e., Shams ad-Dīn Muhammad), The *Dīwan* (collection of poems by the Persian lyrical poet – probably the greatest Persian poet next to Firdausī).

1369 Timur gains control of the Khanate of Chaghadai (i.e., Turkestan, with its capital Samarqand).

March: 23rd, Henry of Trastamare kills Pedro I the Cruel, the former King of Castile; Henry (II) now in uncontested control.

May: 21st, Charles V declares war on England.

June: 3rd, Edward III reassumes the title 'King of France'.

Society, Education, and Religion
Further outbreaks of the Black Death in England, France, etc.

1370 **Sept:** **27th**, Pope Urban V returns to Avignon.

Nov: **5th**, death of Casimir III the Great, King of Poland, the last of the Piast dynasty.

Politics, Government, Law, and Economy
First established example of insurance in northern Europe, at Bruges, involving a Genoese trader.

Science, Technology, and Discovery
Henri de Vick installs a mechanical clock in the Palais Royal, Paris.

1371 **Sept:** **26th**, Murād defeats and kills King Vukašin of Serbia at Črnomen, on the Marica; he conquers Macedonia, while Constantinople and Bulgaria become Turkish tributaries.

1372 **Science, Technology, and Discovery**
Al-Damīrī writes *Kitāb hayāt al-Hayāwan/The Lives of Animals*, an encyclopedia of animals, real and mythical; the greatest zoological work in Arabic.

Literature
'Sir John de Mandeville' (a *nom-de-plume ?; alias* 'John of Burgundy' ?), *Voiage and Travaile* (purports to describe the author's travels to Jerusalem, India, Java, China ('Cathay') and island utopias, and the wonders and monsters he saw; a largely derivative compilation; it enjoys great popularity in western Europe, being translated into several languages (the earliest manuscript, in a Paris dialect, is dated 1371); printed from 1480).

1373 **June:** **16th**, in the Treaty of London, England and Portugal make a perpetual alliance.

Art, Sculpture, Fine Arts, and Architecture
The two La Grange chapels, Amiens (first appearance of the 'Flamboyant' style of Gothic architecture).

1374 **Literature**
Ibn-al-Khatīb, *History of Granada*; numerous poetic, philosophical and geographical works.

1375 **June:** **27th**, English and French embassies, in conference at Bruges, conclude a general treaty of truce; Edward now holds only Calais, Brest, Bordeaux and Bayonne in France.

Oct: —, Florence organizes a league in the Papal States, causing rebellions against the Pope there.

Science, Technology, and Discovery
Abraham Cresques (?), a Jewish mapmaker of Las Palmas, makes the first world map showing Marco Polo's travels, as a gift from Pedro of Aragon to Charles of France.

Literature
Pearl (remarkable elegiac poem, written in north western English dialect; anon., but perhaps by the poet who also wrote the narrative poem *Gawain and the Green Knight*).

1376 **June:** **4th**, formation of the League of Swabian Towns.

Politics, Government, Law, and Economy
The 'Good Parliament' in England is the first to impeach the king's ministers, and the first when the Commons are known to have elected a Speaker; thereafter election of the Speaker became normal practice.

Art, Sculpture, Fine Arts, and Architecture
Town Hall, Bruges (–1421).

1377 Death of Olgierd, Grand Prince of (eastern) Lithuania, who had conquered Podolia and the Ukraine, expelling the Mongols; succeeded by Jagiello (–1381).

Hayam Wuruk, Emperor of Mājapāhit (Java), destroys the last remains of the Hindu Empire of Srīvījaya (Sumatra).

Jan: **17th**, Gregory restores the Papacy to Rome.

Society, Education, and Religion
Gregory XI condemns 19 conclusions in John Wycliffe's political writings.

Art, Sculpture, Fine Arts, and Architecture
Choir of Ulm Minster (–1449; architects: Heinrich and Michael Parler).
Court of Lions, Alhambra, Granada (–1391).

Statistics
Returns of the poll-tax indicate that the English population (aged 14 and over) is 1,361,478.

1378 **April:** **8th**, Bartolomeo Prignano elected as Pope Urban VI (–1389).

July: **28th**, Florence and the Papacy make peace in the Treaty of Tivoli.

Sept: **20th**, dissident cardinals, encouraged by Charles V, elect Robert of Geneva as Pope Clement VII (–1394).

Nov: **—**, Charles IV and England announce their recognition of Urban against Clement.
16th, Charles V declares his acceptance of Clement.
29th, death of the Holy Roman Emperor, Charles IV, King of Bohemia; succeeded by his son, Wenceslas (–1419, and see Aug 1400) with his younger sons, Sigismund and John, being respectively endowed with the Mark of Brandenburg and the newly formed Duchy of Görlitz.

Society, Education, and Religion
Beginning of the Great Schism, with papal courts at Rome and Avignon (–1417).
St. Catherine of Siena, *Dialogo* (treatise on the spiritual life, in Italian).

Art, Sculpture, Fine Arts, and Architecture
Nave of Canterbury Cathedral (architect: Henry Yevele; –1411).

1379 **June:** **20th**, Pope Clement VII establishes his papacy at Avignon.

1380 Death of Haakon VI of Norway; succeeded by his son, Olaf (V), King of Denmark (–1387). Albert of Sweden also claims Norway, and in the war following there develops the organization of the 'Vitalian Brethren' which plunders Baltic shipping for the next 50 years.

Sept: **8th**, Dmitri of Moscow leads the Russians to victory over 'the Golden Horde' at Kulikova Pole, on the upper Don; Moscow's supremacy in Russia was thus confirmed.
16th, death of Charles V the Wise, King of France; succeeded by his son, Charles VI (–1422).

Politics, Government, Law, and Economy
Hung-wu, in suppressing a conspiracy, abolishes the office of Prime Minister and the Central Chancellery; henceforth Chinese emperors assume personal and autocratic rule.

Society, Education, and Religion
John Wycliffe, English translation of the Bible.

1381 Tokhtamysh (–1397), Timur's vassal ruling part of 'the Golden Horde', defeats Mamay (ruling the western part) on the Kalka and thus reunites the Horde.

June: **14th**, in the Peasants' Revolt, the rebels occupying London kill Archbishop Sudbury, the Chancellor, and Robert Hales, the Treasurer. The following day, Richard II meets Wat Tyler, the rebel leader, who is killed; the revolt now suppressed.

1382 Establishment of the Burji line (of Circassian origin) of Mamlūk Sultans of Egypt; its history is one of intrigue and murder, with a total of 23 sultans.
Timur conquers Khurāsān.
Hung-wu completes the conquest of China and expulsion of the Mongols.

May: **3rd**, the weavers of Ghent, led by Philip van Artevelde, take Bruges; other Flemish towns revolt.

Aug: **26th**, Tokhtamysh sacks Moscow and then withdraws, having restored his suzerainty over Russia.

Sept: **11th**, death of Lewis the Great, King of Hungary and Poland; one of his two daughters, Jadwiga, is elected as 'King' of Poland (–1399); the Hungarians elect the elder, Mary (–1395), betrothed to Sigismund of Bohemia, but Charles of Durazzo claims as the Angevin male heir and invades.

Nov: **27th**, a French army defeats Flemish rebels at Roosebeke; Philip van Artevelde is killed.

Society, Education, and Religion
An English church council at Blackfriars condemns John Wycliffe's theological opinions; he is expelled from Oxford.

Humanities and Scholarship
Nicholas Oresme, translations into French of Aristotle's *Politics* and *Ethics*.

1383 Poland and Lithuania united by the Treaty of Volkovysk, whereby Jadwiga marries Jagiello; Lithuania now accepts Christianity, so ending the Crusades of the Teutonic Knights, whose expansion had prompted this union.

Oct: **—**, death of Ferdinand I of Portugal; he had recognized his son-in-law, John of Castile, as his heir.

1384 **Jan: 30th**, death of Louis de Maële, Count of Flanders; succeeded by his son-in-law, Philip the Bold of Burgundy (–1404).

Literature

Kan'ami, founder of a hereditary line of performers of the Japanese *Nō* drama.

1385 The Turks take Sofia.

Timur partially conquers Azerbaijan.

March: 23rd, the nobles of Siena overthrow its democratic government.

May: 6th, Gian Galeazzo seizes his uncle, Bernabò Visconti, and takes control of Milan.

Aug: 14th, John of Portugal, with English support, decisively defeats John of Castile at Aljubarrota.

Dec: 18th, the Peace of Tournai, between Philip the Bold of Burgundy and the weavers of Ghent, ends a period of social upheaval in Flanders.

Society, Education, and Religion

Foundation of Heidelberg University.

1386 Timur completes his conquest of Persia and sacks Tiflis, where he captures Bagrat V of Georgia. He is, however, compelled to withdraw from Azerbaijan after Tokhtamysh takes Tabriz.

May: 9th, the Treaty of Windsor, between Kings Richard and John, makes a perpetual alliance of England and Portugal.

July: 9th, the Swiss defeat and kill Duke Leopold III of Austria at Sempach.

Oct: 24th, Richard II of England is compelled by the magnates to replace his senior ministers and appoint a commission of reform.

Art, Sculpture, Fine Arts, and Architecture

Gian Galeazzo Visconti lays the foundation stone of Milan Cathedral.

1387 Louis II of Anjou gains the Kingdom of Naples following the flight, because of a revolt, of Ladislas and his mother, Margaret, the regent.

Oct: 19th, Gian Galeazzo takes Verona and then Vicenza.

Nov: —, Timur destroys Isfahan.

Society, Education, and Religion

Sāyana, commentaries on the Veda (?same as Mādhava, author of *Sarvadarśana-samgraha*; summary of Hindu philosophies).

Literature

Geoffrey Chaucer begins *The Canterbury Tales.*

1388 **Feb: 3rd**, the 'Merciless Parliament' meets and convicts Richard's courtiers accused by the Lords Appellant (Gloucester, Warwick, Arundel, Derby and Norfolk), who take control of the government.

April: 9th, the Swiss defeat Duke Albert III of Austria at Näfels.

Society, Education, and Religion

Cologne University founded.

1389 Death of Rajasanagara, King of Java (from 1350); his empire – almost the whole of modern Indonesia – now collapses.

April: 1st, Albert of Austria recognizes the recent Swiss conquests in the Treaty of Zurich.

May: 5th, Wenceslas promulgates a Public Peace for south Germany to end the wars between princes and towns.

June: 15th, Murād I killed in defeating the Serbians at Kossovopolje (or Kosova); succeeded by his son, Bāyezīd I (–1403). Lazar of Serbia also killed; in the disintegration of his dominions, Montenegro becomes independent.

Society, Education, and Religion

Foundation of Buda University.

Art, Sculpture, Fine Arts, and Architecture

Claus Sluter, Portal and Well of Moses (sculpture), Champmol Charterhouse, Dijon (–1404).

1390 **Feb: —**, assassination of Che Bong Nga, King of Champa; his conquests in Dai Viet are abandoned by his successor, La Khai.

Society, Education, and Religion

Matthias of Cracow, *Speculum aureum de titulis beneficiorum; De squaloribus curiae Romanae* (anti-papal treatises by a Bohemian reformer).

Literature

Miracles de Nôtre-Dame par personnages (collection of 42 French miracle plays by different anonymous authors).

1391

June: 18th, Timur defeats Tokhtamysh on the Kondurcha but does not pursue him west of the Volga.

Society, Education, and Religion

Jews in Spain massacred or forcibly converted to Christianity.
Ferrara University founded.

Humanities and Scholarship

Manuel Chrysoloras of Constantinople holds the first west European chair of Greek, at Florence (–1400).

1392

Timur takes Baghdād.

A period of feudal warfare in Japan (since 1336) ends with the abdication of the southern emperor in favour of the northern emperor (at Kyōto), who is still controlled by the Ashikaga Shoguns (–1568).

Yi Sŏng-gye, a Korean general, usurps the throne, ending the Koryō dynasty and founding the Yi dynasty (–1910); he recognizes Chinese supremacy.

April: 11th, Florence, Bologna, Padua, Ferrara, etc., form the League of Bologna for mutual defence against Gian Galeazzo.

Aug: —, Charles VI of France becomes insane while leading an expedition towards Brittany; the Dukes of Burgundy and Berri take control of his government.

Society, Education, and Religion

Tsong Kapa founds the reformed order of Tibetan Lamas, the S'a-ser ('Yellow Hats').

Science, Technology, and Discovery

Earliest known use, in Korea, of metal movable type for printing.

1393

The Turks complete their conquest of Bulgaria.

Timur campaigns against 'the Golden Horde' in Russia, reaching Moscow; he also completes his conquest of Persia and Iraq, extinguishing the last independent Mongol dynasties.

March: 8th, Sikandar dies and is succeeded by his brother, Mahmūd (–1413); the kingdom of Delhi is dissolving in feudal anarchy.

Politics, Government, Law, and Economy

'The Great Statute' of *Praemunire*, anti-papal legislation in England.

Statistics

The Ming army consists of 493 guard units (of 5,600 men each) under the Ministry of War.
Population registers record 60,000,000 Chinese in 10,000,000 households, and land registers show 129,000,000 acres in use.

1394

Bāyezīd's conquest of the Karamans of Rūm is recognized in the grant to him of the title of Sultan by the Caliph of Egypt.

Yi Sŏung-gye establishes the Korean capital at Seoul.

April: 12th, the Turks take Salonika.

May: —, Malik Sarvar founds the Muslim kingdom of Jaunpur, on the middle Ganges (–1479).

Society, Education, and Religion

Matthias of Janov, a famous Czech preacher, *De regulis veteris et novi testamenti* (critical of the Church).

Art, Sculpture, Fine Arts, and Architecture

Westminster Hall (architect: Henry Yevele; –1400).

1395

April: 15th, Timur defeats Tokhtamysh on the Terek.

May: 11th, Wenceslas sells the title of Duke of Milan to Gian Galeazzo.
17th, the Hungarians and Wallachians defeat the Turks at Rovine; but Wallachia becomes tributary to the Turks, who also conquer the Dobrudja.

Aug: 26th, Timur abandons his campaign against Moscow, having destroyed the economy of 'the Golden Horde'.

1396 **Sept: 25th**, the Turks destroy the crusading army of Sigismund and his western allies at Nicopolis.

Society, Education, and Religion

Walter Hilton, the *Scale of Perfection* (religious instructions written in the vernacular for laymen by an English mystic).

1397 'The Golden Horde' deposes Tokhtamysh as Khan and elects Timur-Kutlugh (–1400), with Edigey actually ruling. Vitold of Lithuania invades the Ukraine as Tokhtamysh's ally (–Aug 1399).

June: 17th, Margaret holds an assembly of Scandinavian nobles at Calmar for the coronation of her grand-nephew, Eric (VII) of Pomerania, as King of Denmark, Norway and Sweden – the 'Calmar Union'.

Aug: —, the League of Bologna defeats the Milanese at Governolo.

Sept: 29th, Richard holds a Parliament which condemns the actions of the Lords Appellant in 1387–8; Arundel is executed and Warwick imprisoned; Gloucester had already (presumably) been murdered.

Politics, Government, Law, and Economy

First publication of *Ta-Ming lü* (*Laws of the Great Ming*; comprehensive code of Chinese criminal and administrative law).

Humanities and Scholarship

Gasparino da Barzizza, considered the greatest Latin scholar of his time, appointed professor of rhetoric at Padua (–1422).

Music

Francesco Landino, composer and organist; he invents a new type of clavier, the *serena serenorum*.

1398 **Sept: —**, Timur invades the Punjab and subsequently sacks Delhi.

Society, Education, and Religion

Gian Galeazzo Visconti suppresses Pavia University (refounded 1412) and refounds Piacenza University.

1399 Emperor Manuel II begins his journey from Constantinople to Venice, Paris and London to seek western aid against the Turks.

Aug: 5th, 'the Golden Horde' defeats Vitold's Lithuanian and Russian army on the Vorskla.

Sept: 29th, Richard II abdicates and is declared deposed in a quasi-parliamentary assembly; Henry of Lancaster claims and receives the crown, as Henry IV (–1413).

Society, Education, and Religion

Christine de Pisan, *Épitre au dieu d'amour* (in defence of women).

1400 Timur defeats the Egyptians at Aleppo and Damascus, and sacks the cities of Syria.

Death of Timur-Kutlugh, Khan of 'the Golden Horde'; succeeded by Shadibeg, with Edigey continuing to rule (–1407).

Le Quy Ly deposes the last Tran Emperor of Dai Viet and becomes Emperor with the name Ho Quy; after eight months he abdicates in favour of his son, Ho Han Thuong (–1407).

Aug: 21st, the Rhenish Electors elect Rupert III of the Palatinate as King of the Romans (–1410) in place of Wenceslas IV, whom they declare deposed.

Politics, Government, Law, and Economy

The introduction of herring curing enables the Dutch of Brill to rival the Hanseatic merchants' fish trade; the Hanse is also hampered by the migration of herring from the Baltic during the fifteenth century.

Humanities and Scholarship

Jean Froissart, *Chronicles* (1307–1400; continued to 1467 by two others; translated by Lord Berners as *The Cronycles of England, Fraunce, Spayne* –1525).

Everyday Life

Hops introduced to England.

1401 **Spring:** Wenceslas, after being besieged in Prague Castle by the 'League of the Lords', accepts a permanent committee of nobles to govern Bohemia with him.

Jan: 18th, Jagiello agrees that his lieutenant-governor of Lithuania, Vitold, son of Kiejstut, should be its Grand Duke, as his vassal, for life (–Oct 1430).

July: 9th, Timur destroys Baghdād to punish its revolt.

Aug: —, Sigismund released by the Hungarians who had imprisoned him for a few months.

Society, Education, and Religion

(2nd March) Statute *De Heretico Comburendo*; William Sawtry is the first Lollard to be burnt at Smithfield.

1402 The Teutonic Knights purchase the Neumark of Brandenburg from Sigismund; the Order's lands now extend from the Oder to the Narva.

July: 28th, Timur defeats the Ottoman Turks near Ankara; Bāyezīd captured. Timur next takes Brusa.

Society, Education, and Religion

John Hus appointed to the Bethlehem Chapel, Prague.

1403 **Autumn:** After his imprisonment by his brother Sigismund, Wenceslas escapes from Vienna to Bohemia and regains authority there.

Yung-lo, son of Hung-wu, usurps the Chinese throne (–1424).

July: 21st, Henry defeats and kills Henry 'Hotspur' at Shrewsbury, so ending his revolt.

Aug: 5th, Ladislas of Naples crowned as King of Hungary, but soon withdraws from Hungary.

Sept: 29th, Henry recovers Carmarthen Castle.

Humanities and Scholarship

Yung-lo Ta-tien (traditional date for completion of this Chinese encyclopedia in 22,937 volumes, none of which is extant; 2,000 scholars employed on this compilation of all Chinese knowledge).

Art, Sculpture, Fine Arts, and Architecture

Lorenzo Ghiberti, bronze doors of the Baptistery, Florence.

1404 Timur leaves Anatolia, having reinstated the Turkish princes and thus dismembered the Ottoman Empire.

April: 27th, death of Philip the Bold, Duke of Burgundy; succeeded by his son, John the Fearless (–1419).

Science, Technology, and Discovery

First notice of an Archimedean screw driven by a windmill for drainage, in Holland.

1405 **Feb: 19th**, Timur dies while leading an expedition to China; his heirs retain only Transoxiana and Khurāsān, with his son, Shāh Rūkh, ruling (eventually) from Herat (–1447). The Mamlūks recover Syria, the dynasty of Black Sheep Turkomans from Azerbaijan establish a dominion from eastern Anatolia to Baghdād, and the Safawi dynasty appears in Persia.

Literature

Johann von Tepl, *Ackermann aus Böhmen (Death and the Ploughman;* dialogue influenced by Italian humanist models).

1406 **June: 18th**, Innocent VII excommunicates Ladislas of Naples and declares him deprived of his kingdom.

Dec: 22nd, Henry dismisses parliament, called 1st March, the longest ever held in medieval England; it had withheld grants of taxation until Henry announced the names of his councillors and accepted regulations for their conduct.

Humanities and Scholarship

Ibn-Khaldūn, *Muqaddamah* (unique work on philosophy of history); history of the Arabs, Persians and Berbers.

1407 Edigey deposes Shadibeg and appoints Bulat-Saltan Khan of 'the Golden Horde' (–1410).

Yung-lo, Emperor of China, occupies Hanoi and annexes Dai Viet, extinguishing the Ho dynasty; Vietnamese resistance continues despite savage reprisals (–1418).

Nov: 23rd, Louis, Duke of Orleans, murdered at the instigation of John, Duke of Burgundy.

1408 **Jan: 28th**, Gregory XII reaches Lucca but evades a meeting with the rival pope, Benedict XIII, who is at Porto Venere.

April: 25th, Ladislas of Naples occupies Rome; Gregory therefore breaks off his negotiations with Benedict.

Dec: 23rd, Edigey unsuccessfully besieges Moscow but restores the 'Tartar Yoke'.

Literature

Bogurodzico (a Battle Song – the beginning of Polish literature).

1409 **June: 5th**, the Council of Pisa declares the deposition of Popes Benedict XIII and Gregory XII; the latter holds a council at Cividale.

26th, the cardinals at Pisa elect Cardinal Peter Philarges as Pope Alexander V (–1410).

Oct: —, Ladislas expelled from the Papal States. Alexander supports Louis II of Anjou in an attempt to recover Naples.

1410 Yung-lo campaigns in Mongolia, securing the neutrality of the (western) Oirats and defeating the (eastern) Tatars.

July: **15th**, in the Great Northern War, Jagiello of Poland and Vitold of Lithuania defeat the Teutonic Knights at Tannenberg (Grunwald).

Sept: **20th**, Following the death of Rupert of Wittelsbach, Sigismund of Brandenburg, King of Hungary, elected as King of the Romans (–1437).

Society, Education, and Religion

Archbishop Zbyněk of Prague burns works by John Wycliffe and excommunicates John Hus.

Art, Sculpture, Fine Arts, and Architecture

Paul, Hans and Hermann Limburg, *Les très riches heures du Duc de Berry.*

1411 Timur-Khan assumes personal power and defeats Edigey, but is soon expelled by Jalāl ad-Dīn, son of Tokhtamysh, who is supported by Vitold of Lithuania; the disintegration of 'the Golden Horde' thus continues (–1502).

Feb: **1st**, by the Treaty of Thorn (Toruń), the Teutonic Knights make peace with Poland and Lithuania, ceding Samogitia to the latter.

Nov: **8th**, John of Burgundy, supported by an English contingent, defeats the Armagnacs attempting to take Paris at St. Cloud.

Art, Sculpture, Fine Arts, and Architecture

Donatello, *St. Mark* (statue), the first of several figures for Or San Michele, Florence (–1412).

1412 Vitold fortifies the Dnieper to control its passage to the Black Sea; he employs in his garrisons some Mongol groups calling themselves Cossacks, a name also adopted by Russian Ukrainians of this area.

May: **18th**, by the Treaty of Eltham, Henry IV makes an alliance with the Armagnacs against Burgundy.

Society, Education, and Religion

A papal interdict on Bohemia causes John Hus to leave Prague; he writes *Adversus indulgentias and Contra bullam pape.*

1413 **Feb:** **—**, death of Mahmūd, (nominal) King of Delhi, so ending the Tughluq dynasty; Dawlat Khān Lōdī elected as his successor (–1414).

March: **20th**, death of Henry IV, King of England; succeeded by his son, Henry V (–1422).

July: **—**, Muhammad I, the youngest son to Bāyezid, with support from the Greeks, defeats and kills his brother, Mūsa, at Jamurlu, in Serbia; he thus reunites the Ottoman dominions.

Oct: **—**, John XXIII's envoys accept Sigismund's demand that a general council of the Church should be called.

2nd, the Union of Horodlo, a charter of Jagiello of Poland and Vitold of Lithuania, reaffirms the unity of the two states but makes the autonomy of Lithuania permanent and cedes new privileges to its nobility.

Society, Education, and Religion

John Hus, *De Ecclesia; Exposition of Belief* (in Czech).
Juliana of Norwich, an English mystic, *Revelations of Divine Love.*
Henry Wardlaw, Bishop of St. Andrews, founds St. Andrews University.

1414 Fresh outbreak of war between the Teutonic Knights and Poland and Lithuania.
Yung-lo invades and defeats the Oirats of western Mongolia.

May: **28th**, Khizr Khān, the Mongol ruler of the Punjab, takes Delhi and establishes the Sayyid dynasty of Delhi (–Apr 1451).

Aug: **6th**, death of King Ladislas of Naples, thus ending his attempt to conquer the Papal States.

Nov: **5th**, John XXIII opens the General Council of Constance (–1418).

Humanities and Scholarship

Al-Fīrūzābādī, *Al-Qāmūs* (*The Ocean*; Arabic dictionary).

Art, Sculpture, Fine Arts, and Architecture

Quercia, *Fonte Gaia* (public fountain), Siena (–1419).

1415 **March:** **14th**, Henry V's second embassy to demand the French throne ends its negotiations in Paris with its minimum terms refused.

20th, John XXIII flees from Constance.

May: **29th**, the Council of Constance deposes John XXIII from the papacy.

July: **4th**, Gregory XII's representatives announce his abdication to the Council of Constance.

Aug: **13th**, Henry invades France.

Sept: **2nd**, the nobility of Bohemia and Moravia protest against the execution of Hus. **5th**, they form an association to oppose the Church authorities.

Oct: **25th**, Henry V defeats the French at Agincourt.

Society, Education, and Religion

Christine de Pisan, *Le Livre de trois vertus* (didactic assertion of the right of women to receive a full education, and, as writers of their right to be regarded on equal terms with male authors).

(6th July) In the decree of *Haec Sancta*, the Council of Constance declares the supremacy of general councils in the Church. The Council also condemns John Hus as a heretic and he is burnt.

1416 The Venetians defeat the Turks off Gallipoli.

Society, Education, and Religion

Sikander Butshikan (the Iconoclast), King of Kashmīr, destroys Hindu temples and forces conversions to Islam.

1417 **July:** **26th**, the Council of Constance deposes Benedict XIII.

Aug: **1st**, Henry V lands at Trouville to begin his campaign to conquer Normandy.

Nov: **11th**, The Great Schism ends with the election of Pope Martin V at the Council of Constance.

Politics, Government, Law, and Economy

Yung-lo has definitive editions of the Confucian classics published in order to exclude heterodox ideas; the restoration of traditional Confucianism is accompanied by the revival of the associated examination system for the Chinese civil service.

1418 Le Loi, a Vietnamese peasant, organizes national resistance to the Chinese occupation (–1428).

Dec: **26th**, the Dauphin Charles proclaims himself Regent of France.

Politics, Government, Law, and Economy

The Hanseatic League makes its first legislative act, regulating the alliance and its trading operations; Lübeck recognized as its leading member.

Society, Education, and Religion

Establishment of the reformed religious community at Melk, Austria (beginning of 'Melk Reforms').

Science, Technology, and Discovery

(–1419) Madeira discovered by seamen sent by Henry the Navigator.

Art, Sculpture, Fine Arts, and Architecture

Ghiberti, model of the dome for Florence Cathedral.

1419 **Jan:** **19th**, Rouen surrenders to Henry V, whose conquest of Normandy is thus complete.

July: **30th**, a crowd of Hussites murders anti-Hussite town councillors of Prague by defenestration.

Sept: **10th**, John the Fearless, Duke of Burgundy, murdered at Montereau during a conference with the Dauphin Charles; succeeded by his son, Philip the Good (–1467).

Science, Technology, and Discovery

Henry the Navigator founds the nautical school at Sagrez.

1420 Yung-lo transfers the capital of China from Nanking to Peking, which is rebuilt.

Feb: **21st**, the Hussite extremists seize Austi and found Tabor, whence their sect is named (Taborites).

March: **1st**, Martin V declares a crusade against the Hussites.

May: **21st**, by the Treaty of Troyes, Charles VI recognizes Henry V as Duke of Normandy and his own heir to the French throne.

June: **2nd**, Henry marries Charles' daughter, Catherine.

July: **14th**, the Taborites, led by John Žiška, defeat a crusading army led by Sigismund on the Vitkow (now Žiška's) Hill outside Prague. The 'Four Articles of Prague' defining the principles common to the Hussites, now published.

Sept: **30th**, Martin V enters Rome; the papal residence restored here following the partial pacification of the Papal States.

Nov: **1st**, the Hussites again defeat Sigismund under the Heights of Vyšehrad, near Prague: the first anti-Hussite crusade fails. Four further unsuccessful crusades follow (–1431).

Politics, Government, Law, and Economy

Establishment of the Tung-ch'ang, Peking (the 'Eastern Yard', where the eunuchs in the Emperor's service kept secret files on official personnel).

Science, Technology, and Discovery

Feuerwerkbuch (manual on manufacture and use of cannon and gunpowder; describes a nitro-explosive, shrapnel, etc.).

1421 **June:** **1st**, the estates of Bohemia and Moravia, meeting at Čáslav, renounce Sigismund as their king and form a government.

Society, Education, and Religion

The Jews expelled from Austria.

Establishment of the reformed monastic congregation of Santa Giustina, Padua.

1422 **Jan:** **6th**, John Žižka defeats Sigismund at Kutná Hora.

Aug: **31st**, death of Henry V, King of England; succeeded by his infant son, Henry VI, with the lords establishing a council to rule in his minority (–1471).

Sept: **27th**, by the Treaty of Melno, the Teutonic Knights end their war with Poland and Lithuania.

Oct: **21st**, death of Charles VI, King of France; succeeded, according to the Treaty of Troyes, by Henry VI of England.

30th, the Dauphin Charles, son of Charles VI, assumes the title of King (Charles VII) of France (–1461).

Society, Education, and Religion

Banda Nawāz, *Mi'raj al-'ashiqin* and *Hidāya nāma* (treatises on Muslim mysticism; earliest examples of Urdū prose).

1423 Florence declares war on Milan; hostilities continue until 1454.

April: **27th**, Žižka defeats the moderates at Hořic in the first battle of the Bohemian civil war.

Science, Technology, and Discovery

Earliest illustration, in a Munich manuscript, of a crank and connecting-rod (operating a hand-mill); wood-boring apparatus also shown.

1424 Death of Yung-lo, the Chinese Emperor.

Oct: **11th**, death of John Žižka; his followers take the name of 'the Orphans'.

1425 Portugal begins the conquest of the Canary Islands.

Dec: **3rd**, Venice and Florence make an alliance against Milan.

Society, Education, and Religion

Thomas à Kempis (i.e., Thomas Hemerken), *De imitatione Christi/The Imitation of Christ*; revised 1441).

Foundation of Louvain University.

Art, Sculpture, Fine Arts, and Architecture

Jan van Eyck appointed court painter of Philip of Burgundy.

Masaccio, Frescoes in Brancacci Chapel and, of the *Trinity*, in Sta. Maria Novella, Florence.

1426 Giovanni Francesco Gonzaga of Mantua takes Brescia from Milan.

Feb: **—**, Venice declares war on Milan.

Art, Sculpture, Fine Arts, and Architecture

Hubert and Jan van Eyck, *The Adoration of the Lamb* (painted polyptych, St Bavo, Ghent; –1432).

1427 **July:** **11th**, Eric of Denmark defeats the Hanse off Copenhagen; the war followed Eric's imposition of dues on ships passing the Sound between Sealand and Scania.

Oct: **11th**, Venetian forces led by Francesco Carmagnola defeat the Milanese at Maclodio, thus winning Bergamo.

1428 Le Loi, having defeated the Chinese, declares himself Emperor of Dai Viet (as Le Thaito; –1433), establishing the Le dynasty (–1786); the Ming recognize him on his admission of Chinese suzerainty.

April: **19th**, by the Peace of Ferrara, Milan cedes Brescia and Bergamo to Venice.

July: **3rd**, by the Treaty of Delft, Jacqueline of Bavaria recognizes Philip of Burgundy as governor and her heir in Holland, Zeeland and Hainault.

1429 **Jan:** **10th**, Philip of Burgundy establishes the Order of the Golden Fleece.

Feb: **23rd**, Joan of Arc arrives at Chinon to meet Charles VII.

April: **29th**, Joan relieves the English siege of Orléans.

July: **17th**, Charles VII crowned as King of France at Reims.

1430 **Dec:** **2nd**, Niccolò Piccinino, the condottiere serving Milan, defeats Florentine forces under the Count of Urbino on the Serchio.

Society, Education, and Religion

Moses Arragel, *Bible of the House of Alba* (translation of the Bible from Latin and Hebrew into Castilian).

Art, Sculpture, Fine Arts, and Architecture

Capella Pazzi, Florence (–1443; architect: Brunelleschi).

1431 John of Castile defeats the Moors of Granada at La Higuera.
Paramaraja II of Ayudhya sacks Angkor, capital of Cambodia.

May: **17th**, Niccolò Piccinino and Francesco Sforza, the Milanese condottieri, defeat the Venetian forces under Carmagnola at Soncino.

July: **23rd**, opening of the General Council of Basel.

Dec: **16th**, Henry VI crowned as King of France in Paris.

Science, Technology, and Discovery

(–1432) Portuguese discovery of the Azores.

Art, Sculpture, Fine Arts, and Architecture

Luca della Robbia, Cantoria ('Singing Gallery'), Florence Cathedral (sculpture).

1433 **Jan:** **4th**, After a preliminary meeting with representatives of the Council of Basel at Cheb (1432), Bohemian delegates arrive in Basel to discuss Hussite doctrines with the Council.

May: **31st**, Eugenius IV crowns Sigismund as Holy Roman Emperor.

Nov: **30th**, the delegates of the Council of Basel in Prague make terms for a settlement with the Bohemian moderates – the 'Compacts of Prague'.

Society, Education, and Religion

Nicholas of Cusa, *Concordantia Catholica* (a moderate conciliarist's plea for unity and tolerance in the Church).
Juan de Torquemada, *Summa de Ecclesia* (defending papal supremacy).

Art, Sculpture, Fine Arts, and Architecture

Donatello, Cantoria, Florence Cathedral (–1439).

1434 The capital of Cambodia transferred to Phnom Penh.

May: **30th**, in the Battle of Lipany, the Bohemian Catholics and Utraquists (moderate Hussites) defeat the extremist Taborites led by Andrew Prokop, who is killed.

Oct: **5th**, Cosimo de' Medici returns from exile to Florence, becoming its effective ruler (–1464). Palla Strozzi is banished.

Nov: **15th**, death of Louis III, Duke of Anjou and claimant to Naples; succeeded by his brother, Réné of Provence, Duke of Bar and Lorraine (–1480).

Art, Sculpture, Fine Arts, and Architecture

Donatello, *David* (bronze).
Jan van Eyck, *Arnolfini marriage group* (painting).

1435 **July:** **17th**, by the Treaty of Vordingborg, the Hanse makes peace with Eric of Denmark, Norway and Sweden.

Sept: **21st**, by the Treaty of Arras, Philip of Burgundy makes peace with Charles VII of France.

Science, Technology, and Discovery

First known dredger, called the *Scraper*, built at Middelburg.

Art, Sculpture, Fine Arts, and Architecture

Jan van Eyck, *Madonna of the Chancellor Rolin* (painting; –1436).
Roger van der Weyden, *The Descent from the Cross* (painted altarpiece).

1436 **April:** **13th**, Paris taken from the English for Charles VII.

Oct: **—**, (?)the minority of Henry VI ends and his personal rule begins.

Politics, Government, Law, and Economy
The Hanse suspends trade with Flanders following an anti-German riot in Sluys.

Science, Technology, and Discovery
Fei Hsin, *Hsing-cha-sheng-Ian (Description of the Star Raft*; eye-witness account of Cheng Ho's voyages).

1437 Philip of Burgundy acquires the Duchy of Luxemburg by purchase.

Nov: —, The Greek Emperor John VIII leaves Constantinople for Rome on a mission to seek assistance against the Turks.

Dec: 9th, death of Sigismund, the Holy Roman Emperor; succeeded as King of Hungary by Duke Albert V of Austria (–1439). The Bohemians, however, refuse to accept him as their King.

Politics, Government, Law, and Economy
The Libel of English Policy (poem describing English trade and urging its expansion and the exploitation of sea-power).

Science, Technology, and Discovery
Astronomers of Samarqand make the *Tables of Ulūgh Beg.*

Art, Sculpture, Fine Arts, and Architecture
Fra Filippo Lippi, *The Tarquinia Madonna; Barbaderi Altarpiece* (paintings).

1438 **Jan: 5th**, Eugenius IV opens a General Council at Ferrara; he had transferred the General Council here from Basel, but most of its members refuse to comply.
24th, the Council of Basel decrees the suspension of Eugenius from the exercise of papal authority.

March: —, John VIII and a Greek delegation arrive to attend the Council of Ferrara.

July: 7th, publication of the Pragmatic Sanction of Bourges, a declaration by a council of the French church held by Charles VII restricting papal authority in France.

Politics, Government, Law, and Economy
The Hanse raises its embargo on trade with Flanders when Bruges cedes its demands.

Society, Education, and Religion
Margery Kemp, *Her Book (The Book of Margery Kempe*; the earliest 'autobiography' in English literature, by a mystic).

1439 **Jan: 10th**, the Council of Ferrara reassembles in Florence.

June: 25th, the Council of Basel declares Eugenius deposed from the Papacy.

July: —, English and French embassies meeting in the Congress of Calais fail to make peace as the English will not renounce Henry VI's title to be King of France; but the English make a truce with Philip of Burgundy (on 28th Sept).
6th, in the Council of Florence, the union of the Latin and Greek Churches is proclaimed; despite the subscription of John VIII and his delegation to the union, the citizens of Constantinople refuse to accept it.

Nov: 5th, the Council of Basel elects Amadeus VIII, Duke of Savoy, as Pope Felix V.

Society, Education, and Religion
Georgios Gemistos Plethon, a Greek delegate to the Council of Florence, prompts Cosimo de' Medici to found the Florentine Academy.

Art, Sculpture, Fine Arts, and Architecture
The spire of Strasbourg Cathedral completed, then the tallest in Europe (142 m).

1440 Death of Itzcoatl, fourth Aztec king; he had established his primacy in the valley of Mexico; succeeded by Montezuma I (–1469).

Feb: 2nd, Frederick (III) Habsburg, Duke of Styria, elected as King of the Romans (–1493).
15th, Charles calls his last meeting of the Estates-General of northern France to Bourges, but it is not held because of 'the Praguerie'. This baronial revolt headed by the Dauphin Louis and the Dukes of Bourbon, Brittany and Alençon, is defeated in a two months' campaign. Charles hereafter regularly raises taxes without calling for assent from the estates-general.

Nov: 2nd, the canton of Schwyz begins a war against the city of Zurich, which it prevents from seizing from Schwyz the lands of the last Count of Toggenburg.

Society, Education, and Religion
Aeneas Silvius Piccolomini, *De Gestis Concilii Basiliensis (History of the Council of Basel*).

Science, Technology, and Discovery
Johann Gensfleisch (Gutenberg) invents printing by movable metal type, at Mainz.

Art, Sculpture, Fine Arts, and Architecture
Fra Angelico, frescoes and altarpiece, S. Marco, Florence.

1441 Mayapán destroyed in a revolt; the New Mayan Empire disintegrates and its cities are abandoned.

Sept: 19th, the French take Pontoise, completing their recovery of the Île-de-France from the English.

Politics, Government, Law, and Economy
Frederick III declares a public peace for Germany.
The Peace of Copenhagen ends a commercial war between the Hanse and Flanders.

1442 **June: 14th**, Zurich allies with Frederick against the Swiss Confederation.

Society, Education, and Religion
First report of gipsies in Europe, as having landed at Barcelona.

Humanities and Scholarship
Al-Maqrīzī, *Al-Mawā'iz w-al-I'tibār fi Dhikr al-Khitat w-al-Āthār/Sermons and Learning by Example on an Account of the New Settlements and Remains*; on Egyptian topography, history and antiquities).

1443 Skanderbeg (George Castriota) (–1468) begins the revolt of Albania against the Turks.

May: 16th, the Council of Basel holds its last general session.

Sept: 28th, Eugenius returns to Rome. The General Council is transferred there from Florence (but its later history is not known).

Nov: 10th, a crusading army led by John Hunyadi, Voivode of Transylvania, defeats the Turks at Niš; it also takes Sofia.

Politics, Government, Law, and Economy
The Parlement of Toulouse (temporarily established in 1420) reorganized as a court of appeal for south west France; it is thus the first provincial parlement.

Art, Sculpture, Fine Arts, and Architecture
Fra Filippo Lippi, *The Annunciation* (painting).

Literature
Bāisunqur Mirzā, son of Shah Rūkh, great patron of Persian artists and founder of library at Herat.
Zeami Motokiyo, writer and performer of Nō dramas, *Kadensho/Book of the Flowery Tradition*; chief theoretical work on this classic Japanese drama.

Everyday Life
Ashikaga Yoshimasa, Shogun of Japan, has rules made for the Tea Ceremony.

1444 **June: 12th**, at Szeged, Murād makes a truce for ten years with the crusaders, with Skanderbeg, and with George Barnković, who is restored as Despot of Serbia.

Aug: 26th, at St. Jakob on the Birs, the Swiss are defeated by French freebooters ('écorcheurs') sent by Charles VII to assist Frederick of Austria.

Oct: 21st, by the Treaty of Zofingen, Charles makes peace with the Swiss Confederation.

Nov: 10th, Murād destroys the crusading army at Varna; Hunyadi escapes, Cesarini disappears, and Vladislav III of Poland and Hungary is killed.

Science, Technology, and Discovery
Niccolò de Conti returns to Venice after travelling in Asia, including Java, for 25 years.

Art, Sculpture, Fine Arts, and Architecture
Konrad Witz, *Christ walking on the Water* (painting).

1445 By a secret ordinance, Charles VII establishes a regular army of cavalry ('*compagnies de Grande Ordonnance*') which is first employed to clear unoccupied France of the '*écorcheurs*'.

April: 23rd, Henry VI marries Margaret of Anjou.

July: 7th, Vasili of Moscow defeated and captured by forces of Ulug-Mahmed, Khan of 'the Golden Horde'; he is released and confirmed as Grand Duke; Ulug-Mahmed is subsequently murdered and succeeded by his son, Mahmudek.

Literature
Juan Alfonso de Baena, *Cancionero* (de Baena; anthology of about 600 Spanish poems; a standard work of classic status).

1446 **June:** **12th**, by the Treaty of Constance, Frederick of Austria makes peace with the Swiss Confederation.

Society, Education, and Religion

Onmum ('vernacular writing'; phonetic system for writing) officially adopted in Korea.

Science, Technology, and Discovery

Denis Fernandez discovers Cape Verde and the Senegal.

Art, Sculpture, Fine Arts, and Architecture

Roger van der Weyden, *The Last Judgement* (painting).

1447 Death of Shah Rūkh, followed by dissolution of the Tīmūrid house of Herat; the Turkoman dynasty of the White Sheep now rules Persia (except for Khurāsān) from Tabriz.

Feb: **23rd**, death of Humphrey, Duke of Gloucester, while under arrest; it is soon rumoured that he has been murdered.

June: **25th**, Casimir, the Grand Prince, is crowned as Casimir IV, King of Poland (–1492).

1448 **Feb:** **—**, envoys of Nicholas V conclude the Concordat of Vienna with Frederick III and other German princes; in return for the right to exercise some papal powers in their territories, they abandon the Council of Basel.

Oct: **17th**, (–19th) Murād II defeats Hunyadi at the (second) battle of Kossovopolje and thus regains control of the Balkans (excluding Albania).

Art, Sculpture, Fine Arts, and Architecture

Donatello, *Gattamelata* (equestrian statue) in Padua.

1449 Cheng-t'ung, the Chinese Emperor, defeated and captured while attacking the Oirats (western Mongols); they briefly besiege Peking, but withdraw when the defenders elect a new emperor.

March: **24th**, English forces sack Fougères, in Brittany, and so give Charles VII cause to renew the war.

Oct: **29th**, the English surrender Rouen to Charles VII.

1450 **May:** **2nd**, the Duke of Suffolk murdered on his way into exile.

June: **—**, rebellion in Kent and Sussex led by 'Jack Cade'. The rebels later seize London before 'Cade' is killed in July.

July: **13th**, Zurich rejoins the Swiss Confederation.

Aug: **12th**, the English holding Cherbourg surrender; Charles VII's conquest of Normandy thus completed.

29th, the formal union of Denmark and Norway, under Christian, enacted at Bergen.

Art, Sculpture, Fine Arts, and Architecture

The Jubilee in Rome finances the buildings (including the new St. Peter's) and library of Nicholas V.

Literature

Volksbücher (prose sagas in German) started.

1451 **Aug:** **20th**, the capture of Bayonne completes the French conquest of Gascony; England's only French possession now is Calais.

Oct: **—**, Frederick III, as guardian of Ladislas Posthumus, appoints George of Poděbrady governor of Bohemia and John Hunyadi governor of Hungary.

Politics, Government, Law, and Economy

Commercial war of the Hanse against France and Burgundy.

Science, Technology, and Discovery

Ma Huan, *Ying-yai-sheng-lan (Description of the Coasts of the Ocean*; eye-witness account of Cheng Ho's voyages).

Humanities and Scholarship

Koryŏ sa (History of Korea under the Koryŏ dynasty, 936–1392; an official compilation on the Chinese model).

Art, Sculpture, Fine Arts, and Architecture

Jean Fouquet, *The Melun Diptych* (painting).

1452 Ladislas assumes personal rule in Hungary but Hunyadi remains as viceroy and captain-general.

March: **19th**, Pope Nicholas V crowns Frederick III as Holy Roman Emperor.

Society, Education, and Religion

Foundation of Valence University, with Grenoble University incorporated.

Art, Sculpture, Fine Arts, and Architecture
Fra Filippo Lippi, *Virgin and Child*; Frescoes at Prato (–1464).
Piero della Francesca, *The True Cross* (frescoes in S. Francesco, Arezzo; –1459?).

1453 Vasili II of Moscow establishes his authority over Novgorod.

Jan: 6th, Frederick III erects Austria into an Archduchy.

April: 7th, Muhammad begins the siege of Constantinople.
29th, he takes the city by storm. Emperor Constantine XI is killed and the Greek Empire finally extinguished. Constantinople becomes the Ottoman capital.

July: 17th, the French victory at Châtillon ends the Hundred Years War; the English are expelled from all French soil except Calais.

Aug: —, Henry VI becomes insane.

Oct: 28th, Ladislas Posthumus crowned as King of Bohemia; he appoints George of Poděbrady as governor.

1454 **Feb: —**, Casimir IV of Poland incorporates Prussia into Poland at the request of the union of Prussian nobles and towns revolting against the Teutonic Order.

March: 27th, Following the insanity of Henry VI the lords in Parliament appoint Richard of York as protector of England.

April: 9th, the Peace of Lodi ends the war between Milan and Venice and Florence.

Aug: —, Milan, Venice, and Florence make a league for 25 years, to which the Papacy and Alfonso of Aragon and Sicily accede; the need of these states for permanent representatives with each other initiates the modern type of diplomacy.

Dec: 25th, Henry VI recovers his sanity; York is consequently dismissed from the protectorate.

Politics, Government, Law, and Economy
Charles VII's ordinance establishing a *chambre des comptes* completes his reforms of the French financial system.

Art, Sculpture, Fine Arts, and Architecture
Uccello, the three *Battles* (paintings; –1457).

1455 **May: 22nd**, Richard of York and the Nevilles attack the court at St. Albans, capturing Henry VI and killing Edmund Beaufort, Duke of Somerset. First battle of the 'Wars of the Roses' (–1485).

Science, Technology, and Discovery
Antoniotto Usodimare and Alvise da Cá da mosto explore the rivers Senegal and Gambia and discover five of the Cape Verde Islands (–1456).

Art, Sculpture, Fine Arts, and Architecture
Ghiberti, *Commentarii* (important for information on fourteenth-century Florentine art; also includes his autobiography, the first by an artist).

1456 The Turks take Athens, ending its Latin Duchy.

July: 7th, a French ecclesiastical court rehabilitates Joan of Arc, declaring her trial in 1430–1 to be irregular.
22nd, Hunyadi defeats the Turks besieging Belgrade, forcing them to withdraw. He dies soon afterward.

Politics, Government, Law, and Economy
The castle built at Yedo (now Tokyo), one of the first in Japan, symbolizes the development of 'feudal' anarchy.

Literature
François Villon, *Le Petit Testament*.

1457 **June: 6th**, the Poles take Marienburg; the Teutonic Knights then make Königsberg their headquarters.

Politics, Government, Law, and Economy
The Treaty of Lübeck ends a commercial dispute between the Hanse and Philip of Burgundy.

Society, Education, and Religion
Foundation of Freiburg University.

Humanities and Scholarship
Lorenzo Valla, 'founder of critical scholarship', *Elegantiae Latinae linguae* (printed 1471).

1458 **Jan:** **24th**, After the death of Ladislas V Posthumus (23rd Nov 1457), Matthias Corvinus Hunyadi elected as King of Hungary (–1490).

Art, Sculpture, Fine Arts, and Architecture
Pitti Palace, Florence (partly designed by Brunelleschi; –1470).
Jean Fouquet, illuminated ms. of *Les Grandes Chroniques de France*, completed.

1459 Turkish conquest of Serbia.
AbūSaʿīd (–1469) reunites the Timūrid kingdoms of Transoxiana and Khurāsān.

1460 The Turks take the Greek principality of the Morea.

March: **5th**, Christian of Denmark becomes Duke of Schleswig and Holstein on terms favourable to their nobility and guaranteeing the perpetual union of the two provinces.

July: **10th**, Henry VI captured in the defeat of his supporters by the Nevilles at Northampton.

Oct: **31st**, Henry accepts Richard of York as his heir to the English throne.

Dec: **30th**, York killed in his defeat by 'Lancastrian' forces at Wakefield.

Society, Education, and Religion
Foundation of Universities of Basel and Nantes.

Sport and Recreation
(–1465) René of Anjou, *Livre des tournois* (on tournaments, etc).

1461 **Feb:** **17th**, Henry VI rescued by Queen Margaret at her victory over Warwick at St. Albans.

March: **4th**, Edward of York assumes the English crown as Edward IV.

July: **22nd**, death of Charles VII of France; succeeded by his son, Louis XI (–1483).

Sept: **—**, the Turks conquer the Greek Empire of Trebizond.

Society, Education, and Religion
St. Jonas, the first Metropolitan of Russia (from 1448) independent of the Greek Church.

Literature
François Villon, *Le Grand Testament; Ballades.*

1462 **March:** **28th**, death of Vasili II of Moscow; succeeded by his son, Ivan III (–1505). For the first time, the Khan of 'the Golden Horde' is not asked to confirm the succession, nor is tribute now paid to him; the 'Tartar Yoke' has ended.

May: **9th**, by the Treaty of Bayonne, John of Aragon pledges the counties of Roussillon and Cerdagne to Louis in return for French military assistance against the Catalans; this army is destroyed by the climate.

June: **11th**, The *Generalitat* (government) of Catalonia declares war on John.

Politics, Government, Law, and Economy
Alum discovered at Tolfa, in the Papal States; Pius II claims a monopoly of supply in Europe.

1463 By overrunning Austria, Matthias Corvinus compels Frederick III to cede his claims to Hungary and end his intervention there; although their treaty of peace recognizes that the Habsburgs might inherit Hungary if Matthias' issue should fail.

Jan: **9th**, the French take Perpignan in Louis' forcible annexation of Rouissillon and Cerdagne, which its people oppose.
13th, Louis persuades Henry of Castile and John of Aragon to make a truce.

Oct: **22nd**, Pius II publishes the last bull calling a crusade against the Turks.

Humanities and Scholarship
Flavio Biondi of Forli, founder of classical archaeology, *Roma triumphans; Roma instaurata.*

Art, Sculpture, Fine Arts, and Architecture
Mosque of Sultan Muhammad II, Constantinople (–1470).

1464 **Aug:** **1st**, death of Cosimo de'Medici; succeeded, as virtual ruler of Florence, by his son, Piero (–1469).

Society, Education, and Religion
Establishment at Bursfelde, Brunswick, of the first regular monastic congregation in Germany.

Science, Technology, and Discovery
Alvise da Cá da mosto, Portuguese navigator, *El libro de la prima navigatione per l'oceano a le terre de Negri della bassa Etiopa* (printed 1507).

Humanities and Scholarship

Andrea di Bossi, Bishop of Leira, first uses the term 'Middle Ages' with reference to the period between classical times and his own.

1465 Murder of 'Abd-al-Haqq II, last of the Marīnid rulers of Morocco; succeeded by the Wattāsids (–1549), who had been regents since his accession (in 1428).

Politics, Government, Law, and Economy

Matthias of Hungary establishes a standing army, universal conscription and permanent taxation.

Literature

The Ballad of William Tell appears in Switzerland.

1466 **July:** —, Henry VI captured and imprisoned in the Tower of London.

Oct: **19th**, the Peace of Toruń (Thorn) ends the Teutonic Knights' disastrous war (since 1454) with Poland; the Order accepts Polish sovereignty and cedes Pomerania, etc., retaining Königsberg.

Dec: **23rd**, Paul II excommunicates George of Poděbrady and declares his deposition.

Science, Technology, and Discovery

Earliest dated illustration of a ship (carrack) with three masts, the third having a lateen sail.

1467 Muhammad II conquers the Duchy of Herzegovina.

June: **15th**, death of Philip the Good, Duke of Burgundy; succeeded by his son, Charles the Bold (–1477).

Politics, Government, Law, and Economy

Louis XI founds the silk industry at Lyons with a settlement of Italian workmen.

Society, Education, and Religion

The Unity of the Brotherhood institutes its own church organization in Bohemia.

1468 Sunni Ali, ruler of Gao (on the middle Niger) takes Timbuktu; he founds the great African Empire of Gao (–1492).

Outbreak in Japan of the Ōnin War, 'feudal' warfare on an extensive scale (–1477); the Shogunate now has little real power.

July: **3rd**, Charles of Burgundy marries Margaret, sister of Edward IV, who thus joins the confederation of French magnates against Louis.

Oct: **9th**, Louis arrives in Péronne for an interview with Charles of Burgundy; when Liège revolts – at his instigation – Louis is virtually placed under arrest.

30th, Louis is compelled to attend Charles at the sack of Liège, and is soon afterwards released.

Politics, Government, Law, and Economy

Statute of Edward IV against livery and maintenance ('bastard feudalism'); another statute, designed to encourage archery, renewed the prohibition of dice, quoits and football and extended it to 'divers new imagined plays'.

1469 Yādigār Muhammad succeeds Abū Sa'īd as the Tīmūrid ruler of Khurāsān (Herat; –1470); while Ahmad succeeds in Transoxiana (Samarqand: –1494).

Death of Montezuma I, the fifth Aztec King; he had extended his dominions to the Gulf of Mexico.

May: **3rd**, Matthias Corvinus of Hungary, invading Bohemia at the instigation of Paul II, declared King of Bohemia by rebels against King George.

9th, by the Treaty of St. Omer, Sigismund, Count of Tyrol, mortgages to Charles of Burgundy Upper Alsace and other lands already pledged to the Swiss.

July: **11th**, Warwick seals his alliance with George, Duke of Clarence, by the latter's marriage to his daughter, Isabel Neville.

28th, Warwick completes his *coup d'état* with the arrest of Edward.

Oct: **17th**, Ferdinand, son of John of Aragon, marries Isabella, sister of Henry of Castile.

Dec: **2nd**, death of Piero de'Medici; succeeded, as virtual rulers of Florence, by his sons Lorenzo (–1492) and Giuliano (–1478).

Society, Education, and Religion

Birth of Gurū Nānak, founder of the Sikhs (–1533).

Science, Technology, and Discovery

(–1471) Fernáo Gomes crosses the Equator, reaching Cape Catherine.

Humanities and Scholarship
Ibn-Taghri-Birdi, *Al-Nujūm al-Zāhirah fi Muluk Misr w-al-Qāhirah/The Brilliant Stars regarding the Kings of Egypt and Cairo*; history of Egypt, 640–1453.

Art, Sculpture, Fine Arts, and Architecture
Tomb of Frederick III, St. Stephen's, Vienna (–1480; sculptor: Nicholas of Leyden).

1470 **March:** **12th**, Edward disperses a Lincolnshire rising at Empingham ('Loosecoat Field'); learning of Warwick's implication, he turns against the Earl, who flees to France.

Oct: **6th**, the Earl of Warwick restores Henry VI as King; Edward flees to Holland.

Art, Sculpture, Fine Arts, and Architecture
S. Andrea, Mantua (architect: Alberti).
Piero della Francesca, *Duke and Duchess of Urbino* (painted diptych).
Giovanni Bellini, *Pietà* (Milan); Altarpiece, S. Francesco, Pesara.

Literature
Sir Thomas Malory?; *Le Morte d'Arthur* ('reduced into Englysshe' from the French Arthurian epical romances; printed by Caxton 1485).

1471 Le Thanh-tong, Emperor of Dai Viet, annexes the northern provinces of Champa.
Death of Inca Pachacuti; he had established the Inca Empire in Peru, Bolivia, Ecuador and northern Chile and Argentina (–1533).

March: **21st**, death of George of Poděbrady, King of Bohemia; succeeded by Vladislav II (–1516).

April: **14th**, Edward defeats and kills Warwick at Barnet, thus regaining the English throne.

May: **4th**, Edward defeats Margaret's forces at Tewkesbury, capturing her and killing Edward, Prince of Wales, her and Henry VI's son.
21st, murder of Henry VI.

June: **—**, Frederick holds a Reichstag at Regensburg which grants a tax to defend Germany against the Turks.

July: **3rd**, Lorenzo de' Medici secures control of Florence when its Signoria appoints his nominees as the ten Accoppiatori to hold full powers of government.

Oct: **11th**, the Republic of Novgorod, after its defeat by Ivan III, becomes subject to the Dukes of Moscow.

Society, Education, and Religion
Niccolò di Malermi, Italian translation of the Bible (from the Vulgate) first printed at Venice (revised 1477).
Denis the Carthusian, mystic, *Speculum conversionis peccatorum* (printed 1473).

Art, Sculpture, Fine Arts, and Architecture
Mosque of Khwāja Mahmūd Gāwān, Bīdar.

1472 **Oct:** **17th**, Barcelona surrenders to John of Aragon; Catalonia makes peace and is reunited to Aragon.

Society, Education, and Religion
The Florentine *studium* (university) transferred to Pisa.

1473 Charles occupies Guelders and Zutphen.

Feb: **1st**, John of Aragon enters Perpignan in his recovery of Roussillon and Cerdagne following their revolt against French occupation.

Oct: **15th**, Charles compels René II, the new Duke of Upper Lorraine, by the Treaty of Nancy, to allow passage to Burgundian troops.

Society, Education, and Religion
Gedun-dub, the first Dalai Lāma of Tibet.

1474 **March:** **30th**, by Louis' mediation, Sigismund of Austria recognizes the independence and territories of the Swiss Confederation in return for its promise of assistance.

April: **4th**, in the Union of Constance, Sigismund, the Swiss and the 'Basse-Union' (Strasbourg, Schlettstadt, Colmar and Basel) make a defensive alliance (against Charles of Burgundy).

Dec: **13th**, Isabella (–1504), and her husband, Ferdinand of Aragon, are proclaimed as Queen and King of Castile.

Politics, Government, Law, and Economy
Edward IV, in the Peace of Utrecht, ends war with the Hanse and restores its privileges in England.

Music
Guillaume Dufay, Flemish composer of sacred and secular music.

Literature
William Caxton prints and publishes, at Bruges, his first book in English, his own translation of *Recuyell of the Histories of Troye* (a French romance by Raoul le Fèvre).

1475 Kaffia, the Genoese colony in the Crimea, taken by the Turks; the Mongol Khan of the Crimea becomes an Ottoman vassal.

March: **10th**, Perpignan recovered for France; so ends a savage war (since 1473) by which Louis reconquered Roussillon and Cerdagne.

Nov: **—**, Charles conquers the Duchy of Lorraine.

Art, Sculpture, Fine Arts, and Architecture
Uspensky Cathedral, the Kremlin, Moscow (–1479; architect: Aristotle of Florence).
Hugo van der Goes, *The Portinari Altarpiece* (painting).

Literature
Garcia de Montalvo, *Amadis de Gaula/Amadis of Gaul*; prose Spanish romance of chivalry written down about now from lost originals of the fourteenth century; 'A new age of Romance began' – Hallam).

1476 Ivan III refuses to pay tribute to Ahmad, Khan of 'the Golden Horde', and defeats him.

March: **22nd**, the Swiss defeat the Burgundian army at Grandson.

June: **22nd**, the Swiss again defeat Charles at Morat. René recovers his Duchy of Lorraine.

Society, Education, and Religion
Foundation of Upsala University.

1477 End of the Ōnin War because of general exhaustion; civil warfare, however, remains endemic in Japan.

Jan: **5th**, the Swiss defeat and kill Charles the Bold, Duke of Burgundy at Nancy. His heir is his daughter, Mary, but Louis rapidly seizes the Duchy and County of Burgundy and the Somme towns.

Aug: **19th**, Mary of Burgundy marries Maximilian of Austria; he now leads the defence of the Low Countries against Louis.

Society, Education, and Religion
Foundation of Mainz and Tubingen Universities.
Ferdinand and Isabella establish the Inquisition in Spain.

Art, Sculpture, Fine Arts, and Architecture
Botticelli, *Primavera* (painting).

1478 The Turks conquer Albania.

Jan: **24th**, Maximilian and Mary of Burgundy make peace with the Swiss, at Zurich.

Feb: **18th**, George, Duke of Clarence, murdered after being convicted in Parliament for treason against his brother, Edward IV.

April: **26th**, in the Pazzi Conspiracy, supported by Pope Sixtus IV, Giuliano de' Medici is murdered but his brother Lorenzo escapes.

June: **1st**, Sixtus IV excommunicates Lorenzo de' Medici; he allies with Naples in a general war against Florence, Venice and Milan.

Dec: **7th**, by the Treaty of Olomuc, Matthias of Hungary recognizes Vladislav II as King of Bohemia, so ending their war over the Bohemian succession.

Society, Education, and Religion
Christian I founds Copenhagen University.

1479 Le Thanh-tong of Dai Viet takes Luang Prabang, capital of Laos.

Jan: **19th**, death of John II of Aragon; succeeded by his son, Ferdinand II (–1516), and in Navarre by his daughter Eleanor.

26th, Muhammad II makes peace with Venice in the Treaty of Constantinople.

Sept: **4th**, by the Treaty of Trujillo, Alfonso of Portugal recognizes Isabella as Queen of Castile.

Literature
Francesco Colonna, *Hypnerotomachia Polophili* (a prose allegory, a romance, a miscellany of classical archaeology written in a hybrid language – Lombardic Italian, Latin, Greek, Hebrew and Arabic. When printed and illuminated by Aldus (1499) one of the most beautiful books in the world).

1480 **March: 6th**, by the Treaty of Toledo, Ferdinand and Isabella recognize Alfonso's African conquests, while he cedes the Canaries to Spain.

6th, by a personal mission to Ferrante, Lorenzo de' Medici makes a peace between Naples and Florence, to which the Papacy, Milan and Venice accede.

July: 10th, death of René II the Good, Duke of Anjou; Louis XI thus gains possession of Provence, Anjou, Maine and Bar.

28th, the Knights Hospitallers finally repulse the siege of Rhodes.

Science, Technology, and Discovery

First attempt by a ship from Bristol to discover the 'Isle of Brasil' (in mid-Atlantic).

Leonardo da Vinci designs a parachute.

Humanities and Scholarship

Rudolphus Agricola (Roelof Huysmann), *De Inventione Dialectica* (philosophical work by the greatest Dutch humanist and scholar of his age).

Art, Sculpture, Fine Arts, and Architecture

King's College Chapel, Cambridge (–1515).

Hieronymus Bosch, *The Crucifixion; Christ Mocked; The Epiphany* (paintings).

1481 Death of Muhammad II, the Ottoman Sultan; succeeded by his son, Bāyezīd II (–1512), who is opposed by his brother, Djem.

Ahmad, Khan of 'the Golden Horde', murdered after abandoning a campaign against Moscow to restore the 'Tartar Yoke'.

Dec: 22nd, Nicholas von Flüe, a hermit, intervenes in a diet at Stanz and averts a breach of the Swiss Confederation; Fribourg and Solothurn join it.

Politics, Government, Law, and Economy

Louis XI, on gaining possession of Marseilles, proposes to make it an emporium for oriental merchandise.

Art, Sculpture, Fine Arts, and Architecture

Leonardo, *Adoration of the Kings* (painting).

Botticelli, Ghirlandaio and Perugino, Frescoes in the Sistine Chapel, Rome (–1482).

Verrocchio, Statue of Bartolomeo Colleone, Venice.

1482 Boabdil rebels against his father, Abū-al-Hasan, and seizes Granada (as Muhammad XI; –1483).

Feb: 26th, the Castilians win Alhama from Granada.

Sept: 1st, Kiev (then in Lithuania) sacked by the Crimean Tartars, as Ivan's allies.

Dec: 23rd, by the Treaty of Arras, Louis makes peace with Maximilian, who recognizes the French occupation of Burgundy, Picardy and Artois, and himself remains in possession of the Low Countries.

Science, Technology, and Discovery

Diego Cão, a Portuguese mariner, reaches the Congo. The Portuguese make a settlement on the Gold Coast.

1483 **April: 9th**, death of Edward IV of England; succeeded by his son, Edward V.

23rd, the Castilians defeat the army of Granada besieging Lucena and capture Boabdil; Abū-al-Hasan then resumes the throne of Granada (–1485).

June: 26th, Richard, Duke of Gloucester, begins to rule as Richard III (–1485), having deposed his nephew, Edward V; the latter and his brother, Richard, Duke of York, are soon afterwards murdered in the Tower of London.

Aug: 30th, death of Louis XI of France; succeeded by his son, Charles VIII (–1498), whose sister, Anne of Beaujeu, acts as regent.

Politics, Government, Law, and Economy

Code of Hong-duc (Vietnamese law-code).

Society, Education, and Religion

Tommaso de Torquemada appointed inquisitor-general of Castile and Aragon.

Ferdinand of Aragon founds Palma University, Majorca.

Art, Sculpture, Fine Arts, and Architecture

Ashikaga Yoshimasa, the retired Shogun, builds the Silver Pavilion, Kyōto.

Leonardo, *The Virgin of the Rocks* (Louvre).

1484 Ivan annexes the principality of Tver.

The Turks take Kilia (in Moldavia) and Bialgorod.

1485 **June:** **1st**, Matthias Corvinus of Hungary takes Vienna in his conquest of Austria (from Frederick III) and makes the city his capital.

Aug: **22nd**, Richard III killed at the Battle of Bosworth; Richmond succeeds as Henry VII (–1509), founding the Tudor dynasty (–1603).

Society, Education, and Religion

In the Treaty of Kutná Hora, Vladislav II confirms the Compacts of Prague (–Nov. 1433) and other concessions to Hussite opinion.

Art, Sculpture, Fine Arts, and Architecture

Ivan III rebuilds the Kremlin.

Mantegna, *The Triumph of Caesar* (cartoons; –1494).

1486 Sāluva Narasimha, a virtually independent ruler of Chandragirirājya, in the disintegrating Vijayanagar Empire, deposes Praudharāya and founds the Sāluva dynasty (–1505).

Feb: **10th**, the Breton Estates plan the marriage of Anne, the heir of Duke Francis, to Maximilian; he consequently attempts to invade France.

16th, Maximilian I of Habsburg elected as King of the Romans (–1519); he proclaims a peace in Germany for ten years.

Dec: **—**, Louis of Orléans, René of Lorraine and other French nobles ally with the lords of Brittany in a new league against the Regent Anne.

Humanities and Scholarship

Giovanni Pico della Mirandola, *De omni re scribili (Concerning All Things Knowable)*; and *Oratio de hominis dignitate* (a treatise on Free Will).

Erik Olai, *Chronica Regni Gothorum* (a chronicle, by the father of Swedish historical writing).

1487 **June:** **16th**, Henry defeats and captures the pretender Simnel at East Stoke, near Newark; this is the last battle in 'The Wars of the Roses'.

July: **—**, Frederick and Maximilian form the Swabian League of prelates, lords and towns to oppose the aggressions of the Wittelsbach Dukes of Bavaria.

—, Ivan the Great subdues the Mongol khanate of Kazan and installs a vassal khan.

Politics, Government, Law, and Economy

Henry VII's (subsequently misnamed) 'Star Chamber Act' establishes a judicial subcommittee of his council.

Adoption of a set form for writing examination papers for the Chinese civil service.

Society, Education, and Religion

Henricus Insitoris, *Malleus Maleficarum* (*The Hammer of Witches*; infamous work encouraging the zeal of witch-hunters).

1488 **Aug:** **20th**, by the Treaty of Sablé, Charles VIII makes peace with Francis of Brittany.

Sept: **9th**, death of Francis II; succeeded by his daughter, Anne (–1491). Charles claims custody of the Duchy but the Bretons oppose him.

Politics, Government, Law, and Economy

Boromo Trailokanet, King of Ayudhya (Siam, from 1448), has formed a centralized administration, codified laws, and organized society by now.

Science, Technology, and Discovery

Bartholomew Diaz, a Portuguese mariner, rounds the Cape of Storms (renamed the Cape of Good Hope by John II of Portugal).

1489 **Nov:** **25th**, Muhammad XII of Granada surrenders to Ferdinand and Isabella at their capture of Baza; Boabdil resumes the Kingdom of Granada (–1492).

Humanities and Scholarship

Philippe de Commynes, *Mémoires* (completed in 1498; more than a chronicle of events in the times of Charles the Bold and Louis XI, as the author was the first critical and philosophical historian in European literature).

Art, Sculpture, Fine Arts, and Architecture

Hans Memling, *The Shrine of St. Ursula* (painted relic shrine).

1490 The Muslim kingdom of Kulbarga (the Deccan) disintegrates with the establishment of kingdoms by the governors of Bījāpur, Berar, Bīdar, and Ahmadnagar.

April: **6th**, death of Matthias Corvinus, King of Hungary, without lawful issue; the Habsburgs recover Austria in the disintegration of his empire.

Dec: **—**, Maximilian marries Anne of Brittany by proxy.

1491 **Nov: 25th**, Boabdil concludes a treaty to surrender the city of Granada to Ferdinand and Isabella, which they have besieged since the spring.

Dec: 6th, Anne of Brittany marries Charles VIII and so ends the Duchy's independence of France.

Science, Technology, and Discovery

? Seamen from Bristol possibly discover Newfoundland.

(17th April) Ferdinand and Isabella sign their contract with Christopher Columbus concerning his proposed voyage of discovery.

1492 **Jan: 2nd**, the Spanish complete the conquest of Granada.

Feb: —, Charles VIII of France abandons Anne of Beaujeu and takes control of affairs.

March: 31st, Jews in Spain are given three months to accept Christianity or leave.

April: 8th, Piero de' Medici succeeds as ruler of Florence (–1495) on the death of his father, Lorenzo the Magnificent.

Aug: 3rd, Christopher Columbus sails from Palos, Spain.
10th, Roderigo Borgia is elected Pope Alexander VI (–1503).

Sept: —, Perkin Warbeck, a Fleming claiming to be Richard, Duke of York (the second son of Edward IV), is accepted at the French court as rightful claimant to the English throne.

Oct: 2nd, Henry VII of England invades France.
12th, Christopher Columbus reaches the Bahamas.

Nov: 3rd, by Peace of Étaples, Charles VIII of France undertakes to expel Perkin Warbeck.

Science, Technology, and Discovery

Leonardo Da Vinci draws a flying machine.

Art, Sculpture, Fine Arts, and Architecture

Carlo Crivelli, *The Immaculate Conception.*

Bramante starts building the choir and cupola of S. Maria delle Grazie, Milan (–1498).

Literature

Diego de San Pedro, *La Cárcel de amor.*

Sport and Recreation

Mont Aiguille in the Alps is ascended by a party of Frenchmen on the orders of Charles VIII of France, to destroy the peak's reputation for inaccessibility.

The Expansion of Europe

1493–1789

1493 Turks invade Dalmatia and Croatia.

April: **25th**, Alfonso Fernández de Lugo begins Spanish conquest of Tenerife (–1496).

May: **3rd**, (–4th) Pope Alexander VI publishes first bull *Inter cetera* dividing New World between Spain and Portugal (revised by second bull, 28th June).

Aug: **19th**, on Frederick III's death, Maximilian I assumes the title of Holy Roman Emperor elect (–1519).

Sept: **18th**, Henry VII banishes Flemings from England and the Merchants' Adventurers move their staple from Antwerp to Calais.

Science, Technology, and Discovery

(4th March) Christopher Columbus returns to Lisbon from the West Indies.

1494 **Jan:** **25th**, Alfonso II succeeds to the throne of Naples on the death of Ferdinand I.

June: **7th**, by Treaty of Tordesillas, Spain and Portugal agree to divide the New World.

Sept: **1st**, Charles VIII of France invades Italy to claim the throne of Naples.

Nov: **17th**, Charles VIII enters Florence, where the Republican Party, influenced by Savonarola, expels Piero de' Medici.

Dec: **1st**, Edward Poynings opens a Parliament at Drogheda which passes legislation ('Poynings Law') making Irish legislature dependent on England.
31st, Charles VIII enters Rome; the Pope takes refuge in the Castle of St. Angelo.

Science, Technology, and Discovery

Luca Pacioli's *Algebra*, includes a study of the problems of cubic equations.

Art, Sculpture, Fine Arts, and Architecture

Leonardo da Vinci, *Madonna of the Rocks* (painting).

Literature

Sebastian Brandt, *Das Narrenshiff* (*The Ship of Fools*; translated 1509).

1495 **Feb:** **22nd**, Charles VIII enters Naples; Alfonso II has already fled, leaving his kingdom to his son Ferrante, who takes the title Ferdinand II.

March: **31st**, Pope Alexander VI forms the Holy League with the Empire, Spain, Venice and Milan, ostensibly to fight the Turks but aiming at expelling Charles VIII from Italy.

May: **12th**, Charles VIII is crowned King of Naples.

July: **—**, Ferdinand II reconquers Naples, with the help of the Spanish fleet, under Gonzalo de Cordova.
3rd, Perkin Warbeck fails to land at Deal in Kent.
5th, Charles VIII defeats forces of the Holy League at the Battle of Fornovo.

Aug: **7th**, the Imperial Diet of Worms proclaims Perpetual Peace within the Empire; the right of private warfare is abolished.

Nov: **27th**, James IV of Scotland receives Perkin Warbeck at Stirling.

Humanities and Scholarship

Aldine Press (founded by Aldus Manutius at Venice in 1490) begins publication of celebrated editions of the Greek classics.

Art, Sculpture, Fine Arts, and Architecture

Hieronymus Bosch, *Adoration of the Magi* (painting); also *Garden of Worldly Delights* (painting).
Leonardo da Vinci, *The Last Supper* (painting) (–1498).

1496 **March:** **5th**, Henry VII commissions John and Sebastian Cabot to discover new lands.

Sept: **—**, James IV of Scotland invades Northumberland in support of Perkin Warbeck.

Politics, Government, Law, and Economy

Marino Sanudo the younger begins his 'diaries' of affairs in Venice (–1535).
John Alcock founds Jesus College, Cambridge.

Science, Technology, and Discovery

(11th June) Columbus returns to Spain after a second voyage, on which he has discovered Dominica, Puerto Rico, Antigua, and Jamaica, and circumnavigated Hispaniola, where he has founded a settlement at Isabella.

Literature

Sir John Mandeville (pseudonym), *Travels*.
Johann Reuchlin, *Sergius* (Latin play, introducing comedy into Germany).

1497 **May:** **—**, Rising breaks out in Cornwall. James Tutchet, Lord Audley, leads an army of 15,000 to attack London.

June: **7th**, Henry VII defeats the Cornish rebels under Lord Audley at Blackheath.

Sept: **30th**, Anglo-Scottish truce is signed at Ayton.

Oct: **5th**, Perkin Warbeck is captured; the West Country submits.
28th, John II of Denmark defeats the Swedes at Brunkeberg and enters Stockholm, reviving the Scandinavian Union.

Science, Technology, and Discovery

(2nd May) John Cabot sails from Bristol and reaches the American coast at Cape Breton Island (24th June) and explores the coast of Newfoundland.
(9th July) Vasco da Gama leaves Lisbon on a voyage to India; he rounds the Cape of Good Hope in Dec.

Art, Sculpture, Fine Arts, and Architecture

Albrecht Dürer, *The Artist's Father*.

1498 **April:** **7th**, Louis XII, Duke of Orléans, the last of the direct line of the house of Valois, succeeds as King of France (–1515) on the death of his cousin Charles VIII.

May: **—**, English merchants return to Antwerp.

Aug: **5th**, Louis XII and Ferdinand II sign the treaty of Marcoussis.

Society, Education, and Religion

Girolamo Savonarola is strangled, then burnt, at Florence for continuing to preach and for sedition and 'religious errors'.

Science, Technology, and Discovery

(20th May) Vasco da Gama discovers the sea route to India, arriving at Calicut on the Malabar coast.
(30th May) Christopher Columbus sets out on his third voyage of exploration (–25th Nov, 1500), on which he discovers Trinidad (31st July), and South America (1st Aug).

Humanities and Scholarship

The Aldine Press, Venice, begins production of octavo editions of the Greek and Latin classics at 'popular' prices.

Art, Sculpture, Fine Arts, and Architecture

Albrecht Dürer, *Self-Portrait*; *The Knight, Death and the Devil*; *Apocalypse*.
Michelangelo, *Pietà*, St. Peter's, Rome (–1500).

Everyday Life

The first known cases of syphilis in Europe.

1499 Cesare Borgia begins conquest of the Romagna (–Jan 1501), reducing the papal estates to central control.

Feb: **—**, War between the Swabian League and the Swiss Cantons flares up in the Rhine.

July: **—**, outbreak of war between the Turks and Venice.
22nd, decisive victory of the Swiss over the Swabian League at Dornach.

Sept: **11th**, the French take Milan, meeting with little opposition.
22nd, the Peace of Basle ends the Swabian War; the Swiss establish their independence from imperial jurisdiction and taxation.

Nov: **21st**, Perkin Warbeck is tried for treason and, 23rd, executed.

Science, Technology, and Discovery
(May) (–June 1500) Alonso de Ojeda and Amerigo Vespucci leave Spain on a voyage of discovery in South America on which they discover the mouth of the river Amazon.

Humanities and Scholarship
Francesco Colonna, *Hypnerotomachia Poliphili.*

Art, Sculpture, Fine Arts, and Architecture
Luca Signorelli, fresco cycle at Orvieto Cathedral (begun by Fra Angelico in 1447).

Everyday Life
First known political cartoon (on the subject of Louis XII of France and the Italian war).

1500 **Feb:** **5th**, Ludovico Sforza with the aid of German and Swiss mercenaries recovers Milan from the French.
24th, Joanna, wife of Philip of Austria, Duke of Burgundy, gives birth to the future Emperor Charles V.

April: **8th**, a French army reconquers Milan; Ludovico Sforza (–1508) is sent as a prisoner to France.

May: **—**, Ferdinand of Aragon suppresses a Moorish revolt in Granada.

June: **1st**, Pope Alexander VI proclaims a Year of Jubilee and calls on all princes to support a crusade against the Turks, for which he imposes a tithe.

Science, Technology, and Discovery
(21st April) Pedro Álvarez Cabral discovers Brazil.

Humanities and Scholarship
Desiderius Erasmus, *Adagia.*

Art, Sculpture, Fine Arts, and Architecture
Hieronymus Bosch, *Ship of Fools.*
Sandro Botticelli, *Mystic Nativity*; also *The Miracles of St. Zenobius.*

Literature
The first edition of the oldest German *Schwank* (see 1509) collection of tales known as *Till Eulenspiegel* published about this time in Lübeck.

1501 Ivan the Great of Russia invades Polish Lithuania.
Ismail the Sofi, Sheikh of Ardabil, conquers Persia at the Battle of Shurnur and founds the Safavid dynasty (–1736).

June: **—**, French enter Rome and, 25th, Pope Alexander VI confirms the Franco-Spanish Treaty of Granada (Nov 1500) for the partition of Naples.

July: **—**, In the conquest of Naples (see 1503), the French, with the help of Cesare Borgia, take Capua, while the Spanish take Apulia and Calabria.

Nov: **7th**, Edmund, Earl of Suffolk, a Yorkist claimant to the throne, is denounced by Henry VII as a traitor (Suffolk is attainted in 1504 and executed in 1513).
15th, Arthur, Prince of Wales, marries Catherine of Aragon.

Art, Sculpture, Fine Arts, and Architecture
Michelangelo, Statue of *David* (–1504, Florence).

1502 **March:** **2nd**, Maximilian I demands the resignation of Berthold of Henneberg from the archchancellorship of the Empire.

April: **2nd**, Arthur, Prince of Wales dies.

July: **—**, Open warfare breaks out between the French and Spanish in Italy over the partition of Naples (–May 1503).

Aug: **7th**, James IV of Scotland marries Margaret Tudor.

Politics, Government, Law, and Economy
Vasco da Gama founds a Portuguese Colony at Cochin, Malabar, in India.

Science, Technology, and Discovery
(11th May) (–7th Nov) 1504 Christopher Columbus sails on his final voyage of exploration, visiting Honduras and Panama. He plants a short-lived colony at Nombre de Dios (Nov).

Art, Sculpture, Fine Arts, and Architecture
Gerard David, St. John the Baptist triptych, Bruges (–1507).
Raphael, *Coronation of the Virgin.*

Music
First book of Masses by Josquin, published by Petrucci. Others follow in 1512 and 1516.

1503

Poland surrenders the left bank of the R. Dnieper to Russia.

Jan: 20th, the Casa Contratacion (or Board of Trade) is founded in Spain for dealing with the affairs of America.

Feb: 4th, Queen Elizabeth, consort of Henry VII of England, dies in childbed.

March: —, Venice signs peace treaty with the Turks.

Aug: 18th, Pope Alexander VI dies.

Sept: 3rd, Ferdinand II sends an army to North Africa against the Moors; Mers-el-Kebir falls to the Spanish.
22nd, Francesco Todeschini is elected Pope Pius III.

Nov: 1st, Giuliana della Rovere is elected Pope Julius II (–1513) on the death of Pius III.

Dec: 1st, war of succession between Bavaria and the Palatinate, on the death of George, Duke of Bavaria-Landshut (–Aug 1504).
26th, Pope Julius II grants dispensation for the marriage of Henry, Prince of Wales and Catherine of Aragon (married in 1509).
29th, Gonzalo de Cordova defeats the French at the battle of Garigliano.

Politics, Government, Law, and Economy
The Portuguese send African slaves to South America.

Society, Education, and Religion
The first English translation (Anon.) of Thomas à Kempis, *The Imitation of Christ.*

Science, Technology, and Discovery
Pedro di Navarro first uses explosive mines, during the siege of Naples.

Art, Sculpture, Fine Arts, and Architecture
Leonardo da Vinci, *Mona Lisa.*
Henry VII's chapel, Westminster Abbey, is begun (–1519).

1504

Venice sends an ambassador to the Sultan of Turkey, proposing the construction of a Suez Canal.
The Constitution of Radom makes the Diet the legislative organ of Poland.

Jan: 25th, English Parliament meets (–1st April) and passes statutes against retainers and liveries, to curb private warfare.
31st, by Treaty of Lyons, Louis XII of France finally cedes Naples to Ferdinand of Aragon (confirmed 31st Mar; Naples remains under Spanish control until 1713).

Aug: —, Albert of Bavaria-Munich, with the backing of Maximilian I, defeats Rupert of the Palatinate and so acquires the Landshut domains.

Sept: 22nd, Treaty of Blois is signed by Louis XII of France with Maximilian I and his son, Philip the Handsome of Burgundy.

Society, Education, and Religion
University of Santiago de Compostela, in Spain, is founded by bull of Pope Julius II.

Art, Sculpture, Fine Arts, and Architecture
Michelangelo, *Madonna and Child* (Florence); *Little St. John.*

1505

June: 27th, Henry, Prince of Wales, denounces his marriage contract with Catherine of Aragon.

Nov: —, Ferdinand II of Aragon signs Treaty of Salamanca, undertaking to rule jointly with his daughter Joanna and her husband Philip the Handsome.

Society, Education, and Religion
Christ's College, Cambridge, is founded by Lady Margaret Beaufort.

Science, Technology, and Discovery
The Portuguese establish a fort at Sofala in East Africa.
Scipio Ferro solves a form of cubic equation.

Art, Sculpture, Fine Arts, and Architecture
Giovanni Bellini, altarpiece, San Zaccaria.
Raphael, *Madonna del Granduca.*

Everyday Life
A regular mail service is established between Brussels and Vienna.

1506 **Jan: 16th**, Joanna and Philip the Handsome, on passage from the Netherlands to Castille to claim their inheritance, are driven by storms to the English coast.

March: —, Maximilian I secures the betrothal of Anne of Hungary to his grandson, the Archduke Ferdinand, which guarantees Habsburg succession to Hungary and Bohemia.

Sept: 25th, Philip the Handsome dies at Burgos. Because of the insanity of his widow, Joanna (who is confined until her death in 1555), the grandees of Castille nominate a council of regency under Cardinal Ximenéz de Cisnéros.

Oct: 7th, Julius II deposes the Duke of Bologna and with French help takes Bologna.

Politics, Government, Law, and Economy

N. Machiavelli forms the Florentine militia, the first national army in Italy.

Humanities and Scholarship

Laocoon group is unearthed at Rome.

Art, Sculpture, Fine Arts, and Architecture

Lucas Cranach, St. Catherine altar-piece.
Bramante begins to rebuild St. Peter's, Rome.

1507 **April: —**, the Diet of Constance restores the imperial chamber and places imperial taxation and armed levies on a permanent basis.
—, the States-General of the Netherlands appoint Margaret of Austria as Regent during the minority of the Archduke Charles.

Society, Education, and Religion

Pope Julius II proclaims an indulgence for aiding the rebuilding of St. Peter's, Rome.

Science, Technology, and Discovery

Martin Waldseemüller in *Cosmographie introductio* proposes the new world should be called 'America' after Amerigo Vespucci, the first navigator to be convinced this was a new continent, not an outlying part of Asia.

Art, Sculpture, Fine Arts, and Architecture

Albrecht Dürer, *Adam and Eve.*

1508 **Feb: —**, Maximilian I attacks Venice for refusing to give him a free passage to Rome.
4th, Maximilian I issues Proclamation of Trent, assuming the imperial title without being crowned.

June: —, Maximilian I is defeated by Venice and forced to sign a three-year truce with the Republic.

Dec: 10th, Margaret of Austria and the Cardinal of Rouen form the League of Cambrai with Ferdinand II, for despoiling Venice; the papacy and other Italian states subsequently join.

Politics, Government, Law, and Economy

Maximilian I creates the financier Jacob Fugger of Augsburg, a Knight of the Holy Roman Empire.

Humanities and Scholarship

Regular courses in Greek under Girolamo Aleandro begin at Paris University.

Art, Sculpture, Fine Arts, and Architecture

Giorgione, *The Tempest.*
Michelangelo begins to paint the roof of the Sistine Chapel, Rome (–1512), and Raphael enters the service of Pope Julius II.

Literature

William Dunbar, *Lament for Makaris; The Thrissil and the Rois* (a political allegory) and five other poems, printed at Edinburgh by Chepman and Myllar.
Garci Rodriguez de Montalvo, *Amadis de Gaula* in 4 bks.

1509 Francisco d'Almeida, the Portuguese viceroy of the Indies, defeats the Moslem princes of northwest India.
Almeida defeats the combined Indian and Egyptian fleets at the battle of Diu (Gujarat), establishing Portuguese supremacy in the Indian Ocean.

April: 7th, France declares war on Venice.
21st, Henry VIII succeeds as King of England (–1547) on the death of Henry VII.

May: —, Spanish troops under Cardinal Ximénez de Cisnéros take Oran from the Moors.
14th, the French defeat the Venetians at Agnadello and become masters of north Italy.

June: —, Florence takes Pisa.
11th, Henry VIII marries Catherine of Aragon.

Society, Education, and Religion
Brasenose College, Oxford, and St. John's College, Cambridge, are founded.

Science, Technology, and Discovery
Peter Henle of Nuremberg invents the watch (the 'Nuremberg Egg').

Art, Sculpture, Fine Arts, and Architecture
Matthias Grünewald paints the Isenheim triptych.

1510 Shah Ismail of Persia drives the Uzbeks from Khorasan.

Feb: —, Pope Julius II detaches himself from the League of Cambria and establishes good relations with Venice.

Aug: —, Pedro Navarro, having taken Algiers and Tripoli for Spain, is killed in an ambush in North Africa.

17th, Richard Empson and Edmund Dudley, Henry VII's finance ministers, having been found guilty of constructive treason, are beheaded.

Sept: —, Louis XII summons a synod of French bishops at Tours to condemn the conduct of Pope Julius II.

Politics, Government, Law, and Economy
The Portuguese acquire Goa.

Literature
Everyman (morality play; based probably on a Dutch morality of 1495).

1511 Ships of the Lübeck Hansa capture a Netherlands trading fleet for infringing the Hansa monopoly in the Baltic.

May: —, French under Gian Trivulzio capture Bologna and expel the papal troops.

Oct: **5th**, Pope Julius II forms the Holy League of Ferdinand II of Aragon, Venice and the Papacy to drive the French out of Italy.

Nov: **13th**, Henry VIII joins the Holy League and thus enters European politics.

Politics, Government, Law, and Economy
Diego de Valasquez occupies Cuba.

Society, Education, and Religion
A Patriarch of Moscow is appointed by Vassili III.

Science, Technology, and Discovery
The Portuguese discover Amboyna and conquer Malacca.

Humanities and Scholarship
Desiderius Erasmus, *Encomium Moriae (In Praise of Folly)* published in Paris.

Literature
Gil Vicente, *Four Seasons* (Portuguese *auto* – sacred play).

1512 Polish war with Russia over White Russian region (–1526).
By Peace of Malmoe, Netherlands vessels are permitted by the German Hanseatic League to trade in the Baltic provided they carry no contraband of war.

April: —, Maximilian I and the Swiss join the Holy League against France.
—, Gaston de Foix defeats the Spanish and Papal forces at Ravenna but Gaston's death in battle checks the French advance into Italy.
—, Bayazid II, Sultan of Turkey, abdicates in favour of his youngest son, Selim, Governor of Trebizond, who becomes Selim I (–1520), following a civil war.

July: —, Pope Julius II recovers Bologna.

Aug: —, at Congress of Mantua the Swiss restore the duchy of Milan to Maximilian Sforza and the rule of the Medici is restored in Florence (–May 1527).

Society, Education, and Religion
(10th April) (–16th Mar, 1517) The Fifth Lateran Council, at which the Immortality of the Soul is pronounced a dogma of the Church.

Art, Sculpture, Fine Arts, and Architecture
Raphael, fresco of Galatea, Rome.

1513 Peasants' Revolts in the Black Forest and Württemberg (–1514).

Feb: **21st**, Pope Julius II dies.

March: **9th**, Giovanni de' Medici elected Pope Leo X (–1521).

April: **5th**, by the Treaty of Mechlin Maximilian I, Henry VIII, Ferdinand II and Pope Leo X form alliance for a joint invasion of France.

June: **6th**, French army is defeated at Novara by the Swiss and returns to France.

July: **—**, James IV of Scotland declares war against England.

Aug: **—**, Henry VIII and Maximilian I rout the French at the Battle of the Spurs.

Sept: **9th**, the Earl of Surrey defeats the Scots at the Battle of Flodden; heavy casualties include King James IV. James V, an infant of 17 months, succeeds as King of Scotland (–1542); his mother, Margaret Tudor, assumes the Regency.

Dec: **—**, Louis XII makes peace with Pope Leo X.

Politics, Government, Law, and Economy

Niccolò Machiavelli begins writing *The Prince* (published 1532).

Science, Technology, and Discovery

A Portuguese expedition under Jorge Alvarez reaches Canton.

(April) Juan Ponce de Leon discovers Florida.

(26th Sept) Vasco Nuñez de Balboa crosses the Panama Isthmus to discover the Pacific Ocean, which he sights from Darien.

Humanities and Scholarship

Raphael makes plans for the excavation of ancient Rome.

Art, Sculpture, Fine Arts, and Architecture

Giovanni Bellini, altarpiece, St. John Chrysostom.

Michelangelo, *Moses* (Rome); also *Dying Captive* and *Heroic Captive* (Paris, –1516).

1514

Peasants' revolt in Hungary, led by George Dózsa, is suppressed by John Zápolya.

April: **—**, Maximilian I and Ferdinand II sign truce with Louis XII of France.

July: **—**, Anglo-French truce, followed by a full peace treaty April 1515.

Aug: **23rd**, Selim I defeats Shah Ismail of Persia at Tchadiran.

Sept: **5th**, Selim I of Turkey enters Tabriz.

8th, Polish-Lithuanian armies crush Russians at Orsza.

Oct: **—**, Louis XII of France marries Mary Tudor, sister of Henry VIII.

Politics, Government, Law, and Economy

Santiago is founded by Diego Velasquez and becomes the capital of Cuba.

Humanities and Scholarship

The first book to be printed in Arabic type, *septem horae canonicae*, is published at Fano in Italy.

Art, Sculpture, Fine Arts, and Architecture

Antonio Allegri da Correggio discovers chiaroscuro; and Correggio paints *Madonna of St. Francis* (–1516).

1515

The Sultan Selim I conquers eastern Anatolia and Kurdistan.

Jan: **—**, the Infante Charles of Austria takes over as Governor of the Netherlands.

1st, Francis, Duke of Angoulême succeeds as Francis I of France (–1547), on the death of his uncle Louis XII.

Aug: **—**, Spanish Navarre is incorporated with Castille.

Sept: **13th**, at the battle of Marignano, Francis I defeats the Swiss and Venetian armies and conquers Milan; the supremacy of the Swiss mercenaries is ended.

Dec: **24th**, Thomas Wolsey is appointed Lord Chancellor of England.

Humanities and Scholarship

The Lateran Council's decree (*De impressione librorum*), by which no work could be printed without previous examination by the relevant ecclesiastical authority.

Art, Sculpture, Fine Arts, and Architecture

Raphael, tapestry cartoons for the Sistine Chapel, Rome (–1516; now at Hampton Court).

Hampton Court Palace is completed for Cardinal Wolsey.

1516

Jan: **—**, Archduke Charles (later Emperor Charles V) succeeds as King of Spain on the death of Ferdinand II of Aragon (–1556), founding the Habsburg dynasty in Spain.

Aug: **13th**, by the Peace of Noyon between France and Spain, Francis I retains Milan but renounces his claim to Naples.

18th, Concordat of Bologna between France and the Papacy.

24th, the Sultan Selim I defeats the Mameluke Sultan of Egypt, Kansu-al-Guari, near Aleppo and annexes Syria.

Nov: **29th**, Francis I signs the Treaty of Freiburg of perpetual peace with the Swiss (this remains in force to 1789).

Politics, Government, Law, and Economy

Sir Thomas More, *Libellus ... Insula Utopiae* (original Latin text of *Utopia*, printed at Louvain; trans. 1551).

Society, Education, and Religion

The *New Testament* in Greek and Latin (the first published Greek text, with the annotations of Erasmus; Basle).

Art, Sculpture, Fine Arts, and Architecture

Titian, *The Assumption*, Frari Church, Venice (–1518).

Literature

Ludovico Ariosto, *Orlando Furioso* (romantic epic; sequel to Boiardo's work of 1495).

1517 **Jan:** **22nd**, the Turks take Cairo. The Sherif of Mecca subsequently surrenders to Selim I and Arabia comes under Turkish suzerainty.

Oct: **31st**, Martin Luther nails his 95 theses at Wittenberg Palace church, denouncing the sale of papal indulgences by Johann Tetzel and others.

Politics, Government, Law, and Economy

The Portuguese establish a factory at Colombo, Ceylon.

Society, Education, and Religion

Corpus Christi College, Oxford, is founded by Richard Fox, Bishop of Winchester.

Pope Leo X closes the Lateran Council, declaring that all reforms of the Church have been accomplished.

(31st Oct) In protest against the sale of Indulgences, Martin Luther posts on the door of the Palace Church in Wittenberg, his *Ninety-five Theses*, following the usual custom for giving notice of disputations.

Science, Technology, and Discovery

The wheel-lock musket is invented by a Nuremberg gunsmith.

Everyday Life

Coffee is first brought to Europe.

1518 Foundation of the Barbary States of Algiers and Tunis.

Oct: **12th**, Martin Luther, summoned to the Diet of Augsburg, refuses to recant.

Politics, Government, Law, and Economy

The Emperor Charles V grants Lorens de Gominot the first licence (or *asiento*) to import 4,000 African slaves into the Spanish American colonies during eight years.

Society, Education, and Religion

P. Melanchthon is appointed Professor of Greek at Wittenberg University.

Art, Sculpture, Fine Arts, and Architecture

Albrecht Altdorfer, St. Florian altarpiece.
Raphael, *Pope Leo X with Two Cardinals*.

1519 **Jan:** **12th**, the Emperor Maximilian I dies.

June: **28th**, Charles I of Spain, Sicily and Sardinia, is elected Holy Roman Emperor as Charles V (–1556), thanks to the money of the Fuggers of Augsburg.

Nov: **8th**, Hernando Cortes enters Tenochtitlán, Mexico, and is received by Montezuma the Aztec ruler.

Politics, Government, Law, and Economy

The Sherifs found the Moorish Empire of Morocco.

Society, Education, and Religion

The Leipzig Disputation, in which Martin Luther gives evidence of his determination to question such fundamental ideas as the infallibility of papal decisions.

Science, Technology, and Discovery

(2nd May) Leonardo da Vinci dies (aged 67).

(20th Sept) Ferdinand Magellan, a Portuguese in the service of Spain, leaves Europe. In 1520, he rounds Cape Horn. Though Magellan is killed in the Philippines, the expedition continues under Sebastien del Cano, completing the circumnavigation of the globe.

1520 **Jan:** **18th**, Christian II of Denmark and Norway with an army of mercenaries defeats the Swedes under Sten Sture at Lake Asunden and subsequently conquers Sweden.

June: **4th**, (–24th) Henry VIII and Francis I meet at the Field of Cloth of Gold.
15th, Pope Leo X excommunicates Martin Luther by the bull *Exsurge*.

July: **—**, during Charles's absence the Spanish *communeros* in Toledo and Castille revolt.

Sept: **20th**, Suleiman I (the Magnificent) succeeds as Sultan of Turkey (–1566).

Oct: **23rd**, Charles V is crowned Holy Roman Emperor at Aachen.

Nov: **4th**, Christian II of Denmark is crowned King of Sweden in Stockholm.

8th, in the Stockholm Bloodbath, Christian II massacres Eric Vasa and leading Swedish bishops and nobles, provoking a national revolt under Gustavus Vasa (–June 1523).

Dec: **10th**, Martin Luther publicly burns the bull *Exsurge*.

Society, Education, and Religion

Luther attacks all sacraments except Baptism and the Lord's Supper.

(15th June) Martin Luther is declared a heretic.

Science, Technology, and Discovery

Gaspard Koller invents rifling on firearms.

Humanities and Scholarship

The Royal Library of France is founded by Francis I in the Palace of Fontainebleu, with Guillaume Budé, the scholar and humanist, as Librarian.

Art, Sculpture, Fine Arts, and Architecture

Michelangelo, Medici Chapel, St. Lorenziana, Florence.

Everyday Life

Chocolate in slab form is on sale in Spain.

1521

Peasants in Majorca massacre the nobility.

April: **17th**, (–18th) Martin Luther appears before the Diet of Worms.

23rd, (–24th) the Spanish *communeros* are defeated at Villalar.

28th, Charles V grants his brother, the Archduke Ferdinand, the Habsburg possessions in Lower Austria, Carinthia, Styria and Carinola.

May: **26th**, the Edict of Worms imposes on Martin Luther the ban of the Empire.

Sept: **13th**, Spanish force under Cortes takes Tenochtitlan, the Aztec capital, after 8-week siege, assuming his control of Mexico.

29th, Suleiman I conquers Belgrade and begins his advance into Hungary.

Oct: **11th**, Pope Leo X confers the title 'Defender of the Faith' on Henry VIII.

Nov: **19th**, war between Habsburg and Valois (–1526) breaks out in Italy.

Dec: **1st**, Pope Leo X dies.

Politics, Government, Law, and Economy

The Portuguese establish a trading post in Amboyna.

Society, Education, and Religion

Henry VIII, King of England, *Assertio Septem Sacramentorum* ('The Assertion of the Seven Sacraments' in opposition to Martin Luther; see 1520, 1522).

Art, Sculpture, Fine Arts, and Architecture

Michelangelo, tombs of Guiliamo de' Medici and of Lorenzo de' Medici, Florence (–1534).

Everyday Life

Silk manufacture is introduced to France.

1522

Shih Tsung becomes Emperor of China (–1566).

Spanish force under Pedro de Alvardo conquers Guatemala (–1524).

Jan: **9th**, Adrian of Utrecht, Regent of Spain, is elected Pope Adrian VI (–Sept 1523).

July: **9th**, Charles V visits England and signs the Treaty of Windsor with Henry VIII.

March: **—**, Martin Luther returns to Wittenberg and condemns the religious riots in Saxony.

April: **27th**, Spanish and imperial troops defeat the French and Swiss at Bicocca, three miles from Milan; Francesco Sforza is restored to the duchy.

May: **—**, England declares war against France and Scotland.

Aug: **24th**, Gustavus Vasa accepts the office of Administrator of Sweden from an assembly at Vadstena and pledges himself to free the rest of Sweden from Danish control.

Oct: **15th**, Charles V appoints Cortes Governor of New Spain (Mexico).

Dec: **—**, the Turks under Suleiman I take Rhodes from the Knights of St. John.

Society, Education, and Religion

Martin Luther introduces a liturgy in German and communion in both kinds for the laity at Wittenberg.

Zwingli condemns fasting and the celibacy of priests, at Zurich.

(Sept) Martin Luther's translation of the *New Testament* ('The Bible of the Reformation'; his complete Bible is available in 1534).

Science, Technology, and Discovery
Pascual de Andagoya leads an expedition by land from Panama to discover Peru (Biru).
Francisco Montaño ascends Mount Popocatepetl, Mexico.

1523 The Portuguese are expelled from China, where they formed a settlement in 1520.

March: —, Danish nobles depose Christian II. His uncle Frederick of Schleswig-Holstein becomes Frederick I of Denmark and Norway (–1533).

June: **7th**, Gustavus Vasa is elected Gustavus I of Sweden (–1560).

Aug: —, Charles of Bourbon, Constable of France, defects to Charles V.

Sept: **14th**, Pope Adrian VI dies.

Nov: **19th**, Guilio de' Medici is elected Pope Clement VII (–1534).

Society, Education, and Religion
Hans Sachs, *Die Wittenbergische Nachtigall* (an allegory in verse, *The Nightingale of Wittenberg*, in praise of Luther and his doctrines).

Science, Technology, and Discovery
[Anthony] Fitzherbert, *Book of Husbandry*, the first manual of agricultural practice.

Art, Sculpture, Fine Arts, and Architecture
Titian, *Bacchus and Ariadne.*

Music
Keyboard music printed in Italy with right- and left-hand staves and bar lines.

1524 Zwingli establishes control over Zurich, and Bucer over Strassburg.
By the Treaty of Malmö, Denmark confirms the independence of Sweden.

Jan: —, Lorenzo Campeggio, the papal legate, at the Diet of Nuremberg orders the Edict of Worms (of May 1521) to be carried out as far as possible.

April: **30th**, the exiled Duke of Bourbon, in the service of the Emperor Charles V, drives the French from Lombardy.

June: —, The Peasants' Revolt in southern Germany (–May 1525) begins at Stühlingen.
28th, the Duke of Bourbon invades Provence.

July: **26th**, James V of Scotland, aged 12, is 'erected' King at Edinburgh.

Aug: —, the Peasants' Revolt, led by Thomas Müntzer, extends to Swabia, Franconia, Bavaria, the Tyrol, Carinthia, Thuringia and Alsace.

Sept: **29th**, Bourbon retires from Provence, having abandoned the siege of Marseilles.

Oct: —, Francis I crosses the Mount Cenis Pass, to attack the retreating imperialists.
26th, the Spanish surrender Milan, stricken by the plague, to the French.

Nov: **6th**, Francis I lays siege to Pavia.

Science, Technology, and Discovery
Giovanni de Verrazano, sent on an expedition to the New World by Francis I discovers New York Bay and the Hudson River.

Humanities and Scholarship
Philippe de Comines (or Commynes), *Memoirs.*
Desiderius Erasmus, *Colloquies.*
The *Gesta Romanorum* translated anon; printed by Wynkyn de Worde.

Art, Sculpture, Fine Arts, and Architecture
Lucas Cranach, *Judgement of Paris*; also *Luther and his wife* (roundels).

Music
Martin Luther, *Geistliche Leider* (a German hymnal, expanded 1549).

1525 Sultan Suleiman I of Turkey is urged by France to attack Germany.
The Mogul Emperor Barbar invades the Punjab.

Feb: **24th**, the Duke of Bourbon and the Marquis of Pesara lead an imperialist-Spanish army to rout the French and Swiss at the battle of Pavia. Francis I of France is taken prisoner to Spain. In the battle the Spanish infantry first use muskets.

April: **10th**, Albert of Brandenburg, Grand Master of the Teutonic Knights, surrenders the lands of his order to the King of Poland to form a duchy of Brandenburg.

May: —, the Peasants' Revolt in south Germany is suppressed and Müntzer is executed.

July: **—**, German Catholic princes meet at Dessau to consider the formation of a Catholic League.

Aug: **30th**, Peace is signed between England and France.

Society, Education, and Religion

William Tyndale's translation of *The New Testament* published at Worms (see May 1530 and 1536).

Ulrich Zwingli, *Commentarius* ('de vera et falsa religione').

Humanities and Scholarship

Pietro Bembo, *Prose della vulgar lingua* (influential argument in favour of the use of Italian as a literary and scholarly language instead of Latin).

Everyday Life

Hops are introduced to England from Artois.

1526

Russo-Polish Twenty Years' War is concluded; Russia retains Smolensk (conquered in 1514).

Jan: **—**, Anglo-Scottish Peace is signed.

14th, Francis I of France and the Emperor Charles V sign the Peace of Madrid.

March: **17th**, Francis I of France is released from Spanish captivity.

April: **27th**, Barbar, Mogul Emperor of India, defeats Ibrahim at the battle of Panipat and establishes the Mogul dynasty in Delhi (–1761).

May: **2nd**, The Protestant League or Torgau is formed under Elector John of Saxony.

23rd, Pope Clement VII forms the League of Cognac as an offensive league against the Emperor Charles V; signatories include Venice, Florence, Milan and France.

Aug: **20th**, Cardinal Pompeo Colonna plunders Rome, forcing Pope Clement VII to take refuge in the Castle of St. Angelo.

29th, (–30th) Suleiman I defeats the Hungarian army at the battle of Mohacs, at which Louis II of Hungary is killed.

Sept: **10th**, Suleiman I takes Buda.

Nov: **10th**, John Zápolya is crowned King of Hungary.

Dec: **17th**, Ferdinand of Austria is elected King of Bohemia.

Society, Education, and Religion

Zurich authorities make rebaptizing adults an offence punishable by drowning.

Science, Technology, and Discovery

Sebastian Cabot sails up the Paraná and Paraguay rivers.

Portuguese vessels visit New Guinea.

1527

Jan: **1st**, the Habsburg administration of Austria is reorganized (the system remains basically unchanged to 1848).

March: **16th**, the Mogul Emperor Barbar defeats a Hindu Confederacy at Kanwanha.

May: **6th**, the Sack of Rome, when imperialist troops under Charles, Duke of Bourbon (who is killed), pillage the city and kill some 4,000 of the inhabitants.

16th, the Medicis are expelled from Florence, which reverts to being a republic.

June: **24th**, the Swedish Diet of Västerås effects a Reformation, under which most of the property of the Church passes to the Crown.

July: **—**, A French army under Vicomte de Lautrec invades the Milanese and turns south, aiming at rescuing the Pope.

Aug: **10th**, Ferdinand of Bohemia defeats John Zápolya of Hungary at Tokay.

Nov: **3rd**, Ferdinand is recognized King of Hungary by the Diet at Buda.

1528

Jan: **22nd**, England and France declare war on the Emperor Charles V at Burgos.

Feb: **11th**, the imperial army leaves Rome to meet a French army led by Vicomte Lautrec advancing from Bologna.

24th, John Zápolya makes a treaty with Suleiman I, recognizing the Sultan's suzerainty.

March: **—**, Philip, Landgrave of Hesse, and the Elector John of Saxony form the defensive alliance of Weimar and mobilize troops for withstanding a Catholic attack.

—, the arrest of English merchants in Spain and Flanders provokes a commercial crisis.

—, Widespread distress among weavers in the eastern counties of England.

April: **—**, a truce is signed between England and the Netherlands (–Feb 1529), to ease the commercial crisis.

July: **—**, England experiences the first severe outbreak of the plague.

Aug: **30th**, the French army capitulate at Aversa.

Sept: 12th, Andrea Doria enters Genoa which regains its independence, under the protection of the Emperor, as a republic (–1796).

Politics, Government, Law, and Economy

Baldassare, Count Castiglione, *Il Cortegiano.*

Society, Education, and Religion

P. Melanchthon proposes thoroughgoing educational reforms in Germany.

Order of the Capuchins is organized, as a branch of the Observants.

The Reformation begins to take root in Scotland (–1560).

Science, Technology, and Discovery

P. Paracelsus, *Die Kleine Chirurgie*, the first manual proper of surgery.

Art, Sculpture, Fine Arts, and Architecture

Hans Holbein the younger, *The Artist's Wife and Two Elder Children.*

Literature

Ulrich von Hutten, *Arminius* (posthumous).

1529

April: 19th, the Second Diet of Speyer votes to put in force the Edict of Worms (of 1521); the minority led by the Elector John of Saxony, the Margrave George of Brandalburg and Philip, Landgrave of Hesse, read their 'Protest', giving rise to the term 'Protestant'.

June: 9th, civil war in Switzerland between the Catholic Forest Cantons and the Protestant Civic League. The Catholic Cantons are defeated 24th June.

24th, The Swiss Catholic Forest Cantons are defeated by the Protestant Civic League and the first Peace of Kappel ends the civil war in Switzerland.

29th, Pope Clement VII agrees to the Emperor Charles V's terms by the Treaty of Barcelona.

Aug: 5th, Francis I of France and the Emperor Charles V sign the Treaty of Cambrai.

Sept: 21st, (–Oct 15th) the Turks under Suleiman I lay siege to Vienna, arousing considerable national sentiment in the empire.

Oct: 15th, Suleiman I is forced to raise the siege of Vienna, but Ferdinand fails to recapture Buda.

18th, Cardinal Wolsey falls from power.

26th, Sir Thomas More is appointed Lord Chancellor in succession to Wolsey.

Nov: 4th, (–Dec 17th) the first session of the English 'Reformation Parliament' (–Feb 1536).

Society, Education, and Religion

Francis I of France founds the Collège de France.

Bernardino de Sahagún starts his Franciscan mission in Mexico.

The Short Catechism is published, known as 'Luther's Catechism'.

(Oct) Luther and Zwingli hold disputation on the Eucharist at Marburg.

Humanities and Scholarship

Guillaume Budé, *Commentaries on the Greek Language (Commentarii Linguae Gracecae).*

Media

The Diet of Speyer imposes censorship of the Press in Germany.

1530

The Knights Hospitallers are established in Malta.

Martin Affonso de Souza leads a Portuguese expedition to establish a colony in South America and founds São Vincente.

Feb: 24th, Charles V is crowned Holy Roman Emperor and King of Italy by Pope Clement – the last imperial coronation by a pope.

June: 20th, the Diet of Augsburg meets in the presence of Charles V.

Aug: 12th, Florence is restored to the Medicis by imperial troops after a siege of 10 months.

Sept: 22nd, the Diet of Augsburg rules that the Protestant princes must conform by 15th April 1531.

Nov: 4th, Cardinal Wolsey is arrested as a traitor; he dies at Leicester on the 29th.

Dec: 31st, the Protestant princes of Germany form the Schmalkaldic League in self-defence against the Emperor Charles V and his Catholic allies.

Society, Education, and Religion

P. Melanchthon, *Apologia.*

(25th June) *The Confession of Augsburg* of the German Reformers is accepted as the Creed of the Lutheran Church.

Science, Technology, and Discovery

C Rudolff uses decimals to extend whole-number rules to fractions.

Art, Sculpture, Fine Arts, and Architecture
Angelo Bronzino, *Guidobaldo di Montefeltro.*
Antonio Allegri de Correggio, *Adoration of the Shepherds.*

Music
First extant book of printed songs (printed by Wynkyn de Worde).

1531

Jan: **—**, Charles V appoints his sister, Mary of Hungary, Regent of the Netherlands (–1552).
5th, Ferdinand of Bohemia is elected King of the Romans.

Feb: **11th**, Henry VIII is recognized as Supreme Head of the Church in England.

Sept: **—**, War breaks out in Switzerland between Zurich, dominated by Zwingli, and the Catholic Forest Cantons.

Oct: **11th**, Zwingli is killed at the battle of Kappel, where the Forest Cantons defeat Zurich.
24th, Bavaria, though a Catholic state, joins the Schmalkaldic League.

Nov: **23rd**, the Peace of Kappel ends the second civil war in Switzerland; by its terms each canton and each district have the right to worship as they choose.

Dec: **17th**, Pope Clement VII founds the Inquisition in Lisbon, Portugal, by the bull *Cum ad nihil.*

Politics, Government, Law, and Economy
Sir Thomas Elyot, *The Boke Named the Governour*, a treatise on education for statesmen.
First English Act for Poor Relief.

Society, Education, and Religion
Michael Servetus, *De Trinitatis Erroribus* (denying the Trinity; see 1553).

Science, Technology, and Discovery
Martin Affonso de Souza explores the coastline of Brazil.

1532

March: **19th**, Henry VIII confiscates annates (or first fruits of benefices).

April: **15th**, the Submission of the Clergy is made to Henry VIII, beginning the political Reformation in England.
26th, Suleiman I invades Hungary and advances towards Vienna.

May: **16th**, Sir Thomas More resigns as Lord Chancellor.

July: **23rd**, the Turkish invasion forces Charles V to agree to the peace of Nuremberg with the German Protestants; the Edict of Augsburg is revoked.

Aug: **7th**, (–28th) Suleiman I fails to take Güns and retires, ravaging Carinthia and Croatia (Sept).

Sept: **—**, the Emperor Charles V invades Italy (–Apr 1533).

Oct: **—**, Henry VIII visits Francis I to sign the Treaty of Boulogne.

Nov: **—**, Francisco Pizarro leads expedition from Panama for the conquest of Peru (–1534), and, 16th, takes the Inca Atahualpa prisoner.

Politics, Government, Law, and Economy
The Diet of Ratisbon approves the Caroline Code for reforming the criminal law in Germany.
Sugar-cane is first cultivated in Brazil.

Society, Education, and Religion
Jean Calvin lays the foundation of the French Reformation in Paris.

Art, Sculpture, Fine Arts, and Architecture
Romano Giulio, frescoes, Palazzo del Tè.

Literature
François Rabelais, *Pantagruel.*

1533

Accession of Ivan IV (The Terrible) of Russia, aged three, on the death of Basil III.
Lithuanian-Russian War (–1536).
Pizarro executes the Inca of Peru, Atahualpa, and occupies Cuzco.
Cortes attempts to found a colony in Lower California (–1535).
Spanish colonization of La Plata by Pedro de Mendoza.
Spanish conquest of Yucatan.

Jan: **—**, Henry VIII secretly marries Anne Boleyn.

March: **—**, Thomas Cranmer is consecrated Archbishop of Canterbury.

April: **—**, death of Frederick I of Denmark leads to a civil war ('The War of the Counts'; Christian III succeeds in 1534).

May: **28th**, Archbishop Cranmer pronounces Anne Boleyn's marriage to Henry VIII lawful.

June: **1st**, coronation of Queen Anne Boleyn.
22nd, Ferdinand of Austria and Suleiman I of Turkey sign a peace treaty.

July: **11th**, Pope Clement VII excommunicates Henry VIII.

Sept: **7th**, Queen Anne Boleyn gives birth to Princess Elizabeth.

Nov: **—**, the Catholic League of Halle is formed.

Politics, Government, Law, and Economy
Pedro de Heredia founds Cartagena.

Art, Sculpture, Fine Arts, and Architecture
Hans Holbein the younger, *The Ambassadors.*
Giorgio Vasari, *Lorenzo the Magnificent.*

Music
Earliest published madrigals printed in Rome.

1534 **Jan:** **—**, John of Leyden joins the Anabaptizts at Münster, Westphalia, where a 'Communist state' is established (–June 1535), following an insurrection on 9th Feb.

March: **16th**, final severance of England from Rome; Acts are passed forbidding the payment of annates and Peter's Pence to the Pope.

April: **20th**, Elizabeth Barton, the Maid of Kent, is executed for treason.

May: **11th**, Henry VIII makes peace with his nephew, James V of Scotland.

Sept: **25th**, Pope Clement VII dies. Alessandro Farnese is subsequently elected Pope Paul III (–1550), and appoints a number of reforming cardinals.

Oct: **18th**, 'Placards' appear in Paris describing the Mass in offensive terms.

Nov: **3rd**, English Parliament meets (–18th Dec) and passes a new Act of Supremacy.

Society, Education, and Religion
Martin Luther completes his translation of the Holy Bible.
(10th Aug) The Jesuit Order is founded in Paris by Ignatius Loyola.

Science, Technology, and Discovery
Jacques Cartier sights Labrador (10th May), and explores the Gulf of St. Lawrence.

Literature
François Rabelais, *Gargantua.*

1535 **Jan:** **15th**, Henry VIII assumes the title 'Supreme Head of the Church'.

Feb: **—**, France and Turkey sign an offensive and defensive alliance.

June: **—**, Charles V leads an expedition to conquer Tunis from Barbarossa (–Aug); he completes the Spanish conquest of the North African coast (begun in 1494).

24th, Münster capitulates to the Hessian army; the Anabaptizt leaders John of Leyden and Burgomaster Knipperdollinck are tortured to death.

July: **1st**, Sir Thomas More is tried for treason in refusing the oath of Supremacy.
6th, More is executed.

Nov: **1st**, on the death of Francesco Sforza II of Milan, the last of the House of Sforza, the duchy is occupied by Charles V.

Society, Education, and Religion
Miles Coverdale's translation of the *Holy Bible*; not printed in England until 1537.
(Nov) Angela Merici founds the Order of Ursulines at Brescia.

Science, Technology, and Discovery
Jacques Cartier sails up the St. Lawrence River (–1536).

Art, Sculpture, Fine Arts, and Architecture
Hans Holbein the younger, *Henry VIII.*

1536 **Feb:** **—**, Francis I of France conquers Savoy, occupies Turin and by April completes conquest of Piedmont, seeking to gain the duchy of Milan for his third son.

April: **14th**, Henry VIII dissolves the 'Reformation Parliament'. The royal assent is given to an Act for the dissolution of the lesser monasteries. The Court of Augmentations is established to administer former monastic property.

May: **15th**, Anne Boleyn and her brother, Lord Rochford, are tried and found guilty of adultery and incest.
19th, Anne Boleyn is executed.
30th, Henry VIII marries Jane Seymour.

June: **29th**, Thomas Cromwell is appointed Lord Privy Seal.

July: **14th**, France signs the Treaty of Lyons with Portugal, for an attack on Spain.

25th, Spain invades Provence, but the campaign ends in failure.
29th, Copenhagen surrenders to Christian III, who subsequently establishes his authority in Denmark and Norway.

Oct: 9th, the Pilgrimage of Grace, a popular rising in the north country against the dissolution of the monasteries and religious innovations, begins (–1537).

Politics, Government, Law, and Economy
Spain founds Asunción on the Paraguay River.
(2nd Feb) Pedro de Mendoza founds Buenos Aires on the La Plata estuary.

Society, Education, and Religion
John Calvin, *Christianae Religionis Institutio.*
The Ten Articles are authorized by Henry VIII, and approved by Convocation.
(July) Calvin settles in Geneva.
(6th Oct) William Tyndale is strangled and burnt.

Science, Technology, and Discovery
Alvar Nuñez Cabeza de Vaca reaches Sonora in Arizona.

Art, Sculpture, Fine Arts, and Architecture
Michelangelo, *Last Judgement* on altar wall of Sistine Chapel (–1541).

1537 **Jan: —**, Francis I secures an agreement with Suleiman I of Turkey for a joint attack on Charles V.
7th, Alessandro de' Medici is assassinated; Cosmo de' Medici succeeds him in Florence.

Feb: 10th, the Pilgrimage of Grace in Yorkshire is effectively ended with the capture of Sir Francis Bigod; Aske and other leaders of the uprising are subsequently executed.

March: 10th, the French invade Italy and advance as far as Rivoli.

Sept: —, Henry VIII creates the Council of the North to govern the northern counties.
2nd, Christian III issues Ordinance for the Danish Church, with Luther's approval.

Oct: 24th, Queen Jane Seymour dies, following the birth of Prince Edward, on the 12th.

Politics, Government, Law, and Economy
The Portuguese obtain Macao as a trading settlement (permanently settled in 1557).
Calvin founds his system of government in Church and State for Geneva.

Science, Technology, and Discovery
Niccolò Tartaglia explains the trajectory of bullets in *La Nova Scientia* (Venice).

Humanities and Scholarship
Marcus Tullius Cicero, *Opera Omnia*, 4 vols., ed. with notes by Pietro Victorius.

Art, Sculpture, Fine Arts, and Architecture
Sansovino, façade, Doge's Palazzo Loggietta, Venice (–1540).

1538 Destruction of relics, images and shrines in churches and abbeys in southern England in a wave of anti-papal iconoclasm, notably of Thomas à Becket's shrine at Canterbury.

Jan: —, The visitation of the greater monasteries in England is begun (they are dissolved 1539).

July: 14th (–16th), Charles V and Francis I meet at Aigues Mortes to discuss the repression of Protestant heresies and a crusade against the Turks.

Dec: 16th, Francis I issues an edict, at the Parlement of Toulouse, for the persecution of French Protestants.
17th, Pope Paul III issues a further bull excommunicating and deposing Henry VIII.

Politics, Government, Law, and Economy
Philip Melanchthon, *Ethica Doctrinae Elementa*, stating the Protestant theory of Natural Right.

Art, Sculpture, Fine Arts, and Architecture
Titian, *The Urbino Venus.*

1539 **Jan: —**, Cardinal David Beaton, Archbishop of St. Andrews, enemy of the pro-English faction, becomes chief adviser to James V of Scotland.

Feb: —, Joachim II, Elector of Brandenburg, becomes a Protestant, and with the accession later in the year of Henry, Duke of Saxony (–1541), a Lutheran, on the death of his elder brother, Duke George, a Catholic, all the states of northern Germany, except Brunswick, accept the Reformation.
1st, the Emperor Charles V and Francis I of France sign the Treaty of Toledo.

May: —, Royal assent is given to the Six Articles of Religion.

Aug: —, Ghent breaks into open rebellion against Mary of Hungary, Regent of the Netherlands, refusing to contribute a subsidy to the Emperor.

Nov: **—**, The Abbots of Reading and Colchester are executed for treason in denying the King's supremacy and (Dec) the Abbot of Glastonbury for felony.

Society, Education, and Religion

The Great Bible (or *Cranmer's Bible*), a revision of Tyndale's and Coverdale's versions, is issued in England.

Science, Technology, and Discovery

Hernando de Soto begins the exploration of Florida (–1542).

1540 Hamayun is expelled from India by Afghans under Sher Shat, who becomes Emperor of Delhi.

Jan: **6th**, Henry VIII marries Anne of Cleves (–July 9th).

Feb: **14th**, Charles V enters Ghent without resistance, executes the leaders of the revolt and abrogates the city's liberties.

May: **—**, Charles V appoints René of Chalons *stadtholder* in Holland, Zeeland and Utrecht.
4th, treaty between Venice and Turkey is signed at Constantinople.

June: **18th**, Thomas Cromwell, Earl of Essex, is arrested at the Council table for treason (he is executed 28th July). Lord Treasurer Norfolk becomes Henry VIII's principal minister.

July: **9th**, Henry VIII's marriage to Anne of Cleves is annulled.
23rd, the infant John Sigismund Zápolya succeeds as King of Hungary (–1571) on the death of his father, John Zápolya; Archduke Ferdinand sends troops into Hungary to claim the whole country and lays siege to Buda.
28th, Henry VIII marries Katherine Howard.

Science, Technology, and Discovery

G L de Cardenas discovers the Grand Canyon, Arizona.

1541 The Spanish begin the conquest of Peru (–1542).

April: **5th**, the Diet of Ratisbon meets (–July) in the presence of the Emperor Charles V. He is forced to admit Protestants to the Imperial Chamber.

May: **—**, Francis I of France, to embarrass Charles V, reaches an undertaking with Suleiman I, Sultan of Turkey.

Aug: **26th**, Suleiman I, Sultan of Turkey, having invaded Hungary to dispute the Archduke Ferdinand's claim to that kingdom, takes Buda and annexes Hungary.

Oct: **—**, The expedition of Charles V to Algiers fails, largely as a result of storms.

Nov: **9th**, Queen Katherine Howard is sent to the Tower of London.

Science, Technology, and Discovery

Hernando de Soto discovers the Mississippi River and crosses Arkansas and Oklahoma.
Francisco de Coronada leads an expedition from New Mexico across the buffalo plains of Texas, Oklahoma and Eastern Kansas.
Francisco de Orellana first descends the R. Amazon.
Gerardus Mercator's terrestrial globe.

Sport and Recreation

English Act of Parliament for the maintenance of archery and debarring of unlawful games, such as slide thrift.

1542 **Feb:** **13th**, Queen Katherine Howard is executed.

July: **—**, further war breaks out between Francis I of France and the Emperor Charles V (–Sept 1544).
21st, Pope Paul III establishes the Inquisition in Rome.

Aug: **—**, The Schmalkaldic League attacks the Catholic Duke Henry of Brunswick and sequester his land.

Nov: **25th**, the Scots under James V are routed at the battle of Solway Moss.

Dec: **14th**, accession of Mary Queen of Scots, born on 8th Dec, following the death of James V at Falkland.

Society, Education, and Religion

Magdalene College, Cambridge, is founded.
St. Francis Xavier arrives at Goa as a Jesuit missionary.

Science, Technology, and Discovery

Antonio da Mota is the first European to reach Japan.
Andreas Vesalius writes *De Fabrica Corporis Humani* and founds the modern study of anatomy.

1543 Portuguese seamen land on the island of Tanegashima, Japan.

Jan: 10th, Scottish lords depose Cardinal Beaton from the regency; they approve the appointment as Regent of the Earl of Arran.

Feb: 11th, Henry VIII signs a treaty of alliance with the Emperor Charles V against France (confirmed 20th May).

June: 22nd, Henry VIII's ultimatum to France serves as a declaration of war.

July: 12th, Henry VIII marries Catherine Parr, widow of Lord Latimer.

Aug: 5th, the French and Turkish combined fleets capture Nice.

Sept: 3rd, the Earl of Arran submits to Cardinal Beaton, who assumes the regency.

Society, Education, and Religion

Index Librorum Prohibitorum is issued by Pope Paul III (see 1557, 1559, 1564).

The first Protestant is burned in Spain.

Science, Technology, and Discovery

Nicolaus Copernicus writes *De Revolutionibus Orbium Coelestium* and explains the heliocentric theory for the movement of the planets (which he formed 1506–12).

1544 **May: 1st**, the Turks again invade Hungary, take Wischegrad and seize the Hungarian crown jewels. Suleiman I subsequently organizes the country into 12 sanjaks.

3rd, an English military and naval expedition is sent to Scotland; it captures Leith and burns Edinburgh.

July: 14th, Henry VIII crosses to Calais to join with the Emperor in the campaign against Francis I in Picardy.

Sept: 18th, Peace of Crécy is signed between Francis I and Charles V, who has not consulted his ally, Henry VIII. The English continue the war with France.

Science, Technology, and Discovery

Lourenço Marques and Antonio Calderia explore the rivers in the region of Delagoa Bay, East Africa.

Georg Agricola (or Bauer) writes *De ortu et causis subterraneis* and founds the study of geology.

Literature

Margaret of Navarre, *Heptameron*.

1545 **April: 12th**, Francis I authorizes a further massacre of the Vaudois Protestants; the first had taken place in 1540.

July: —, A French fleet under Admiral d'Annebault enters the Solent; the *Mary Rose*, England's finest warship, keels over in Portsmouth harbour and sinks.

Nov: —, Charles V and Ferdinand make the Truce of Adrianople with Suleiman I, Sultan of Turkey; the Emperor is thus free to turn to German affairs.

Politics, Government, Law, and Economy

The opening of the silver mines at Potosi, Peru, leads to the Price Revolution in Europe, spreading from Spain.

Society, Education, and Religion

(13th Dec) The Council of Trent meets and inaugurates the Counter-Reformation (see also 1551, 1562, 1564).

Science, Technology, and Discovery

The earliest botanical garden is established in Padua.

Ambrose Paré writes *Manière de traitez les Plaies* and founds the study of modern surgery.

Humanities and Scholarship

Philippe de Commines, *Mémoires* (–1548; posthumous).

Art, Sculpture, Fine Arts, and Architecture

Benvenuto Cellini, *Perseus* (Florence; –1554).

Benvenuto Cellini writes his *Autobiography*.

1546 In Mexico the Spaniards put down a serious Maya rising.

May: 29th, Cardinal Beaton is assassinated at St. Andrews.

June: 7th, the Peace of Ardres ends England's war with France and Scotland.

Oct: 27th, Charles V formally assigns the Saxon electorate from John Frederick to Maurice of Saxony, who has agreed to aid him against the Schmalkaldic League.

30th, Bohemian troops invade Saxony; Maurice and Frederick fight for control of the duchy.

Dec: 23rd, Ulm and, 29th, Frankfurt, formerly strongholds of the Schmalkaldic League, submit to Charles V.

Society, Education, and Religion

Henry VIII founds Trinity College, Cambridge.

(Aug) Étienne Dolet, printer of learned books, charged with publishing heretical books (i.e. Protestant translations of the Scriptures). He is pardoned by the King, then rearrested, convicted, hanged and burnt in the Place Maubert, Paris.

Science, Technology, and Discovery

Gerardus Mercator states the earth has a magnetic pole.

Art, Sculpture, Fine Arts, and Architecture

Michelangelo designs the Dome and undertakes the completion of St. Peter's, Rome, begun by Bramante (–1564).

Pierre Lescot begins constructing the Louvre, Paris.

Literature

Hans Sachs, *Lisabetha* (tragedy).

1547

Final union of the Crown of Brittany with the Crown of France.

The Inquisition is finally established at Lisbon.

Jan: —, the cities of Augsburg and Strasbourg submit to the emperor Charles V.

—, the Council of Trent's decrees on justification by faith end Charles V's chances of reconciliation with the German Protestant princes.

16th, Ivan IV (the Terrible), who had ascended the throne in 1533 at the age of three, is crowned Tsar of Russia in Moscow, the first tsar to assume the crown formally.

28th, Edward VI, aged nine, succeeds as King of England (–1553) on the death of Henry VIII.

31st, Edward Seymour, Earl of Hertford (later Duke of Somerset), is appointed Lord Protector.

March: **31st**, Henry II succeeds as King of France (–1559) on the death of his father, Francis I.

April: **24th**, Charles V defeats the army of the Schmalkaldic League at Mühlberg.

June: **13th**, a truce between Hungary and Turkey is signed for five years: the Sultan Suleiman I restores most of western Hungary to the Archduke Ferdinand.

Sept: **1st**, Charles V, at the height of his power, meets the Diet of Augsburg and proposes constitutional reforms to strengthen the executive of the Empire.

10th, Protector Somerset, who has invaded Scotland to enforce the marriage treaty of 1543 (for Mary's betrothal to Edward VI), defeats the Scots army at Pinkie.

Oct: —, *La Chambre Ardente* is created in Paris as a criminal court for the trial of heretics.

Nov: —, the Bohemian Crown is proclaimed hereditary in the house of Habsburg.

4th, English Parliament meets (–15th April, 1552) and repeals the Henrican Act of Six Articles (of 1539) as the first stage of a Protestant Reformation.

Sport and Recreation

Torquemada publishes a treatise on draughts.

1548

Pedro de la Gasca defeats Gonzalo Pizarro at the battle of Xaquixaguana to end the separatist movement in Peru.

May: **15th**, the Turks occupy Tabriz, Persia.

Aug: **15th**, Mary Queen of Scots, aged six, betrothed to the Dauphin, lands in France.

Politics, Government, Law, and Economy

The silver mines of Zaatecar, Mexico, are exploited by the Spanish.

Society, Education, and Religion

St. Ignatius Loyola, *Spiritual Exercises* printed (*Ejercicios espirituales*, written in 1522).

St. Francis Xavier founds a Jesuit mission in Japan.

1549

Tsar Ivan IV calls the first national assembly in Russia (*Zemski Sobor*).

The Audiencia of New Grenada is created, with Santa Fé (now Bogotá) the provincial capital.

Feb: —, Maximilian, son of the Archduke Ferdinand, is recognized as the next King of Bohemia.

July: —, Robert Kett leads a revolt in Norfolk in protest at the enclosure movement.

Aug: **8th**, France declares war on England.

26th, John Dudley, Earl of Warwick, defeats Robert Kett's Norfolk rebels at the Battle of Dussindale, near Norwich.

Oct: **10th**, fall of Protector Somerset.

12th, Protector Somerset is sent to the Tower.

Nov: **1st**, Pope Paul III dies (Julius III is elected Feb 1550, after a prolonged conclave).

Society, Education, and Religion

(15th Jan) Act of Uniformity orders the use of the Common Prayer Book.

Science, Technology, and Discovery

The first anatomical theatre is established in Padua.

Literature

Joachim Du Bellay, *La Déffense et illustration de la langue française* (the first statement of the theory of the poetic group known as *La Pléiade.*

Joachim Du Bellay, *L'Olive* (the first sonnet-sequence in the French language).

Everyday Life

In this year a Prayer Book (unbound) cost 2/2d.; bound, 3/8d.

1550 **March: 24th**, the Peace of Boulogne ends England's war with France and Scotland: England returns Boulogne to France on payment of 400,000 crowns.

Society, Education, and Religion

Thomas Cranmer, *A Defence of the Catholic Doctrine of the Sacrament.*

Science, Technology, and Discovery

Siegmund von Herberstein, *De Natura Fossilium.*

Art, Sculpture, Fine Arts, and Architecture

Giorgio Vasari, *Lives of the Artists.*

Palladio, Villa Rotunda, Vicenza (–1551).

Music

Jean Calvin compiles a complete psalter, including 'The Old Hundredth', for developing metrical pointing for congregational singing.

Literature

Pierre de Ronsard, *Odes* (bks. I–IV). *Les Bocages.*

1551 **June: —**, Henry II of France begins campaigning in Italy against Charles V.

July: —, the Turkish fleet fails to capture Malta.

Aug: 14th, the Turks capture Tripoli.

Society, Education, and Religion

(27th June) Edict of Châteaubriant is issued by Henry II of France, to combat Calvinism.

Science, Technology, and Discovery

Konrad von Gesner writes *Historia Animalium*, a pioneer study of zoology (–1558).

Music

Giovanni Pierluigi da Palestrina is appointed director of music at St. Peter's, Rome.

Everyday Life

First licensing of alehouses and taverns in England and Wales.

1552 Ivan IV of Russia begins the conquest of Kazan and Astrakhan from the Tartars.

Jan: —, Treaty of Friedewalde between Protestant German princes and Henry II of France, who is to support the princes against Charles V.

March: —, the Turks invade Hungary to win the battle of Szegedin, but fail to capture Erlau. **13th**, Henry II invades Lorraine with 35,000 men.

April: —, Maurice of Saxony secedes from Charles V and (4th) takes Augsburg and (18th) Linz. **19th**, Maurice fails to capture Charles V at Innsbruck and the Emperor escapes across the Brenner Pass to take refuge in Villach in Carinthia.

Aug: 2nd, by the Treaty of Passau Lutherans are assured of the free exercise of their religion in Germany.

Society, Education, and Religion

Christ's Hospital and some 35 grammar schools are founded in the name of King Edward VI.

Thomas Cranmer, *The Second Prayer Book* of Edward VI (see 1549).

Humanities and Scholarship

Francesco López de Gómara (secretary to Cortéz), *Historia general de las Indias.*

1553 A Turkish fleet, aided by the French, ravages the Mediterranean.

Sultan Suleiman I makes peace with Persia.

Jan: 1st, Charles V abandons an attempted siege of Metz and returns to Brussels, leaving Germany to its own fate. The bishoprics of Metz, Toul and Verdun pass to the French Crown.

March: —, the League of Heidelberg is formed by both Catholic and Protestant princes in Germany to preserve peace and prevent the election of Philip of Spain as Holy Roman Emperor.

July: 6th, on the death of Edward VI, Lady Jane Grey is unwillingly proclaimed Queen of England by the Duke of Northumberland, 10th.
9th, Maurice of Saxony is killed at the Battle of Sievershausen. The Saxon electorate is united in the Albertine branch, descending to Maurice's brother, Augustus.
19th, Lady Jane Grey is deposed and Mary proclaimed Queen of England (–1558).

Aug: 3rd, Queen Mary I enters London. The Roman Mass is celebrated at Court.
22nd, the Duke of Northumberland is executed.

Nov: —, a marriage treaty is signed between Mary I and Philip of Spain.

Society, Education, and Religion
Lima University, Peru, is founded.
Michael Servetus, *Christianismi Restitutio* (denying the belief that Christ is the eternal Son of God); he is burnt at the stake in Geneva.
The Act of Uniformity of 1549 is repealed (restored, 1559).

Science, Technology, and Discovery
Hugh Willoughby and Richard Chancellor set out to discover a north-east passage to China. Willoughby dies while wintering on the Kola Peninsula. Chancellor reaches the site of Archangel and travels to Moscow (–1554).
Michael Servetus in *Christianismi Restitutio* relates his discovery of the pulmonary circulation of the blood.

Art, Sculpture, Fine Arts, and Architecture
Titian, *Danae*.

Literature
[Diego Hurtado de Mendoza], *Lazarillo de Tormes* (the first Spanish picaresque novel).
Hans Sachs, *Tristan und Isolde*.

1554

Jan: 25th, Sir Thomas Wyatt gathers an army of 2,000 at Rochester, in Kent, to raise rebellion, in opposition to Mary I's projected Spanish marriage.

Feb: 7th, Wyatt crosses Kingston Bridge, marches on London, and (9th) is defeated.
12th, Lady Jane Grey is executed.

March: 15th, Wyatt is tried (executed 11th April).
18th, Princess Elizabeth is imprisoned for suspected complicity in Wyatt's rebellion.

April: 12th, Mary of Guise, the Queen Mother, succeeds the Earl of Arran as Regent of Scotland (–1560).

May: —, Henry II of France invades the Netherlands.

July: 25th, Queen Mary I marries Philip of Spain at Winchester.

Nov: 12th, (–Jan 1555) Parliament meets and re-establishes Roman Catholicism.

Politics, Government, Law, and Economy
São Paulo, Brazil, is founded.

Humanities and Scholarship
John Knox flees to Dieppe and thence to Geneva, where he meets John Calvin.
Palladio, *L'Antichita di Roma*, a guidebook to Roman antiquities.

Music
Palestrina writes his first book of Masses.

1555

In Geneva an anti-Calvinist rising is ruthlessly put down.
Japanese pirates besiege Nanking.

Aug: 26th, Philip of Spain leaves England for the Low Countries.

Sept: 25th, by the Peace of Augsburg, the princes and free cities of the Empire who acknowledge the Confession of Augsburg are free to worship and introduce Lutheranism within their territories; at the Diet of Augsburg, Philip of Spain renounces his claim to the Imperial Crown in favour of Maximilian, son of the Archduke Ferdinand.

Oct: 16th, Bishops Latimer and Ridley are burnt at the stake.
21st, (–9th Dec) Parliament meets and opposes the idea that Philip be crowned King.
25th, the Emperor Charles V resigns the government of the Netherlands, Milan, and Naples to Philip of Spain at a ceremony in Brussels.

Politics, Government, Law, and Economy
Foundation of the English Muscovy Company for trade with Russia.

Society, Education, and Religion
John Knox returns to preach in Scotland (returning to Geneva in July 1556).

Science, Technology, and Discovery
Pierre Belon, *L'Histoire de la nature des oyseaux.*

Humanities and Scholarship
An Aztec dictionary is published.

Art, Sculpture, Fine Arts, and Architecture
Tintoretto, *St. George's Fight with the Dragon* and *Christ Washing the Disciples' Feet.*

Everyday Life
Tobacco is first brought to Spain from America.

1556

Jan: 16th, Charles V resigns Spain to Philip II (–1598).

March: 22nd, Cardinal Pole is consecrated Archbishop of Canterbury, following Thomas Cranmer's deposition and execution, 21st.

July: —, the secretary of the Spanish ambassador is seized in Naples; this starts a conflict between the Pope and Spain that lasts until Sept 1557.

Sept: 7th, Charles V resigns the Holy Roman Empire to his brother, Ferdinand I (–1564).

Oct: 17th, Charles V leaves the Low Countries, to retire into the monastery of Yuste, Spain.

Nov: 5th, Akbar (–1605), who has succeeded as Mogul Emperor of India on the death of Humayun, defeats the Afghans at Panipat.

Dec: —, The French under François, Duke of Guise, invade Italy.

Humanities and Scholarship
George Colvile translates *The Consolation of Philosophy* of Boethius.

Music
De Lassus writes his first book of Masses.

1557

Bankruptcy in France and Spain, caused by the influx of American silver;
Russians invade Livonia in a war of succession to the Baltic lands of the German knights (–1571); Poland, Russia, Sweden and Denmark make conflicting claims.

Feb: 28th, an Anglo-Russian commercial treaty is signed in London.

Dec: 3rd, the First Covenant is signed in Scotland.

June: —, the Scots invade England.
7th, England declares war on France, as ally of Spain.

Aug: 10th, the French under Gaspard de Coligny are defeated by a Spanish force under Philibert Emmanuel of Savoy, aided by English troops, at St. Quentin.

Politics, Government, Law, and Economy
The Portuguese establish trading factories at Macao.

Science, Technology, and Discovery
Robert Record writes *Whetstone of Wit*, the first English treatise on algebra.

Literature
Henry Howard, Earl of Surrey, translates Books I and IV of Virgil's *Aeneid* (posthumous); he was the first poet to use blank verse in English.

1558

Akbar, Mogul Emperor of India, conquers Gwalior.

Jan: 7th, The French under François, Duke of Guise, capture Calais from England.

March: 14th, Ferdinand I assumes the title of Holy Roman Emperor without being crowned by the Pope.

April: 24th, Mary Queen of Scots marries the Dauphin, the future Francis II.

Sept: 21st, the ex-Emperor Charles V dies.

Nov: 17th, accession of Elizabeth I, Queen of England (–1603), on the death of Mary I.

Politics, Government, Law, and Economy
Thomas Gresham formulates 'Gresham's Law'.

Society, Education, and Religion
John Knox, *The First Blast of the Trumpet against the Monstrous Regiment of Women.*

Science, Technology, and Discovery
Anthony Jenkinson journeys to Bokhara (–1559).

Literature
Joachim du Bellay, *Les Antiquités de Rome* and *Les Regrets* (sonnet sequences).

Everyday Life

Jean Nicot, French Ambassador in Spain, sends samples of tobacco ('Nicotine') to Paris. The Portuguese introduce the habit of taking snuff to Europe.

1559 **April:** **2nd**, (–3rd) peace treaty is signed at Cateau-Cambrésis between England, Spain and France.

May: **—**, Selim and Bayazid, sons of Suleiman I, Sultan of Turkey, fight for the future succession at Konya in Asia Minor; the defeated Bayazid flees to Persia, where he is murdered.

2nd, John Knox returns to Scotland.

10th, Knox preaches a defiant sermon at Perth, inciting the Protestant Lords of the Congregation to rise.

July: **10th**, accession of Francis II of France (–1560) on the death of his father Henry II in a tournament; François, Duke of Guise, and his brother, the Cardinal of Lorraine, seize power. Francis's wife, Mary Queen of Scots, assumes the title Queen of England.

Oct: **—**, the Swedes take Estonia from Livonia.

21st, the Scottish Lords of the Congregation depose the Regent, Mary of Guise.

Dec: **18th**, Elizabeth I sends to the Scottish Lords of the Congregation aid by land and sea for driving the French from Scotland; aid confirmed by the Treaty of Berwick, Feb 27th 1560.

Society, Education, and Religion

(8th May) Elizabeth's *Act of Supremacy* passed; and *Act of Uniformity* ordains the Elizabethan *Prayer Book*.

Humanities and Scholarship

James Amyot's translation of Plutarch's *Parallel Lives* from the Greek into French (translated into English 1579).

1560 Madrid becomes the capital of Spain.

In India the Mogul Emperor Akbar conquers the Rajput kingdom and Lower Bengal.

Feb: **—**, Turkish galleys rout Spanish fleet under Duke of Medina Celi off Tripoli.

March: **15th**, Huguenot conspiracy at Amboise fails to rescue King Francis II of France from the Guise faction. The Prince of Condé is subsequently imprisoned by the Duke of Guise.

July: **6th**, by Treat of Edinburgh between England and Scotland the claims of Mary Queen of Scots to the English throne are annulled; but Mary refuses to ratify the treaty.

Dec: **5th**, Charles IX succeeds as King of France (–1574), on death of Francis II, with Catherine de' Medici as Regent.

Society, Education, and Religion

Parliament in Scotland adopts the Calvinistic Confession.

Science, Technology, and Discovery

Battista Porta in *Magia Naturalis* discusses the structure of the eye and invents the camera obscura.

Art, Sculpture, Fine Arts, and Architecture

Pieter Breughel, *Adoration of the Magi* (I).

Titian, *Venus with a Mirror*.

Literature

Hsü Wei, *Ching P'Ing Mei* (the first classic Chinese novel of social realism).

1561 The Baltic states of the Order of the Teutonic Knights are secularized.

Jan: **28th**, by the Edict of Orléans, persecution of the Huguenots is suspended.

Aug: **19th**, Mary Queen of Scots lands at Leith in Scotland.

Society, Education, and Religion

The first Calvinist refugees from Flanders settle in England.

Scottish Church Ministers draw up the *Confession of Faith*, for the establishment of Protestantism (largely the work of John Knox).

Science, Technology, and Discovery

Italian physician Gabriello Fallopius writes *Observationes anatomicae*, a pioneer study of anatomy which describes the inner ear and female reproductive organs.

Portuguese monks at Goa introduce printing into India.

Art, Sculpture, Fine Arts, and Architecture

Cornelius Floris, Antwerp town hall (–1565).

1562 Ribault establishes a Huguenot colony at Charlesfort and claims Florida.

Jan: **6th**, Shane O'Neill, Earl of Tyrone, ends his first rebellion by surrendering to Queen Elizabeth. (He rebels again, 26th May).

17th, Michel de l'Hôpital promulgates the Edict of St. Germain, which recognizes the Huguenots in France.

March: 1st, 1,200 French Huguenots are slain by order of the Guises at the Massacre of Vassy, which provokes the First War of Religion.

May: 26th, Shane O'Neill leads a second rebellion in Ireland (–June 1567).

Sept: 22nd, Queen Elizabeth signs the Treaty of Hampton Court with the Huguenot leader, Louis I de Bourbon, Prince of Condé.
22nd, Maximilian, son of the Emperor Ferdinand I, succeeds as King of Bohemia.

Nov: 5th, the rebellion of George Gordon, Earl of Huntly, in Scotland is crushed by the Earl of Moray at Corrichie.

Dec: 19th, at the Battle of Dreux in the French Civil War, Condé and Montmorency are taken prisoners.

Politics, Government, Law, and Economy
Earliest English slave-trading expedition under John Hawkins.

Society, Education, and Religion
The Articles of Religion of 1552 in England are reduced to the *Thirty-Nine Articles*.

Art, Sculpture, Fine Arts, and Architecture
Paul Veronese, *Marriage of Cana*.

Literature
Rabelais, *Pantagruel* continued (bk. V; posthumous; begun 1532).

1563 **Feb: 24th**, François, Duke of Guise, is killed before Orléans.

March: 19th, the Peace of Amboise ends the First War of Religion in France; under its terms the Huguenots are granted limited toleration.

May: —, Ivan IV of Russia conquers Polotski in Eastern Livonia, taking it from Poland (intermittent warfare between Russia and Poland continues to 1582).

Society, Education, and Religion
General outbreak of plague in Europe, spreading to England, kills over 20,000 inhabitants of London.
John Foxe, *Actes and Monuments* (popularly known as *Foxe's Book of Martyrs*; first English edition; illustrated).

Science, Technology, and Discovery
Gerardus Mercator surveys Lorraine to make the first detailed, accurate map.

Art, Sculpture, Fine Arts, and Architecture
Pieter Breughel, *Tower of Babel*.
Herrera begins to build the Escorial for Philip II of Spain.

1564 **April: 11th**, the Peace of Troyes ends the war between England and France.

June: —, Ivan IV of Russia, in the course of a struggle for power against the boyars, led by Prince Kurbsky, is forced to withdraw from Moscow.

July: 25th, Maximilian II succeeds as Holy Roman Emperor and as King in Austria, Bohemia and Hungary (–1576) on the death of Ferdinand I; the rest of the Habsburg dominions pass to the Archduke Charles.

Society, Education, and Religion
The Council of Trent's *Professio Fidei* is confirmed by Pope Pius IV, together with Rules *De Libris Prohibitis* (see 1545, 1562, 1564).
(25th May) Philip Neri founds the *Congregation of the Oratory* in Rome.

Art, Sculpture, Fine Arts, and Architecture
Jacopo Tintoretto, Paintings for the Scuolo Grande di San Rocco (–1587).
Philibert Delorme designs the Tuileries, Paris.

Music
One of the earliest extant violins made by Andrea Amati is dated to this year.

1565 **May: —**, (–Sept) the Knights of St. John, under La Valette, defend Malta from the Turks.

July: 29th, Mary Queen of Scots marries Henry, Lord Darnley, in Edinburgh.

Politics, Government, Law, and Economy
Sir Thomas Gresham founds the Royal Exchange, London.

Science, Technology, and Discovery
The Royal College of Physicians, London, is empowered to carry out human dissections.

Art, Sculpture, Fine Arts, and Architecture
Pieter Breughel, *A Country Wedding*; *Hunters in the Snow*, and *Stormy Days*.

Music
Palestrina, *Missa Papae Marcelli*.

Everyday Life
Sir John Hawkins introduces tobacco to England.

1566
March: 9th, David Rizzio, Mary Queen of Scots' confidential secretary, is murdered in Holyrood House on Darnley's orders.

April: 5th, by the Compromise of Breda, a confederacy of lesser nobility, nicknamed *Les Gueux*, organizes resistance to Spanish persecution in the Netherlands.

Sept: 5th, Selim II (The Sot) succeeds as Sultan of Turkey (–1574) on the death of Suleiman I; henceforward the Janissaries become a hereditary caste.

Humanities and Scholarship
William Adlington translates *The Golden Ass* of Apuleius.

1567
In Japan Nobunaga deposes the Shogun and acquires dictatorial powers.

Feb: 10th, Darnley is murdered at Kirk o'Field, Edinburgh, on the orders of James Hepburn, Earl of Bothwell.

March: 13th, Margaret of Parma, Regent of the Netherlands, with German mercenaries, annihilates 2,000 Calvinist sectaries led by John de Marnix at Austruweel.

May: 15th, Mary Queen of Scots marries Bothwell in Edinburgh.

June: —, at the battle of Carberry Hill, the Lords of the Covenant rout Bothwell's supporters; Mary is taken captive, and, 17th, is imprisoned in Lochleven Castle.
2nd, Shane O'Neill, Earl of Tyrone, the Irish rebel, is assassinated.

July: 24th, Mary Queen of Scots is forced to abdicate and appoint the Earl of Moray as Regent for the infant James.

Aug: 8th, the Duke of Alva arrives in the Netherlands as military governor with 10,000 veteran Spanish and Italian troops.
22nd, the Duke of Alva establishes the Council of Blood, and begins a reign of terror.

Sept: 29th, the Huguenot Conspiracy of Meaux, to capture Charles IX, provokes the Second War of Religion in France.

Oct: 6th, Margaret of Parma resigns the regency of the Netherlands.

Society, Education, and Religion
Martin Chemnitz, a Lutheran, draws up *Corpus doctrinae Prutenicum*.

1568
Feb: 17th, Sultan Selim II makes peace with the Emperor Maximilian II.

March: 23rd, the Treaty of Longjumean ends the Second War of Religion in France.

May: 2nd, Mary Queen of Scots escapes from Lochleven.
16th, Mary takes refuge in England.
23rd, William of Orange with German mercenaries defeats a Spanish force under Count Aremberg at Heiligerlee.

June: 2nd, Counts Egmont and Hoorn are pronounced guilty of high treason and, 6th, are beheaded in Brussels.

July: 21st, the Duke of Alva defeats Louis of Nassau at Jemmingen.

Nov: —, The Moors in Spain revolt against oppressive treatment, desecrating churches in Granada. In retaliation Philip II orders the slaughter of the Moorish population.

Dec: —, Three Spanish treasure ships with pay for the Duke of Alva's troops, driven by storm into Plymouth, are impounded by Elizabeth; commercial relations between England and Philip II's dominions are severed (until Aug 1574).

Society, Education, and Religion
The first Eisteddfod, for Welsh music and literature, is held at Caerwys.
Seminary (the English College) founded at Douai by William Allen to train Jesuit missionaries for work in England (see 1580).

Literature
John Skelton, *Works* ... newly collected ('Pithy, pleasaunt and profitable workes of maister Skelton, Poete Laureate ...').

Everyday Life
Alexander Nowell, Dean of St. Paul's, invents bottled beer.

1569 **Jan:** —, desultory fighting in Périgord leads to the Third War of Religion in France.

March: —, The Duke of Anjou defeats the Huguenots at Jarnac; the Prince of Condé is killed.
20th, the Duke of Alva requires the States-General at Brussels to grant burdensome taxes, including the Tenth Penny.

July: —, William of Orange begins issuing letters of marque to the 'Beggars of the Sea' for plundering Spanish shipping.
1st, Sigismund II of Poland achieves the Union of Lithuania with Poland and Lublin.

Nov: **9th**, the Northern Rebellion breaks out in England under the Roman Catholic Earls of Northumberland and Westmorland.

Dec: **15th**, the Earls of Northumberland and Westmorland flee to Scotland. The rebels are defeated 20th Feb, 1570.

Science, Technology, and Discovery
Gerardus Mercator's Map of the World for navigational use, on 'Mercator's' projection, with parallels and meridians at right angles, published.

1570 Don John of Austria clears the Moriscos from Andalusia.
The Japanese open the port of Nagasaki to overseas trade.

Jan: **23rd**, assassination of the Earl of Moray, Regent of Scotland, leads to civil war with the Marians.

Feb: **25th**, Pope Pius V issues the bull *Regnans in Excelsis*, excommunicating Elizabeth I.

May: —, Turkey declares war on Venice for refusing to surrender Cyprus.

Aug: **8th**, the Peace of St. Germain-en-Laye ends the Third Civil War in France. The Huguenots gain greater concessions; Admiral Coligny becomes all-powerful at the French court (but see Aug 1572).

Dec: **13th**, by the Peace of Stettin Denmark recognizes the independence of Sweden, confirming the Treaty of Brömsebro (1541); Sweden surrenders her claim to Norway.

Society, Education, and Religion
Roger Ascham, *The Scholemaster*.

Science, Technology, and Discovery
Abraham Ortelius of Antwerp publishes *Theatrum Orbis Terrarum*, with 53 maps, the first modern atlas.

Art, Sculpture, Fine Arts, and Architecture
Nicholas Hilliarde, portrait of *Queen Elizabeth I*.
Palladio publishes *Quattro Libri dell' Architettura*.

Everyday Life
The potato is introduced to Europe from Spanish America.

1571 **May:** **20th**, Pope Pius V signs a league with Spain and Venice to combat the Turks.

Aug: **3rd**, the Turks take Famagusta, Cyprus, after a siege of eleven months; they massacre many of the inhabitants.

Sept: **4th**, the Marian Party in Scotland, led by the Hamiltons and William Maitland, makes a successful *coup d'état* at Stirling, where the Regent Lennox is killed.

Oct: **7th**, Don John of Austria decisively defeats the Turkish fleet off Lepanto.

Society, Education, and Religion
Harrow School is founded by John Lyon.

Music
Giovanni Pierluigi da Palestrina, five-part Mass.

1572 **Jan:** **16th**, the Duke of Norfolk is tried for treason for complicity in the Ridolfi plot to restore Catholicism in England (executed 2nd June).

April: **1st**, the Dutch 'Beggars of the Sea' capture Brill, following their expulsion from English ports: the effective beginning of the Dutch War of Independence.

July: **7th**, the Estates of Poland declare the monarchy elective on the death of Sigismund II; the Duke of Anjou is elected King of Poland in May 1573.
18th, William of Orange is elected Stadtholder by Holland, Friesland, Zeeland and Utrecht at the Dort Assembly.

Aug: **18th**, Henry of Navarre marries Margaret of Valois, sister of Charles IX of France.
22nd, (–24th) the Massacre of St. Bartholomew's Day in Paris where Coligny and many

Huguenots are killed. The massacre spreads to the provinces and provokes the fourth War of Religion (–July 1573).

Society, Education, and Religion

Act for poor relief and punishment of vagrants.

Humanities and Scholarship

Henri Estienne, *Thesaurus Linguae Graecae.*

Music

Andrea Amati in Cremona makes one of earliest known cellos.

Literature

Luis Vaz de Camoens, *Os Lusiados.*

1573

Feb: (–May) the Pacification of Perth ends the fighting in Scotland between the Regent and the faction supporting Mary Queen of Scots.

March: **7th**, the Peace of Constantinople ends the war between Turkey and Venice: Venice cedes Cyprus.

July: **6th**, the Pacification of Boulogne ends the Fourth War of Religion in France.
11th, Haarlem falls to the Spanish under Don Frederick of Toledo.

Dec: **18th**, the Duke of Alva is succeeded as Governor of the Netherlands by Don Louis Requesens.

Music

Orlando di Lasso, *Patrocinium Musices* (–1576).

Literature

Torquato Tasso, *Aminta* (pastoral, not published until 1580).

1574

The Spaniards lose Tunis to the Turks.
The Portuguese settlement at Angola is begun with the foundation of São Paulo.

Feb: **23rd**, the Fifth War of Religion breaks out in France (–May 1576).

May: **30th**, Henry III succeeds as King of France (–1589) on the death of Charles IX.

June: **30th**, William of Orange persuades the Estates of Holland to open the dykes to hinder the Spanish siege of Leyden; the siege is raised, 3rd Oct.

Politics, Government, Law, and Economy

Jean Bodin, *Discours sur les causes de l'extreme cherté qui est aujourdhuy en France.*

Society, Education, and Religion

The first *auto-da-fé* (held in Mexico).

Humanities and Scholarship

Justus Lipsius edits *The Histories* and *The Annals* of Tacitus.

Art, Sculpture, Fine Arts, and Architecture

Longleat House, Wiltshire, is completed.

1575

Financial crisis in Spain becomes more acute. In Sept, Philip II suspends all payments. Requesens, Governor of the Netherlands, has no money to pay his soldiers.
The Mogul Emperor Akbar conquers Bengal.

May: (–July) a series of conferences is held at Breda between Requesens and William of Orange to reach an accommodation, but Philip II refuses to grant any concessions to the rebels.

Nov: **14th**, Elizabeth I refuses to accept the sovereignty of the Netherlands, which William of Orange, in desperation at the course of the war, had agreed to have offered to her.

Dec: **14th**, Stephen Báthory is elected King of Poland (–1586) in succession to Henry (now King of France) whom the Estates had deposed in his absence.

Society, Education, and Religion

The plague breaks out in Sicily and spreads to Italy, where casualties are heavy in Milan and Florence.
Leyden University is founded, to commemorate the siege.

Science, Technology, and Discovery

Danish astronomer Tycho Brahe constructs an observatory for the King of Denmark.
The first European imitation of Chinese porcelain is made at Florence.

Music

William Byrd and Thomas Tallis, *Cantiones Sacrae.*

1576 **Feb:** **3rd**, Henry of Navarre escapes from Paris and 5th, abjures Catholicism at Tours.

March: **3rd**, death of Don Louis Requesens, Governor of the Netherlands (in April Philip II appoints his half-brother, Don John of Austria, as Governor).

May: **6th**, the Fifth War of Religion in France is ended by the Peace of Monsieur (after the Duke of Anjou), promulgated by the Edict of Beaulieu. The Edict provokes Henri of Lorraine, Duke of Guise to form a Catholic League to overthrow the Huguenots.

Oct: **12th**, accession of the Emperor Rudolf II (–1612) on the death of his brother Maximilian II.

Nov: **4th**, the Spanish army mutinies and sacks Antwerp – 'the Spanish Fury'.
8th, by the Pacification of Ghent all 17 Provinces of the Netherlands are united. They agree to require Philip II to recall Spanish troops, grant religious toleration and summon a representative assembly.

Politics, Government, Law, and Economy
Jean Bodin, *Les Six livres de la République*, advocating a limited monarchy.

Society, Education, and Religion
Another English statute for the punishment of vagrants, ordering the establishment of houses of correction to set vagrants and pilferers to hard labour.
The League of Torgau draws up Articles of Faith (*The Torgau Book*).

Science, Technology, and Discovery
Martin Frobisher discovers Frobisher Bay.

Humanities and Scholarship
Académie du Palais founded by Henry III in Paris.

Literature
(13th April) James Burbage obtains a twenty-one-year lease of land in Shoreditch, London. *The Theatre* opens on the site at the end of the year.

1577 **Feb:** **6th**, Henry of Navarre becomes recognized as head of the Huguenot Party.
12th, Don John of Austria, the new Governor of the Netherlands, issues the Perpetual Edict to settle the civil war. William of Orange refuses to publish the Edict.

March: **—**, The Sixth War of Religion breaks out in France (–Sept).

Aug: **17th**, the Peace of Bergerac ends the Sixth War of Religion.

Sept: **23rd**, William of Orange enters Brussels. The States-General depose Don John of Austria.

Nov: **15th**, Francis Drake leaves on his voyage round the world, via the Cape of Good Hope, to attack Spanish settlements and shipping (–Nov 30th, 1580).

Humanities and Scholarship
Ralph Holinshed and others, *Chronicles* (2nd edn. 1587).

1578 Ōtomo Yoshishige, one of the chief rulers in Japan, is converted to Christianity.

March: **12th**, the Earl of Morton resigns the regency and James VI takes over the government of Scotland.

June: **—**, Swedish army defeats the Russians at Wenden in the battle for the Baltic.

Aug: **4th**, Sebastian, King of Portugal, invades Morocco, but he is killed at Alcazar in 'The Battle of the Three Kings'; Cardinal Henry, aged 67, accedes as King of Portugal (–1580).
13th, François, Duke of Anjou is proclaimed Defender of Liberties in the Netherlands by the States-General.

Oct: **1st**, Alessandro Farnese, Duke of Parma, is appointed Governor of the Netherlands by Philip II on the death from a fever of Don John of Austria.

Humanities and Scholarship
(31st May) The Catacombs of Rome discovered by accident.

Literature
John Lyly, *Euphues, the Anatomy of Wit*, pt. I (pt. II – *Euphues and His England*, 1580; complete 1617).
Pierre de Ronsard, *Sonnets pour Hélène* (addressed to Hélène de Surgères).

1579 **Jan:** **25th**, the Union of Utrecht is signed by Holland, Zeeland, Utrecht, Gelderland, Friesland, Groningen and Overyssel. The Union marks the foundation of the Dutch Republic.

May: **17th**, by the Peace of Arras the southern provinces of the Netherlands are formally reconciled to Philip II.

July: **—**, Lord Grey, Lord Deputy of Ireland, massacres the force of Spaniards, Italians and Portuguese who have invaded in support of the rebels at Smerwick, Kerry.

Society, Education, and Religion

St. John of the Cross, *Dark Night of the Soul* (–1583).

Humanities and Scholarship

Sir Thomas North translates Plutarch's *Lives* into English from the French of Jacques Amyot (1559).

Art, Sculpture, Fine Arts, and Architecture

Palladio, Teatro Olimpico, Vicenza (–1580).

Literature

Edmund Spenser, *The Shepheards Calender* (twelve eclogues).

1580 **April:** **—**, the Seventh War of Religion breaks out in France (–Nov).

July: **5th**, Proclamation to restrict the growth of London forbids new building.

Aug: **25th**, Spanish invasion of Portugal under the Duke of Alva, who defeats the supporters of Don Antonio at the battle of Alcántana, near Lisbon.

Nov: **26th**, the Peace of Fleix ends the Seventh War of Religion in France.

Humanities and Scholarship

Jean Bodin, *Démonomanie des sorciers* (against witchcraft).
John Stow, *The Chronicles of England* (–1592; in later editions called 'Annals').
Michel de Montaigne, *Essais*, 2 vols. (see 1588).

Music

'Greensleeves', traditional English tune, is first mentioned.

1581 Beginnings of the Russian Conquest of Siberia (completed 1598).
The Mogul Emperor Akbar conquers Afghanistan.

April: **1st**, the Portuguese Cortes at Thomar submit to Philip II.
4th, Queen Elizabeth knights Francis Drake at Deptford.

May: **—**, Stephen Báthory, King of Poland, invades Russia. Poland gains Livonia and Estonia, 15th Jan 1582.

July: **17th**, Edmund Campion is seized; he is tried for treason and, 1st Dec, executed.

Nov: **7th**, (–11th) a marriage treaty is signed between François, Duke of Anjou and Elizabeth I (but further proceedings peter out).

Politics, Government, Law, and Economy

The English Levant (or Turkey) Company is founded.

Science, Technology, and Discovery

Galileo Galilei discovers the principle of the pendulum, that the time of the swing is independent of the size of the swing.

Art, Sculpture, Fine Arts, and Architecture

Caravaggio, *Martyrdom of St. Maurice.*

Music

Baltasar de Beaujoyeux's *Balet de la Royne* (earliest ballet with music extant) performed at French court.

Literature

Torquato Tasso, *Gerusalemme Liberata.*

1582 The Venetian Constitution is amended to restrict the authority of the Council of Ten.
Nobunaga, ruler of Japan, is assassinated by Akechi Mitsuhide.

March: **18th**, attempted assassination of William of Orange.

Aug: **22nd**, in the Ruthven Raid, the English Party in Scotland capture James VI while hunting at Ruthven Castle. James remains in captivity until June 1583.

Oct: **4th**, (–15th) the Gregorian Calendar is adopted in the Papal States, Spain and Portugal; adopted throughout Catholic Europe by 1584.

Society, Education, and Religion

Edinburgh University is founded.
Jesuit Mission in China is started.

Everyday Life

Graduated pay, according to rank, is introduced into the Royal Navy.

1583 **Jan: 7th**, (or 17th) François, Duke of Anjou, sacks Antwerp, but fails to seize the city – 'The French Fury'.

July: —, Ivan the Terrible kills his son Ivan in a fit of rage.

Aug: —, William of Orange accepts the sovereignty of the northern Netherlands.

Oct: —, The Somerville Plot to assassinate Elizabeth I is discovered (John Somerville is executed 20th Dec).

Dec: —, The Throgmorton Plot, for a Spanish invasion of England, is discovered and Francis Throgmorton arrested; he is executed 10th July, 1584.

Humanities and Scholarship

Joseph Justus Scaliger, *Opus De Emendatione Temporum* (the foundation of modern chronology).

Everyday Life

(18th June) First-known life insurance policy in England made, on the life of William Gibbons for one year at eight per cent premium.

1584 **March: 18th**, Feodore succeeds as Tsar of Russia (–1598) on the death of Ivan the Terrible. Feodore is dominated by his brother-in-law, Boris Godunov.

June: 15th, François, Duke of Anjou dies at Château-Thiery, leaving the Protestant Henry of Navarre as heir to the French throne.

July: —, William of Orange is assassinated by Balthazar Gérard, at the instigation of Philip II. William is succeeded as Stadholder by his son, Maurice of Nassau.

Politics, Government, Law, and Economy

Banco di Rialto is established in Venice.

Humanities and Scholarship

Reginald Scott, *The Discoverie of Witchcraft*, an attack on superstition.

1585 Hideyoshi is appointed Dictator in Japan.

May: 19th, English shipping in Spanish ports is confiscated.

June: 29th, Queen Elizabeth delines to take the sovereignty of the Low Countries.

July: 7th, Henry III is forced to sign the Treaty of Nemours with the Guises, in which he capitulates to their demands for revoking all toleration to Huguenots; this provokes the War of the Three Henries (Henry III, Henry of Navarre and Henry of Guise).
7th, An expedition lands at Roanoke, Virginia, to plant Raleigh's first colony.

Aug: 14th, Elizabeth I issues a Declaration taking the Netherlands under her protection.

Sept: 3rd, Treaty of Nonsuch between England and the States-General.

Dec: —, The Earl of Leicester takes up his command in the Netherlands (–Nov 1586; resumes command Aug 1587, resigns March 1588).

Politics, Government, Law, and Economy

(17th Aug) The Sack of Antwerp by Spanish troops ends the days of Antwerp as an international port and as the hub of the international money market.

Society, Education, and Religion

Elizabethan Act against the Jesuits and Seminarists (see 1568).

Literature

Miguel de Cervantes Saavedra writes *Galatea* (pastoral romance).
Battista Guarini writes *Pastor Fido* (pastoral drama).
Lord Chamberlain's Men; and then Lord Admiral's Company of actors formed.

1586 Abbas I accedes as Shah of Persia (–1629).

July: 1st, by the Treaty of Berwick, Elizabeth I and James VI form a league of amity.
17th, Sir Francis Walsingham succeeds in unravelling the Babington Plot to murder Elizabeth I, establishing that Mary Queen of Scots was implicated in the plans.
27th, the English plantation of Munster is attempted.

Sept: 13th, Anthony Babington and his fellow conspirators are tried, and, 20th, executed.
22nd, Sir Philip Sydney is fatally wounded at the attack on Zutphen (dies Oct 17th).

Oct: 11th, (–14th) Mary Queen of Scots is tried for treason at Fotheringhay.
25th, sentence is pronounced against Mary Queen of Scots in the Star Chamber.

Nov: —, the Sixteen establish a revolutionary government in Paris, pledged to support the Duke of Guise and the Catholic League.

Politics, Government, Law, and Economy
Pope Sixtus V, by the bull *Detestabilis,* forbids usury.

Science, Technology, and Discovery
(21st July) Thomas Cavendish leaves Plymouth on a voyage of circumnavigation, west to east (he returns to Plymouth, Sept 10th, 1588).

Art, Sculpture, Fine Arts, and Architecture
El Greco, *Burial of Count Orgaz.*

1587 Raleigh's second settlement in Roanoke, Virginia under John White (–1591).
Portuguese missionaries are banished from Japan.

Feb: 1st, Elizabeth I signs warrant for the execution of Mary Queen of Scots, and, 8th, she is executed at Fotheringhay.

April: 19th, Sir Francis Drake singes the King of Spain's beard by sacking Cadiz.

Aug: —, Pope Sixtus V proclaims a Catholic Crusade for the invasion of England.

Oct: 20th, Henry of Navarre defeats Catholic League at Battle of Coultras.

Society, Education, and Religion
John Knox, *History of the Reformation in Scotland* [to 1567] (posthumous 1586/7).

Science, Technology, and Discovery
Rialto Bridge, Venice, is built (–1591).

Literature
Historia von D Johann Fausten (anon.).

1588 **April: —**, Henry III summons Swiss mercenaries under Biron to the suburbs of Paris to defend him against the Catholic League; in alarm the Parisians send for the Duke of Guise.

May: 12th, at the Day of Barricades, Guise makes himself master of Paris.
30th, (or 9th June), the Duke of Medina Sidonia sets sail from Lisbon with the Spanish Armada.

July: 27th, (or 6th Aug), after a running fight up the English Channel the Armada anchors in Calais Roads.
28th, (or 7th Aug), Lord Admiral Howard of Effingham sends in fire ships to destroy many of the Spanish galleons off Calais.
29th, the Spanish Armada is sighted off the Cornish coast.
29th, (or 8th Aug), defeat of the Armada at the Battle of Gravelines.

Oct: 16th, the States-General meet at Blois and suggest the surrender of the French Crown to the Duke of Guise.

Dec: 23rd, Henry III arranges for the assassination of Henry, Duke of Guise, at Blois.

Society, Education, and Religion
Luis de Molina, *Liberi Arbitrii cum Gratiae Donis...Concordia* (leads to a dispute on free will by Jesuits and Dominicans – Molinists and Thomists).
The *Martin Marprelate Tracts* (seven extant) are issued from a secret press, in defence of Presbyterianism. Suspected authors John Penry and John Udall are arrested; Penry executed in 1593; Udall dies whilst awaiting punishment in prison.

Humanities and Scholarship
Michel de Montaigne, *Essais*, vol. 3 (see 1580).

Art, Sculpture, Fine Arts, and Architecture
Fontana completes cupola and lantern of St. Peter's, Rome (–1590).

Music
William Byrd, *Psalmes, sonets, and songs.*

1589 **Jan: 5th**, Catherine de' Medici, Queen Mother of France, dies.

April: 13th, (–July) Sir Francis Drake and Sir John Norris lead an expedition to Portugal. They destroy Corunna but fail to take Lisbon.
3rd, Henry III and Henry of Navarre sign a truce, to oppose the designs of the Catholic League (the two Kings meet outside Tours 30th April).

Society, Education, and Religion
Metropolitan Patriarch of Moscow asserts independence from Constantinople.

Science, Technology, and Discovery
Richard Hakluyt, *The Principall Navigations, Traffiques and Discoveries of the English Nation* (enlarged 1598, 1600).
Rev William Lee of Cambridge invents the stocking frame, the first knitting machine.

Art, Sculpture, Fine Arts, and Architecture
Caravaggio, *Bacchus*.

1590 Shah Abbas I of Persia makes peace with the Turks, abandoning Tabriz, Shirva and Georgia, to enable him to deal with the Uzbeks under Abdullah II.
The Emperor of Morocco annexes Timbuctoo and the Upper Niger.
Jan: —, Philip II of Spain agrees to support the Holy League in France.
—, the Cardinal of Bourbon is proclaimed Charles X of France by the Leaguers (he dies May 10th).
May: **7th**, Henry IV begins to invest Paris from the north, causing famine in the capital.
Sept: —, The Duke of Parma, advancing from the Spanish Netherlands, forces Henry IV to raise the siege of Paris.

Politics, Government, Law, and Economy
Coalmining is begun in the Ruhr.

Science, Technology, and Discovery
Zacharias Jansen invents the compound microscope which uses two lenses.

Humanities and Scholarship
José de Acosta, *Historia natural y moral de las Indias*.

Literature
Christopher Marlowe, *Tamburlaine the Great* (tragedy).
Sir Philip Sidney, The Countess of Pembroke's *Arcadia* (posthumous).
Edmund Spenser, *The Faerie Queene*, bks. 1–3 (see 1596).

Births and Deaths
Ambrose Paré dies (aged 80).

1591 Navarre and the counties of Foix and Albret are annexed to the Crown of France.
Aug: —, Robert Earl of Essex is sent with an army to France to aid Henry IV in the siege of Rouen.
—, the *Revenge* is captured by the Spaniards in an action off the Azores and Sir Richard Grenville is mortally wounded.
Sept: **21st**, French bishops meeting at Rouen accept Henry IV as King of France.

Society, Education, and Religion
Trinity College, Dublin, is founded by Queen Elizabeth I.

Humanities and Scholarship
Giordano Bruno, *De immenso et innumerabilis seu de universo et mundis*.

Literature
Sir John Harington translates Ariosto's *Orlando Furioso* into English heroical verse.
The Troublesome Raigne of King John of England (anon., attributed to Shakespeare).

1592 The Mogul Emperor Akbar takes Sind.
The Portuguese settle at Mombasa.
Hideyoshi, Shogun of Japan, invades Korea.
Aug: —, Sir John Burrows captures the Portuguese galleon *Madre de Dios* at Flores.

Society, Education, and Religion
The plague kills 15,000 inhabitants of London (–1593).
The Parliament in Edinburgh ratifies the Presbyterian Order of the Church of Scotland.
The Vulgate (Latin translation of the Bible see 1590), issued in a definitive text with the approval of Clement VIII.

Science, Technology, and Discovery
A windmill is used to drive a mechanical saw in Holland.
Galileo writes *Scienza Mechanica* (*On the Mechanical Sciences*) which discusses the problems of raising weights.

Humanities and Scholarship
The ruined Roman city of Pompeii is discovered.

Art, Sculpture, Fine Arts, and Architecture
Tintoretto, *The Last Supper* (–1594).

Literature
Robert Greene, *A Groatsworth of Wit Bought with a Million of Repentance*.
Thomas Kyd, *The Spanish Tragedy*.

1593 **July:** **25th**, Henry IV becomes a Roman Catholic, hearing Mass at St. Denis.
Oct: —, Sigismund III's attempt to restore Roman Catholicism in Sweden is successfully opposed by the Convention of Uppsala.

Science, Technology, and Discovery

Giacomo della Porta writes *De Refractione, optices parte*, including an account of binocular vision.

Purana Pul bridge of 23 arches is built across the R. Musi in Hyderabad.

Literature

William Shakespeare, *Venus and Adonis* (poem). *The Comedy of Errors* is acted between 1592 and 1594, including a performance at Gray's Inn, 28th Dec, 1594.

1594 Henry IV issues the Edict of St. Germain-en-Laye granting Huguenots liberty of worship.

The Mogul Emperor Akbar takes Kandahar.

The Lisbon spice market is closed to Dutch and English merchants.

Period of harvest failure and high grain prices (–1597).

Feb: 27th, Henry IV is crowned King of France at Chartres.

March: 22nd, Henry IV enters Paris; the rest of the country gradually submits to him.

Aug: —, Hugh O'Neill, Earl of Tyrone, in alliance with O'Donnell, Earl of Tyrconnell, leads a rising in Ulster against Queen Elizabeth I and appeals to Philip II for aid.

Society, Education, and Religion

Richard Hooker, *Of the Laws of Ecclesiastical Polity*, bks. 1–4 (8th bk. see 1648), a defence of the Church of England under the Elizabethan settlement.

Art, Sculpture, Fine Arts, and Architecture

Giovanni de Bologna, equestrian statues of Cosimo I and Ferdinando (Florence).

Music

Queen Elizabeth sends an organ, made by Thomas Dallam, to the Sultan of Turkey.

1595 Sir Walter Raleigh explores 300 miles up the R. Orinoco.

Jan: 17th, Henry IV of France declares war on Spain.

July: 23rd, the Spanish land in southwest Cornwall and burn Mousehole and Penzance before taking to their ships.

Oct: 28th, Sigmund Báthory defeats the Turks at Giurgevo and subdues Wallachia.

Nov: —, the Treaty of Teusina ends Sweden's war with Lithuania; Sweden acquires Estonia and Narva.

Society, Education, and Religion

(2nd Feb) Robert Southwell, Jesuit priest and poet, is hanged at Tyburn after prolonged torture and imprisonment.

Science, Technology, and Discovery

The bow is finally abandoned as a weapon by the English army.

Literature

Sir Philip Sidney, *An Apologie for Poetrie* (sometimes entitled *The Defence of Poetry*).

1596 The Spanish coinage is further devalued to stave off bankrupcy.

Jan: 31st, the decrees of Folembray end the war of the Catholic League.

June: 30th, (–July 5th) English expedition under Lord Howard of Effingham and the Earl of Essex sacks Cadiz, ravages the Spanish coast and captures much booty.

Oct: 23rd, (–26th) the Turks under Mohammed III defeat the Imperialist army under the Archduke Maximilian at Keresztes, near Erlau, North Hungary.

25th, Spanish expedition leaves Lisbon with men and arms to support the Earl of Tyrone in Ireland, but subsequently founders off Cape Finistère.

Science, Technology, and Discovery

Willem Barents discovers Spitzbergen.

Rheticus' *Opus palatinum de triangulis* is published posthumously; it gives the values of the six standard trigonometric functions.

Literature

Edmund Spenser, *Faerie Queene*, bks. 4–5 (see 1590).

1597 Persian army defeats the Uzbeks to prevent further invasion of Khorasan.

Jan: —, Maurice of Nassau, aided by the English contingent under Sir Francis Vere, defeats the Spanish at Turnhout, freeing north Brabant and Zeeland from further attack.

Aug: 1st, (or 11th) English merchants are expelled from the Empire in retaliation for the treatment of the Hansa in London.

Sept: 25th, Amiens, captured by Archduke Albert of Austria in March, is retaken by Henry IV.

Oct: —, Spanish Armada leaves Ferrol for England, but is scattered by storms.

Society, Education, and Religion
James VI of Scotland, *Demonologie* (on witchcraft).

Humanities and Scholarship
Sir Francis Bacon (Lord Verulam), *Essays: Civil and Moral* (10 essays; increased in edition of 1612; increased again (to 58) in 1625, the final edition).

Music
Jacopo Peri's *Dafne* (the first opera) performed in Florence.

Literature
John Dowland, *First Book of Songs*.
William Shakespeare, *King Richard the Second*; *Romeo and Juliet*; *Richard the Third*.

1598
The Dutch take Mauritius and send traders to Guiana.
On the death of Hideyoshi, Jeyasu Tokugawa restores the Shogunate in Japan (–1868).

Jan: **7th**, on the death of Feodore I of Russia, last surviving son of Tsar Ivan the Terrible, Boris Godunov seizes the throne (–1605).

March: **20th**, by the Treaty of Ponts de Cé, the Duke of Mercoeur in Brittany submits to Henry IV, effectively ending the civil war in France.

May: —, By the Peace of Vervins between Henry IV and Philip II, Spain restores Calais, Blavet and all conquests except Cambrai.
—, Philip II assigns the Spanish Netherlands to the Archduke Albert of Austria and the Infanta Isabel, who agree to marry.

Aug: **4th**, the Steelyard, London headquarters of the Hanseatic League, is closed.
14th, the Earl of Tyrone, Irish rebel, annihilates an English force at the Yellow Ford on the Blackwater River. The disaster prompts the appointment of the Earl of Essex as Lord Lieutenant of Ireland in Mar 1599.

Sept: **13th**, Philip III succeeds as King of Spain (–1621) on the death of Philip II.
25th, Charles IX of Sweden defeats Sigismund III at Stangebro.

Politics, Government, Law, and Economy
Poor Law in England and Wales provides the basic structure and patterns of poor relief that is to obtain until 1834 (confirmed with minor modifications in 1601).

Society, Education, and Religion
(15th April) Edict of Nantes issued by Henry IV of France granting toleration to the Huguenots (this is revoked by Louis XIV, Oct 22nd, 1685).

Science, Technology, and Discovery
Tycho Brahe gives an account of his discoveries in *Astronomiae Instauratae Mechanica*.
Lindschoten publishes maps and charts of the Far East.

Humanities and Scholarship
George Chapman translates seven books of the *Iliad*.
The Oxford University Library is refounded and enriched by Sir Thomas Badley (opened, 1602); henceforth known as The Bodleian Library.

Literature
Christopher Marlowe, *Hero and Leander* (poem on the classical story completed after Marlowe's death by George Chapman).
William Shakespeare, *Henry IV*, part I; *Love's Labour's Lost*.

1599
A final Armada is collected in Spain for sending against England, but is scattered by storms and returns to port.
Rosnay, Duke of Sully, is appointed Superintendent of Finances in France.

Sept: **7th**, the Earl of Essex signs a truce with the Irish rebel Tyrone and, 24th, leaves Ireland, arriving at the court at Nonsuch, 28th, where he is arrested.

Dec: —, Henry IV of France obtains a divorce from Queen Margaret of Valois.

Politics, Government, Law, and Economy
James VI of Scotland, *Basilikon Doron*.
Sully creates the office of 'grandvoyer', to begin the reform of the French road system.
Duke of Lerma introduces copper coinage into Spain.

Literature
Mateo Alemán, *Guzmán de Alfarache* (picaresque novel; trans. 1622, as *The Rogue*).
The Globe Theatre, Bankside, Southwark, is built.
(21st Sept) William Shakespeare's *Julius Caesar* is acted.

1600 Ieyasu defeats his rivals in Japan at the Battle of Sekigahara.

June: —, Robert Earl of Essex is tried for misdemeanours in Ireland and sentenced to lose his offices at court.

July: **2nd**, Maurice of Nassau defeats the Archduke Albert's Spanish and Italian troops at the battle of Nieuport.

Aug: **5th**, the Gowrie Conspiracy in Scotland.
6th, Henry IV of France invades Savoy.

Oct: **5th**, Henry IV of France marries Marie de' Medici.

Politics, Government, Law, and Economy
The English East India Company is founded.
Edward Coke, *Law Reports*.

Society, Education, and Religion
(17th Feb) Giordano Bruno burnt for his belief in the plurality of inhabited worlds in Campo di Fiori, Rome (aged 52).

Science, Technology, and Discovery
English physician William Gilbert writes *De magnete*, a pioneer study of electricity and magnetism.

Humanities and Scholarship
Philemon Holland translates Livy's *Roman History*.

Literature
William Shakespeare, *As You Like It*; *Henry IV, part 2*; *Henry V*; *The Merchant of Venice*; *A Midsummer-Night's Dream*; *Much Ado About Nothing*.

Statistics
Approximate populations (in millions): France, 16; German states, etc., 14½; Poland, 11; Spain, 8; Austrian Habsburg dominions, 5½; England and Ireland, 5½; Holland, 3; Portugal, 2; Sweden, 1½; Scotland, 1.

1601 The False Dmitri, claiming to be a son of Tsar Ivan IV, appears in Poland where he wins support for an invasion of Russia.

Jan: —, the capital of Spain is transferred from Madrid to Valladolid.
7th, (–8th) Robert Earl of Essex leads a revolt in London against Queen Elizabeth which is swiftly crushed.
17th, the Treaty of Lyons ends the war in Savoy.

Feb: **19th**, the Earl of Essex is tried for treason and, 25th, executed.

Sept: —, a force of 3,000 Spaniards lands at Kinsale, Ireland, to support the Earl of Tyrone's rebellion (it capitulates to the Earl of Mountjoy in Jan 1602).

Nov: **20th**, Queen Elizabeth's 'Golden Speech' to Parliament.

Humanities and Scholarship
Philemon Holland translates Pliny (the Elder), *Natural History*.

Art, Sculpture, Fine Arts, and Architecture
Caravaggio, *Conversion of St. Paul*.

Music
Thomas Morley, *Triumphs of Oriana*.

Literature
Ben Jonson, *Every Man in His Humour* (comedy).
William Shakespeare, *Twelfth Night*.

1602 A fresh war breaks out between Persia and Turkey (–1627).
Spanish traders arrive in eastern Japan.

April: —, The Counter-Reformation is enforced with repression in the Habsburg lands of Styria, Carinthia and Carniola.

Politics, Government, Law, and Economy
The Dutch East India Company is founded.

Science, Technology, and Discovery
Tycho Brahe's *Astronomia Instauratae Progymnasmata* is published posthumously, giving the plans of 777 fixed stars and a description of the 1572 supernova.

1603 **March:** **24th**, James VI King of Scotland accedes as James I of England and Ireland (–1625) on the death of Queen Elizabeth I.

30th, the Earl of Tyrone, Irish rebel, submits to Lord Mountjoy at Mellifort.

July: —, 'the Main Plot', for the dethronement of James I and the succession of Arabella Stuart, is discovered and, 17th, Sir Walter Raleigh is arrested for suspected complicity.

—, the Imperial Diet at Ratisbon is prorogued by the Archduke Matthias after acrimonious debates between Catholic and Protestant representatives.

Sept: —, Henry IV recalls the Jesuits to France.

Nov: **12th**, Sir Walter Raleigh's trial for high treason at Winchester; he is found guilty and sentenced to imprisonment.

Politics, Government, Law, and Economy

Johannes Althusias, *Politica methodice digesta et exemplis sacris et profanis illustrata.*

Science, Technology, and Discovery

Hieronymus Fabricius of Acquapendente discovers that the veins contain valves.

Literature

Francisco Gomez de Quevedo, *La vida del buscón* (picaresque novel).
William Shakespeare, *Hamlet* (in the 'bad' quarto see 1604).

1604 Protestants in Hungary revolt against the Habsburgs.
Abbas the Great of Persia takes Tabriz from the Turks.
Sir Henry Middleton leads an English East India Company voyage to Java and the Moluccas, while John Mildenhall arrives at Agra, India.

Jan: **21st**, the False Dmitri who has invaded Russia, is defeated by Tsar Boris Godunov.

March: **19th**, the first Parliament of James I meets (–Feb 1611). Parliament opposes the King's plans for a Union with Scotland.

Aug: **18th**, (or 28th) peace is signed between England and Spain and the Archdukes.

Sept: **25th**, Ambrogio de Spinola captures Ostend from the Dutch after a siege of 3½ years.

Politics, Government, Law, and Economy

Oxford and Cambridge Universities are granted Parliamentary representation (revoked 1948).
Samuel de Champlain founds a French settlement at Port Royal in Acadia (later Annapolis Royal, Nova Scotia), the first French colony in North America.
The Cossacks found Tomsk.

Society, Education, and Religion

Conference of English Clergy at Hampton Court Palace, resulting in the decision to prepare an Authorized Version of the Bible (published 1611).

Science, Technology, and Discovery

Sully begins constructing a canal to link the R. Loire with the R. Seine.
Johannes Kepler publishes *Optics*, which describes how the eye focuses light and how the intensity of the light varies with its distance from the source.

Music

Orlando di Lasso, *Magnum Opus Musicum* (posthumous).

Literature

Lope de Vega Carpio, *Comedias* (25 vols; completed 1647).

Everyday Life

James VI and I, *Counterblast to Tobacco.*

1605 The Dutch seize Amboyna, Malaysia.
Hidetada succeeds as Shogun of Japan (–1623) on the retirement of his father, Ieyasu.

April: **13th**, Theodore II succeeds as Tsar of Russia (–June 20th) on the death of his father Boris Godunov.

June: **20th**, the False Dmitri enters Moscow; Tsar Theodore II is assassinated by the boyars.

July: **2nd**, a General Assembly of Presbyterian ministers meets at Aberdeen in defiance of James VI; the leaders are subsequently imprisoned.

Oct: —, Jehangir succeeds as Mogul Emperor of India (–1627) on the death of his father, Akbar.

Nov: **5th**, Gunpowder Plot, to blow up the House of Lords during James I's state opening of Parliament, is discovered.

Politics, Government, Law, and Economy

Santa Fé, New Mexico, is founded.

Humanities and Scholarship
Sir Francis Bacon, *The Advancement of Learning.*

Music
John Dowland, *Lachrymae, or Seaven Teares, in Seaven Passionate Pavans.*

Literature
Miguel de Cervantes Saavedra, *Don Quixote*, part 1 (part 2, 1615).
William Shakespeare, *Macbeth.*

1606 Episcopacy is restored in Scotland by Act of the Scottish Parliament.

Jan: 27th, trial of Guy Fawkes and his fellow conspirators; executed, Jan 31st.

April: —, the Habsburg archdukes rebel against the Emperor Rudolf II and recognize the Archduke Matthias as leader (see June 1608).

May: 17th, the False Dmitri murdered in Russia by Basil Shuisky.

Nov: 11th, treaty of peace is signed at Zsitva-Torok between the Turks and the Austrians; the House of Habsburg ceases paying tribute for the Habsburg part of Hungary.

Science, Technology, and Discovery
The Spanish navigator Torres sails between New Guinea and Australia.

Humanities and Scholarship
Joseph Scaliger, *Thesaurus Temporum* (a chronology of the ancient world).

1607 **May: 13th**, foundation of Jamestown, Virginia, as an English colony under the leadership of Captain John Smith.

Aug: —, The Bank of Genoa fails, following national bankruptcy in Spain.

Sept: 14th, the 'Flight of the Earls' when Hugh O'Neill, Earl of Tyrone, and Rory O'Donnell, Earl of Tyrconnel, flee from Ireland for Spain.

Music
Claudio Monteverdi, *Orfeo.*

Literature
Ben Jonson, *Volpone, or The Fox* (comedy).
Cyril Tourneur, *The Revenger's Tragedy.*
Honoré D'Urfé, *Astrée*, part 1 (pastoral romance, completed 1627 by Baro).

1608 **April: 18th**, Cahir O'Dogherty of Tyrone raises rebellion in Ulster.
27th, Protestants break up the Diet of Ratisbon, denying the right of the Catholic majority to bind the minority.

May: 12th, a Protestant Union of German princes opposing the Catholic *bloc* is formed.
20th, O'Dogherty's rebellion in Ulster collapses (he is slain July 20th).

June: 25th, the Emperor Rudolf II is compelled by the Archdukes to cede Austria, Hungary and Moravia to his brother Matthias and to promise him the succession to Bohemia.

Politics, Government, Law, and Economy
Captain John Smith, *A True Relation of Virginia.*
(July) Samuel de Champlain founds a French settlement at Quebec.

Science, Technology, and Discovery
Galileo invents the microscope.

Art, Sculpture, Fine Arts, and Architecture
El Greco, *Golgotha*; *View of Toledo*; *Assumption of the Virgin Mary* (–1613).

Literature
Thomas Middleton, *A Mad World my Masters* (satirical comedy).
William Shakespeare, *King Lear*; *Coriolanus.*

1609 The Jesuits, given complete control of the Indian missions by Philip III of Spain, establish their first mission at San Ignacio Guazu in Paraguay.

Feb: —, Charles IX of Sweden signs an alliance at Viborg to aid Tsar Basil Shuisky of Russia against Sigismund III of Poland, who advances to Smolensk.

April: 9th, Spain signs a nine years' truce with Holland, which implies the virtual independence of the seven United Provinces.

July: 10th, a Catholic League of German princes is formed at Munich under Maximilian, Duke of Bavaria, in opposition to the Protestant Union (of May 1608).

Sept: 22nd, the Duke of Zerma expels 500,000 Moors and Moriscoes from Spain.

Society, Education, and Religion
St. Francis de Sales, *Introduction à la vie dévote* (revised 1619).

Science, Technology, and Discovery
Johann Kepler, *De Motibus Stellae Martis.*

Humanities and Scholarship
G de la Vega, *History of the Conquest of Peru* (–1617).

Art, Sculpture, Fine Arts, and Architecture
Rubens, *The Artist and his first wife, Isabella Brant.*

Everyday Life
Tea from China is first shipped to Europe by the Dutch East India Company.

1610

Feb: **12th**, Henry IV of France signs an alliance with the German Protestant Union (of 1608).

May: **14th**, François Ravaillac, a fanatic, assassinates Henry IV of France, who is succeeded by Louis XIII, then aged 9 (–1643), with Marie de' Medici, the Queen Mother, as Regent (–1617).

July: **19th**, Basil Shuisky, Tsar of Russia, is deposed, after a Swedish army under Jacob de la Gardie, sent against the Polish invaders of Russia, is forced to surrender.

Science, Technology, and Discovery
Jean Beguin publishes *Tyrocinium Chymicum*, the first textbook on chemistry rather than alchemy.
(7th Jan) Galileo observes Jupiter's satellites.
(3rd Aug) Henry Hudson discover Hudson's Bay.

Literature
Ben Jonson, *The Alchemist* (comedy).
William Shakespeare, *Cymbeline*; *A Winter's Tale*; *The Tempest.*

1611

Sir Thomas Sherley arrives in England as ambassador from the Shah of Persia.

Jan: **26th**, the Duke of Sully resigns as French Superintendent of Finances.

April: **4th**, Christian IV of Denmark declares war on Sweden – the War of Kalmar (–Jan 1613).
13th, proclamation for English 'undertakers' for the plantation of Ulster to assemble at Dublin.

May: **23rd**, Matthias is crowned King of Bohemia (the Emperor Rudolf does not formally resign the crown until 11th Aug).

Oct: **30th**, Charles IX of Sweden dies.

Dec: **—**, The Swedish estates meet at Nyköping to elect Gustavus II (Gustavus Adolphus) king (–1632).

Politics, Government, Law, and Economy
First English settlement on the east coast of India, at Masulipatam, Madras.

Society, Education, and Religion
The Authorised Version of the Holy Bible.

Science, Technology, and Discovery
Thomas Harriott, Johannes Fabricius, Father Scheiner, and Galileo discover sunspots around the same time.
Simon Sturtevant patents the use of mineral coal for smelting iron, but his process is not adopted for many years.

Art, Sculpture, Fine Arts, and Architecture
Rubens, *Descent from the Cross* (–1614).

Music
Gibbons, William Byrd and John Bull, *Parthenia* (anthology of music for virginals).

Literature
Thomas Coryate, *Crudities.*
Thomas Middleton, *The Roaring Girl* (comedy).

1612

Dutch first use Manhattan Island as a centre for the fur trade.
Earliest colonization of the Bermudas from Virginia, under Sir George Somers.

Jan: **20th**, Matthias, King of Bohemia succeeds as Holy Roman Emperor (–1619) on the death of Rudolf II (formal election in June).

July: **—**, Trial of the witches in Pendle, Lancashire (–Aug).

Nov: **5th**, Henry, Prince of Wales, 'the Hope of Protestantism', dies.

Politics, Government, Law, and Economy
Tobacco is first planted in Virginia.

Society, Education, and Religion
Bartholomew Legate of London and Edward Wightman of Lichfield are the last persons to be burnt for their religious opinions in England.

Science, Technology, and Discovery
Bartholomew Pitiscus first uses a decimal point in his trigonometrical tables.

Humanities and Scholarship
Jakob Boehme, *Aurora; oder, Morgenröte im Aufgang* (mystical philosophy condemned by the Lutherans).

Music
Orlando Gibbons, *First set of Madrigals and Motets of five parts, apt for Viols and Voices.*

Literature
John Webster, *The White Devil* (tragedy).

1613 **Jan: 20th**, the Peace of Knärod, mediated by James I of England, ends the War of Kalmar between Denmark and Sweden.

Feb: 14th, Elizabeth, daughter of James I, marries Frederick V of the Palatinate.

Aug: 13th, the German Diet meets at Ratisbon. The Catholic and Protestant princes are in deadlock on the religious issue.

Sept: —, the Turks invade Hungary.

Politics, Government, Law, and Economy
Copper coins are introduced to England.

Science, Technology, and Discovery
Hugh Myddelton constructs the 'New River' cut to bring water to London.

Music
Claudio Monteverdi is appointed maestro di capello at St. Mark's, Venice.

Literature
Francis Beaumont and John Fletcher, *The Knight of the Burning Pestle.*
Don Luis de Góngora y Argote, *Soledades* (–1614).
Lope de Vega, *Fuenteovejuna.*
The Globe Theatre, Southwark, London, destroyed by fire (see 1599).

1614 **Feb: 19th**, (–May) the Prince of Condé, supported by the Dukes of Nevers, Mayenne and Longueville, rebels, plunging France into civil war.

April: 5th, James I's second Parliament ('The Addled Parliament') meets (–7th June).

May: 15th, French Civil War ends with the Peace of St. Menehould.

June: 7th, James I dissolves Parliament; not a single Act is passed. The King subsequently imprisons four members of the Commons who had opposed the Crown.

Oct: —, the French States-General assemble at Paris (–Mar 1615).
—, The Third Estate attacks the *Taille* and the sale of offices and demands a declaration that no person can depose the King.

Science, Technology, and Discovery
John Napier devises his logarithmic tables (*Mirifici Logarithmorum Canonis Descriptio*).

Humanities and Scholarship
George Chapman translates Homer's *Odyssey*, books 1–12 (completed 1615).
Sir Walter Raleigh, *The History of the World.*

Music
Girolamo Frescobaldi, *Toccate di Cembalo.*

Literature
Ben Jonson, *Bartholomew Fayer* (comedy) acted (published 1631).
Sir Thomas Overbury, *Characters.*

1615 English fleet defeats the Portuguese off the coast of Bombay.
The Dutch seize the Moluccas from the Portuguese.

Jan: —, Sir Thomas Roe is sent from England on an embassy to the Mogul of India (he arrives in Sept).

Aug: 9th, Second Civil War in France (–May 1616), in which the Prince of Condé is in league with the Huguenots, led by Henry Duke of Rohan.

Nov: 9th, exchange of Bourbon and Habsburg brides at Burgos after proxy marriages of Louis XIII to Anne of Austria and of Philip of Asturias to Elizabeth of Bourbon.

Politics, Government, Law, and Economy
Montchrestien, *Traité de l'Économie Politique*, expounds mercantilist principles.

Art, Sculpture, Fine Arts, and Architecture
Salomon de Brosse, Palais de Luxembourg, Paris (–1624).

Literature
Miguel de Cervantes Saavedra, *Don Quixote*, part 2 (part 1, 1605).

1616 The Tartars of Manchu invade China (–1620).

Jan: 3rd, Sir George Villiers, James I's new favourite, is appointed Master of the Horse; he becomes Earl of Buckingham Jan 1617.

March: 20th, as a result of Villiers' intervention with James I, Sir Walter Raleigh is released from the Tower to search for gold in Guiana (he sails 1617).

July: —, To improve his serious financial position James I begins to sell peerages.

Sept: 1st, the Prince of Condé is arrested at the Louvre and imprisoned in the Bastille.

Oct: —, Catholic oppression in Bohemia is intensified and rouses national sentiment against the Emperor Matthias.

Nov: 1st, James I removes Sir Edward Coke, Chief Justice of the Common Pleas, for refusing to suspend an action in which the Crown is an interested party.
20th, Richelieu, in France, becomes Minister of State for foreign affairs and war.

Politics, Government, Law, and Economy
John Smith, *A Description of New England.*

Society, Education, and Religion
St. Francis de Sales, *On the Love of God.*

Science, Technology, and Discovery
Galileo is threatened by the severest penalties of the Inquisition unless he agrees not to teach the Copernican system.
William Baffin discovers Baffin Bay in his search for a North West Passage.

Humanities and Scholarship
Johann Valentin Andraea, *Chymische Hochzeit Christiani Rosenkreutz.*

Art, Sculpture, Fine Arts, and Architecture
Inigo Jones, Queen's House, Greenwich (–1618).

1617 The Dutch purchase the island of Goree, off Cape Verde, from the natives.

Feb: 27th, the Peace of Stolbovo is signed between Russia and Sweden. Poland remains at war with Sweden (–Nov 1618)

April: 24th, Concino Concini, Marquis d'Ancre, is assassinated by order of Louis XIII. Charles d'Albret, Duke of Luynes, favourite of Louis XIII, takes charge of the government of France (–1621).

June: 29th, the Archduke Ferdinand of Styria, cousin and imperial heir of the Emperor Matthias, is recognized by the Bohemian Estates as heir to the Bohemian throne.

July: 9th, Maurice of Nassau declares himself the champion of the Contra-Remonstrants in Holland, in opposition to Johan van Oldenbarneveldt.

Politics, Government, Law, and Economy
Francis Bacon is appointed Lord Keeper of the Great Seal of England (elevated to the Lord Chancellorship 1618).

Science, Technology, and Discovery
Willibrord Snell establishes the technique of trigonometrical triangulation for cartography.

1618 **April: —**, Richelieu is ordered into exile in Avignon for intriguing with the Queen Mother of France, Marie de' Medici.

May: —, Count Thurn leads the Bohemians to revolt against the Regents in Prague.
23rd, the Defenestration of Prague, when the Regents, Martinitz and Slawata, are overthrown by the Bohemian rebels, begins the Thirty Years War (–Oct 1648).

June: —, Count Mansfeld is sent to assist the rebels by the Protestant Union.

July: 1st, Ferdinand of Styria is crowned King of Hungary.

Aug: —, on the death of Albert II, Duke of Prussia, without heirs, his possessions pass to the electorate of Brandenburg, though remaining under Polish suzerainty.
23rd, Johan van Oldenbarneveldt, Advocate of Holland, is arrested on a charge of treason.

27th, James VI's five Articles of Religion, for introducing Anglican principles into the Church of Scotland, are approved by the General Assembly of that Church.

Oct: 29th, Sir Walter Raleigh is executed.

Dec: 24th, Poland signs a two-year truce with Sweden (afterwards extended to July 1621).

Society, Education, and Religion

Catherine de Vivonne, Marquise de Rambouillet, starts a literary *salon* as a centre of wit and letters in her Hotel Rambouillet, Paris (–1650).

Sport and Recreation

King James issues the 'Book of Sports' permitting a variety of popular sports to be played, which provokes Puritan objections.

1619 The first Africans in North America arrive in Virginia, as indentured servants.

March: 20th, Emperor Matthias dies; the Archduke Ferdinand assumes the crown of Bohemia.

May: 13th, the execution of Oldenbarneveldt at the Hague, regarded by some as judicial murder, leaves Maurice Prince of Orange supreme in Holland.

July: 30th, a representative colonial assembly – the first in America – is held at Jamestown, Virginia, under the new governor of the colony, Sir George Yeardley.

Aug: 26th, the Bohemian Diet elects Frederick V, the Elector Palatine, King of Bohemia.
28th, Ferdinand II is elected Holy Roman Emperor (–1637).

Sept: —, The Treaty of Angouléme ends the dispute between Louis XIII and the Queen Mother, Marie de' Medici.

Nov: —, Frederick V of the Palatinate is crowned King of Bohemia in Prague.

Politics, Government, Law, and Economy

Jan Pieters Coen founds Batavia.

Science, Technology, and Discovery

Johannes Kepler publishes *Harmonia Mundi* which contains his third planetary law.
English physician William Harvey announces his discovery of the circulation of the blood.

Art, Sculpture, Fine Arts, and Architecture

Inigo Jones, Banqueting House, Whitehall (–1622).

1620 **April: 27th** (or 8th May), secret treaty between England and Spain for Charles, Prince of Wales, to marry the Infanta Maria of Spain.

June: —, War between Sweden and Poland is resumed.
19th, the Protestants in the Valtelline are massacred.

July: 3rd, the Catholic League and the Protestant Union sign an agreement at Ulm.

Aug: —, Richelieu negotiates peace in France between the rebellious nobles and the Crown. Marie de' Medici, the Queen Mother, is reconciled to her son.

Sept: 6th (or 16th), the Pilgrim Fathers, members of a Separatist Congregation, leave Plymouth in the *Mayflower* for North America.

Nov: 8th, the Catholic League under Count Tilly defeats the army of Frederick of Bohemia, led by Christian of Anhalt, at the Battle of the White Mountain, near Prague. The Bohemian revolt against Emperor Ferdinand II is suppressed.

Dec: 26th, the Pilgrim Fathers land at New Plymouth, Massachusetts, to found Plymouth Colony, with John Carver as Governor.

Art, Sculpture, Fine Arts, and Architecture

Rubens, *Chapeau de Paille.*
Gianlorenzo Bernini, *Neptune and Triton.*

Literature

Jacob Cats, *Selfsrijt.*

1621 The Scots settle at Acadia (Nova Scotia, 1632).

Feb: —, the Huguenot Assembly at La Rochelle declares for rebellion against Louis XIII.

April: —, the Protestant Union in Germany is dissolved.
19th, charges are drawn up in Parliament against Francis Bacon, Lord Verulam, the Lord Chancellor, for corruption; he is imprisoned in May, but then pardoned by James I in Nov.
23rd, William Bradford becomes Governor of Plymouth Colony, on the death from sunstroke of John Carver.

May: 31st, accession of Philip IV of Spain (–1665) on the death of Philip III.

Aug: —, The Twelve Years Truce (of April 1609) between the United Provinces and Spain comes to an end and war is resumed.

Oct: —, Sir Francis Wyatt, the new Governor, arrives in Virginia with fresh regulations for the administration of the colony by a governor, council of state and an elected assembly.

Politics, Government, Law, and Economy

(3rd June) The Dutch West India Company is chartered.

Science, Technology, and Discovery

Cornelius Vermuyden begins to drain the Fens.

Humanities and Scholarship

Robert Burton, *Anatomy of Melancholy.*

Pietro della Valle visits Persepolis and sends to Europe the first cuneiform signs.

Media

(24th Sept) *Corante; or newes from Italy, Germany, Hungarie, Spaine and France* is issued in London, the first periodical publication with news.

1622 An English force captures Ormuz from the Portuguese.

Jan: —, Richelieu is recalled to the Council of Louis XIII; he becomes a cardinal, 5th Sept.

—, James I places John Pym, the Parliamentary leader, under house arrest for criticism of royal policy in the recent Parliamentary session.

1st, the Papal Chancery adopts 1st Jan as the beginning of the New Year (instead of 25th Mar).

June: —, Sigismund of Poland makes an armistice with Gustavus II of Sweden.

—, Count Tilly defeats Christian of Brunswick, brother of the Duke, at the battle of Höchst, effectively ending the conquest of the Palatinate and Frederick V.

Aug: —, Count Olivares becomes Chief Minister in Spain (–1643).

Oct: **18th**, the Treaty of Montpellier ends the rebellion of the Huguenots. The Edict of Nantes (of 1598) is confirmed.

Politics, Government, Law, and Economy

First turnpike act in England, for the road between Biggleswade and Baldock.

(9th March) James VI and I grants land in New Hampshire to John Mason.

Science, Technology, and Discovery

Francis Bacon, *Historia Naturalis et Experimentalis.*

Humanities and Scholarship

Jacob Boehme, *De signatura rerum.*

Art, Sculpture, Fine Arts, and Architecture

Rubens, *The Medici Cycle of Paintings*; and paintings for the Luxembourg Palais, Paris (–1625).

Media

(23rd May) *Weekeley Newes* ... printed by Nicholas Bourne and Thomas Archer is issued in London.

1623 **Feb:** —, Dutch massacre English colonists at Amboyna.

25th, Maximilian Duke of Bavaria is granted the Upper Palatinate.

Aug: **30th**, Prince Charles and the Duke of Buckingham leave Madrid in disgust at the breakdown of negotiations over the prince's betrothal to the Infanta.

Dec: —, James I finally breaks off the Spanish marriage treaty.

Politics, Government, Law, and Economy

First English settlement at New Hampshire, by David Thomas.

(June) New Netherlands in America is formally organized as a province.

Humanities and Scholarship

Tommaso Campanella, *La Città de Sole* (*The City of the Sun*) (an Italian Utopia).

Art, Sculpture, Fine Arts, and Architecture

Guido Reni, *Baptism of Christ.*

Literature

Jacob Cats, and others, *De Zeewsche Nachtegaal.*

William Drummond, *Flowers of Sion.*

John Webster, *The Duchess of Malfi* (tragedy); *The Devil's Law Case* (tragi-comedy).

1624 The first English settlement is made in East India.

Dutch settle in New Amsterdam.

Jan: **31st**, Count Mansfeld leaves Dover with 12,000 men to aid the Elector Palatine, Frederick V; the expedition is a failure.

March: **10th**, England declares war on Spain.

June: **24th**, dissolution of the Virginia Company; Virginia becomes a Crown colony.

Aug: **13th**, Louis XIII appoints Cardinal Richelieu as First Minister of France (–1642).

Science, Technology, and Discovery
Antonio de Andrade leaves the Jesuit mission at Agra to explore beyond the Himalayas and Tibet.

Art, Sculpture, Fine Arts, and Architecture
Frans Hals, *The Laughing Cavalier.*
Nicolas Poussin, *Rape of the Sabine Women.*
Bernini, Baldacchino, St. Peter's, Rome.

Music
Claudio Monteverdi, *Combattimento di Tancredie Clorinda.*

Literature
Thomas Middleton's satirical comedy, *A Game at Chess* (–1625).

1625 **March:** **27th**, accession of Charles I of England and Scotland (–1649) on the death of James I (James VI of Scotland).

April: **7th**, Wallenstein is appointed General of the Imperial Forces by Ferdinand II.
23rd, Frederick Henry succeeds as Stadtholder of Holland on the death of Maurice of Nassau.

June: **—**, Ambrogio de Spinola takes Breda from the Dutch after a siege of 11 months.
13th, Charles I marries Henrietta Maria, daughter of Henri IV.

Politics, Government, Law, and Economy
Hugo Grotius, *De jure belli et pacis.*
First English settlement on Barbados is made under Sir William Courteen.

Society, Education, and Religion
Vincent de Paul founds in Paris a sisterhood of charity: the Order of Sisters of Mercy.

Art, Sculpture, Fine Arts, and Architecture
Inigo Jones, Covent Garden Church and Square, Westminister.

Music
Heinrich Schütz, *Cantiones Sacrae.*

1626 **Jan:** **—**, Charles I, in need of revenue, requires all Englishmen with property over £40 a year to undertake the dignity of Knighthood, with fines for exemptions.

April: **25th**, Wallenstein defeats Count Mansfeld at the Bridge of Dessau, proceeds to occupy Pomerania and pursues Mansfeld through Silesia to Hungary.

July: **—**, The Ordinance of Nantes requires all castles and fortresses to be dismantled in France.

Aug: **27th**, Tilly defeats Christian IV of Denmark at Lutter in the Harz mountains. North Germany is placed at the mercy of the Catholic League.

Dec: **20th**, the Emperor Ferdinand II is forced to sign the Treaty of Pressburg with Gabor Bethlen of Transylvania, who is threatening Vienna.

Politics, Government, Law, and Economy
Cardinal Richelieu declares the publication of works against religion or the state a capital offence.

Society, Education, and Religion
Louis XIII publishes an edict condemning to death anyone who kills his adversary in a duel.
Congregation of Priests of the Mission founded by Vincent de Paul.

Science, Technology, and Discovery
Jardin des Plantes, Paris, is established.

Humanities and Scholarship
William Roper, *The Life of Sir Thomas More* (posthumous).

Art, Sculpture, Fine Arts, and Architecture
Jacques Le Mercier, Le Sorbonne, Paris.

1627 Korea becomes a tributary state of China.

March: **—**, Huguenots again rise, fearing their freedom of worship will be further curtailed.

June: **—**, the Duke of Buckingham sails from Portsmouth with a fleet to aid the Huguenots in the defence of La Rochelle; he returns defeated, 12th Oct.

Oct: **—**, Christian IV withdraws to Denmark, in the face of the advance of Tilly and Wallenstein, who by the end of the month subdue Holstein, Schleswig and Jutland.

Science, Technology, and Discovery
Johannes Kepler, employed by Rudoph II, complies the 'Rudolphine Tables', giving the places of 1,005 fixed stars.

Literature
Francisco Gomez de Quevedo, *Los Sueños.*

1628 The Dutch seize the Spanish treasure fleet and also occupy Java and Malucca.
Shah Jahan becomes Mogul Emperor of India (–1658).

April: —, Sweden and Denmark sign a treaty for the defence of Stralsund against Wallenstein, which brings Gustavus II into the Thirty Years War.

June: **7th**, Charles I is forced to accept the Petition of Right which declares arbitrary imprisonment, martial law, forced loans and the billeting of troops illegal.

Aug: —, Wallenstein raises the siege of Stralsund (begun in May), his first reverse.
23rd, the Duke of Buckingham, about to embark at Portsmouth with a further expedition to La Rochelle, is assassinated by John Felton.

Sept: **28th**, John Endecott leads an English party of colonists to settle at Salem, Massachusetts, later Massachusetts Bay Colony.

Oct: **28th**, La Rochelle capitulates to the French Crown.

Society, Education, and Religion
Gregory XV canonizes Ignatius Loyola.

1629 **March:** **2nd**, the House of Commons passes resolutions, proposed by Sir John Eliot, against innovators in religion and against tonnage and poundage. Charles I dissolves Parliament the same day (Parliament does not meet again until Apr 1640).
5th, Sir John Eliot and eight other M.P.s are imprisoned.
29th, Edict of Restitution of Church property in Germany, for all property secularized since the Peace of Augsburg, 1555, to be restored to the Catholic Church. The Edict is rigorously enforced by Wallenstein and the Catholic League.

April: —, (–June) last rising of French Huguenots under Rohan, aided by Spain.

Politics, Government, Law, and Economy
Cardinal Richelieu forms the Company of New France for the monopoly of trade in Canada.

Society, Education, and Religion
Lancelot Andrewes, *Sermons*, edited by W Laud and J Buckeridge.

Art, Sculpture, Fine Arts, and Architecture
Velazquez, *Los Borrochos.*

1630 **July:** **6th**, Gustavus II lands in Pomerania and marches his army into Germany.

Aug: **13th**, Ferdinand II dismisses Wallenstein. Count Tilly assumes command of his army. The Emperor is no longer able to dictate to the Catholic League.

Nov: **10th**, in the 'Day of Dupes', Cardinal Richelieu overthrows the conspiracy of Marie de' Medici and Gaston of Orléans against him.

Politics, Government, Law, and Economy
(April) John Winthrop sails with the Plymouth Company's expedition to settle in Massachusetts Bay. Boston, Mass., is laid out (17th Sept).

Art, Sculpture, Fine Arts, and Architecture
Georges de la Tour, *Magdalene with the Lamp.*
Rubens, *Blessings of Peace.*

Literature
François de Malherbe, *Oeuvres poétiques*
Tirso de Molina, *El Burlador de Sevilla y convidado de Piedra* introduces the story of Don Juan to literature.

1631 **Feb:** **20th**, (–12th Apr) the German Protestant Princes hold a Convention at Leipzig and decide to form an alliance with Gustavus II.

April: **3rd**, (or 13th) Gustavus II takes Frankfort-on-Oder, displaying great brutality.

May: **20th**, Count Tilly's imperialist army sacks Magdeburg; terrible carnage ensues and the city catches fire, leaving only the cathedral standing.

July: —, Pope Urban VIII annexes Urbino.

Sept: **17th**, Gustavus II, supported by the Saxons under Arnim, defeats Count Tilly at the battle of Breitenfeld, near Leipzig.

Politics, Government, Law, and Economy
The Dutch West India Company makes a settlement on the Delaware River.

Humanities and Scholarship

John Stow, *The Annals of England*, complete edition by E Howes.

Media

(May) Théophraste Renaudot establishes the *Gazette* in Paris (from 1752 it takes the title *Gazette de France*).

1632 The Scottish settlement at Acadia (Nova Scotia) fails.

April: —, Charles I issues a charter for the colony of Maryland, under the control of Lord Baltimore, a Roman Catholic.

13th, Ferdinand II formally reinstates Wallenstein as Supreme Imperial Commander with an army of 50,000 men.

14th, Gustavus II defeats Count Tilly's imperialist army at the Lech, near the confluence of the Rivers Lenz and Danube. Tilly is mortally wounded (dies, 30th).

Nov: 6th (or 16th), Gustavus II, supported by Arnim's Saxon troops, defeats Wallenstein at the battle of Lützen, but is killed in action.

6th (or 16th), accession of Queen Christina of Sweden (–1654).

Society, Education, and Religion

John Donne, *Death's Duell* (his last sermon).

Science, Technology, and Discovery

Galileo publishes *Dialogo sopra i due massimi sistemi del mondo/Dialogue concerning the two chief world systems*.

The Botanic Gardens, Oxford, are established.

Humanities and Scholarship

Famianus Strada writes *De bello belgico* at the request of Alessandro Farnese.

Art, Sculpture, Fine Arts, and Architecture

Rembrandt, *The Anatomy Lesson of Dr. Tulp*.

Music

Claudio Monteverdi, Great Mass, to mark the end of the plague in Venice.

1633 Trial of the Lancashire witches.

An English trading post is founded in Bengal.

June: 18th, Charles I is crowned King of Scotland at Edinburgh. He orders the Scottish Parliament to prepare a liturgy on Anglican lines.

Aug: 6th, William Laud is elected Archbishop of Canterbury (–1645).

Oct: 18th, Charles I reissues his father's 'Book of Sports' which may be indulged in on Sundays, angering the Puritans.

Nov: —, the Infanta Isabella dies in Brussels; henceforth the Spanish Netherlands are governed direct from Spain. A rising in Brussels is easily suppressed.

Politics, Government, Law, and Economy

The Dutch settle in Connecticut.

Society, Education, and Religion

William Prynne, *Histriomastix: the Players Scourge or Actors Tragedie* (for which the author was fined £5,000, pilloried and mutilated).

Francis Quarles, *Divine Poems*.

Science, Technology, and Discovery

(20th Sept) Galileo is condemned by the Inquisition at Liège and forced to retract his Copernican views.

Art, Sculpture, Fine Arts, and Architecture

Jacques Callot, *Les Grandes Misères de la Guerre*;

Jacques Le Mercier, Palais Cardinal (now Palais Royal), Paris.

Literature

John Donne, *Poems* (posthumous).

John Ford, *The Broken Heart* (tragedy); *'Tis Pity She's a Whore* (tragedy).

George Herbert, *The Temple; or Sacred Poems* (posthumous).

Philip Massinger, *A New Way to Pay Old Debts* (comedy).

1634 Cardinal Richelieu reforms the office of Intendant to centralize French administration.

Jan: 24th, the Emperor Ferdinand II secretly deprives Wallenstein of his command for a second time, and declares him a traitor.

Feb: 25th, Wallenstein is murdered by his own officers.

Sept: 5th (–6th), the Swedes under Bernhard of Saxe-Weimar are defeated by the imperial general Matthias Gallas at the battle of Nördlingen; 17,000 Swedes are slain.

Oct: **20th**, Charles I issues first writs for the collection of Ship Money from London and the ports, ostensibly to provide a fleet for the protection of merchant shipping.

Politics, Government, Law, and Economy

An English settlement is made at Cochin, Malabar (–1663).

Literature

The Oberammergau Passion Play is inaugurated (see 1662).

1635 The colonization of Connecticut begins.

The French occupy Martinique and Guadeloupe.

The Dutch take Pernambuco from the Portuguese and occupy Formosa.

May: **19th**, France declares war on Spain and sends armies against the Spanish Netherlands and against Franche-Comté.

30th, the Peace of Prague is signed between the Emperor Ferdinand II and the Elector John George of Saxony. The treaty is subsequently accepted by Brandenburg and most Lutheran states.

Politics, Government, Law, and Economy

Charles I extends the incidence of Ship Money from coastal towns to the entire realm.

Society, Education, and Religion

(10th Feb) Académie Française is founded in Paris.

Humanities and Scholarship

The discovery of the tomb of the Merovingian king, Childeric, in the Spanish Netherlands starts an interest in archaeology.

Art, Sculpture, Fine Arts, and Architecture

Philippe de Champaigne, portrait of Cardinal Richelieu.

Rubens, ceiling of Banqueting Hall, Whitehall; and *Infanta Isabella.*

Velazquez, *Surrender of Breda.*

François Mansart, Château Blois (–1638).

Literature

Pedro Calderón de la Barca, *La Vida es sueño.*

Everyday Life

The sale of tobacco in France is limited to apothecaries, who may supply only on a doctor's prescription.

1636 Ceylon is settled by the Dutch.

The Manchus proclaim the Ch'ing dynasty at Mukden.

July: **—**, Prince Octavio Piccolomini invades France with a Spanish army and reaches as far as Corbie before he is repulsed. His advance creates alarm in Paris.

Oct: **9th**, Charles I issues the third writs for the collection of Ship Money. Payment is subsequently refused by Lord Saye and John Hampden.

Politics, Government, Law, and Economy

(June) Roger Williams and other refugees from Massachusetts settle at Providence, Rhode Island. Dutch colonists settle in Brooklyn by the shore of Gowanns Bay.

Society, Education, and Religion

Harvard College (so called from 1639) is founded at Newe Towne, Cambridge, Mass.

Art, Sculpture, Fine Arts, and Architecture

Van Dyck, *Charles I on Horseback.*

Rembrandt, *Danae*; and *Portrait of an 83-year-old Woman.*

Literature

Pedro Calderón de la Barca, *Comedias*, vol. 1.

Pierre Corneille, *Le Cid* (tragedy).

The Italian Fedeli Company play *Harlequin*: pantomime, at the French court.

1637 English traders establish a factory at Canton.

French traders from Dieppe found a settlement at St. Louis at the mouth of the Senegal River.

Feb: **15th**, Ferdinand III succeeds as Holy Roman Emperor (–1657) on the death of Ferdinand II.

July: **23rd**, Jenny Geddes leads a riot when the new Laudian Prayer Book is first used in St. Giles' Cathedral, Edinburgh.

Politics, Government, Law, and Economy

(June) Prynne, Burton and Bastwick are condemned in the Court of Star Chamber for seditious writings (14th June) and are sentenced to be pilloried and mutilated (30th June).

(11th June) Ten of the 12 judges to whom Charles I referred the legality of Ship Money give judgment for the Crown, but John Hampden still refuses to pay his levy.

Humanities and Scholarship
René Descartes, *Discours de la méthode.*
Literature
John Milton, *A Masque* (that is, *Comus*), presented at Ludlow Castle, 1634.

1638 Murad IV of Turkey recovers Baghdad from Shah Abbas I of Persia.
Feb: 19th, Charles I's proclamation, defending the Scottish Prayer Book, is tantamount to a declaration of war.
March: 1st, the Scottish National Covenant is signed by the clergy of Edinburgh, and, 2nd, by the people, and is circulated throughout the northern Kingdom for signatures.
Nov: 21st, the General Assembly of the Church of Scotland meets at Glasgow.
28th, The Assembly of the Church of Scotland continues to sit until Dec 20th, and abolishes episcopacy.
Dec: —, Père Joseph (François du Tremblay), Richelieu's secret agent, dies.
17th, Bernhard of Saxe-Weimar takes Breisach, the key to Alsace. The fall of Breisach is a turning-point in the struggle between Bourbon and Habsburg.
Society, Education, and Religion
Mrs Anne Hutchinson, leader of the New England Antinomians, is banished from Boston, Mass, and sets up a community among the Indians of Rhode Island.
Science, Technology, and Discovery
Galileo investigates the motion of falling bodies and publishes *Discorsi e Dimostrazioni Matematiche.*
Art, Sculpture, Fine Arts, and Architecture
Nicolas Poussin, *Et in Arcadia Ego.*
Literature
John Milton, *Lycidas.*

1639 **March: —**, The Scottish Covenanters take Edinburgh and other principal towns.
June: 18th, since Charles I dare not give battle against the superior Scottish army, he signs the Pacification of Berwick to end the war and returns to London.
Sept: 22nd, Thomas Lord Wentworth arrives in London from Ireland and becomes Charles I's principal adviser.
Oct: 11th, (or 21st) the Dutch fleet, under Van Tromp defeats the Spanish fleet, carrying troops for Flanders, that had taken refuge in the Downs.
31st, the Scottish Parliament is dissolved.
Science, Technology, and Discovery
Quinine is increasingly used for medicinal purposes following the cure of the Countess of Chinchou in Peru.
(24th Nov) Jeremiah Horrocks observes the transit of Venus, as he had predicted. He is the first person to have observed the transit.
Humanities and Scholarship
(7th Feb) Académie Française begins the Dictionary of the French Language (see 1694).
Art, Sculpture, Fine Arts, and Architecture
Rubens, *Judgment of Paris*; and *Self-Portrait with a Sword.*
Media
First printing press in North America operates at Cambridge, Mass.

1640 Foundation of Fort St. George in Bengal.
April: 13th (–5th May), Short Parliament, Charles I's fourth, meets but is dissolved when it refuses to vote money and attacks Charles's Church policy.
May: 12th, revolts break out in Barcelona and spread throughout Catalonia.
Aug: 20th, Scots cross the Tweed into England in the Second Bishops' War.
30th, Scots enter Newcastle.
Nov: 3rd, the Long Parliament meets (–20th Apr, 1653).
11th, John Pym leads attack on Thomas Wentworth, Earl of Strafford, who is subsequently impeached and sent to the Tower of London.
Dec: —, Elector George William of Brandenburg dies and is succeeded by Frederick William ('the Great Elector' – 1688).
1st, revolt in Portugal which becomes independent under John IV of the Braganzas.
7th, Commons proclaim Ship Money to be an illegal tax.
11th, 'Root and Branch' petition to abolish Episcopacy.
18th, Archbishop Laud is impeached.

Politics, Government, Law, and Economy
[John Selden], *De jure Naturali et Gentium*, a discourse on the powers of the peers and the commons.

Society, Education, and Religion
John Eliot, *Bay Psalm Book*; the oldest surviving book printed in North America.
Cornelius Jansen, *Augustinus* (posthumous), 4 vols.

Humanities and Scholarship
Edward Dacres translates *The Prince* of Machiavelli (first published 1532).

Art, Sculpture, Fine Arts, and Architecture
Rembrandt, *Self-portrait at the age of 34.*

Literature
Thomas Carew, *Poems.*
Izaak Walton, *The Life of Donne.*

1641
Body of Liberties codifying 100 laws is set up by General Court of Massachusetts Bay Company.

Jan: —, Portuguese finally surrender Malacca to Dutch.

Feb: **16th**, Charles I consents to Triennial Bill.

March: **22nd**, the trial of Strafford opens.

April: **21st**, Commons votes Bill of Attainder for execution of Strafford.

May: **2nd**, Mary, Charles I's daughter, marries William, son of the Prince of Orange.
12th, Strafford is beheaded.

Aug: **20th**, English Treaty of Pacification with Scotland ratifies agreement of 1640.

Oct: **23rd**, outbreaks of Catholic Irish rebellion; Ulster Protestants are massacred.

Nov: **23rd**, Grand Remonstance is carried in Parliament by 11 votes.

Society, Education, and Religion
Théophraste Renaudot's plan for free medical treatment of the needy in Paris (leads in 1644 to the Faculty of Medicine forbidding him to practise).

Science, Technology, and Discovery
Vincenzio Galileo, the son of Galileo, makes a clock with a pendulum and a pin-wheel escapement.

Humanities and Scholarship
John Evelyn begins his *Diary* (–1706).

Art, Sculpture, Fine Arts, and Architecture
Claude, *Embarkation of St. Ursula.*
Frans Hals, *The Governors of St. Elizabeth Hospital.*

1642
Dutch obtain monopoly of foreign trade in Japan on final exclusion of Portuguese (since 1637) but severe limitations are imposed on their activities.

Jan: **4th**, Charles I marches to Westminster to arrest 5 members of the Commons, but they seek refuge in the City of London at the Guildhall, and his attempt fails.

Aug: **22nd**, Royal Standard is raised at Nottingham, and Civil War begins.

Oct: **23rd**, indecisive battle of Edgehill.

Dec: **4th**, on death of Cardinal Richelieu, Mazarin becomes Chief Minister.

Society, Education, and Religion
Cornelius Jansen's *Augustinus* is condemned by Urban VIII (see 1640).

Science, Technology, and Discovery
Italian mathematician and physicist Evangelista Torricelli invents the barometer using mercury in a glass tube sealed at the top.
French mathematician Blaise Pascal builds an adding machine.
Van Diemen, governor of the Dutch East India Company sends Tasman on a voyage from Batavia, in which he discovers Tasmania and New Zealand.

Humanities and Scholarship
Thomas Hobbes, *De Cive* (translated edition, 1651).

Art, Sculpture, Fine Arts, and Architecture
Rembrandt, *The Night Watch.*

Music
Monteverdi's opera *L'incoronazione di Poppea* is performed in Venice.

Literature
Theatres in England are closed by order (reopened, 1660).

1643 **March:** (–Apr 15th) Parliamentary Commissioners meet Charles I at Oxford for unsuccessful peace negotiations.

May: 13th, Oliver Cromwell defeats Royalists at Grantham.
14th, Louis XIII dies, and is succeeded by Louis XIV (–1715).
18th, Anne of Austria, the Queen Mother, is invested with supreme power in France at a *Lit de Justice*; she confirms Mazarin as First Minister.
19th, French under Enghien defeat Spanish at Rocroi which marks end of supremacy of Spanish forces.
19th, Confederation of New England formed by Connecticut, New Haven, Plymouth and Massachusetts Bay.

Sept: 15th, 'First Cessation' ends Irish rebellion enabling royalists to bring troops to England.
20th, first battle of Newbury ends in Royalists' defeat.
25th, Assembly of Westminster, meeting since July, adopts Presbyterianism by the Solemn League and Covenant between Parliament and Scotland.

Dec: —, William Dowsing receives a Parliamentary commission to engage in a campaign of iconoclastic destruction of church images in East Anglia.

Politics, Government, Law, and Economy
William Prynne, *The Soveraigne Power of Parliaments and Kingdomes.*

Humanities and Scholarship
John Milton, *The Doctrine and Discipline of Divorce.*
François Eudes de Mézeray, *Histoire de France.*

Literature
Sir Thomas Browne, *Religio Medici* (preceded in 1642 by an unauthorized edition).

Everyday Life
Coffee is first drunk in Paris.

1644 Ming dynasty in China ends and is succeeded by the Ch'ing dynasty.
Dutch establish settlement in Mauritius.
Providence is united by Charter with Newport and Portsmouth, Rhode Island.
Matthew Hopkins begins witch-hunt in the eastern counties of England (–1646).

Jan: —, the Scots invade England.
22nd, Charles I's Parliament meets at Oxford.

July: 2nd, Royalists under Prince Rupert are defeated by Oliver Cromwell at Marston Moor.

Aug: 3rd (–5th), Enghien's successes at Freiburg lead to French occupation of the Rhineland.

Sept: 2nd, the Earl of Essex's army surrenders to Charles near Fowey.

Politics, Government, Law, and Economy
John Milton pleads for uncensored printing in *Areopagitica.*

Society, Education, and Religion
English Parliament forbids merriment or religious festivities at Christmas.

Humanities and Scholarship
René Descartes publishes *Principia Philosophicae.*

Art, Sculpture, Fine Arts, and Architecture
Claude, *Landscape – Narcissus*; and *A Seaport.*
G Bernini, *Vision of St. Teresa*, Rome.

1645 Turkish-Venetian war breaks out when the Turks attempt to take Crete.
Portuguese in Brazil rebel against Dutch.
Capuchin monks ascend River Congo.

Jan: 10th, Archbishop Laud is beheaded.

Feb: 2nd, the royalist Montrose is victorious over Argyll's Covenanters at Inverlochy.

April: —, beginning of parliament's New Model Army.
3rd, Self-Denying Ordinance is passed by the House of Lords.

June: 1st, peace negotiations finally open between Empire and France at Münster and Empire and Sweden at Osnabrück (culminating in Treaty of Westphalia, 1648).
14th, Cromwell defeats Royalists at Naseby.

Sept: —, Mazarin, following the French victory at Nördlingen on 3rd Aug, is in a strong enough position to force the Paris *Parlement* to yield.

10th, General Fairfax forces Prince Rupert to surrender Bristol.
13th, Montrose is defeated at Philiphaugh and flees to Continent.
24th, The King's depleted army is defeated at Rowton Heath, near Chester.

Politics, Government, Law, and Economy

John Lilburne founds the Leveller movement in Southwark.

Art, Sculpture, Fine Arts, and Architecture

Jacob van Campen, Nieuwe Kerk, Haarlem.

Music

Lully is appointed violinist and kitchen boy at the French court.
Heinrich Schütz, *Die Sieben Worte Christi am Kreuz* (oratorio).

Literature

John Milton, *L'Allegro*; *Il Penseroso*; *Sonnets* and other poems.
Paul Scarron, *Jodelet; ou, Le Maître Valet* (comedy).

1646 English occupy Bahamas.

May: 5th, Charles surrenders to Scots at Newark.

June: 25th, surrender of Oxford to Roundheads virtually signifies end of Civil War.

July: 7th, Levellers publish *Remonstrance of Many Thousand Citizens* proclaiming the sovereignty of the people.
30th, Parliamentary Commissioners present Charles I at Newcastle with the Newcastle Propositions, demanding he consent to religious reforms.

Dec: 24th, Charles I attempts to escape but the plan fails.

Society, Education, and Religion

The schools at Port Royal, France, are fully organized, with special series of text books on logic, grammar and mathematics.

Science, Technology, and Discovery

The German Athanasius Kircher invents the magic lantern.

Literature

Sir Thomas Browne, *Pseudodoxia Epidemica;*.
Henry Vaughan, *Poems*.
Vida y hechos de Estebanillo González (anon. autobiographical picaresque novel).

1647 Tsar Alexis is faced with revolt in Moscow.

Jan: 30th, Scots agree to sell Charles I to Parliament for £400,000.

May: 18th, Commons vote to disband most of the army.

June: 4th, Cornet Joyce seizes Charles I at Holmby House as a prisoner for the army.
14th, 'Representation of Army' sets out the army's grievances.

July: 7th, Naples revolts against Spain under Mananiello but, 16th, he is assassinated. Don John of Austria restores Spanish rule April 1648.

Aug: 7th, the army marches into London.

Nov: 11th, Charles I escapes but is captured and, 14th, imprisoned at Carisbrooke Castle.

Dec: 26th, Charles I concludes 'Engagement' with Scots to abolish Episcopacy and restore Presbyterianism. The Scots agree to restore the King by force if necessary.

Politics, Government, Law, and Economy

(Oct) John Lilburne and others draft the Levellers' Manifesto.

Science, Technology, and Discovery

Johann Hevel first charts the lunar surface in *Selenographia*.

1648 Arabs take Muscat from Portuguese.

Jan: 30th, Peace between Spain and Netherlands at Münster.

May: 1st, Scots begin Second Civil War.

Aug: 17th (–20th), Oliver Cromwell defeats Scots at Preston.
26th (–27th), Paris mob rises, which signifies outbreak of Fronde (–Apr 1649).

Sept: 18th, Parliament opens negotiations with Charles I at so-called Treaty of Newport.

Oct: 2nd, Parliament rejects Charles I's concessions (of Sept 28th).
24th, Peace of Westphalia ends 30 Years War: the independence of the Netherlands, the German states and Swiss cantons is guaranteed and France gains Alsace.

Dec: 6th, Colonel Pride's Purge of the House of Commons, removing many Presbyterian members; the remainder is known as the 'Rump'.
23rd, Parliament votes to bring Charles I to trial.

Society, Education, and Religion
Jeremy Taylor, *Of the Liberty of Prophesying* (i.e. of Preaching).
George Fox starts his Society of Friends.

Science, Technology, and Discovery
Jan Baptista van Helmont in *Ortus medicinae* (posthumous) invents the term 'gas', for describing carbon monoxide.

Art, Sculpture, Fine Arts, and Architecture
Jacob Van Campen, Town Hall, Amsterdam (–1655).

Literature
Robert Herrick, *Hesperides.*

1649

Jan: 15th, the French Court leaves Paris; opening of the 12-weeks war in the Fronde.
19th, trial of Charles I opens.
30th, Charles I is beheaded.

Feb: 5th, Scots proclaim Charles II as King in Edinburgh and later in the year the Irish rise in his favour under Ormonde.

March: 11th, Treaty of Ruel ends first Fronde after the rebels have been forced to treat.
17th, English Parliament abolishes House of Lords and, 19th, abolishes the monarchy.

May: 15th, the Levellers are defeated at Burford.
19th, England is declared to be a Commonwealth.

Aug: —, Sultan Ibrahim is deposed and murdered; he is succeeded by Mohammed IV (–1687).

Sept: 11th, Oliver Cromwell sacks Drogheda.

Oct: 11th, Cromwell sacks Wexford.

Dec: —, Unrest in France, including riots in Paris, signify outbreak of second Fronde.

Politics, Government, Law, and Economy
John Gauden, *Eikon Basilike*, compiled partly from Charles I's notes, defends monarchy and the image of the late King, but is answered by Milton, *Eikonoklastes.*
The Diggers begin to work at St. George's Hill, Surrey, and on being prosecuted denounce the institution of private property.
English becomes the language of all legal documents in place of Latin (until 1660; reintroduced 1733).
Providence (later Annapolis, Maryland) is settled by Puritan exiles from Virginia.

Literature
Richard Lovelace, *Lucasta.*

1650

Jan: 18th, Fronde leaders, including Condé, are imprisoned.

April: 27th, Montrose is defeated at Carbisdale and is subsequently executed (21st May).

Sept: —, Cromwell defeats the Scots at Dunbar
29th, French *parlement* imposes peace on Bordeaux, ending the second Fronde.

Society, Education, and Religion
James Usher, *Annales Veteris et Novi Testamenti* (–1654; fixes Creation at 4004 BC, in a scriptural chronology).

Science, Technology, and Discovery
German physicist Otto von Guericke invents the air pump and proves that the air presses with equal force in all directions.

Humanities and Scholarship
René Descartes, *Traité des Passions de L'ame.*

Literature
Anne Bradstreet, *The Tenth Muse Lately Sprung Up in America* (poems).

1651

Ietsuna becomes Shogun of Japan and subsequently overcomes two revolts in Edo.

Jan: 1st, Scots crown Charles II at Scone.

Feb: 6th (–7th), Cardinal Mazarin is forced to flee from Paris during the night after *Parlement* votes for release of Condé and other Fronde leaders.

July: —, The Poles defeat the Cossacks and their allies, the Tartars.

Sept: 3rd, Oliver Cromwell defeats Charles at Worcester and Charles flees to France (17th Oct).
7th, Louis XIV attains majority and at the same time charges against Condé are withdrawn; but he leaves Paris and subsequently allies with Spain.

Oct: —, first English Navigation Act passed.
27th, surrender of Limerick after long siege.

Politics, Government, Law, and Economy
Thomas Hobbes, *Leviathan.*

Science, Technology, and Discovery
William Harvey writes *Exercitationes de generatione animalium*, a treatise on generation, which founds the study of embryology.

Literature
Paul Scarron, *Le Roman comique.*

1652 **Feb: —**, English Parliament passes Act of Pardon and Oblivion to reconcile Royalists.

May: 19th, (–29th) English defeat Dutch at battle of the Downs off Folkestone.

July: 2nd, Turenne defeats Condé in the Faubourg St. Antoine, Paris, but has to withdraw. Provisional Fronde government is set up in Paris after rising of June.

Oct: 21st, King Louis XIV returns to Paris and government is re-established.

Politics, Government, Law, and Economy
Gerrard Winstanley, *The Law of Freedom in a Platform*, expounds a system of communism, with the prohibition of buying and selling and the institution of civil marriage.
Maine is joined to Massachusetts Colony.
(April) The Dutch found Cape Town.

Society, Education, and Religion
Henry Vaughan, *The Mount of Olives* (devotions).

Humanities and Scholarship
Sir Fulke Greville (Lord Brooke), *The Life of Sir Philip Sidney.*

Art, Sculpture, Fine Arts, and Architecture
Rembrandt, *Hendrickje Stoffels.*

Everyday Life
Christopher Bowman opens London's first Coffee House in Cornhill.

1653 John de Witt becomes Grand Pensionary in Holland.

April: 20th, Cromwell expels Long Parliament for trying to pass Perpetuation Bill.
29th, Cromwell sets up small council of ten members.

July: 31st (or 9th Aug), English are victorious against Dutch fleet off Texel.
4th (–12th Dec), Little, or Barebones, Parliament meets.

Aug: 5th, Brandenburg establishes standing army; the Great Elector suppresses his Diet.

Sept: 26th, 'Act of Satisfaction' for distribution of forfeited lands in Ireland.

Dec: 16th, by the Instrument of Government a Protectorate is set up in England with a Council of State and Oliver Cromwell as Protector.

Society, Education, and Religion
James Naylor is recognized by his English followers as the Messiah. The rise of the 'Fifth Monarchy' men.

Music
Lully, music for Bensarade's ballet *La Nuit*, in which Louis XIV dances the part of 'Le Roi Soleil'.

Literature
Thomas Middleton, *The Changeling*; *The Spanish Gipsie.*

Sport and Recreation
Isaak Walton, *The Compleat Angler* (–1676).

1654 Dutch are finally driven out of Brazil by Portuguese.

March: —, Surrender of Breisach signifies end of Fronde.

April: 5th, (or 15th) peace Treaty of Westminster ends first Anglo-Dutch War.

May: —, The Cossacks place themselves under the protection of Tsar John Alexis.

June: 6th, Christina of Sweden abdicates and is succeeded by Charles X (–1660).
7th, coronation of Louis XIV at Rheims.

July: 10th, (or 20th) Anglo-Portuguese treaty placing Portugal under English control.

Society, Education, and Religion
Blaise Pascal retires to Port-Royal.

Science, Technology, and Discovery
Blaise Pascal and Pierre de Fermat found the theory of probabilities.

Art, Sculpture, Fine Arts, and Architecture
Pieter de Hooch, *Delft after the Explosion.*

Literature
Savinien Cyrano de Bergerac, *Le Pédant joué* (comedy).

Everyday Life
John Amos Comenius (Komensky) publishes the first picture-book for children in Nuremberg, *Orbis Sensualium Pictus*, the world in pictures with a Latin-German text.

1655 **April:** **28th**, Blake destroys pirate fleet from Bey of Tunis and releases prisoners in Algiers.

May: **4th**, English capture Jamaica.

July: —, outbreak of First Northern War when Charles X invades Poland.

Aug: **23rd**, Charles X defeats John Casimir of Poland and, 30th, takes Warsaw.

Nov: **24th**, Cromwell prohibits Anglican services.

Society, Education, and Religion
(14th Dec) Jews readmitted into England by Cromwell (–1656).

Science, Technology, and Discovery
English mathematician John Wallis writes *Arithmetica Infinitorum*, a treatise on conic sections.

Humanities and Scholarship
William Drummond, *A History of the Five Jameses.*

Art, Sculpture, Fine Arts, and Architecture
Nicholaes Maes, *Woman Scraping Parsnips*; and *The Idle Servant.*

Music
Lully bans shawms in favour of oboes for indoor performances at the French court.

1656 **Feb:** —, Spain declares war on England and subsequently signs treaty with Charles II.

July: **29th**, (–31st) Poles under John Casimir are defeated at Warsaw by combined Swedish-Brandenburg force.

Sept: **9th**, (or 19th) Spanish treasure ships are captured off Cadiz by Robert Blake.

Politics, Government, Law, and Economy
James Harrington, *Commonwealth of Oceana.*

Society, Education, and Religion
[Blaise Pascal] *Lettres Provinciales* (–1660).

Science, Technology, and Discovery
Dutch scientist Christian Huygens observes the satellites of Saturn.
Christian Huygens invents the cycloidal pendulum and makes a pendulum clock.

Art, Sculpture, Fine Arts, and Architecture
Velazquez, *Las Meninas.*
Vermeer, *The Procuress.*
Bernini, Piazza, St. Peter's, Rome; also façade St. Maria della Pace, Rome (–1657)

Literature
Abraham Cowley, *Poems.*

1657 **March:** **31st**, Humble Petition and Advice, offers title of King to Oliver Cromwell who subsequently rejects offer (3rd April).

May: **25th**, New Humble Petition and Advice creates new House of Lords.

July: —, Denmark attacks Charles X of Sweden, who is already campaigning against Russia, Poland and Austria.

Sept: **19th**, by Treaty of Wehlau, Poland renounces sovereignty of Prussia on behalf of Brandenburg.

Nov: **6th**, by Treaty of Bromberg, Brandenburg allies with Poland against Sweden.
10th, Brandenburg makes an offensive alliance with Denmark.

Art, Sculpture, Fine Arts, and Architecture
Velazquez, *Las Hilanderas.*

Everyday Life
Drinking chocolate is first sold in London.

1658 Dutch take Jaffnapatam, the last Portuguese possession in Ceylon.

June: —, Aurangzeb imprisons his father the Shah, after winning battle at Samgarh.
4th, (or 14th) Anglo-French army defeats Spaniards at the battle of the Dunes.

July: **31st**, Aurangzeb is proclaimed Mogul Emperor.

Aug: (–Sept) Charles X begins second war with Denmark and besieges Copenhagen.

Sept: **3rd**, Oliver Cromwell dies and is succeeded as Lord Protector by his son, Richard (–May 1659).

Society, Education, and Religion

Société des Missions Étrangères (Roman Catholic) founded in Paris.

Literature

Molière forms the company of actors at the *Théâtre du Petit-Bourbon* which eventually becomes the company to be known as *La Comédie-Française* (see 1680).

Everyday Life

Palmstruck devises the first banknote, for issue by the Riksbank, Stockholm.

1659 The Great Elector drives out the Swedes from Pomerania and Prussia.

Jan: **14th**, Portuguese defeat Spanish at Elvas.

April: **22nd**, Richard Cromwell dissolves Parliament after peaceful army *coup d'état*.

May: **7th**, Restoration of the Rump Parliament.
25th, Richard Cromwell resigns; the Rump Parliament re-establishes the Commonwealth.

Oct: **12th**, army expels the Rump Parliament.

Nov: **7th**, Peace of the Pyrenees, between Spain and France.

Dec: **26th**, the Long Parliament meets again.

Science, Technology, and Discovery

English scientist Rupert Boyle makes observations on the elastic pressure of the air in all directions, with the combination of his 'pneumatical engine'.

Literature

Molière, *Les Précieuses ridicules* (comedy).

1660 **Jan:** **1st**, General George Monck crosses R. Tweed, and, 3rd Feb, leads his army into London.

March: **—**, Virginia proclaims Charles II king and restores governor Sir William Berkeley.
16th, Long Parliament dissolves itself (elected Nov 1640, restored May 1659).

April: **4th**, Charles II issues Declaration of Breda, promising amnesty and religious toleration.
25th, (–29th Dec) Convention Parliament meets and invites Charles II to return.

May: **3rd**, through French mediation, the Peace of Oliva is signed, ending war between Brandenburg, Poland, Austria and Sweden.
29th, Charles II enters London.

June: **—**, Louis XIV of France marries Maria Teresa, Infanta of Spain.
6th, Peace of Copenhagen ends war between Sweden and Denmark.

Politics, Government, Law, and Economy

Parliament passes the Navy Discipline Act and strengthens the Navigation Act.

Society, Education, and Religion

Blaise Pascal's *Lettres Provinciales* are placed on the Index.

Humanities and Scholarship

(1st Jan) Samuel Pepys begins his *Diary* (–1669).

Art, Sculpture, Fine Arts, and Architecture

The Great Elector begins to build Potsdam Palace (–1682).

Literature

Patents are granted for reopening theatres in London (closed since 1642).

1661 Famine in India, where no rain has fallen for two years.

March: **9th**, Cardinal Mazarin dies and Louis XIV begins his personal rule.
23rd (or 3rd July), Portugal cedes Tangier and Bombay to Charles II as dowry of his Queen.

April: **23rd**, coronation of Charles II.

June: **21st**, the Peace of Kardis is signed between Russia and Sweden, ending the northern war.

Aug: **6th**, by treaty with the Dutch, the Portuguese retain Brazil, the Dutch keep Ceylon.

Sept: **5th**, in France, Colbert becomes principal financial minister (–1683).

Dec: **20th**, Royal Assent is given to Corporation Act.

Society, Education, and Religion

John Graunt, *National and Political Observations on the Bills of Mortality*, provides statistical information for life insurance in England.
John Eliot, translation of the Holy Bible into Algonquin.

Science, Technology, and Discovery
Robert Boyle publishes *The Sceptical Chemist* which introduces the modern concept of an element, alkali, and acid. He refutes many of the earlier ideas on the composition of matter.

Art, Sculpture, Fine Arts, and Architecture
Jan Steen, *Easy Come, Easy Go.*
Velazquez, *The Rokeby Venus.*
Le Vau, Galerie d'Apollon, Louvre (–1662) and Collège des Quatre Nations, Paris.

Music
The Académie Royale de Danse is founded by Louis XIV (enlarged, 1672).

1662
Accession of K'ang-hsi, Emperor of China, aged 8 years. He begins personal rule at the age of 15 (–1722).
The Dutch lose Formosa, which becomes autonomous (–1683).

May: **21st**, Charles II marries Catherine de Braganza, daughter of John IV of Portugal.

Oct: **27th**, Charles II sells Dunkirk to France for 2½ million livres (£400,000).

Politics, Government, Law, and Economy
The last silver pennies are minted in England.

Society, Education, and Religion
Episcopal Ordination Act of Scotland; Presbyterian assemblies are forbidden.
(19th May) *The Book of Common Prayer* of the Church of England; the final text is approved and it is enforced by the Act of Uniformity.

Science, Technology, and Discovery
(15th July) The Royal Society receives its charter.

Art, Sculpture, Fine Arts, and Architecture
Louis XIV begins to build Versailles Palace and appoints Le Brun his principal painter.
Le Nôtre, gardens and park, Versailles.

Literature
Samuel Butler, *Hudibras*, part 1 (part 2 1663, part 3 1678).
Molière, *L'École des femmes* (comedy).

1663
Colbert forms the colony of New France into a province, with Quebec as its capital.

March: **24th**, grant of Carolina to the eight proprietors.

April: **18th**, Turks declare war against Emperor Leopold I; the war lasts until Aug 1664.

July: **8th**, a Charter is granted by Charles II to Rhode Island.

Politics, Government, Law, and Economy
The gold guinea-piece is first coined in England.
Turnpike tolls are first levied in England.

Science, Technology, and Discovery
Otto von Guericke makes a frictional electrical machine.

Humanities and Scholarship
Gottfried von Leibniz, *De principio individui*, a defence of nominalistic philosophy.
Académie des Inscriptions et Belles Lettres founded in Paris by Jean Baptiste Colbert.

Literature
Andreas Gryphius, *Horribilicribrifax* (satirical comedy on the Thirty Years War).

1664
April: **5th**, Triennial Act is repealed.

June: **—**, War breaks out between England and Holland in the colonies and at sea.

Aug: **29th**, English annexe New Netherlands from Connecticut to Delaware, and rename New Amsterdam, surrendered two days earlier by Peter Stuyvesant, as New York.

Dec: **15th**, union of Connecticut and New Haven.

Politics, Government, Law, and Economy
Colbert abolishes many internal tariff-duties in France.
The French Compagnie des Indes Occidentales is formed.

Society, Education, and Religion
Armand de Rancé founds the Trappist Order (*La Trappe*) at La Trappe, Normandy.
Conventicle Act forbids general meetings of Nonconformists in England.

Art, Sculpture, Fine Arts, and Architecture
Pieter de Hooch, *Young woman weighing gold*; and *Woman at a window reading a letter.*
Literature
Jean de La Fontaine, first book of *Contes et Nouvelles.*
Molière, *Le Tartuffe* (comedy; Acts 1–3 first performed).
Jean Racine, *La Thébaide* (his first tragedy, produced by Molière).
Everyday Life
J Forster, *England's happiness increased ... by a plantation of the roots called potatoes.*

1665 Maine is restored to the heirs of Sir Ferdinando Gorges.
June: 6th, (or 17th) Spanish are defeated by the Portuguese and English at Montes Claros. A further victory at Villa Viciosa secures Portugal's independence.
Sept: —, (–Sept 1666) Great Plague of London, bubonic in nature.
17th, Philip IV of Spain dies and is succeeded by Charles II, his son (–1700).
Politics, Government, Law, and Economy
A census is taken in Quebec, the first of modern times.
Society, Education, and Religion
An Native American, Caleb Cheeshateaumuck, takes an AB degree at Harvard.
John Bunyan, *The Holy City.*
Pope Alexander VII orders the Jansenists to submit to the Bull of 1653.
Science, Technology, and Discovery
Francis Grimaldi announces his discovery of the diffraction of light in *Physico-Mathesis de Lumine*, published posthumously.
Robert Boyle proves that air is necessary for candles to burn and for animals to live.
Robert Hooke describes the microscope in his *Micrographia.*
Humanities and Scholarship
Jacques Godefroy edits *Codex Theodosianus.*
Art, Sculpture, Fine Arts, and Architecture
Murillo, *The Rest on the Flight to Egypt* (–1670).
Vermeer, *The Artist's Studio.*
Literature
La Rochefoucauld, *Maximes* (first Paris edition).
Molière, *Don Juan* (comedy).

1666 **Jan: 16th**, (or 26th) France, in alliance with Holland, declares war against England.
July: 25th, (or Aug 4th) Lord Albemarle defeats the Dutch fleet at battle of St. James' Fight, off Foreland.
Sept: 2nd, (–6th) Great Fire of London virtually destroys the city.
Nov: 18th, Scottish Covenanters are crushed at the battle of Pentland Hills.
Politics, Government, Law, and Economy
Newark, New Jersey, is settled by Puritans from Connecticut.
Society, Education, and Religion
The Great Plague of London is at its height (May–Sept), killing 68,596 persons.
Science, Technology, and Discovery
Académie des Sciences, Paris, is founded by Colbert.
Isaac Newton uses the infinitesimal calculus and measures the moon's orbit.
Art, Sculpture, Fine Arts, and Architecture
Rembrandt, *Portrait of Titus.*
Colbert establishes the Gobelin Tapestry workshops in Paris.
Literature
Molière, *Le Médecin malgré lui* and *Le Misanthrope* (comedies).

1667 Revolt in Portugal when Alfonso VI is banished to the Azores by his brother, Pedro.
Jan: 20th, the Truce of Andrussov between Russia and Poland ends the Thirteen Years War; Poland cedes Smolensk and Kiev to Russia.
May: 24th, French troops invade the Spanish Netherlands to begin the War of Devolution (–May 1668); the Turks begin the siege of Candia (–Sept 1669).
June: 12th, (or 13th) the Dutch fleet under Admiral de Ruyter burns Sheerness, sails up the R. Medway, and raids Chatham dockyard; this humiliating defeat represents the nadir of English naval power.

July: —, Turenne completes the French conquest of Flanders and Hainault.
21st, (or 31st) Peace of Breda between Holland and France with England, which obtains Antigua, Monserrat, St. Kitts, Cape Coast Castle and New Netherlands.

Science, Technology, and Discovery
The National Observatory, Paris, is founded.

Literature
John Milton, *Paradise Lost* (enlarged edn. 1674).
Molière, *Le Tartuffe* (comedy; in part performed in 1664).
Jean Racine, *Andromaque* (tragedy).

1668 The government of Maine again passes to the control of Massachusetts.

Feb: **13th**, by the Treaty of Lisbon, Spain recognizes the independence of Portugal.

March: **10th**, Charles II issues a proclamation to enforce the Act of Uniformity, provoking riots in London 23rd–27th.
27th, Bombay passes to the control of the English East India Company.

Science, Technology, and Discovery
Isaac Newton constructs the first reflecting telescope.
Anthony van Leeuwenhoek first describes red corpuscles accurately.

Literature
Mrs. Aphra Behn, *Oroonoko* (novel).
Jean de La Fontaine, *Fables choisies mises en vers* (vol 2 1678, vol 3 1693).
Molière, *Amphitryon*, *George Dandin* and *L'Avare* (comedies).

1669 The Hindu religion is banned in India by Aurangzeb.

June: **19th**, Michael Wisniowiecki, a Lithuanian, is elected King of Poland (–1673) after nine months of struggle over the succession to John Casimir (abdicated 19th Sept 1668).

July: **21st**, John Locke's Constitution for Carolina is approved.

Sept: —, The Venetians surrender Crete to the Turks, after a siege begun in 1648.

Politics, Government, Law, and Economy
Vauban, *La Conduite des Sièges.*

Science, Technology, and Discovery
Marcello Malpighi's treatise on the silkworm is the first description of the anatomy of an invertebrate.
Jan Swammerdam writes a History of Insects which describes the reproductive parts of insects and correctly describes metamorphosis.

Humanities and Scholarship
Jacques-Bénigne Bossuet, *Oraison funèbre de la reine Angleterre*, the first of his series of funeral orations.
(31st May) The last entry in the *Diary* of Samuel Pepys (see 1660).

1670 The Bahamas are granted to the proprietors of Carolina.

Aug: —, France occupies Lorraine.

Dec: **21st**, (or 31st) Boyne treaty between France and England makes public the secret Treaty of Dover (22nd May).

Politics, Government, Law, and Economy
An English settlement is made at Charles Town (Charleston), South Carolina.

Society, Education, and Religion
Uniforms are introduced to the French Army by Louvois.

Humanities and Scholarship
Blaise Pascal, *Pensées* (posthumous).
Benedict de Spinoza, *Tractatus Theologico-Politicus.*
John Dryden is appointed Historiographer Royal and Poet Laureate.

Music
Académie Royale des Opéra (original home of the Paris Opéra) is founded.

Literature
Marie-Madeleine de La Fayette, *Zaïde.*

1671 The French Senegal company is founded.

Jan: —, English buccaneers under Sir Henry Morgan destroy Panama.
Sept: —, Vauban begins construction of forts in the Netherlands.

Society, Education, and Religion

Jacques Bénigne Bossuet, *Exposition de la foi catholique.*

Science, Technology, and Discovery

Gottfried von Leibniz adapts an adding-machine to facilitate multiplication.

Art, Sculpture, Fine Arts, and Architecture

Lionel Bruant, Hôtel des Invalides, Paris (–1675).

Literature

John Milton, *Paradise Regained*; *Samson Agonistes.*
Marie, Marquise de Sévigné, *Letters* (to her married daughter, Madame de Grignan), first series.

1672 The French occupy Pondicherry and Coromandel Coast in India.

March: **15th**, Charles II issues Declaration of Indulgence towards Roman Catholics and Nonconformists (withdrawn 8th Mar 1673).
17th, England declares war on Holland; France subsequently declares war on the Dutch.
May: **2nd**, Great Elector concludes alliance with Dutch; the First Coalition against France.
June: **7th**, Admiral de Ruyter defeats the English and French fleets in Southwold Bay.
15th, the Sluices are opened in Holland to save Amsterdam from the French.
July: **4th**, William of Orange is elected Stadtholder of Holland.
Aug: **20th**, the De Witt brothers, republican statesmen, are assassinated at the Hague.
Oct: **18th**, Poland is forced to cede Podolia and Ukraine to Turkey.

Politics, Government, Law, and Economy

Charles II grants a charter to the Royal Africa Company.
S. Pufendorf, *De jure naturae et gentium*, places international law on an ethical basis.

Society, Education, and Religion

Synod of Jerusalem revives the *Confession of Faith* of the Greek Orthodox Church.

Science, Technology, and Discovery

Jan van der Heyde and his son make a flexible hose for fighting fires.

Literature

Molière, *Les Femmes Savantes.*

Everyday Life

John Banister holds first public concerts in London at Whitefriars (–1678); seats 1/- each.

1673 Marquette and Joliet descend Mississippi to Arkansas.
Frontenac founds Fort Frontenac, with La Salle as commandant, and conciliates Iroquois.

Feb: —, Abrogation of French *Parlement*'s rights to object to Royal Edicts.
March: **29th**, the Test Act excludes Roman Catholics from office in England.
June: **6th**, Peace of Vossem between Brandenburg and France ending the First Coalition against Louis XIV.
12th, James, Duke of York, is forced by Test Act to retire as Lord High Admiral.
Aug: —, Dutch capture New York.
11th, (or 21st) English fleet is defeated off Texel by the Dutch.

Music

J B Lully, *Cadmus and Hermonie*, first performed in Paris.
Buxtehude starts the Abendmusiken performances at Lubeck.

Literature

John Dryden, *Marriage à la mode* (comedy); *Amboyna* (tragedy).
Molière, *Le Malade imaginaire* (comedy).
Jean Racine, *Mithridate* (tragedy).
Pedro Calderon de la Barca, *La vida es sueno* (tragi-comedy).

1674 The United Provinces declare the office of Stadtholder hereditary in the family of Orange.
Native Madagascans expel the French from Madasgascar.
Sivaji, founder of the Mahratta State, concludes a treaty with England and declares himself independent of the Mogul Emperor Aurangzeb.

Feb: **9th**, (or 19th) Treaty of Westminster by which English withdraw from the Dutch War, and New York and New Sweden are definitely recognized as English.
May: **21st**, John Sobieski is elected King of Poland as John III.
28th, at the German Diet of Ratisbon, Emperor Leopold I declares war on France.
June: **28th**, (–Oct) French successes in Franche-Comté, Flanders and western Germany.

Humanities and Scholarship
Nicolas Boileau, *L'Art poétique.*
Nicolas Malebranche, *De la recherche de la vérité.*
Anthony à Wood, *Historia et Antiquitates Universitatis Oxoniensis.*

Music
J B Lully, *Alceste* (opera).

1675 Guru Gobind Singh organizes political power of Sikhs.

Jan: 5th, Turenne defeats the Great Elector of Brandenburg at Colmar.

July: 27th, Turenne is killed at Sassbach, marking the end of great French victories.

Aug: —, French defeat Dutch and Spanish fleets in Bay of Palermo and take Sicily.
8th, (–12th) London silk-weavers riot against engine looms.

Sept: 9th, New England Confederation declares war aginst Wampanoag Indians, for breaking truce (–Aug 1676).

Oct: —, War breaks out between Denmark and Sweden.

Science, Technology, and Discovery
Danish astronomer Olaus Römer discovers the finite velocity of light.
Isaac Newton proposes the corpuscular theory of light.
Gottfried von Leibniz makes important advances in differential and integral calculus. He discovers the product rule for differentiation and invents the modern notation for an integral.
(Aug) In England, the Greenwich Observatory is established.

Humanities and Scholarship
Philosophical Transactions of the Royal Society of London are initiated.

Art, Sculpture, Fine Arts, and Architecture
Sir Christopher Wren begins rebuilding St. Paul's Cathedral, London.

Literature
William Wycherley, *The Country Wife* (comedy).

1676 **Dec: —**, Charles XI of Sweden defeats the Danes at Lunden.

Science, Technology, and Discovery
Nehemiah Grew in the Anatomy of Plants, describes the functions of stamens and pistils (published 1682).

1677 **Feb: —**, Lord Shaftesbury and others are imprisoned in the Tower.

March: —, Louis XIV takes Valenciennes and St. Omer.
—, Massachusetts buys most of Maine from the heirs of Sir Ferdinando Gorges.

Nov: 4th, (or 14th) William of Orange marries Mary, daughter of James, Duke of York.

Dec: 12th, Great Elector takes Stettin and (in 1678) Rugen.

Politics, Government, Law, and Economy
Increase Mather, *The Troubles That Have Happened in New England.*

Humanities and Scholarship
Benedict de Spinoza, *Ethics.*

Art, Sculpture, Fine Arts, and Architecture
Pieter de Hooch, *Musical Party in a Courtyard.*

Literature
Jean Racine, *Phèdre* (tragedy).

1678 Russo-Swedish war breaks out.

Feb: —, The Earl of Shaftesbury is released from the Tower.

March: —, Louis XIV captures Ghent and Ypres.

Aug: 10th, Peace of Nijmegen between France and Holland.
13th, the Popish Plot, in which it is alleged that the Pope has required the Jesuits to overthrow Charles II with French and Spanish aid, is brought to the King's notice.

Sept: 17th, Franco-Spanish peace Treaty of Nijmegen.

Nov: 5th, Greifswald, Sweden's last possession in Pomerania, falls to the Great Elector.
30th, Roman Catholics are excluded from both Houses of Parliament.

Society, Education, and Religion
John Bunyan, *The Pilgrim's Progress, part 1* (part 2, 1684).
David Calderwood, *History of the Kirk of Scotland* (1514–1625).

Science, Technology, and Discovery
La Salle explores the Great Lakes of Canada (–1679).

Art, Sculpture, Fine Arts, and Architecture
(July) Architecture: Jules Hardouin-Mansart, Versailles, Marly Trianon, etc. (–1699).

Literature
Anne Bradsheet, *Contemplations.*
Marie-Madeleine, Comtesse de La Fayette, *La Princesse de Clèves.*

1679 **Jan: 24th**, the 'Cavalier Parliament' (sitting since 1661) is dissolved.

June: 22nd, the Duke of Monmouth subdues insurrection of Scottish Covenanters at Bothwell Bridge.

July: 12th, Charles II dissolves third Parliament for attempting to exclude the Duke of York from the throne.

Sept: 18th, New Hampshire is created a separate province from Massachusetts.

Oct: 7th, fourth Parliament of Charles II meets but is immediately prorogued over the Exclusion Bill, and does not meet again for a year.

Dec: 17th, the effective ruler of Spain, Don John, dies and the Queen Mother, Marie of Austria, regains power; Habsburg influence is again established in Madrid.

Politics, Government, Law, and Economy
Sir William Petty, *A Treatise on Taxes and Contributions.*
Louis XIV issues a stringent edict against duelling.

Literature
P'U Sungling, *Liao Chai* (collection of short stories).
(18th Dec) John Dryden is attacked by hired ruffians in Rose Alley, Covent Garden, London.

Everyday Life
Serious fire at Boston, Massachusetts, destroys the dockyard and many dwellings.

1680 The Great Elector incorporates the Archbishopric of Magdeburg with Brandenburg.
French colonial empire from Quebec to the mouth of the R. Mississippi is organized.
French factory is founded in Siam.

Nov: 30th, Lord Stafford is tried for treason.

Dec: 29th, Lord Stafford is executed.

Politics, Government, Law, and Economy
Sir William Temple, *An Essay on Government*; and *A Survey of the Constitution.*

Humanities and Scholarship
François de Salignac de La Mothe-Fénelon, *Dialogues sur l'éloquence.*

Art, Sculpture, Fine Arts, and Architecture
Jules Hardouin-Mansart, Chapel des Invalides, Paris (–1719).
Sir Christopher Wren, St. Clement Dane's Church, London.

Music
Stradivari makes his earliest known cello.

Literature
La Comédie-Française formed.

1681 Large-scale emigration of Huguenots from northern and western France begins.

March: 4th, royal charter for Pennsylvania.

Politics, Government, Law, and Economy
Sir Stephen Fox persuades Charles II to found Chelsea Hospital.

Science, Technology, and Discovery
Canal du Midi (Languedoc Canal), joining the Bay of Biscay to the Mediterranean, is completed.

Humanities and Scholarship
Jacques-Bénigne Bossuet, *Discours sur l'histoire universelle.*

Literature
John Dryden, *Absalom and Achitophel*, part 1 (part 2, 1682).
Andrew Marvell, *Miscellaneous Poems* (posthumous).

1682 **March: —**, The Assembly of the French Clergy endorse Louis XIV's Declaration of Four Articles to secure the independence of the Gallican Church.

April: 9th, La Salle claims the entire area of Louisiana for France.

May: 15th, (–18th) Revolt of the Streltzy in Russia.

July: 5th, on the death of Tsar Feodore, Tsaritza Sophia becomes Regent (–1689) for her infant brothers, Ivan and Peter, who are to rule jointly.

Oct: —, Pennsylvania adopts a Constitution (the Great Charter), and Philadelphia is laid out.

Politics, Government, Law, and Economy

A weaving-mill with 100 looms is established at Amsterdam.

Society, Education, and Religion

Elias Ashmole founds the Ashmolean Museum, Oxford, on the collections of the Tradescants.

Science, Technology, and Discovery

P. Bayle publishes *Thoughts on the Comet of 1680*, ends the superstitious fear about comets.

Music

Archangelo Corelli's concerti grossi played in Rome (published 1746).

Literature

Thomas Otway, *Venice Preserv'd* (tragedy).

1683 Manchus conquer Isle of Formosa (which remains in Chinese possession until 1895).

March: 31st, Polish alliance with Emperor against the Turks.

June: —, Turks begin siege of Vienna.

Sept: 12th, John III of Poland and Charles of Lorraine raise Turkish siege of Vienna.

Oct: 17th, Charter of franchises and liberties is drawn up in New York.

Dec: 25th, the Duke of Monmouth flees to Holland, following the discovery of the Rye House plot to assassinate Charles II and his brother James (June 12th).

Politics, Government, Law, and Economy

William Penn, *A General Description of Pennsylvania.*

Science, Technology, and Discovery

Dampier begins his voyage round the world.

Music

Henry Purcell is appointed composer to Charles II.

1684 English abandon Tangiers to the Moors.

Jan: 12th, Louis XIV marries Mme. de Maintenon.

May: —, James, Duke of York, is restored as Lord Admiral.

June: —, French take Trier, Courtrai, Oudenarde and Luxemburg.

Oct: —, Charter of Massachusetts is annulled by the English Court of Chancery.

Dec: —, Arrival at Versailles of Embassy from Siam.

Society, Education, and Religion

John Bunyan, *The Pilgrim's Progress*, part 2 (part 1, 1678).
Increase Mather, *Remarkable Providences.*

Science, Technology, and Discovery

Kämpfer travels to the Persian Gulf, Java and Japan.

Literature

Takemoto Gidayu starts a Japanese puppet play theatre in Tokio.

Everyday Life

London streets are first lit.

1685 K'ang-hsi opens all Chinese ports to foreign trade.

Feb: 6th, Charles II dies and is succeeded by James II (–1688).

June: 11th, outbreak of the Duke of Monmouth's rebellion.

July: 6th, Monmouth is defeated at Sedgemoor and (15th) is beheaded.

Sept: —, Judge Jeffreys conducts 'Bloody Assizes', sentencing adherents of Monmouth in West Country.

Oct: 18th, Louis XIV revokes Edict of Nantes; thousands of French Protestant refugees flee to England, Holland, and Brandenburg.

1686 Louis XIV proclaims annexation of Madagascar.
Aurangzeb annexes the Kingdom of Bijapur; he conquers Golkonda 1687.

June: —, James II introduces Roman Catholics into the Church and the army.

July: 9th, League of Augsburg is formed between the Emperor, Spain, Sweden, Saxony, the Palatinate and Brandenburg against Louis XIV.

Sept: 2nd, Charles, Duke of Lorraine, takes Buda from the Turks after a lengthy siege.

Oct: —, Russia declares war on Turkey, having secured Kiev by a treaty with Poland.

Politics, Government, Law, and Economy
First European settlement is made in Arkansas by the French.

Society, Education, and Religion
Maison de St. Cyr is founded as a convent school for daughters of poor gentlefolk by Louis XIV for Mme. de Maintenon.

Humanities and Scholarship
Bernard Le Bovier, Sieur de Fontenelle, *Entretiens sur la pluralité des mondes*.

1687 The French build Fort Niagara to prevent English reaching the Upper lakes of Canada.
French Huguenots settle at the Cape of Good Hope.

March: **19th**, La Salle is murdered by his colleagues.

April: **4th**, Declaration of Indulgence for Liberty of Conscience is issued by James II.

Sept: **26th**, Venetians bombard Athens and destroy the Parthenon and Propyleiea and, 28th, Turks surrender the city; the Morea is subjugated.

Oct: **11th**, Hungarian Diet of Pressburg renounces rights of resistance and recognizes the Crown as a hereditary possession of the male line of Habsburgs.

Nov: **2nd**, Mohammed IV is deposed in a revolution in Constantinople and succeeded by Suleiman III with Mustafa Kiuprili as Grand Vizier.

Society, Education, and Religion
François de Salignac de la Mothe-Fénelon, *Traité de l'éducation des filles*.

Science, Technology, and Discovery
Isaac Newton publishes *Principia Mathematica*, establishing the laws of motion and gravitation.

Humanities and Scholarship
Jacques Bénigne Bossuet, *Oraison funèbre du Grand Condé*.

Literature
John Dryden, *The Hind and the Panther*, and *Song for St. Cecilia's Day*.

1688 Revolution in Siam against French influence.

June: **10th**, birth of a son to James II – the 'Warming-pan Incident'.
30th, seven Whig Lords invite William of Orange to England.

Sept: **6th**, Turks lose Belgrade to the Emperor Leopold I.
24th, Louis XIV begins war against the Empire, the War of the League of Augsburg.

Nov: **5th**, William of Orange lands at Torbay.
26th, Louis declares war on Holland.

Dec: **19th**, William of Orange enters London.
25th, James II escapes to France.

Politics, Government, Law, and Economy
London underwriters begin to meet regularly in Lloyd's Coffee House.

Science, Technology, and Discovery
Plate glass is first cast.

Humanities and Scholarship
Jean de la Bruyère, *Caractères*.
Charles Perrault, *Parallèle des anciens et des modernes* (–1697).

1689 Natal becomes a Dutch colony.
Louis XIV appoints de Frontenac Governor of Canada.

Feb: **13th**, Bill of Rights is drawn up by a Committee of Commons (enacted July).

March: **12th**, James arrives in Ireland (and, May, holds a Parliament in Dublin).

April: **—**, Coronation of William and Mary.
20th, siege of Londonderry (–July).

May: **2nd**, England and Holland join the League of Augsburg, which is generally ratified and becomes the Grand Alliance.

July: **1st**, Episcopacy is abolished in Scotland.
27th, Scottish Jacobites defeat the Covenanters at Killiekrankie.

Aug: —, Lewis of Baden defeats the Turks, takes Nissa, and occupies Bulgaria.

Oct: **11th**, Peter the Great becomes Tsar of Russia.

Politics, Government, Law, and Economy
John Locke, *Two Treatises on Civil Government.*
The Dutch hold the first modern trade fair, at Leyden.

Society, Education, and Religion
(24th May) Act of Toleration (for Dissenters).

Science, Technology, and Discovery
Baron La Hontau first describes the Great Salt Lake, Utah.

Humanities and Scholarship
Cotton Mather, *Memorable Providences relating to Witchcraft and Possessions.*

Art, Sculpture, Fine Arts, and Architecture
Hobbema, *Avenue at Middleharnis.*

Music
Henry Purcell, *Dido and Aeneas* (opera).

1690 Louis XIV restores Avignon to the Pope (seized in 1663)

March: **16th**, Louis XIV sends troops to Ireland to fight for James II.

June: **30th** (or 10th July), French under Admiral Tourville defeat English and Dutch fleets at the battle of Beachy Head.

July: —, French, under the Duke of Luxemburg, defeat the allies at Fleurus.
1st, William III defeats James II at the battle of the Boyne.

Oct: **8th**, the Turks reconquer Belgrade and reoccupy Bulgaria.

Politics, Government, Law, and Economy
Sir William Petty, *Political Arithmetic*, an essay in comparative statistics.
(24th Aug) Job Charnock founds Calcutta.

Science, Technology, and Discovery
Christiaan Huygens propounds a theory of the undulation of light.
Denis Papin devises a pump with a piston raised by steam.

Humanities and Scholarship
John Locke, *An Essay Concerning Human Understanding.*

1691 **July:** —, Capitulation of Limerick; many Irish enter the services of Louis XIV.

Sept: **17th**, the colony of Massachusetts is given a new charter.

Politics, Government, Law, and Economy
Act of Parliament refines Settlement Laws to ease labour mobility while increasing the effective discretionary and monitoring powers of local authorities (basic grounds of settlement and removal).

Society, Education, and Religion
Claude Fleury, *Histoire ecclésiastique* started (completed in 20 volumes, 1720).
Anthony à Wood, *Athenae Oxonienses*, 2 vols.

Everyday Life
A society for the Reformation of Manners (the first of many in the 1690s) is set up in Tower Hamlets, for the prosecution of swearing, drunkenness and immorality.

1692 Witch-hunt in Salem, Massachusetts: in all 160 persons are accused between Feb and Oct 1692; last trials take place May 1693.

Feb: **13th**, massacre of MacDonalds by the Campbells at Glencoe, on government orders.

May: **19th**, (or 29th) English defeat French navy at La Hogue.

June: —, the French capture Namur, in Louis XIV's presence.

Politics, Government, Law, and Economy
Queen Mary founds Greenwich Hospital for wounded sailors and pensioners.

Society, Education, and Religion
William and Mary College, Virginia, is founded.

Science, Technology, and Discovery
Ijsbrand Iders explores the Gobi Desert (–1694).

Humanities and Scholarship
The Anglo-Saxon Chronicle, edited by Edmund Gibson.

Music
Henry Purcell, *The Fairy Queen* (opera).

1693 Carolina is divided into North and South Carolina.
Dutch take Pondicherry after siege.

Feb: —, The National Debt is established in England.

March: **23rd**, Lord Somers is appointed Lord Keeper, the head of the 'Whig' Junta.

Aug: —, Louis XIV fails to take Liège and never appears in the field with his troops again.

Dec: —, Louis XIV puts out feelers for peace – the turning-point in his foreign policy.

Politics, Government, Law, and Economy
William Penn, *An Essay on the Present and Future Peace of Europe*, suggests federation.

Science, Technology, and Discovery
Edmund Halley compiles tables for calculating the distance from the sun.

1694 **Dec:** **3rd**, Triennial Bill becomes law.
28th, Queen Mary II dies.

Politics, Government, Law, and Economy
(27th July) The Bank of England is founded.

Science, Technology, and Discovery
Rudolf Camerarius discusses the reproductive organs of plants in *De sexu plantarum epistola*.

Humanities and Scholarship
Dictionnaire de l'Académie française, 2 vols.
George Fox, *Journal* (posthumous), edited by Thomas Ellwood.

Art, Sculpture, Fine Arts, and Architecture
Sir Christopher Wren, Greenwich Hospital.

1695 **April:** —, Government censorship of the Press is ended in England.

May: **3rd**, an Act is passed to prevent bribery in Parliamentary elections.

Politics, Government, Law, and Economy
Window Tax is enforced in England.

Science, Technology, and Discovery
Nehemiah Grew isolates magnesium sulphate ('Epsom Salts') from spring water.

Music
Henry Purcell, *The Indian Queen* and *The Tempest* (operas).

Literature
William Congreve, *Love For Love* (comedy).

1696 **Feb:** **27th**, (–May) the Oath of Association to defend William III and preserve the Protestant settlement is taken throughout England and Wales.

July: **29th**, Peter the Great takes Azov from the Turks.

Sept: —, The Russian Tsar Peter the Great conquers Kamchatka.

Politics, Government, Law, and Economy
Re-coinage of British silver money is carried out under John Locke and Isaac Newton.

1697 China conquers West Mongolia.

March: **21st**, (–Sept 1698) Peter the Great visits Prussia, Holland, England and Vienna, prompting him to introduce reforms in Russia.

May: **1st**, the English ministry becomes wholly Whig in composition.

June: **27th**, the Elector Augustus of Saxony is elected King of Poland in succession to John III.

Sept: **10th**, (or 20th) the Treaty of Ryswick is signed between France, England, Holland and Spain, to end the war (Austria signs 30th Oct).

Politics, Government, Law, and Economy
Daniel Defoe, *An Essay upon Projects*, recommends income tax.
English statute lays down that the poor are to be distinguished by wearing badges.

Humanities and Scholarship
Pierre Bayle, *Dictionnaire historique et critique*, 2 vols. (biographical).
John Dryden translates Virgil's *Pastorals*; *Georgics*; and the *Aeneid*.

Music

John Blow, anthem for opening service of St. Paul's Cathedral, London.

Literature

John Dryden, *Alexander's Feast*; or *The Power of Musique*.
Charles Perrault, *Contes de ma mère l'Oye*.

1698 The French establish a legation in China.

June: 17th, Peter the Great's foreign mercenaries scatter the Streltzy rebels in Moscow.

Sept: —, Peter the Great executes the Streltzy rebels (–Oct). He imposes a tax on beards in Russia.

Politics, Government, Law, and Economy

Last poll tax in England until 1989, abandoned because of unpopularity, difficulties of collection and low yield.

Science, Technology, and Discovery

Thomas Savery patents a pumping-machine, the first practical steam engine.

Art, Sculpture, Fine Arts, and Architecture

Jules Hardouin-Mansart, Place Vendôme.

1699 Jan: 26th, the Peace of Karlowitz is signed by Austria, Russia, Poland and Venice with Turkey; it cedes Hungary, Transylvania, Croatia and Slavonia to the Habsburgs.

Dec: 20th, Peter the Great decrees that the New Year in Russia is to begin on 1st Jan (instead of 1st Sept), and introduces administrative reforms.

Politics, Government, Law, and Economy

Pierre Lemoyne founds the first European settlement in Louisiana at Fort Maurepas.

Science, Technology, and Discovery

Dampier explores the north-west coast of Australia.

Art, Sculpture, Fine Arts, and Architecture

John Vanbrugh, Castle Howard (–1726).

Literature

François de Salignac de la Mothe Fénelon, *Télémaque* (suppressed; –1717).

1700 Administrative reorganization of Bengal under Sir Charles Eyre.

May: —, Saxon troops invade Livonia, which marks the start of the Great Northern War (–1721).

Aug: 18th, Charles XII enforces the peace of Travendal on Denmark.

Oct: 3rd, Charles II of Spain appoints Philip of Anjou his heir.

Nov: 1st, Charles II dies.
30th, Charles XII defeats Peter the Great at Narva.

Politics, Government, Law, and Economy

Sewall, *The Selling of Joseph*, the first American protest against slavery.
Approximate populations (in millions): France 19; Austrian Habsburg dominions 7½; Great Britain and Ireland 7½; Spain 6.

Science, Technology, and Discovery

Berlin Academy of Science is founded, with Gottfried von Leibniz as president.
Henry Winstanley completes Eddystone lighthouse (the tower is destroyed by gale, 20th Nov, 1703).

Humanities and Scholarship

Sir John Cotton bestows his grandfather's collection of books and manuscripts to the nation. Transferred to British Museum, 1753.
The Gregorian Calendar adopted by German Protestants.

Literature

William Congreve, *The Way of the World* (comedy).

1701 A fort and settlement at Detroit is founded by Antoine de la Mothe Cadillac.

Jan: 18th, Frederick III of Brandenburg is crowned Frederick I, King of Prussia.

Feb: —, War of Spanish Succession begins; Philip of Anjou enters Madrid as Philip V of Spain while French troops also occupy Southern Spanish Netherlands.

June: 12th, Act of Settlement provides for Protestant succession in Britain of House of Hanover by Sophia, Princess of Hanover.

Aug: 27th, (or 7th Sept) the Treaty of the Hague, known as the Grand Alliance, is signed, by which Britain, Holland and the Emperor ally against France.

Sept: 6th, James II dies and Louis XIV recognizes the Old Pretender as James III.

Politics, Government, Law, and Economy
William III's charters to weavers in Axminster and Wilton for making carpets.
Yale College, New Haven, Connecticut, founded.

Society, Education, and Religion
Society for Propagating the Gospel in Foreign Parts founded (SPG), London.
Father Francisco Ximénez collects and translates the *Popul Vah*, the sacred national book of the Quiché Indians of Guatemala (–1721).

Science, Technology, and Discovery
Jethro Tull invents a machine-drill for sowing crops in drills.
A terrestrial globe is made at Lyons showing the lakes of Africa.

Everyday Life
(23rd Feb) Capt. Kidd is hanged for piracy.

1702 Rebellion of Camisards Protestant peasants, in Cévennes.

Feb: 24th, Act of Abjuration of the Pretender.

March: 8th, (or 19th) William III dies and is succeeded by Queen Anne in Britain (–1714).
24th, the Earl of Marlborough becomes Captain-General of the English armed forces.

April: 23rd, (–4th May) Britain, Holland and the Emperor declare war against France.

May: 14th, Charles XII of Sweden takes Warsaw and subsequently (July) Cracow.

Politics, Government, Law, and Economy
The Asiento Company is founded to transport negroes to Spanish America.

Humanities and Scholarship
Edward Hyde, the Earl of Clarendon, *The History of the Rebellion* (posthumous).
Daniel Defoe, *The Shortest Way With Dissenters.*

Media
(2nd March) *The Daily Courant*, the first daily paper is issued in London (–1735).

1703 **Jan: —**, Delaware becomes a separate colony from Pennsylvania.

May: —, the Chushingura Incident in Japan when Kiva Yoshinaka is murdered by supporters of the dead Lord of Ako.

Sept: 12th, Archduke Charles is proclaimed King of Spain in Madrid.

Nov: —, Queen Anne's Bounty to increase the incomes of small benefices.

Politics, Government, Law, and Economy
(June) Peter the Great lays the foundations of St. Petersburg.

Everyday Life
(16th Dec) Following the reduction of duties on port, brought about by the Methuen Treaty with Portugal, port becomes popular in England.

1704 Peter the Great fortifies Kronstadt to protect St. Petersburg.

April: —, the French ally with the Indians and massacre inhabitants of Deerfield, in the Connecticut Valley.

June: 21st, (or 2nd July) Marlborough is victorious at Donauwörth.

July: —, Stanislaus Lesczcynski is elected King of Poland as Stanislaus I (–1709) at Charles XII's instigation after Augustus II is deported (Jan).
24th, (or 4th Aug) British, under Sir George Rooke, take Gibraltar.

Aug: 2nd, (or 13th) Marlborough and Prince Eugène of Savoy defeat the French and Bavarians at Blenheim.

Science, Technology, and Discovery
Isaac Newton publishes *Optics*, which defends the corpuscular theory of light.

Humanities and Scholarship
Antoine Galland, translates into French *The Arabian Nights Entertainment* (–1708).

Music
J S Bach writes his first cantata.

Literature
Jonathan Swift, *A Tale of a Tub* and *The Battle of the Books.*

Everyday Life
Beau Nash becomes master of ceremonies at Bath.

Media
Boston News-Letter, the first newspaper in America is issued weekly from 24th April.

1705 Husseinite dynasty of Beys becomes ruler of Tunis and throws off Turkish suzerainty.

July: **—**, Revolution in Russia at Astrakhan, against Peter's westernization.

Oct: **4th**, (or 15th) British navy, under Lord Peterborough, takes Barcelona.

Science, Technology, and Discovery
Edmund Halley conjectures that a comet seen in 1682 was identical with comets observed in 1607, 1531 and earlier; he correctly predicts its return in 1758.
Thomas Newcomen improves the steam-engine by using a vacuum to drive the piston.

Humanities and Scholarship
Bernard de Mandeville, *The Grumbling Hive* (–1714).

Art, Sculpture, Fine Arts, and Architecture
Sir John Vanbrugh, Blenheim Palace.

Music
(8th Jan) G F Handel, *Almira* (opera) produced in Hamburg.

Literature
Prosper Jolyot Crébillon (*père*), *Idoménée* (tragedy).
Sir John Vanbrugh, *The Confederacy* (comedy).

1706 Riots in Scotland over proposed union with England.

May: **12th**, (or 23rd) Marlborough defeats French at Ramillies and conquers Spanish Netherlands.

June: **—**, British and Portuguese enter Madrid.

Politics, Government, Law, and Economy
The Sun Fire Office is founded in London.

1707 **March:** **3rd**, Aurangzeb dies in India and is succeeded by Bahadur, but his Empire falls apart.

May: **1st**, Union between England and Scotland under the name of Great Britain.

Aug: **—**, 'Perpetual' Alliance between Prussia and Sweden is signed.

Politics, Government, Law, and Economy
Vauban in *Díme Royal* attacks exemptions from taxation in France and pleads for uniform land and income taxes; it is burnt on Louis XIV's orders.

Science, Technology, and Discovery
English physician John Floyer introduces the practice of counting the rate of pulse-beats of patients.

Literature
George Farquhar, *The Beaux' Stratagem* (comedy).

1708 War of Emboabas in Brazil between Portuguese and Paulistas (Portuguese slave-raiding parties).

March: **23rd**, the Old Pretender arrives at Firth of Forth but, 27th, returns to Dunkirk.

June: **30th**, (or 11th July) Duke of Marlborough and Prince Eugène defeat French at Oudenarde.

Aug: **—**, British take Sardinia.
18th, (or 29th) British capture Minorca.

Science, Technology, and Discovery
The first accurate map of China is made as a result of surveys by Jesuit missionaries.

1709 First Russian prisoners are sent to Siberia.
Rising of Afghans at Kandahar under Mir Vais.

May: **—**, first mass emigration of Germans from the Palatinate to North America.

July: **8th**, Peter I of Russia defeats Charles XII at Poltava.

Aug: **31st**, (–11th Sept) Marlborough and Prince Eugène defeat the French at Malplaquet.

Politics, Government, Law, and Economy
First Copyright Act in Britain, to operate from 1st April, 1710.

Science, Technology, and Discovery
George Berkeley publishes *New Theory of Vision*.
Abraham Darby constructs first successful experiment, at Coalbrookdale, Shropshire, for using coke in a blast-furnace to smelt iron.

Humanities and Scholarship
Remaining Port-Royalists forcibly removed and the buildings destroyed.

Music
Bartolomeo Cristofori makes the first pianoforte.

1710 Mauritius, which was formerly part of Dutch East Indies, becomes French.
War of Mascates between Portuguese and Brazilian Indians begins.

Aug: 8th, fall of Whig Ministry; Robert Harley and Henry St. John form Tory Ministry.

Nov: 30th, Turkey declares war against Russia at the instigation of Charles XII.

Politics, Government, Law, and Economy
Fénelon recommends the summoning of the States-General in France.

Science, Technology, and Discovery
The dye, Prussian blue, is first made.

Humanities and Scholarship
George Berkeley, *A Treatise Concerning the Principles of Human Knowledge.*
Cotton Mather, *Essays to Do Good.*

1711 **April: 17th**, Joseph I dies and is ultimately succeeded by his brother, Charles III of Spain, as the Emperor Charles VI, but he does not leave Spain until September.

May: 1st, Peace of Szathmar, an agreement between the Hungarian rebels and the Emperor, is signed. Charles VI promises to respect the Hungarian Constitution.

Aug: 1st, Peter I, surrounded by Turks at the Pruth, makes peace and restores Azov.

Sept: —, the Tuscarura War in North Carolina.
22nd, Rio de Janeiro is captured by the French.

Dec: 31st, Duke of Marlborough is dismissed as Commander-in-Chief.

Humanities and Scholarship
Berlin Academy started, under the Presidency of Leibniz.
London Academy of Arts opened.

Music
Johann Adolf Hasse introduces the clarinet into the orchestra in his opera *Croesus.*
John Shore invents the tuning fork.

Media
(1st March) Joseph Addison and Richard Steele found *The Spectator* (–Dec 6th, 1712).

1712 War of Succession between Bahadur's four sons in India.

Jan: 1st, (or 12th) Peace Congress opens at Utrecht.

July: 8th, (or 19th) Anglo-French truce.
24th, the Dutch are defeated by Villars at Denain and join the truce.

Sept: 7th, the Danes and Russian troops defeat Swedes in Baltic and Scandinavia.

Politics, Government, Law, and Economy
The last execution for witchcraft in England.
(1st Aug) The Stamp Act in England imposes a tax of 1d. on a whole sheet.

Humanities and Scholarship
Biblioteca National, Madrid, founded.

Literature
Alexander Pope, *The Rape of the Lock.*

1713 **Feb: —**, Charles XII of Sweden is taken prisoner by the Turkish Sultan (until Sept 1714).
25th, Frederick I of Prussia dies and is succeeded by Frederick William I (–1740).

March: 31st, (–11th April) Peace of Utrecht between France, Britain, Holland, Savoy, Portugal and Prussia. Philip V, a Bourbon, is recognized as King of Spain, but Spain and France are never to be united under one king.

April: 19th, the Emperor Charles VI issues the Pragmatic Sanction setting out female rights of succession to Habsburg domains.

July: 27th, the Peace of Adrianople between Turkey and Russia.

Politics, Government, Law, and Economy
Abbé Saint Pierre, *Projet pour la Paix Perpétuelle.*

Music

The School of Dance is established at the Paris Opéra.

Literature

The Scriblerus Club founded in London (by Alexander Pope, Jonathan Swift, William Congreve, John Gay and others).

Joseph Addison, *Cato.*

1714 **March: 13th**, Battle of Storkyro leads to Russian domination of Finland.

Aug: 1st, Queen Anne dies and is succeeded by George Lewis, Elector of Hanover, as George I (–1727) (the Electress Sophia had died 28th May).

Science, Technology, and Discovery

Jethro Tull introduces the horse-hoe to England from France.

Humanities and Scholarship

Gottfried Wilhelm von Leibniz, *Monadologie.*

Art, Sculpture, Fine Arts, and Architecture

Thomas Archer, St. John's Church, Smith Square, Westminister (–1728).

James Gibbs, St. Mary-le-Strand Church, London (–1717).

1715 Venetians are expelled from the Morea by Turks.

Large-scale German and Scots-Irish immigrations to N. America begins.

March: 27th, Lord Bolingbroke flees to James III in France.

April: —, Prussia, Saxony, Poland, Hanover and Denmark form an alliance against Sweden and war is declared.

15th, rising of Yamassees and other Indian tribes in S. Carolina takes place.

Sept: 1st, Louis XIV dies and is succeeded by Louis XV (–1774), his 5-year-old great-grandson, under the regency of the Duc d'Orléans, his nephew, until 1723.

6th, Jacobite rising begins at Braemar in Scotland, under the Earl of Mar.

Oct: 12th, (–10th April 1717) Robert Walpole becomes First Lord of the Treasury and Chancellor of the Exchequer.

Nov: 13th, the Jacobites are defeated at Sheriffmuir.

13th, (–14th) the Jacobites are also defeated at the Battle of Preston.

Dec: 22nd, James III, the 'Pretender', arrives at Peterhead having sailed from France.

24th, Prussians take Stralsund from Sweden and Charles XII attacks Norway.

Science, Technology, and Discovery

John Lethbridge devises a water-tight suit for diving.

Humanities and Scholarship

Alexander Pope's verse translation of Homer's *Iliad*, vol. 1 (–1720).

Art, Sculpture, Fine Arts, and Architecture

Giovanni Tiepolo, *Sacrifice of Isaac.*

Literature

Alain-René Lesage, *Gil Blas de Santillane* (–1735).

1716 Moldavia and Wallachia obtain Phanariot governors.

Feb: 10th, James III returns to France and subsequently dismisses Bolingbroke.

April: 13th, the Emperor declares war on Turkey.

26th, British Parliament passes the Septennial Act.

Dec: 24th, (or 24th Jan 1717) Triple Alliance of England France and Holland against intrigues of the Pretender, Charles XII of Sweden and Alberoni, the Parmesan Minister at Madrid.

Politics, Government, Law, and Economy

John Law establishes the Banque Générale in France.

Art, Sculpture, Fine Arts, and Architecture

Antoine Watteau, *La leçon d'amour.*

Music

François Couperin, *L'Art de toucher le clavecin.*

1717 The Act of Grace provides for the release of the Jacobite rebels in British prisons.

Stanhope puts into force Walpole's Sinking Fund to reduce the national debt.

Feb: —, James III, the Pretender, is forced to leave France because of the Triple Alliance.

Aug: —, John Law's Mississippi Company is given the monopoly of trade with Louisiana.

16th, Prince Eugène defeats the Turks at Belgrade, which he subsequently occupies.

22nd, Spain attacks Sardinia and it is taken by the end of Nov.

Society, Education, and Religion

The *Bangorian Controversy* leads to the indefinite prorogation of Convocation.

Science, Technology, and Discovery

Lady Mary Wortley Montague introduces the practice of inoculation for smallpox into England; the inoculation of the Princess of Wales makes it fashionable.

Humanities and Scholarship

Joseph Simon Assemani sent by the Pope to Egypt and Syria to search for manuscripts.

Art, Sculpture, Fine Arts, and Architecture

Antoine Watteau, *Embarkation for the Isle of Cytheria.*

Music

G F Handel, first performance of *Water Music* suite of 21 pieces, by a band of 50 musicians in a barge alongside King George's barge at a water concert on the Thames.

1718

New Orleans is founded by the Mississippi Company.
Spain founds Pensacola, Florida.
Chinese troops are annihilated by the western Mongols in an attempt to obtain Lhasa.

July: 7th, Alexis, heir to Peter the Great of Russia, is murdered at the instigation of his father.

21st, the Peace of Passarowitz ends the war between the Empire and Turkey; the Empire retains Belgrade; Turkey keeps the Morea.

22nd, (or 2nd Aug) the Quadruple Alliance is signed between France, the Emperor, England and Holland against Spain, after the Spanish seizure of Sicily.

31st, (or 11th Aug) Admiral Byng defeats Spain off Cape Passaro.

Dec: 11th, Charles XII of Sweden is killed at Frederikshall in an expedition against Norway and is succeeded, after a revolution, by his sister Ulrica Eleanor (–1720).

Politics, Government, Law, and Economy

Transportation Act in England provides for transportation of felons.

Science, Technology, and Discovery

Etienne Geoffroy presents tables of affinities (*tables des rapports*) to the French Academy.
(9th Sept) Thomas Lombe's patent for a machine to make thrown silk.

1719

Mohammed Shah, grandson of Bahadur, Great Mogul (–1748).

June: —, Emperor Charles VI expels Spaniards from Sicily.

Dec: 15th, Cardinal Alberoni falls in Spain and is banished by Philip V.

Literature

Daniel Defoe, *Robinson Crusoe* (and *The Further Adventures of Robinson Crusoe*).

Media

The Boston Gazette is founded by William Brooker (21st Dec) and *The American Mercury* is issued in Philadelphia (22nd Dec).

1720

Spain occupies Texas (–1722) under Marquis of Aguayo.

Feb: 6th, Peace treaty is signed between the Quadruple Alliance and Spain; the Duke of Savoy becomes King of Sardinia.

Sept: 10th, The 'South Sea Bubble' begins to burst.

Dec: —, John Law flees from France after his financial schemes, in particular those of his Mississippi Company, lead to wave of speculation resulting in national banruptcy.

Politics, Government, Law, and Economy

The French government establishes a body of technical civil servants to oversee roads and bridges.

Science, Technology, and Discovery

Fahrenheit uses mercury in a thermometer.

Humanities and Scholarship

Bernard de Montfaucon, *L'Antiquité Expliquée* (–1724, 15 vols.).

Art, Sculpture, Fine Arts, and Architecture

Giovanni Tiepolo, *Martyrdom of St. Bartholomew.*
Nicholas Hawksmoor, Church of St. George's, Bloomsbury, London (–1730).

1721

China suppresses a revolution in Formosa.

April: 3rd, Robert Walpole becomes First Lord of the Treasury and Chancellor of the Exchequer (–1742).

Sept: 10th, Treaty of Rystad is signed between Sweden and Russia; the latter acquires Livonia, Estonia, Ingria and East Karelia, but restores Finland.

Nov: 2nd, Peter I is proclaimed Emperor of All the Russias.

Humanities and Scholarship
Nathaniel Bailey, *An Universal Etymological English Dictionary* (–1731).

Music
J S Bach completes *The Brandenburg Concertos.*
G F Handel, *Acis and Galatea* (opera).

Literature
Charles de Secondat, Baron de la Brède et de Montesquieu, *Lettres Persanes.*

1722 Yung Cheng dynasty in China with the accession of Shih Tsung (–1735).

March: **8th**, Mir Mahmud of Afghanistan begins war against Persia (which capitulates by Sept, and he becomes Shah).

Sept: **12th**, Russians take Baku and Derbent on the Caspian Sea from Persia.

Art, Sculpture, Fine Arts, and Architecture
James Gibbs Church of St. Martin-in-the-Fields, London (–1726).

Music
J S Bach, *Das Wohltemperierte Clavier*, pt. 1.
Jean-Philippe Rameau, *Traité de l'harmonie.*

Literature
Daniel Defoe, *A Journal of the Plague Year*, *Colonel Jacque*, *Moll Flanders.*

1723 Prussia establishes a General Directory of War, Finance and Domains.

Feb: **16th**, Louis XV attains his majority.

Politics, Government, Law, and Economy
The Waltham Black Act adds at least 50 capital offences to the English statute book.
Workhouse Test Act authorizes the establishment of parish workhouses.

Science, Technology, and Discovery
M A Capeller publishes *Prodromus Crystallographie*, the earliest treatise on crystallography.

Humanities and Scholarship
T' U Shu Chi Ch'êng – a Chinese Encyclopaedia, compiled by Imperial Mandate (–1736).

Art, Sculpture, Fine Arts, and Architecture
Nicholas Hawksmoor, Christ Church, Spitalfields (–1739).

Literature
Voltaire, *La Henriade* (first published as *La Ligue*).

1724 The Afghan ruler Mahmud becomes insane and orders the massacre of the Persian nobility and royal family.
Congress of Cambrai meets throughout the year.

Jan: **14th**, Philip V of Spain abdicates, during a fit of religious mania, in favour of Don Luis, as Luis 1; he resumes the throne after Luis dies 31st Aug.

Science, Technology, and Discovery
Jacapo Francesco Riccati propounds his equation, an important type of differential equation.
Hermann Boerhaave publishes *Elements of Chemistry*, a pioneer study of organic chemistry.

Music
J S Bach, *St. John Passion* (oratorio).
The Three Choirs Festival is founded for choirs in Gloucester, Hereford and Worcester.

Literature
Jonathan Swift, *Drapier's Letters.*

1725 Ashraf Shah, an Afghan, succeeds Mahmud in Persia.

Feb: **—**, Louis XV dismisses the Spanish Infanta who was due to marry him, which angers Spain. As a result Spain draws nearer to the Emperor.
8th, Peter the Great of Russia dies and is succeeded by his wife, Catherine (–1727).

Science, Technology, and Discovery
John Flamsteed publishes *Historia coelestis* (posthumous).

Humanities and Scholarship
Alexander Pope, *The Odyssey of Homer* translated.
Giambattista Vico, *Scienza nuova intorno alla natura* (revised 1730, 1744).

Art, Sculpture, Fine Arts, and Architecture
Antonio Canaletto, *Four views of Venice*, for Stefano Conti of Lucca.

Music
Joseph Fux, *Gradus ad Parnassum* (treatise on counterpoint) published in Vienna.

1726

Science, Technology, and Discovery
General George Wade begins building military roads in Scottish Highlands.

Humanities and Scholarship
Real Academia Española, Madrid (founded 1714) publishes vol. I of a *Diccionario* (–1739).
(May) Voltaire lands in England on liberation from the Bastille (returns to France 1729).

Art, Sculpture, Fine Arts, and Architecture
Giovanni Tiepolo, frescoes in the Bishop's Palace, Udine (–1728).

Music
G F Handel becomes a British subject by Act of Naturalisation.
Jean-Philippe Rameau, *Nouveau système de musique théorique.*

Literature
Jonathan Swift, *Gulliver's Travels.*
James Thomson, *Winter* (part I of *The Seasons*, other volumes published 1727, 1728, 1730).

1727

England first engages Hessian mercenaries for the defence of Hanover.

Feb: —, Without a formal declaration, war begins between England and Spain by the latter's siege of Gibraltar (–24th Feb 1727).

June: **11th**, George I dies and is succeeded by his son George II (–1760).

Science, Technology, and Discovery
Stephen Hales obtains oxygen, but fails to recognize he has discovered a new element. His *Statical Essays* explain the nutrition of plants.
J A de Peyssonel discovers the animal nature of red coral.

1728

Feb: **24th**, (or 6th Mar) Convention of the Pardo ends the Anglo-Spanish war.

Science, Technology, and Discovery
Fauchard publishes *Le Chirurgien Dentiste ou traité des dents.*
Payn and Hanbury constructs a rolling-mill for sheet iron.
Virus Behring discovers Behring Strait.

Humanities and Scholarship
Ephraim Chambers, *Cyclopaedia; or An Universal Dictionary of Arts and Sciences*, 2 folio vols.

Music
John Gay, *Beggar's Opera*, first performed in Lincoln's Inn Fields Theatre, London.

Literature
Alexander Pope, *The Dunciad*, bks. 1–3.
Allan Ramsay, *Poems.*

1729

Baltimore is founded.
Corsica becomes independent of Genoa after a series of revolutions (Genoa regains the island 1732).
North and South Carolina become Crown colonies.

Nov: —, Portugal loses Mombasa to the Muscat Arabs.

Science, Technology, and Discovery
Stephen Gray discovers that some bodies are conductors of electricity.

Art, Sculpture, Fine Arts, and Architecture
John Wood, Queen's Square, Bath (–1736).

Music
J S Bach, *St. Matthew Passion* (oratorio).

Literature
Jonathan Swift, *A Modest Proposal.*

Everyday Life
The Emperor Yung Cheng prohibits opium smoking in China.

Media
James and Benjamin Franklin publish *The Pennsylvania Gazette* (–1765).

1730

Kuli Khan expels Afghans from Persia; Ashraf is murdered.

Sept: **17th**, Ahmad XII is deposed and succeeded by Mahmoud I in Turkey (–1754).

Politics, Government, Law, and Economy
Townshend introduces a four-course system of husbandry in Norfolk, cultivating clover and turnips.

Science, Technology, and Discovery
René-Antoine Ferchault de Réaumur invents alcohol thermometer and temperature scale in which the freezing point of water is 0° and the boiling point 80°.

Media
The Daily Advertiser started in London (–1807).

1731 Spanish *guarda-costas* mutilate Jenkins, an English captain, for trading in defiance of their monopoly.

Dec: —, The Empire, Russia and Prussia agree to act together to oppose Stanislaus I in Poland.

Art, Sculpture, Fine Arts, and Architecture
William Hogarth, *Harlot's Progress* (–1732).

Music
Lodovico Giustini di Pistoia composes 12 sonatas for *cimbalo di piano e forte*, probably the first works written specially for piano.

Literature
Pierre Carlet de Chamblain de Marivaux, *La Vie de Marianne* .

1732 Genoa regains Corsica.

July: —, 139 members of the Paris *Parlement* are exiled by order of the King, but are eventually triumphant over the Crown, and secure their recall in Dec

Humanities and Scholarship
George Berkeley, *Alciphron*; or *The Minute Philosopher*.

Art, Sculpture, Fine Arts, and Architecture
J B S Chardin, *Kitchen table with shoulder of mutton.*
Salvi, The Trevi Fountain, Rome.

Literature
Benjamin Franklin, *Poor Richard's Almanack* started (–1757).

1733 Conscription is introduced in Prussia.

Feb: **1st**, Augustus II of Poland (and Saxony) dies.

Aug: **14th**, outbreak of War of Polish Succession.

Nov: **7th**, by the Treaty of Escurial, France and Spain declare the Union of the two branches of the Bourbon family indivisible.

Politics, Government, Law, and Economy
James Oglethorpe makes first settlement in Georgia, at Savannah.

Science, Technology, and Discovery
(26th May) John Kay patents his Flying Shuttle.

Art, Sculpture, Fine Arts, and Architecture
The Serpentine Lake, Hyde Park, London, is laid out for Queen Caroline.

Music
J P Rameau, *Hippolytus and Aricio* (opera), first performed in Paris.

Literature
Alexander Pope, *Essay on Man.*
Antoine François Prévost, *Manon Lescaut.*
Voltaire, *English Letters.*

1734 8,000 Protestants from Salzburg settle in Georgia.

Feb: —, Turkish-Persian war (–Oct 1735).

May: —, The Spanish army, under Don Carlos, conquers Naples.

June: **17th**, French troops take Philipsburg, but the Duke of Berwick is killed.
30th, Russian troops take Danzig which had been besieged since Oct 1733.

Oct: —, Risings of Servian and Hungarian peasants are ruthlessly suppressed.

Science, Technology, and Discovery
René Réaumur publishes *History of Insects*, a founding work of entomology.

Humanities and Scholarship
Charles-Louis de Secondat, Baron de Montesquieu, *Considérations sur la cause de la grandeur des Romains et de leur décadence.*

Art, Sculpture, Fine Arts, and Architecture
Nicholas Hawksmoor, West Towers, Westminster Abbey.

Music
J S Bach, *Christmas Oratorio.*

Sport and Recreation
First horse-race in America, at Charleston Neck, South Carolina.

1735 Chien Lung becomes Emperor of China.

Aug: —, A Russian army reaches the Rhine; Fleury in alarm hastens his peace overtures.

Oct: **3rd**, preliminary peace accord at Vienna.

Society, Education, and Religion
The Wesleys (Charles and John) start their Methodist Revival in Georgia, America (see 1738).

Science, Technology, and Discovery
Carlous Linnaeus introduces the modern system for classifying plants and animals in *Systema Naturae.*
Benoît de Maillet in *Telliamed* puts forward the evolutional hypothesis.
A French scientific expedition under Charles de la Condamine is sent to South America to explore the R. Amazon.

Art, Sculpture, Fine Arts, and Architecture
William Hogarth, *Rake's Progress.*

Music
Rameau, *Les Indes Galantes* (ballet).

Literature
Marivaux, *Le Paysan parvenu.*

1736 **Jan:** **26th**, Stanislaus I formally abdicates as King of Poland.

Feb: —, Nadir Shah becomes King of Persia (–1747).

May: —, Russia attacks Turkey in order to regain Azov (the war lasts till 1739).

Sept: **7th**, Porteous Riots in Edinburgh.

Politics, Government, Law, and Economy
English Statutes against witchcraft are repealed.

Society, Education, and Religion
Pope Clement XII condemns freemasonry.

Science, Technology, and Discovery
The French Academy sponsors an expedition to Lapland under Andreas Celsius to measure the arc of meridian.
Leonhard Euler founds the study of mechanics based on differential equations.

Music
G Pergolese, *Stabat Mater* (oratorio).

1737 Turkish army defeats Maria Theresa's forces which are supporting the Russians; Seckendorf, Austrian Field Marshal, is recalled and imprisoned until 1740.

April: —, William Byrd founds Richmond, Virginia.

Society, Education, and Religion
John Wesley, *Psalms and Hymns* (published in Charleston).

Science, Technology, and Discovery
J Swammerdam's *Biblia naturae* is re-issued. It describes his microscopic studies of insects.

Art, Sculpture, Fine Arts, and Architecture
J B S Chardin, *The Draughtsman.*
James Gibbs, Radcliffe Camera, Oxford (–1749).

1738 The *Corvée*, a system of forced labour to construct and repair roads, is organized in France.

March: **28th**, debate in Parliament urging war on Spain, as the debate on 'Jenkins' Ear' (Walpole delays a declaration of war until Oct 1739).

Nov: **18th**, France recognizes the Pragmatic Sanction at the Peace Treaty of Vienna.

Society, Education, and Religion

George Whitefield follows John Wesley to Georgia as 'Leader of the Great Awakening'.
(24th May) John Wesley's evangelical conversion.

Science, Technology, and Discovery

Daniel Bernoulli in *Hydrodynamica* studies the pressure and velocities of fluids.

Humanities and Scholarship

Excavation of Herculaneum begins under Colonel D Rocco de Alcubierre (see 1753).

Music

G F Handel, *Israel in Egypt* (oratorio) and *Saul* (oratorio).
Imperial Ballet School is founded in St. Petersburg.

1739 Nadir Shah of Persia sacks Delhi and conquers the Punjab.

July: 22nd, Turks defeat Emperor's troops at Crocyka and threaten Belgrade.

Sept: 18th, Peace of Belgrade between the Emperor Charles VI and Turkey, by which Austria cedes Orsova, Belgrade and Serbia.

23rd, Treaty of Belgrade between Russia and Turkey by which the Tsar restores all conquests except Azov and agrees not to maintain vessels in the Black Sea.

Oct: 8th, England declares war against Spain after Spain refuses to adhere to the Convention of Pardo (of 3rd Jan).

Society, Education, and Religion

The Foundling Hospital, London, is founded.
Moravian Church in America founded by Bishop August Gottlieb Spangenberg.

Humanities and Scholarship

David Hume, *A Treatise on Human Nature* (–1740).
Bernard de Montfaucon compiles *Bibliotheca Bibliothecarum*, a catalogue of manuscripts in European libraries.

1740 Frederick II abolishes torture and introduces liberty of the Press and freedom of worship in Prussia.
Nadir Shar extends his influence in Balkh and Bokhara.

May: 31st, Frederick William I of Prussia dies and is succeeded by Frederick II ('the Great' –1786).

Sept: 18th, (–15th June, 1744) George Anson sets out on voyage around the world.

Oct: 20th, Charles VI dies and is succeeded by his daughter Maria Theresa (–1780). The succession is disputed.

28th, Anne, daughter of Peter the Great, dies and is succeeded by Ivan VI (–1741), grandson of Anne's sister Catherine. Ivan's mother acts as Regent.

Dec: 16th, Frederick II of Prussia enters Silesia and begins the first Silesian War.

Politics, Government, Law, and Economy

Frederick the Great founds the Berlin Academy of Science.

Science, Technology, and Discovery

The dye 'Saxony blue' (Indigo extract) is made.
Anson's voyage round the world in *Centurion.*

Humanities and Scholarship

William Stukeley, *Stonehenge.*

Art, Sculpture, Fine Arts, and Architecture

Antonio Canaletto, *Return of the Bucentoro.*
François Boucher, *Morning Toilet.*

Music

T. Arne, *Alfred* (masque, with words by James Thomson) first performed, containing the song 'Rule Britannia'.

Literature

Samuel Richardson, *Pamela; or Virtue Rewarded.*
Louis de Rouvroy, Duc de Saint-Simon, *Memoirs* (–1752).

1741 Russian expedition to Alaska opens fur trade under Behring.

April: 10th, Frederick II defeats Maria Theresa's forces at Mollwitz and conquers Silesia.

Aug: 15th, French troops cross Rhine to invade south Germany, Austria and Bohemia.

Nov: 26th, French, Bavarian and Saxon troops take Prague.

Dec: —, Elizabeth becomes Empress of Russia after a bloodless revolution (–1762).

Society, Education, and Religion
Jonathan Edwards publishes *Sinners in the Hands of an Angry God*: sermon delivered at Enfield, Massachusetts and published (a notable event in 'The Great Awakening').

Art, Sculpture, Fine Arts, and Architecture
Bartolomeo Rastrelli, Summer Palace, St Petersburg.

Music
G F Handel, *Messiah*; first performed in Dublin 8th April 1742.

Literature
(19th Oct) David Garrick's début in London, as Richard III.

1742 Dupleix becomes Governor-General of French possessions in India.

Jan: **24th**, Charles Albert, Elector of Bavaria, is elected Emperor; crowned 12th Feb.

Feb: **9th**, Robert Walpole becomes Earl of Orford.
11th, Walpole resigns his offices.

July: **28th**, Peace of Berlin between Maria Theresa and Prussia ends first Silesian War.

Dec: **12th**, the French evacuate Prague and return to France.

Science, Technology, and Discovery
Anders Celsius invents the centigrade (or Celsius) temperature scale.

Art, Sculpture, Fine Arts, and Architecture
François Boucher, *Bath of Diana* and *La Toilette*.

Literature
Henry Fielding, *Joseph Andrews*.
Edward Young, *The Complaint, or Night Thoughts on Life, Death and Immortality* (–1745).

1743 **April:** —, Maria Theresa is crowned at Prague.

June: **16th**, George II defeats French at Dettingen.

Aug: **17th**, Peace of Aæringåbö ends war between Russia and Sweden.

Society, Education, and Religion
(5th Jan) George Whitefield's meeting at Wadford, Glamorgan, at which the Welsh Calvinistic Methodists form the first Methodist Association.

Science, Technology, and Discovery
Sevington Savary invents a chronometer for measurement by double image.

Art, Sculpture, Fine Arts, and Architecture
William Hogarth, *Marriage à la Mode*.

1744 **March:** **4th**, France declares war on England.

April: **26th**, France declares war on Maria Theresa.

June: **6th**, France allies with Prussia against Maria Theresa.

Aug: —, Louis XV is dangerously ill at Metz.
15th, second Silesian War begins with Frederick II's invasion of Saxony.

Sept: **16th**, Frederick II takes Prague but is driven back into Saxony.

Dec: —, Clive arrives in Madras.
28th, Quadruple Alliance, between Great Britain, Maria Theresa, Saxony-Poland and Holland against Prussia.

Science, Technology, and Discovery
Jean d'Alembert publishes *Traité de l'équilibre et du mouvement des fluides*, applying his principle to fluid motion.
Eruption of Mount Cotopaxi in S. America.

Music
J S Bach, *Das Wohltemperierte Clavier*, Pt. 2.
Gluck, *Iphigénie en Aulide* (opera) performed in Paris.

1745 **Jan:** **20th**, Emperor Charles VII dies.

April: **22nd**, Peace of Füssen between Maria Theresa and Bavaria, which renounces its claim to the Empire and Maria Theresa restores all her conquests in Bavaria to Maximilian Joseph.
30th, French under Marshal Saxe defeat English led by the Duke of Cumberland at Fontenoy, and conquer the Austrian Netherlands.

June: **16th**, British take Cape Breton Island.

July: **23rd**, Charles Edward, the Young Pretender, lands on Eriskay Island, Scotland.

Sept: —, Mme. de Pompadour is installed at Versailles as Louis XV's recognized mistress.
2nd, Charles Edward defeats English army under General Cope at Prestonpans.
11th, Jacobites enter Edinburgh.
12th, Francis Stephen, husband of Maria Theresa is elected Holy Roman Emperor (–1765), the first of the Lorraine-Tuscany line.

Dec: **4th**, Charles Edward advances as far south as Derby but 6th, is forced to retreat.
18th, Jacobite victory at Penrith.
25th, by the Peace of Dresden with Maria Theresa and Saxony, Prussia retains Silesia and in return recognizes the Pragmatic Sanction and Francis I as Emperor.

Science, Technology, and Discovery
Ewald Georg von Kleist invents the Leyden jar.

Humanities and Scholarship
Julien Offroy de Lammettrie, *L'Histoire naturelle de l'âme* (published and burnt in public in France).

Art, Sculpture, Fine Arts, and Architecture
Giovanni Tiepolo, frescoes on the theme of Antony and Cleopatra for Labia Palace, Venice; also begins painting 137 etchings of Rome.

Music
'The Campbells are Coming', Scottish tune, is published.

Literature
Claude-Prosper Jolyot de Crébillon, *fils, Le Sopha.*

1746 Persecution of Christians in China.

Jan: **16th**, Prince Charles Edward is victorious at Falkirk.

Feb: **20th**, Brussels falls to Marshal Saxe, after a siege since the end of Jan.

April: **16th**, the final defeat of the Jacobites at Culloden by the Duke of Cumberland, who subsequently abolishes the Clan organization.

June: **16th**, victorious at the Battle of Piacenza, Maria Theresa and Sardinia are able to expel the French and Spanish forces from Lombardy and Sardinia.

Sept: **10th**, the French, under Labourdonnais and Dupleix, conquer Madras after a short siege.
20th, with the help of Flora MacDonald the Young Pretender escapes to France.

Oct: **11th**, the French, under Marshal Saxe, are victorious at Raucoux and Maria Theresa loses the Austrian Netherlands.

Society, Education, and Religion
Jonathan Edwards, *A Treatise Concerning the Religious Affections.*
(22nd Oct) The College of New Jersey is founded (becomes Princeton University in 1896).

Science, Technology, and Discovery
Albert von Haller publishes *Disputationes Anatomicae Selectiones*, a pioneer work of anatomy, which includes his discovery of the contraction of muscles.
Jean Étienne Guettard makes first geological map (of France).

Humanities and Scholarship
Étienne Bonnot, Abbé de Condillac, *Essai sur l'origine des connaissances humaines.*

Everyday Life
Lock Hospital for venereal diseases is founded in London.

1747 After the murder of Nadir Shah, Ahmad Shah proclaims himself King of Afghanistan which becomes independent of Persia.

July: **6th**, France and Spain, having tried to relieve Genoa since Feb, finally break the combined blockade of the English fleet and troops of Maria Theresa.

Politics, Government, Law, and Economy
Benjamin Franklin, *Plain Truth.*

Society, Education, and Religion
George Whitefield, *God's Dealings with George Whitefield.*

Humanities and Scholarship
Biblioteca Nazionale founded in Florence in memory of Antonio Magliabecch (d. 1714), who bequeathed his library of 30,000 volumes to the Grand Duke of Tuscany.

Literature
William Collins, *Odes* (*Odes to a Lady*; *Ode to Evening*; *How Sleep the Brave*).
Thomas Gray, *Ode on Eton College.*

1748 Shah Rukh, grandson of Nadir Shah, becomes ruler of Persia and, despite being blinded by a rival, immediately establishes his rule.

Oct: 6th, French raise English siege of Pondicherry.

7th, by the Peace of Aix-la-Chapelle there is a general recognition of Francis I as Holy Roman Emperor and of Frederick II's conquest of Silesia.

Politics, Government, Law, and Economy

Montesquieu, *De l'esprit des lois.*

Science, Technology, and Discovery

Leonhard Euler publishes *Analysis Infinitorum*, an introduction to pure analytical mathematics.

John Fothergill publishes *Account of the Sore Throat, attended with Ulcers*, an early description of diphtheria.

Lewis Paul invents a hand machine for wool-carding.

Humanities and Scholarship

David Hume, *Philosophical Essays Concerning Human Understanding.*

The buried Roman city of Pompeii is discovered under lava from Vesuvius as excavations on the site begin.

Literature

Friedrich Gottlieb Klopstock, *The Messiah* (–1773).

Samuel Richardson, *Clarissa*; or *The History of a Young Lady*, 7 vols.

Tobias George Smollett, *The Adventures of Roderick Random*, 2 vols.

Marie-Thérèse Geoffrin (*née* Rodet) opens her *salon* in Paris.

1749 Halifax, Nova Scotia, is established as a fortress.

Dupleix secures French control of the Carnatic after the battle of Ambur.

Oct: 22nd, the first settlement is founded by the Ohio Co.

Science, Technology, and Discovery

G L L de Buffon publishes *Theory of the Earth.*

Denis Diderot publishes *Lettre sur les aveugles à l'usage de ceux qui voient*, gives expression to the doctrine of relativity, for which he is imprisoned.

Humanities and Scholarship

Étienne Bonnet, Abbé de Condillac, *Traité des systèmes.*

Art, Sculpture, Fine Arts, and Architecture

Thomas Gainsborough, *Mr. and Mrs. Robert Andrews.*

Bartolmeo Rastrelli, Great Palace, Tsarkoie Selo (–1756).

Music

J S Bach, *Die Kunst der Fuge.*

Literature

Henry Fielding, *The History of Tom Jones, A Foundling.*

Ewald Christian von Kleist, *Der Frühling.*

1750 Spain and Portugal exchange colonies in Paraguay and San Sacramento, which leads to a war in Paraguay lasting six years.

Science, Technology, and Discovery

Nicolas de Lacaille leads French expedition to the Cape of Good Hope to observe 10,000 stars in the southern heavens and determines the lunar and solar parallax.

Humanities and Scholarship

Benedictines of Saint-Maur, *Dictionnaire de l'art de vérifier les dates des faits historiques.*

Frederick the Great, *Oeuvres du Philosophe de Sanssouci.*

J J Rousseau, *Discours sur les lettres: Sur les arts et les sciences.*

Literature

John Cleland, *The Memoirs of a Woman of Pleasure.*

(20th March) Samuel Johnson, *The Rambler* started.

Sport and Recreation

The English Jockey Club is founded.

Hambledon Cricket Club is founded, playing on Broad Halfpenny Down, Hampshire.

Statistics

The population of Europe reaches 140,000,000.

1751 China invades Tibet.

May: —, Pombal curbs power of the Inquisition in Portugal.

Politics, Government, Law, and Economy
Code Fredéric, drawn up by Cocceji, replaces Roman law in Prussia.

Society, Education, and Religion
Pennsylvania Academy founded by Benjamin Franklin.

Science, Technology, and Discovery
Carl Linné (Linnaeus) publishes *Philosophia Botanica.*

Humanities and Scholarship
Denis Diderot and Jean le Rond d'Alembert, *Encyclopédie; ou Dictionnaire Raisonné des Sciences, des Arts et des Métiers, par une société de gens de lettres*, Paris.
David Hume, *Enquiry Concerning the Principles of Morals.*
(2nd Nov) Society of Antiquaries, London, granted a royal charter (refounded 1707).

Art, Sculpture, Fine Arts, and Architecture
Lancelot ('Capability') Brown, Croom Court Gardens and House.

Literature
Thomas Gray, *An Elegy Wrote in a Country Churchyard.*
Tobias Smollett, *The Adventures of Peregrine Pickle*, 4 vols.

1752 **June:** **9th**, the French, before Trichinopoly, surrender to Clive and Lawrence.
Sept: **14th**, Britain adopts the Gregorian Calendar (the dates 3rd–13th Sept are omitted).

Politics, Government, Law, and Economy
Murder Act lays down that murderers are not to receive burial but be either hung in chains or handed over to surgeons for dissection.

Science, Technology, and Discovery
Benjamin Franklin performs his famous kite-flying experiment to investigate the nature of lightning.

Music
Gluck completes his opera *La Clemenza de Tito.*

Literature
Henry Fielding, *Amelia*, 4 vols.
Henry St. John (Viscount Bolingbroke) *Letters on the Study and Uses of History*, 2 vols. (posthumous).

1753 France faces bankruptcy.
Louis XV supports the Archbishop of Paris and exiles the Paris *Parlement.*
July: **7th**, Act for the naturalization of Jews in England.
Aug: **—**, Duquesne, French Governor of Canada, seizes the Ohio Valley.

Politics, Government, Law, and Economy
Lord Hardwicke's Marriage Act in Britain ends 'Fleet Prison' and other weddings by unlicensed ministers and requires notice to be given by the calling of banns.

Science, Technology, and Discovery
Carl Linné (Linnaeus) publishes *Species Plantarum.*

Humanities and Scholarship
Georges-Louis Leclerc, Comte de Buffon, *Discours sur le style.*
The Villa dei Papiri is discovered at Herculaneum, and scrolls are found there (see 1738).
Sir Robert Bruce Cotton's Library transferred to the British Museum Library (see 1700).

Art, Sculpture, Fine Arts, and Architecture
J B Pigalle, Tomb Maréchal de Saxe, Strasburg (–1776).

Literature
Samuel Richardson, *Sir Charles Grandison*, vols. 1–4 (–1754).

1754 **June:** **—**, delegates from New England colonies accept Benjamin Franklin's scheme for American Union; the scheme is later rejected by colonial and home governments.
—, Anglo-French war breaks out in North America.
July: **—**, To end the dispute on ecclesiastical affairs, Louis XV recalls the *Parlement.*

Humanities and Scholarship
Étienne Bonnot, Abbé de Condillac, *Traité des sensations.*
Jonathan Edwards, *Inquiry into Freedom of the Will.*
David Hume, *History of Great Britain* (Vol. 1; Vol. 2, 1757; Vols. 3 and 4, 1759; Vols. 5 and 6, 1762).
J J Rousseau, *L'inégalité parmi les hommes: discours* (–1755).

Art, Sculpture, Fine Arts, and Architecture
William Hogarth, *The Election.*
Thomas Chippendale publishes *The Gentleman and Cabinetmaker's Directory.*
Bartolomeo Rastrelli, Winter Palace, St. Petersburg.

Sport and Recreation
St. Andrews Royal and Ancient Golf Club founded.

1755 **April:** —, Pasquale de' Paoli is elected a general in Corsica and subsequently leads revolt against Genoa (–1769).

July: **9th**, British army under General Braddock is crushed by French near Fort Duquesne.

Nov: **1st**, Lisbon earthquake kills 30,000 inhabitants.

Politics, Government, Law, and Economy
R. Cantillon, *Essai sur la nature du commerce en général* founds Physiocratic School of French economists.
Aloung P'Houra Alompra founds Rangoon.

Humanities and Scholarship
Samuel Johnson, *Dictionary of the English Language* (revised –1773).
Johann Joachim Winckelmann, *Gedanken über die Nachahmung der griechischen Werke.*

Art, Sculpture, Fine Arts, and Architecture
Thomas Gainsborough, *The Artist's Daughter chasing a Butterfly* (–1756).

Music
Haydn composes his first string quartet.

Literature
Gotthold Ephraim Lessing, *Miss Sara Sampson.*

1756 **May:** **1st**, Alliance of Versailles between France and Austria constitutes the Diplomatic Revolution, achieved by the Austrian Chancellor, Kaunitz.
17th, Britain declares war on France.

June: **4th**, end of the Quaker supremacy in Pennsylvania, when six leading Quakers resign from the Assembly.
20th, Black Hole of Calcutta, in which over 120 British soldiers are imprisoned and die.

Aug: —, Montcalm, French commander, drives the British from the Great Lakes.
29th, Frederick II invades Saxony. This marks the outbreak of the Seven Years' War.

Oct: **15th**, Saxon army capitulates to Prussia at Pirna.

Politics, Government, Law, and Economy
Victor, Marquis de Mirabeau, *Ami des hommes ou traité de la population.*

Science, Technology, and Discovery
Joseph Black gives the first detailed description of chemical action in *Experiments upon Magnesia, quicklime and other alkaline substances.*

Humanities and Scholarship
Voltaire completes *Siècle de Louis XIV* (begun in 1735).

Art, Sculpture, Fine Arts, and Architecture
Joshua Reynolds, *Admiral Holbourne and his Son ; also Mrs. Francis Beckford.*

Literature
Voltaire, *Désastre de Lisbonne.*

1757 **Jan:** **5th**, J-F Damiens attempts to assassinate Louis XV and is subsequently executed.
17th, Empire declares war on Prussia.

March: **14th**, Admiral Byng is shot for neglect of duty resulting in loss of Minorca to France in May 1756.

May: **6th**, Frederick II defeats Charles of Lorraine at Prague.

June: **18th**, Emperor's forces defeat Frederick II at Kollin and he loses 13,000 of his 33,000 troops.
23rd, Clive takes Plassey, after the Nawab breaks alliance, and recovers Calcutta.

Sept: **8th**, British under the Duke of Cumberland capitulate at Kloster Seven and surrender Hanover and Brunswick. George II refuses to ratify the Convention of Kloster Seven.

Nov: **5th**, Frederick II defeats French and Imperial troops at Rossbach.

Dec: **5th**, Frederick II defeats Imperial troops at Leuthen.

Science, Technology, and Discovery

John Baskerville prints first volume in his new type at Birmingham.

Humanities and Scholarship

Johann Jakob Bodmer edits *Nibelungenlied.*

Denis Diderot, *Entretiens sur Le Fils naturel.*

Art, Sculpture, Fine Arts, and Architecture

J B S Greuze, *La Paresseuse Italienne.*

Jacques Soufflot, St. Geneviève (later the Panthéon), Paris.

Literature

Friedrich Gottlieb Klopstock, *Der Tod Adams* (tragedy).

1758 Robert Clive becomes Governor of Bengal, as President of ruling council of 10 members.

China occupies East Turkestan.

June: **23rd**, the French are defeated at Crefeld by Ferdinand of Brunswick.

30th, Prussian blockade of Olmütz (since 8th May) is ended.

Aug: **25th**, undecided battle of Zorndorf between Prussians, led by Frederick the Great, and Russian troops under Fermor.

27th, Despite the indecisive nature of the battle of Zorndorf, Russian troops withdraw.

Sept: **3rd**, revolution in Portugal, led by Marquis of Tavora and his wife, who wound King Joseph, but plotters soon arrested. Tavora and his wife are executed 13th Jan 1759.

Nov: **25th**, John Forbes and George Washington take Fort Duquesne, which is subsequently renamed Pittsburg.

Politics, Government, Law, and Economy

Quesnai, *Tableau Économique.*

Society, Education, and Religion

Magdalen House is established in London as a reformatory for repentant prostitutes.

Science, Technology, and Discovery

Jedediah Strutt invents a ribbing-machine for the manufacture of hose.

Humanities and Scholarship

Claude Adrien Helvétius, *De l'esprit*; it is published, condemned, and publicly burnt.

Art, Sculpture, Fine Arts, and Architecture

John and Robert Adam, Harewood House (–1771).

Literature

Samuel Johnson, *The Idler* (Universal Chronicle, weekly, –1760).

1759 **July:** **23rd**, Russians under Saltikóv defeat Prussians at Kay.

Aug: **1st**, French are decisively defeated at Minden by Ferdinand of Brunswick.

12th, Russian and Austrian troops, led by Laudon, defeat Frederick II at Kunersdorf.

17th, Boscawen defeats French off Cape St. Vincent.

Sept: **3rd**, expulsion of Jesuits begins in Portugal as a result of the conspiracy of 1758.

18th, British victory at Quebec, but both Montcalm and Wolfe (who scaled the Heights of Abraham, 13th) are killed.

Nov: **20th**, Royal Navy under Admiral Hawke defeats French at Quiberon Bay.

Politics, Government, Law, and Economy

The Annual Register is first issued, edited by Robert Dodsley and Edmund Burke.

Étienne de Silhouette, French Controller-General of Finances, is forced to resign through public outcry at his land tax.

Science, Technology, and Discovery

Alexis Clairault and Jean Bailly calculate the perihelion of Halley's comet. Observations of the return of the comet verify Newton's law.

Humanities and Scholarship

Gotthold Ephraim Lessing, *Die Litteraturbriefe* (–1765).

Adam Smith, *Theory of Moral Sentiments.*

(16th Jan) British Museum opened.

Literature

Samuel Johnson, *Rasselas.*

Voltaire, *Candide.*

1760 Jacobus Coetsee leads a party of Hottentots beyond the Orange River.

Feb: 25th, Robert Clive leaves India, to return to England.

June: 23rd, Prussian army at Landshut suffers crushing defeat.

Aug: 15th, Frederick II, against all odds, defeats Austrian forces at Leignitz.

Sept: 8th, British troops under Jeffrey Amherst take Montreal, and control Canada.

Oct: 9th, (–13th) Russians burn Berlin which is occupied by them, together with Imperial troops, until Frederick's advance from Silesia.
25th, George II dies and is succeeded by his grandson George III (–1820), then aged 22.

Nov: 3rd, Frederick II defeats Austrian troops under Daun at Torgau.

Science, Technology, and Discovery
M. Brisson publishes *Ornithologie.*

Art, Sculpture, Fine Arts, and Architecture
Robert Adam, Interior, Syon House (–1769).

Literature
Denis Diderot writes *La Religieuse* (not published until 1790).
Laurence Sterne, *Tristram Shandy* (vols. 1 and 2) (–1767).

Everyday Life
The silk hat is invented in Florence.

1761 Whiteboys societies founded in Ireland, due to discontent caused by evictions.

Jan: 7th, Afghans defeat Mahrattas at Panipat.
16th, Eyre Coote takes Pondicherry after a siege (since Sept 1760) and this marks the end of French dominion in India.

Oct: —, Austrian troops under Laudon take Schweidnitz and blockade Frederick II at Bunzelwitz.

Politics, Government, Law, and Economy
J P. Süssmilch makes pioneer study of the science of statistics.

Science, Technology, and Discovery
James Brindley completes the Duke of Bridgwater's Canal between Manchester and the Worsley collieries.
The Danish government sponsors an expedition under C Niebuhr to explore Arabia (–1763)

Humanities and Scholarship
Paul Heinrich Dietrich, Baron d'Holbach, *Le Christianisme dévoilé.*

Art, Sculpture, Fine Arts, and Architecture
Lancelot ('Capability') Brown, Bowood gardens.

Music
(1st May) Haydn is engaged as second kapellmeister to Paul Esterházy of Galántha.

Literature
Carlo Goldoni, *Una delle ultime sere di Carnevale* (comedy).
J-J Rousseau, *Julie; ou La Nouvelle Héloise* started (–1765).

1762 **Jan: 5th**, Tsarina Elizabeth of Russia dies and is succeeded by Peter III (–July), who aims at peace.

May: —, Spanish invasion of Portugal, after Portuguese refuse to close ports to British ships.
5th, Treaty of St. Petersburg between Russia and Prussia.

July: 17th, Peter III is assassinated and is succeeded by Catherine II (–1796).

Oct: 29th, battle of Freiburg, in which Austrian troops are defeated by Prince Henry.

Nov: 1st, the French capitulate at Cassel and evacuate the right bank of the Rhine.
3rd, peace preliminaries of Fontainebleau are signed between France, Spain and Britain.
24th, truce between Prussia, Saxony and Empire.

Politics, Government, Law, and Economy
J-J Rousseau, *Du Contrat Social; ou principes du droit politique.*

Science, Technology, and Discovery
Matthew Boulton opens Soho Engineering works at Handsworth Heath, Birmingham.
John Roebuck devises method for converting cast iron into malleable iron at his Carron ironworks in Stirlingshire.

Humanities and Scholarship
The Library of the Sorbonne, Paris, founded; Annapolis Circulating Library opened.

Art, Sculpture, Fine Arts, and Architecture
George Stubbs, *Mares and Foals*.

Music
C Gluck, *Orpheus and Euridice* (opera) is first performed in Vienna in Italian.
W A Mozart and his sister (aged six and ten) begin touring Europe giving concerts.

Literature
Denis Diderot, *Le Neveu de Rameau* (–1773).
Carlo Goldoni, *Le Baruffe chiozzotte* (comedy of the lower classes).
James Macpherson ('Ossian'), *Fingal.*

Media
The North Briton, ed. by John Wilkes and Charles Churchill (–1763).

1763 **Feb: 10th**, the Peace of Paris between Britain, France and Spain ends the Seven Years' War (called in America the French and Indian War), the last of the series of dynastic wars; by its terms (1) Britain secures Canada, Nova Scotia, Cape Breton, St. Vincent, Tobago, Dominica, Grenada, Senegal and Minorca from France, and Florida from Spain; (2) France regains Martinique, Guadaloupe, St. Lucia and Goree and is guaranteed fishing rights off Newfoundland; (3) the French settlements in India are restored, but no fortifications are to be built there; (4) Spain acquires Louisiana from France, exchanges Florida for Havana and recovers Manila and the Philippines.

April: 7th, Earl of Bute's ministry falls in Britain.
16th, George Grenville becomes prime minister and chancellor of Exchequer.
23rd, John Wilkes attacks the King's Speech, commending the terms of peace, in No. 45 of the *North Briton* and a week later is arrested on a general warrant.

May: 6th, chief justice Pratt discharges Wilkes on ground of Parliamentary privilege and declares general warrants illegal.

July: —, 'Whiteboys' revolt against agrarian hardships in Ireland.

Oct: 7th, British proclamation provides for government of the new colonies of Quebec, East and West Florida and Grenada, while assignment of region west of the Alleghenies as an Indian reserve halts westward expansion and imperial government takes over regulation of trade with the Indians.

Literature
(16th May) James Boswell meets Samuel Johnson.

1764 **Jan: 19th**, John Wilkes is expelled from Commons for having written seditious libel; riots in London in favour of Wilkes.

April: 11th, treaty between Russia and Prussia guarantees the present constitutions of Poland and Sweden, and provides for controlling election to Polish monarchy and joint action against Nationalists.

May: 18th, British Parliament amends Sugar Act from a commercial to a fiscal measure, to tax American Colonists and establish a single Vice-Admiralty court for the thirteen colonies.

Science, Technology, and Discovery
James Hargreaves invents the spinning jenny.

Humanities and Scholarship
J J Winckelmann, *History of Ancient Art.*
Thomas Reid's *Inquiry in the Human Mind on the Principles of Common Sense* founds the philosophical school of natural realism.
F M A de Voltaire publishes *Philosophical Dictionary.*

Art, Sculpture, Fine Arts, and Architecture
Robert Adam, Kenwood House, Middlesex.
The Panthéon, Paris (–1790).

1765 **March: 23rd**, British Parliament passes Stamp Act, devised by Grenville for taxing the American colonies.

May: —, Robert Clive begins administrative reforms in Bengal (–1767).
29th, In the Virginian assembly Patrick Henry challenges the right of Britain to tax the colonies.

July: 16th, Grenville resigns on collapse of ministry over a Regency bill, and Marquess of Rockingham forms a government.

Aug: 18th, Joseph II of Austria succeeds as Holy Roman Emperor on death of Francis I, but is co-regent with Maria Theresa in Bohemia and Hungary.

Oct: 19th, 27 delegates from nine colonies attend Stamp Act Congress in New York and draw up a declaration of rights and liberties.

Politics, Government, Law, and Economy

William Blackstone's *Commentaries on the Laws of England* (–1769).

Science, Technology, and Discovery

Italian biologist Lazzaro Spallanzani pioneers preserving through hermetic sealing and argues against spontaneous generation.

Scot James Watt invents a condenser (which leads to his construction of a very efficient steam engine 1774, improved 1775).

Literature

Horace Walpole's *The Castle of Otranto* founds the English romantic school of fiction.

1766

March: —, British Parliament repeals the Stamp Act by 275–161 votes but, 18th, passes Declaratory Act, declaring Britain's right to tax the American colonies.

July: 12th, on Rockingham's dismissal by George III, Pitt, becoming Earl of Chatham, forms a ministry with Duke of Grafton; Henry Conway and Shelburne becoming secretaries of state and Charles Townshend chancellor of Exchequer (dubbed by Burke 'a tessellated pavement without cement').

Art, Sculpture, Fine Arts, and Architecture

J H Fragonard, *The Swing* (painting).

Literature

G E Lessing, *Laocoön*.

Heinrich Gerstenberg, *Letters on the Curiosities of Literature* (–1770), formulates the principles of *Sturm und Drang*.

Oliver Goldsmith, *The Vicar of Wakefield*.

1767

Jan: —, Robert Clive leaves India, where chaos soon prevails, until the arrival of Warren Hastings in 1772.

May: —, Townshend introduces taxes on imports of tea, glass, paper and dyestuffs in American colonies to provide revenue for colonial administration.

Sept: —, at public meeting in Boston a non-importation agreement is framed in protest at the new taxes.

Science, Technology, and Discovery

Nautical Almanac first issued. It is edited by Nevil Maskelyne, Astronomer Royal, and gives the position of heavenly bodies at specific times.

Music

C W Gluck, *Alceste* (opera).

1768

March: 28th, John Wilkes is elected MP for Middlesex.

July: —, Massachusetts Assembly is dissolved for refusing to assist collection of taxes.

Aug: —, Confederation founded in Poland at Bar, aided by France, to counter Russian designs; attempts are made by the Confederates to kidnap King Stanislas and Civil War breaks out.

Oct: —, Turkey, instigated by France, declares war on Russia in defence of Polish liberties.

Science, Technology, and Discovery

(25th May) James Cook sails on first voyage of discovery, on which he explores the Society Islands and charts the coasts of New Zealand and West Australia (–June 1771).

Art, Sculpture, Fine Arts, and Architecture

The Royal Academy is founded, with Joshua Reynolds as president, who begins delivering fifteen discourses on art (–1790).

Music

Wolfgang Amadeus Mozart, *Bastien and Bastienne* (opera).

1769

Feb: 4th, Wilkes is expelled from Parliament and, though thrice re-elected for Middlesex, the Commons declare his opponent to be the successful candidate (15th April).

May: 1st, Privy Council decides to retain the tea duty in American colonies after weeks of argument.

Oct: —, Prusso-Russian alliance is renewed until 1780; Joseph II guaranteeing Frederick II the reversion of Ansbach and Bayreuth, while Prussia guarantees to uphold the Swedish constitution.

Science, Technology, and Discovery

Richard Arkwright's spinning machine, or water frame, invented. It is one of the key inventions of Britain's Industrial Revolution.

Humanities and Scholarship

E Forcellini, *Totius Latinitatis Lexicon.*

Charles Bonnet, *Palingénésie philosophique* (–1770) .

Literature

J G Herder, *Kritische Wälder.*

G E Lessing, *Wie die Alten den Tod gebildet.*

Media

The Morning Chronicle, London, issued.

1770 **Jan: 28th**, North becomes prime minister on Grafton's resignation, forming the ministry of 'The King's Friends'.

March: 3rd, brawl between civilians and troops in Boston (annually celebrated as Boston Massacre).

April: —, British Parliament repeals duties on paper, glass and dyestuffs in American colonies, but retains tea duty.

May: 16th, Dauphin of France marries Marie Antoinette, daughter of the Empress Maria Theresa of Austria.

Dec: 5th, Struensee abolishes the Council in Denmark and becomes supreme; begins far-reaching programme of reforms, introducing freedom of worship and of press.

Politics, Government, Law, and Economy

E Burke, *Thoughts on the Cause of the Present Discontents.*

Society, Education, and Religion

Paul Holbach, *Système de la Nature*, attacking Christianity, is refuted by Voltaire and by Frederick the Great.

Science, Technology, and Discovery

(28th April) James Cook discovers Botany Bay.

1771 **Jan: 22nd**, Maupeou overthrows the French Parlements, which he replaces by a simplified system of courts.

June: —, Russia completes conquest of the Crimea.

Society, Education, and Religion

Encyclopædia Britannica, first edition.

Science, Technology, and Discovery

Italian anatomist Luigi Galvani discovers the electric nature of nervous impulse.

Humanities and Scholarship

A H Anquetil Duperron translates *The Zenda Avesta.*

1772 **Feb: 28th**, Boston assembly threatens secession from Britain unless rights of colonies are maintained.

April: 13th, Warren Hastings appointed governor of Bengal (–1785).

Aug: 5th, Frederick the Great, fearing Austria's concern at Russian conquests in Turkey will lead to a general war, engineers First Partition of Poland, Prussia taking West Poland (except Danzig) and Ermland, Austria taking East Galicia and Lodomerica and Russia taking lands east of Dvina and Dnieper.

19th, Gustavus III re-establishes full authority of the monarchy in Sweden.

Politics, Government, Law, and Economy

Lord Mansfield's decision that a slave is free on landing in England (Somerset's Case).

Science, Technology, and Discovery

Scottish chemist Daniel Rutherford discovers nitrogen.

Joseph Priestley discovers that plants give off oxygen.

Humanities and Scholarship

J G Herder's *On the Origins of Speech* begins the study of comparative philology.

Literature

P A F Choderlos de Laclos writes *Les Liaisons Dangereuses.*

Media

(2nd Nov) *The Morning Post*, London, issued.

1773 **March: 12th**, Virginia House of Burgesses appoints a Provincial Committee of Correspondence for mutual action against British, and other colonies follow this lead.

May: —, British East India Company Regulating Act provides for a governor-general and a council in India and officers are forbidden to trade for themselves.

July: 21st, Pope Clement XIV by the bull *Dominus ac Redemptor* dissolves the Jesuits.

Sept: —, Warren Hastings, first governor-general of India, makes alliance with the state of Oudh for campaign against the Mahrathas.

Dec: 16th, Boston Tea Party.

Science, Technology, and Discovery
T F Pritchard's cast-iron bridge at Coalbrookdale, Shropshire.

Literature
Drama J W Goethe, *Goetz von Berlichingen.*
O Goldsmith, *She Stoops to Conquer.*

1774 **March: 28th**, British Parliament passes Coercive Acts against Massachusetts, which include act closing port of Boston from 1st June.

May: 10th, accession of Louis XVI of France, who appoints Jean Maurepas premier and Vergennes foreign secretary.

July: —, Russians rout Turks at battle of Shumla.
21st, Following the battle of Shumla, the peace of Kutchuk-Kainardji is signed, by which Turkey cedes to Russia the Crimea and mouth of River Dnieper, grants her free navigation for trade in Turkish waters and promises to protect Christians in Constantinople.

Aug: —, Louis XVI recalls the Parlements and appoints Turgot controller-general of France.

Sept: 5th, (–26th Oct) first Continental Congress of the thirteen American Colonies meets at Philadelphia with representatives from each colony except Georgia.
9th, Suffolk Convention in America resolves that the Coercive legislation of 28th March be disregarded.
13th, Turgot reintroduces free trade in corn in France (suspended since 1766, but abolished again 1776).
14th, the pretender Pugachoff is delivered by Cossacks to the Russian government, following a decisive defeat (executed Jan 1775).

Science, Technology, and Discovery
Joseph Priestley discovers oxygen which he calls 'dephlogisticated air'.
Antoine Lavoisier demonstrates the conservation of mass in chemical reactions.

Music
C W Gluck, *Iphigénie en Aulide* (opera).

Literature
J W Goethe, *Clavigo* and *Sorrows of Werther.*

1775 **Feb: 1st**, Chatham introduces bill to conciliate American colonists, which is rejected, and repressive legislation follows.

April: 19th, War of American Independence opens with defeat of British under Thomas Gage at Lexington and Concord.

June: 15th, George Washington is appointed Commander-in-Chief of American forces (takes up command at Cambridge, Mass., 3rd July).
17th, British victory at Bunker Hill.

Politics, Government, Law, and Economy
The study of Danish language and literature supplants German in Danish schools.

Science, Technology, and Discovery
James Watt perfects the steam engine at Matthew Boulton's Birmingham works.
(25th July) James Cook returns to England after second voyage in South Seas, during which he discovered the Sandwich Islands and conquered scurvy.

Art, Sculpture, Fine Arts, and Architecture
Denis Diderot's accounts of the Salon, Paris, begin modern art criticism.

Literature
Drama P A C Beaumarchais' *Barber of Seville* produced in Paris after two years' prohibition.
R B Sheridan, *The Rivals.*

1776 Unified administration for Portuguese S American colonies under viceroyalty of River Plate, with capital in Rio de Janeiro.

March: **4th**, Washington occupies Heights of Dorchester.
15th, Congress resolves that the authority of the British Crown be suppressed.

May: **12th**, Turgot is dismissed by Louis XVI for attempting to make further financial reforms.

June: **7th**, Lee frames proposal that the United Colonies are of right independent states.
12th, Virginia publishes its Bill of Rights.

July: **4th**, American Declaration of Independence, drafted by Thomas Jefferson with revisions by Benjamin Franklin and Samuel Adams, is carried by Congress.

Sept: **—**, free trade in corn (reintroduced 1774) abolished in France.

Politics, Government, Law, and Economy
Jeremy Bentham, *A Fragment on Government.*
Adam Smith, *An Inquiry into the Nature and Causes of the Wealth of Nations.*

Science, Technology, and Discovery
James Cook begins his third voyage of discovery to the Pacific.

Humanities and Scholarship
Edward Gibbon, *Decline and Fall of the Roman Empire* (–1788).
Denis Diderot's *Encyclopédie* completed by D'Alembert.

Sport and Recreation
Col. St. Leger establishes the St. Leger at Doncaster Races.

1777 **Oct:** **4th**, Washington is defeated at Germantown, Pennsylvania.
7th, Burgoyne loses second battle of Bemis Heights and
17th, capitulates to Americans under Horatio Gates at Saratoga, New York.

Nov: **15th**, Congress adopts Confederation Articles of perpetual union of United States of America, which are sent to states for ratification (completed 1781) as first US constitution.

Politics, Government, Law, and Economy
E Burke, *A Letter to the Sheriffs of Bristol*, on Parliamentary representation, and *Address to the King.*

Science, Technology, and Discovery
K F Wenzel's work on atomic theory.

Music
J Haydn, *La Roxolane* Symphony (No. 63 in C).
C W Gluck, *Armide* (opera).

1778 **Feb:** **6th**, France and American Colonists sign offensive and defensive alliance and also a commercial treaty.
6th, Britain declares war on France.

June: **17th**, US Congress rejects British peace offer.
28th, Washington defeats British at Monmouth, New Jersey.

July: **3rd**, Prussia declares war on Austria, with whom Saxony is allied, in the war of Bavarian Succession (lasting with minor skirmishes until May 1779).

Sept: **4th**, the States of Holland sign treaty of amity and commerce with American Colonies.

Science, Technology, and Discovery
Friedrich Mesmer first practises 'mesmerism' in Paris.

Literature
Fanny Burney (pseudonym), *Evelina.*
J G Herder's collection of folk songs (–1779) leads to study of folklore in Germany.
(30th May) Voltaire dies (aged 83).
(2nd July) J J Rousseau dies (aged 66).
Drama R B Sheridan, *The School for Scandal.*

1779 **June:** **16th**, Spain declares war on Britain (after France has undertaken to assist her in recovering Gibraltar and Florida), and the siege of Gibraltar opens (–1783).

Science, Technology, and Discovery
Lazzaro Spallanzani shows that semen is necessary to fertilization.
Samuel Crompton's spinning mule is invented. It is a cross between a spinning jenny and a water-frame spinning machine.
A 'velocipede', a type of early bicycle, is constructed in Paris.

Art, Sculpture, Fine Arts, and Architecture
Antonio Canova, *Daedalus and Icarus* (sculpture).
James Gillray's earliest satirical cartoon.

Music
C W Gluck, *Iphigénie en Tauride* (opera).

Literature
S Johnson, *Lives of the Poets* (–1781).
Drama G E Lessing, *Nathan the Wise.*
R B Sheridan, *The Critic.*

Sport and Recreation
The Derby is established at Epsom Racecourse, Surrey; first winner is Sir C Bunbury's 'Diomed'.

1780 **March: 10th**, Russia's declaration of armed neutrality, to prevent British ships from searching neutral vessels for contraband of war, which is subsequently confirmed by France, Spain, Austria, Prussia, Denmark and Sweden.

April: —, Dunning's resolution deploring the increased influence of the Crown leads Commons to affirm the principle of periodical scrutiny of the civil list.
19th, Harry Grattan demands Home Rule for Ireland.

June: 2nd, (–8th), Gordon riots in London, when Lord George Gordon heads procession for presenting petition to Parliament for repealing Catholic Relief Act of 1778, and Roman Catholic chapels are pillaged.

Oct: —, Serfdom in Bohemia and Hungary abolished.

Nov: 29th, Maria Theresa of Austria dies, succeeded by Joseph II (–1790).

Dec: 13th, Ireland is granted free trade with Britain and is to enjoy advantages of the colonial trade.

Art, Sculpture, Fine Arts, and Architecture
J Reynolds' portrait of Mary Robinson as 'Perdita'.

Music
Sébastien Erard makes the first pianoforte.
Haydn, *Toy* Symphony.

Literature
Frederick the Great, *De la Littérature allemande.*

Media
(26th March) *The British Gazette and Sunday Monitor*, the first Sunday newspaper issued.

1781 **Feb: —**, Conclusion of Russia's treaty with Austria, for driving the Turks out of Europe, restoring a Greek Empire under Catherine's grandson Constantine, forming a Kingdom of Dacia under an Orthodox prince and allocating Serbia and the western Balkans to Austria and the Morea, Candia and Cyprus to Venice.

Oct: 13th, Joseph II grants patent of religious tolerance in Austrian Empire and freedom of the press.
19th, Cornwallis capitulates at Yorktown with 7,000 men; the British evacuate Charleston and Savannah and land operations are virtually over.

Nov: 26th, Joseph II abolishes serfdom in Austria and (28th) makes monastic orders independent of Rome.

Politics, Government, Law, and Economy
J H Pestalozzi expounds his educational theory in *Leonard and Gertrude.*

Science, Technology, and Discovery
(13th March) William Herschel discovers the planet Uranus.

Humanities and Scholarship
Clarendon Press, Oxford, founded.
Immanuel Kant, *Critique of Pure Reason.*

Music
Wolfgang Amadeus Mozart, *Idomeneo* (opera).

Literature
J H Voss, translation of Homer's *Odyssey.*
J.-J Rousseau, *Confessions.*
Drama F Schiller, *Die Räuber*, produced at Mannheim.

1782 Rama I founds new dynasty in Siam, with capital at Bangkok.

March: 19th, Lord North resigns and, 27th, Marquess of Rockingham forms Whig Coalition ministry with C J Fox, E Burke, Lord Shelburne and, on George III's insistence, Thurlow.

April: —, Gratton makes Irish Declaration of Rights, demanding complete legislative freedom.
12th, Admiral George Rodney defeats de Grasse at battle of The Saints, saving the West Indies.

May: 3rd, Commons vote the earlier resolution rejecting Wilkes as an MP to be subversive of the electors' rights.
17th, Fox introduces repeal of Ireland Act, 1720, thus granting Ireland legislative independence (–1800), but Gratton's Parliament is elected solely by Protestants.
17th, treaty of Salbai ends Mahratta War.
July: 11th, Shelburne forms ministry, following Rockingham's death, (1st) with William Pitt the Younger, chancellor of Exchequer and leader of Commons, but Fox and Burke are excluded from office.
Nov: 30th, peace preliminaries, arranged by Franklin and Adams, are accepted by Britain and America.

Humanities and Scholarship

Dugald Stewart, *Elements of the Philosophy of the Human Mind.*

Art, Sculpture, Fine Arts, and Architecture

H Fuseli, *The Nightmare* (painting).
F Guardi, *Fêtes for the Archduke Paul of Russia* and *The Concert* (paintings).

Music

Wolfgang Amadeus Mozart, *Haffner* Symphony (K 385 in D) and *Il Seraglio* (opera).

Literature

William Cowper, *Poems* and *Table Talk.*

1783 **Feb: 14th**, British proclamation for cessation of arms, followed by Americans (20th Feb).
20th, American proclamations for cessation of arms, following British proclamation on 14th Feb.
24th, Lord Shelburne resigns, following resolution censuring the peace preliminaries and lengthy negotiations begin in which William Pitt and Lord North in turn decline to form ministry.
April: 1st, Duke of Portland becomes nominal premier of a Fox-North coalition.
Sept: 3rd, by Peace of Versailles between Britain, France, Spain and USA Britain recognizes independence of USA and recovers her West Indian possessions; France recovers St. Lucia, Tobago, Senegal, Goree and East Indian possessions; Spain retains Minorca and receives back Florida; France may fortify Dunkirk (a separate treaty between Britain and Holland is signed 20th May, 1784).
Dec: 19th, William Pitt forms ministry (–1801) and as chancellor of Exchequer is sole member of cabinet in Commons.

Politics, Government, Law, and Economy

Civil marriage and divorce established in Austrian Empire.

Science, Technology, and Discovery

William Herschel writes *Motion of the Solar System in Space.*
The first human flight, by Jean F Pilâtre de Rozier and the Marquis d'Arlandes in Paris, using a hot-air balloon made by Joseph and Étienne Montgolfier.
Marquis Jouffroy d'Abbans sails a paddle-wheel steamboat on the river Sâone.

Humanities and Scholarship

Moses Mendelssohn pleads for freedom of conscience in *Jerusalem* .

Music

Wolfgang Amadeus Mozart, *Mass in C Minor.*
Ludwig van Beethoven publishes first composition (*Variations on a march of Dressler*).

Literature

William Blake, *Poetical Sketches.*

1784 **Jan: 6th**, by treaty of Constantinople, Turkey acquiesces in Russia's annexation of the Crimea and Kuban.
Aug: 13th, Pitt's India Act places East India Company under a government-appointed Board of Control (–1858) and forbids interference in native affairs, to check territorial expansion.

Science, Technology, and Discovery

Henry Cavendish discovers that water is a compound of hydrogen and oxygen.
Rene Haüy publishes *Essai d'une théorie sur la structure des cristaux.*
Henry Cort's puddling process revolutionizes the manufacture of wrought iron.

Humanities and Scholarship

William Jones founds the Bengal Asiatic Society and his discourses (–1794) mark a turning-point in the study of Sanskrit.
J G Herder, *Ideas towards a Philosophy of History* (–1791).
(28th Feb) John Wesley signs deed of declaration as the charter of Wesleyan Methodism, and ordains two 'Presbyters' for the American Mission (1st Sept).

Art, Sculpture, Fine Arts, and Architecture

T Rowlandson's first political cartoon.

Literature

Drama P A C Beaumarchais, *Mariage de Figaro.*

1785 Parlement of Paris begins series of attacks on Charles de Calonne.

Jan: —, Joseph II begins unsuccessful attempts to exchange Bavaria with Charles Theodore for the Austrian Netherlands, excepting Luxembourg and Namur.

Nov: **10th**, alliance between France and Holland, despite the efforts of the British envoy at The Hague.

Science, Technology, and Discovery

Steam engine with rotary motion installed by Matthew Boulton and James Watt in a cotton-spinning factory at Papplewick, Nottinghamshire.

Art, Sculpture, Fine Arts, and Architecture

J L David, *Oath of the Horatii* (painting).

J A Houdon visits US to sculpt George Washington.

Music

Wolfgang Amadeus Mozart, six string quartets dedicated to J Haydn.

1786 **March:** **29th**, William Pitt appoints commissioners for reducing the national debt through establishing a sinking fund (abolished 1828).

May: —, Annapolis convention, under James Madison and Alexander Hamilton, attended by New York, Pennsylvania, Virginia, New Jersey and Delaware, draws attention to weakness of the Confederation.

Aug: **11th**, Penang ceded to Britain by Rajah of Kedah.

17th, Frederick the Great dies, succeeded by Frederick William II (–1797), brother of the Princess of Orange.

Sept: —, Rebellion of Daniel Shays in Massachusetts, aiming to prevent further judgments for debt until next state election; state troops are used to protect the arsenal and (Nov) the revolt peters out.

Politics, Government, Law, and Economy

Thomas Clarkson, *Essay on Slavery.*

Society, Education, and Religion

Members of the Mennonite sect from Central Europe settle in Canada.

Music

Wolfgang Amadeus Mozart, *The Marriage of Figaro* (opera).

Literature

Robert Burns, *Poems chiefly in the Scottish Dialect.*

William Bilderdijck's *Elias* starts the Dutch Romantic Revival.

Sport and Recreation

Baseball is first played, at Princeton.

1787 **Jan:** —, Joseph II constitutes Austrian Netherlands as a province of the Austrian monarchy, provoking riots in Louvain and Brussels, led by Van der Noot.

—, Catherine II visits the Crimea where she is joined, in Feb, by Joseph II, with whom she forms a defensive alliance.

May: **14th**, Philadelphia convention meets under Washington to frame a constitution.

Aug: **10th**, Turkey declares war against Russia, fearing designs on Georgia.

Sept: **17th**, US constitution is signed.

Science, Technology, and Discovery

Antoine Lavoisier, with collaborators, publishes *Méthode de nomenclature chimique*, a system for naming chemicals based on scientific principles.

(2nd Aug) Horace Saussure reaches the summit of Mt. Blanc.

Music

Wolfgang Amadeus Mozart, *Don Giovanni*, *Prague* Symphony and *Eine Kleine Nachtmusik.*

Literature

Drama F Schiller, *Don Carlos.*

J W Goethe, *Iphigenie auf Tauris.*

1788 **Jan:** **20th**, Parlement of Paris presents a list of grievances.

28th, first British penal settlement is founded at Botany Bay.

30th, death of Charles Edward Stuart, the Young Pretender, in Rome.

Feb: 9th, Joseph II of Austria declares war on Turkey.

June: —, Sweden declares war on Russia, invading Russian Finland.
21st, US constitution comes into force, when ratified by the 9th state, New Hampshire.

Aug: 22nd, foundation of British settlement in Sierra Leone as an asylum for slaves.

Society, Education, and Religion

American Presbyterians revise the Westminister Catechism and introduce principles of religious liberty.

Humanities and Scholarship

John Lemprière, *Classical Dictionary*. I Kant, *Critique of Practical Reason*.

Music

Wolfgang Amadeus Mozart, Symphonies 39 (E flat), 40 (C minor) and 41 (*Jupiter*).

Literature

Drama J W Goethe, *Egmont*.

Sport and Recreation

MCC codifies the laws of cricket.

Media

(1st Jan) John Walter founds *The Times*.

1789

March: 4th, first Congress meets at New York and during the session ten of the proposed twelve amendments to the constitution are made and sent to the states for ratification.

April: 30th, George Washington inaugurated as President of US with John Adams vice-president, Thomas Jefferson secretary of state and Alexander Hamilton secretary of Treasury.

May: 5th, States-General meet at Versailles.

June: —, Spaniards attack British fishing vessels at Nootka Sound, W Canada.
17th, third estate in France declares itself a National Assembly and undertakes to frame a constitution (–Sept 1791).
20th, third estate takes tennis court oath, undertaking not to depart until a constitution is drawn up.
27th, Union of the three estates in France.

July: 11th, Louis XVI's dismissal of Jacques Necker implies a royalist *coup d'état* and provokes the Paris mob.
14th, In Paris, the mob sacks the Bastille.

Aug: 4th, French feudal system is abolished.
27th, French National Assembly adopts Declaration of the Rights of Man.

Nov: 2nd, nationalization of property of church in France.

Dec: 13th, Austrian Netherlands declare independence as Belgium.

Politics, Government, Law, and Economy

J Bentham, *Introduction to the Principles of Morals and Legislation*.
E J Sièyes, *Qu'est-ce que le Tiers État?* and *Exposition des Droits de l'Homme*.
Journal des Débats founded in Paris.

Science, Technology, and Discovery

Antoine Lavoisier publishes *Traité élémentaire de chimie* which establishes the oxygen theory of combustion and the new chemical nomenclature.

Luigi Galvani annouces his observations on the muscular contraction of dead frogs, which he infers was caused electrically.

Art, Sculpture, Fine Arts, and Architecture

François Gérard, *Joseph and his Brothers* (painting).

Music

Wolfgang Amadeus Mozart, *Così fan tutte* (opera).

Literature

William Blake, *Songs of Innocence*.
Drama J W Goethe, *Tasso*.

The European Ascendancy

1790–1945

1790 **Feb: —**, In British Parliament, Edmund Burke condemns and Charles James Fox welcomes the developments in France.

20th, Leopold II of Austria becomes Holy Roman Emperor on Joseph II's death.

July: 14th, festival of Champ de Mars, Paris; Louis XVI accepts the constitution.

Oct: —, Wolfe Tone founds Society of United Irishmen as a political union of Roman Catholics and Protestants to further Irish Parliamentary reform.

Dec: 2nd, Austrians re-enter Brussels and suppress revolution.

Politics, Government, Law, and Economy

E Burke, *Reflections on the Revolution in France.*

Society, Education, and Religion

Civil constitution of the clergy in France (12th July). Jews in France are admitted to civil liberties.

Science, Technology, and Discovery

Firth-Clyde and Oxford-Birmingham canals begun.
George Vancouver explores the northwest coast of America.

Humanities and Scholarship

I Kant, *Critique of Judgment.*

1791 **March: 4th**, Vermont becomes a state of US.

May: 6th, by Canada Constitution Act Canada is divided into two provinces, Upper (Ontario) and Lower (Quebec), with separate legislative assemblies.

June: 20th, (–25th) Louis XVI attempts to leave France, but is turned back at Varennes and taken to Paris.

Aug: 27th, by declaration of Pillnitz Austria and Prussia state they are ready to intervene in French affairs with consent of other powers, but William Pitt announces Britain will remain neutral; France interprets the declaration as a threat.

Sept: 3rd, French Constitution is passed by National Assembly, making France a constitutional monarchy.

Oct: 1st, Legislative Assembly meets at Paris (–Sept 1792); Jacques Brissot and others of the Girondist Party in France urge war against Austria.

Politics, Government, Law, and Economy

Thomas Paine, *The Rights of Man*, part I.

Science, Technology, and Discovery

Ordnance Survey established in Britain.

Art, Sculpture, Fine Arts, and Architecture

Karl Langhans, Brandenburg Gate, Berlin.

Music

Wolfgang Amadeus Mozart, *Magic Flute* (opera) and *Requiem.*
J Haydn, *Surprise* Symphony.

Literature

Boswell, *Life of Johnson.*
Drama Joseph Chénier's plays *Henry VIII* and *Jean Calas* produced in Paris.
Goethe becomes director of the Weimar theatre (–1817).

Media

The Observer founded.

1792 Sierra Leone company formed.

Differences in US arising from Alexander Hamilton's financial policy lead to formation of political parties, namely Republican (Thomas Jefferson) and Federal (Hamilton and John Adams).

Feb: **5th**, Tippoo of Mysore, defeated in his war with British and Hyderabad, cedes half Mysore to Britain.

March: **1st**, Francis II of Austria succeeds his brother Leopold II as Holy Roman Emperor (–1835).

24th, Girondins under Jean Roland and Charles Dumouriez form ministry in France.

29th, Gustavus III of Sweden is assassinated.

April: **20th**, France declares war on Austria (the War of the First Coalition).

May: **19th**, Russia invades Poland, where the constitution is abrogated.

July: **8th**, France declares war on Prussia.

Aug: **—**, Prussian and Austrian troops invade France.

9th, revolutionary Commune established in Paris.

10th, mob invades Tuileries, massacring the Swiss guard; the Legislative Assembly is suspended.

13th, French royal family is imprisoned.

Sept: **21st**, French National Convention meets.

22nd, French Republic proclaimed; the Revolutionary Calendar comes into force.

Nov: **—**, The Jacobins, under G J Danton, wrest power from the Girondins.

Dec: **5th**, trial of Louis XVI before the Convention opens.

Politics, Government, Law, and Economy

Mary Wollstonecraft, *Vindication of the Rights of Women.*

Dollar coinage introduced in US, with the opening of a mint at Philadelphia.

(Feb) T Paine, *Rights of Man*, part II.

Society, Education, and Religion

In France the religious orders are dissolved and civil marriage and divorce is instituted.

Humanities and Scholarship

Dugald Stewart, *Elements of the Philosophy of the Human Mind*, Vol. I (continued 1814 and 1827).

Art, Sculpture, Fine Arts, and Architecture

James Hoban begins the White House, Washington.

Music

C J Rouget de Lisle, 'La Marseillaise' ('Chant de guerre de l'armée du Rhin').

1793 **Jan:** **21st**, Louis XVI is executed.

Feb: **1st**, France declares war on Britain and Holland.

13th, first Coalition against France is formed by Britain, Austria, Prussia, Holland, Spain, and Sardinia.

March: **7th**, France declares war on Spain; the Spanish invade Roussillon and Navarre.

26th, Holy Roman Empire declares war on France.

26th, Royalist revolt in La Vendée.

April: **6th**, Committee of Public Safety established in France with dictatorial power, dominated by G J Danton.

May: **7th**, second partition of Poland effected, Russia taking Lithuania and W Ukraine, and Prussia taking Danzig, Thorn, Posen, Gnesen, and Kalisz.

June: **2nd**, final overthrow of Girondins and arrest of Jacques Brissot begins Reign of Terror.

24th, revised French constitution is framed.

Oct: **5th**, Christianity is abolished in France.

16th, Marie Antoinette is executed.

Politics, Government, Law, and Economy

M J Condorcet, *Tableau du Progrès de l'Esprit humain.*

William Godwin, *The Inquiry Concerning Political Justice.*

Science, Technology, and Discovery

Eli Whitney invents the cotton gin in US, which leads to the rapid growth of cotton exports from the southern states.

Humanities and Scholarship

I Kant, *Religion within the Boundaries of Reason.*

Art, Sculpture, Fine Arts, and Architecture

J L David, *Marat* (painting).

The Louvre, Paris, becomes a national art gallery.

1794 Abolition of slavery in French colonies.

June: **—**, French force invades Spain.

July: **28th**, Conspiracy by Moderates of the Mountain and Dantonists against M Robespierre, succeeds in abolishing the Commune of Paris (founded Aug 1792) and Robespierre and A St. Just are executed.

Sept: **28th**, alliance of St. Petersburg, of Britain, Russia, and Austria against France.

Dec: **27th**, French troops under Charles Pichegru invade Holland.

Society, Education, and Religion

École Normale founded in France.
W Paley, *A View of the Evidences of Christianity.*
(8th June) M Robespierre presides over the Feast of the Supreme Being in Paris.

Science, Technology, and Discovery

Erasmus Darwin publishes *Zoonomia, or the laws of Organic Life*, expressing his ideas on evolution (which he assumes has an environmental cause).

Humanities and Scholarship

James Stuart and Nicholas Revett, *The Antiquities of Athens, measured and delineated.*

Literature

W Blake, *Songs of Experience.*
Anne Radcliffe, *The Mysteries of Udolpho.*
W Godwin, *Caleb Williams, or Things as They are.*
Xavier de Maistre, *Voyage autour de ma chambre.*

1795 **April:** **5th**, by Peace of Basle France cedes to Prussia her conquests on the right bank of the Rhine, Frederick William II defends the interests of the N German princes and subsequently Saxony, Hanover, the Bavarian Palatinate and Hesse-Cassel make terms with France.
23rd, Warren Hastings is acquitted of high treason.

Aug: **23rd**, third French constitution, vesting power in Directory (effective 3rd Nov).

Oct: **24th**, in third Partition of Poland Prussia takes Warsaw and land between R Bug and R Niemen, Austria takes Cracow and Galicia, and Russia the area between Galicia and R Dvina.

Dec: **19th**, (and 31st) Austria signs armistice with France.

Politics, Government, Law, and Economy

École Polytechnique, Paris.

Science, Technology, and Discovery

Mungo Park explores the course of the River Niger.

Art, Sculpture, Fine Arts, and Architecture

F Goya, *The Duchess of Alba* (painting).
John Soane begins the Bank of England (–1827).

Music

Haydn *Drum Roll* Symphony and first performance of *London* Symphony (composed 1791).

Literature

M G Lewis, *The Monk.*
J W Goethe, *Wilhelm Meister.*

1796 **March:** **19th**, freedom of the press in France.

April: **13th**, Napoleon Bonaparte assumes command in Italy defeating Austrians at Millesimo and, 22nd, the Piedmontese at Mondovi.

Nov: **—**, John Adams defeats Thomas Jefferson in US presidential election by three votes; Jefferson elected vice-president.
16th, Paul I succeeds as Emperor of Russia on Catherine II's death (–1801).

Politics, Government, Law, and Economy

Jean Cambacérès *Projet de Code Civil* (taken as the basis for the Napoleonic Code in 1801).

Science, Technology, and Discovery

Pierre Laplace enunciates the 'nebular hypothesis', that the solar system formed from a cloud of gas, in *Exposition du système du monde.*
Edward Jenner performs the first inoculation against smallpox.
Georges Cuvier's lectures at École Centrale du Panthéon found the science of comparative zoology.

Art, Sculpture, Fine Arts, and Architecture
F Goya's *Los Caprichos*, which satirize the government and religion, are seized by the Inquisition.

1797 **Jan: 4th**, Napoleon Bonaparte defeats Austrians under Joseph Alvintzi at Rivoli.
26th, final treaty of Polish partition.

Feb: 14th, John Jervis and Horatio Nelson defeat Spanish fleet off Cape St. Vincent.

March: 4th, John Adams inaugurated President of US.

Oct: 17th, by Peace of Campo Formio between France and Austria, Austria cedes Belgium and Lombardy to France and obtains Istria, Dalmatia and Venice; and by a secret agreement Austria agrees to future cession of left bank of Rhine, from Basle to Andernach, to France and the free navigation of the Rhine in return for French help to acquire archbishopric of Salzburg and part of Bavaria.

Nov: 16th, Frederick William III succeeds as King of Prussia and continues policy of neutrality (–1840).

Society, Education, and Religion
William Wilberforce, *A Practical View of the Prevailing Religious System of Professed Christians.*

Science, Technology, and Discovery
Henry Maudslay invents the carriage lathe which permits the operator to use the lathe without holding the metal-cutting tool.

Humanities and Scholarship
I Kant, *Metaphysical Foundations of the Theory of Right.*
F Schelling, *Philosophy of Nature.*

Music
J Haydn, *Emperor* quartet.

Literature
S T Coleridge, *Kubla Khan* (published 1816).
Drama August Kötzebue, *Menschenhass und Reue* (produced in London as *The Stranger*).
Ugo Foscolo, *Tieste.*

1798 Following the passage of the Aliens and Seditions Acts, the Virginia and Kentucky legislatures pass resolutions, framed by James Madison and Thomas Jefferson respectively, to nullify any act of Congress in any state which considers it to be unconstitutional.

Feb: 11th, French take Rome.
15th, Roman Republic proclaimed and Pius VI, refusing to surrender his temporal power, leaves Rome for Valence.

March: 5th, France occupies Bern and
9th, annexes left bank of Rhine.
29th, Helvetian Republic proclaimed.

July: 21st, Napoleon Bonaparte, having occupied Alexandria, becomes master of Egypt at battle of the Pyramids.

Aug: 1st, Horatio Nelson destroys French fleet off Aboukir (battle of the Nile), cutting Bonaparte's communications with Europe.

Dec: 24th, Anglo-Russian alliance, the foundation of a Second Coalition against France, is signed.

Politics, Government, Law, and Economy
T R Malthus, *Essay on the Principle of Population.*

Science, Technology, and Discovery
Henry Cavendish determines the mean density of the earth; it is 5.5 times as dense as water.
Count Rumford discovers heat is generated by friction.
Alois Senefelder invents lithography.

Music
J Haydn, *The Creation* (oratorio).

Literature
W Wordsworth and S T Coleridge, *Lyrical Ballads* (including *The Rime of the Ancient Mariner*).

Media
Johann Cotta founds *Allgemeine Zeitung* in Leipzig.

1799 **June: 1st**, William Pitt concludes formation of Second Coalition of Britain, Russia, Austria, Turkey, Portugal, and Naples against France.

July: 24th, Napoleon Bonaparte defeats the Turks at Aboukir.

Aug: 15th, French are defeated at Novi by A Suvorov, who then crosses the Alps.
22nd, Bonaparte leaves Egypt.

Oct: 22nd, Russia, disgusted with Austria, leaves Coalition.

Nov: 9th, Bonaparte overthrows the Directory.

Dec: 24th, Constitution of Year VIII establishes the Consulate, with Napoleon Bonaparte First Consul for ten years; Britain and Austria reject French offers of peace.

Society, Education, and Religion
F Schleiermacher, *Reden über die Religion.*
Church Missionary Society and Religious Tract Society founded in London.

Art, Sculpture, Fine Arts, and Architecture
J L David, *Rape of the Sabine Women* (painting).

Music
L van Beethoven, *Pathétique* Sonata in C Minor (op. 13).

Literature
Drama F Schiller, *Wallenstein.*

1800 **March: 28th**, Act of Union with England passes Irish Parliament.

June: —, US Departments of State are moved from Philadelphia to Washington, the new seat of government.
14th, Napoleon Bonaparte defeats Austrians at battle of Marengo and reconquers Italy.

Nov: —, In US presidential election Thomas Jefferson and Aaron Burr (Republican) each secure 73 votes against John Adams, 65 and Charles Pinckney, 64 (Federalist) and House of Representatives determines election of Jefferson; downfall of Federalist Party.

Dec: 16th, Second Armed Neutrality of the North agreed between Russia, Sweden, Denmark, and Prussia and St. Petersburg, to counter British right of search, imposes new criteria for a valid blockade.

Politics, Government, Law, and Economy
Robert Owen's model factory at New Lanark.

Society, Education, and Religion
Library of Congress, Washington, established.
Church of United Brethren in Christ founded in US.

Science, Technology, and Discovery
Humphry Davy publishes *Researches, Chemical and Philosophical, Chiefly Concerning Nitrous Oxide.*
William Herschel discovers the existence of infra-red solar rays.
Alessandro Volta produces electricity from his cell.

Art, Sculpture, Fine Arts, and Architecture
J L David, *Portrait of Mme Récamier.*

Music
L van Beethoven, 1st Symphony in C major (op.21), and 3rd Piano Concerto in C minor (op.37).
M L C Cherubini, *The Water-Carrier* (opera).

Literature
Maria Edgeworth, *Castle Rackrent.*
Novalis (pseudonym), *To the Night.*
William Wordsworth's manifesto of romanticism as preface to 2nd edition of *Lyrical Ballads.*
Drama F Schiller, *Mary Stuart.*

1801 **Jan: 1st**, Act of Union of England and Ireland comes into force.

Feb: 9th, Peace of Lunéville between Austria and France marks virtual destruction of Holy Roman Empire; France gains the left bank of the Rhine, Tuscany is ceded to Parma to form the new kingdom of Etruria, and recognition is given to Batavian, Cisalpine, Helvetian, and Ligurian Republics.

March: 4th, Thomas Jefferson inaugurated as President of US in new capital of Washington.
14th, William Pitt (having first tendered resignation 5th Feb) resigns over question of Catholic Emancipation, and is replaced by Henry Addington.
23rd, Assassination of Tsar Paul I who is succeeded by Alexander I (–1825).

July: 15th, under French Concordat with Papacy French ecclesiastics are to be appointed by government and merely confirmed by Pope, who is allowed to keep the Papal States, with exception of Ferrara, Bologna , and Romagna (ratified by Napoleon 28th Sept, but not fully ratified by France until 18th April, 1802).

Oct: 1st, peace preliminaries between Britain and France signed whereby Britain to restore all maritime conquests, except Trinidad and Ceylon, to France, Spain and Holland; France agrees to evacuate Naples; the integrity of Portugal is recognized; the independence of the Ionian Islands is agreed upon; both French and English armies are to evacuate Egypt which is to be restored to Turkey, and Malta is to be restored to the Knights by Britain (see Peace of Amiens, March 1802).

Politics, Government, Law, and Economy

Foundation of the Bank of France.

Society, Education, and Religion

J H Pestalozzi, *How Gertrude teaches her children.*

Science, Technology, and Discovery

John Dalton formulates the law of partial pressure in gases, stating that each component of a gas mixture produces the same pressure as if it occupied the container alone.

Karl Friedrich Gauss publishes *Disquisitiones arithmeticae.*

Marie Bichat publishes *Anatomie générale* which investigates the tissues of the body and organs.

Robert Fulton constructs a submarine, *Nautilus*, at Brest.

(1st Jan) Giuseppe Piazzi discovers the first asteroid, Ceres.

Art, Sculpture, Fine Arts, and Architecture

J L David, *Napoléon au Grand Saint-Bernard* (painting).

Elgin marbles brought from Athens to London.

Music

J Haydn, *The Seasons.*

L van Beethoven, 1st (op.15) and 2nd (op.19) Piano Concertos, and six string quartets (op.18).

Statistics

First accurate censuses taken in 1800 and 1801 provide population statistics for Italy, 17.2 mill.; Spain 10.5 mill.; Great Britain, 10.4 mill.; Ireland 5.2 mill.; and US, 5.3 mill.; London, 864,000; Paris, 547,756; Vienna, 231,050; Berlin, 183,294, and New York, 60,515.

1802

Jan: **26th**, Napoleon Bonaparte becomes President of Italian Republic (the former Cisalpine Republic).

March: **27th**, Peace of Amiens between Britain and France which achieves the complete pacification of Europe (for terms, see Oct 1801).

Aug: **2nd**, Napoleon Bonaparte becomes First Consul for life, with right to appoint his successor.

Politics, Government, Law, and Economy

Jeremy Bentham's *Civil and Penal Legislation* introduces the theory of utilitarianism.

Science, Technology, and Discovery

William Herschel discovers that some stars revolve round others, forming binary pairs.

Thomas Wedgwood makes the first photograph in copying paintings on glass.

John Dalton compiles tables of atomic weights and states his atomic theory.

Music

L van Beethoven, *Moonlight* Sonata (op. 27, no. 2); and 2nd Symphony (D major, op 36).

Literature

Vicomte de Chateaubriand, *Le Génie du Christianisme.*

Media

(Oct) *Edinburgh Review* (–1929).

1803

Feb: **19th**, Act of Mediation in Switzerland, whereby Cantons regain independence.

24th, US Supreme Court, in a unanimous decision (*Marbury* v. *Madison*), for the first time declares an act of Congress to be unconstitutional and of no effect.

April: **30th**, US purchases Louisiana and New Orleans from the French.

May: **8th**, renewal of hostilities between Britain and France because of Napoleon's interference in Italian and Swiss affairs, and because of Britain's refusal to part with Malta immediately.

Science, Technology, and Discovery

J-B Lamarck publishes *Recherches.*

Caledonian Canal begun.

Humanities and Scholarship

J L Tieck's translation of *Minnelieder* leads to the study of old Germanic literature.

Art, Sculpture, Fine Arts, and Architecture

J S Cotman and J B Crome found Norwich School of artists.

Music

L van Beethoven, *Kreutzer* Sonata for piano and violin (op. 47).

1804 **May: 10th**, William Pitt forms Cabinet, but finds it necessary to exclude C J Fox.
16th, Napoleon proclaimed Emperor by Senate and Tribunate (–1815).

Sept: 25th, Twelfth Amendment added to American Constitution which provides for separate ballots for the Presidency and the Vice-Presidency.

Dec: 2nd, Napoleon Bonaparte is crowned Emperor as Napoleon I by Pope Pius VII in Paris.

Politics, Government, Law, and Economy
Code Napoléon promulgated in France.

Music
L van Beethoven, 3rd (*Eroica*) Symphony (op. 55).

Literature
William Blake, *Jerusalem.*

1805 **March: 4th**, Thomas Jefferson begins second term as President of US.

April: 11th, by treaty of St. Petersburg, Britain and Russia agree to form a European league for the liberation of the northern German states, the Third Coalition against France.

May: 26th, Napoleon is crowned King of Italy in Milan Cathedral.

Aug: 9th, Austria joins signatories of Treaty of St. Petersburg.

Oct: 21st, Lord Nelson defeats combined Franco-Spanish fleet at Trafalgar, and is mortally wounded in the action.

Dec: 2nd, Napoleon defeats combined Russo-Austrian forces at Austerlitz.
15th, by treaty of Schönbrunn with France, Prussia cedes Cleves, Neuchâtel, and Ansbach, and is allowed to occupy Hanover in order to prevent her joining the coalition against Napoleon.
26th, by Peace of Pressburg between Austria and France, the Austrians give up the Tyrol and all possessions in Italy and in Dalmatia and, in addition, give up all possessions and influence in Southern Germany so that Bavaria and Württemberg become kingdoms, and Baden becomes a Grand Duchy.

Science, Technology, and Discovery
Thomas Telford builds an iron aqueduct over the Ellesmere Canal.

Art, Sculpture, Fine Arts, and Architecture
F Goya, *Doña Isabel Cobos de Porcal* (portrait).
J M W Turner, *Shipwreck* (painting).

Music
L van Beethoven, 4th Piano Concerto in G (op. 58); and *Fidelio* (opera).

Literature
Vicomte Chateaubriand, *René.*
Walter Scott, *The Lay of the Last Minstrel.*
William Wordsworth completes *The Prelude.*

1806 **Jan: 23rd**, death of William Pitt.

Feb: 10th, Formation of 'Ministry of all the Talents' with Lord Grenville as Prime Minister and C J Fox as Foreign Secretary.

March: 30th, Joseph Bonaparte becomes King of Naples.

April: 1st, Britain declares war on Prussia after the seizure of Hanover.

June: 5th, Louis Bonaparte becomes King of Holland.

July: 12th, establishment of Confederation of Rhine under protection of France, uniting Bavaria, Württemberg, Mainz, Baden, and eight lesser principalities.

Oct: 9th, Prussia declares war on France.
14th, Napoleon defeats Prussia at Jena and Saxony at Auerstädt.

Nov: 21st, by the Berlin Decrees, Napoleon begins the 'Continental System', closing continental ports to British vessels and declaring all British ports to be in a state of blockade.

Science, Technology, and Discovery
Humphry Davy discovers the elements potassium and sodium by passing an electric current through the molten compounds.

Art, Sculpture, Fine Arts, and Architecture
Claude Clodion begins Arc de Triomphe, Paris.

Music
L van Beethoven, *Rasoumoffsky* string quartets (op. 59), 4th Symphony in B flat (op. 60) and Violin Concerto (op. 61).

1807 **March:** **24th**, fall of 'Ministry of all the Talents' over Lord Grenville's refusal to grant Catholic Emancipation at a future date, and the Whigs surrender seals of office, never to take office again under George III.

31st, Duke of Portland becomes Prime Minister with George Canning and Lord Castlereagh as Secretaries of State.

July: **7th**, Napoleon meets Tsar Alexander and Frederick William II on the R Niemen, and by Treaty of Tilsit with France, Russia agrees to establishment of Duchy of Warsaw, recognizes Confederation of Rhine, agrees to close all ports to British ships, and, by a secret agreement, the Tsar agrees to coerce Denmark, Sweden, and Portugal into joining alliance against Britain, and is given a free hand in Finland.

9th, by a separate Treaty of Tilsit with France, Prussia loses all possessions west of Elbe and all Polish territories, which are to form Duchy of Warsaw under King of Saxony, and by a secret agreement, agrees to join the 'Continental System' and to exclude British ships from Prussian ports.

Sept: **7th**, Napoleon suppresses Tribunate, thus ensuring his dictatorship.

Oct: **9th**, Emancipation of Prussian serfs.

Nov: **7th**, Russia breaks off relations with Britain, amounting to declaration of war (as result of Treaty of Tilsit of 7th July).

Politics, Government, Law, and Economy

Comte de Saint-Simon, *Introduction aux Travaux Scientifiques du xix Siècle.*

Science, Technology, and Discovery

Alexander von Humboldt and Aimé Bonpland, in *Voyage aux régions équinoxiales du Nouveau Continent, 1799–1804*, study climate, volcanoes, etc., of Spanish America.

Charles Bell publishes *System of Comparative Surgery.*

Humanities and Scholarship

First Convention of US Evangelical Association, or 'New Methodists', founded by Jacob Albright.

Art, Sculpture, Fine Arts, and Architecture

J M W Turner, *Sun Rising in a Mist* (painting).

J L David completes *Coronation of Napoleon* (painting).

Music

L van Beethoven, *Leonora No. 3* and *Coriolanus* overtures; *Appassionata* sonata.

Literature

B Constant, *Adolphe* (published 1815).

William Wordsworth, *Ode on Intimations of Immortality.*

Sport and Recreation

Horse-racing: Ascot Gold Cup first given.

1808 **Jan:** **1st**, US prohibits import of slaves from Africa.

Feb: **16th**, France invades Spain.

28th, Austria joins Napoleon's 'Continental System'.

June: **15th**, Joseph of Naples becomes King of Spain (subsequently Joachim Murat becomes King of Naples).

Aug: **1st**, British expedition is sent to Portugal.

Science, Technology, and Discovery

John Dalton publishes *New System of Chemical Philosophy* (–1827).

Art, Sculpture, Fine Arts, and Architecture

Antonio Canova, *Pauline Bonaparte Borghese as Venus* (sculpture).

Kaspar Friedrich, *The Cross on the Mountains* (painting).

J D Ingres, *La Grande Baigneuse* (painting).

Music

L van Beethoven, 5th Symphony (op. 67) and 6th, *Pastoral* Symphony (op. 68).

Literature

W Scott, *Marmion.*

Drama J W Goethe, *Faust*, pt. I.

1809 **Jan:** **6th**, Sir John Moore is killed at Corunna, having created a diversion to distract Napoleon.

March: **4th**, James Madison becomes the fourth President of US.

29th, Gustavus IV of Sweden is forced to abdicate after military defeats in war with Denmark; he is succeeded (June 5th) by Charles XIII (–1818).

May: **12th**, Arthur Wellesley defeats French under Soult at Oporto and forces them to retreat from Portugal.

13th, French army takes Vienna.
17th, Napoleon issues Imperial Decree annexing Papal States.

July: 5th, (–6th) Napoleon defeats Austrians at Wagram.
6th, Pope Pius VII, having excommunicated Napoleon, is taken prisoner by the French.
28th, Arthur Wellesley is victorious at Talavera and is subsequently created Duke of Wellington.

Aug: 4th, Prince Metternich becomes Chief Minister of Austria.

Oct: 4th, Spencer Perceval forms an administration in Britain.
14th, by Peace of Schönbrunn, Austria cedes Trieste and Illyria to France, Galicia to Saxony and Russia, Salzburg and Inn District to Bavaria, and joins the Continental System.

Dec: 16th, Napoleon is divorced from Josephine by an act of Senate.

Society, Education, and Religion
Evangelical revival begins in Germany.
Elizabeth Seton founds Sisters of Charity of St. Joseph in US.

Science, Technology, and Discovery
Pall Mall, London, is lit by gas.

Music
L van Beethoven, 5th Piano Concerto, (*Emperor*) in E flat (op. 73).

Literature
J W Goethe, *The Elective Affinities.*

1810 **Feb: 11th**, Napoleon marries Marie-Louise of Austria.

April: 19th, under influence of Simon Bolivar, the Junta in Venezuela breaks from Spain, refusing to recognize Joseph Bonaparte, and proclaiming allegiance to Ferdinand VII.

July: 9th, Napoleon annexes Holland.

Sept: 16th, Revolt in Mexico in favour of independence from Spain.
18th, Junta in Chile revolts against Joseph Bonaparte and assumes authority.

Society, Education, and Religion
K W von Humboldt as Prussian minister of education reforms the gymnasia and institutes pre-university matriculation.

Science, Technology, and Discovery
J W Goethe rejects Newton's theory of light in *Theory of Colours.*

Art, Sculpture, Fine Arts, and Architecture
Francisco Goya engraves *Los Desastres de la Guerra* (–1813).
J F Overbeck founds the 'Nazarenes' to regenerate German religious art.

Music
G Rossini, *La Cenerentola* (opera).

Literature
Heinrich von Kleist, *Das Kätchen von Heilbronn* and Prinze Friederick von Hambourg (published 1821).

1811 **Feb: 5th**, George III's insanity necessitates Regency Act, whereby Prince of Wales becomes Prince Regent, but with limited powers for twelve months.

May: 8th, Duke of Wellington defeats French at Fuentes d'Onoro.

July: 5th, Venezuela becomes independent and adopts constitution under influence of Simon Bolivar and Francisco de Miranda, having disavowed allegiance to Ferdinand VII of Spain (lasts until July 1812).

Aug: 14th, Paraguay declares itself independent of Spain (and of Buenos Aires, 12th Oct).

Politics, Government, Law, and Economy
Civil Code is introduced into Austrian Empire, excepting Hungary, after 50 years of preparation.

Humanities and Scholarship
Berthold Niebuhr, *Roman History* (–1832).
J P A Récusat, *Essai sur la langue et la littérature chinoises.*

Art, Sculpture, Fine Arts, and Architecture
J Nash begins Regent Street.

Literature
Jane Austen, *Sense and Sensibility.*

1812 **Feb:** **11th**, British Act of Parliament removes the restrictions on the Prince Regent (of Feb 1811).

March: **19th**, Spanish Cortes passes liberal constitution under a hereditary monarch.

April: **14th**, Louisiana becomes a state of the US.

May: **11th**, Spencer Perceval is assassinated in House of Commons, and Lord Liverpool agrees to form an administration.
21st, Lord Liverpool resigns after vote of no confidence.
28th, by Treaty of Bucharest with Turkey, Russia obtains Bessarabia and withdraws demand for Moldavia and Wallachia, and the peace enables the Tsar to act against Napoleon.

June: **8th**, Tory administration under Liverpool resumes office.
18th, US Congress approves war against Britain (the formal declaration is made 19th).
24th, Napoleon crosses the R Niemen and enters Russian territory.

Sept: **7th**, following their defeat at Borodino the Russians are obliged to retreat, and abandon Moscow.
14th, Napoleon enters Moscow and occupies it until the 18th; the city burns until 19th Oct.

Oct: **19th**, Napoleon's retreat from Moscow begins.

Nov: **—**, In US presidential election James Madison (128 electoral votes) defeats De Witt Clinton (89 votes).

Society, Education, and Religion
Jews in Prussia emancipated.

Science, Technology, and Discovery
Humphry Davy publishes *Elements of Chemical Philosophy*.
Pierre Laplace publishes *Théorie Analytique* (the first complete theory of probability).
Georges Cuvier, in *Recherches sur les ossements fossiles de quadrupèdes*, founds comparative vertebrate paleontology.
Henry Bell's steamship *Comet* (25 tons) plies on the Clyde, maximum speed 7 knots.

Humanities and Scholarship
G W Hegel, *Logic*.
J G Fichte, *Transcendental Philosophy*.

Art, Sculpture, Fine Arts, and Architecture
Francisco Goya, *Duke of Wellington* (painting).

Music
L van Beethoven, 7th (op. 92) and 8th Symphonies (op. 93).

Literature
Lord Byron, *Childe Harold's Pilgrimage* (–1818).
J and W Grimm, *Fairy Tales*.

1813 **March:** **17th**, Frederick William III of Prussia declares war against the French, appeals to the people to support the campaign, and begins formation of *Landwehr* and *Landsturm*.

May: **2nd**, Napoleon defeats the Prussian and Russian armies at Lützen (Gross-Gorschen).

June: **21st**, Wellington completely routs the French at Vittoria, forcing Joseph Bonaparte to flee from Spain to France.

July: **—**, Venezuela becomes independent for second time with Simon Bolivar as virtual dictator.

Aug: **12th**, Austria declares war against Napoleon.
26th, French are defeated at Katzbach by Gebhard von Blücher.
26th, (–27th) in battle of Dresden, Napoleon defeats the allied army from Bohemia.

Sept: **9th**, Treaty of Teplitz confirms Reichenbach agreement (of 27th June) uniting Russia, Prussia and Austria against France.

Oct: **16th**, (–19th) Napoleon's defeat in the 'Battle of the Nations' at Leipzig and retreat leads to dissolution of Confederation of the Rhine and of Kingdom of Westphalia.

Nov: **6th**, Mexico declares itself independent.

Dec: **1st**, by Declaration of Frankfurt the allies resolve to invade France because of vague reply to peace terms by Napoleon.

Politics, Government, Law, and Economy
Robert Owen, *A New View of Society*.

Science, Technology, and Discovery
Hedley's steam locomotive 'Puffing Billy', with smooth wheels running on smooth rails, installed at Wylam colliery.

Music
G Rossini, *Tancredi* and *The Italian Girl in Algiers* (operas).

Literature
Jane Austen, *Pride and Prejudice.*

1814 **Feb: 1st**, in battle of La Rothière, Blücher first attacks the French and the Russians complete the victory.

March: 30th, (–31st) allies triumphantly enter Paris.

April: 8th, National Assembly in Norway meets to discuss constitution, as Norway has declared itself independent, in defiance of Treaty of Kiel (14th Jan), and decides on limited monarchy (Christian Frederick of Denmark is elected King on 17th May).
11th, by Treaty of Fontainebleau, Napoleon abdicates unconditionally and is banished to Elba.

May: 3rd, Louis XVIII enters Paris.
4th, Ferdinand of Spain annuls Constitution of the Cortes.
30th, by First Peace of Paris, the French recognize frontier of 1792 and agree to recognize independence of the Netherlands and the Italian and the German States.

Aug: 24th, a British force takes Washington and burns main buildings.

Nov: 1st, Congress of Vienna formally opens.

Science, Technology, and Discovery
J J Berzelius publishes *Theory of Chemical Proportions and the Chemical Action of Electricity.*
(25th July) George Stephenson constructs the first effective steam locomotive, capable of hauling 30 tons faster than a horse.

Art, Sculpture, Fine Arts, and Architecture
Dulwich Gallery is opened, the first collection accessible to the public in Britain.

Music
Franz Schubert, *Gretchen am Spinnrade.*
L van Beethoven, *Fidelio*, final two-act form.

Literature
Jane Austen, *Mansfield Park.*
Walter Scott, *Waverley.*

1815 **Jan: 3rd**, by secret treaty, Austria, Britain, and France form defensive alliance against Prusso-Russian plans to solve the Saxon and Polish problems.

March: 1st, Napoleon lands in France forcing Louis XVIII to flee (19th).
20th, Napoleon enters Paris and the 'Hundred Days' begin (–29th June).
23rd, Corn Law is passed, prohibiting imports of foreign corn into Britain when average home price of wheat is below 80 shillings per quarter, but allowing duty-free imports when that price is exceeded.
25th, Austria, Britain, Prussia, and Russia form new alliance against Napoleon in order to maintain the established order in Europe.

June: 9th, Congress of Vienna closes after Final Act is passed; Holland, Belgium and Luxembourg are united to form the Netherlands (by Act of 31st May), Switzerland is to be neutral, East Poland is ceded to Russia and the Western Provinces of Poland to Prussia, Cracow becomes an independent republic, Lombardy and Venetia are restored to Austria, Prussia gains the Rhineland and the northern region of Saxony, Hanover obtains East Friesland and Hildesheim, the German Confederation is established under Presidency of Austria (by Act of 8th June), the Bourbon monarch Ferdinand VII is restored in Spain, the Braganza dynasty returns to the Portuguese throne, Ferdinand IV is recognized as King of Two Sicilies, the Pope and the minor Italian princes are restored, and Britain retains the majority of her overseas conquests, including Malta and Heligoland.
18th, Duke of Wellington and Gebhard von Blücher defeat Napoleon at Waterloo.
22nd, Napoleon abdicates for second time, after being given choice of resignation or deposition by the French Chambers.

July: 7th, Allies enter Paris, enabling Louis XVIII to return, 8th, to Tuileries.

Aug: 2nd, by agreement between Prussia, Austria, Britain, and Russia, the imprisonment of Napoleon is left as a British decision and he is banished to St. Helena (where he arrives 17th).

Sept: 26th, anti-Liberal Holy Alliance is formed between Austria, Russia and Prussia to maintain Vienna settlement.

Nov: 20th, by Second Peace of Paris, France yields territory to Savoy and to Switzerland, and agrees to restore captured art treasures, while the Quadruple Alliance between Austria, Prussia, Russia, and Britain is renewed.

Science, Technology, and Discovery

Jean Lamarck develops a number of new features in the classification of animals in *Histoire naturelle des animaux*.

Humphry Davy invents miner's safety lamp.

John Macadam's method of constructing roads of broken stone officially adopted in England.

1816 **Jan: 16th**, Brazil made an Empire under John, Prince Regent of Portugal.

March: 20th, Maria I, the insane Queen of Portugal, dies, and is succeeded by her son, John VI (–1826).

May: 5th, Carl August of Saxe-Weimar grants first German Constitution.

July: 9th, at Congress of Tucuman, independence of United Provinces of La Plata (Argentina) is declared.

Nov: 5th, Diet of German Confederation opened at Frankfurt-am-Main under Prince Metternich.

Dec: 11th, Indiana becomes an American state.

Society, Education, and Religion

Friedrich Froebel starts an educational community at Keilhau, Thuringia.

Music

Franz Schubert, *Erl King* and 5th Symphony in B flat.

G Rossini, *Barber of Seville* (opera).

Literature

Jane Austen, *Emma.*

S T Coleridge, *Kubla Khan* (written 1797).

Count Leopardi, *Alle Pressamente alle Morte.*

Media

William Cobbett's *Political Register*, published at 2d., the first cheap periodical.

1817 **March: 4th**, James Monroe is inaugurated fifth President of US.

4th, Habeas Corpus Act is suspended after secret Parliamentary committee's report that insurrection is imminent (extended by Act of Parliament, 30th June to last until 1st March 1818).

31st, Act to prevent seditious meetings is passed.

Dec: 10th, Mississippi is admitted to the Union as an American state.

Politics, Government, Law, and Economy

David Ricardo, *Principles of Political Economy and Taxation.*

Society, Education, and Religion

Joseph de Maistre, *Du Pape.*

Science, Technology, and Discovery

Karl Ritter publishes *Geography in its relation to Nature and History* (–1818).

Humanities and Scholarship

H F R de Lamennais, *Essai sur l'indifférence.*

Art, Sculpture, Fine Arts, and Architecture

John Constable, *Flatford Mill* (painting).

Francis Chantrey, *Sleeping Children* (sculpture).

T Jefferson, University of Virginia, Charlottesville (–1826).

1818 **Jan: 6th**, by Treaty of Mundoseer, the dominions of Holkar of Indore are annexed with the Rajput States and come under British protection.

Feb: 5th, on the death of Charles XIII of Sweden, Bernadotte succeeds to throne as Charles XIV, founding a new dynasty.

12th, Independence of Chile proclaimed in Santiago (and is safeguarded by defeat of Spanish Royalist forces, 5th April).

June: 3rd, Baji Rao, Peshwa of Poona and his dominions come under British control in Bombay presidency.

Sept: 27th, (–21st Nov) Conference at Aix-la-Chapelle is held between Austria, Prussia, Russia, France, and Britain to discuss French indemnity.

Oct: 20th, by convention between US and Britain, the border between Canada and US is defined as the 49th Parallel, and a joint occupation of Oregon is to take place for 10 years.

Nov: 15th, France is invited to join European Concert.

15th, the Quadruple Alliance between Russia, Austria, Prussia and Britain is renewed to watch over France in order to protect her against revolution; Britain refuses to make a formal alliance with her allies and with France.

20th, Simón Bolívar formally declares Venezuela independent of Spain.

Dec: 3rd, Illinois becomes US state, with population of approximately 40,000.

Art, Sculpture, Fine Arts, and Architecture

Prado Museum, Madrid.

Music

Franz Schubert, 6th Symphony in C.

Literature

Jane Austen, *Northanger Abbey* and *Persuasion* (posthumous).
Lord Byron, *Don Juan* (–1823).
Walter Scott, *Heart of Midlothian* and *Rob Roy*.
Mary Wollstonecraft Shelley, *Frankenstein*.

Sport and Recreation

First professional horse-racing in US.

1819 **Feb: 6th**, East India Company, represented by Stamford Raffles, establishes a settlement at Singapore by treaty with local ruler (preliminary treaty having been concluded, 30th Jan).

22nd, US Congress ratifies treaty (Adams-Onis Treaty) that obtains Florida from Spain by purchase; after delays, ratifications are exchanged 24th Feb 1821.

Aug: 16th, 'Peterloo' Massacre takes place when a crowd which has gathered in St. Peter's Fields, Manchester, to listen to speeches on parliamentary reform and on repeal of Corn Laws, is charged on by the militia.

Sept: 20th, after A von Kötzebue's murder the Frankfurt Diet, instigated by Prince Metternich, sanctions the Carlsbad Decrees, whereby freedom of press is abolished, universities are placed under State supervision, all political agitation is to be suppressed, and a meeting to investigate rumours of conspiracy is to take place in attempt to check revolutionary and liberal movements in the German Confederation.

Oct: —, first step towards *Zollverein* (Customs Union) taken when Prussia concludes tariff treaty with Schwarzburg-Sonderhausen.

Dec: 7th, Hanover given Constitution with two Chambers by Ordinance of Prince Regent of Britain.

14th, Alabama is admitted as a US state.

17th, Simón Bolívar becomes President of newly-formed Republic of Colombia, created from Venezuela and New Granada.

Politics, Government, Law, and Economy

Simón Bolívar, *Discourse Before the Congress of Angostura*.
In *McCulloch* v. *Maryland*, Chief Justice John Marshall gives judicial sanction to doctrine of centralization of power, at expense of states.

Science, Technology, and Discovery

Hans Christian Oersted discovers electromagnetism.
First ship fitted with steam engine to cross the Atlantic, the *Savannah*, makes crossing in 26 days.

Humanities and Scholarship

Jakob Grimm's *German Grammar* establishes the permutation of consonants.
Arthur Schopenhauer, *World as Will and Idea*.

Art, Sculpture, Fine Arts, and Architecture

Théodore Géricault, *Raft of the Medusa* (painting).
K F Schinkel, Schauspielhaus, Berlin (–1823).

Music

Franz Schubert, *Trout* Quintet (op. 114).

Literature

John Keats, *Hyperion* (published 1856).

1820 **Jan: 1st**, Revolution in Spain begins due to Ferdinand VII's failure to adhere to Constitution of 1812, also his sending troops to Spanish America to put down risings with which Spanish rebels are in sympathy.

29th, George III dies and is succeeded by Prince Regent as George IV (–1830).

Feb: 13th, Duc de Berry, heir presumptive to French throne, is assassinated when proposals to modify Louis XVIII's Charter are being discussed.

23rd, Cato Street Conspiracy to murder Cabinet ministers is discovered and leaders later executed.

28th, following the accession of George IV Parliament is dissolved; the subsequent elections of 6th March–14th April are mainly favourable to the Tory government).

March: 3rd, Maine enters the Union as a free state to counteract impending entrance of Missouri as slave state.

6th, 'The Missouri Compromise' is decided by Congress, whereby Missouri to enter Union as slave state, but slavery is to be abolished in the remainder of Louisiana purchase.

7th, Ferdinand VII of Spain is forced to restore the Constitution of 1812 and to abolish Inquisition.

May: 15th, Final Act of the Conference at Vienna under Metternich (which has been meeting since Nov 1819) is passed authorizing the German Confederation to interfere in the affairs of those states unable to maintain public order and the principles of despotic government (this is passed as law by Frankfurt Diet, 8th June).

July: 2nd, revolt begins in Naples, due to misrule of Ferdinand IV, at the instigation of the Carbonari and other secret societies, resulting in promise of Constitution similar to that in Spain (by royal decree, 7th).

Aug: 24th, revolution in Portugal begins in Oporto and spreads to Lisbon (29th), caused by discontent at King John VI living in Brazil and at the Regency under English influence; the leaders demand a constitution.

Nov: 19th, Preliminary Protocol issued by Austria, Russia, and Prussia at Troppau, expelling those nations undergoing revolutions from the Concert of Europe and allowing other States to intervene to crush revolts by force if necessary (an agreement repudiated by Britain, 16th Dec).

Society, Education, and Religion

Thomas Erskine, *Internal Evidence for the Truth of Revealed Religion.*

Science, Technology, and Discovery

First iron steamship is launched (makes maiden voyage 1822).

Humanities and Scholarship

Thomas Brown, *Lectures on the Philosophy of the Human Mind.*

Art, Sculpture, Fine Arts, and Architecture

William Blake's illustrations to the Book of Job.

The Venus de Milo is discovered.

Music

Franz Schubert, *Wanderer* fantasia.

Literature

John Keats, *The Eve of St. Agnes* and *Ode to a Nightingale.*

Alexander Pushkin, *Ruslan and Ludmila.*

P B Shelley, *Prometheus Unbound* and *Ode to the West Wind.*

Walter Scott, *Ivanhoe.*

1821

Jan: 26th, Portuguese Cortes is established and discusses basis of Constitution whereby feudalism and the Inquisition are to be abolished; a single elective Chamber is to be established and the King is to have only a suspensory vote (this basis is decreed 9th May).

Feb: 13th, at Laibach, Austria agrees to Ferdinand IV's request to send army into Naples to suppress revolt.

March: 5th, James Monroe begins second term as US President.

6th, revolt in Moldavia (after earlier outbreak in Wallachia in Feb) against oppressive rule of the Turks; the rebels appeal to Tsar Alexander I for help, thus beginning Greek War of Independence.

10th, Revolution, influenced by the Carbonari, begins in Piedmont to put Charles Albert Carignan on the throne.

16th, Charles Felix issues decree forcing Charles Albert to renounce claim to throne of Piedmont.

May: 7th, Africa Company is dissolved because of heavy expenses incurred, and Sierra Leone, Gambia, and Gold Coast are taken over by the British government to form British West Africa.

28th, repeal of customs duties on certain timber imports begins British free trade legislation.

June: 24th, Simón Bolívar ensures independence of Venezuela by defeating Spanish army at Carabobo, but the subsequent Constitution of the Cortes severely curtails power of the President.

July: 19th, Coronation of George IV, but Queen Caroline not admitted to ceremony.

28th, Independence of Peru from Spain formally proclaimed.

Aug: 10th, Missouri finally becomes member of the Union as a slave state (see March 1820).

Sept: 15th, Guatemala is declared independent of Spain and aligns itself with Mexico.

Nov: 28th, Panama is declared independent of Spain and joins Republic of Colombia.

Dec: 1st, Republic of San Domingo is established independent of Spain.

Politics, Government, Law, and Economy

Comte de St. Simon, *Du Système industriel.*

Society, Education, and Religion
École des Chartes, Paris, founded for the study of historical documents.

Science, Technology, and Discovery
Michael Faraday builds the first electric motor.

Humanities and Scholarship
G W Hegel, *Philosophy of Right.*

Art, Sculpture, Fine Arts, and Architecture
John Constable, *Hay Wain* (painting).

Music
C M von Weber, *Der Freischütz* (opera).

Literature
Thomas de Quincey, *Confessions of an English Opium Eater.*
J W Goethe, *Wilhelm Meisters Wanderjahre.*
Heinrich Heine, *Poems.*

Media
Manchester Guardian founded.

Statistics
Populations (in millions): France, 30.4; Great Britain, 20.8 (of which Ireland, 6.8); Italian states, 18; Austria, 12; US 9.6; combined populations of Prussia, Bavaria, Saxony, the duchies, principalities and free cities of Germany, 26.1.
Coal Production: UK 8 mill. tons; US 3,650 tons.

1822 Liberia is founded as a colony for freed American slaves.

Jan: 27th, Greek independence formally proclaimed.

Sept: 23rd, Portuguese Constitution is decreed, providing for liberty, legal equality, a single Chamber which the King may not dissolve until its period of four years has expired, and a constitutional monarchy.

Oct: 12th, Brazil becomes formally independent of Portugal and Dom Pedro is proclaimed Emperor.

Dec: 14th, Congress of Verona ends, having ignored Greek War of Independence.

Science, Technology, and Discovery
Streets of Boston, Mass., lit by gas.

Music
Franz Schubert, Symphony No. 8 in B minor (*Unfinished*).

Literature
Alexander Pushkin, *Eugene Onegin* (–1832).

Media
The *Sunday Times* founded.

Statistics
UK textile trade: raw cotton imports 145 mill. lb. exports of cottons 304 mill. yds. exports of woollens 1.7 mill. pieces exports of linen 33.8 mill. yds. exports of silks 287,000 lb.

1823 **March: 19th**, Augustus de Iturbide forced to abdicate in Mexico (and Mexico becomes a republic, Oct 1824).

June: 11th, Ferdinand VII of Spain refuses to leave Madrid in the face of French invasion and is declared to be temporarily incapacitated, a provisional Regency of the Cortes being established.
18th, John VI annuls Portuguese Constitution of 1822 after risings against his rule and against the loss of Brazil.

Oct: 1st, Ferdinand VII of Spain, having been restored by the French who have crushed Spanish rebellion, issues a Decree for execution of his enemies and reign of tyranny begins.

Dec: 2nd, Monroe Doctrine excludes European powers from interfering in politics of American Republics and closes American continent to colonial settlements by them.

Society, Education, and Religion
Friedrich Schleiermacher, *Christian Dogma.*

Science, Technology, and Discovery
Michael Faraday liquefies chlorine.
Giovanni Battista Amici observes pollen approaching plant ovary.
Charles Babbage begins construction of calculating machine.
Charles Macintosh invents waterproof fabric.
Lake Chad, Central Africa, discovered by Walter Oudney on an expedition from Tripoli.

Sport and Recreation

William Webb Ellis originates Rugby Football.

1824 **Feb: 24th**, Governor-General of India declares war against Burmese after the latter have violated territory of East India Company by capturing island of Shahpuri.

May: 11th, British take Rangoon.

Sept: 16th, Louis XVIII dies and is succeeded by Charles X (–1830).

Nov: —, in US presidential election none of the four candidates has a majority; House of Representatives elect John Adams as president.

Humanities and Scholarship

Leopold von Ranke's *History of the Roman and Teutonic People, 1494–1514*, founds modern historiography.

Art, Sculpture, Fine Arts, and Architecture

Eugène Delacroix, *Les Massacres de Chios* (painting).

National Gallery, London, founded with the collection of J J Angerstein.

Music

L van Beethoven's 9th (*Choral*) Symphony performed in Vienna; quartets (op. 127, 130, 131 and 135).

Literature

Count Leopardi, *Canzoni e Versi.*

1825 **Feb: 28th**, Anglo-Russian Treaty over the latter's territory on north-west coast of America, and over respective rights in Pacific Ocean (similar to US-Russian Treaty 17th April 1824).

July: 5th, Acts of Parliament passed modifying Navigation Acts permitting European goods to enter Britain in ships of country of origin.

Aug: 6th, Bolivia (Upper Peru) becomes independent of Peru.
25th, Uruguay becomes independent of Brazil.
29th, Portugal recognizes Brazilian independence under Dom Pedro.

Sept: 19th, Hungarian Diet reopened after 13 years, and Austrian Emperor, in face of discontent in Hungary, agrees to triennial meetings.

Dec: 1st, Tsar Alexander I dies (aged 47) and is succeeded by Nicholas I, his younger son (–1855).
26th, Decembrist Rising in Russian army, aiming at assembly of national representatives, is easily crushed.

Society, Education, and Religion

Joe Smith, founder of Mormons, claims he had his vision.

Comte de St.-Simon, *Nouveau Christianisme.*

Science, Technology, and Discovery

Michael Faraday isolates benzene by distilling whale oil.

In England, George Stephenson builds the first public railway to carry steam trains – the Stockton to Darlington line.

Music

Franz Schubert, *Death and the Maiden* quartet (–1826).

Literature

Alessandro Manzoni, *I Promessi Sposi.*

Aleksandr Pushkin, *Boris Godunov.*

1826 **March: 25th**, promulgation of Brazilian Constitution with hereditary monarchy and general assembly of two chambers (which convenes 6th May).

April: 4th, St. Petersburg Protocol between Britain and Russia respecting Greek problem, on the basis of complete autonomy of Greece under Turkish suzerainty (but does not become treaty until July 1827 when France also joins).

Science, Technology, and Discovery

First railway tunnel (Liverpool–Manchester railway).

Music

F Mendelssohn, music for *A Midsummer Night's Dream.*

Literature

James Fenimore Cooper, *The Last of the Mohicans.*

1827 **Jan:** **26th**, Peru secedes from Colombia in protest against Simón Bolívar's alleged tyranny.

Feb: **17th**, Lord Liverpool suffers a stroke and is forced to resign as Prime Minister.

April: **10th**, George Canning forms ministry of liberal Tories and moderate Whigs.

July: **6th**, Treaty of London whereby Russia, Britain, and France agree to recognize autonomy of Greece and to force truce on Sultan.

Aug: **8th**, death of George Canning (aged 56).
31st, Lord Goderich forms Tory administration in Britain.

Oct: **20th**, Turkish and Egyptian fleets are destroyed at Battle of Navarino by allied squadrons (the Egyptians had arrived in Sept).

Society, Education, and Religion
John Darby secedes from Church of England to found Plymouth Brethren.

Science, Technology, and Discovery
George Ohm formulates Ohm's Law relating current and voltage in an electric circuit.
French doctor Joseph Niepce produces photographs on a metal plate using a camera obscura and eight-hour exposure.
John James Audubon begins publication of *Birds of America*.
Robert Brown observes the motion of tiny particles on a liquid surface (Brownian motion).

Music
Franz Schubert, *Die Winterreise*.

Media
The Evening Standard, London, founded.

1828 **Jan:** **25th**, Duke of Wellington forms Tory administration, following resignation of Goderich, 8th, on question of appointing chairman of finance committee.

April: **26th**, Russia declares war on Turkey.

May: **9th**, repeal of British Test and Corporation Acts so that Catholic and Protestant Nonconformists now allowed to hold public office in Britain.

July: **15th**, new Corn Law allowing imports of corn at any price and using sliding scale.
19th, London Protocol issued by Britain, Russia, and France, allowing France to intervene in the Morea to evacuate hostile troops in order to secure Greek independence.

Nov: **—**, In US presidential election, Andrew Jackson (178 electoral votes) defeats John Quincy Adams (83 votes).
16th, London Protocol, issued by France, Britain, and Russia, recognizes independence of Greece when Morea and Cyclades Isles are guaranteed by those powers.

Society, Education, and Religion
S T Coleridge, *Constitution of Church and State*.

Science, Technology, and Discovery
Karl von Baer, in *Ueber die Entwickelungsgeschichte der Thiere* (–1837), establishes science of comparative embryology.

Humanities and Scholarship
Dugald Stewart, *Philosophy of the Active and Moral Powers of Man*.

Art, Sculpture, Fine Arts, and Architecture
William Dyce's *Madonna* introduces ideas of 'Nazarener' artists to Britain.

Music
Franz Schubert, C Major Symphony (*Great*) and Klavierstücke.

Literature
Thomas Carlyle's *Essay on Goethe* draws attention of English readers to German literature.

1829 **April:** **13th**, Roman Catholic Relief Bill passed in the House of Lords (House of Commons, 5th March) allowing Catholics to sit and vote in Parliament, giving them right of suffrage and making them eligible for all military, civil and corporate offices except those of Regent, Lord Chancellor of England, and Lord Lieutenant of Ireland; they are to take an oath denying the Pope has power to interfere in domestic affairs and recognizing Protestant succession.

Aug: **8th**, Charles X appoints Prince de Polignac Prime Minister in France, an Ultra Conservative who does not possess the confidence of the Chamber, which constitutes a departure from ministerial responsibility.

Sept: 14th, treaty of Adrianople ends Russo-Turkish War and Sultan Mahmud II recognizes London Protocol (March) which guarantees territory of Greece, the independence of Danubian Provinces and of Serbia, while Tsar Nicholas I obtains land south of Caucasus.

Politics, Government, Law, and Economy
Robert Peel founds the Metropolitan Police force.
Governor-General Lord Bentinck secures abolition of 'Suttee' in Bengal (extended to Bombay and Madras in 1830).

Science, Technology, and Discovery
Thomas Graham formulates law on diffusion of gases.
(Oct) George and Robert Stephenson's *Rocket* wins Liverpool and Manchester Railway competition.

Art, Sculpture, Fine Arts, and Architecture
E Delacroix, *Sardanapalus* (painting).

Music
G Rossini, *William Tell* (opera).

Literature
Honoré de Balzac, *Les Chouans* and *La Comédie Humaine* (–1848).

Sport and Recreation
Oxford and Cambridge boat race first rowed.

Media
Revue des Deux Mondes first issued (re-founded 1831).

1830

Feb: 3rd, at London Conference, Greece is declared independent under the protection of France, Russia and Britain.

June: 26th, George IV dies and is succeeded by William IV (–1837).

July: 5th, French begin invasion of Algeria and take Algiers.
19th, French elections finally held, after delays caused by Charles X, and the Liberal opposition obtains majority.
25th, Charles X issues five ordinances, for controlling press, dissolving Chambers and changing electoral system.
27th, (–29th) Revolution in Paris and other areas of France on news of Charles's law.
31st, Louis Philippe is appointed Lieutenant-General of France.

Aug: 2nd, abdication of Charles X.
7th, Louis Philippe is elected King of France by Chambers, and, 9th, accepts throne (–1848).
14th, Constitutional Charter in France, based on an elective monarchy, allowing for initiation of legislation in Chambers, for the permanent suppression of press censorship, and for end to Catholicism as State religion of France.
25th, Revolution in Belgium, against union with Dutch.

Sept: —, Revolts in Saxony, Hesse and Brunswick where rulers are dethroned and constitution granted.
11th, Republic of Ecuador established and granted Constitution by Colombia under which it is to be part of Confederation of Colombia.
22nd, Venezuela secedes from Colombia and becomes an independent sovereign state.

Nov: 15th, Duke of Wellington resigns over the civil list and Lord Grey is asked to form a Liberal-Whig ministry, with Lord Palmerston as Foreign Secretary.

Politics, Government, Law, and Economy
Count Mikhail Speranski codifies Russian law (45 vols. with commentaries).

Society, Education, and Religion
Joseph Smith, *Book of Mormon*; a Mormon church is established at Fayette, New York.

Science, Technology, and Discovery
Charles Lyell publishes the first volume of *Principles of Geology* (–1833) which describes the Earth as being several million years old.

Humanities and Scholarship
Auguste Comte, *Course of Positive Philosophy* (–1842).

Music
Hector Berlioz, *Symphonie Fantastique*.

Literature
Stendhal (pseudonym), *Le Rouge et le Noir*.

1831 **Jan: 25th**, Polish Diet declares independence of Poland, dethrones Nicholas and deposes Romanovs.

Feb: 3rd, revolutionary outbreaks in Modena, Parma and Papal States influenced by French Revolution (of July 1830), and crisis worsens after election of a reactionary Pope, Gregory XVI.

Sept: 4th, Saxony is granted constitution after revolt of Sept 1830.

8th, Russia takes Warsaw after two-day battle and Polish revolt collapses (Tsar proclaims peace Oct 18th).

Nov: 15th, treaty incorporating 24 Articles for separation of Holland and Belgium is accepted by Austria, France, Britain, Prussia, Russia, and Belgium (ratified 31st Jan 1832).

Politics, Government, Law, and Economy

William L Garrison begins publishing *The Liberator*, an abolitionist periodical, in Boston.

Science, Technology, and Discovery

Michael Faraday discovers electromagnetic induction and makes the first dynamo. Joseph Henry makes the same discovery independently of Faraday and shortly before him, but does not publish his work.

Charles Darwin begins his two-year voyage on the *Beagle*.

Art, Sculpture, Fine Arts, and Architecture

'Barbizon School' of artists, including Jean Millet and Pierre Rousseau, first exhibit in the salon.

Music

V Bellini, *La Sonnambula* and *Norma* (operas).

Literature

V Hugo, *Notre-Dame de Paris*. .

1832 **April: 10th**, French law excludes families of Charles X and of Napoleon from France.

June: 7th, Reform Bill becomes law (after King has agreed to create sufficient Whig Peers to out-vote Tory opposition in Lords if necessary). Over 140 seats redistributed, and in the boroughs all antiquated forms of franchise are eliminated and the franchise is extended to include leaseholders paying minimum of £10 rent per annum, while in counties the 40-shilling freehold qualification is retained and certain lease-holders acquire the vote.

28th, Prince Metternich's Six Articles to maintain despotic government in face of opposition within the German Confederation.

Aug: 8th, Greek National Assembly elects Prince Otto of Bavaria King as Otto I (–1862).

Nov: —, In US presidential election, Andrew Jackson, who was nominated as candidate at the first Democratic Convention to be held, defeats Henry Clay (219 electoral votes to 49).

Politics, Government, Law, and Economy

Giuseppe Mazzini founds 'Young Italy' movement.

Slavery Abolition Society founded in Boston, Mass.

Music

F Chopin, Mazurkas (op. 6).

G Donizetti, *L'Elisir d'Amore* (opera).

Literature

Aleksandr Pushkin, *Eugene Onegin* completed.

Book jackets are first used by British publishers.

Drama Goethe, *Faust*, pt. II.

1833 Beginning of Whig Party in US which absorbs the National Republican Party, the former opposition, and attacks Andrew Jackson's democratic policies.

Jan: 1st, Britain proclaims sovereignty over Falkland Islands.

March: 23rd, Prussia establishes *Zollverein* (customs union) in Germany by a series of treaties, but Austria is excluded.

May: 3rd, Turkey recognizes independence of Egypt and cedes Syria and Aden to Mehemet Ali.

July: 8th, by treaty of Unkiar-Skelessi, a defensive alliance between Turkey and Russia, Sultan agrees to close Dardanelles to all but Russian warships.

Oct: 15th, at Berlin, Prussia, Russia and Austria agree to support the integrity of the Ottoman Empire and to further the Holy Alliance by promising to aid one another in the event of attack.

Society, Education, and Religion

John Keble, *National Apostasy* (Assize sermon at Oxford) begins Oxford Movement.

Science, Technology, and Discovery

Diastase, the first enzyme, is separated from barley by Anselme Payen.

Wilhelm Weber and Karl Friedrich Gauss construct an electric telegraph at Göttingen.

Music
F Mendelssohn, 4th Symphony in A (*Italian*).
F Chopin, 12 Études (op. 10).

Literature
Thomas Carlyle, *Sartor Resartus*.
Nicolai Gogol, *The Government Inspector*.
Aleksandr Pushkin, *Queen of Spades*.

1834 **April: 9th**, revolt of silk-weavers in Lyons, lasting four days, after attempts by French government to suppress trade union activities.

12th, 150 Republicans arrested in Paris from fear of insurrection and, 14th, rising crushed by army under Adolphe Thiers.

22nd, Britain, France, Spain, and Portugal form Quadruple Alliance in support of liberal constitutions in Iberian Peninsula.

July: —, Beginning of civil war in Spain when Don Carlos, brother of late Ferdinand VII of Spain, claims throne (the Carlists are finally defeated, Aug 1839).

9th, Lord Grey resigns over problem of tithes and coercion act in Ireland , and is succeeded, 16th, by Melbourne.

Aug: 15th, South Australia Act is passed allowing for establishment of colony there.

Nov: —, Lord Melbourne resigns after the King's refusal to allow Lord Russell to become leader of House of Commons and Robert Peel is asked to form Tory administration (he accepts, 9th Dec).

Dec: 17th, Robert Peel issues Tamworth Manifesto giving Tory Party a policy of liberal Conservatism, accepting Reform Act of 1832 and agreeing to pass more equitable reforms.

Politics, Government, Law, and Economy
(1st Aug) Abolition of slavery in British Empire.

Science, Technology, and Discovery
Louis Braille perfects system of characters for the blind to read.
Cyrus McCormick's reaping machine.

Music
R Schumann, *Carnaval* (op. 9).

1835 **April: 8th**, Robert Peel resigns after defeat when voting against resolution to appropriate surplus revenues of Irish Church for non-ecclesiastical objects and 18th, Lord Melbourne forms Whig ministry.

Sept: —, 'September Laws' in France severely censor the press and suppress the radical movement.

9th, British Municipal Corporations Act abolishes all old Charter privileges and establishes new governing body of councillors elected by ratepayers with aldermen elected by councillors, and a mayor elected for one year.

Society, Education, and Religion
D F Strauss, *Life of Jesus*.

Science, Technology, and Discovery
Samuel Colt's revolver patented.

Music
G Donizetti, *Lucy of Lammermoor* (opera).

Literature
Hans Andersen, *Fairy Tales* (–1872).
Georg Büchner, *Danton's Death*.
N Gogol, *Dead Souls*.

1836 **April: 21st**, Texan independence is ensured by defeat of Mexico at battle of San Jacinto.

June: 15th, Arkansas becomes US state.

16th, formation of London Working Men's Association begins Chartist Movement.

Politics, Government, Law, and Economy
Communist league formed in Paris.

Science, Technology, and Discovery
Acetylene is made.

Humanities and Scholarship
R W Emerson's *Nature* founds Transcendentalism.

Art, Sculpture, Fine Arts, and Architecture
Arc de Triomphe, Paris, completed.

Literature
Charles Dickens, *Sketches by Boz* and *Pickwick Papers* (–1837).

Media
Beginnings of cheap press in France with *La Presse* and *Le Siècle.*

1837 **Jan:** **26th**, Michigan becomes a US state.

March: **4th**, Martin Van Buren is inaugurated President of US.

June: **—**, Natal Republic founded by Dutch settlers and a Constitution is proclaimed.

18th, liberal Constitution is proclaimed in Spain providing for national sovereignty, House of two Chambers, absolute veto of crown and restricted suffrage.

20th, on death of William IV Queen Victoria succeeds to British throne (–1901).

20th, Hanover is automatically separated from Britain, as Salic Law forbids female succession, and the throne is taken up by Ernest Augustus, Duke of Cumberland, eldest surviving son of George III (–1851).

Nov: **—**, Louis Joseph Papineau's rebellion in Lower Canada, result of conflicts between governor and legislative councils, and the popularly-elected assemblies, and also due to opposition between French and British elements; the rebels are successful, 22nd, at St. Denis, but are routed, 24th, at St. Charles.

Dec: **5th**, similar revolt in Upper Canada under William Lyon Mackenzie.

Politics, Government, Law, and Economy
F W A Froebel opens first kindergarten near Blankenburg.

Science, Technology, and Discovery
René Dutrochet recognizes that chlorophyll is necessary for photosynthesis.
Isaac Pitman invents shorthand.

1838 **Sept:** **18th**, Anti-Corn Law League is established in Manchester by Richard Cobden.

Oct: **1st**, Britain's First Afghan War, to prevent increased influence of Russia, which constitutes threat to British position in India.

Politics, Government, Law, and Economy
(8th May) The Working Men's Association, led by F O'Connor, draw up the People's Charter, demanding reform, including manhood suffrage, vote by ballot, annual parliaments and payment of members.

Science, Technology, and Discovery
Justus von Liebig demonstrates that animal heat is due to respiration, founding the science of biochemistry.

Art, Sculpture, Fine Arts, and Architecture
National Gallery, London, opened.
The great palace of the Tsars, Moscow, rebuilt (–1849).

Literature
Charles Dickens, *Nicholas Nickleby* (–1839).

1839 **April:** **19th**, treaty of London whereby territorial arrangements between Belgium and Holland are finally accepted by King William I of Holland, so that Belgium is independent, Luxembourg becomes an independent Grand Duchy, and R Scheldt is opened to commerce of both Dutch and Belgian nations.

21st, Turkish army invades Syria in opposition to Mehemet Ali (war continues until Feb 1841).

May: **7th**, Lord Melbourne resigns because of small majority for Jamaican Bill and Robert Peel is asked to form Conservative administration, but he fails to do so because of 'Bedchamber Question' when Queen Victoria refuses to dismiss certain of her Whig ladies-in-waiting, so that, 13th Melbourne's Whig administration returns.

July: **—**, Beginning of Opium War between China and Britain after Chinese authorities seize and burn British cargoes of opium.

Nov: **4th**, Chartist rising in Newport, Monmouth, in attempt to break open jail is easily crushed.

Politics, Government, Law, and Economy
Louis Blanc, *L'Organization du travail*, proposes system of national workshops.

Science, Technology, and Discovery
Theodor Schwann publishes *Microscopic Investigations on the Accordance in the Structure and Growth of Plants and Animals*, founding modern cell theory.
(March) Louis Daguerre perfects process for producing a silver image on a copper plate – the

'daguerreotype' – following William Henry Fox Talbot's production of a photographic negative (25th Jan).

Art, Sculpture, Fine Arts, and Architecture
J M W Turner, *Fighting Téméraire* (painting).

Music
F Chopin, 24 Preludes (op. 28).

Literature
M Y Lermontov, *A Hero of Our Time.*
Stendhal (pseudonym), *La Chartreuse de Parme.*

Sport and Recreation
Henley Royal Regatta instituted.
Grand National first run at Aintree and Cesarewitch at Newmarket.

1840

Feb: **5th**, by treaty of Waitangi, Maori chiefs surrender sovereignty to British.
10th, marriage of Queen Victoria to Prince Albert of Saxe-Coburg-Gotha.

June: **6th**, Carlist Wars in Spain end when Carlist forces finally surrender, due mainly to negotiations of General Espartero.
7th, death of Frederick William III of Prussia, who is succeeded by Frederick William IV (–1861).

July: **15th**, Russia, Britain, Prussia and Austria form Quadruple Alliance in support of Turkey and by treaty of London offer Mehemet Ali Egypt, as hereditary possession, and southern Syria for life, provided he gives up Crete and northern Syria (but he refuses in hope of French aid).
23rd, act of Parliament for union of Upper and Lower Canada with equal representation for both of these former provinces.

Politics, Government, Law, and Economy
P J Proudhon, *Qu'est-ce-que la Propriété?*
(10th Jan) Rowland Hill introduces penny post in Britain.

Science, Technology, and Discovery
John William Draper photographs the moon.

Art, Sculpture, Fine Arts, and Architecture
Charles Barry, Houses of Parliament (–1852).

Music
R Schumann, *Dichterliebe* song cycle.
A Sax invents saxophone.

1841

Jan: **26th**, British sovereignty proclaimed over Hong Kong.

Feb: **13th**, Sultan finally accepts treaty with regard to Mehemet Ali who obtains Egypt as a hereditary possession.

March: **4th**, W H Harrison inaugurated President of US.

April: **4th**, on Harrison's death, John Tyler becomes President of US.

May: **3rd**, New Zealand is formally proclaimed as British colony.

July: **13th**, France joins Quadruple Alliance of July 1840 with regard to Turkey.
13th, by Convention of the Straits the powers guarantee Ottoman independence and the Dardanelles and Bosphorus are closed to warships of all nations in peacetime (thus overthrowing treaty of Unkiar Skelessi, 1833).

Aug: **30th**, Robert Peel forms Conservative ministry when Lord Melbourne resigns after defeat over amendment to Address.

Society, Education, and Religion
Ludwig Feuerbach, *Essence of Christianity.*
Oratory of St. Francis de Sales founded in Italy for work among poor youths.
David Livingstone begins missionary work in Africa.

Science, Technology, and Discovery
Robert Wilhelm Bunsen invents carbon-zinc battery.
David Livingstone discovers Lake Ngami.

Media
Punch is issued, with Mark Lemon editor and John Leech chief illustrator.

Statistics
Populations: Great Britain, 18,534,000; Ireland, 8,175,000; US 17,063,353. Principal cities: London, 2,235,344; Paris, 935,261; Vienna, 356,870 ; New York, 312,710; Berlin, 300,000.

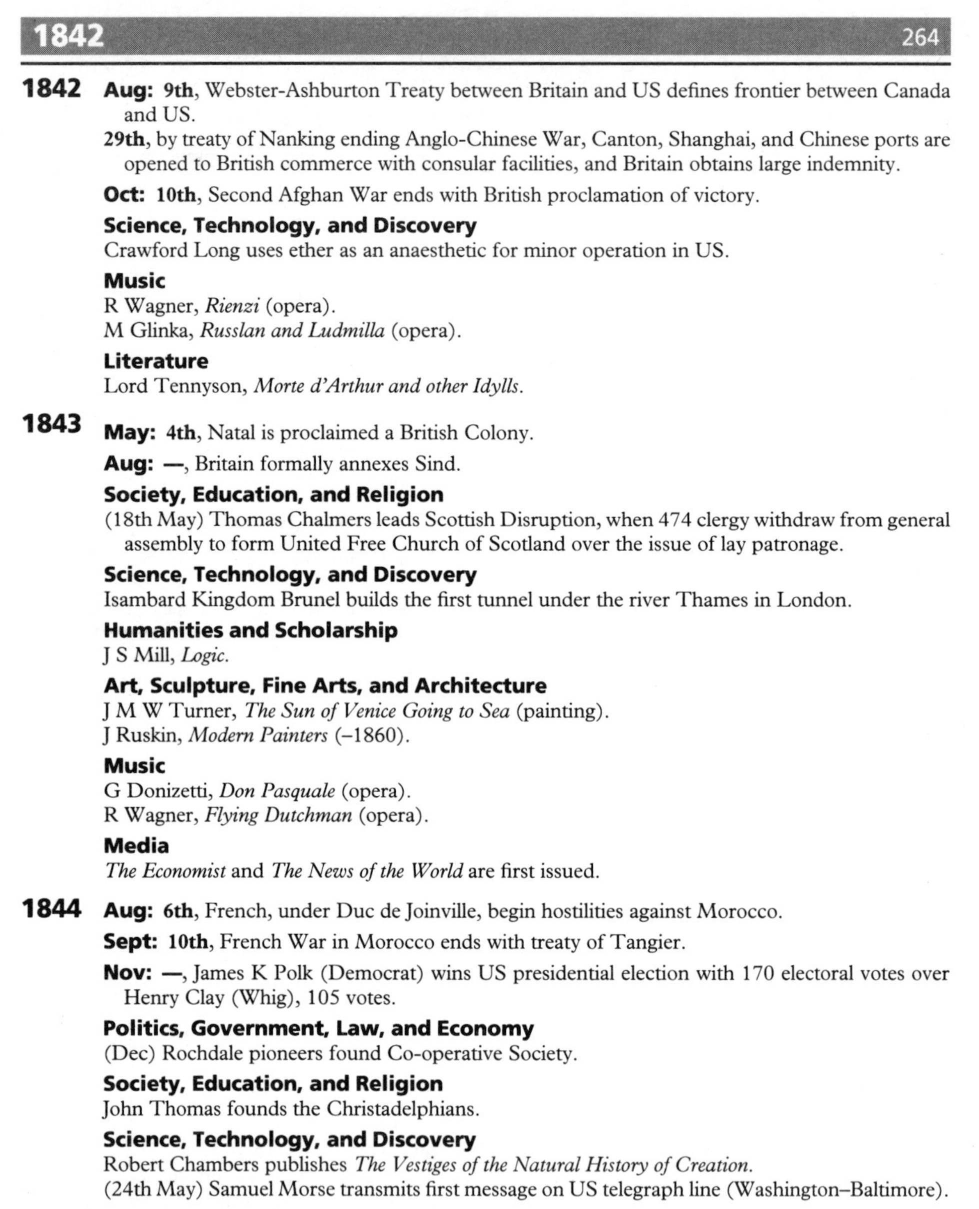

1842 **Aug:** **9th**, Webster-Ashburton Treaty between Britain and US defines frontier between Canada and US.

29th, by treaty of Nanking ending Anglo-Chinese War, Canton, Shanghai, and Chinese ports are opened to British commerce with consular facilities, and Britain obtains large indemnity.

Oct: **10th**, Second Afghan War ends with British proclamation of victory.

Science, Technology, and Discovery

Crawford Long uses ether as an anaesthetic for minor operation in US.

Music

R Wagner, *Rienzi* (opera).
M Glinka, *Russlan and Ludmilla* (opera).

Literature

Lord Tennyson, *Morte d'Arthur and other Idylls*.

1843 **May:** **4th**, Natal is proclaimed a British Colony.

Aug: **—**, Britain formally annexes Sind.

Society, Education, and Religion

(18th May) Thomas Chalmers leads Scottish Disruption, when 474 clergy withdraw from general assembly to form United Free Church of Scotland over the issue of lay patronage.

Science, Technology, and Discovery

Isambard Kingdom Brunel builds the first tunnel under the river Thames in London.

Humanities and Scholarship

J S Mill, *Logic*.

Art, Sculpture, Fine Arts, and Architecture

J M W Turner, *The Sun of Venice Going to Sea* (painting).
J Ruskin, *Modern Painters* (–1860).

Music

G Donizetti, *Don Pasquale* (opera).
R Wagner, *Flying Dutchman* (opera).

Media

The Economist and *The News of the World* are first issued.

1844 **Aug:** **6th**, French, under Duc de Joinville, begin hostilities against Morocco.

Sept: **10th**, French War in Morocco ends with treaty of Tangier.

Nov: **—**, James K Polk (Democrat) wins US presidential election with 170 electoral votes over Henry Clay (Whig), 105 votes.

Politics, Government, Law, and Economy

(Dec) Rochdale pioneers found Co-operative Society.

Society, Education, and Religion

John Thomas founds the Christadelphians.

Science, Technology, and Discovery

Robert Chambers publishes *The Vestiges of the Natural History of Creation*.
(24th May) Samuel Morse transmits first message on US telegraph line (Washington–Baltimore).

Music

G Verdi, *Ernani* (opera).

Literature

Alexandre Dumas, *The Three Musketeers* and *The Count of Monte Cristo*.
E Sue, *The Wandering Jew* (–1845).

1845 **March:** **3rd**, Florida becomes US state.

Dec: **6th**, Robert Peel resigns, as Conservatives are not in favour of free trade, but he returns, 20th as Russell is unable to form government.

11th, outbreak of Anglo-Sikh war when Sikhs cross Sutlej and surprise British.

29th, Texas becomes US state.

Politics, Government, Law, and Economy

F Engels, *The Condition of the Working Classes in England* (Leipzig).

Society, Education, and Religion

(9th Oct) J H Newman is received into the Roman Catholic Church and explains his step in *Essay on the Development of Christian Doctrine*.

Humanities and Scholarship
A H Layard begins excavations at Nineveh.

Music
R Wagner, *Tannhäuser* (opera).

Sport and Recreation
Knickerbocker Club codifies rules of baseball.

1846

The Irish potato crop again fails and famine increases despite organized relief.

May: 13th, formal declaration of war by US against Mexico.

26th, Robert Peel repeals the Corn Laws (royal assent given 26th June), splitting the Conservative Party.

June: 30th, Robert Peel resigns on failing to secure passage of Coercion bill for preserving public order in Ireland, and Lord John Russell forms Liberal government, with Lord Palmerston as Foreign Secretary.

Aug: 22nd, US annexes New Mexico.

Dec: 28th, Iowa becomes a state of US.

Politics, Government, Law, and Economy
Smithsonian Institution, Washington, founded.

Society, Education, and Religion
F C Baur traces the composition of the synoptic Gospels.
Evangelical Alliance founded in London to oppose Romanism.

Science, Technology, and Discovery
A Sobrero prepares nitroglycerine.
Christian Schönbein invents gun-cotton.

Humanities and Scholarship
William Whewell, *Elements of Systematic Morality*.

Music
H Berlioz, *Damnation of Faust*.
F Mendelssohn, *Elijah* (oratorio, in Birmingham).

Literature
Edward Lear, *Book of Nonsense*.
J G Whittier, *Voices of Freedom*.
Honoré de Balzac, *La Cousine Bette*.

Media
(21st Jan) *Daily News*, first cheap English newspaper founded, with C Dickens.

1847

July: 4th, Adolphe Thiers holds first reform banquet held in Paris, demanding wider franchise.

Oct: 21st, *Sonderbund* War begins in Switzerland after Catholic Cantons refuse to dissolve union in face of liberal majority in Diet (20th July), the *Sonderbund* is dissolved after defeat of Catholic Cantons (29th Nov).

Politics, Government, Law, and Economy
(Sept) Gold is discovered in California and leads to the first 'gold rush'.

Science, Technology, and Discovery
Sir James Simpson uses chloroform as an anaesthetic during childbirth.

Humanities and Scholarship
Karl Marx attacks P J Proudhon in *The Poverty of Philosophy*.
The Mormons found Salt Lake City.

Music
G Verdi, *Macbeth* (opera).

Literature
Charlotte Brontë, *Jane Eyre*.
Emily Brontë, *Wuthering Heights*.
A H Hoffmann, *Struwwelpeter*.
W M Thackeray, *Vanity Fair* (–1848).

1848

Jan: 12th, revolt in Palermo, Sicily, against corruption of Bourbons; it is completely successful by end of month.

Feb: 2nd, treaty of Guadaloupe Hidalgo ends Mexican–US War.

22nd, (–24th) revolt in Paris due to failure of Louis Philippe's reign, the economic depression and prohibition of reform banquets.

24th, Louis Philippe abdicates in favour of grandson, Comte de Paris, but Republican Provisional government is proclaimed under Alphonse de Lamartine.
27th, National Workshops are erected in France on Louis Blanc's plan to provide relief in Paris.

March: 12th, (–15th) revolution in Vienna begins with university demonstrations.
13th, Prince Metternich resigns and calling of States-General is promised.
14th, Constitution in Rome promulgated by Pope Pius IX.
17th, revolution in Venice under Daniele Manin, after knowledge of success of Italian, French and Viennese Revolts, and Republic is proclaimed (22nd).
17th, (–19th), in revolution in Berlin, Frederick William IV agrees to grant constitution, but, 21st, is forced to parade in streets of Berlin.
18th, (–22nd) five-day revolution in Milan (*Cinque Giornate*) against Austrian rule, and Joseph Radetzky forced to abandon city.
20th, revolt in Parma.
20th, Second Sikh War begins, arising out of Sikh aristocracy's discontent at British administration and murder of two British officers.
31st, German Ante-Parliament (*Vorparlement*) meets at Frankfurt (–4th April).

April: 13th, Sicily is declared independent of Naples.

May: 15th, Communist rising in Paris, after news of suppression of Polish revolt; workmen overturn government and set up provisional administration which immediately collapses.
18th, German National Assembly meets at Frankfurt and suspends German Confederation.
29th, Wisconsin becomes US state.
30th, Treaty of Guadaloupe Hidalgo (2nd Feb) ratified by Mexico so that US obtains Texas, New Mexico, California, Nevada, Utah, Arizona, parts of Colorado and of Wyoming from Mexico in return for large indemnity.

June: 17th, Austrian troops under Prince Windischgrätz suppress Czech revolt in Prague.
23rd, (–24th) 'June Days' in France, when Louis Cavaignac suppresses Paris workmen in effort to close workshops, killing thousands.

July: 27th, formal union of Venice, Sardinia, and Lombardy.

Sept: 7th, abolition of serfdom in Austria.
12th, new constitution by which Switzerland becomes federal union with strong central government.

Oct: 6th, third revolution in Vienna at news that government is to crush revolt in Hungary.

Nov: 4th, Republican Constitution in France is promulgated with single Chamber, strong President and direct election under universal suffrage.

Dec: 10th, Louis Napoleon is elected President of France by a massive majority.

Politics, Government, Law, and Economy

J S Mill, *Principles of Political Economy.*
(Feb) Karl Marx and Friedrich Engels issue *Communist Manifesto.*

Humanities and Scholarship

Lord Macaulay, *History of England* (–1861).

Art, Sculpture, Fine Arts, and Architecture

H Holman Hunt, J Millais and D G Rossetti found the Pre-Raphaelite Brotherhood.

Literature

Vicomte de Chateaubriand, *Mémoires d'Outre-tombe.*
Alexandre Dumas, *La Dame aux Camélias.*

1849

Feb: 9th, Rome proclaimed Republic under Giuseppe Mazzini.

March: 4th, Zachary Taylor inaugurated President of US.
12th, Sardinia ends truce with Austria (of Aug 1848).
23rd, on Austrian victory at Novara, Charles Albert of Sardinia abdicates in favour of Victor Emmanuel II.
29th, Britain annexes Punjab by treaty with Maharajah of Lahore.

June: 5th, liberal Constitution in Denmark provides for limited monarchy, and civil liberties are guaranteed.
6th, German National Assembly (a 'rump') moves to Stuttgart and, 18th, is dissolved by troops; marks failure of attempt at German unification under a Parliamentary system.

Aug: 6th, Peace of Milan ends war between Sardinia and Austria.

Society, Education, and Religion

Charles Kingsley and F D Maurice teach Christian Socialism.

Science, Technology, and Discovery
Joseph Monier's reinforced concrete developed.

Art, Sculpture, Fine Arts, and Architecture
Alfred Rethel's wood-engravings, *The Dance of Death.*

1850 **March:** —, Further Anglo-Kaffir war breaks out (–1853).
20th, a German Parliament is summoned by Frederick William IV of Prussia to Erfurt to form a new confederation in opposition to Austria.

April: **12th**, French troops restore Pius IX and garrison Rome; Pius revokes the Constitution.
29th, Erfurt Parliament is prorogued.

July: **9th**, death of US President Zachary Taylor who is succeeded by Millard Fillmore.

Aug: **5th**, Australia Government Act grants representative government to South Australia, Tasmania, and Victoria (which is separated from New South Wales).
12th, California is admitted to the Union as a free state.

Oct: —, Taiping rebellion in China under Hung Siu-tsuen, who takes Nanking and Shanghai, proclaims himself emperor and attacks Peking.
11th, Camillo Cavour is appointed minister in Piedmont where he begins economic reforms.

Society, Education, and Religion
(Sept) Re-establishment of the Roman Catholic hierarchy in Britain.

Science, Technology, and Discovery
Rudolf Clausius generalizes the second law of thermodynamics and founds the kinetic theory of gases.
Robert Wilhelm von Bunsen invents the burner that bears his name.
J W Brett lays first submarine cable between Dover and Calais.

Art, Sculpture, Fine Arts, and Architecture
Gustave Courbet, *The Stone-Breakers* (painting).
J E Millais, *Christ in the House of his Parents* (painting).

Literature
N Hawthorne, *The Scarlet Letter.*
Lord Tennyson publishes *In Memoriam* and succeeds William Wordsworth as poet laureate.

1851 **Dec:** **2nd**, Louis Napoleon carries out *coup d'état* in order to change constitution of France; risings break out 3rd (–4th), but are easily suppressed.

Science, Technology, and Discovery
Isaac Singer's sewing machine built.

Art, Sculpture, Fine Arts, and Architecture
J Ruskin, *The Stones of Venice* (–1853).

Music
G Verdi, *Rigoletto* (opera).

Literature
H Melville, *Moby Dick.*

Everyday Life
The Great Exhibition, Hyde Park.

1852 **Feb:** **23rd**, Lord John Russell resigns, after defeat on amendment to Militia Bill and, 27th, a Conservative administration is formed under Lord Derby, with Benjamin Disraeli chancellor of Exchequer (–Dec 20th).

May: **8th**, treaty of London by Britain, France, Russia, Prussia, Austria and Sweden guarantees integrity of Denmark.

June: **30th**, British Act of Parliament gives new Constitution providing for representative government for New Zealand.

Nov: —, In US presidential election Franklin Pierce (Democrat) defeats Winfield Scott (Whig) by 254 electoral votes to 42.
4th, Count Cavour becomes Prime Minister of Piedmont.

Dec: **2nd**, French (Second) Empire is proclaimed with Napoleon III Emperor.
20th, Following defeat of Disraeli's budget, Derby's government resigns, and a Coalition of Whigs and Peelites is formed under Lord Aberdeen, with Gladstone as chancellor of Exchequer.

Science, Technology, and Discovery
Herbert Spencer coins the term 'evolution' in *The Development Hypothesis.*

Literature
H Beecher Stowe, *Uncle Tom's Cabin.*

1853 **March:** **4th**, Franklin Pierce inaugurated President of US.

April: **18th**, W E Gladstone introduces first Budget which abolishes most of duties on partially manufactured goods and foodstuffs and halves most duties on manufactured products.
19th, Prince Alexander Menshikov, Russian emissary to Turkey, claims protectorate for Russia over Christian subjects of Ottoman Empire.

May: **21st**, Turks reject Russian ultimatum (of 19th April) and Menshikov leaves Constantinople.
31st, Tsar Nicholas I orders occupation of the Danubian Principalities.

Humanities and Scholarship
T Mommsen, *History of Rome* (–1856).

Art, Sculpture, Fine Arts, and Architecture
Georges Haussmann begins reconstruction of Paris and lays out the Bois de Boulogne.

Music
G Verdi, *Il Trovatore* and *La Traviata* (operas).

1854 **Feb:** **23rd**, at Convention of Bloemfontein, British agree to leave territory north of Orange River which allows for establishment of Constitution for Orange Free State.

March: **27th**, France and, 28th, Britain declare war on Russia.

May: **30th**, Kansas-Nebraska Act repeals Missouri Compromise (of 1820) and provides for settlement of these territories under popular sovereignty, a situation which immediately leads to 'War for Bleeding Kansas' between free-states and pro-slavery elements.

July: **6th**, Republican Party formally established in US in opposition to Kansas-Nebraska Act (title having first been adopted 28th Feb).

Aug: **8th**, Vienna Four Points by Britain, Austria and France state conditions of peace to be Russia's abandonment of claim to protectorate over Sultan's Christian subjects, revision of Straits settlement in interests of European powers, free passage of mouth of Danube and guarantee of integrity of Danubian principalities and of Serbia.

Oct: **25th**, battle of Balaclava is begun by Russians and results in allied victory at great loss after Charge of the Light Brigade and also of the Heavy Brigade.

Society, Education, and Religion
(8th Dec) Pius IX declares the dogma of Immaculate Conception of Blessed Virgin Mary to be an article of faith.

Science, Technology, and Discovery
Elisha Otis installs first safety elevator which, with the development of cheaper steel, makes possible the skyscraper.

Music
H Berlioz, *The Childhood of Christ* (oratorio).

Literature
Coventry Patmore, *Angel in the House.*

Media
Le Figaro, Paris, issued.

1855 **Feb:** **6th**, Lord Palmerston undertakes to form Liberal ministry after resignation of Lord Aberdeen (1st), due to popular dissatisfaction with war policy.

March: **—**, End of Taiping Rebellion in China.
2nd, Tsar Nicholas I of Russia dies (aged 58) and is succeeded by Alexander II (–1881).

July: **16th**, British Parliament establishes responsible government throughout Australian States, except for Western Australia.

Science, Technology, and Discovery
(Nov) D Livingstone discovers Victoria Falls of the Zambesi River.

Literature
H W Longfellow, *The Song of Hiawatha.*
G de Nerval's *La Rève et la Vie* (posthumous) begins the Symbolist Movement.

Media
Foundation of *The Daily Telegraph* (29th June) and *The Saturday Review.*

1856 During the year Britain grants self-government to Tasmania and allows responsible government in New Zealand.

Feb: 13th, Britain annexes Oudh, which increases hostility of India to British rule.

March: 30th, the integrity of Turkey is recognized by the powers in the Treaty of Paris who guarantee Danubian Principalities, Russia cedes Bessarabia, the Black Sea is to be neutral, and the R Danube is to be free.

April: 15th, Britain, France and Austria guarantee integrity and independence of Turkey in a further treaty.

16th, Declaration of Paris abolishes privateering, defines nature of contraband and blockade and recognizes principle of 'free ships, free goods'.

July: 12th, Natal is established as a separate British Crown Colony with an elected assembly.

Oct: 8th, *Arrow* Incident, when ship flying British flag is boarded by Chinese, who arrest members of crew; provokes second Anglo-Chinese War (–June 1858).

Nov: —, James Buchanan (Democrat) wins US presidential election (174 electoral votes) over John C Frémont (Republican, 114 votes) and Millard Fillmore (Whig, 8 votes).

Dec: 6th, The South African Republic (Transvaal) is organized under Marthinius Pretorius.

Science, Technology, and Discovery

Nathaniel Pringsheim observes sperm entering ovum.

Henry Bessemer's process for making steel brings down prices.

Richard Burton and John Speke set out to find source of the Nile and (1858) discover Lake Tanganyika and Lake Victoria Nyanza.

Literature

Gustave Flaubert, *Madame Bovary* (–1857).

Sport and Recreation

Thomas Cook leads first travel tour to Europe.

Media

Frankfurter Zeitung.

1857 **March: 7th**, the decision of the Supreme Court in the Dred Scott case in connection with position of a slave in a free state renders the Missouri compromise unconstitutional.

Aug: —, Italian National Association formed by Giuseppe Garibaldi for unification under Piedmont.

Oct: —, Irish Republican Brotherhood (Fenians) founded in New York; soon spreads to Ireland.

Humanities and Scholarship

'Rolls Series' of edited texts of chronicles and memorials of the Middle Ages is begun.

Art, Sculpture, Fine Arts, and Architecture

J F Millet, *The Gleaners* (painting).

Literature

Charles Baudelaire, *Les Fleurs du Mal.*

E B Browning, *Aurora Leigh.*

Anthony Trollope, *Barchester Towers.*

1858 **Feb: 26th**, Lord Derby forms Conservative administration.

May: 12th, Minnesota becomes US state.

June: 26th, Treaty of Tientsin ends Anglo-Chinese War; China opens further ports to British commerce and legalizes opium trade (similar treaty with France by Chinese 27th June).

July: 20th, Napoleon III and Cavour begin meetings at Plombières to plan unification of Italy.

Aug: 2nd, powers of East India Company are transferred to the British Crown.

26th, Anglo-Japanese commercial treaty providing for unsupervised trade and for setting up British residency.

Society, Education, and Religion

Blessed Virgin Mary is reputed to have appeared to Bernadette Soubirous at Lourdes, which becomes a centre of pilgrimage.

Art, Sculpture, Fine Arts, and Architecture

Édouard Manet, *Le Concert aux Tuileries* (painting).

Covent Garden Opera House built by Charles Barry.

Ringstrasse, Vienna, is begun.

Music
Jacques Offenbach, *Orpheus in the Underworld* (opera).
César Franck, *Messe Solennelle.*

1859 **Feb: 14th**, Oregon becomes a US state.

March: 31st, Lord Derby's ministry is defeated over B Disraeli's Reform Bill.

April: 19th, Austrian ultimatum to Sardinia to disarm (rejected by Count Cavour, 26th).

June: 10th, Lord Derby resigns after further defeat and Lord Palmerston subsequently forms Liberal administration.
24th, Austrians defeated at Solferino by French and Sardinian forces.

July: 11th, preliminary Peace of Villafranca (confirmed Nov) by which Austria is to cede Parma and Lombardy to France, for subsequent cession to Sardinia; Tuscany and Modena are to be restored and Venice is to remain Austrian, a treaty which causes Count Cavour to resign in disgust.

Sept: —, Formation of German National Association by Rudolf von Bennigsen to work for German unity under Prussia.

Oct: 16th, (–18th) John Brown, American abolitionist, makes abortive raid on Harper's Ferry, site of a federal arsenal (he is hanged 2nd Dec).

Politics, Government, Law, and Economy
J S Mill, *On Liberty.*
K Marx, *Criticism of Political Economy.*

Science, Technology, and Discovery
Charles Darwin publishes *The Origin of Species by Natural Selection* expounding his theory of evolution by natural selection.
Edwin Drake drills the first oil well, at Titusville, Pennsylvania.

Art, Sculpture, Fine Arts, and Architecture
J A Ingres, *Le Bain Turc* (painting).
É Manet, *Absinthe Drinker* (painting).

Music
C F Gounod, *Faust* (opera).
R Wagner, *Tristan und Isolde* (opera).

Literature
George Eliot (pseudonym), *Adam Bede.*
Edward Fitzgerald, *Rubaiyat of Omar Khayyam.*

1860 **Jan: 23rd**, Cobden-Chevalier Treaty establishes substantial degree of free trade between Britain and France.

March: 11th, (–15th) Plebiscites in Tuscany, Emilia, Parma, Modena and Romagna in favour of union with Sardinia.

April: 2nd, first Italian Parliament meets in Turin.

Oct: 21st, (–22nd) plebiscites in Naples and Sicily in support of union with Sardinia.

Nov: 4th, (–5th) plebiscites in Umbria and Legations for union with Sardinia.
6th, in US presidential election, Abraham Lincoln (Republican) opposing further extension of slavery secures a majority of popular votes, but only 180 out of 303 electoral votes; John C Breckinidge (Southern Democrat) has 72 votes, John Bell (Constitutional Union), 39, and Stephen A Douglas (Northern Democrat), 12 votes.

Society, Education, and Religion
Frederick Temple, Mark Pattison and others contribute to *Essays and Reviews*, which is condemned by Convocation.

Science, Technology, and Discovery
Chemical congress at Karlsruhe settles problem of atomic weights.

Art, Sculpture, Fine Arts, and Architecture
J Burckhardt, *The Culture of the Renaissance in Italy.*

Literature
Wilkie Collins, *The Woman in White.*
George Eliot (pseudonym), *The Mill on the Floss.*
Ivan Turgeniev, *On the Eve.*

Sport and Recreation
Open Golf Championship started (first won by W Park).

Media

The Cornhill Magazine founded under W M Thackeray's editorship.

1861

Jan: 2nd, Frederick William IV of Prussia dies and is succeeded by William I (–1888).
29th, Kansas is created US state.

Feb: 4th, Congress of Montgomery at which South Carolina, Georgia, Alabama, Mississippi, Florida, and Louisiana decide, 8th, to elect Jefferson Davis as President of Confederate States of America which is formed 9th (five more states join April–May).
18th, Italian Parliament proclaims Victor Emmanuel King (and Kingdom of Italy proclaimed 17th March).

March: 3rd, emancipation of Russian serfs proclaimed (19th Feb old style).
4th, Abraham Lincoln inaugurated President of US.

April: 12th, (–13th) Confederates take Fort Sumter, Charleston, S Carolina after 40-hour bombardment, marking outbreak of American Civil War.

Dec: 14th, death of Prince Consort (aged 42).

Politics, Government, Law, and Economy

Paper duties in UK are repealed.

Science, Technology, and Discovery

Louis Pasteur develops the germ theory of disease.
William Siemens in UK and Pierre and Émile Martin in France simultaneously develop the open-hearth process for making steel with a regenerative gas-fired furnace, which effects a rapid rise in steel production and a reduction in the coal used.
Pierre Michaux and his son Ernst construct the first 'bone-shaker' pedalled bicycle.

Humanities and Scholarship

H Maine, *Ancient Law*.

Art, Sculpture, Fine Arts, and Architecture

Jean Garnier builds Paris Opera House (–1875).
William Morris begins to make wallpapers and tapestries.

Literature

Charles Dickens, *Great Expectations*.
George Eliot (pseudonym), *Silas Marner*.

1862

Aug: 29th, (–30th), second battle of Bull Run, where Thomas ('Stonewall') Jackson defeats Union Army.

Sept: 22nd, Abraham Lincoln declares all slaves to be free from 1st Jan 1863.
22nd, Otto von Bismarck becomes Prussian premier.
29th, Bismarck's 'Blood and Iron' speech.

Politics, Government, Law, and Economy

J S Mill, *Utilitarianism*.
F Lassalle's *The Working Man's Programme* advocates a system of State socialism.
Foundation of colleges in each US state in which science and technology is placed on a par with arts subjects.

Music

G Verdi, *La Forza del Destino* (opera).

Literature

V Hugo, *Les Misérables*.
Ivan Turgeniev, *Fathers and Sons*.

1863

Jan: 22nd, Polish insurrection begins when National Committee publishes manifesto.

Feb: 8th, Prussia allies with Russia to suppress Polish Revolt at Convention made by Count Alvensleben.
24th, Arizona organized as territory of US.

March: 3rd, Idaho organized as territory of US.
30th, William, Prince of Denmark, recognized as King of Greece and takes title of George I (–1919).

June: 20th, West Virginia created US state.

July: 1st, (–3rd) Robert E Lee's Confederate army defeated by General Meade's force at Gettysburg, Pennsylvania.

Nov: 23rd, (–25th) Confederates defeated at Chattanooga, Tennessee.

Science, Technology, and Discovery
Thomas Graham's process for separating gases by atmolysis.

Humanities and Scholarship
T Mommsen issues first part of *Corpus Inscriptionum Latinum.*
Paul Littré, *Dictionnaire de la langue française* (–1872).
E Renan, *Vie de Jésus* and *Histoire des origines du christianisme.*

Art, Sculpture, Fine Arts, and Architecture
É. Manet, *Luncheon on the Grass* (painting).
C Baudelaire's essay on Constantin Guy, 'Le Peintre de la vie moderne'.

Music
H Berlioz, *The Trojans*, pt. I – *The Trojans at Carthage* (opera).

Sport and Recreation
Football Association founded.

1864

May: 26th, territory of Montana organized in US.

Sept: 1st, Confederates abandon Atlanta, Georgia, which is occupied, 2nd, by Sherman.
5th, (–8th) British, French and Dutch fleets attack Japan in Shimonoseki Straits in reprisal for closing ports and expelling foreigners (a truce, 14th, is followed by peace convention, 22nd Oct, when Japan pays indemnity).
15th, Franco-Italian Treaty whereby Italy renounces claim to Rome and Florence becomes Italian capital (–1870) in place of Turin.

Oct: 30th, Peace of Vienna by which Denmark cedes Schleswig, Holstein and Lauenburg to Austria and Prussia.
31st, Nevada created US state.

Nov: 8th, re-election of Abraham Lincoln as US President.

Politics, Government, Law, and Economy
Geneva Convention prescribes immunity for the Red Cross League, founded by Henri Dunant, in time of war.

Society, Education, and Religion
J H Newman, *Apologia pro vita sua.*
(8th Dec) Pius IX issues Syllabus of Errors, claiming the Church's control over culture, science, and education, and provokes a discussion of papal infallibility.

Science, Technology, and Discovery
Louis Pasteur invents pasteurization (for wine).
Robert Whitehead constructs torpedo.

Humanities and Scholarship
N Fustel de Coulanges, *La Cité Antique.*

Music
Anton Bruckner, Mass No. I in D minor.

Literature
Charles Dickens, *Our Mutual Friend.*
Leo Tolstoy, *War and Peace* (–1869).

Media
Neue Freie Presse, Vienna.

1865

April: 9th, Lee, Confederate commander in chief, capitulates to Ulysses S Grant at Appomattox.
14th, Abraham Lincoln assassinated by J W Booth and is succeeded by Andrew Johnson as President of US.

May: 26th, surrender of last Confederate army at Shreveport, near New Orleans, ends US Civil War.

Aug: 14th, Convention of Gastein by which Austria receives Holstein, whereas Prussia obtains Schleswig and Kiel, and purchases Lauenburg.

Oct: 4th, (and 11th) Otto von Bismarck and Napoleon III meet at Biarritz when the French Emperor agrees to Prussian supremacy in Germany, and to a united Italy.
18th, Lord Palmerston dies (aged 80) and Lord John Russell becomes Prime Minister, with W E Gladstone leader of House of Commons.

Dec: 10th, Leopold I of Belgium dies and is succeeded by his son, Leopold II (–1909).

Politics, Government, Law, and Economy
Foundation of Massachusetts Institute of Technology and of Odessa University.

Society, Education, and Religion
William Booth founds Salvation Army.

Science, Technology, and Discovery
First carpet sweeper and first mechanical dishwasher invented.
Atlantic cable finally successful.
Gregor Mendel's papers published. They establish the laws of heredity.

Art, Sculpture, Fine Arts, and Architecture
É. Manet, *Olympia* (painting).

Music
R Wagner's opera *Tristan und Isolde* is performed in Munich.

Literature
Lewis Carroll (pseudonym), *Alice's Adventures in Wonderland.*

1866 **June: 13th**, US 14th Amendment incorporates Civil Rights Act and gives states the choice of Negro enfranchisement or reduced representation in Congress.
14th, Federal Diet in Germany votes for mobilization against Prussian intervention in Holstein, at which Prussian delegates declare the German Confederation at an end.
15th, (–16th) Prussia invades Saxony, Hanover and Hesse during the night.
20th, Italy declares war on Austria.
24th, Austrian forces under Archduke Albert defeat Italians at Custozza, northern Italy.

July: 3rd, Prussians defeat Austrians at Sadowa (Königgrätz).
6th, Lord Derby forms Conservative administration, with B Disraeli leader of the House of Commons.

Aug: 23rd, Peace of Prague confirms preliminary peace of Nikolsburg (26th July), whereby Austria to be excluded from Germany, while Hanover, Hesse, Nassau and Frankfurt are to be incorporated with Prussia, South German States to be independent, but States north of the Main to form Confederation under Prussia, which also obtains Austrian Silesia and territory from Saxony and from South German States.

Oct: 3rd, war between Austria and Italy ended by treaty of Vienna.
21st, (–22nd) plebiscites in Venezia result in support for union with Italy.

Society, Education, and Religion
Dr. T J Barnardo opens home for waifs in Stepney.

Science, Technology, and Discovery
Alfred Nobel invents dynamite.

Art, Sculpture, Fine Arts, and Architecture
Edgar Degas begins to paint scenes of ballet dancers.

Music
Friedrich Smetana, *The Bartered Bride* (opera).

Literature
Fyodor Dostoevsky, *Crime and Punishment.*

1867 **Feb: 17th**, Hungarian Diet is opened, and subsequently the Constitution of 1848 is restored so that *Ausgleich* (Compromise) takes place allowing for Dual Monarchy, whereby Magyars dominate Hungary and German element dominates rest of Austrian territories, though there were to be single foreign and war policies.

March: 1st, Nebraska becomes a US state.
2nd, Basic Reconstruction Act in US dividing southern states into five military districts; to re-enter Union these districts are to draw up constitutions passed by Congress, and they must recognize 14th Amendment (of June 1866).
29th, British North America Act establishes Dominion of Canada comprising Quebec, Ontario, Nova Scotia and New Brunswick.
30th, US purchases Alaska from Russia.

April: 16th, formation of North German Confederation with Prussia at head.

Aug: 15th, Parliamentary Reform Act in Britain extends suffrage in boroughs to all householders paying rates and all lodgers paying £10 rent annually, in counties to landowners with land at value of £5 p.a. and tenants paying £12 rent annually; redistribution of seats takes place.

Oct: 27th, Garibaldi begins march on Rome.

Dec: 13th, Fenian outrage at Clerkenwell kills 12 people.

Politics, Government, Law, and Economy
Karl Marx, *Das Kapital*, vol. I.

Science, Technology, and Discovery
Pierre Michaux manufactures bicycles.
Joseph Lister announces practice of antiseptic surgery using phenol (carbolic acid).
George Westinghouse invents the air brake for railways.

Art, Sculpture, Fine Arts, and Architecture
The Paris World Fair introduces Japanese art to the West.

Music
G Verdi, *Don Carlos* (opera).
J Strauss, The *Blue Danube* Waltz.

Literature
Anthony Trollope, *Last Chronicle of Barset*.
Drama H Ibsen, *Peer Gynt*.

1868 **Jan: 3rd**, Shogunate abolished in Japan and restoration of Meiji dynasty.

Feb: 25th, Lord Derby resigns through ill health and
28th, B Disraeli replaces him as Prime Minister.

March: 12th, Britain annexes Basutoland.

Sept: 17th, Liberal revolution against Queen Isabella II in Spain under Marshal Juan Prim and, 18th, Admiral Topete issues a Liberal manifesto in Cadiz.
30th, Queen Isabella of Spain flees to France, and is declared deposed.

Nov: —, In US presidential election Ulysses S Grant (Republican) has 214 electoral votes over Horatio Seymour (Democrat), with 80 votes.

Dec: 2nd, following Liberal victory (387 seats) over Conservatives (272 seats) in British general election, B Disraeli resigns without waiting for Parliament's reassembly. W E Gladstone, who lost his seat in south-west Lancashire, forms a Liberal ministry with Lord Clarendon as Foreign Secretary and Robert Lowe as chancellor of Exchequer.

Art, Sculpture, Fine Arts, and Architecture
Renoir and Manet begin to paint continually out of doors.

Music
J Brahms, *A German Requiem*, op. 45 (additions made, 1872).
E Grieg, *Piano Concerto in A minor* (op. 16).
R Wagner, *The Mastersingers of Nuremberg* (opera).

Literature
W Collins, *The Moonstone*.
Fyodor Dostoevsky writes *The Idiot*.

1869 **June: 1st**, new Spanish Constitution promulgated, providing for continuation of monarchical form of government.

Oct: 11th, Red River Rebellion begins in Canada when half-breeds, led by Louis Riel, stop survey team near Winnipeg.

Politics, Government, Law, and Economy
J S Mill, *The Subjection of Women*.
The State of Wyoming enfranchises women and gives them the right to hold office.

Society, Education, and Religion
Girton College, Cambridge, founded.
(Dec) The Vatican Council meets and H E Manning advocates a definition of papal infallibility.

Science, Technology, and Discovery
Dimitri Mendeléev expounds his periodic law for the classification of the elements.
John Wesley Hyatt invents celluloid (the first plastic) independently of Alexander Parkes.
Johann Frederick Miescher discovers the genetic material DNA in cells.

Music
R Wagner, *The Rhinegold* (opera).

Literature
G Flaubert, *L'Éducation sentimentale*.

Everyday Life
H Mège-Mouries invents margarine.

1870 **May:** **12th**, Manitoba made Canadian province, which helps to end Red River Rebellion.

July: **2nd**, news reaches France of acceptance of Spanish throne by Leopold, Prince of Hohenzollern.
13th, French ultimatum to Prussia not to renew Spanish candidature results in 'Ems Telegram'.
19th, France declares war on Prussia.

Sept: **1st**, French defeated at battle of Sedan, France.
4th, defeat leads to revolt in Paris, provisional government of national defence is set up and a Republic proclaimed.

Oct: **2nd**, Rome made capital of Italy by Decree of 9th, and King of Italy formally incorporates Rome and Roman provinces in Italy.

Politics, Government, Law, and Economy
W E Forster's Education Act establishes board schools.

Society, Education, and Religion
(May) Convocation of Church of England appoints committees to revise the Old and New Testaments, which lead to the 'Revised Version'.
(18th July) Vatican Council declares dogma of papal infallibility in matters of faith and morals by 533 votes to 2.

Science, Technology, and Discovery
Zénobe Théophile Gramme invents dynamo with ring armature, the first commercially practical generator for direct current electricity.

Music
Clément Delibes, *Coppélia* (ballet).
R Wagner, *Die Walküre* (opera).

Literature
Fyodor Dostoevsky, *The House of the Dead.*

1871 **Jan:** **18th**, William I of Prussia proclaimed German Emperor at Versailles.

March: **13th**, London Conference between great powers repudiates Black Sea clauses of 1856 (after Russian repudiation of clauses, Oct 1870).
18th, rising of Commune begins in Paris.
26th, Commune is formally set up.

April: **16th**, German Empire receives Constitution remodelled from that of North German Confederation.

May: **10th**, Franco-German Peace of Frankfurt by which France cedes Alsace-Lorraine, pays indemnity of 5 milliards of francs, and is to be subjected to army of occupation until payment completed.
13th, Law of Guarantees in Italy declares the Pope's person inviolable and allows him the possession of the Vatican.
21st, (–28th) 'Bloody Week' in Paris ends with defeat of the Commune.

June: **16th**, University Test Acts allow students to enter Oxford and Cambridge without religious tests.
29th, British Act of Parliament for legalizing trade unions.

July: **—**, Germany begins *Kulturkampf* (cultural struggle) with Catholic Church, when Otto von Bismarck suppresses the Roman Catholic Department for spiritual affairs.
20th, British Columbia joins Dominion of Canada (after Imperial Order-in-Council of May).

Politics, Government, Law, and Economy
Purchase of commissions in British Army abolished.

Society, Education, and Religion
Jehovah's Witnesses founded.

Science, Technology, and Discovery
Charles Darwin publishes *The Descent of Man*, discussing the evolution of humans.
(10th Nov) H M Stanley meets D Livingstone at Ujiji.

Humanities and Scholarship
Heinrich Schliemann begins to excavate Troy.
T Mommsen, *Roman Constitutional Law* (–1888).

Music
G Verdi *Aïda* (opera).

Literature
L Carroll (pseudonym), *Through the Looking-Glass.*
George Eliot (pseudonym), *Middlemarch* (–1872).
É. Zola, *Les Rougon-Macquart* series of novels (–1893).

Sport and Recreation
FA Cup established.

Statistics
Populations (in millions): Germany, 41; US, 39; France, 36.1; Japan, 33; Italy, 26.8; Great Britain, 26, and Ireland, 5.4.
Coal production (in mill. tons): Great Britain, 117.4; US, 35; Germany, 29.4; France, 13.3; Austria, 12.5.
Iron production (in mill. tons): Great Britain, 6.6; France, 2.5; Germany, 1.4.

1872 **Sept: 7th**, meeting of the three emperors in Berlin leads to an *entente* between Germany, Russia and Austria-Hungary.

Nov: 5th, re-election of Ulysses Grant, the Republican candidate (286 electoral votes) as President, over Horace Greeley, Liberal Democrat (62 votes), who dies, 30th.

Science, Technology, and Discovery
Thomas Edison perfects the 'duplex' telegraph.

Literature
Thomas Hardy, *Under the Greenwood Tree.*
Ivan Turgeniev, *A Month in the Country.*

Sport and Recreation
(30th Nov) First International Association football match, England *v.* Scotland.

1873 **Feb: 11th**, abdication of Amadeo I of Spain.
16th, Republic proclaimed in Spain.

April: —, Ashanti War breaks out.

May: 24th, L A Thiers falls and M MacMahon is elected French president.
24th, Financial crisis begins in Vienna, spreading to other European capitals and leading to withdrawal of foreign investments from USA.

Sept: —, Financial panic in US caused by speculation, over-production and withdrawal of foreign capital.

Oct: 22nd, alliance of the emperors of Germany, Russia and Austria-Hungary.

Science, Technology, and Discovery
First oil well sunk in Baku.
Philo Remington's company produce a typewriter designed by Christopher Latham Scholes.
Introduction of colour sensitizing makes colour photography possible.

Humanities and Scholarship
Walter Pater, *Studies in the History of the Renaissance.*
D L Moody and I Sankey begin revivalist meetings in England (–1875).

Literature
Leo Tolstoy, *Anna Karenina* (–1875).

1874 **Feb: 4th**, Garnet Wolseley burns Kumasi, ending Ashanti War and, 13th, by treaty of Fommenah King Koffee of Ashanti promises free trade, an open road to Kumasi and undertakes to pay indemnity to Britain and stop human sacrifices.
17th, British general election results in Conservative majority of 83 (the first clear Conservative majority since 1841), W E Gladstone resigns and
18th, B Disraeli forms ministry, with Stafford Northcote chancellor of Exchequer, 15th Earl of Derby as foreign secretary and Richard Cross as home secretary.

May: —, At the Gotha Conference German Marxists and Lassalleans unite to form Socialist Working-Men's Party.

Nov: 24th, Alfonso, son of Queen Isabella, comes of age and declares for a constitutional monarchy in Spain.

Dec: 29th, (–31st) Spanish generals rally to Alfonso who is proclaimed King as Alfonso XII (–1885).

Politics, Government, Law, and Economy
Union Générale des Postes established at Berne.

Science, Technology, and Discovery
Solomon introduces pressure-cooking method for canning foods.

Humanities and Scholarship
Henry Sidgwick, *Methods of Ethics.*
Art, Sculpture, Fine Arts, and Architecture
First Impressionist Exhibition, Paris, includes works by P Cézanne, E Degas, C Pissarro and A Sisley.
Music
M P Moussorgsky, *Boris Godunov* (opera), and *Pictures from an Exhibition.*
J Strauss, *Die Fledermaus* (opera).
R Wagner completes *Götterdämmerung.*
G Verdi, *Requiem.*
F Smetana, symphonic poem *My Fatherland.*
Sport and Recreation
Wingfield invents lawn tennis ('Sphairistike').

1875 **Jan:** **12th**, Kwang-su becomes Emperor of China (–1908).
13th, W E Gladstone resigns Liberal leadership in House of Commons.
30th, Republican Constitution in France, with Wallon amendment, is passed by one vote.
July: **—**, Risings in Bosnia and Herzegovina against Turkish rule.
Nov: **25th**, Britain buys 176,602 shares in Suez Canal from the Khedive of Egypt.
Science, Technology, and Discovery
London's main-drainage system completed.
Humanities and Scholarship
F Max Müller edits *The Sacred Books of the East* (51 vols. –1903).
Mary Baker Eddy, *Science and Health.*
Art, Sculpture, Fine Arts, and Architecture
Claude Monet, *Boating at Argenteuil* (painting).
The *Hermes* of Praxiteles is found at Olympia (see 364 BC).
Music
P I Tchaikovsky, 1st Piano Concerto in B flat minor (op. 23).
G Bizet, *Carmen* (opera).
Trial by Jury begins W S Gilbert and A Sullivan partnership.
Literature
M Twain (pseudonym), *The Adventures of Tom Sawyer.*
Statistics
Production of pig iron (in thousand tons): Great Britain, 6,365; Germany, 2,029; France, 1,416.
Production of steel (in thousand tons): Great Britain, 536; Germany, 370; France, 258.
Strength of armies: Russia, 3,360,000; Germany, 2,800,000; France, 412,000; Great Britain, 113,649.

1876 **Feb:** **26th**, China declares Korea to be an independent state.
March: **8th**, rule of National Assembly in France ends with summoning of a new Senate (Conservative) and a Chamber (overwhelmingly Republican).
9th, (–16th) Turkish troops massacre Bulgarians.
Nov: **—**, G J Goschen and Joubert visit Egypt to establish dual control.
7th, in US Presidential election S J Tilden, Democrat, secures 184 out of the 185 electoral votes required, against R B Hayes, Republican, with 165, but 20 votes are in dispute (settled by electoral commission, Jan 1877).
Dec: **23rd**, proclamation of Ottoman Constitution, embodying parliamentary government, freedom of worship and a free press.
Politics, Government, Law, and Economy
M Bakunin organizes Land and Liberty, a secret society in Russia, which becomes spearhead of the Populist Movement.
German Conservative Party founded.
Science, Technology, and Discovery
Alexander Graham Bell invents the telephone.
Humanities and Scholarship
F H Bradley, *Ethical Studies.*
Music
J Brahms, 1st Symphony in C Minor (op. 68).
R Wagner, *Siegfried* (opera).
Bayreuth Festspielhaus opens for first complete performance of Wagner's *The Ring.*

Literature
S Mallarmé, *L'Après-midi d'un faune.*

1877 **Jan: 1st**, Queen Victoria proclaimed Empress of India.
20th, failure of the powers at the Constantinople Conference to effect accord between Russia and Turkey in the Balkans.

March: 4th, R B Hayes inaugurated US President.

April: 12th, Theophilus Shepstone annexes South African Republic of Transvaal for Britain on grounds of bankruptcy and danger from Basutos and Zulus, but annexation violates Sand River convention of 1852.
24th, Russia declares war on Turkey and invades Romania.

May: 2nd, Porfirio Diaz becomes President of Mexico (–1911).
16th, crisis of *Seize Mai* in France when M MacMahon, annoyed at Jules Simon's failure to stand up to the anti-clerical Left, dismisses him, appointing de Broglie to form a Monarchist ministry, which, 19th, is given a vote of no confidence in the Chamber.

Science, Technology, and Discovery
Thomas Alva Edison invents the phonograph.
Frozen meat is shipped from Argentina to France.
Nikolaus August Otto develops the four-stroke internal combustion engine.

Art, Sculpture, Fine Arts, and Architecture
P Cézanne shows 16 pictures at third Impressionist Exhibition.

Music
Alexander Borodin, Symphony No. 2 in B minor.
P I Tchaikovsky, Symphony No. 4 in F minor (op. 36).

Literature
É. Zola, *L'Assommoir.*

Sport and Recreation
All-England Lawn Tennis championships first played at Wimbledon; 1st champion, Spencer Gore.

1878 **Jan: 9th**, Turks capitulate at Shipka Pass and appeal to Russia for an armistice.

July: 13th, by Treaty of Berlin Bulgaria is split into (a) autonomous Bulgaria, north of Balkans, (b) Eastern Rumelia with a special organization under Turkey and (c) Macedonia where reforms are to be undertaken; Austria is given mandate to occupy Bosnia and Herzegovina; Roumania is awarded Dobrudja but has to hand over South Bessarabia to Russia; Montenegro is given Antivari; Montenegro, Roumania and Serbia become independent states; Russia receives Batum, Kars and Ardahan; British occupation of Cyprus is confirmed; Italian and Greek demands are shelved; promises for reforms in Macedonia and Asia Minor lead to agitation.

Oct: 18th, anti-Socialist law in Germany (–1890), prohibits public meetings, publications and collections, thus driving Socialism underground.

Politics, Government, Law, and Economy
Flemish becomes the official language in Flanders.

Science, Technology, and Discovery
Swan's carbon filament lamp.
David Hughes invents the microphone.
Earliest electric street lighting in London.

Humanities and Scholarship
William Booth founds Salvation Army in Britain.

Art, Sculpture, Fine Arts, and Architecture
James Whistler awarded a farthing damages in libel action with John Ruskin for disparaging remarks on his painting, *Nocturne in Black and Gold.*

Music
P I Tchaikovsky, *Swan Lake* (ballet).

Literature
A C Swinburne, *Poems and Ballads.*

Sport and Recreation
Bicycle Touring Club founded in England.

1879 **Jan: 12th**, (–July) British-Zulu War.

30th, on M MacMahon's resignation, Jules Grévy, a Conservative Republican, is elected President of France.

July: 12th, protectionist laws for industry and agriculture in Germany split the Liberal Party.

Aug: —, Count Taaffe forms Austrian ministry (–1893) and ends German predominance in Austria-Hungary in favour of Slavs.

Sept: 1st, Britain signs peace with Zulu chiefs.

Nov: 24th, (–9th Dec) W E Gladstone in Midlothian Campaign denounces Conservative government for imperialism and mishandling of domestic affairs.

Politics, Government, Law, and Economy

Henry George, *Progress and Poverty.*

W L Blackley proposes scheme for old-age pensions.

The radical, terrorist, Will of the People Society is founded in Russia.

Society, Education, and Religion

(4th Aug) Papal Encyclical protesting against modern metaphysics.

Science, Technology, and Discovery

W E Ayrton pioneers electricity as a motive power.

Werner von Siemens demonstrates an electric tram in Berlin.

Music

J Brahms, Violin Concerto in D (op. 77) played by H Joachim.

P I Tchaikovsky, *Eugen Onegin* (opera).

A Bruckner, 6th Symphony.

Literature

Drama H Ibsen, *The Doll's House.*

A Strindberg, *The Red Room.*

1880 **April: 18th**, in British elections Liberals secure majority of 137 over Conservatives and Irish Nationalists win 65 seats, so Beaconsfield resigns.

28th, W E Gladstone forms Liberal ministry in which he is also chancellor of Exchequer, with Lord Granville foreign secretary, William Harcourt home secretary and Joseph Chamberlain president of Board of Trade.

Dec: 30th, Transvaal Boers under Kruger declare a Republic.

Politics, Government, Law, and Economy

Employers' Liability Act grants workmen compensation for accidents caused by employers' negligence.

Society, Education, and Religion

Owens College becomes Manchester University.

First girls' high schools in England.

Science, Technology, and Discovery

Louis Pasteur discovers streptococcus.

Thomas Alva Edison and J W Swan independently make the first practical electric light.

Beginning of street lighting by electricity in New York.

Music

A Dvořák, Symphony No. 1 in D (op. 60).

P I Tchaikovsky, *1812 Overture* and *Italian Capriccio.*

Literature

Fyodor Dostoevsky, *The Brothers Karamazov* (–1881).

É. Zola, *Nana.*

Statistics

Coal production (in mill. tons): Great Britain, 149; US, 64.9; Germany, 59; France, 19.4; Russia, 3.2.

Pig-iron production (in mill. tons): Great Britain, 7.8; US, 3.9; Germany, 2.5; France, 0.5; Russia, 0.4.

Railway mileage in operation: US, 87,801; Great Britain, 17,935; France, 16,430; Russia, 12,200.

1881 **Feb: 27th**, Boers defeat British under G Colley at Majuba Hill.

March: 4th, James A Garfield, Republican, is inaugurated US President.

12th, following raids of Krumir tribes into Algiers, France occupies Tunis.

13th, Alexander II signs Ukase calling an assembly of Russian nobles and the same day is assassinated by terrorists. Alexander III succeeds (–1894).

April: 5th, Britain concludes treaty of Pretoria with Boers, recognizing independence of South African Republic of Transvaal.

19th, on death of Lord Beaconsfield, Lord Salisbury becomes leader of Conservatives in Lords, Stafford Northcote in Commons.

May: 12th, by treaty of Bardo with the Bey Tunis accepts French protectorate.

June: 18th, Three Emperors' League, a secret alliance between Germany, Austria and Russia for three years.

July: —, Rising against the French in Algeria (–1883).

2nd, President Garfield is shot; he dies Sept 19th, and is succeeded by Chester Arthur.

Aug: 16th, W E Gladstone's Irish Land Act fixes tenures, and establishes a land court to deal with excessive rents.

Sept: 9th, Nationalist rising in Egypt under Arabi Pasha.

Politics, Government, Law, and Economy

American Federation of Labor founded at Pittsburgh.

Society, Education, and Religion

University College, Liverpool, founded.

B F Westcott and F J A Hort publish *Greek New Testament.*

Revised Version of New Testament.

Science, Technology, and Discovery

Louis Pasteur attenuates anthrax virus to produce a vaccine.

Music

Jacques Offenbach, *The Tales of Hoffmann* (opera).

Literature

A France (pseudonym), *Le Crime de Sylvestre Bonnard.*

H James, *Portrait of a Lady.*

Drama H Ibsen, *Ghosts.*

Statistics

Population (in millions): US, 53; Germany, 45.2; France, 37.6; Great Britain, 29.7; Italy, 28.4; Ireland, 5.1.

Populations of chief cities: London, 3.3; Paris, 2.2; New York, 1.2; Berlin, 1.1; Vienna, 1.0; Tokio, 0.8; St. Petersburg, 0.6; Brussels, 0.1.

1882

During the year there are 2,590 agrarian outrages in Ireland and 10,457 families are evicted.

March: 29th, primary education in France to be free, compulsory and non-sectarian.

May: 6th, Fenians murder new Irish chief secretary, Lord Frederick Cavendish, and T H Burke, Irish under-secretary, in Phoenix Park, Dublin.

20th, Italy joins Austro-German alliance, which becomes Triple Alliance, for five years (renewed until 1915); this assures Italy of support in event of French attack, but secures no guarantee of her possession of Rome.

Sept: 13th, Garnet Wolseley defeats Egyptians at Tel-el-Kebir, Lower Egypt, and proceeds to occupy Egypt and the Sudan.

15th, British force occupies Cairo; Arabi surrenders and is banished to Ceylon.

Nov: 9th, Franco-British dual control of Egypt established.

Politics, Government, Law, and Economy

Married Women's Property Act in Britain gives married women the right of separate ownership of property of all kinds.

Science, Technology, and Discovery

Gottlieb Daimler builds petrol engine.

Thomas Alva Edison's generating station at Pearl Street, New York, and the first hydro-electric plant at Appleton, Wisconsin.

Art, Sculpture, Fine Arts, and Architecture

É. Manet, *Le Bar aux Folies-Bergères* (painting).

O Wilde's *Lectures on the Decorative Arts* explains the aesthetic movement.

Music

A Sullivan, *Iolanthe* (opera).

R Wagner, *Parsifal* (opera).

Media

Berliner Tageblatt.

1883

April: 16th, Paul Kruger becomes President of South African Republic.

Nov: 5th, the Mahdi defeats Egyptian force under William Hicks at El Obeid and Britain decides to evacuate the Sudan.

Science, Technology, and Discovery
First skyscraper built in Chicago.

Humanities and Scholarship
F Nietzsche, *Thus Spake Zarathustra.*

Music
J Brahms, Symphony No. 3 in F (op. 90).
A Dvořák, *Stabat Mater* (oratorio).

Literature
R L Stevenson, *Treasure Island.*

1884 **Nov:** **—**, In US presidential election Grover Cleveland, Democrat, wins 219 electoral votes against James G Blaine, Republican, with 182, who is deserted by the Mugwumps, the reformist Republicans.
15th, Berlin conference of 14 nations on African affairs, organized by Otto von Bismarck and Jules Ferry, provides for free trade on Congo river and the abolition of slavery and the slave trade.

Dec: **—**, British Franchise bill passes, after W E Gladstone undertakes to meet Conservative demands to introduce a further measure for redistributing seats, with uniform male suffrage in counties and boroughs for householders and lodgers, increasing the electorate to 5 million.
10th, Porfirio Diaz becomes President of Mexico (–1911).

Politics, Government, Law, and Economy
Fabian Society founded.

Science, Technology, and Discovery
Charles Parsons constructs first practical steam turbine for making electricity.
Hiram Maxim's recoil-operated gun invented.

Humanities and Scholarship
Oxford English Dictionary (ed. James Murray –1928).

Art, Sculpture, Fine Arts, and Architecture
'Les Vingt' exhibiting society founded by James Ensor in Brussels, supported by Georges Seurat, Paul Gauguin, Paul Cézanne and Vincent van Gogh (–1894).
G Seurat, *Bathers at Asnières* (painting).
A Rodin, *Burghers of Calais* (sculpture) (–1895).

Music
J Massenet, *Manon* (opera).

Literature
G D'Annunzio, *Il Libro delle Vergini.*
Mark Twain (pseudonym), *Huckleberry Finn.*
Drama H Ibsen, *The Wild Duck.*

1885 **Jan:** **26th**, the Mahdi takes Khartoum and General Charles Gordon dies.
28th, British relief force arrives at Khartoum; the Sudan is evacuated.

Feb: **5th**, Congo State is established under Leopold II of Belgium, as a personal possession.
25th, Germany annexes Tanganyika and Zanzibar.

June: **9th**, W E Gladstone resigns, following hostile amendment to budget.
25th, Lord Salisbury forms Conservative ministry (–Jan 1886), himself taking foreign secretaryship, with Michael Hicks Beach chancellor of Exchequer and Richard Cross home secretary.

Oct: **22nd**, Britain sends ultimatum to King Thibaw of Burma concerning his interference with trade and his refusal to comply leads to Third Burmese War.

Nov: **23rd**, in British general election Liberals win 335 seats, Conservatives 249, Irish Home-Rulers 86; Lord Salisbury remains premier.

Politics, Government, Law, and Economy
Karl Marx, *Das Kapital*, vol. 2.

Science, Technology, and Discovery
Gottlieb Daimler develops a successful lightweight petrol engine and fits it to a bicycle to create the prototype of the present-day motorcycle. Karl Benz fits his lightweight petrol engine to a three-wheeled vehicle, pioneering the development of the motor-car.

Humanities and Scholarship
Dictionary of National Biography is begun under Leslie Stephen.

Music
J Brahms, Symphony No. 4 in E minor (op. 98).

Literature
Richard Burton, *The Arabian Nights* (–1888).
G de Maupassant, *Bel Ami.*
George Meredith, *Diana of the Crossways.*

1886 First Indian National Congress meets, but lacks Moslem support.

Jan: 27th, Lord Salisbury resigns, after defeat on 'three acres and a cow' amendment of Jesse Collings to Address.

Feb: 1st, W E Gladstone forms third Liberal ministry (–July 20th), with Lord Rosebery foreign minister and W V Harcourt chancellor of Exchequer.

April: 8th, Gladstone introduces Home Rule bill for Ireland.

June: 8th, W E Gladstone's Liberal government is defeated on second reading of Irish Home Rule bill, with 93 Liberals, including John Bright, Joseph Chamberlain and the Marquess of Hartington, voting with the Opposition.

July: 24th, In British general election Conservatives win 316 seats, dissident Liberals 78; Liberals 191 and Irish Nationalists 85; and, 26th, Lord Salisbury forms Conservative ministry (–Aug 1892).

Politics, Government, Law, and Economy
Karl Marx, *Capital* (first English edition of vol. 1).
(8th Dec) American Federation of Labor founded.

Science, Technology, and Discovery
Carl von Welsbach invents gas mantle.
Niagara Falls hydro-electric installations begun.

Humanities and Scholarship
English Historical Review founded under Mandell Creighton 's editorship.
A Harnack, *History of Dogma.*
(Nov) British School of Archaeology, Athens, opened.

Art, Sculpture, Fine Arts, and Architecture
G Seurat, *Sunday on the Island of Grande Jatte* (painting).
Eighth and last Impressionist Exhibition.
J Whistler, P W Steer and W Sickert found New English Art Club.
Statue of Liberty.

Literature
H Rider Haggard, *King Solomon's Mines.*
F Nietzsche, *Beyond Good and Evil.*
R L Stevenson, *Dr. Jekyll and Mr. Hyde.*

Media
Jean Moréas and Gustave Kahn found *Le Symboliste*, a literary review of the Symbolist Movement.

1887 **Jan: 11th**, Otto von Bismarck advocates a larger German army.

Feb: 4th, US Interstate Commerce Act regulates railways.
8th, H L Dawes's Act empowers US President to terminate tribal government and divide lands amongst Indians.
20th, Triple Alliance between Germany, Austria, and Italy renewed for three years.

April: 4th, first Colonial Conference in London opens.

June: 18th, Germano-Russo Reinsurance treaty (–1890) to replace expiring Three Emperors' Alliance, which Russia had refused to renew.
21st, Queen Victoria's Golden Jubilee.
21st, Britain annexes Zululand, blocking the attempt of Transvaal to gain communication with coast.

July: 31st, Francesco Crispi forms ministry in Italy (–1891) on A Depretis's death.

Oct: —, G Boulanger's *coup d'état* fails in France, but his popularity increases with revelations of scandals connected with President Grévy's family.

Society, Education, and Religion
Canonization of Sir Thomas More, John Fisher and other English Roman Catholic martyrs.

Science, Technology, and Discovery

Emil Fischer and Tafel synthesize fructose.

Heinrich Hertz produces radio waves and demonstrates that they are reflected in a manner similar to light waves.

Hilaire Comte de Chardonnet invents a process for making artificial silk.

Music

A Borodin, *Prince Igor* (opera – unfinished).

G Verdi, *Otello* (opera).

J Stainer, *The Crucifixion* (oratorio).

1888 **Jan: 28th**, military agreement between Germany and Italy provides for use of Italian troops against France in the event of a Franco-German war.

March: 9th, Frederick III succeeds as Emperor of Germany on William I's death.

May: 12th, British protectorate over North Borneo and Brunei.

13th, serfdom abolished in Brazil.

June: 15th, William II becomes Emperor of Germany, on death of his father, Frederick III.

Nov: —, In US presidential election, fought on tariff issue, Benjamin Harrison, Republican, wins 233 electoral votes, Grover Cleveland, Democrat, 168 and Cleveland's loss is ascribed to treachery of Tammany Hall, the Democratic organization in New York.

Science, Technology, and Discovery

Nikola Tesla invents an AC electric motor which is manufactured by George Westinghouse.

George Eastman's 'Kodak' box camera, the first commercial roll-film camera.

John Boyd Dunlop invents pneumatic tyre.

Music

N Rimsky-Korsakov, symphonic suite *Scheherezade* (op. 35).

Richard Strauss, tone poem *Don Juan*.

Hugo Wolf, *Der Gärtner* and other lieder.

Literature

Edward Bellamy, *Looking Backwards, 2000–1887*.

A France (pseudonym), *La Vie littéraire* begins.

R Kipling, *Plain Tales from the Hills*.

É. Zola, *La Terre*.

Drama A Strindberg, *Miss Julie*.

Sport and Recreation

Football League founded.

Lawn Tennis Association established.

Media

The Financial Times, *The Star* (ed. O'Connor – 1960), and *Collier's Weekly* are first issued.

Statistics

Value of World Production: percentages contributed by US, 31.8; Great Britain, 17.8; Germany, 13.3; France, 10.7; Russia, 8.1; Austro-Hungary, 5.6; Italy, 2.7; Belgium, 2.2; Spain, 1.9; other countries, 5.9.

1889 **Jan: 10th**, France establishes protectorate over Ivory Coast.

Feb: 11th, Constitution granted in Japan, with two-chamber Diet, but Emperor retains extensive powers.

22nd, North and South Dakota, Montana and Washington are created US states.

April: 8th, G Boulanger, fearing trial for treason, flees from France and in the subsequent elections the Republicans triumph.

May: 31st, Naval Defence Act in Britain inaugurates extensive naval building programme.

Oct: 29th, British South Africa Company, headed by Cecil Rhodes, is granted royal charter with extensive powers for expanding its territory at the expense of Transvaal.

Nov: 15th, on Pedro II's abdication Brazil is proclaimed a republic.

Politics, Government, Law, and Economy

G B Shaw, *Fabian Essays*.

London County Council is formed (–1965). Lord Rosebery is elected first chairman (12th Feb).

'The Red Flag' is written in London after a dock strike.

Science, Technology, and Discovery

Frederick Abel invents cordite, a smokeless gunpowder.

George Eastman produces a celluloid roll-film.

Humanities and Scholarship

H Bergson, *Les Données immédiates et la conscience.*
T H Huxley, *Agnosticism.*

Art, Sculpture, Fine Arts, and Architecture

Eiffel Tower, Paris, built.

Music

R Strauss, symphonic poem *Death and Transfiguration* (op. 31).

1890

March: 20th, Otto von Bismarck is dismissed by William II and Georg Caprivi becomes German chancellor (–1894).

27th, universal suffrage in Spain.

May: 24th, by Mackinnon treaty between Leopold of Belgium and British East Africa Company, the latter recognizes Leopold's rights on the west bank of the Upper Nile in return for territory near Lake Tanganyika.

June: 18th, Germany allows Reinsurance treaty (see June 1887) with Russia to lapse, despite Russian attempts to open negotiations for a renewal.

July: 2nd, John Sherman's anti-trust law enacted in US.

2nd, Brussels act passed by international conference to eradicate African slave trade and liquor traffic with primitive peoples.

3rd, Idaho becomes a US state.

10th, Wyoming becomes a US state.

Oct: 1st, German anti-socialist law of 1878 expires and, 21st, Social Democrats adopt Marxist programme at Erfurt congress.

Nov: 14th, Anglo-Portuguese agreement on Zambesi and the Congo grants Britain the control of the Lower Zambesi and the right to colonize central territory up to the Congo.

Politics, Government, Law, and Economy

Alfred Marshall, *Principles of Economics.*
First May Day labour celebrations in Germany.

Society, Education, and Religion

Free elementary education in England.
Lux Mundi, edited by Charles Gore.

Science, Technology, and Discovery

First 'tube' railway opens: the City and South London Railway, passing beneath River Thames.
Entirely steel-framed building erected in Chicago.

Humanities and Scholarship

J G Frazer, *The Golden Bough* (–1914).
William James, *The Principles of Psychology.*

Art, Sculpture, Fine Arts, and Architecture

P Cézanne, *The Cardplayers* (painting).
William Morris founds Kelmscott Press.

Music

P I Tchaikovsky, *Queen of Spades* (opera).

Literature

Leo Tolstoy, *The Kreutzer Sonata.*
Drama H Ibsen, *Hedda Gabler.*

Media

Stefan George founds *Blätter fur die Kunst.*
(4th Jan) *Daily Graphic,* first fully-illustrated English newspaper.

Statistics

Railway mileage in operation: US, 125,000; France, 20,800; Great Britain, 20,073; Russia, 19,000.
Coal production (in mill. tons): Great Britain, 184; US, 143; Germany, 89; France, 26.1; Austro-Hungary, 26; Russia, 6.
Steel production (in mill. tons): US, 4.3; Great Britain, 3.6; Germany, 2.3; France, 0.7; Austro-Hungary, 0.5; Russia, 0.4.
Emigration to US (1881–90): from Great Britain, 807,357; from Ireland, 655,482.

1891

May: 6th, Triple Alliance of Germany, Austria and Italy is renewed for twelve years.

June: 11th, further Anglo-Portuguese convention on territories north and south of Zambesi: Portugal assigns Barotseland to Britain. Nyasaland is subsequently proclaimed a British Protectorate.

Aug: 27th, Franco-Russian *entente.*

Oct: —, British Liberal party adopts the 'Newcastle Programme', advocating Irish Home Rule, Disestablishment of Welsh Church, reform of Lords, triennial parliaments, abolition of plural franchise and local veto on sales of liquor.

Politics, Government, Law, and Economy

Charles Booth, *Life and Labour of the People in London* (–1903).

(April) Pan-German League is founded.

Humanities and Scholarship

(15th May) Papal encyclical *Rerum novarum* on condition of working classes, earns Leo XIII the name of 'the working man's Pope'.

Art, Sculpture, Fine Arts, and Architecture

P Gauguin settles in Tahiti.

Henri Toulouse-Lautrec's first posters for Montmartre music halls.

Giovanni Segantini, *Ploughing of the Engadine* (painting).

Music

P I Tchaikovsky's *Casse-Noisette* ballet music.

Literature

A C Doyle's *Adventures of Sherlock Holmes* begin in *Strand Magazine.*

J K Huysmans, *Là-bas.*

F Wedekind, *Spring's Awakening.*

O Wilde, *The Picture of Dorian Gray.*

Media

Il Mattino issued.

Statistics

Populations (in mills.): US 65; Germany, 49.4; Japan, 40.7; France, 38.3; Great Britain, 33; Ireland, 4.7; Italy, 30.3; Austria, 23.8.

1892 **May:** —, Giovanni Giolitti replaces Marquis di Rudin as premier of Italy.

Aug: 11th, Lord Salisbury resigns and W E Gladstone forms Liberal ministry (–9th March 1893), with Lord Rosebery foreign secretary, W V Harcourt chancellor of exchequer and H H Asquith home secretary.

Nov: 8th, Grover Cleveland, Democrat, wins US presidential election with 277 electoral votes, on platform opposing the McKinley tariff and the Force bill, against Benjamin Harrison, Republican, 145, and James B Weaver, Populist, 22.

10th, the Panama scandal breaks in France and Ferdinand de Lesseps and associates are committed for trial for corruption and mismanagement.

Science, Technology, and Discovery

Charles Cross discovers viscose, making the manufacture of rayon possible.

Rudolf Diesel patents a new type of internal combustion engine.

Humanities and Scholarship

James Darmesteter edits the Zend-Avesta (–1893).

Art, Sculpture, Fine Arts, and Architecture

Claude Monet begins pictures of Rouen Cathedral (–1895).

Music

R Leoncavallo, *I Pagliacci* (opera).

Literature

Drama M Maeterlinck, *Pelléas et Mélisande*, with C Debussy 's music.

1893 France acquires protectorate over Laos.

Jan: —, Franco-Russian alliance is signed.

13th, Independent Labour Party formed at conference in Bradford under Keir Hardie.

March: —, Gerald Portal hoists British flag in Uganda, which British East Africa Company evacuates.

10th, French colonies of French Guinea and Ivory Coast formally established.

May: 10th, Natal is granted self-government.

Sept: 1st, the Second Irish Home Rule bill, proposing that 80 Irish representatives should sit at Westminster, passes the Commons but is rejected, 8th, by the Lords.

Politics, Government, Law, and Economy

Franchise in New Zealand is extended to women.

Universal suffrage in Belgium with plural voting, on basis of wealth and education.

Society, Education, and Religion
Imperial Institute, South Kensington, and the University of Wales are founded.

Science, Technology, and Discovery
Karl Benz's four-wheel car.
Egbert Judson invents zip fastener.

Humanities and Scholarship
F H Bradley, *Appearance and Reality.*

Art, Sculpture, Fine Arts, and Architecture
The Studio, with Aubrey Beardsley's drawings, spreads the ideas of *art nouveau* in architecture and interior decoration.

Music
A Dvořák, Symphony no. 5 (*From the New World*, op. 95).
P I Tchaikovsky, Symphony no. 6 in B minor (*Pathétique*, op. 74).

Literature
Drama A W Pinero, *The Second Mrs. Tanqueray.*
O Wilde, *A Woman of No Importance.*

Everyday Life
Chicago World Exhibition.

1894 **Jan:** —, L Starr Jameson completes occupation of Matabeleland.

March: **3rd**, W E Gladstone resigns, having split Liberal Party over Home Rule, and Lord Rosebery, a Liberal Unionist, becomes prime minister, with W V Harcourt as leader of the Commons.

April: —, H V Harcourt introduces death duties in budget.
11th, Uganda is declared a British protectorate.

Aug: **1st**, Japan declares war on China over question of Korea.

Oct: **15th**, Alfred Dreyfus is arrested on treason charge.
26th, Prince Hohenlohe succeeds Count Caprivi as German chancellor; the unpopularity of the commercial treaty with Russia (Feb) contributes to Caprivi's fall.

Nov: **21st**, Japanese victory over Chinese at Port Arthur.
26th, On Alexander III's death Nicholas II becomes Tsar (–1917).

Dec: **22nd**, A Dreyfus is convicted by a court martial *in camera*, and imprisoned in Devil's Island, French Guiana.

Science, Technology, and Discovery
Lord Rayleigh and William Ramsay discover argon.

Music
Claude Debussy, *L'Après-midi d'un Faune.*

Literature
R Kipling, *The Jungle Book.*
Drama G B Shaw, *Arms and the Man.*

1895 Risings in Cuba against Spain, aiming at independence.

Feb: **12th**, resounding Japanese victory at Wei-hai-wei.

April: **17th**, by treaty of Shimonoseki, China and Japan recognize independence of Korea,

May: **2nd**, British South Africa Company territory South of Zambesi is organized as Rhodesia.
8th, by revised treaty Japan surrenders Liao Tung peninsula and Port Arthur to China in return for huge indemnity.

June: **25th**, Lord Salisbury forms Unionist ministry, with Joseph Chamberlain as colonial secretary (–July 1902).

Dec: **29th**, L Starr Jameson's Raid into Transvaal from Bechuanaland.

Politics, Government, Law, and Economy
K Marx, *Das Kapital*, volume 3.

Society, Education, and Religion
London School of Economics and Political Science founded.
Bible Conference of conservative evangelicals at Niagara defines 'fundamentalism'.

Science, Technology, and Discovery
Wilhelm Röntgen discovers X-rays.
Guglielmo Marconi invents wireless telegraphy.
Auguste and Louis Lumière invent the cinematograph.

Music
G Mahler, Symphony no. 2.
Robert Newman arranges first series of Promenade Concerts at Queen's Hall, under Henry J Wood.

Literature
H G Wells, *The Time Machine.*
W B Yeats, *Poems.*
Drama O Wilde, *The Importance of Being Earnest.*

Everyday Life
National Trust founded.

1896 Revival of Young Turk movement.

Jan: 2nd, L Starr Jameson surrenders at Doornkop.
3rd, William II sends 'Kruger telegram', congratulating Transvaal leader on suppressing the Raid, which provokes crisis in Anglo-German relations.
4th, Utah becomes a US state.
6th, Cecil Rhodes resigns premiership of Cape Colony; a committee of Cape Assembly reports, subsequently, that Rhodes engineered the Jameson Raid. Transvaal orders munitions from Europe and fortifies Pretoria and Johannesburg.

Feb: —, Beginning of Cretan revolution against Turkey, inspired by Greeks.

March: 1st, Ethiopians defeat Italians at Adowa, forcing Italy to sue for peace.
5th, F Crispi's ministry falls in Italy, through indignation at failure of Ethiopian War, and Antonio Rudini forms ministry with support from Radicals under Felice Cavalotti.
12th, Britain decides on reconquest of Sudan, to protect the Nile from French advance.

June: 3rd, treaty signed in Moscow by which China and Russia form defensive alliance for 15 years and China grants Russia the right to operate railway in North Manchuria.
9th, Russo-Japanese agreement recognizes Russia's position in Korea.

Sept: 30th, Russia and China sign convention over Manchuria.

Oct: 4th, Lord Rosebery resigns Liberal leadership on account of party's view of Armenian question, being succeeded in Lords by Lord Kimberley and in Commons by W V Harcourt.

Nov: 26th, In US presidential election William McKinley, Republican, on gold-standard platform, gains 271 electoral votes against William Jennings Bryan, Democratic and Populist candidate, standing for policy of free silver coinage, with 176 votes.

Society, Education, and Religion
Nobel Prizes established.

Science, Technology, and Discovery
(6th May) Samuel Pierpont Langley 's flying machine makes first successful flight; it makes another 28th Nov.

Music
G Puccini, *La Bohème* (opera).

Literature
A France (pseudonym), *L'Histoire contemporaine* (–1901).
T Hardy, *Jude the Obscure.*
Drama H Ibsen, *John Gabriel Borkman.*

Media
Alfred Harmsworth founds the *Daily Mail*, selling at a halfpenny.

1897 **Feb: 6th**, Crete proclaims union with Greece.

April: 5th, the Czech language is granted equality with German in Bohemia.
7th, Turkey declares war on Greece.

May: 8th, Greece begs powers to intervene; intervention follows Turkish defeat of Greeks, 12th, in Thessaly.

July: 10th, French force under Marchand occupies Fashoda.

Dec: 16th, Peace of Constantinople between Greece and Turkey (the problem of Crete settled in Nov 1898).

Science, Technology, and Discovery
Ronald Ross discovers malaria parasite in the anopheles mosquito.
Monotype type-setting machine invented.

Art, Sculpture, Fine Arts, and Architecture
Tate Gallery, London, opened.
Bing's *Art Nouveau* Gallery opens in Paris with exhibition of Edvard Munch's paintings.

Literature
Joseph Conrad, *The Nigger of the Narcissus.*
Stefan George, *Das Jahr der Seele.*
A Strindberg, *Inferno.*
Drama Edmond Rostand, *Cyrano de Bergerac.*

1898 **Jan: 11th**, acquittal of Major M C Esterhazy in trial for alleged forgery of document in Dreyfus case, provokes Zola's *J'accuse*, 13th, an open letter to the French President (for which, Feb 23rd, he is imprisoned).

March: 27th, Russia obtains lease of Port Arthur and Britain is leased Wei-hai-wei and Kowloon.
28th, First German navy bill, introduced by Alfred von Tirpitz, begins Germany's naval expansion.

April: 19th, US ultimatum to Spain to relinquish authority in Cuba.
24th, US declares war on Spain, retroactive to April 21st.

May: 3rd, (–8th) bread riots in Milan are put down with heavy loss of life.

June: 11th, (–Sept 16th) Emperor Te Tsung of China's 100 days of Reform, under guidance of K'ang Yu-wei.

Aug: 12th, transfer of islands of Hawaii to US.

Sept: 2nd, Horatio Kitchener defeats Dervishes at Omdurman.
21st, Tzu-hsi, Dowager Empress of China, seizes power and revokes reforms.

Society, Education, and Religion
London University bill establishes a teaching university.

Science, Technology, and Discovery
Pierre and Marie Curie discover radium and polonium.

Art, Sculpture, Fine Arts, and Architecture
A Rodin, *The Kiss* (sculpture).

Literature
H James, *The Turn of the Screw.*
H G Wells, *The War of the Worlds.*

1899 Revisionist German Social Democrats abandon strict Marxism.

May: 18th, (–21st July) at first Peace Conference 26 nations meet at the Hague, at the Tsar Nicholas II's suggestion, to extend Geneva Convention to naval warfare, explosive bullets and poison gas and authorize the establishment of a permanent Court of Arbitration.

June: 22nd, René Waldeck-Rousseau, a moderate, becomes French premier.

Aug: 9th, Britain purchases the possessions of the Niger Company (protectorate proclaimed, Jan 1900).

Sept: 9th, at retrial at Rennes court martial Alfred Dreyfus is condemned 'with extenuating circumstances', but, 19th, is pardoned by presidential decree, which with premier Waldeck-Rousseau's intervention in the Le Creusot strike, helps to heal divisions in France.

Oct: 9th, Paul Kruger's ultimatum, which is supported, 11th, by Orange Free State, provokes, 12th, Anglo-Boer War.
17th, Bohemian language ordinances of April 1897 are repealed.

Dec: 23rd, Germany secures Baghdad Railway contract.
24th, Netherlands adopts Proportional Representation.

Politics, Government, Law, and Economy
H S Chamberlain, *The Foundations of the XIXth Century* (published in Vienna).
London Borough Councils are established.

Society, Education, and Religion
John Dewey, *School and Society.*

Science, Technology, and Discovery
The magnetic recording of sound is devised.
Aspirin is invented.

Humanities and Scholarship
T H Green's *Prolegomena to Ethics* is published posthumously.
James Ward, *Naturalism and Agnosticism.*

Music
H Berlioz, *The Taking of Troy*, being pt. 2 of *The Trojans* (opera).
Edward Elgar, *Enigma Variations*.

Literature
Stefan George, *Der Teppich des Lebens*.
R Kipling, *Stalky and Co*.
Drama A W Pinero, *The Gay Lord Quex*.

1900 **Feb: 27th**, in Britain, at conference in London, the Independent Labour Party, Fabian Society, Social Democratic Federation, and trade unions found the Labour Representation Committee to work for independent representation of working people in parliament; Ramsay MacDonald is appointed secretary.

28th, Redvers Buller relieves Ladysmith in Natal (under siege by Boers since 30th Oct 1899).

28th, Count Muraviev, Russian foreign minister, suggests that France and Germany put joint pressure on Britain to end South African War, but Germany rejects this (3rd March) while France takes advantage of Britain's plight to advance its interests in Morocco.

April: 7th, US President William McKinley appoints commission with Judge W H Taft as president to extend US civil power in the Philippines (commences work in Sept, with appropriations for the construction of roads and harbours).

May: 17th, in South Africa, British forces relieve the besieged town of Mafeking.

19th, the Tonga Islands become a British protectorate.

24th, Lord Roberts announces the annexation of the Orange Free State as the Orange River Colony.

June: 13th, (–14th Aug), in China, rising of Boxers (supporters of the Society of Harmonious Fists) against Europeans.

Sept: 1st, Lord Roberts formally proclaims the annexation of the Transvaal.

Oct: 16th, in the 'Khaki' election in Britain, the Conservatives, organized by Joseph Chamberlain, remain in power, with a majority of 134 (Conservatives and Unionists, 334 seats; Liberal Unionists, 68; Liberals, 184; Irish Nationalists, 82; Labour, 2). Lord Salisbury reconstructs his ministry, appointing Lord Lansdowne foreign secretary.

Nov: 6th, in US presidential election William McKinley, Republican, defeats William Jennings Bryan, Democrat, on an anti-imperialist platform, with 292 electoral votes to Bryan's 155; popular vote: McKinley, 7,207,923; Bryan, 6,358,133.

Politics, Government, Law, and Economy
Civil Law Code introduced in Germany; similar codes are later adopted elsewhere in Europe and Japan.

Society, Education, and Religion
Sigmund Freud publishes *The Interpretation of Dreams* suggesting that dreams reveal the unconscious mind.
(31st Oct) Union of Free and United Presbyterian Churches in Scotland.

Science, Technology, and Discovery
Max Planck in Germany begins quantum theory by suggesting that some physical processes are discontinuous.
(2nd July) In Germany, first trial flight of Zeppelin airship by Count Ferdinand von Zeppelin.

Humanities and Scholarship
British archaeologist Arthur Evans discovers an unknown Bronze Age civilization at Knossos on Crete; Evans names it 'Minoan' after the legendary king of Crete.

Art, Sculpture, Fine Arts, and Architecture
Architecture Charles Rennie Mackintosh designs the Glasgow School of Art, Scotland.
Edwin Lutyens, Deanery Gardens, Sonning, England.
Sculpture Auguste Rodin's reputation is established by exhibition at La Place de l'Alma, Paris.

Music
Gustave Charpentier, *Louise* (opera).
Edward Elgar, *The Dream of Gerontius* (oratorio).
Gustav Mahler, Symphony No. 4.
Giacomo Puccini, *Tosca* (opera).
Jean Sibelius, *Finlandia*.

Literature
Colette, first of five 'Claudine' novels (–1907).
Joseph Conrad, *Lord Jim*.
Drama Anton Chekhov, *Uncle Vanya*.

Everyday Life

In USA, the Eastman Kodak Company launches the Brownie Box Camera, selling for just $1.
'Cakewalk' dance craze.
(30th April) US engine driver Casey Jones dies on the footplate, trying to slow his engine before it hits another engine at Vaughan, Mississippi.
(19th July) In France, opening of the Métropolitain or 'Métro' underground railway in Paris.

Sport and Recreation

(20th May) (–28th Oct) The 2nd Olympic Games are held in Paris, in connection with the Paris International Exhibition. France wins 29 gold medals; USA, 20; Britain, 17; Belgium, 8; Switzerland, 6; Austria, 4; Germany, 3.
(8th Aug) (–10th) In USA, Dwight Filley Davis presents an international challenge cup for lawn tennis (the Davis Cup); the USA wins the trophy, beating Great Britain 3–0 in Boston, Massachusetts.

1901

Jan: 1st, Commonwealth of Australia comes into being with Edmund Barton, federalist and protectionist, as prime minister.
22nd, death of Queen Victoria (at Osborne House, Isle of Wight, S England), after a brief illness; those present at her death include the German Kaiser, Wilhelm II; the Prince of Wales accedes to the throne as Edward VII (proclaimed, 23rd).

May: 29th, a confidential memorandum by British prime minister Salisbury upholds the policy of isolation, marking the end of discussions for a British–German alliance.

June: 12th, new constitution for Cuba is agreed, reserving rights to the USA that make the country virtually a US protectorate.

Aug: 17th, as expression of imperialist sentiment the Royal Titles Act adds the words 'and of the British Dominions beyond the Seas' to Edward VII's title.

Sept: 6th, in USA, the anarchist Leon Czolgosz shoots President McKinley at a reception at Buffalo, New York (McKinley dies on 14th Sept, when Vice-President Roosevelt is sworn in as president; aged 42, he is the youngest man to hold the presidency).
7th, Peace of Beijing formally ends the Boxer Rising; China is to pay an indemnity to the great powers.

Nov: 18th, second Hay–Pauncefote Convention between the USA and Britain provides for the USA to construct a canal across the Isthmus of Panama; the canal zone will be under US jurisdiction (ratified by US Senate 16th Dec).

Politics, Government, Law, and Economy

Mass production of cars begins in Detroit, USA, with the introduction of the Oldsmobile.
(Feb) In USA, J P Morgan buys Andrew Carnegie's steel companies for $250 million, forming the US Steel Corporation.
(22nd July) In Britain, the House of Lords rules on the Taff Vale Case: a trade union can be liable for damages caused by its members during a strike (the Taff Vale Railway Company had sued the Amalgamated Society of Railway Servants; the Society is fined £23,000).

Society, Education, and Religion

(16th Oct) In USA, President Roosevelt entertains the African-American teacher Booker T Washington to dinner at the White House, arousing protest in southern states; Roosevelt seeks Washington's advice on African-American and southern appointments.

Science, Technology, and Discovery

Guglielmo Marconi receives radio signals transmitted across Atlantic from Poldhu, SW England, to Newfoundland.
First petrol-engined motor-bicycle in Britain.

Humanities and Scholarship

Max Weber, *The Protestant Ethic and the Birth of Capitalism*.

Music

Eduardo di Capua, 'O Sole Mio!'.
Antonin Dvořák, *Rusalka* (opera).

Literature

Rudyard Kipling, *Kim*.
Thomas Mann, *Buddenbrooks*.
Drama August Strindberg, *Dance of Death*.
Anton Chekhov, *Three Sisters*.

Everyday Life

Invention of instant coffee.

Statistics

Populations (in millions): China, 350; India, 294; Russia, 146; US, 75.9; Germany, 56.3; Japan, 45.4; Great Britain and Ireland, 41.4; France, 38.9; Italy, 32.4; Austria, 26.1.

Coal production (in million tons): US, 268; Great Britain, 219; Germany, 112; Austria, 34; Belgium, 23; Russia, 15.

Steel production (in million tons): US, 10.1; Germany, 6.2; Great Britain, 4.9; France, 1.5.

1902

Jan: 30th, Britain qualifies its isolationist foreign policy by signing a treaty with Japan, to safeguard their common interests in China and Korea; in the event of Britain or Japan being at war with a foreign power in East Asia, the other shall maintain strict neutrality, but shall assist its ally if a second foreign power should join the first.

May: 31st, signing of Peace of Vereeniging ends Boer War, in which British casualties numbered 5,774 killed (and 16,000 deaths from disease) against 4,000 Boers killed in action; Boers accept British sovereignty but are promised self-government in the Orange River Colony and Transvaal, and £3 million from Britain for restocking farms.

June: 3rd, in France René Waldeck-Rousseau resigns, despite his majority in the Chamber, through lack of sympathy with extremists, and is succeeded by Émile Combes who directs a vigorous anti-clerical policy.

28th, renewal of Triple Alliance between Germany, Austria, and Italy for six years (originally agreed in 1882).

28th, US Congress passes Isthmian Canal Act which authorizes the president to purchase the rights of the French Panama Company and to acquire from Colombia perpetual control of the canal zone.

30th, (–11th Aug) Colonial Conference in London supports the principle of Imperial Preference (i.e. Britain and the colonies setting preferential tariffs for each other's goods).

July: 11th, Lord Salisbury retires as British prime minister; succeeded by his nephew Arthur Balfour on the following day.

Politics, Government, Law, and Economy

J A Hobson, *Imperialism*.

Society, Education, and Religion

Immigration Restriction Act in Australia.

Australia introduces universal suffrage in federal elections (with voting age of 21); women hold a preponderance of votes in Melbourne and Sydney constituencies.

Education Act for England and Wales provides for secondary education, places schools under Committees of local authorities and brings denominational schools into the State system.

William James, *The Varieties of Religious Experience*.

Science, Technology, and Discovery

British physicist Oliver Heaviside and US engineer Arthur Edwin predict the existence of an electrified layer in the atmosphere that reflects radio waves.

William Bayliss and Ernest Starling in England discover hormones.

Ernest Rutherford and Frederick Soddy discover Thorium X and publish *The Cause and Nature of Radioactivity* containing the atomic disintegration theory of radioactivity.

Art, Sculpture, Fine Arts, and Architecture

Painting Claude Monet, *Waterloo Bridge*.

Music

Gustav Mahler, Symphony No. 5 ('The Giant').

Scott Joplin, 'The Entertainer' rag.

Claude Debussy, *Pelléas et Mélisande* (opera).

Literature

Joseph Conrad, *The Heart of Darkness* (published in *Youth and Other Stories*).

Hilaire Belloc, *The Path to Rome*.

Arthur Conan Doyle, *The Hound of the Baskervilles*.

Rudyard Kipling, *Just So Stories*.

Drama Gabriele D'Annunzio, *Francesca da Rimini*.

Anton Chekhov, *Three Sisters*.

Everyday Life

Teddy bears start to become popular after an incident in which US President Theodore Roosevelt refused to shoot a bear cub.

Advances in refrigeration enable fish and chips to become a popular delicacy in London.

Media

In Britain, *The Times Literary Supplement* is published.

1903 **Feb:** —, Publication in Britain of report by Consul Roger Casement alleging atrocious treatment of African and Indian labourers in the Belgian Congo by white traders; a British government commission confirms the findings.

July: 6th, (–9th) visit to London of President Émile Loubet and Théophile Delcassé begins conversations leading to *Entente Cordiale.*

20th, following death of Pope Leo XIII, Giuseppe Sarto is elected Pope Pius X.

25th, in Britain, Arthur Henderson wins parliamentary by-election at Barnard Castle, NE England, for the Labour Party in three-cornered fight.

Aug: —, At London Congress the Russian Social Democratic Party splits into Mensheviks ('minority'), led by G V Plecharoff, and Bolsheviks ('majority'), led by V I Lenin.

Dec: 18th, USA–Panama treaty places Panama Canal Zone in US hands in perpetuity for annual rent.

Politics, Government, Law, and Economy

Krupp metal-working industries founded in the Ruhr region of Germany.

Society, Education, and Religion

In USA, regulation of child labour is introduced.

In Britain, Mrs Emmeline Pankhurst founds the Women's Social and Political Union (WSPU), a nonparty organization to campaign for female suffrage.

Foundation of Letchworth Garden City in S England, an attempt by Ebenezer Howard to realize his 'garden city' ideal of well-planned urban centres which would include agricultural activities.

(18th March) Dissolution of most French religious orders.

Science, Technology, and Discovery

(17th Dec) Orville and Wilbur Wright make the first successful flight in an aeroplane with a petrol engine at Kitty Hawk, North Carolina, USA.

Humanities and Scholarship

G E Moore, *Principia Ethica.*

Art, Sculpture, Fine Arts, and Architecture

Architecture New York Chamber of Commerce and Stock Exchange built.

Charles Reed and Allen Stem, Grand Central Station, New York, USA (–1913).

Antonio Gaudí begins work on upper transept of Sagrada Familia church, Barcelona (church still unfinished).

Literature

Samuel Butler, *The Way of All Flesh* (posthumous).

Drama George Bernard Shaw, *Man and Superman.*

Sport and Recreation

The Tour de France, organized by Henri Desgrange, editor of the French cycling magazine *L'Auto*, is run for the first time. The first winner is Maurice Garin, an Italian chimney sweep.

The Marylebone Cricket Club (MCC) takes over responsibility for English teams touring abroad.

Media

(Nov) In Britain, Alfred Harmsworth founds the *Daily Mirror*, a women's paper sold for a penny; Jan 1904, renamed the *Daily Illustrated Mirror* and published as an illustrated tabloid sold for a halfpenny.

1904 **Feb: 8th**, (–9th) start of Russo–Japanese War: Japanese fleet makes surprise attack on Russian squadron at Port Arthur (Russian treaty port in NE China), damaging two battleships and a cruiser, and then blockades the port.

April: 8th, *Entente Cordiale* settles British–French differences in Morocco, Egypt, and Newfoundland fishery; Britain recognizes Suez Canal Convention and surrenders claim to Madagascar.

Aug: 25th, (–3rd Sept) Japanese defeat Russians at Liaoyang, China.

Nov: —, Zemstvo Congress at St Petersburg demands a republican constitution and civil liberties.

8th, in US presidential election, President Theodore Roosevelt (Republican) defeats Alton B Parker (Democrat) with 336 electoral votes to 140; popular vote: Roosevelt, 7,623,486; Parker, 5,077,911.

Politics, Government, Law, and Economy

Canada passes a protectionist tariff.

Society, Education, and Religion

Émile Combes introduces bill for separation of Church and State in France, ending the 1801 Concordat (promulgated Dec 1905).

In England, foundation of the Workers' Educational Association by Albert Mansbridge.

Science, Technology, and Discovery

In Germany, Johann Phillip Ludwig Elster devises the photo-electric cell.

An ultraviolet lamp is made.

Humanities and Scholarship

Discovery of a Viking ship burial at Oseberg, Norway.

Benedetto Croce founds *La Critica* to reinvigorate Italian thought and to unite it with European idealist philosophy.

Henry Adams, *Mont St. Michel and Chartres.*

Art, Sculpture, Fine Arts, and Architecture

Architecture

Charles Rennie Mackintosh, The Willow Tea Rooms, Glasgow, Scotland.

Painting Paul Cézanne, *Mont Sainte-Victoire* (–1906).

Music

Giacomo Puccini, *Madama Butterfly* (opera).

Literature

G K Chesterton, *The Napoleon of Notting Hill.*

Joseph Conrad, *Nostromo.*

Jack London, *Sea Wolf.*

Henry James, *The Golden Bowl.*

Drama J M Barrie, *Peter Pan.*

Anton Chekhov, *The Cherry Orchard.*

Thomas Hardy, *The Dynasts.*

Luigi Pirandello, *Il fu Mattia Pascal/The Late Mattia Pascal.*

J M Synge, *Riders to the Sea.*

The Abbey Theatre, Dublin, opened by Miss E F Horniman.

Everyday Life

In the USA, the St Louis exposition popularizes the hamburger and the ice cream cone.

Invention of the teabag by Thomas Sullivan in the USA.

Sport and Recreation

(1 July) (–23rd Nov) The 3rd Olympic Games are held in St Louis, Missouri, USA, to coincide with the World Fair. The United States wins 80 gold medals; Germany and Cuba, 5 each; Canada, 4; Hungary, 2.

1905

Sun Yat-Sen (Sun Zhong Shan) organizes Combined League Society of Chinese in Japan to work for the expulsion of Manchu rulers and administrators from China.

Jan: 2nd, Russian commander of Port Arthur surrenders the port to the Japanese.

22nd, 'Bloody Sunday' in St Petersburg, when a procession of workers and their families, led by a priest (Father Gapon) and carrying a petition to the tsar, is fired on by guards outside the Winter Palace; over 100 are killed and riots break out elsewhere in Russia.

March: 3rd, Tsar Nicholas II promises to undertake religious and other reforms and to call a consultative assembly.

31st, Emperor William II's visit to Tangier sets off the 'First Moroccan Crisis', being seen as a test of the British–French Convention of 1904 which arranged for French predominance over Morocco.

June: 7th, Norwegian Storting (parliament) decides on separation from Sweden (ratified by plebiscite, Aug).

28th, mutiny by sailors on the Russian battleship *Potemkin*, anchored off Odessa; unrest spreads through the Russian navy.

Aug: 19th, Tsar Nicholas II issues an Imperial Manifesto, proposing to create an Imperial Duma (parliament), elected on limited franchise, and with only deliberative powers.

Sept: 5th, Treaty of Portsmouth (New Hampshire, USA), mediated by US president Roosevelt, ending Russo–Japanese War: Russia to cede Port Arthur and the Guangdong Peninsula, evacuate Manchuria and half of Sakhalin Island, and to recognize Japan's interests in Korea (Japan's demand for indemnity is not granted).

Oct: 20th, (–30th) general strike in Russia.

26th, delegates of strike committees in St Petersburg form the first Soviet ('council').

26th, by Treaty of Separation between Norway and Sweden, Oscar II abdicates Norwegian crown.

30th, in Russia, Tsar Nicholas II issues the 'October Manifesto' capitulating to demands for the Duma to have legislative powers, a wider franchise for its election, and civil liberties.

Dec: 4th, British Conservative prime minister Arthur Balfour resigns.

5th, Sir Henry Campbell-Bannerman forms Liberal ministry with Sir Edward Grey as foreign secretary, Herbert Asquith as chancellor of exchequer and R B Haldane as war secretary; King Edward issues a warrant giving official recognition to the office of prime minister and according the holder precedence after the Archbishop of York.

Science, Technology, and Discovery

In Switzerland, Albert Einstein develops his special theory of relativity, his mathematical analysis of Brownian motion, and his theory of the photoelectric effect.

Edwin Brandenberger invents cellophane.

Humanities and Scholarship

George Santayana, *The Life of Reason.*

Art, Sculpture, Fine Arts, and Architecture

Louis Vauxcelles coins the name *Les Fauves* ('Wild Beasts') for the group of French artists led by Henri Matisse.

Die Brücke ('The Bridge') group of artists is formed in Dresden by Ernst Kirchner and revives interest in the graphic arts; the group's style is expressionism (–1913).

Architecture Antonio Gaudí, Casa Milà and Casa Batlló, Barcelona (–1910).

Painting Paul Cézanne, *Les Grandes Baigneuses.*

Henri Matisse, *Portrait of Madame Matisse (The Green Line), Bonheur de Vivre* (–1906).

Pablo Picasso, *Acrobat and Young Harlequin, Boy With Pipe.*

Music

Claude Debussy, *La Mer.*

Franz Léhar, *The Merry Widow* (operetta).

Richard Strauss, *Salome* (opera).

Literature

Drama George Bernard Shaw, *Major Barbara.*

Everyday Life

Neon signs are first displayed.

Statistics

Religious denominations (in thousands): (a) *Britain:* Roman Catholics, 5,800; Church of England, 2,450; Presbyterian Church of Scotland, 1,170; Wesleyan Methodists, 521; Primitive Methodists, 212; Congregationalists, 498; Baptists, 426; Presbyterians, 80; Unitarians, 75; Episcopal Church of Scotland, 50; Quakers, 18; Jews, 240. (b) *US:* Roman Catholics, 12,079; Baptists, 6,166; Episcopal Methodists, 6,305; Congregational Methodists, 296; Presbyterians, 1,830; Mormons, 350; Unitarians, 90; Quakers, 90; Jews, 177.

1906

Jan: **12th**, Liberal landslide in British general election (Liberals, 400 seats, with majority of 130 over all parties; Unionists, 157; Irish Nationalists, 83; Labour, 30); Sir Henry Campbell-Bannerman's cabinet embarks on sweeping social reforms.

16th, (–8th April) in southern Spain, Algeciras conference of great powers to settle their dispute over position of Morocco; cooperation of Britain and France isolates Germany.

April: **8th**, 'Act of Algeciras' signed, ending the Moroccan Crisis; it gives France and Spain chief control in Morocco (under a Swiss inspector and respecting the sultan's authority).

18th, (–19th) major earthquake in San Francisco, USA; the quake and subsequent fires devastate the city, leaving over 200,000 people homeless and over 1,000 dead.

May: **5th**, fall of Count Witte in Russia, who is succeeded by the Conservative Ivan Goremykin.

10th, first Duma meets in Russia, resulting in deadlock through the Cadets' Party's criticism of Fundamental Laws (see 21st July).

30th, Giovanni Giolitti forms ministry in Italy (– Dec 1909).

July: **21st**, on dissolution of Duma the Cadets adjourn to Finland and issue the Viborg Manifesto, calling on Russians to refuse to pay taxes.

Dec: **6th**, Britain grants self-government to Transvaal and Orange River Colonies.

Politics, Government, Law, and Economy

Aga Khan III founds All India Muslim League.

Society, Education, and Religion

The Azusa Street revival begins in Los Angeles, USA, under the leadership of William Seymour, the starting point for the worldwide spread of Pentecostalism.

International prohibition on night-shift working for women.

Confederazione Generale de Lavoro founded in Italy.

The English Hymnal (edited by Percy Dearmer and Ralph Vaughan Williams).

Science, Technology, and Discovery

Launch in Britain of the battleship HMS *Dreadnought*, with entirely large-calibre armament.

Humanities and Scholarship

Excavations by German and Turkish scholars at Boghazköy (–1908) reveal that the city was ancient Hattusas, capital of the Hittites.

P S Allen, *Erasmi Epistolae* (–1958).

Music

Invention of Gabel's 'Automatic Entertainer', i.e., the jukebox.

Literature

Bodleian Library, Oxford, England, repurchases (for £3,000) a copy of the First Folio of Shakespeare which it had sold in 1664.

John Galsworthy, *The Man of Property*, the first volume in The Forsyte Saga (–1922).

Foundation of 'Everyman's Library', cheap editions of important literary works published in Britain by Edward Dent.

Everyday Life

W K Kellogg Toasted Corn Flake Company launch their new breakfast cereal.

Sport and Recreation

(22nd April) (–2nd May) The Interim Olympic Games are held in Athens; France wins 18 gold medals; USA, 12; Greece and Britain, 8 each; Italy, 7; Switzerland, 5; Germany and Norway, 4 each.

Media

Radio Richard Aubrey Fessenden first transmits speech by wireless, using amplitude modulation.

Statistics

Populations (in millions): China, 438; Russia, 149.2; US, 85; Germany, 62; Great Britain, 38.9; Ireland, 4.3; France, 39.2.

Army strengths (in millions): Russia, 13; Germany, 7. 9; Austro-Hungary, 7.4; France, 4.8; Italy, 3.1; Great Britain, 0.8, with 0.4 from colonial forces.

1907

Jan: 10th, in Austria, passing of bill extending suffrage to all males aged 24 or over (first election held on 14th May).

April: 21st, in Ireland, political clubs merge to form the Sinn Féin League.

June: 14th, female suffrage adopted in Norway (on same terms as for municipal elections).

15th, (–18th Oct) reassembly of peace conference of great powers at the Hague, originally called at US President Roosevelt's suggestion in 1904, but postponed owing to the Russo–Japanese War in Far East; attempt at stopping the arms race fails, but progress is made in direction of voluntary arbitration of disputes, despite German opposition.

16th, reactionary party in Russia forces Tsar Nicholas II to dissolve the Second Duma; an electoral edict increases representation of propertied classes and reduces representation of national minorities.

July: —, Triple alliance between Germany, Austria, and Italy is renewed for six years, despite the reserved attitude of Italy.

25th, Korea agrees convention giving Japan control over its government (through presence of Japanese vice-ministers in major departments).

Sept: 26th, following a royal proclamation, the Colony of New Zealand is known as the Dominion of New Zealand.

Nov: 16th, in USA, Oklahoma is admitted to the union as the 46th state.

Society, Education, and Religion

Famine in Russia kills several million people.

Bubonic plague in India kills 1.3 million people.

In Britain, Robert Baden-Powell founds the Boy Scouts.

In USA, controversy over magnitude of immigration from southern Europe and immigrants' effects on US jobs and wage rates.

Pope Pius X condemns Modernism in encyclical *Pascendi gregis*.

(1st Nov) First women councillors elected in England in local elections.

Art, Sculpture, Fine Arts, and Architecture

National League of Handicrafts Societies leads to extension of the 'arts and crafts' movement in the USA.

Painting Pablo Picasso, *Les Demoiselles d'Avignon*.

Henri Matisse, *Blue Nude*, *Luxe, Calme et Volupté*, *Memory of Biskra*.

Edvard Munch, *Amor and Psyche*.

Music

Frederick Delius, *A Village Romeo and Juliet* (opera).

Literature

Joseph Conrad, *The Secret Agent.*

Rainer Maria Rilke, *Neue Gedichte* (New Poems).

Drama J M Synge, *The Playboy of the Western World.*

Everyday Life

The Hurley Machine Co. of Chicago markets the first electric washing machine in the USA.

Sport and Recreation

The Association Football Players' Union (later the Professional Footballers' Association) is founded at a meeting in Manchester, England.

(11th June) Northamptonshire are dismissed for 12 by Gloucestershire in the County Championship match at Gloucester; it remains the lowest total in first-class cricket.

(3rd June) (–6th July) In billiards, Tom Reece of Oldham compiles a record break of 499,135 points using the cradle cannon (later outlawed) in 85 hours 49 minutes, spread over five weeks.

1908

April: 8th, King Edward VII, holidaying at Biarritz in SW France, appoints Herbert Asquith as British prime minister (12th, new ministry announced, with David Lloyd George as chancellor of the exchequer).

May: —, In Australia the government is defeated in a confidence vote; a Labour government takes office under Andrew Fisher.

July: 6th, Young Turks under Niazi Bey stage revolt at Resina in Macedonia; the government troops sent to quell them desert.

Oct: —, The Australian parliament agrees to the establishment of a new federal capital at Canberra near Sydney.

5th, King Ferdinand I of Bulgaria declares Bulgaria's independence and assumes the title of tsar.

6th, Austria annexes Bosnia and Herzegovina by decree.

7th, Crete proclaims union with Greece.

12th, South Africa constitutional convention meets at Durban, later removes to Capetown (–Feb 1909), agreeing on a Union of South Africa.

27th, The *Daily Telegraph* publishes remarks by Kaiser Wilhelm II of Germany in which he states the German people are hostile to Britain while he is a friend; strong feelings are aroused in Germany, both against Britain and against the Kaiser for making policy pronouncements without consulting the chancellor.

Nov: 3rd, in US presidential election William Howard Taft, Republican, with 231 electoral votes, defeats William Jennings Bryan, Democrat, with 162 votes; popular vote: Taft, 7,678,908; Bryan, 6,409,104.

10th, (–11th) in Germany, the Reichstag debates the *Daily Telegraph* interview, further embittering British–German relations.

Politics, Government, Law, and Economy

Frederick Meinecke, *Cosmopolitanism and the National State.*

Henry Ford of the Ford Motor Company, USA, announces the production of the Model T car, which will sell for only $850.

(26th July) In USA, foundation of the Bureau of Investigation (renamed, 1st July 1935, Federal Bureau of Investigation, or FBI).

Society, Education, and Religion

First observation of Mother's Day, at Philadelphia, Pennsylvania, USA.

Foundation of the Graduate School of Business Administration at Harvard University, USA.

Science, Technology, and Discovery

Hermann Minkowski elaborates four-dimensional geometry, the mathematics of relativity.

Humanities and Scholarship

Georges Sorel, *Reflections on Violence.*

Art, Sculpture, Fine Arts, and Architecture

Painting Marc Chagall, *Nu Rouge.*

Maurice Utrillo, white period (–1914).

Sculpture Jacob Epstein, controversial figures for the building of the British Medical Association, London.

Music

Béla Bartók, String Quartet No. 1.

Literature

E M Forster, *A Room With a View.*

Anatole France, *L'ile des pingouins/Penguin Island.*

Kenneth Grahame, *The Wind in the Willows.*

Everyday Life

In USA, introduction of the electric iron and the paper cup.

Sport and Recreation

(20th April) (–22nd) W G Grace plays his last first-class cricket match, for the Gentlemen of England v. Surrey, at the age of 59.

(27th April) (–31st Oct) The 4th Olympic Games are held in London; Britain wins 56 gold medals; USA, 23; Sweden, 8; France, 5; Germany, Hungary, and Canada, 3 each.

Media

Film In USA, filming of *The Count of Monte Cristo* is completed near Los Angeles, California; in the next few years more film-makers are attracted to the low costs and reliable climate of California.

1909

Feb: 13th, Kiamil Pasha, grand vizier of Turkey, forced to resign by the Turkish nationalists.

April: 19th, army of liberation captures Constantinople from rebels.

27th, Young Turks depose Sultan Abdul Hamid who is succeeded by his brother as Mohammed V (–1918).

29th, British chancellor Lloyd George introduces his 'People's Budget'; to raise money for defence and social expenditure it proposes taxes on land values, profits on land sales, and a 'super-tax' on high incomes.

Nov: 5th, after six months of debate, the British House of Commons gives a final reading to Chancellor Lloyd George's 'People's Budget', which then goes to the House of Lords.

30th, the British House of Lords rejects the 'People's Budget' by 350 votes to 75, thereby creating a major constitutional crisis in Britain.

Politics, Government, Law, and Economy

(21st Dec) In Britain, the Osborne Judgement: the House of Lords rules on the Osborne case, making compulsory union political levies illegal (resulting from an action by Walter Osborne to restrain his union from making a political donation to the Labour Party; principle reversed by legislation in 1913).

Society, Education, and Religion

Trade Boards Act provides for the regulation of wages in the 'sweated trades' of British industry.

Girl Guide movement founded in Britain.

(18th April) Pope Pius X beatifies Joan of Arc.

Science, Technology, and Discovery

Leo Baekeland in the USA invents Bakelite, the first totally synthetic plastic.

Louis Blériot crosses the English Channel by monoplane in 36 minutes.

Art, Sculpture, Fine Arts, and Architecture

Filippo Tommaso Marinetti, Italian poet and publicist, 'First Futurist Manifesto', published in *Le Figaro*, Paris, France.

Architecture Frank Lloyd Wright, Robie House, Chicago, USA.

Music

Richard Strauss, *Elektra* (opera).

Literature

Rabindranath Tagore, *Gitanjali*.

Drama Maurice Maeterlinck, *The Blue Bird*.

Everyday Life

US businessman H G Selfridge opens the first department store in Britain (Selfridge's in London).

Sport and Recreation

The Jugendherbergen, a national network of hostels providing overnight accommodation for students, is established in Germany.

Media

In Britain, publication of the *Daily Sketch* (a halfpenny tabloid).

1910

Jan: 15th, in Britain, general election held on Chancellor Lloyd George's budget, the power of the Lords, and Irish Home Rule, resulting in reduced Liberal majority (Liberals, 275 seats; Labour, 40; Irish Nationalists, 82; Unionists, 273).

May: 6th, death of King Edward VII at Buckingham Palace, London, after brief illness; succeeded by George V (–1936).

10th, British House of Commons resolves that the House of Lords should have no power to veto money bills, only limited powers to postpone other bills, and that the maximum lifetime of Parliament should be reduced from seven to five years.

July: 1st, Union of South Africa becomes a dominion.

Aug: **22nd**, Japan formally annexes Korea.

Sept: **15th**, South African party wins first South African elections and Louis Botha becomes prime minister.

Oct: **4th**, King Manuel II of Portugal flees to England on outbreak of revolution in Lisbon and, 5th, Portugal is proclaimed a republic under Theophilo Braga.

Dec: **—**, In British general election Liberals win 272 seats; Labour, 42; Irish Nationalists, 84; Unionists, 272 (making a majority for a Parliament Bill and Home Rule 126, an increase of 4 since Jan).

Politics, Government, Law, and Economy

Norman Angell, *The Great Illusion: A Study of the Relation of Military Power in Nations to their Economic and Social Advantage.*

Germany's machine-tool industry overtakes Britain's.

Society, Education, and Religion

First of the twelve volumes of *The Fundamentals* published, with contributions from many conservative Evangelical scholars in Europe and the USA.

Albert Schweitzer, *The Quest of the Historical Jesus.*

E Underhill, *Mysticism.*

(1st Feb) First Labour Exchanges for the unemployed opened in Britain.

(1st May) Foundation of the National Association for the Advancement of Colored People (NAACP), an organization of US black radicals and liberals; it publishes *Crisis*, edited by W E B Du Bois.

(19th June) In USA, first celebration of Father's Day, founded by Mrs Dodd at Spokane, Washington.

Science, Technology, and Discovery

Marie Curie, *Treatise on Radiography*, published in France.

Art, Sculpture, Fine Arts, and Architecture

Manet and the Post-Impressionists, exhibition of recent French painting at the Grafton Galleries, London, organized by Roger Fry.

Painting Henri Matisse, *La Danse II.*

Music

Giacomo Puccini, *The Girl of the Golden West* (opera).

Ralph Vaughan Williams, Symphony No. 1, *A Sea Symphony.*

Igor Stravinsky, *The Firebird* (ballet).

Literature

Paul Claudel, *Cinq grandes odes.*

E M Forster, *Howard's End.*

Charles Péguy, *Le Mystère de la charité de Jeanne d'Arc.*

Everyday Life

(19th May) Return of Halley's comet – the Earth passes through the comet's tail; in the USA comet parties are held and there is a brisk sale for 'Comet Pills', allegedly an antidote to the poisonous gases thought to be in the comet's tail.

Sport and Recreation

The first Rugby Union Five Nations Championship is held, following the admission of France (to join England, Wales, Scotland, and Ireland).

Statistics

Defence estimates (in £ million): Great Britain, 68; Germany, 64; Russia, 63; France, 52; Italy, 24; Austria-Hungary, 17.

Battleships in commission (and under construction): Great Britain, 56 (9); Germany, 33 (8); US, 30 (4); France, 17 (6); Japan, 14 (3); Italy, 10 (2); Russia, 7 (8).

1911

May: **15th**, British House of Commons passes the Parliament Bill.

July: **1st**, arrival of German gunboat *Panther* in Agadir, Morocco, allegedly to protect German interests threatened by French involvement in Morocco; an international crisis ensues.

Aug: **10th**, the British House of Lords passes the Parliament Bill, deciding (by 131–114 votes) not to insist on their amendments; the House of Lords' power to veto bills is converted into the power to suspend money bills for one month and other bills for a maximum period of two years; the maximum length of a parliament is reduced from seven to five years (except in an emergency situation).

Sept: **14th**, assassination of Peter Stolypin, Russian prime minister (19th, Vladimir Kokovtsoff appointed prime minister).

29th, Italy declares war on Turkey and Italian fleet bombards Tripoli coast.

Oct: 26th, Chinese Republic proclaimed.

Nov: 4th, convention ending the 'Agadir Crisis' by which Germany allows France a free hand in Morocco in return for territory in the Congo.

5th, Italy annexes Tripoli and Cyrenaica.

8th, A J Balfour resigns leadership of British Conservative and Unionist Party (13th, succeeded by Andrew Bonar Law).

Politics, Government, Law, and Economy

Copyright Act in Britain provides for copyright in a work to last for 50 years after the author's death; books no longer have to be registered at Stationers' Hall.

Official Secrets Act passed in Britain; it becomes a criminal offence for government officials to disclose certain categories of information.

Science, Technology, and Discovery

(15th Dec) Norwegian explorer Roald Amundsen reaches the South Pole.

Humanities and Scholarship

Cambridge Medieval History (–1936).

Art, Sculpture, Fine Arts, and Architecture

At the Salon des Indépendents, Paris, cubism becomes a public phenomenon but Picasso and Braque do not exhibit.

Wassily Kandinsky and Franz Marc found *Blaue Reiter* (Blue Rider) group of artists in Munich.

Architecture Walter Gropius and Adolph Meyer, Fagus Factory, Alfeld, Germany.

Music

Richard Strauss, *Der Rosenkavalier* (opera).

'Alexander's Ragtime Band', by Irving Berlin.

Igor Stravinsky, *Petrushka* (ballet).

Literature

Max Beerbohm, *Zuleika Dobson.*

D H Lawrence, *The White Peacock.*

Katherine Mansfield (pseudonym), *In a German Pension.*

Everyday Life

(21st Aug) *Mona Lisa* by Leonardo da Vinci is stolen from the Louvre, Paris.

Media

In Britain, founding of the *Daily Herald* as a daily Labour paper (formally taken over by the Labour Party in 1922).

Film First Keystone comedy film, produced by Max Sennett.

Statistics

Populations (in millions): China, 325; India, 315; Russia, 167; US, 94; Germany, 65; Japan, 52; Great Britain, 40.8; Ireland, 4.3; France, 39.6; Italy, 34.6.

Steel production (in million tons): US, 23.6; Germany, 14.7; Great Britain, 6.4; France, 3.8; Russia, 3.8; Austria-Hungary, 2.3; Belgium, 1.9.

1912

Jan: 3rd, Ulster Unionists resolve to repudiate the authority of any Irish parliament set up under Home Rule Bill.

6th, in USA, New Mexico is admitted to the union as the 47th state.

Feb: 12th, Manchu dynasty abdicates in China and a provisional republic is established.

14th, in USA, Arizona is admitted to the union as the 48th state.

March: 28th, British House of Commons rejects women's franchise bill.

April: 15th, the British liner *Titanic*, carrying 2,224 people on its maiden trans-Atlantic voyage, hits an iceberg S of Newfoundland and sinks; 1,513 are lost for want of sufficient lifeboats.

Sept: 18th, in northern Ireland, Anti-Home Rule demonstrations begin at Enniskillen under Edward Carson.

Oct: 8th, Montenegro declares war on Turkey.

17th, Turkey declares war on Bulgaria and Serbia.

Nov: 3rd, Turkey asks powers to intervene to end Balkan war.

5th, in US presidential election, Woodrow Wilson, Democrat, wins with 435 electoral votes against Theodore Roosevelt, Progressive, with 88, and President W H Taft, Republican, with 8 votes; popular vote: Wilson, 6,293,454; Roosevelt, 4,119,538; Taft, 3,484,980.

Dec: 3rd, armistice between Turkey, Bulgaria, Serbia, and Montenegro (Greece abstains).

20th, at London peace conference between Turkey and Balkan states, ambassadors of great powers accept principle of Albanian autonomy, providing Serbia has canal access to Adriatic.

Society, Education, and Religion

Ernst Troeltsch, *Socialism and the Christian Church.*

C J Jung, *The Psychology of the Unconscious.*

(24th July) (–30th) First International Eugenics Congress held at the University of London.

(5th Nov) In USA, the states of Arizona, Kansas, and Wisconsin adopt women's suffrage.

Science, Technology, and Discovery

In Germany Max von Laue demonstrates that crystals are composed of regular, repeated arrays of atoms by studying the patterns in which they diffract X-rays; this is the start of X-ray crystallography.

Henry Brearley invents a type of stainless steel.

(18th Jan) British explorer Robert Falcon Scott reaches the South Pole.

Humanities and Scholarship

At Piltdown in southeast England Charles Dawson discovers 'Piltdown Man', a human skull with an ape-like jaw (exposed as a forgery in 1953).

Art, Sculpture, Fine Arts, and Architecture

Painting Marcel Duchamp, *Nude Descending A Staircase, II.*

Music

Maurice Ravel, *Daphnis et Chloé* (ballet).

Arnold Schoenberg, *Pierrot Lunaire.*

Literature

'New Poetry' movement in USA.

Everyday Life

London has 400 cinemas (90 in 1909); in USA, five million people visit cinemas daily.

Sport and Recreation

(5th May) (–22nd July) The 5th Olympic Games are held in Stockholm. Sweden wins 24 gold medals; USA, 23; Britain, 10; Finland, 9; France, 7; Germany, 5. Races are timed electronically for the first time.

Media

In Russia, foundation of the socialist paper *Pravda.*

Foundation in Britain of the *Daily Herald*, published by members of the Labour movement.

Film Formation of the British Board of Film Censors.

1913

Jan: 16th, Irish Home Rule bill passes British House of Commons (but on 30th Jan is rejected by Lords).

Feb: 3rd, Bulgarians renew Turkish War (–16th April).

March: 18th, King George I of Greece is assassinated by a Greek in newly occupied Salonika.

May: 6th, British House of Commons rejects a women's franchise bill.

June: 18th, British House of Commons debates the Marconi Report which acquits Chancellor Lloyd George and other ministers of corruption in assigning the imperial wireless contract to the Marconi Company.

30th, Second Balkan War opens, with Bulgaria attacking Serbian and Greek positions.

July: 7th, British House of Commons passes Irish Home Rule bill (but rejected on 15th July by Lords).

23rd, outbreak of rebellion in Yangzi Valley and southern China (–Sept).

Aug: 7th, French army bill, imposing three years' military service.

Oct: 6th, Yuan Shikai is elected president of the Chinese Republic.

Nov: 6th, Mahatma Gandhi, leader of Indian Passive Resistance movement, is arrested.

Politics, Government, Law, and Economy

(25th Feb) The 16th Amendment to the US constitution takes effect, empowering the Congress to collect income tax.

(31st May) The 17th Amendment to the US constitution transfers election of senators from state legislators to a popular vote.

(23rd Dec) US Congress passes the Federal Reserve Bank Act, establishing a Federal Reserve Board with power over monetary policy and 12 district Federal Reserve banks.

Society, Education, and Religion

Rockefeller Foundation established in USA, to promote human well-being worldwide.

US automobile manufacturer Henry Ford introduces the conveyor-belt assembly technique into his Detroit-based company.

(26th May) Miss Emily Duncan appointed first woman magistrate in England.

(4th June) In Britain, Emily Wilding Davison, a member of the Women's Social and Political Union, an organization of militant suffragettes, dies after throwing herself at the King's horse Anmer, during the Derby at Epsom.

Science, Technology, and Discovery

Bela Schick discovers test for immunity from diphtheria.

In USA, Elmer McCollum isolates vitamin A.

Humanities and Scholarship

Dictionary of the Irish Language (–1976).

Art, Sculpture, Fine Arts, and Architecture

International Exhibition of Modern Art (exhibition of post-impressionist and cubist art), known as the 'Armory Show', held in New York.

Architecture Edwin Lutyens, Viceroy's House, New Delhi, India.

Painting Harold Gilman, Walter Sickert, and Wyndham Lewis form the London Group of artists, an exhibiting association (first exhibition, March 1914).

Music

Igor Stravinsky, *The Rite of Spring* (ballet).

Literature

Alain-Fournier, *Le Grand Meaulnes/The Lost Domain.*

D H Lawrence, *Sons and Lovers.*

Thomas Mann, *Death in Venice.*

Marcel Proust, *Du côté de chez Swann*, the first part of *À la recherche du temps perdu* (–1927).

Drama George Bernard Shaw, *Androcles and the Lion, Pygmalion.*

Everyday Life

Foxtrot popular.

(11th Jan) Last horse-drawn omnibus in Paris.

(Dec) Recovery of Leonardo da Vinci's *Mona Lisa*, missing since 1911; the thief, Vincenzo Perugia, claimed he was retaliating against France for taking Italian art works from Italy.

Media

Foundation of *New Statesman* periodical in Britain.

Statistics

Industrial output: increases percent, since 1893:

	US	Germany	Great Britain
Coal	210	159	75
Pig iron	337	287	5
Steel	715	522	136
Exports of raw materials	196	243	238
Exports of manufactures	563	239	121

Steel production (in million tons): Germany, 14; US, 10; Great Britain, 6; Russia, 4.2; France, 2.8.

1914

April: 22nd, US forces bombard and seize the port of Veracruz, Mexico (to prevent Germans landing munitions for President Huerta's forces; withdrawn 23rd Nov).

May: 10th, in Britain, the Liberal Unionists unite with Conservatives.

25th, British House of Commons passes the Irish Home Rule bill.

June: 28th, Archduke Franz Ferdinand of Austria-Hungary and his wife are assassinated at Sarajevo in Bosnia by Gavrilo Princip, an 18-year-old Bosnian Serb student linked with the Serbian nationalist society the 'Black Hand'.

July: 16th, announcement that President Huerta of Mexico has gone into exile and replaced by Carbajal as provisional president (Aug, Carbajal flees).

23rd, Austria-Hungary, suspecting Serbian involvement in the assassination of Franz Ferdinand, issues ultimatum to Serbia.

26th, Austria-Hungary mobilizes army on Russian frontier.

26th, clash in Dublin between troops and Irish nationalists involved in gun-running.

28th, Austria-Hungary declares war on Serbia.

Aug: 1st, Germany declares war on Russia.

4th, Germany declares war on France and invades Belgium and France.

4th, Britain declares war on Germany and establishes naval blockade of North Sea, Channel and Mediterranean to stop access to Central Powers.

4th, President Wilson of the USA declares US neutrality in the European war.

6th, Austria-Hungary declares war on Russia.

6th, Serbia and Montenegro declare war on Germany.

10th, France declares war on Austria.

12th, Britain declares war on Austria-Hungary.

24th, (–7th Sept) British and Belgians retreat from Mons.
28th, Austria-Hungary declares war on Belgium.

Sept: 1st, in Russia, the name of St Petersburg is changed to Petrograd.
5th, (–10th) Battle of the Marne; 10th (–13th), Germans retreat, stabilizing their line along the River Aisne.

Oct: 12th, (–11th Nov) on Western Front, First Battle of Ypres (Belgium), when Germans attempt to break the Allied line.

Nov: 2nd, Russia declares war on Turkey.
5th, France and Britain declare war on Turkey.

Politics, Government, Law, and Economy

Currency and Bank Notes Act, repealing Bank Charter Act, 1844, empowers Bank of England to issue £1 and 10-shilling notes.

(Aug) Defence of the Realm Act passed in Britain, conferring emergency powers on the government.

(15th Aug) Opening of the Panama Canal; about 6,000 workers died during its construction.

Society, Education, and Religion

Education (Provision of Meals) Act in England places a duty on local education authorities to provide school dinners.

Germany enacts a system of maternity benefits.

Science, Technology, and Discovery

Edward Calvin Kendall isolates thyroxine from thyroid gland.

Music

Gustav Holst, *The Planets* (–1916; first performed, 1918).

Literature

James Joyce, *Dubliners*.
Miguel de Unamuno, *Niebla*.

Everyday Life

Elastic brassiere invented in New York by Mary Phelps Jacob; it finds much more commercial favour than previous bra designs.

Statistics

Defence estimates (in £ millions): Germany, 110.8; Russia, 88.2; Great Britain, 76.8; France, 57.4; Austria-Hungary, 36.4; Italy, 28.2.

Army strengths (at mobilization in millions): Germany, 4.2; France, 3.7; Russia, 1.2; Austria-Hungary, 0.8; Great Britain, 0.7; Italy, 0.7.

1915

Jan: 12th, in USA, the House of Representatives defeats proposal for women's suffrage.

Feb: 19th, British and French fleets bombard Turkish forts at the entrance to the Dardanelles.

April: 22nd, (–27th May) on Western Front, Second Battle of Ypres: a German offensive pushes the Front in SW Belgium forward by 5 km/3 mi.
22nd, on Western Front, at Langemark near Ypres, Germans use poison gas from cylinders for the first time.
25th, in Turkey, Allied landings on the Gallipoli Peninsula (British and French at Cape Helles; Australians and New Zealanders or ANZACS at Anzac Cove).
26th, secret Treaty of London between Britain, France, and Italy; Italy to join war and at its end to be awarded land and reparations from Germany and Austria-Hungary.

May: 1st, US vessel *Gulflight* sunk by German submarines without warning.
2nd, (–30th Sept) on Eastern Front, Austro-German offensive in Galicia (NE Austria-Hungary) breaks Russian lines.
4th, Italy denounces its Triple Alliance with Germany and Austria-Hungary (which had been renewed in Dec 1912).
7th, Germans sink the British liner *Lusitania* off the S coast of Ireland; 1,198 perish, including 128 US citizens.
23rd, Italy declares war on Austria-Hungary and seizes several areas of land belonging to Austria-Hungary.
26th, British Prime Minister Asquith forms a coalition government, with A J Balfour as first lord of the admiralty and Reginald McKenna chancellor of the exchequer; Winston Churchill leaves the admiralty for the chancellorship of Duchy of Lancaster; a new Ministry of Munitions is created with Lloyd George as minister.

June: 23rd, (–7th July) First Battle of the Isonzo: Italians try to force bridgeheads held by Austrians on River Isonzo beyond NE Italy.

Aug: 25th, Italy declares war on Turkey.

Sept: 8th, Tsar Nicholas II takes personal command of the Russian armies.

Oct: 12th, Germans execute the British nurse Edith Cavell in Brussels for harbouring British and French prisoners and aiding escapes.

12th, Allies declare they will assist Serbia under Bucharest treaty of 10th Aug 1913.

Dec: 18th, (–19th) Allied troops withdraw from Suvla and Anzac on the Gallipoli Peninsula.

Society, Education, and Religion

Women's Institute (WI) founded in Britain.

In Georgia, USA, William J Simmons revives the anti-black Ku Klux Klan.

Science, Technology, and Discovery

Albert Einstein in Germany proposes his general theory of relativity which explains the origin of gravity.

Art, Sculpture, Fine Arts, and Architecture

Painting Marcel Duchamp, *The Large Glass* or *The Bride Stripped Bare by her Bachelors, Even* (–1923).

Pablo Picasso, *Harlequin*.

Music

'Pack Up Your Troubles in Your Old Kit Bag', words by George Asaff, music by Felix Powell.

Literature

Rupert Brooke, *1914 and Other Poems*.

John Buchan, *The Thirty-Nine Steps*.

D H Lawrence, *The Rainbow*.

Ezra Pound, *Cathay* (poems).

Media

Lord Beaverbrook buys the *Daily Express* in Britain.

1916

Feb: 21st, (–18th Dec) on Western Front, Battle of Verdun: Germans try to capture the French city of Verdun, but meet determined resistance; the Germans and French suffer about 400,000 casualties each.

March: 17th, (–4th April) in Scotland, strike of workers in munitions factories along River Clyde.

20th, Allies agree on partition of Turkey.

April: 24th, (–29th) Easter Rising in Dublin by members of the Irish Republican Brotherhood supported by Sinn Féin (15 leaders are later executed).

May: 31st, (–1st June) in North Sea, Battle of Jutland: major clash of British and German surface fleets; British lost most ships, but the German fleet remained in harbour for the rest of the war.

June: 4th, (–10th Aug) on Eastern Front, the Brusilov offensive: Russian armies commanded by Alexei Brusilov push back the Austro-Hungarian line south of the Pripet Marshes; German reinforcements blunt the attack.

23rd, Convention of Ulster Nationalists agrees to exclude Ulster under Government of Ireland Act.

July: 1st, (–19th Nov) on Western Front, Battle of the Somme: massive offensive by French and British troops, which gains 8 km/5 mi; the British army suffers 60,000 casualties (including 20,000 dead) on the first day; during the campaign British and French casualties exceed 620,000 and German casualties amount to about 450,000.

Aug: 27th, Romania joins the Allies and declares war on Austria-Hungary; it starts an offensive in Transylvania (then in Hungary).

28th, Italy declares war on Germany.

30th, Turkey declares war on Russia.

Oct: 16th, Allies occupy Athens.

Nov: 7th, Woodrow Wilson, Democrat, is re-elected US president with 277 electoral votes against Charles E Hughes, Republican, with 254 votes; popular vote: Wilson, 9,129,606; Hughes, 8,538,221; A L Benson, 585,113.

29th, the Sheriff of Mecca, Hussein, is proclaimed King of the Arabs.

Dec: 7th, in Britain, David Lloyd George is appointed prime minister, forms a coalition government, and (on 10th Dec) forms war cabinet, including the Conservatives A J Balfour, Andrew Bonar Law, Lord Curzon, and Lord Milner, and the Labour leader Arthur Henderson.

20th, President Wilson of USA issues 'peace note' to belligerents in European war.

Society, Education, and Religion

In Britain, the first Military Service Act (given royal assent on 27th Jan) introduces compulsory military service for single men; a second act (royal assent, 25th May) extends conscription to married men.

Wilfredo Pareto, *Treatise of General Sociology*.
Foundation of the School of Oriental and African Studies, London University.
(1st June) War Food Office established in Germany to rationalize price controls; the disastrous harvest of 1916 leads to severe rationing and the 'turnip winter' of early 1917.
(7th Dec) In elections to the US Congress, Miss Jeanette Rankin is the first woman to be returned, as a member of the House of Representatives for Montana.

Science, Technology, and Discovery

Development of the first effective military tanks (first used in battle at the Somme, France, 15th Sept).
The British government establishes a Department of Scientific and Industrial Research.
Treatment of war casualties stimulates development of plastic surgery.
F W Mott develops the theory of shell-shock.

Art, Sculpture, Fine Arts, and Architecture

The term 'Dada' is coined in Zurich, possibly by Tristan Tzara; the Dada movement (producing iconoclastic 'anti-art' works) lasts until 1922.
Painting Claude Monet, *Water Lilies* (murals at the Musée d'orangerie, Paris).

Music

Richard Strauss, *Ariadne auf Naxos* (opera, second version).
Period of emergence of term 'jazz' for syncopated, improvizational, highly rhythmic music of black origin, originating in the southern USA.

Literature

James Joyce, *Portrait of the Artist as a Young Man.*
Drama Harold Brighouse, *Hobson's Choice.*
Eugene O'Neill, *Bound East.*

Everyday Life

National Savings movement launched in Britain to raise money for the war effort.
British Summer Time (daylight saving) introduced in Britain.

Sport and Recreation

The 6th Olympic Games, scheduled for Berlin, are cancelled due to the War.

Media

Forward, British Labour newspaper, suppressed for inciting Clydeside workers to refuse making munitions.

1917

Jan: 16th, Greece accepts Allied ultimatum of Dec 1916, demanding withdrawal of forces from Thessaly.

Feb: 1st, Germany declares policy of unrestricted submarine warfare.
12th, US President Wilson refuses to reopen negotiations with Germany until it abandons unrestricted naval warfare.

March: 8th, (–14th) (old style, 23rd Feb–1st March) the 'February Revolution' in Russia: striking workers are joined, 10th, by soldiers; 14th the Duma establishes a provisional government, headed by Prince G E Lvov.
15th, in Russia, Tsar Nicholas II abdicates throne for himself and son; his brother Grand Duke Michael refuses the throne, ending the Romanov dynasty's rule.
16th, on Western Front, German troops withdraw to the specially constructed 'Hindenburg Line' between Arras and Soissons.

April: 6th, USA declares war on Germany.

May: 18th, Prince Lvov reforms cabinet in Russia to include socialists; Alexander Kerensky becomes minister of war.

June: 14th, American Expeditionary Force, commanded by General John J Pershing, arrives in France.
16th, first all-Russian congress of Soviets ('councils') held in Petrograd.
18th, (–13th July) on Eastern Front, Russian minister of war, Alexander Kerensky, launches the Kerensky offensive: a series of attacks against the Germans, which are quickly repulsed.
19th, British royal family renounces German names and titles, having adopted name of Windsor.
24th, Russian Black Sea fleet mutinies at Sebastopol.
29th, Greece declares war on the Central Powers.

July: 16th, (–17th) in Petrograd, mass demonstrations against the provisional government; Bolsheviks attempt to encourage an insurrection, but crowds melt away.
19th, (–4th Aug) on Eastern Front, counteroffensive by Germans and Austro-Hungarians; the Russian line is pushed back.
21st, in Russia, Alexander Kerensky replaces Prince Lvov as prime minister.

31st, (–10th Nov) on Western Front, Third Battle of Ypres (or Battle of Passchendaele): British forces in Belgium advance about 13 km/8 mi at cost of massive casualties.

Aug: 14th, China declares war on Germany and Austria.

Sept: 9th, General Lavr Kornilov, dismissed as Russian commander in chief, sends cavalry force to Petrograd; submits to delegates from soviets and workers (Kornilov is later arrested).

14th, in Russia, prime minister Kerensky declares a republic.

Oct: 24th, (–10th Nov) on the Italian Front, the Battle of Caporetto: Austro-Hungarians and Germans break the Italian line; Italians regroup along the River Piave.

Nov: 2nd, British foreign secretary A J Balfour issues the 'Balfour declaration' on Palestine in a letter to Lord Rothschild: Britain favours the establishment of a national home for the Jewish people without prejudice to non-Jewish communities.

6th, on Western Front, in SW Belgium, Canadians and British capture Passchendaele Ridge.

7th, (old style, 26th Oct) in Russia, the 'October Revolution': Lenin and Bolsheviks seize the Winter Palace in Petrograd, overthrowing the provisional government.

7th, at meeting of All-Russian Congress of Soviets in Petrograd, most Menshevik and other socialists walk out, leaving the Bolsheviks in control; Lenin forms a Soviet of People's Commissars (composed of Bolsheviks) to be the new government.

Dec: 5th, German and Russian delegates sign armistice at Brest-Litovsk (in modern Belarus).

Society, Education, and Religion

Maude Royden becomes Assistant Preacher at the City Temple, London, the first Englishwoman to have a permanent pulpit.

(18th May) The Selective Service Act passed in the USA; it requires every male between 21 and 30 to register for the draft 5th June; local boards will select about half a million men for service.

Science, Technology, and Discovery

In USA, Clarence Birdseye develops freezing as a method for preserving food.

Art, Sculpture, Fine Arts, and Architecture

Pablo Picasso's sets and costumes for Sergei Diaghilev's ballet *Parade* are described by Guillaume Apollinaire as 'Surrealist' – first use of the term.

Piet Mondrian launches *de Stijl* magazine in Holland.

Literature

P G Wodehouse, *The Man with Two Left Feet* (collection of stories in which Jeeves and Wooster first appear).

In USA, Pulitzer Prizes are first awarded (for literature, journalism, and music).

T S Eliot, *Prufrock and Other Observations* (poems).

Drama Guillaume Apollinaire, *Les Mamelles de Tirésias*.

Everyday Life

Women's need to cut hair short for work in factories leads to a fashion for the 'bob'.

Media

In Russia, following the Bolshevik Revolution, *Pravda* becomes the leading newspaper, as mouthpiece of the Bolshevik (Communist) Party; *Izvestiya* is also founded.

1918

Jan: 8th, in message to US Congress, Woodrow Wilson propounds his 'Fourteen Points' for peace settlement (including principles of national self-determination, free trade, open diplomacy, and foundation of a league of nations).

18th, Russian Constituent Assembly opens in Petrograd but, 19th, is dispersed by Bolsheviks.

28th, Bolsheviks occupy Helsinki, Finland.

March: 3rd, peace treaty of Brest-Litovsk between Russia and the Central Powers (Germany and Austria-Hungary): Russia cedes Baltic Provinces and Russian Poland to Central Powers and recognizes independence of Finland and the Ukraine; Turkey to take former Russian districts of Kars, Ardahan, and Batum.

21st, (–17th July) on Western Front, German Spring offensive begins with the Second Battle of the Somme: Germans make great advance towards Paris.

23rd, Lithuania proclaims independence from Russia.

May: 7th, Romania signs the Peace of Bucharest with Germany and Austria-Hungary; Romania is allowed to annexe Bessarabia (but Russia refuses to recognize the annexation).

June: 9th, (–13th) on Western Front, German offensive near Compiègne.

15th, (–23rd) Battle of the Piave: Austro-Hungarians attack the Italian line but are repulsed.

21st, British government announces abandonment of Home Rule and conscription for Ireland.

July: 6th, Montagu–Chelmsford Report on Constitution of India published, advocating that Indian ministers be given charge of aspects of provincial government.

16th, in Russia, execution at Ekaterinburg (now Sverdlovsk) of ex-Tsar Nicholas II and family on orders of Ural Regional Council.

18th, (–10th Nov) on Western Front, Allied counteroffensive against Germans (with strong forward movement from 8th Aug).
22nd, on Western Front, Allies cross the River Marne.

Sept: 15th, Allied breakthrough in Bulgaria.
29th, the German quartermaster general, Ludendorff, and commander in chief, Hindenburg, advocate that Germany should become a constitutional monarchy and approach the Allies for an armistice.
30th, Bulgaria signs armistice with Allies.
30th, George, Count Hertling, German chancellor, resigns.

Oct: 12th, Germany and Austria agree to Woodrow Wilson's terms and that their troops should retreat to their own territory before an armistice is signed.
28th, mutiny of German sailors at Kiel.
30th, Allies sign armistice with Turkey on the warship *Agamemnon* at Mudros.
30th, Czechoslovakia proclaimed as an independent republic in Prague.

Nov: 3rd, Allies sign armistice with Austria-Hungary (to come into force on 4th).
4th, Allied conference at Versailles agrees on peace terms for Germany.
7th, Republic proclaimed in Bavaria, Germany.
9th, to forestall the proclamation of a communist republic in Germany, the Social Democrat Philipp Scheidemann proclaims a republic; Max Ebert replaces Prince Max as chancellor; Kaiser Wilhelm II flees to the Netherlands.
10th, in Germany, Ebert's government receives the support of the armed forces and of the workers' and soldiers' councils of Berlin.
11th, armistice between Allies and Germany in force (from 11 am).
13th, Soviet government annuls treaty of Brest-Litovsk.
18th, National Council proclaims independence of Latvia.

Dec: 4th, National Council proclaims formation of Kingdom of Serbs, Croats, and Slovenes with Alexander I (son of King Peter of Serbia) as prince-regent (country renamed Yugoslavia in 1929).
14th, in British general election, Coalition has majority of 249: Coalition Conservatives, 335, Coalition Liberals, 133, Coalition Labour, 10 (total Coalition, 478); Irish Unionists, 25; Irish Nationalists, 7; Conservatives, 23; Liberals, 28; Labour, 63; Sinn Féin, 73; others, 10.

Politics, Government, Law, and Economy

Oswald Spengler, *The Decline of the West*, Volume 1 (Volume 2 published in 1922).
(Feb) In Britain, the Labour Party adopts a constitution (drafted by Sidney Webb and Arthur Henderson), which includes 'clause IV' seeking 'Common Ownership of the Means of Production'.
(10th July) New constitution adopted in Russia, as basic document of the new Russian Soviet Federated Socialist Republic (RSFSR).

Society, Education, and Religion

'Fisher' Education Act raises school leaving-age in Britain to 14 and advocates part-time Day Continuation classes for school leavers.
Women over 30 achieve the right to vote in Britain, as do all men aged over 21 previously barred by residence and property qualifications.
Food shortage in Britain leads to establishment of National Food Kitchens (March) and rationing (14th July); the prime minister appeals to women to help with the harvest (25th June).
(–Spring 1919) 'Spanish flu' epidemic kills at least 20 million people in Europe, America, and India.

Humanities and Scholarship

Lytton Strachey, *Eminent Victorians*.

Art, Sculpture, Fine Arts, and Architecture

Amédée Ozenfant and Le Corbusier, *Après le Cubisme*, a manifesto on 'Purism'.
Painting Paul Klee, *Gartenplan*.
Paul Nash, *We are making a New World*.

Music

US soprano Rosa Ponselle makes her debut at the Metropolitan Opera, New York.
Establishment around this time of 78 revolutions per minute as the standard playing speed for records.
Béla Bartók, *Duke Bluebeard's Castle* (opera).
The Original Dixieland Jazz Band records 'Tiger Rag'.
First visit by a US jazz band to Britain, The Jazz Boys.

Literature
Alexander Blok, *The Twelve.*
Rupert Brooke, *Collected Poems* (posthumous).
Gerard Manley Hopkins, *Poems* (posthumous).
Drama Luigi Pirandello, *Six Characters in Search of an Author.*

Everyday Life
Three-colour traffic lights installed in New York.

Media
Film *Tarzan of the Apes* (the original version, starring Elmo Lincoln).

Statistics
Casualties, 1914–18 (in thousands):

	Killed	Wounded	Missing
British Empire	767	2,090	132
France	1,383	2,560	
Germany	1,686	4,211	991
Italy	564	1,030	
Russia*	1,700	2,500	
US	81	179	1

* to Peace of Brest-Litovsk.

1919 **Jan: 5th**, (–15th) Communist (Spartacist) revolt in Berlin.
5th, in Germany, formation of German Workers' Party (later National Socialist German Workers' Party) in Munich (12th Sept, Adolf Hitler attends for first time).
10th, (–4th Feb) Soviet Republic of Bremen, NW Germany.
15th, volunteer soldiers suppress the Spartacist rising in Berlin; the Spartacist leaders, Karl Liebknecht and Rosa Luxemburg, are arrested and shot.
18th, opening of Paris Peace Conference under chairmanship of Georges Clemenceau.
21st, Sinn Féin MPs elected to the Westminster parliament meet in Dublin as a constituent assembly for Ireland (the Dáil Eireann); they proclaim an Irish Republic and elect a president (Éamon de Valera) and ministers; meanwhile the Irish Republican Army (IRA) attacks British authorities in Ireland.
25th, Paris Peace Conference adopts principle of founding League of Nations.

Feb: 14th, Woodrow Wilson lays League of Nations Covenant before Paris Peace Conference (adopted 25th March).

March: 22nd, Soviet government formed in Budapest, Hungary.
23rd, in Italy, Benito Mussolini founds Fasci d'Italiani di Combattimento; i.e., the Italian Fascist movement.

April: 4th, Soviet Republic established in Bavaria (–1st May).
30th, Paris Peace Conference grants German concession in Shandong peninsula to Japan, whereupon China leaves the Conference.

May: 6th, Paris Peace Conference disposes of Germany's colonies, assigning German East Africa as a League of Nations mandate to Britain, and German South-West Africa as a mandate to South Africa.
7th, at Paris Peace Conference, Allies present terms to Germany without giving opportunity for negotiation: Germany to lose large areas of land; Rhineland to be demilitarized and part occupied for 5–15 years; Germany to pay reparations; limits placed on size of Germany's armed forces; Germany to accept the 'war guilt' clause acknowledging responsibility for World War.

June: 22nd, German national assembly at Weimar authorizes signature of peace treaty.
28th, German representatives sign the peace treaty in the Hall of Mirrors of the Palace of Versailles near Paris.

July: 12th, Irish MP Edward Carson demands repeal of Home Rule and threatens to call out Ulster Volunteers.
12th, Britain and France authorize resumption of commercial relations with Germany.
23rd, congress of Turkish nationalists convened at Erzurum, under leadership of Mustafa Kemal, to resist Allied dismemberment of Turkey (second congress held 4th Sept).

Aug: 9th, British–Persian agreement at Tehran to preserve integrity of Persia.
11th, in Germany, the national assembly promulgates the 'Weimar constitution'.

Sept: 10th, Allied peace treaty agreed with Austria at St Germain-en-Laye, near Paris.
12th, Gabriele d'Annunzio leads unofficial Italian army to seize Fiume before it is incorporated in Yugoslavia.

Oct: 28th, dissolution of British war cabinet.

Nov: 11th, two minutes' silence in memory of war victims first observed in Britain.
19th, US Senate votes against ratification of the Treaty of Versailles, thereby leaving the USA outside the League of Nations.
27th, Peace of Neuilly between the Allies and Bulgaria.

Dec: 20th, US House of Representatives moves to curtail immigration.

Politics, Government, Law, and Economy

Communist Third International founded to encourage world revolution; affiliation to this body marks the split between socialist and communist movements and Parties.
J M Keynes, *The Economic Consequences of the Peace.*
(28th June) The Treaty of Versailles requires Germany to pay reparations for damage caused during the war and establishes the League of Nations and the International Labour Organization.

Society, Education, and Religion

Women over 20 are enfranchised by the 'Weimar' German constitution.
Henri Bergson, *L'Energie spirituelle.*
Karl Barth, *The Epistle to the Romans.*
(29th Jan) In USA, the States ratify the 18th Amendment to the Constitution, which outlaws the manufacture, transport, and sale of alcoholic drinks (to take effect on 16th Jan 1920).
(15th March) Delegates from American Expeditionary Force, meeting in Paris, found the American Legion organization of veterans, to support veterans' welfare and the defence of the USA.
(27th July) Race riots in Chicago, USA, cause the deaths of 38 people; followed by riots and lynchings throughout the USA.
(29th Oct) International Labour Conference, inaugurating the International Labour Organization, opens in Washington, DC, USA.
(28th Nov) In Britain, Lady Nancy Astor is elected in a by-election as the first woman Member of Parliament to take her seat.

Science, Technology, and Discovery

First successful helicopter flight.
First motor scooter.
(14th June) (–15th June) British aviators John William Alcock and Arthur William Brown make the first non-stop trans-Atlantic flight, in 16 hrs 27 mins.

Art, Sculpture, Fine Arts, and Architecture

The Bauhaus (School of Design, Building, and Crafts) founded by Walter Gropius in Weimar (transferred to Dessau, 1925).
Painting Pablo Picasso, *Pitcher and Compotier with Apples*, sets for *The Three-Cornered Hat.*

Music

Manuel de Falla, *The Three Cornered Hat* (ballet).
(7th April) The Original Dixieland Jazz Band makes its debut in London.

Literature

Drama George Bernard Shaw, *Heartbreak House.*

Media

Film:
The Cabinet of Dr Caligari (director, Robert Wiene).

1920

Jan: 10th, ratification of the Treaty of Versailles brings the League of Nations into existence, with 29 initial members (out of 32 Allied signatories to the Versailles Treaty; the exceptions are the USA, China, Ecuador, and Nicaragua).
16th, in USA, Prohibition comes into force.
16th, US Senate votes against joining the League of Nations.

Feb: 2nd, in treaty signed at Tartu in Estonia, Russia recognizes independence of Estonia and renounces claims.
26th, in accordance with the Treaty of Versailles, the League of Nations takes over the Saar area between France and Germany; France takes control of the Saar's coal deposits.

March: 19th, the US Senate rejects the Versailles Treaty (and attached reservations).
28th, Bolsheviks take Novorossiisk on Black Sea; collapse of Anton Denikin's White Russian army.

April: 6th, (–17th May) while German troops are suppressing a rebellion in the Ruhr (a demilitarized area) French troops occupy Frankfurt, Darmstadt, and Hanau until German forces have withdrawn.
25th, Supreme Allied Council disposes of territories formerly in the Ottoman (Turkish) Empire: it assigns mandates over Mesopotamia and Palestine to Britain and over Syria and the Lebanon to France.

May: 20th, assassination of President Carranza of Mexico (in response the US government suspends diplomatic relations); Adolfo de la Huerta takes office as provisional president.

June: 4th, Treaty of Trianon between the Allies and Hungary: removes various territories from Hungary; imposes limits on Hungary's armed forces; requires Hungary to pay reparations.
21st, Supreme Allied Council agrees that Germany shall make 42 annual reparations payments largely to France, Britain, Italy, and Belgium.

July: 8th, Britain annexes East African Protectorate as Kenya Colony (a crown colony).

Aug: 10th, New States treaty between Allies, Romania, Czechoslovakia, and Poland; and frontier treaty with Romania, Czechoslovakia, and the Kingdom of the Serbs, Croats, and Slovenes (Yugoslavia).
10th, Treaty of Sèvres between the Allies and Turkey; the Treaty awards part of eastern Thrace, the district of Smyrna (modern Izmir) and other territory to Greece.
14th, Yugoslav–Czechoslovak alliance, which is joined, 17th, by Romania to form the 'Little Entente'.

Nov: 2nd, in US presidential election, Warren G Harding, Republican, wins with 404 electoral votes against James M Cox, Democrat, with 127; popular vote: Harding, 16,152,200; Cox, 9,147,353; Eugene V Debs, Socialist (in prison), 919,799.
12th, by treaty of Rapallo, Italy obtains Istria and cedes Dalmatia to the Kingdom of the Serbs, Croats, and Slovenes (Yugoslavia); Fiume is to be independent.
15th, Danzig (modern Gdańsk) is proclaimed a free city (in early Dec its constitutional assembly is proclaimed the city parliament).
16th, end of Russian civil war, with victory to the Bolsheviks.
19th, convention between Nicaragua, Honduras, and Costa Rica.

Dec: 23rd, British Parliament passes the Government of Ireland Act: Southern Ireland (26 counties) and Northern Ireland (6 counties) each to have own parliament.

Politics, Government, Law, and Economy

Following the establishment of the League of Nations, numerous countries become members (Argentina, 13th Jan; Switzerland, 13th Feb; Norway, 5th March; Denmark, 8th March; Netherlands, 10th March; Austria, 3rd Dec; Bulgaria, Costa Rica, Finland, and Latvia, 16th Dec; Albania, 17th Dec).

In USA, the 'Ponzi swindle' is exposed: Charles Ponzi defrauds over 20,000 investors of over $10 million with a scheme for using International Reply Coupons to make large profits; no money was in fact invested.

A deflationary Budget and a rise in Bank Rate halt the economic boom in Britain and prices and output fall steeply while unemployment rises over one million, where it remains for the entire interwar period; the US economy also suffers a sharp slump.

(25th June) The Hague is selected as seat of the International Court of Justice.

Society, Education, and Religion

(26th Aug) Ratification in USA of the 19th Amendment to the Constitution, permitting women to vote.

(7th Nov) (–21st Dec) Widespread famine in China.

Science, Technology, and Discovery

US gunsmith John T Thompson invents the sub-machine gun.

Art, Sculpture, Fine Arts, and Architecture

Spectators at the Exhibition of Dadaist art in Cologne, Germany, are provided with an axe to smash paintings.

Bernard Leach establishes Leach Pottery at St Ives, Cornwall, England.

Music

Marie Rambert founds the Rambert School of Ballet in London, leading to the establishment of the Marie Rambert Dancers.

French critic Henri Collet refers to the group of composers comprising Darius Milhaud, Francis Poulenc, Arthur Honegger, Louis Durey, Germaine Tailleferre, and Georges Auric as 'Les Six'.

Literature

Franz Kafka, *The Country Doctor.*

Katherine Mansfield (pseudonym), *Bliss.*

Wilfred Owen, *Collected Poems.*

Sigrid Undset, *Kristin Lavransdatter* (–1922).

Everyday Life

(7th Sept) First 'Miss America' beauty competition held in Atlantic City, New Jersey; winner is Miss Margaret Gorman.

Sport and Recreation

(20th April) (–12th Sept) The 7th Olympic Games are held in Antwerp, Belgium; the USA wins 41 gold medals; Sweden, 19; Britain and Finland, 15 each; Belgium, 14; Norway and Italy, 13.

(26th Aug) In England, cricketer Percy Fender, batting for Surrey, scores a century in 35 minutes against Northamptonshire in the County Championship match at Northampton.

Media

Press Association in Britain leases telegraph wires for news distribution.

Radio The Westinghouse Company in the USA establishes the KDKA station in East Pittsburgh, Pennsylvania (first broadcast, 2nd Nov 1920, of presidential election returns).

(Feb) In Britain, the Marconi company makes radio broadcasts from Chelmsford in Essex.

Statistics

Coal production (in million tons): US, 645.5; Great Britain, 229.5; Germany, 107.5.

Petroleum production (in million barrels): US, 443; Mexico, 163; Russia, 25; Dutch East Indies, 17; Persia, 12; India, 7; Roumania, 7; Poland, 5.

Motor vehicles licensed: US, 8,887,000; Great Britain, 663,000.

1921

Jan: 24th, (–29th) Paris conference of wartime Allies fixes Germany's reparation payments.

Feb: 9th, in India, state opening of central parliament (established under Government of India Act of 1919).

March: 8th, French troops occupy Düsseldorf and other towns in Ruhr because of Germany's failure to make preliminary reparations payment.

17th, in Britain, Andrew Bonar Law resigns leadership of Conservatives in Commons (21st, Austen Chamberlain elected leader).

20th, plebiscite held in Upper Silesia, part of pre-War Germany; 63% vote for incorporation with Germany.

23rd, Germany announces that it will be unable to pay £600 million due as reparations on 1st May.

April: 27th, Reparations Commission fixes Germany's liability at 132,000 million gold marks (£6,650 million).

May: 5th, Allied Supreme Council warns Germany that failure to accept the reparations figure, by 12th May, will lead to occupation of Ruhr.

6th, peace treaty signed between Germany and Russia.

10th, in German cabinet crisis Karl Joseph Wirth, Catholic Centre Party, becomes chancellor (11th, Reichstag votes to accept Allies' ultimatum on reparations).

14th, in Italian elections, 35 Fascists are returned.

June: 7th, opening of new Parliament of Northern Ireland in Belfast, with Sir James Craig as first prime minister of Northern Ireland (–1940, from 1927 as Viscount Craigavon).

July: 25th, Belgium and Luxembourg sign 50-year economic pact.

Aug: 29th, (–16th Dec) state of emergency proclaimed in Germany in the face of economic crisis.

Sept: 30th, French troops evacuate Ruhr.

Nov: 12th, (–6th Feb 1922) in USA, Washington Conference on disarmament.

12th, rapid fall of the German Mark.

Dec: 13th, USA, British Empire, France, and Japan sign Washington Treaty to respect each other's rights over insular possessions in the Pacific; by this treaty the USA is drawn into consultation with other powers in matters of common concern.

29th, USA, British Empire, France, Italy, and Japan sign Washington Treaty to limit naval armaments.

Politics, Government, Law, and Economy

In Britain, Lord and Lady Lee of Fareham donate the 'Chequers' house and estate near London for use by the prime minister, with an endowment to maintain the estate and pay for the minister's weekend visits (Lloyd George holds house-warming on 8th Jan 1921).

(17th March) At the 10th Congress of the Russian Communist Party, Lenin introduces his New Economic Policy (NEP), which restores some private business and freedom of trade, and affirms peasant ownership of land.

Society, Education, and Religion

(24th May) Foundation of British Legion, to provide care for ex-servicemen and women.

Science, Technology, and Discovery

Ernest Rutherford and James Chadwick disintegrate all elements, except carbon, oxygen, lithium and beryllium, as a preliminary experiment to splitting the atom (–1924).

In Canada, Frederick Banting and C H Best isolate insulin and a diabetic patient in Toronto receives an insulin injection.

Humanities and Scholarship

Institute of Historical Research, London, founded, with A F Pollard as director.

Art, Sculpture, Fine Arts, and Architecture

Painting Henri Matisse, *The Moorish Screen, Odalisque with Red Culottes* – first Matisse bought by a French museum.

Georges Braque, *Still Life with Guitar.*

Music

In Austria, Salzburg Festival established.

Arthur Honegger, *Le Roi David* (dramatic oratorio).

Sergey Prokofiev, *The Love for Three Oranges* (opera).

Literature

Aldous Huxley, *Crome Yellow.*

D H Lawrence, *Women in Love.*

John Dos Passos, *Three Soldiers.*

Italo Svevo, *The Confessions of Zeno.*

Drama Eugene O'Neill, *Anna Christie, The Emperor Jones.*

Everyday Life

(5th May) Chanel No. 5 perfume launched.

Sport and Recreation

Batting against South Africa in the second cricket Test at Johannesburg, Jack Gregory of Australia scores the fastest century in Test cricket history: in 70 minutes off 67 deliveries.

Media

Film *The Sheik* (starring Rudolph Valentino).

The Kid (starring Charlie Chaplin).

Radio First medium-wave wireless broadcast, in USA.

Statistics

Populations (in millions): USSR, 136; US, 107; Japan, 78; Germany, 60; Great Britain, 42.7; France, 39.2; Italy, 38.7.

1922

Jan: 7th, in Ireland, the Dáil Eireann ratifies the British–Irish Treaty by 64 to 57 (Éamon de Valera resigns as president; 9th, replaced by Arthur Griffith).

15th, Michael Collins becomes the first prime minister of the Irish Free State and forms a provisional government.

Feb: 1st, in USA, Washington conference approves treaties restricting submarine warfare and poison gas.

11th, nine-power Treaty of Washington for securing China's independence and maintaining the 'open door'.

11th, USA–Japan naval agreement.

March: 10th, in South Africa, strikes and martial law in Johannesburg.

15th, modified reparations agreement, for Germany to pay with raw materials, signed by France and Germany (31st, approved by Reparations Commission).

15th, in Ireland, Éamon de Valera organizes a Republican Society, to fight the Pro-Treaty Party (Cumann na nGaedheal).

15th, the Sultan of Egypt assumes the title of king as Fuad I; Sudan comes under joint British–Egyptian sovereignty.

18th, in India, Mahatma Gandhi sentenced to six years' imprisonment for civil disobedience.

April: 16th, Rapallo Treaty between Germany and Russia: Germany recognizes Russia as 'a great power' and both sides waive reparations claims; the treaty leads to the resumption of diplomatic and trade relations, and to cooperation between the two countries' armies.

June: 16th, election in the Irish Free State gives majority to Pro-Treaty candidates (58, against 35 anti-Treaty Republicans); anti-Treaty Republicans continue to oppose the new government, with the IRA taking large areas under its control.

28th, in Dublin, anti-Treaty Republicans seize the assistant chief of staff of the Irish army and hold him hostage in the Four Courts building; the Irish army besieges the building, destroying the Irish public records (30th, rebel forces surrender).

July: 2nd, (–5th) in Irish Free State, heavy fighting in Dublin.

20th, Council of League of Nations approves mandates for the former German colonies Togoland (now Togo), the Cameroons, and Tanganyika (now Tanzania) and (24th) for Palestine.

31st, general strike begins in Italy, protesting at weakness of state in face of Fascist agitation;

Fascists use the strike as the opportunity to seize power in several cities (including Milan and Genoa).

Aug: 22nd, Michael Collins (aged 31), prime minister of the Irish provisional government, killed by Republican ambush in west Cork.

Sept: 11th, British mandate proclaimed in Palestine while Arabs declare a day of mourning.

27th, King Constantine of Greece abdicates for second time (departs, 30th); succeeded by crown prince George.

Oct: 19th, in Britain, following the 'Chanak Crisis' of Sept–Oct (when Lloyd George reinforced British troops at Chanak on the Dardanelles and threatened Turkey), Conservatives withdraw from the coalition government; Lloyd George resigns as prime minister (23rd, Andrew Bonar Law forms Conservative ministry).

24th, in Ireland, the Dáil adopts a constitution for Irish Free State, which provides for a governor-general to represent the British crown.

28th, in Italy, Fascists march on Rome; Prime Minister Facta proposes state of emergency, but King Victor Emanuel refuses to sign the decree (30th, Mussolini goes to Rome at the king's invitation and, 31st, forms government composed of Liberals and Nationalists as well as Fascists).

Nov: 1st, Kemal Pasha (Mustafa Kemal) proclaims Turkish republic and abolition of the Sultanate.

1st, civil war renewed in China.

17th, in British general election, Conservatives win 345 seats, Labour 142, Lloyd George Liberals 62, and Asquith Liberals 54.

Dec: 6th, the Dáil of the Irish Free State and the British Parliament ratify the British–Irish Treaty; Tim Healy is appointed governor-general.

7th, Northern Ireland Parliament votes against inclusion in Irish Free State.

30th, establishment of the Union of Soviet Socialist Republics (USSR) through confederation of Russia, Belarus, the Ukraine, and the Transcaucasian Federation.

Politics, Government, Law, and Economy

In Britain the budget makes expenditure cuts of £64 million, mainly in military spending but also in the civil service, following recommendations made by the Committee on National Expenditure chaired by Sir Eric Geddes (the reductions are popularly known as the 'Geddes Axe').

Fordney–McCumber tariff passed in USA, raising tariffs to the highest level ever.

Austin Seven production begins, making it the first British mass-produced car.

USA sets up the 'Prohibition Navy' to prevent widespread liquor smuggling.

Society, Education, and Religion

Marie Stopes holds meetings in London to campaign for birth control.

In Britain the 'Geddes Axe' expenditure cuts include £6 million from education, curtailing the implementation of provisions of 1918 Education Act ('Fisher Act').

(6th Feb) Following the death of Pope Benedict XV (22nd Jan), Ambrogio Ratti is elected Pope and takes the name Pius XI.

Humanities and Scholarship

Ludwig Wittgenstein, *Tractatus Logico-Philosophicus.*

(4th Nov) Howard Carter, supported by Lord Carnarvon, discovers the tomb of Pharaoh Tutankhamun at Luxor, the only ancient Egyptian pharaoh's tomb discovered complete with grave goods.

Art, Sculpture, Fine Arts, and Architecture

Clive Bell publishes *Since Cézanne.*

David Low, *Lloyd George and Co.* (a book of political cartoons).

Music

William Walton, *Façade* ('entertainment' to poems by Edith Sitwell).

Literature

T S Eliot, *The Waste Land.*

James Joyce, *Ulysses* (published in Paris).

Katharine Mansfield, *The Garden Party.*

Rainer Maria Rilke, *Sonette an Orpheus.*

Drama Bertolt Brecht, *Drums in the Night.*

Media

Radio (14th Nov) Following a decision that radio broadcasting should come within control of the Post Office, the British Broadcasting Company makes its first broadcast, on station 2LO (though the company is not licensed until 18th Jan 1923); John Reith is appointed general manager; the broadcasts include commercials.

1923 **Jan:** **11th**, because of Germany's failure to meet reparations payments, French and Belgian troops occupy the Ruhr; Germans respond with passive resistance and sabotage; the occupiers make arrests and deportations, and cut off the Rhineland from the rest of Germany.

March: **3rd**, US Senate rejects proposal to join International Court of Justice.

May: **20th**, British prime minister Andrew Bonar Law resigns because of ill health; 22nd, Stanley Baldwin forms Conservative ministry, with Neville Chamberlain as chancellor of exchequer.

29th, Palestine constitution suspended by British order in council because of Arabs' refusal to cooperate.

July: **6th**, the USSR (and its new constitution) formally comes into existence.

24th, Treaty of Lausanne between Greece, Turkey, and the Allies; Greece to give up Eastern Thrace; Turkey obtained the islands of Imbros and Tenedos.

Aug: **2nd**, in USA, President Harding dies suddenly (aged 57); succeeded, 3rd, by Vice President Calvin Coolidge.

Sept: **1st**, severe earthquake in Japan destroys all of Yokohama and most of Tokyo; about half a million people are killed.

14th, Miguel Primo de Rivera assumes dictatorship in Spain (ruling under King Alfonso XIII).

27th, state of emergency declared in Germany, under article 48 of the constitution.

29th, British mandate in Palestine begins.

Oct: **1st**, failure of Black Reichswehr *coup d'état* in Germany.

11th, value of German Mark drops to rate of 10,000 million to £.

26th, (–8th Nov) British Empire conference in London; recognizes the right of Dominions to make treaties with foreign powers.

29th, amendment to Turkish constitution passed: Turkey to be a republic; Mustafa Kemal is elected president.

Nov: **8th**, (–9th) the 'Munich Putsch': Adolf Hitler and National Socialists attempt a *coup d'état* in Munich.

Dec: **6th**, in British general election the Conservatives, standing on platform of using a protective tariff to relieve unemployment, lose heavily (Conservatives, 258 seats, Labour, 191, Liberal, 159).

Politics, Government, Law, and Economy

Interpol police coordination body founded at a Vienna conference.

A Marshall, *Money, Credit and Commerce.*

Science, Technology, and Discovery

British metallurgist John B Tytus invents continuous hot-strip rolling of steel.

Humanities and Scholarship

J B Bury (ed.), *The Cambridge Ancient History*; the first volume published is Bury's *History of the Later Roman Empire.*

Georg Lukács, *History and Class Consciousness.*

Music

Opening of the Cotton Club in Harlem, New York, providing black music and entertainment for a white audience.

Zoltán Kodály, *Psalmus Hungaricus.*

Literature

Drama James Elroy Flecker, *Hassan.*

Luigi Pirandello, *The Late Mattia Pascal.*

Everyday Life

The first recognizable supermarket is opened in San Francisco, USA.

Sport and Recreation

(28th April) In Britain, the Football Association Cup Final is held at Wembley Stadium, London, for the first time; a crowd estimated at 200,000 sees Bolton Wanderers beat West Ham United 2–0.

Media

In the USA, Henry A Luce and Briton Hadden found the weekly news magazine *Time.*

Film *Safety Last* (starring Harold Lloyd).

1924 **Jan:** **21st**, death of Soviet leader Lenin (3rd Feb, Alexei Rykoff becomes prime minister).

21st, in China, Congress of the Guomindang, the Chinese nationalist party, in Guangzhou, which admits communists to the party and welcomes Soviet advisers.

22nd, following defeat of Conservatives in general election (Dec 1923), British prime minister Stanley Baldwin resigns.

23rd, Ramsay MacDonald forms first Labour government (without an overall majority) in Britain, with Philip Snowden as chancellor of the exchequer.

March: 3rd, the Turkish national assembly expels the Ottoman dynasty, abolishes the caliphate and other religious institutions, and establishes a commissariat of public instruction.

9th, Italy annexes the independent city of Fiume but abandons claims to Yugoslavia's Dalmatian coast.

25th, Greece is proclaimed a republic (confirmed by plebiscite 13th April; Admiral Pavlos Koundouriotis becomes president).

May: 4th, in elections to the German parliament, the Reichstag, Nationalists (95 seats) and Communists (62 seats) strengthen their position against the Social Democrats (100) and Centre Party (65); for the first time, the National Socialists/Nazi Party enter the Reichstag with 32 seats.

June: 10th, abduction of Giacomo Matteotti, an Italian Socialist deputy who had attacked Mussolini's government; during June, when it becomes clear that Matteotti has been murdered, opposition deputies withdraw from the Chamber (the 'Aventine Secession'); Matteotti's corpse is found on 15th Aug.

30th, in South Africa, J B Hertzog, Nationalist Party leader, forms ministry with Labour support, following defeat of J C Smuts' South African Party in elections.

July: 11th, (–15th) rioting between Hindus and Muslims in Delhi.

16th, at London conference on reparations, attended by Gustav Stresemann and Édouard Herriot, the Dawes Report (or Dawes Plan), which removes reparations from the sphere of political controversy, is approved.

Aug: 16th, French delegates at London conference agree to evacuate the Ruhr within a year (18th, French troops leave Offenburg region).

Oct: 9th, in Britain, Parliament is dissolved following defeat of Labour on question of prosecution of the acting editor of *Workers' Weekly*, J R Campbell, for inciting soldiers to mutiny rather than be used to break strikes.

25th, the British Foreign Office publishes the 'Zinoviev Letter', a document inciting revolutionary activity in the army and Ireland, which was said to be by Grigori Zinoviev, chairman of the External Committee of the Comintern (the Soviet-controlled Communist International).

29th, Conservatives win British general election with 415 seats against Labour, 151, and Liberals, 44.

Nov: 4th, Calvin Coolidge, Republican, wins US presidential election with 382 electoral votes, over J W Davis, Democrat, 136, and Robert M LaFollette, Progressive, 13; popular vote: Coolidge, 15,725,016; Davis, 8,386,503; LaFollette, 4,822,856.

4th, Ramsay MacDonald resigns as British prime minister; a week later Stanley Baldwin forms a Conservative government with Austen Chamberlain as foreign secretary and Winston S Churchill as chancellor of the exchequer.

Politics, Government, Law, and Economy

In USA, J Edgar Hoover is appointed acting director of the Bureau of Investigation (later the Federal Bureau of Investigation).

In USA, the Computing-Tabulating-Recording Company is renamed International Business Machines (IBM).

Society, Education, and Religion

(26th May) The Johnson–Reed Act in the USA reduces the maximum number of European immigrants permitted each year to 164,000 and bans Japanese.

Science, Technology, and Discovery

Louis de Broglie in France argues that particles can also behave as waves, laying the foundations for wave mechanics.

The first insecticide is developed.

Humanities and Scholarship

Ancient Monuments Society founded in England.

Art, Sculpture, Fine Arts, and Architecture

Fernand Léger makes film *Ballet Mécanique*.

Painting Stanley Spencer, *The Resurrection, Cookham* (–1926).

Gwen John, *The Convalescent*.

Music

George Gershwin, *Rhapsody in Blue*.

Literature

E M Forster, *A Passage to India*.

Thomas Mann, *The Magic Mountain*.

Drama George Bernard Shaw, *St. Joan.*

Sport and Recreation

(25 Jan) (–4th Feb) 1st Winter Olympic Games are held at Chamonix, France.

(4 May) (–27th July) The 8th Olympic Games are held in Paris. The USA wins 45 gold medals; Finland, 14; France, 13; Britain and Italy, 9 each; Switzerland, 7; Norway, 5. Paavo Nurmi of Finland wins a record 5 golds, for the 1,500-m, 5,000-m, 10,000-m (both individual and team), and the 3,000-m team event.

Media

Film *Alice's Wonderland* (first cartoon by Walt Disney).

'Fonofilm' system of talking pictures is developed.

Statistics

Coal production (in million tons): US, 485; Great Britain, 267.1; Germany, 124.6; France, 44.9.

Steel production (in million tons): US, 45; Germany, 9.3; Great Britain, 8.2; France, 6.9.

1925

Jan: 1st, Christiania, the Norwegian capital, resumes name of Oslo (disused in 1624).

3rd, in Italy, Mussolini announces that he will take dictatorial powers.

April: 25th, Paul von Hindenburg, the former military leader, is elected president of Germany; he entered the contest only in the second ballot and wins 48.5% of the popular vote against 45.2% for Wilhelm Marx of the Centre Party.

Oct: 12th, Soviet–German commercial treaty.

5th, (–16th) Locarno Conference, discussing question of security pact, strikes a balance between French and German interests by drafting treaties (a) guaranteeing the French–German and Belgian–German frontiers; (b) between Germany and France, Belgium, Czechoslovakia, and Poland respectively; (c) a mutual guarantee between France, Czechoslovakia, and Poland. Britain is involved in the guarantee of Franco–Belgian–German frontiers but not in the arrangements in Eastern Europe.

Dec: 1st, Locarno treaties signed in London.

Politics, Government, Law, and Economy

Lord Beaverbrook, *Politicians and the Press.*

Adolf Hitler, *Mein Kampf/My Struggle*, Vol. 1.

Society, Education, and Religion

Songs of Praise (edited by Percy Dearmer).

(1st Jan) Mrs Ross of Wyoming becomes first woman state governor in USA, when she takes office to complete her late husband's term.

(July) Trial of John T Scopes in Dayton, Tennessee, USA, for teaching evolutionary theory, in contravention of a recent state act; Scope was found guilty but the conviction was later overturned on a legal technicality; the trial seen widely as a humiliation for the Fundamentalist cause.

Science, Technology, and Discovery

Austrian-US physicist Joseph Goldberger isolates vitamins B and B_2.

Art, Sculpture, Fine Arts, and Architecture

Architecture Walter Gropius, The Bauhaus, Dessau (–1926).

Painting Pablo Picasso, *Three Dancers.*

Sculpture Alfred Gibert, The Shaftesbury Memorial ('*Eros*').

Music

Alban Berg, *Wozzeck* (opera).

Dmitry Shostakovich, Symphony No. 1.

Literature

Lion Feuchtwanger, *Jew Süss* (written 1921).

John Dos Passos, *Manhattan Transfer.*

F Scott Fitzgerald, *The Great Gatsby.*

Franz Kafka, *The Trial* (posthumous).

P G Wodehouse, *Carry on Jeeves.*

Virginia Woolf, *Mrs Dalloway.*

Drama Noël Coward, *Hay Fever.*

Sean O'Casey, *Juno and the Paycock.*

Everyday Life

Clarence Birdseye in USA extends deep-freezing process to pre-cooked foods.

The 'Charleston' takes New York dance halls by storm.

Sport and Recreation

(18th Aug) Batting for Surrey against Somerset at Taunton, English cricketer J B Hobbs surpasses W G Grace's record of 126 centuries in first-class cricket.

Media

Publication of *The New Yorker*, founded by Harold Ross.

(10th July) Tass press agency founded in USSR.

Film *The Battleship Potemkin* (director, Sergei Eisenstein).

The Gold Rush (starring Charlie Chaplin).

1926

Jan: 8th, in Mecca, following conquests in Arabia and the abdication of Hussein ibn Ali, king of Hejaz (on 5th Oct 1924), Ibn Saud is proclaimed king of Hejaz.

Feb: 10th, Germany applies for admission to League of Nations (17th March, Brazil and Spain block Germany's admission, protesting against the plan to give Germany a seat on the Council, which they thought they should have instead).

March: 11th, Éamon de Valera resigns as leader of Sinn Féin.

May: 3rd, (–12th) in Britain, first (and only) General Strike.

12th, (–14th) in Poland, Józef Pilsudski and army units march on Warsaw and seize power (14, President Wojciechowski and Prime Minister Witos resign; the speaker of parliament becomes acting president).

16th, in Irish Free State, Éamon de Valera founds Fianna Fáil ('Soldiers of Destiny'), thereby splitting the anti-treaty party.

23rd, France proclaims the Lebanon a republic.

Sept: 6th, in China, the Guomindang nationalist forces led by Chiang Kai-shek reach Hankou at the confluence of the Han and the Yangzi rivers; Hankou becomes the Guomindang capital.

8th, Germany is admitted to the League, and in consequence Spain leaves (11th).

Oct: 19th, (–18th Nov) Imperial Conference in London, which decides that Britain and the Dominions are autonomous communities, equal in status.

19th, in USSR, expulsion of Leon Trotsky and Grigory Zinoviev from the Politburo of the Communist Party, following Joseph Stalin's victory.

Nov: —, in Italy, the Socialist, Republican, and Communist Parties are dissolved and the abstaining anti-Fascist deputies are declared to have forfeited their parliamentary seats.

Politics, Government, Law, and Economy

Beatrice Webb, *My Apprenticeship*.

France returns to the gold standard.

(8th Nov) British Parliament appoints the Simon Commission, to examine the working of the 1919 Government of India Act.

Society, Education, and Religion

Foundation of the Council for the Preservation of Rural England.

Science, Technology, and Discovery

F Lindemann, *The Physical Significance of the Quantum Theory*.

Humanities and Scholarship

M Rostovtzeff, *Social and Economic History of the Roman Empire*.

R H Tawney, *Religion and the Rise of Capitalism*.

Art, Sculpture, Fine Arts, and Architecture

Architecture Le Corbusier, *The Coming Architecture* published.

Painting Stanley Spencer, Murals for Burghclere Chapel, Berkshire (–1932).

Music

Zoltán Kodály, *Háry János* (opera).

Giacomo Puccini, *Turandot* (posthumous opera).

Literature

Franz Kafka, *The Castle* (posthumous).

T E Lawrence, *Seven Pillars of Wisdom*.

A A Milne, *Winnie the Pooh*.

Drama Sean O'Casey, *The Plough and the Stars*.

Media

Film *Metropolis* (director, Fritz Lang).

Ben Hur (starring Ramon Navarro).

Radio Following concern about the control of radio in Britain, the BBC is incorporated by royal charter as the British Broadcasting Corporation (effective from 1st Jan 1927), run by a crown-appointed chairman and governors and financed by a licence fee.

Television (26th Jan) John Logie Baird demonstrates a workable television system in Soho, London, using mechanical scanning by Nipkow disc.

Statistics

Populations (in millions): USSR, 148; US, 115; Japan, 85; Germany, 64; Great Britain, 45; France, 41; Italy, 40.

1927

March: 24th, the Guomindang nationalists take Nanjing on the lower Yangzi.

April: 5th, treaty of friendship between Italy and Hungary.

12th, following the arrival of Guomindang forces in Shanghai, E China, Chiang Kai-shek and conservatives start purging communists and other leftist elements from the Guomindang.

May: 20th, by Treaty of Jiddah, Britain recognizes rule of Ibn Saud in the Hejaz.

26th, Britain annuls trade agreement with USSR and breaks off diplomatic relations after discovery of documents relating to Soviet intrigues against the British Empire.

June: 20th, (–4th Aug) Britain, USA, and Japan confer at Washington, DC, USA, on naval disarmament, but fail to reach agreement.

Sept: 2nd, in Turkish elections Mustafa Kemal is empowered to nominate all candidates, giving the People's Party a monopoly.

16th, President Hindenburg of Germany, dedicating the Tannenburg memorial, repudiates Germany's responsibility for the War (article 231 of the Versailles Treaty).

Nov: 14th, Leon Trotsky and Grigory Zinoviev are expelled from the Soviet Communist Party (expulsion confirmed 2nd Dec by 15th Party Congress).

Dec: 14th, Britain recognizes Iraq's independence and promises to support its application for membership of the League of Nations in 1932.

14th, China and the USSR break off diplomatic relations.

Politics, Government, Law, and Economy

Mustafa Kemal, *The New Turkey*.

Adolf Hitler, *Mein Kampf*, Vol 2.

Science, Technology, and Discovery

(20th May) (–21st) US aviator Charles A Lindbergh flies from New York to Paris in 37 hours.

Humanities and Scholarship

British archaeologist Leonard Woolley makes rich discoveries at the site of ancient Ur (now in Iraq).

Martin Heidegger, *Being and Time*.

Bertrand Russell, *The Analysis of Matter*.

Art, Sculpture, Fine Arts, and Architecture

Sculpture Eric Gill, *Mankind*.

Music

George Antheil's 'ballet mécanique', scored for aeroplane propellers, anvils, motor horns, etc.

Literature

Marcel Proust, *Le Temps retrouvé* (posthumous).

Henry Williamson, *Tarka the Otter*.

Virginia Woolf, *To The Lighthouse*.

Media

Film *October* (director, Sergei Eisenstein).

1928

Feb: 20th, Transjordan becomes self-governing under the British mandate.

May: 3rd, (–11th) in China, clashes between Guomindang nationalists and Japanese troops at Ji'nan in NE China, after which Japan reoccupies part of the Shandong Peninsula.

12th, Italian electoral law reduces electorate from 10 million to 3 million.

20th, in German elections Social Democrats increase their number of seats from 131 to 153 and are the largest party but without an overall majority: Centre, 62; Communists, 54; German National People's Party, 73; German People's Party, 45; Nazis, 12.

June: 28th, Hermann Müller, Social Democrat, is appointed German chancellor (following resignation of Wilhelm Marx's ministry, 13th).

Aug: 8th, Croats withdraw from parliament of the Kingdom of the Serbs, Croats, and Slovenes, and establish a separatist assembly in Zagreb.

27th, the Kellogg–Briand Pact, outlawing war and providing for pacific settlement of disputes, is signed in Paris by 65 states, including USA and USSR.

28th, all-party conference at Lucknow votes for dominion status for India (but, 30th, radical members form the Independence of India League).

Sept: 1st, Albania is proclaimed a Kingdom and Zog (Ahmed Beg Zogu) is elected King.

10th, in Argentina, Chamber of Deputies votes to revoke oil concessions (Senate adjourns before considering the matter).

Oct: **4th**, (–16th) plebiscite in Germany against building new battleships fails.

6th, Chiang Kai-shek is elected President of China.

7th, in US presidential election, Herbert Hoover, Republican, wins with 444 electoral votes against Alfred E Smith, Democrat, with 87; popular vote: Hoover, 21,391,381; Smith, 15,016,443; Norman Thomas (Socialist), 267,835.

Politics, Government, Law, and Economy

A new law in Italy reorganizes the membership of parliament: the 13 state corporations are to submit candidates' names to the Grand Council of Fascism, which then finalizes the lists and submits them to the electorate for ratification or rejection.

Overproduction of coffee causes a price slump and economic crisis in Brazil.

(1st Oct) In USSR, Stalin ends the New Economic Policy and introduces state-directed economic planning and distribution, the development of industry, and collectivization of agriculture in accordance with the first Five-Year Plan.

Society, Education, and Religion

Revised Prayer Book of the Church of England rejected by Parliament.

(9th April) By amendment to Turkish constitution, Islam ceases to be the recognized state religion.

(5th July) Voting age for women in Britain reduced from 30 to 21.

Science, Technology, and Discovery

German physicists H Geiger and W Müller improve the 'Geiger counter'.

In Britain, Alexander Fleming discovers penicillin.

Humanities and Scholarship

Completion of *New English Dictionary* (begun 1884).

Art, Sculpture, Fine Arts, and Architecture

Painting Max Beckmann, *Black Lilies*.

Henri Matisse, *Seated Odalisque*.

Music

George Gershwin, *An American in Paris*.

Maurice Ravel, *Boléro* (ballet).

Kurt Weill, *The Threepenny Opera* (musical).

Literature

Aldous Huxley, *Point Counter Point*.

D H Lawrence, *Lady Chatterley's Lover* (privately printed in Florence), *The Woman Who Rode Away*.

Sport and Recreation

The Squash Rackets Association is formed.

The West Indies play Test cricket for the first time, losing all three matches against England.

(17 May) (–12th Aug) The 9th Olympic Games are held in Amsterdam. The USA wins 22 gold medals; Germany, 10; Finland, 8; Sweden, Italy, and Switzerland, 7 each; France and Holland, 6 each. Women's track and field events are held for the first time. India wins the first of six consecutive hockey golds.

Media

Film George Eastman in USA produces the first colour moving pictures.

Steamboat Willie (director, Walt Disney; featuring Mickey Mouse).

1929

Jan: **5th**, King Alexander I suppresses the constitution of the Kingdom of the Serbs, Croats, and Slovenes (Yugoslavia), and establishes a dictatorship.

Feb: **14th**, in Chicago, USA, the 'St Valentine's Day Massacre': gangsters dressed as policemen, working for Al 'Scarface' Capone, gun down seven members of the gang led by George 'Bugsy' Moran.

March: **24th**, Fascists 'win' single-party elections in Italy.

May: **30th**, in British general election, the first held under universal adult suffrage, Labour wins 287 seats, Conservatives 260, Liberals, 59, others, 9.

June: **5th**, in Britain, Ramsay MacDonald forms Labour ministry, with Arthur Henderson as foreign secretary, Philip Snowden as chancellor of the exchequer, and J R Clynes as home secretary.

7th, Young Committee reviewing German reparations payments recommends that Germany should pay annuities, secured on mortgage of German railways, to an international bank until 1988.

Aug: **6th**, (–13th) at Reparations Conference at the Hague, Germany accepts the Young Plan; the Allies agree to evacuate the Rhineland by June 1930.

11th, Iraq and Iran sign treaty of friendship.

Oct: —, Cessation of US loans to Europe, following Wall Street Crash.
3rd, the name of the Kingdom of the Serbs, Croats, and Slovenes is changed to 'Yugoslavia'.
3rd, Britain resumes relations with the USSR.
24th, (–29th) crashes in share values on Wall Street stock market, New York, starting with 'Black Thursday' and continuing (after closure of the market from noon on 24th until 28th) on 'Black Monday' (28th) and 'Black Tuesday' (29th).

Politics, Government, Law, and Economy

In Mexico, formation of the National Revolutionary Party or PNR (renamed the Party of the Mexican Revolution in 1938, and the Institutional Revolutionary Party in 1946).

Society, Education, and Religion

The Presbyterian Churches in Scotland unite to form the Church of Scotland.
In South Africa, the term 'Apartheid' (separate development) is first used in an Afrikaner text.
(Feb) Lateran Treaties between the Pope and Italy establish the independent Vatican City State in Rome and entail Papal recognition of the state of Italy.

Science, Technology, and Discovery

In USA, the Kodak company develop a 16-mm colour film.
Graf Zeppelin airship flies round the world.
US explorer Richard Byrd flies over the South Pole.

Humanities and Scholarship

Martin Heidegger, *What is Metaphysics?*
14th edition of *Encyclopaedia Britannica.*

Art, Sculpture, Fine Arts, and Architecture

Second Surrealist Manifesto; the Surrealist group is joined by Salvador Dali.
Opening of the Museum of Modern Art, New York, with exhibitions of works by Paul Cézanne, Paul Gauguin, Georges Seurat, and Vincent van Gogh.
Painting Piet Mondrian, *Composition with Yellow and Blue.*

Literature

Jean Cocteau, *Les Enfants terribles.*
William Faulkner, *The Sound and the Fury*, *Sartoris.*
Ernest Hemingway, *A Farewell to Arms.*
Erich Remarque, *All Quiet on the Western Front.*
Virginia Woolf, *A Room of One's Own.*

Media

The Listener issued in Britain, reprinting talks from BBC radio.

1930

Jan: 28th, in Spain, the dictator Primo de Rivera resigns, following the army's withdrawal of support; General Dámaso Berenguer forms ministry.

Feb: 6th, treaty of friendship between Austria and Italy.

March: 12th, in India, Mahatma Gandhi opens civil disobedience campaign in India with his 'salt march' (a march from Ahmedabad to the coast, where on 6th April Gandhi seized salt to protest at the levying of salt tax on poor people).
27th, in Germany, resignation of Hermann Müller's government, because Social Democrats oppose planned cuts in unemployment benefit.
30th, Heinrich Brüning, Centre Party, forms a coalition of the Right in Germany, replacing the Social Democrats, but without a majority in the Reichstag.

April: 22nd, USA, Britain, France, Italy, and Japan end London Conference (held since 21st Jan), with signing of a treaty on naval disarmament, regulating submarine warfare and limiting aircraft carriers.

May: 17th, Young Plan for reparations in force.

June: 24th, in Britain, publication of the Simon Report on India; it recommends self-government at provincial level.
30th, 20-year treaty between Britain and Iraq, regulating relations between the countries.
30th, last Allied troops leave Rhineland.

July: 30th, National Union Party (neo-Fascist) founded in Portugal.

Sept: 6th, in Argentina, demonstrations by crowds in Buenos Aires and revolt by army force President Hipólito Irigoyen to resign; General José Uriburu is appointed president.
8th, (–22nd) special sessions of Canadian parliament to enact emergency laws dealing with depression.
14th, in German elections Social Democrats win 143 seats and Communists 77, but National Socialists (Nazis), denouncing Versailles Treaty, gain 107 seats (Centre Party, 68; National People's Party, 41; others, 137).

Oct: 4th, following Liberal revolt in Brazil, to prevent accession of president-elect Dr Júlio Prestes, martial law is declared in three provinces (23rd Oct, military leaders for President Luis to resign; 4th Nov, Getúlio Vargas is installed as temporary president).

5th, British airship R101 crashes and explodes near Beauvais, NE France, killing 44 people.

Nov: 12th, (–19th Jan 1931) first Round Table Conference on India held in London (without Congress Party representatives).

Politics, Government, Law, and Economy

Harold Laski, *Liberty and the Modern State.*

France begins construction of the Maginot Line defence system along the French–German border.

Farm collectivization programme in the USSR gathers speed.

Society, Education, and Religion

Charles Johnson, *The Negro in American Civilization.*

In Britain, Pilgrim Trust founded.

Sigmund Freud, *Civilization and its Discontents.*

Science, Technology, and Discovery

The photoflash bulb is invented.

Acrylic plastics are invented (Perspex by William Chalmers in Britain, Lucite in USA).

(18th March) Clyde Tombaugh at the Lowell Observatory, Arizona, USA, discovers the planet Pluto.

(5th April) (–24th) British aviator Amy Johnson makes solo flight from Britain to Australia.

Art, Sculpture, Fine Arts, and Architecture

Dutch painter Theo van Doesburg first uses term 'Concrete Art'.

Literature

W H Auden, *Poems.*

T S Eliot, *Ash Wednesday.*

Sigrid Undset, *Burning Bush.*

Drama Noël Coward, *Private Lives.*

Sport and Recreation

Australia regains the Ashes, beating England 2–1 in the five-match series in England; during the series, the Australian batsman Donald Bradman scores a record 974 runs with a Test average of 139.14.

The first football World Cup is held in Uruguay; 11 nations take part in the event, which is won by the host nation (beating Argentina 4–2 in the Final in Montevideo); British teams are unable to participate, having withdrawn from FIFA in 1928.

Media

In Britain, amalgamation of the *Daily Chronicle* and *Daily News* to form the *Daily News and Chronicle.*

Film *The Blue Angel* (starring Marlene Dietrich).

Murder (director, Alfred Hitchcock).

Sous les Toits de Paris (director, René Clair).

Radio (29 Dec) Permission is given for Radio Luxembourg to begin broadcasting.

1931

Feb: —, In Britain, Oswald Mosley breaks away from the Labour Party to form the New Party.

March: 5th, by Delhi Pact between the viceroy of India (Lord Irwin, who becomes Lord Halifax in 1934) and Gandhi, the civil disobedience campaign organized by the Indian National Congress is suspended; the Congress Party promises to participate in the Round Table Conference, and political prisoners are released.

April: 12th, following municipal elections in Spain, in which republicans did well, Niceto Alcalá Zamora, leader of a revolutionary committee in Madrid, demands the abdication of the king (14th, King Alfonso XIII flees Spanish revolution; Alcalá Zamora becomes president of a provisional government).

May: 11th, bankruptcy of Credit-Anstalt in Austria begins financial collapse of Central Europe.

June: 16th, Bank of England advances money to Austria, but France withholds support.

July: —, In Britain, the report of the May Committee estimates that the budget deficit could reach £120 million; proposed economies include cut in unemployment benefits, which divides the Labour cabinet.

9th, in Germany, the Nazi leader Adolf Hitler and Alfred Hugenberg of the German National Party agree to cooperate.

Aug: 24th, British Prime Minister Ramsay MacDonald resigns; 25th, forms National Government with other parties to balance the budget; Labour Party subsequently expels MacDonald, Philip Snowden, and J H Thomas, who serve with him; Arthur Henderson becomes leader of Labour Party.

Sept: 7th, (–1st Dec) second Round Table Conference on India held in London (including attendance of Gandhi), but the Conference fails to reach agreement on the representation of religious minorities.

Oct: 27th, in British general election National Government wins 554 seats, Opposition 61 (government supporters comprise 473 Conservatives, 35 National Liberals, 33 Liberals, 13 National Labour; the opposition comprises 52 Labour, 4 Lloyd George Liberals and 5 others); Oswald Moseley's New Party fails to win a seat.

Nov: —, Ramsay MacDonald forms second National Government, with Neville Chamberlain as chancellor of the exchequer, Sir John Simon as foreign secretary, and Stanley Baldwin (leader of the Conservative Party) as lord president of the council.

Dec: 9th, republican constitution promulgated in Spain (10th, Alcalá Zamora elected president and Manuel Azaña appointed prime minister).

Politics, Government, Law, and Economy

(1st July) In southern Africa, opening of Benguella–Katanga railway, which completes first trans-African railway.

(20th Sept) Britain goes off the Gold Standard.

(17th Oct) In USA, Chicago gang-leader Al 'Scarface' Capone is sentenced to 11 years in prison for tax evasion.

Society, Education, and Religion

Pope Pius XI issues the Encyclical *Quadragesimo Anno*, confirming teaching on social questions.

Science, Technology, and Discovery

Publication of 'Gödel's proof' (*On Formally Undecidable Propositions of Principia Mathematica and Related Systems*), Kurt Gödel's questioning of the possibility of establishing dependable axioms in mathematics. He proves that any formula strong enough to include the laws of arithmetic is either incomplete or inconsistent

US physicist Ernest O Lawrence devises the cyclotron (an 'atom-smasher').

US physicist Karl Jansky pioneers radio astronomy through his detection of radio emissions from the Milky Way.

Art, Sculpture, Fine Arts, and Architecture

Architecture Shreve, Lamb, and Harmon, Empire State Building, New York.

Music

Sergei Rachmaninov's music is banned in the USSR as 'decadent'.

Literature

Antoine de St-Exupéry, *Vol de nuit/Night Flight.*

Media

Film *City Lights* (starring Charlie Chaplin).

Dracula (starring Bela Lugosi).

Frankenstein (starring Boris Karloff).

M (director, Fritz Lang).

The Million (director, René Clair).

1932

Jan: 4th, following Mahatma Gandhi's return to India, and the revival of civil disobedience, the Indian government is granted emergency powers for six months; the Indian National Congress is declared illegal and Gandhi is arrested.

7th, Chancellor Heinrich Brüning declares that Germany cannot, and will not, resume reparations payments.

Feb: 2nd, (–July 1932) 60 states, including USA and USSR, attend Geneva Disarmament Conference, at which French proposal for an armed force under international control is opposed by Germany.

18th, Japanese puppet republic of Manzhouguo proclaimed in Manchuria, with former Chinese emperor Pu Yi as chief executive (1st March, is proclaimed emperor).

May: 15th, murder of Tsuyoshi Inukai, prime minister of Japan, by young naval and military officers (succeeded by Makoto Saito).

June: 15th, start of Chaco War between Bolivia and Paraguay (–June 1935), when Bolivians attack Paraguayan positions in the disputed border territory of Chaco Boreal.

16th, (–9th July) at Lausanne reparations conference, Germany accepts proposal for a final conditional payment of 3,000 million Reichsmarks.

July: 5th, in Portugal, President Carmona appoints Oliveira Salazar as prime minister.

31st, in Reichstag elections Nazis win 230 seats, Social Democrats 133, Centre 75, Communists 89, National People's Party 37 (others, 44), producing stalemate, since neither Nazis nor Social Democrats would enter a coalition.

Sept: 14th, Germany withdraws temporarily from the Geneva Disarmament Conference (until Dec), demanding the principle of being allowed armaments equal to those of other powers.

30th, following a financial crisis and the resignation of Count Károlyi, Julius Gömbös forms ministry in Hungary.

Oct: —, Oswald Moseley founds the British Union of Fascists (renamed the British Union of Fascists and National Socialists in summer 1936).

Nov: 6th, German elections produce further deadlock, with some Communist gains from Nazis (Nazis, 192 seats; Social Democrats, 121; Centre, 70; Communists, 100; National People's Party, 52; others, 45).

8th, F D Roosevelt wins US presidential election in Democrat landslide with 472 electoral votes over Herbert Hoover, Republican, with 59; popular vote: Roosevelt, 22,821,857; Hoover, 15,761,841; Norman Thomas (Socialist), 881,951.

19th, (–24th Dec), third India Round Table Conference in London (concerned with reports on franchise, finance, and the states).

29th, French–USSR nonaggression pact.

Dec: 4th, Kurt von Schleicher forms ministry in Germany, attempting to conciliate the Centre and the Left.

11th, Britain, France, Germany, and Italy make the 'No Force Declaration', renouncing the use of force for settling differences; with signing of Geneva Protocol on Germany's equality of rights with other nations, Germany returns to the Geneva Disarmament Conference.

Politics, Government, Law, and Economy

In the Netherlands, the Zuider Zee drainage scheme is completed.

In Germany, the Cologne–Bonn autobahn is opened, one of the world's first motorways or express highways.

Society, Education, and Religion

Famine in USSR.

Wesleyan Methodists, Primitive Methodists, and the United Methodist Church form the Methodist Church of Great Britain and Ireland.

Publication of the first volume of Karl Barth's *Church Dogmatics* (unfinished at author's death).

Reinhold Niebuhr, *Moral Man and Immoral Society.*

Science, Technology, and Discovery

British physicist James Chadwick discovers the 'neutron'.

Vitamin C (ascorbic acid) isolated by Charles Glen King.

US scientist Carl David Anderson, while analysing cosmic rays, discovers positive electrons ('positrons'). This is the first form of anti-matter to be discovered.

Art, Sculpture, Fine Arts, and Architecture

Architecture Liverpool Metropolitan Cathedral begun on Edwin Lutyens' plans (later abandoned, but Lutyens' crypt was incorporated in the final building).

Sir Giles Scott, Battersea Power Station, London (–1934).

Painting Henri Matisse, *Dance* (–1933).

Sculpture Eric Gill, *Prospero and Ariel* (for Broadcasting House, London; –1937).

Alexander Calder, *Mobile* (–34).

Music

Thomas Beecham founds London Philharmonic Orchestra.

Literature

Aldous Huxley, *Brave New World.*

Jules Romains, *Les hommes de bonne volonté* (–1947).

Drama Bertolt Brecht, *The Mother.*

Everyday Life

In USA, Route 66 from Chicago to Los Angeles is completed; it becomes an American icon.

(1st March) Baby son of aviator Charles Lindbergh and Anne Lindbergh is kidnapped (body found on 12th May); Bruno Hauptmann is executed for the murder 3rd April 1936.

Sport and Recreation

(30 July) (–14th Aug) The 10th Olympic Games are held in Los Angeles, USA; the USA wins 41 gold medals; Italy, 12; France, 10; Sweden, 9; Japan, 7; Hungary, 6; Finland, 5. National flags are used in medal ceremonies for the first time.

Media

Film 127 sound films made (compared with eight in 1929).

Doctor Jekyll and Mr Hyde (director, Rouben Mamoulian).

À nous la liberté (director, René Clair).

A Farewell to Arms (starring Gary Cooper).

Grand Hotel.

Shanghai Express (starring Marlene Dietrich).

Tarzan the Ape Man (starring Johnny Weissmüller).

1933 **Jan:** **28th**, in Germany, Kurt von Schleicher's ministry falls, following failure to conciliate the Centre and Left.

30th, Adolf Hitler is appointed Chancellor of Germany; his cabinet includes only two Nazis, Hermann Goering (Minister without Portfolio) and Wilhelm Frick (Minister of the Interior); Franz von Papen is Vice-chancellor, Constantin von Neurath, Foreign Minister.

Feb: **9th**, in Britain, the Oxford Union debating society carries the motion 'that this House will in no circumstances fight for its King and its Country'.

16th, fearing German threats, the 'Little Entente' (Czechoslovakia, Romania, and Yugoslavia) is reorganized, with a permanent council.

23rd, (–12th March), the Japanese army advances south-west from Manchuria into Jehol (Chengde), NE of the Great Wall, and later advances southwards.

27th, fire destroys the Reichstag (parliament) in Berlin; though it was started by a Dutch worker, Marinus van der Lubbe, the Nazis denounce the fire as a Communist plot and use it as the pretext for suspending civil liberties and freedom of the press.

March: **4th**, inauguration of F D Roosevelt as 32nd President of the USA; he declares that 'the only thing we have to fear is fear itself'; in the evening he addresses the Nation on radio; Cordell Hull is appointed secretary of state.

5th, general election in Germany, in which the Nazis win 288 seats; Social Democrats, 120; Communists, 81; Centre, 74; National People's Party, 52; others, 32.

7th, Engelbert Dollfuss, chancellor of Austria, suspends the Austrian Parliament.

23rd, in Germany, the Enabling Act gives Adolf Hitler dictatorial powers until April 1937.

27th, Japan announces that it will leave the League of Nations (effective from 1935).

April: **1st**, start of official persecution of the Jews in Germany, with a national boycott of Jewish shops, businesses, and professionals.

8th, Western Australia, irritated by federal taxation, votes to secede from the Commonwealth of Australia.

May: **3rd**, oath of allegiance to the British Crown is removed from the Irish Constitution; appeals to the Privy Council are made illegal.

July: **14th**, in Germany, suppression of political parties other than the Nazi Party.

Oct: **14th**, Germany withdraws from the League of Nations and its Disarmament Conference.

Dec: **29th**, in Romania, the fascist Iron Guard murders the Liberal prime minister Ion Duca; succeeded by George Tartarescu.

Politics, Government, Law, and Economy

In the USA, economic legislation under F D Roosevelt's 'New Deal' includes the Agricultural Adjustment Act (12th May), which attempts to raise prices by providing grants to farmers for reducing areas under cultivation and livestock numbers; the Federal Securities Act (27th May), which compels disclosure of information about security issues; the National Industrial Recovery Act (16th June), which encourages joint economic planning by government and business and establishes the National Recovery Administration; and the Glass-Steagall Banking Act, which creates the Federal Bank Deposit Insurance Corporation to guarantee deposits under $5,000 (effective from Jan 1934).

The Tennessee Valley Authority is formed to build dams and hydroelectric plants.

(22nd Jan) USSR launches second Five-Year Plan, envisaging continued growth of heavy industry but also production of more consumer goods (Plan redrafted and adopted by 27th Party Congress in Feb 1934).

Society, Education, and Religion

Germany inaugurates a four-year plan (the Schacht Plan) for abolishing unemployment by expanding public works.

In USA, social legislation under the 'New Deal' extends government involvement in social provision. The Federal Emergency Relief Act, 12th May, provides money to states for unemployment relief projects and establishes the Public Works Administration, which constructs roads and buildings and runs numerous other projects.

Germany opens concentration camps for enemies of the Nazi regime; the first camp is at Dachau, near Munich (opened 20th March).

George Orwell, *Down and Out in Paris and London*.

Humanities and Scholarship

The Warburg Institute is transferred from Hamburg to London (and incorporated in London University in 1944).

Art, Sculpture, Fine Arts, and Architecture

Architecture Ove Arup, Highpoint I, Highgate, London.

Music

Debut in Britain of Duke Ellington's orchestra from the USA.
Richard Strauss, *Arabella* (opera).

Literature

André Malraux, *La condition humaine/Man's Estate.*
Gertrude Stein, *The Autobiography of Alice B Toklas.*
Drama Eugene O'Neill, *Ah, Wilderness!*

Everyday Life

The British Imperial Chemical Industries (ICI) makes the first commercially produced synthetic detergent.

Sport and Recreation

England regains the Ashes on the 'Bodyline' tour of Australia: diplomatic relations between the two countries are threatened when protests are made over the English tactics of bowling short on the line of the batsman's body.

Media

Film Odeon Cinema circuit founded in Britain.
Queen Christina (starring Greta Garbo).
King Kong.

1934

Jan: 8th, in France, death of Alexander Stavisky (by suicide or murder), who had been accused of issuing fraudulent bonds (with official backing).

Feb: 1st, (–16th) in Austria, political parties are forcibly dissolved except for Chancellor Engelbert Dollfuss's Fatherland Front; a general strike called on 12th Feb fails to stop the dissolution.

6th, (–7th) riots in Paris protesting at the corruption implied by the Stavisky affair; 8, Paul Doumergue forms National Union ministry of all parties, except Royalists, Socialists, and Communists, to avert civil chaos.

9th, pact signed between Greece, Turkey, Romania, and Yugoslavia, forming the 'Balkan Entente' as a counterpart to the Little Entente, to prevent Balkans from encroachment by the great powers.

12th, (–13th) general strike in France, in protest at danger posed by rise of Fascism.

March: 8th, for first time the Labour Party wins a clear majority on the London County Council over Municipal Reform and Liberal Parties.

16th, (–17th) Rome protocols signed between Italy, Austria, and Hungary to a form Danubian bloc against Little Entente (Czechoslovakia, Romania, and Yugoslavia).

June: 5th, J C Smuts' South African Party unites with Hertzog's followers in Nationalist Party to form United South African Nationalists, while other Nationalists reform under D F Malan.

8th, Oswald Mosley addresses mass meeting of British Union of Fascists at Olympia, London.

11th, Geneva Disarmament Conference ends in failure.

29th, (–30th) in Germany, 'Night of the Long Knives': a Nazi purge to break the power of the SA or Storm Troopers; those murdered include Ernst Roehm, head of the SA, General Kurt von Schleicher, over 70 leading Nazis, and many others (executions continue until 2nd July).

July: 12th, Belgium prohibits uniformed political parties.

25th, Engelbert Dollfuss, chancellor of Austria, is murdered in attempted Nazi *coup*.

30th, Kurt Schuschnigg is appointed Austrian chancellor.

Aug: 1st, Australia's prohibitive duty on imported cottons provokes boycott of Australian produce in Lancashire, NW England.

2nd, in Germany, death of President Paul von Hindenburg (aged 87); soon afterwards the presidency is merged with the chancellorship and all members of the armed forces take an oath of loyalty to Adolf Hitler as Führer ('Leader').

19th, German plebiscite on vesting of sole executive power in Adolf Hitler as Führer; 89.9% of voters approve the change.

Sept: 9th, Fascist and anti-Fascist demonstrations in Hyde Park, London.

18th, the USSR is admitted to the League of Nations.

Oct: 4th, Alejandro Lerroux forms ministry of Right in Spain, provoking, 5th, strike called by the Left.

24th, Gandhi withdraws from Indian National Congress, disillusioned with its tactical use of disobedience; he invests his efforts in the All-India Village Industries Association.

Nov: —, Moroccan nationalist movement founded.

7th, in Australia, Joseph Lyons, United Australia Party, forms coalition ministry with the Country Party.

Dec: **1st**, in USSR, assassination of Sergei Kirov, the fourth highest communist leader, probably with Stalin's connivance; the assassin, 13 accomplices, and 103 others are summarily executed.
19th, Japan denounces Washington treaties of 1922 and 1930.

Politics, Government, Law, and Economy
British Council founded, to promote British culture overseas.
(26th March) Road Traffic Act introduces driving tests in Britain.

Society, Education, and Religion
Lewis Mumford, *Technics and Civilization.*
Gordonstoun School at Elgin, Scotland, founded by Kurt Hahn.

Science, Technology, and Discovery
French physicists Frédéric Joliot and Irène Curie-Joliot discover induced radioactivity.
Italian physicist Enrico Fermi suggests that neutrons and protons are the same fundamental particles in two different quantum states.
Chilling process for meat cargoes discovered.

Humanities and Scholarship
Arnold Toynbee, *A Study of History* (–1961).
Oxford History of England, edited by G N Clark (–1965).

Music
Dmitri Shostakovich, *The Lady Macbeth of Mtsensk* (opera).
John Christie founds opera festival at his country house of Glyndebourne, S England.
Sergei Rachmaninov, *Rhapsody on a Theme of Paganini.*

Literature
F Scott Fitzgerald, *Tender is the Night.*
Robert Graves, *I, Claudius.*
Henry Miller, *Tropic of Cancer.*
Mikhail Sholokhov, *Quiet Flows the Don.*
Drama Jean Cocteau, *La Machine infernale.*
Sean O'Casey, *Within the Gates.*

Sport and Recreation
The second football World Cup is held in Italy; Italy wins the trophy, beating Czechoslovakia 2–1 in the final in Rome.

Media
Film *The Last Millionaire* (director, René Clair).
The Scarlet Pimpernel (producer, Alexander Korda).
The Thin Man.

1935

Jan: **13th**, plebiscite in the Saarland: 90.8% of voters favour incorporation in Germany.
15th, (–17th) in the USSR, Grigory Zinoviev, Lev Kamenev, and 17 other former leading Communists are tried and imprisoned for 'moral responsibility' for Kirov's murder in 1934; thousands more around the country are arrested.

March: **1st**, restoration of Saarland to Germany.
16th, Germany repudiates disarmament clauses of the Versailles Treaty and introduces conscription.
25th, in Belgium, Paul van Zeeland forms ministry of National Unity and devalues the Belgian franc.

April: **11th**, (–14th) prime ministers of Italy, France, and Britain, confer at Stresa in NW Italy where they issue protest at German rearmament and agree to act together against Germany.
23rd, adoption of new constitution in Poland; President Moscicki signs it to the accompaniment of a 101-gun salute.

May: **2nd**, French–USSR treaty of mutual assistance for five years.
16th, USSR–Czechoslovakia pact of mutual assistance.

June: **7th**, in Britain, Stanley Baldwin, Conservative, succeeds J Ramsay MacDonald as prime minister and forms a new National Government with MacDonald as lord president of the council, Sir John Simon as home secretary, and Sir Samuel Hoare as foreign secretary.
12th, formal truce in Chaco War between Paraguay and Bolivia (treaty agreed in July 1938).

July: **13th**, USSR–USA trade pact.
25th, (–20th Aug) meeting of the Third International (Soviet-controlled international Communist organization) declares that Communists in democratic countries should support their governments against Fascist states.

Aug: **2nd**, Government of India Act reforms governmental system, separates Burma (now

Myanmar) and Aden from India, grants provincial governments greater self-government, and creates a central legislature at Delhi (to come into force on 1st April 1937).

Sept: 15th, in Germany, at the Nuremberg Nazi Party rally, Hitler announces the anti-Jewish 'Nuremberg Laws': legislation will define Jews, ban them from professions, and forbid marriage and sexual intercourse with non-Jews; the Swastika will become Germany's official flag.

Oct: 2nd, Italy invades Ethiopia.
7th, following Italy's invasion of Ethiopia, the League of Nations Council declares and denounces Italy as aggressor.
7th, (–17th) Kurt Schuschnigg's 'bloodless' *coup d'état* in Vienna in collaboration with Prince Starhemberg against Emil Fey, minister of interior, and his Nazi allies.
19th, the League of Nations imposes sanctions against Italy.

Nov: 3rd, French Socialist groups merge as Socialist and Republican Union, under Léon Blum; this soon forms close relations with Radical Socialists and Communists to found a Popular Front.
4th, German–Polish economic agreement.
14th, in British general election Government parties win 429 seats, Opposition, 184 (Conservatives, 388, National Liberal, 33, National Labour, 8; Liberal, 21, Labour, 154, Independent Labour Party, 4, Communist, 1, others 4); Ramsay MacDonald is defeated by Emmanuel Shinwell at Seaham Harbour.

Dec: 1st, Chiang Kai-shek elected president of Chinese (Guomindang) executive.
9th, Hoare–Laval Pact, whereby the British foreign minister (Samuel Hoare) and the French prime minister (Pierre Laval) propose to cede the most fertile part of Ethiopia to Italy; in both countries public outcry denounces the plan and the British prime minister disowns it.

Politics, Government, Law, and Economy

In Britain, publisher Victor Gollancz founds the Left Book Club (first publication May 1936).
In USA, the National Labor Relations Act (or Wagner Act) outlaws unfair practices by employers and creates a new National Labor Relations Board to manage union elections and bargain for workers; the Act concedes the right to join a trade union and to engage in collective bargaining.
George Gallup founds the American Institute of Public Opinion (known as the Gallup Poll) to conduct political and market research by scientific methods.
(14th July) Foundation in Britain of the Peace Pledge Union (after a mass meeting in the Albert Hall, London), to oppose rearmament and resort to war.

Society, Education, and Religion

Sidney and Beatrice Webb, *Soviet Communism: A New Civilization?*
In USA, in a second round of New Deal legislation, President Roosevelt establishes the Resettlement Administration (1st May), to help owners and tenants move to better land; the Works Progress Administration (WPA) to provide public works programmes; the Rural Electrification Administration (REA) to provide loans to companies for the construction of electricity supply networks in rural areas.
Karl Barth, *Credo.*
(14th Aug) The Social Security Act signed; it provides pensions to the over-65s, help for the disabled and blind, and unemployment assistance (from 1942), paid for by contributions rather than from tax revenues.

Science, Technology, and Discovery

British physicist Robert Watson-Watt builds first practical radar equipment for detecting aircraft.
British driver Malcolm Campbell at Daytona Beach, Florida, USA, drives *Bluebird* at 445.4 kph/276.8 mph.
The 35-mm 'Kodachrome' film devised.

Humanities and Scholarship

Brockhaus Encyclopaedia completed.

Music

Count Basie's band achieves fame through performances at the Famous Door Club, New York.
Alban Berg, Violin Concerto.
George Gershwin, *Porgy and Bess* (opera).
Richard Strauss, *Die Schweigsame Frau* (opera).

Literature

Ivy Compton-Burnett, *A House and its Head.*
Christopher Isherwood, *Mr Norris Changes Trains.*
Drama W H Auden and Christopher Isherwood, *The Dog Beneath the Skin.*
T S Eliot, *Murder in the Cathedral.*
Emlyn Williams, *Night Must Fall.*

Media

Film In the USA, the Fox Company merges with Twentieth Century to form the film company Twentieth Century Fox.

The 39 Steps (director, Alfred Hitchcock).

Anna Karenina (starring Greta Garbo).

David Copperfield (director, David O Selznick).

Top Hat (starring Fred Astaire and Ginger Rogers).

Statistics

Illiteracy: percentages of population: Egypt, 85; India, 80; Brazil, 67; Mexico, 58; Turkey, 55; Greece, 32; Spain, 31; Portugal, 30; Poland, 21; Italy, 19; USSR, 13.

1936

Jan: 6th, (–25th March) resumption of London Naval Conference; Japan withdraws on 15th Jan, because other countries refuse to accept its demand for a common upper limit on naval strength.

20th, in Britain, death of King George V (succeeded by Edward VIII).

Feb: 16th, in Spanish elections the Popular Front coalition of Left parties wins 256 seats against 165 for the Right and 52 for the Centre parties; Manuel Azaña becomes prime minister and re-establishes the constitution of 1931; across Spain, land is seized and churches attacked.

26th, military rebellion in Japan: junior officers murder three government ministers; Prime Minister Keisuke Okada resigns and is succeeded by Koki Hirota.

March: 3rd, British defence budget leaps from £122 million to £158 million, to increase Fleet Air Arm, add 250 aircraft for home defence, and to provide four new infantry battalions.

7th, German troops occupy the demilitarized zone of the Rhineland, thereby violating the Treaty of Versailles.

23rd, Italy, Austria, and Hungary sign Rome Pact: none to discuss matters relating to the Danube without first consulting the other two countries.

25th, Britain, USA, and France sign the London Naval Treaty, which defines categories of ship, permitted tonnages and gun sizes, and requires advance notification of building programmes.

May: 5th, Italians occupy the Ethiopian capital, Addis Ababa, ending the Ethiopian war (9th, Ethiopia is formally annexed by Italy).

24th, in Belgian general election, Rexists (Fascist) win seats for the first time (21 out of 202).

June: 4th, Léon Blum, Socialist, forms Popular Front ministry in France.

July: 15th, League of Nations raises sanctions against Italy.

17th, army mutiny in Spanish Morocco, led by Francisco Franco, to uphold religion and traditional values; other mutinies occur throughout Spain, thereby starting the Spanish Civil War.

Aug: 26th, treaty ends British protectorate over Egypt, except for the Canal Zone, and forms British–Egyptian alliance for 20 years.

Oct: 1st, Spanish nationalists appoint General Francisco Franco chief of state.

2nd, France devalues the franc.

5th, Italy devalues the lira.

12th, in Britain, the leader of the British Union of Fascists, Oswald Mosley, leads an anti-Jewish march along the Mile End Road, a Jewish part of London.

22nd, martial law proclaimed in Belgium, to combat the Rexists.

Nov: 1st, following the visit of Italian Foreign Minister Ciano to Berlin, the Italian prime minister Benito Mussolini proclaims the Rome–Berlin axis.

3rd, in US presidential election F D Roosevelt, Democrat, is re-elected, with 523 electoral votes over Alfred M Landon, Republican, with 8, and carries every state except Maine and Vermont; popular vote: Roosevelt, 27,751,597; Landon, 16,679,583; William Lemke (National Union for Social Justice), 882,479.

25th, Germany and Japan sign Anti-Comintern Pact; the countries agree to work together against international communism; Germany also recognizes Japan's regime in Manchuria.

Dec: 5th, new constitution in USSR, with a supreme council and a two-chamber parliament.

11th, in Britain, King Edward VIII abdicates (12th, proclamation of Duke of York's accession as George VI; Edward is created Duke of Windsor).

12th, President Chiang Kai-shek of China is held under arrest in NW China for several days by Marshal Chang Hsüeh-liang, who wanted stronger opposition to the Japanese (Chiang is released after intervention by a British adviser).

Politics, Government, Law, and Economy

In Germany Adolf Hitler announces a second Four-Year Plan to make the country self-sufficient in raw materials.

Public Order Act in Britain bans political uniforms and gives the police more powers in response to Fascist disturbances in London.

France abandons the gold standard.
J M Keynes, *General Theory of Employment, Interest and Money.*
(5th Dec) New constitution in USSR, with a supreme council and a two-chamber parliament.

Society, Education, and Religion

Dale Carnegie, *How to Win Friends and Influence People.*
(12th June) 40-hour working week introduced in France.

Science, Technology, and Discovery

(4th May) (–7th) British aviator Amy Johnson flies from England to Cape Town in 3 days 6 hrs 25 mins.

Humanities and Scholarship

A J Ayer, *Language, Truth, and Logic.*
A J Carlyle completes *History of Medieval Political Theory in the West.*

Art, Sculpture, Fine Arts, and Architecture

Painting Piet Mondrian, *Composition in Red and Blue.*

Music

Sergei Prokofiev, *Peter and the Wolf.*
In USA, start of the 'swing' era of jazz, with band leader and broadcaster Benny Goodman labelled 'The King of Swing'.

Literature

Aldous Huxley, *Eyeless in Gaza.*
British publisher Allen Lane founds Penguin Books, starting the paperback revolution.

Everyday Life

(30th Nov) In London, the Crystal Palace, at Sydenham, is destroyed by fire.

Sport and Recreation

(19th June) Joe Louis, the 'Brown Bomber', loses to Max Schmeling in the 12th round of their non-title fight at the Yankee Stadium, New York.
(1st Aug) (–16th) The 11th Olympic Games are held in Berlin. Germany wins 33 gold medals; USA, 24; Hungary, 10; Italy, 8; Finland and France, 7 each; Sweden and Holland, 6 each; Japan, 5; the US African-American athlete Jesse Owens wins 4 golds, in the 100 m, the 200 m, the Long Jump, and the 4x100 m relay.

Media

Film *Modern Times* (starring Charlie Chaplin).
Television German television broadcasts from the Berlin Olympic Games, including Jesse Owens' victory in the 200-m race.
(2nd Nov) (–1939) The BBC starts the world's first high-definition television service from its transmitter at Crystal Palace, London.

1937

Feb: 8th, in Spanish Civil War, nationalists take Malaga in S with Italian aid.

March: 2nd, in Mexico, nationalization of oil and establishment of the National Petroleum Corporation to administer oil-producing lands.

April: 27th, in Spanish Civil War, aircraft from the German Condor Legion bomb Guernica, the ancient Basque capital in N Spain.

May: 3rd, (–10th) rising of Anarchists and Syndicalists in Barcelona, SE Spain.
6th, the giant German airship *Hindenburg* explodes as it attempts to moor at Lakehurst Naval Station, New Jersey, USA; 36 are killed.
28th, on Stanley Baldwin's retirement Neville Chamberlain forms a National Government, with Sir John Simon as chancellor of the exchequer and Anthony Eden as foreign secretary.

June: —, In USSR, several high-ranking generals are tried, convicted, and shot for collaboration with Germany; there follows a purge of the armed forces.
14th, in Irish Free State, the Dáil approves de Valera's Constitution for Ireland, which changes the name of the Irish Free State, abolishes the governor-general, and provides for a new form of senate, and a president (to be introduced on 29th Dec).
19th, in Spanish Civil War, nationalists capture Bilbao, the Basque capital in the NE.
21st, on French Senate refusing Léon Blum's demands for emergency fiscal powers, he resigns and Camille Chautemps forms Radical–Socialist ministry.

July: 7th, in China, incident at Marco Polo Bridge, SE of Beijing, is followed by Japanese invasion of NE China.
7th, Royal Commission on Palestine recommends end of mandate and partition of country into British area, Jewish State, and Arab area joined with Transjordan.
8th, Afghanistan, Iran, Iraq, and Turkey sign nonaggression pact.
17th, naval agreements between Britain and Germany and Britain and USSR.

Aug: 14th, W L Mackenzie King, prime minister of Canada, announces establishment of commission to re-examine the structure of the confederation.

25th, in Spanish Civil War, nationalists capture Santander in N.

Oct: 16th, Fascist groups in Hungary form National Socialist Party.

21st, in Spanish Civil War, nationalists take Gijón, capturing the last major town in the N.

Nov: 6th, Italy joins German–Japanese Anti-Comintern Pact.

11th, in Japanese–Chinese War, Japanese troops finally capture Shanghai.

17th, (–21st) British cabinet minister Lord Halifax visits Adolf Hitler, to attempt peaceful settlement of Sudeten problem.

Dec: 4th, in Spanish Civil War, republicans launch offensive in Aragon (–Jan 1938).

5th, (–13th) in Japanese–Chinese War, Japanese troops take Nanjing, NW of Shanghai; their victory is followed by the 'rape of Nanjing', when around a quarter of a million Chinese are killed.

11th, Italy withdraws from the League of Nations.

24th, in Japanese–Chinese War, Japanese capture Hangzhou, SW of Shanghai.

29th, new Irish Constitution comes into force; Irish Free State becomes Eire.

Society, Education, and Religion

A wave of strikes takes place in the US car industry (from 30th Dec 1936), in which workers occupy their factories; the dispute ends with an agreement made on 30th March in which General Motors recognizes the United Automobile Workers.

Romansch recognized as fourth national language in Switzerland.

Talcott Parsons, *The Structure of Social Action.*

Pope Pius XI orders the encyclical *Mit brennender Sorge*, branding Nazism as fundamentally anti-Christian, to be read from all Catholic pulpits in Germany.

Pope Pius XI issues the encyclical Divini Redemptoris, on Atheistic Communism.

George Orwell, *The Road to Wigan Pier.*

Science, Technology, and Discovery

British engineer Frank Whittle builds first prototype jet engine.

British biochemists William Ewins and H Phillips synthesize sulphapyridine, the second sulfa drug.

Art, Sculpture, Fine Arts, and Architecture

International Exhibition held in Paris, France, for which Fernand Léger and his students paint mural *Le Transport des Forces*; Pablo Picasso paints *Guernica*; Léger designs sets for the play *Naissance d'une Cité*; Vera Mukhina produces *Worker and Collective Farm Girl*, a monumental Socialist Realist sculpture atop the Soviet Pavilion.

In Germany, Nazi exhibition of 'Degenerate Art' held in Munich.

Painting In London, William Coldstream and Lawrence Gowing found the Euston Road Group of artists, advocating a return to a realistic conception of painting.

Literature

Jean-Paul Sartre, *La Nausée/Nausea.*

John Steinbeck, *Of Mice and Men.*

Drama W H Auden and Christopher Isherwood, *The Ascent of F6.*

Everyday Life

The synthetic fibre 'Nylon' is patented by the US chemicals company Du Pont.

Media

In Britain, the *Morning Post* is absorbed into the *Daily Telegraph*, to form the *Daily Telegraph and Morning Post.*

Film *La Grande Illusion* (director, Jean Renoir).

Snow White and the Seven Dwarfs (producer, Walt Disney).

A Star is Born (starring Judy Garland and James Mason).

1938

Feb: 20th, British Foreign Minister Anthony Eden resigns in protest at Prime Minister Neville Chamberlain's priorities in foreign affairs; Chamberlain had declined President Roosevelt's suggestion of a conference on international relations and was determined to obtain an agreement with Italy; Eden is succeeded on 25th by Lord Halifax.

21st, in British House of Commons, Winston Churchill leads an outcry against Chamberlain and, 22nd, 25 members of the administration vote against the government in censure motion.

March: 2nd, (–14th) in USSR, trial of the former leading Communist Nikolai Bukharin and other political leaders (Bukharin is convicted and shot on 14th March).

12th, German troops enter Austria, which, 13th, is declared part of the German Reich.

13th, Léon Blum forms Popular Front ministry in France (–10th April).

19th, following the failure of US and British oil companies in Mexico to comply with a pay-and-conditions award of Dec 1937, the government declares the expropriation of the companies' Mexican assets.

28th, Japanese install puppet government of Chinese Republic at Nanjing.

April: **10th**, Édouard Daladier, radical socialist, forms ministry in France, supported by Léon Blum.

Sept: **15th**, British Prime Minister Neville Chamberlain visits Adolf Hitler at Berchtesgaden; Hitler states his determination to annex the Sudetenland in Czechoslovakia on the principle of self-determination.

29th, (–30th) the Munich conference, when British Prime Minister Neville Chamberlain, French Prime Minister Édouard Daladier, Adolf Hitler, and Benito Mussolini agree to Germany's military occupation of the Sudetenland, while the remaining frontiers of Czechoslovakia are guaranteed; Germany becomes the dominant power in Europe and both the Little Entente and the French system of alliances in Eastern Europe are shattered; on his return to London, Chamberlain declares that he has brought back 'peace with honour. I believe it is peace in our time.'

Oct: **1st**, Czechs accept Polish ultimatum for the cession of Teschen in north-central Czechoslovakia.

2nd, Japan withdraws from the League of Nations.

4th, end of the Popular Front in France when Socialists and Communists abstain from vote of confidence.

5th, Eduard Beneš, president of Czechoslovakia, resigns.

6th, the Grand Fascist Council in Italy passes antisemitic legislation; Jews are to be excluded from public activities (such as journalism) and are to cede property to the state (confirmed, 10th Nov; Pope Pius XI condemns the legislation).

Nov: **8th**, mid-term elections in the USA result in Democrats having 69 seats in the Senate and 261 in the House of Representatives, while Republicans have 23 in the Senate and 168 in the House.

9th, (–10th) Kristallnacht ('Crystal night'), when Jewish houses, synagogues, and schools in Germany are burnt down and shops looted; attacks continue until 14th.

26th, USSR–Polish declaration of friendship renews nonaggression pact.

Dec: **14th**, Italian Chamber of Deputies is replaced by Chamber of Fasces and Corporations.

Society, Education, and Religion

The Fair Labor Standards Act in the USA sets a minimum wage (40 cents an hour) and a maximum number of hours per week for workers in companies involved in interstate commerce, and prohibits the hiring of children under 16.

Science, Technology, and Discovery

German physicists Otto Hahn and F Strassman discover nuclear fission by bombarding uranium with neutrons.

Humanities and Scholarship

L Mumford, *The Culture of Cities.*

J B Huizinga, *Homo Ludens.*

Art, Sculpture, Fine Arts, and Architecture

Architecture Frank Lloyd Wright, Taliesin West, Phoenix, Arizona, USA.

Literature

Elizabeth Bowen, *The Death of the Heart.*

Graham Greene, *Brighton Rock.*

Evelyn Waugh, *Scoop.*

Drama Patrick Hamilton, *Gaslight.*

Everyday Life

The Hungarians J Ladisla and Georg Biro patent their ballpoint pen; a few more technical refinements are needed for mass-market success.

Sport and Recreation

The third football World Cup is held in France; Italy retains the trophy, beating Hungary 4–2 in the final in Paris.

Media

In Britain, Edward Hulton founds the illustrated news magazine *Picture Post.*

Film *Alexander Nevsky* (director, Sergei Eisenstein).

Pygmalion (starring Leslie Howard and Wendy Hiller).

Snow White and the Seven Dwarfs (director, Walt Disney).

Statistics

Steel production (in million tons): US, 42,906; Germany, including Saar, 20,573; USSR, 17,380; Great Britain, 11,908; France, 6,946; Belgium, 31,103.

Private cars (in millions): US, 19; Great Britain, 1.7; Germany, including Austria, 1.3; Italy, 1.1; France, 0.8.

1939 **Jan: 26th**, in Spanish Civil War, the nationalists take Barcelona.

March: 15th, German troops occupy Bohemia and Moravia in Czechoslovakia; Hitler makes a triumphal entry into Prague in the evening; the regions become a protectorate ruled by Constantin von Neurath.

16th, Slovakia is placed under German 'protection', while Hungary annexes Ruthenia (formerly part of Czechoslovakia).

21st, Germany demands of Poland that Germany should acquire the Free City of Danzig (modern Gdansk) and routes through the 'Polish Corridor' (which provides Poland with access to the Baltic); Poland rejects the demands.

23rd, Germany annexes Memel (modern Klaipeda) from Lithuania and forces Lithuania to sign a treaty.

28th, in Spanish Civil War, Madrid surrenders to nationalists; remaining republican areas and places surrender the next day, ending the War.

28th, Adolf Hitler denounces Germany's nonaggression pact with Poland (of Jan 1934).

31st, Britain and France pledge to support Poland in any attack on Polish independence (pact of mutual assistance agreed on 6th April).

April: 7th, Italy invades Albania.

7th, Spain joins Germany, Italy, and Japan in the Anti-Comintern Pact.

11th, Hungary withdraws from the League of Nations.

13th, Britain and France guarantee the independence of Romania and Greece.

18th, USSR proposes a triple alliance with Britain and France.

28th, Adolf Hitler denounces 1935 British–German naval agreement and repeats demands on Poland.

May: 8th, Spain leaves the League of Nations.

17th, Sweden, Norway, and Finland reject Germany's offer of nonaggression pacts, but Denmark, Estonia, and Latvia accept.

22nd, Adolf Hitler and Benito Mussolini sign 10-year political and military alliance (the 'Pact of Steel').

23rd, the British Parliament approves a plan for an independent Palestine by 1949, which is later denounced by Jews and by Arabs in Palestine.

Aug: 23rd, Nazi–Soviet Pact; the parties agree not to fight each other; secret protocols provide for the partition of Poland and for the USSR to operate freely in the Baltic States, Finland, and Bessarabia.

23rd, British Prime Minister Neville Chamberlain warns Adolf Hitler that Britain will stand by Poland and pleads for settlement of German claims on Danzig.

25th, British–Polish treaty of mutual assistance signed in London.

Sept: 1st, Germany invades Poland and annexes Danzig; Italy declares neutrality.

3rd, Britain and France declare war on Germany, following Germany's failure to reply to ultimata on Poland; Australia and New Zealand also declare war.

28th, Polish army surrenders; Germany and the USSR conclude a treaty partitioning Poland.

Oct: 8th, Germany incorporates western Poland into the Reich.

Dec: 13th, Battle of the River Plate, between British and German warships, ends on 17th with scuttling of *Graf Spee* off Montevideo.

Politics, Government, Law, and Economy

Michael Oakeshott, *The Social and Political Doctrines of Contemporary Europe*.

British Overseas Airways Corporation (BOAC) established.

Society, Education, and Religion

Frank Buchman's revivalist Oxford Group operates under the name 'Moral Rearmament'.

Science, Technology, and Discovery

British Imperial Chemical Industries (ICI) begins the commercial production of polythene.

Music

Béla Bartók, String Quartet No. 6.

William Walton, Violin Concerto.

In Britain, Myra Hess organizes lunch-time concerts at the National Gallery in London, which popularize pianoforte and chamber music and help to sustain morale.

Literature

James Joyce, *Finnegans Wake* (written from 1922).

Thomas Mann, *Lotte in Weimar*.

John Steinbeck, *The Grapes of Wrath*.

Everyday Life

(20th May) Pan-American Airways begin regular commercial flights between USA and Europe.

Media

Film *Gone With the Wind* (producer David O Selznick, starring Vivien Leigh and Clark Gable).
Goodbye Mr Chips (starring Robert Donat).
Stagecoach (director, John Ford, starring John Wayne).
The Stars Look Down.

1940

March: 12th, end of Russo–Finnish War: Finland signs peace treaty with USSR, ceding the Karelian Isthmus and shores of Lake Ladoga.

May: 7th, in Britain, Prime Minister Neville Chamberlain is attacked for the failure of British troops in Norway; 10th, resigns, when Winston Churchill forms a coalition government, including Labour Party members Clement Attlee as lord privy seal, A V Alexander as first lord of the admiralty, and Ernest Bevin as minister of labour; Chamberlain is lord president and Halifax foreign secretary.

10th, (–14th) Germany invades the Netherlands, Belgium, and Luxembourg.

26th, (–2nd June) over 300,000 British and French soldiers trapped in NE France are evacuated from Dunkirk.

28th, Belgian army surrenders; King Leopold III is taken prisoner.

June: 10th, Italy declares war on France and Britain.

14th, Germans enter Paris.

15th, (–17th) USSR occupies the Baltic States (Estonia, Latvia, Lithuania).

16th, Winston Churchill offers France union with Britain, as a means to continue the war after the defeat of France; the French government rejects the idea and Reynaud resigns as prime minister (succeeded by Marshal Pétain).

17th, in France, Pétain announces that France is negotiating an armistice with Germany; General Charles de Gaulle flees from Paris to Britain.

22nd, France concludes armistice with Germany, dividing the country into two zones: a German-occupied zone in the N and SW and a so-called autonomous 'Vichy' French State with responsibility for French overseas territories (French government established in Vichy on 1st July).

26th, USSR demands Bessarabia and Bukovina from Romania; Romania requests German support for rejection of the demand, but Hitler refuses; 27th, Romania cedes the territories which are occupied 28th by Soviet troops.

30th, Germany occupies the Channel Islands.

July: 5th, the government of Vichy France breaks relations with Britain.

Aug: 5th, Britain signs agreements with Polish Government in London and, 7th, with Free French under Charles de Gaulle.

15th, in Battle of Britain, the Royal Air Force shoots down 180 German planes.

20th, in Battle of Britain, the German emphasis shifts to attacking British airports and aircraft factories.

23rd, all-night German bombing raid on London begins the period of intense bombing known as the 'Blitz'.

Sept: 4th, in Romania, Ion Antonescu assumes dictatorial powers (as 'Conducator'); 6th, King Carol II abdicates in favour of his son Michael and flees to Switzerland with his mistress.

Nov: 5th, in USA, F D Roosevelt, Democrat, is re-elected President for an unprecedented third term, with 449 electoral votes, against Wendell L Wilkie, Republican, with 82; popular vote: Roosevelt, 27,244,160; Wilkie, 22,305,198.

11th, (–12th) British attack and cripple Italian fleet at Taranto, SE Italy.

20th, Hungary and, 23rd, Romania, endorse German–Italian–Japanese Tripartite Pact of 27th Sept.

Dec: 9th, (–9th Feb) in North Africa, Operation Compass: Eighth Army under Archibald Wavell advances from Egypt into Libya (crossing the border 15th).

Society, Education, and Religion

(21st Feb) British women to receive old-age pension at 60.

Science, Technology, and Discovery

Swiss chemist Paul Müller invents the insecticide DDT.
In Oxford, England, Howard Florey and Ernst Chain develops penicillin as an antibiotic.

Art, Sculpture, Fine Arts, and Architecture

In Britain, official war artists are appointed: Edward Ardizzone, Muirhead Bone, Henry Lamb, John Nash, Paul Nash, Eric Ravilious, Stanley Spencer.

Painting Wassily Kandinsky, *Sky Blue.*

Literature

Graham Greene, *The Power and the Glory.*
Ernest Hemingway, *For Whom the Bell Tolls.*
Drama Eugene O'Neill, *Long Day's Journey into Night* (first produced in 1956).

Sport and Recreation

The 12th Olympic Games, due to be held in Tokyo, Japan, are cancelled because of the War.

Media

Film *Fantasia* (producer, Walt Disney).
The Great Dictator (starring Charlie Chaplin).
Pinocchio (producer, Walt Disney).
Rebecca (director, Alfred Hitchcock).
The Road to Singapore (the first 'road' film starring Bing Crosby, Bob Hope, and Dorothy Lamour).

1941

Feb: 12th, German General Erwin Rommel arrives in Tripoli, Libya, to take control of German reinforcements and stiffen Italian resistance to the British.

March: 11th, in USA, the Lend-Lease Bill is signed after two months' controversy.
24th, in N Africa, German and Italian forces commanded by General Rommel take El Algheila in Libya from the British; Rommel launches his first offensive.

April: 20th, in N Africa, Axis forces under Erwin Rommel attack Tobruk in NE Libya.

June: 22nd, Operation Barbarossa: Germany invades the USSR, with three army groups aiming to capture, respectively, Leningrad, Moscow, and the Ukraine (Romanian troops support the invasion).

July: 12th, in USSR, British–Soviet agreement of mutual assistance signed in Moscow.
23rd, following Japan's demand for bases in Indochina, Britain and USA freeze Japanese assets.
24th, Japanese troops begin occupation of Central and S Indochina.
27th, in USSR, Germans enter the Ukraine.

Aug: 11th, Winston Churchill and F D Roosevelt, meeting on a ship off Newfoundland (now part of Canada), sign the Atlantic Charter (published 14th); it condemns territorial changes and affirms human rights.

Sept: 8th, in USSR, German forces reach Leningrad (now St Petersburg) but fail to capture the city; they start a siege (–27th Jan 1944).

Oct: 1st, in USSR, Germans advance from Smolensk towards Moscow.
25th, failure of first German offensive against Moscow.

Nov: 16th, in USSR, second German offensive against Moscow.
18th, in N Africa, British forces in Egypt launch Operation Crusader; they relieve Tobruk in Libya (7th Dec) and advance across Libya (–1942).

Dec: 5th, (–5th Jan 1942) in USSR, Soviet forces launch counteroffensive N and S of Moscow to relieve pressure on the capital.
7th, Japanese make surprise air attack on the US naval base at Pearl Harbor, Hawaii; eight battleships and over 300 aircraft are destroyed or damaged.
8th, USA and Britain declare war on Japan.
9th, in NW USSR, Soviet forces recapture Tikhvin, easing the pressure on Leningrad.
10th, Japanese forces start a series of landings on Luzon, Philippines (others on 12th and 22nd).
11th, Germany and Italy declare war on the USA.
19th, British withdraw from island of Penang off the W coast of Malaya.
24th, in N Africa, British reoccupy Benghazi and regain control of Cyrenaica, Libya.
25th, British Chinese territory of Hong Kong surrenders to Japanese.

Politics, Government, Law, and Economy

(April) Rice-rationing introduced in Japan.

Society, Education, and Religion

In the wake of the German invasion of the USSR, German *Einsatzgruppen* ('Action Groups') slaughter 400,000–500,000 Jews.
The Germans transport Jews from Germany to the 'General Government' area of occupied Poland, where they are placed in ghettos or (from Dec) killed. In Vichy France, Jews are rounded up and turned over to the Germans (May–June).
Rudolf Bultmann, *New Testament and Mythology.*

Étienne Gilson, *God and Philosophy*.
(18th Aug) National Fire Service established in Britain.

Science, Technology, and Discovery

(Dec) In USA, the 'Manhattan Project' of atomic research (to develop an atomic bomb) starts in Chicago and Los Angeles under G B Pegram and H C Urey.

Humanities and Scholarship

Cambridge Economic History of Europe.

Art, Sculpture, Fine Arts, and Architecture

Henry Moore makes crayon drawings of refugees in air-raid shelters during the London Blitz.

Literature

Drama Bertolt Brecht, *Mother Courage and her Children*.
Noël Coward, *Blithe Spirit*.

Everyday Life

Double Summer Time introduced in Britain.
(1st June) 'Utility' clothing and furniture in Britain, where clothes are rationed.

Media

(Jan) (–Sept 1942) The British Communist paper, the *Daily Worker*, is suppressed.
Film *Das andere Ich*.
Citizen Kane (director and star, Orson Welles).
Dumbo (producer, Walt Disney).

1942

Jan: 11th, Japanese advancing through Malaya take Kuala Lumpur.

20th, in Germany, the Wannsee Conference: Nazi leaders and senior officials meet in a Berlin suburb to discuss 'the Final Solution of the Jewish Question'; that is, the destruction of European jewry.

20th, Japanese cross Thailand and invade Burma (now Myanmar), capturing Rangoon (now Yangon) 8th March.

21st, (–6th Feb) in N Africa, Rommel launches new offensive against the British forces in Libya; the British retreat eastwards to NE Libya (to a line between Gazala and Bir Hacheim).

Feb: 1st, in Norway, the Fascist leader Vidkun Quisling is appointed prime minister.

15th, Singapore, and over 70,000 British and Commonwealth soldiers and airmen, surrenders to the Japanese; described by Winston Churchill as 'the worst disaster and largest capitulation in British history'.

April: 9th, in Philippines, US and Filipino forces holding out against the Japanese on the Bataan Peninsula surrender (15th–29th, survivors are taken on a forced march, the 'Bataan death march', during which about 10,000 are killed or die).

18th, the Doolittle Raid: 16 US bombers from a carrier make a bombing raid on Tokyo and other Japanese cities, some then flying on to China.

May: 26th, British–USSR 20-year alliance signed in London.

June: 21st, in N Africa, the Axis forces under Rommel retake Tobruk in NE Libya from the British.

28th, in N Africa, British retreat eastwards to El Alamein in N Egypt.

Aug: 7th, in Pacific, US troops capture an airfield (named Henderson Airfield) on the island of Guadalcanal and hold it against a series of Japanese counterattacks (–7th Feb 1943); the US success at Guadalcanal turns the Japanese tide.

12th, (–15th) in USSR, Averell Harriman for the USA and Winston Churchill for Britain confer with Joseph Stalin in Moscow.

Sept: 13th, (–2nd Feb 1943) in USSR, Battle of Stalingrad: Germans try to capture the city of Stalingrad (now Volgograd) on the River Volga against determined Soviet resistance.

Oct: 23rd, (–4th Nov) in N Africa, (second) Battle of El Alamein: British forces in Egypt under General Bernard Montgomery attack the Axis forces under Rommel.

Nov: 4th, in N Africa, Axis forces under Rommel retreat westwards, pursued by the British.

7th, (–8th) in N Africa, Operation Torch: Allied troops under command of US General Dwight D Eisenhower land in Morocco and Algeria.

19th, in USSR, Soviet counteroffensive at Stalingrad surrounds besieging German army.

Politics, Government, Law, and Economy

The USA vastly expands industrial production for the war effort; among items produced is the 'Liberty Ship', a freighter of simple design.

Campaigns started in Britain ('Dig for Victory') and USA ('Victory Gardens'), encouraging cultivation of gardens and public space to increase food production.

Society, Education, and Religion

Following the Wannsee Conference (Jan), the Germans expand the scale of the killing of Jews, using gas; mobile gas vans kill many Jews, but facilities for large-scale murder are established at six 'death camps' (Chelmo; Bergen-Belsen, March; Sobibor, April; Auschwitz, June; Treblinka, July; Majdanek, autumn); Jews are transported by train from occupied Europe (France, Belgium, Netherlands, etc) to the death camps; Auschwitz sends up to 10,000 Jews to the gas chambers every day. 30,000 Jews are arrested by police in Paris (16th July) and sent to German concentration camps.

In USA, Executive Order 9066 (signed by President Roosevelt on 21st March) establishes the War Relocation Authority to move Japanese-Americans away from the Pacific Coast; some 110,000 are interned in WRA camps (most of the 150,000 Japanese in Hawaii are left alone).

(31st July) Foundation in Oxford, England, of the Oxford Committee for Famine Relief (later 'Oxfam').

(Dec) William Beveridge, *Social Security and Allied Services* (the 'Beveridge Plan').

Science, Technology, and Discovery

First launch of the V2 rocket in Germany.

In USA, magnetic tape is invented.

(July) Flight of the first jet fighter, the German Messerschmidt Me 262.

(2nd Dec) Enrico Fermi at Chicago, USA, initiates a controlled chain-reaction in the first nuclear reactor.

Humanities and Scholarship

G M Trevelyan, *English Social History.*

Music

Dmitri Shostakovich, Symphony No. 7 ('Leningrad').

Frank Sinatra makes a sensational first stage appearance in New York.

Literature

Albert Camus, *The Outsider.*

T S Eliot, *Little Gidding.*

Drama Jean Anouilh, *Antigone.*

Media

Film *Casablanca* (starring Ingrid Bergman and Humphrey Bogart).

How Green Was My Valley (director, John Ford).

Mrs Miniver (starring Greer Garson).

Radio *ITMA (It's That Man Again)*, starring Tommy Handley, is broadcast by BBC on 21st April as the first royal command performance of a radio programme.

1943

Jan: 2nd, in USSR, German withdrawal from Caucasus begins.

12th, (–23rd) Casablanca Conference: F D Roosevelt and Winston Churchill confer on grand strategy; they agree that Germany and Japan must surrender unconditionally.

31st, in USSR, the German commander at Stalingrad, Friedrich von Paulus, and his army surrender to the Red Army.

April: 6th, in N Africa, Axis forces under Rommel retreat north from Gabes Gap in Tunisia, enabling US and British armies to link up, 8th.

12th, discovery of the 'Katyn massacre': Germans find the grave of 4,500 Polish officers at Katyn near Smolensk in the USSR; they announce the discovery on 13th, claiming the Poles were murdered by the Soviets; Soviet authorities deny this.

19th, (–16th May) in Poland, uprising in the Warsaw ghetto.

May: 13th, German Army in Tunisia surrenders.

16th, Operation Chastise: British bombers, led by Wing-Commander Guy Gibson, attack three dams in the Ruhr region of Germany using the spinning or 'bouncing' bombs designed by Barnes Wallis; two dams are breached.

22nd, in USSR, Joseph Stalin dissolves the Third Communist International or Comintern (formed in 1919).

June: 3rd, French Committee of National Liberation is formed, led by General Charles de Gaulle and General Henri Giraud.

July: 10th, (–17th Aug) in Italy, Operation Husky: US and British troops land in Sicily.

25th, in Italy, King Victor Emmanuel III dismisses Benito Mussolini as prime minister and asks Marshal Badoglio to form a government.

Aug: 17th, in Italy, US troops occupy Messina in Sicily, at the crossing point to the mainland.

Sept: 3rd, Italy surrenders unconditionally (surrender announced by General Dwight Eisenhower, 8th).

Oct: 13th, the government of Italy, based in Brindisi, declares war on Germany.

18th, (–30th) Moscow Conference of Allied foreign ministers; it decides to establish the European Advisory Council to provide a forum for US, British, and Soviet consultation on the future of Europe.

Nov: 23rd, (–27th and 2nd–7th Dec) Cairo Conference: F D Roosevelt, Winston Churchill, and Chiang Kai-shek agree measures for defeating Japan.

28th, (–1st Dec) Tehran Conference: F D Roosevelt and Winston Churchill outline to Joseph Stalin the plan for an invasion of France in 1944.

Dec: 24th, (–May 1944) in USSR, the Soviet army, having retaken two-thirds of the territory conquered by the Germans, launch an offensive in the Ukraine.

Society, Education, and Religion

United Nations Relief and Rehabilitation Administration (UNRRA) founded in Washington, DC, USA, to provide relief in war-torn countries (relief programmes in Europe continue until 30th June 1947).

Albert Hoffman, a Swiss research chemist, discovers the hallucinogenic properties of the drug LSD.

Jacques Maritain, *Christianity and Democracy.*

Humanities and Scholarship

In Britain, the Pilgrim Trust purchases Sir Isaac Newton's library.

Jean-Paul Sartre, *Being and Nothingness.*

Art, Sculpture, Fine Arts, and Architecture

Sculpture Henry Moore, *Madonna and Child*, Northampton, England.

Music

Oklahoma (musical), music by Richard Rodgers and Oscar Hammerstein (first performed at the St James Theatre, New York, 31st March).

Literature

Ricardo Molinari, *Mundos de la Madrugada* (poems).

Drama Jean-Paul Sartre, *Les mouches/The Flies.*

Media

In Germany, the *Frankfurter Zeitung* (founded 1855) is ordered to cease publication.

Film *For Whom the Bell Tolls.*

1944

Jan: 17th, in Italy, British and US forces attempt to break the Germans' Gustav Line at Monte Cassino.

20th, British air force drops 2,300 tons of bombs on Berlin (provoking, 9th Feb, protests in the House of Lords about the bombing of German cities).

Feb: 15th, (–17th) in Italy, US and British troops make a second attack on the Germans' Gustav Line at Monte Cassino; the monastery is bombed.

April: —, During the month Allies drop 81,400 tonnes of bombs on Germany and occupied Europe.

May: 11th, (–18th) in Italy, Allied forces make a fourth attack on the Gustav Line at Monte Cassino and break through; Poles storm the monastery 18th; the German defeat enables troops at Anzio to break out.

June: 4th, in Italy, Allied forces enter Rome.

6th, 'D-Day', the start of Operation Overlord: Allied forces surprise the Germans with landings on five beaches in Normandy, NW France; the beachheads are joined on 12th.

26th, in USSR, the Soviet army enters Vitebsk, W of Moscow.

July: 3rd, in USSR, the Soviet army takes Minsk, capturing over 150,000 Germans.

18th, in Japan, following the loss of Saipan, General Tojo is forced to resign as prime minister; succeeded by Kuniaki Koiso.

20th, in E Prussia, Germany, attempt to assassinate Adolf Hitler: a bomb explodes near Hitler in his eastern headquarters at Rastenburg, but fails to kill him; the man who placed the bomb, Count Claus von Stauffenberg, is shot the same evening and in the following months 5,000 people are executed for complicity.

28th, in Poland, the Soviet army takes Brest-Litovsk.

Aug: 1st, (–2nd Oct) the Warsaw Rising: Poles in Warsaw rebel against the German occupiers, but the Soviet army does nothing to help and forbids supplies from the West.

24th, in France, a French armoured unit enters Paris; Charles de Gaulle arrives 25th, and 26th organizes a procession along the Champs Elysées (28th, the Provisional Government is transferred from Algiers to Paris).

Sept: 3rd, in Belgium, British troops enter Brussels.

8th, Germans fire first V2 rockets at Britain.

Oct: 22nd, USA, USSR, and Britain recognize General Charles de Gaulle's Provisional Government of France.

Nov: 7th, F D Roosevelt, Democrat, wins US Presidential election, for a fourth term, with 432 electoral votes over Thomas E Dewey, Republican, with 99; popular vote: Roosevelt, 25,602,504; Dewey, 21,969,170; Dewey fails to carry his own state of New York.

11th, end of liberation of Greece from the Germans, but the resistance organization, the National People's Liberation Army (known as ELAS and part of the Communist-controlled National Liberation Front or EAM), refuses to demobilize; ELAS rebels seize part of Athens and Piraeus.

12th, British bombers sink Germany's last battleship, the *Tirpitz*, in Tromsö Fjord, Norway, enabling Britain's large ships to be released for service in the Pacific War.

Dec: 16th, in the Ardennes (Luxembourg and Belgium), the German army launches an offensive, aiming to reach the Meuse at Namur (the 'Battle of the Bulge', –28th Jan 1945).

Politics, Government, Law, and Economy

(10th Feb) Pay-As-You-Earn system for payment of income tax is introduced in Britain.

(July) United Nations Monetary and Financial Conference at Bretton Woods, New Hampshire, USA, establishes a new world economic order based on fixed exchange rates but not a return to the gold standard; the International Monetary Fund (IMF) and the World Bank are founded to provide liquidity and loans to keep international financial transactions viable.

Society, Education, and Religion

In France, the Provisional Government enfranchises women and allows them to sit in parliament.

William Beveridge, *Full Employment in a Free Society*.

Friedrich von Hayek, *The Road to Serfdom*.

In England and Wales, the 'Butler' Education Act (named after R A Butler, president of the Board of Education) raises the Board's status to that of ministry; it divides education into primary, secondary, and further stages (following the *Norwood Report* of 1943); introduces the 'eleven plus' exam; provides for the raising of the school-leaving age to 15 (and 16 as soon as possible); makes religious education and worship compulsory in schools; reduces the number of local education authorities from 315 to 146 and makes them responsible for the education of the handicapped and for the regular medical inspection of children.

Brother Roger Schutz founds ecumenical monastic community at Taizé, near Cluny, France.

C G Jung, *Psychology and Religion*.

Science, Technology, and Discovery

Quinine is synthesized in USA by R B Woodward and W von Doering.

In USA, Selman A Waksman publishes description of the antibiotic streptomycin, which is used as a treatment for tuberculosis.

Music

Michael Tippett, *A Child of Our Time*.

Literature

T S Eliot, *Four Quartets* (poems).

Drama Terence Rattigan, *Love in Idleness*, *The Winslow Boy*.

Jean-Paul Sartre, *In Camera*.

Tennessee Williams, *The Glass Menagerie*.

Sport and Recreation

The 13th Olympic Games, scheduled for London, are cancelled due to the War.

Media

Film *Henry V* (director and star, Laurence Olivier).

1945

Jan: 1st, British army opens new offensive in Burma (Myanmar).

17th, in Poland, the Soviet army takes Warsaw; 19th, captures Kraków; 23rd, Tilsit (now Sovetsk in Russia).

20th, provisional Hungarian government at Debrecen under General Miklós concludes armistice with Allies.

Feb: 4th, (–11th) F D Roosevelt, Winston Churchill, and Joseph Stalin confer at Yalta (in Russia in the Crimea) to plan for Germany's unconditional surrender (and division of the country into four zones of occupation, with four zones in Berlin), to settle the Polish question, and to make arrangements for the first United Nations conference at San Francisco, USA; Stalin agrees that the USSR will enter the war against Japan after the defeat of Germany and receive an occupation zone in Korea (Korea will be divided into two, along the 38th parallel).

April: 12th, in USA, President Roosevelt dies (aged 63) and is succeeded by Vice-President Harry S Truman.

13th, Soviet army takes Vienna and establishes a Provisional Government of Social Democrats, Social Christians, and Communists with Karl Renner as prime minister.

16th, in Germany, Soviet army launches offensive from its bridgehead on the River Oder, aiming to capture Berlin.

25th, (–26th June) founding conference of the United Nations held in San Francisco, California, USA; at the conclusion, 51 countries sign the UN Charter.

28th, in Italy, Benito Mussolini, his mistress Clara Petacci, and members of his entourage are shot by partisans (the bodies of Mussolini and Petacci are displayed in Milan the following day).

29th, surrender of German army on Italian front.

30th, in Germany, Adolf Hitler shoots himself in his bunker in Berlin; Eva Braun takes poison (1st May, Admiral Doenitz announces Hitler's death and declares himself Hitler's successor).

May: 2nd, Berlin surrenders to Soviet army.

4th, in Burma (Myanmar), Rangoon (Yangon) is captured from the Japanese.

7th, near Reims in France, in the presence of General Dwight Eisenhower and other Allied officers, General Alfred Jodl signs surrender of Germany (effective from 8th May); the German state will cease to exist and be replaced by the Allies' zones of occupation.

8th, 'VE' (Victory in Europe) Day in Western Europe and the USA; in Germany, near Berlin, Wilhelm von Keitel and other German military leaders sign surrender document in presence of Marshal Georgi Zhukov of the USSR and other Allied commanders.

9th, 'VE' Day in USSR.

June: 5th, Allied Control Commission proclaims its control of Germany and authority over the definition of Germany's territories and borders.

July: 17th, (–2nd Aug) in Germany, Potsdam Conference is held, attended by Joseph Stalin, Harry Truman, Winston Churchill, and Clement Attlee, to organize the occupation of Germany; German land east of the Oder–Neisse is left under Polish jurisdiction; Austria is to be divided into occupation zones.

26th, Labour landslide in British general election with 393 seats, against Conservatives with 199, Liberals with 12, and National Liberals with 11; other parties, 25. (On 27th, Clement Attlee forms ministry with Ernest Bevin as foreign secretary and Hugh Dalton as chancellor of the exchequer).

Aug: 6th, in Pacific, US plane drops atomic bomb on the Japanese city of Hiroshima.

8th, USSR declares war on Japan and invades Manchuria.

9th, in Pacific, US plane drops atomic bomb on the Japanese city of Nagasaki.

13th, World Zionist Congress demands admission of 1 million Jews to Palestine.

14th, announcement made that the Japanese emperor will formally proclaim Japan's acceptance of the Allies' terms for ending the war; ie, surrender (his recorded message is broadcast on radio at midday on 15th).

24th, President Harry Truman of USA orders cessation of lend-lease which has cost the USA $48.5 billion.

28th, US forces land on the Japanese mainland.

Sept: 2nd, Japan signs capitulation on board USS *Missouri*; Korea is placed under US and Soviet occupation until a democratic government is established; Outer Mongolia is recognized as under Soviet control, while China regains sovereignty over Inner Mongolia and Manchuria, Formosa (modern Taiwan), and Hainan.

2nd, Ho Chi Minh proclaims independent Democratic Republic of Vietnam (the French refuse to recognize the Republic).

20th, (–23rd) All-India Congress Committee under Gandhi and Pandit Nehru rejects British proposals for self-government and calls on Britain to 'quit India'.

27th, in India, the Congress Party and the Muslim League win most seats in elections for Central Legislative Assembly.

Oct: 11th, in China, breakdown of negotiations between Chiang Kai-shek and Communist leader Mao Zedong leads to fighting between Nationalists and Communists in N China for control of Manchuria.

20th, Egypt, Iraq, Syria, and Lebanon warn USA that creation of a Jewish state in Palestine would lead to war; foundation of Arab League.

21st, elections for French Constituent Assembly show swing to left; Communists win 148 seats; Socialists, 134; Radical Socialists, 35 (the Popular Republican Movement wins 141 seats; Conservatives, 62; others, 2).

24th, the United Nations comes into formal existence with ratification of its Charter by 29 nations.

Nov: 10th, Communist-dominated government of Albania, under Enver Hoxha, recognized by Western powers.

11th, Marshal Tito's National Front wins elections to Yugoslav Constituent Assembly.

13th, in France, Charles de Gaulle is elected president of Provisional Government.

20th, in Nuremberg, Germany, opening of trial of 24 leading Nazis before Allied International Military Tribunal (–31st Aug 1946).

29th, Federal People's Republic of Yugoslavia proclaimed.

Politics, Government, Law, and Economy

The International Military Tribunal, sitting at Nuremberg, to judge crimes against peace, war crimes, and crimes against humanity, rules that an individual's obedience to orders is an insufficient defence for having committed such acts.

(22nd March) League of Arab States ('Arab League') founded by a treaty signed at Cairo.

Society, Education, and Religion

Karl Popper, *The Open Society and Its Enemies.*

Foundation of the United Nations Educational, Scientific, and Cultural Organization (UNESCO).

Allied Control Commission in Japan order the disestablishment of State Shinto (state rites conducted by the emperor); replaced by Shrine Shinto (private practices of the imperial family).

Science, Technology, and Discovery

(16th July) First atomic explosion, in the New Mexico desert, USA, reveals the discovery of releasing and controlling atomic energy.

Music

Benjamin Britten, *Peter Grimes* (opera).

Richard Strauss, *Metamorphosen.*

Arts Council of Great Britain established, to encourage performance in the arts (royal charter, 1946).

Literature

Carlo Levi, *Christ Stopped at Eboli.*

George Orwell *Animal Farm.*

Jean-Paul Sartre, *The Age of Reason.*

Evelyn Waugh, *Brideshead Revisited.*

Everyday Life

'Bebop' sweeps the USA.

Media

Film *Ivan the Terrible* (director, Sergei Eisenstein).

Rome, Open City (director, Roberto Rossellini).

Statistics

War casualties, 1939–45: Great Britain, 244,723 killed; 277,090 wounded. Rest of British Commonwealth, 109,929 killed; 197,908 wounded. US, 230,173 killed; 613,611 wounded. Germany, 3,000,000 military and civilian dead or missing; *c.* 1,000,000 wounded. USSR, estimated 20,000,000 military and civilian dead.

Naval losses: Royal Navy: 5 battleships; 8 aircraft carriers; 26 cruisers; 128 destroyers; 77 submarines. US Navy: 2 battleships; 5 aircraft carriers; 6 escort cruisers; 10 cruisers; 71 destroyers; 52 submarines. Germany: 7 battleships; 2 heavy cruisers; 5 light cruisers; 25 destroyers; 974 U-boats. Japan: 12 battleships; 15 aircraft carriers; 4 escort carriers; 16 heavy cruisers; 20 light cruisers; 126 destroyers; 125 submarines.

The Making of Global Civilization

1946–1997

1946 **Jan: 10th**, first session of United Nations General Assembly opens in London, with Paul Spaak of Belgium as president.

20th, in France, Charles de Gaulle resigns presidency of Provisional Government because of continued Communist opposition (succeeded, 22nd, by the Socialist Félix Gouin).

31st, new constitution in Yugoslavia creates six constituent republics (Serbia, Montenegro, Croatia, Slovenia, Bosnia-Herzegovina, Macedonia), but these are subordinated to the central authority, on the model of the USSR.

Feb: 24th, Juan Perón elected president of Argentina.

March: 5th, Winston Churchill, former British prime minister, delivers speech at Fulton, Missouri, USA, in which he declares that Stalin has lowered an 'iron curtain ... from Stettin in the Baltic to Trieste in the Adriatic', and warns that the USSR is aiming for 'the infinite expansion of [its] power and doctrines'; his speech signals for many the formal start of the Cold War.

6th, France recognizes Vietnam as a Democratic Republic within the Indochinese Federation.

29th, new constitution in Gold Coast, which becomes first British African colony with a majority of Africans in the legislature.

April: 27th, in Tokyo, Japan, opening of the main war crimes trial of the International Military Tribunal for the Far East (–12th Nov 1948); charges are brought against Hideki Tojo, the former prime minister, and 27 associates (one defendant is declared unfit to stand trial; two die during the trial).

May: 20th, British House of Commons passes bill for nationalization of coal mines.

26th, general election in Czechoslovakia, in which the Communists win the largest number of votes (about 38%); Communist Klement Gottwald becomes prime minister.

June: 2nd, in Italy, referendum produces majority in favour of a republic.

3rd, King Umberto II leaves Italy; Alcide de Gasperi, the prime minister, becomes provisional head of state.

28th, Enrico de Nicola elected president of Italy.

July: 4th, independent Philippine Republic inaugurated (replacing the Commonwealth of the Philippines).

15th, in USA, President Truman signs bill of credit for $3.75 billion for Britain.

29th, (–15th Oct) Peace Conference of 21 nations that had opposed the Axis meets in Paris to draft peace treaties.

Sept: 30th, in Nuremberg, Germany, the judges of the International Military Tribunal deliver their judgment; on 1st Oct they announce verdicts and sentences: Joachim von Ribbentrop, Hermann Goering, and ten other leading Nazis (including Martin Bormann, tried in absentia) are sentenced to death; Rudolf Hess, Walter Funk, and Erich Raeder are sentenced to life imprisonment; four others receive long sentences, but Dr Hjalmar Schacht, Franz von Papen, and Hans Fritzsche are acquitted.

Politics, Government, Law, and Economy

Frederick Meinecke, *The German Catastrophe*.

Douglas MacArthur purges extreme nationalists in Japan.

Verdicts of the International Military Tribunal at Nuremberg, Germany, establish that individuals can be guilty of war crimes and punished for crimes against international law.

In Britain, the Privy Council rules that a Canadian Bill to stop appeals from Canadian courts to the Council is valid.

In France, the Monnet Plan suggests a technocratic restructuring of industry and agriculture.

Hyperinflation in Hungary is history's most extreme, resulting in the printing of a 100-trillion-pengo note.

(1st March) British government nationalizes the Bank of England (Bank incorporated in 1694).

Society, Education, and Religion

Italian women enfranchised.

Bombay, India, removes discrimination against the harijans ('untouchables').

(3rd June) US Supreme Court rules that the segregation of African-Americans on interstate buses is unconstitutional.

(27th July) British National Insurance Act consolidates social services.

(6th Nov) Foundation of the National Health Service in Britain.

Science, Technology, and Discovery

C Carlson in USA invents xerography.

Discovery of carbon-13, an isotope for curing metabolic diseases.

Humanities and Scholarship

R G Collingwood, *The Idea of History*.

Bertrand Russell, *History of Western Philosophy*.

Jean-Paul Sartre, *Existentialism and Humanism*.

Literature

Jacques Prévert, *Paroles* (poems).

Drama Eugene O'Neill, *The Iceman Cometh*.

Media

Film *La Belle et la Béte* (director, Jean Cocteau).

Radio (29th Sept) The BBC founds the Third Programme.

1947

Jan: 1st, Britain grants Nigeria modified self-government.

Feb: 1st, in Italy, Alcide de Gasperi forms new ministry of Christian Democrats, Communists, and Left Socialists.

7th, British proposal for dividing Palestine into Arab and Jewish zones with administration as a trusteeship is rejected by Arabs and Jews.

10th, by peace treaties, signed in Paris, (i) Italy loses Adriatic Islands and part of Venezia Giulia to Yugoslavia, the Dodecanese Islands to Greece and small frontier regions to France, renounces sovereignty over its North African colonies, agrees to the establishment of Trieste as a free territory, pays reparations, and reduces its forces to 300,000 men; (ii) Romania loses Bessarabia and North Bukovina to the USSR, but regains Transylvania; (iii) Bulgaria retains South Dobrudja; (iv) Hungary is re-assigned 1938 frontiers; and (v) Finland cedes Petsamo to the USSR.

March: 10th, (–24th April) Moscow Conference of foreign ministers, which fails through division between the West and the USSR over problem of Germany.

12th, in USA, President Harry Truman, in speech to Congress announces plan to give aid to Greece and Turkey and thereby outlines the 'Truman Doctrine': he pledges that the USA will support 'free peoples who are resisting attempted subjugation by armed minorities or by outside pressures'.

19th, Chinese Nationalists capture Communist capital of Yan'an.

April: 2nd, Security Council of the UN appoints the USA as Trustee for Pacific islands formerly under Japanese mandate.

May: 31st, in Italy, Alcide de Gasperi forms government of Christian Socialists and Independents (following resignation, 13th, after friction with the Left).

June: 2nd, German Economic Council is established.

5th, in speech at Harvard University, USA, Secretary of State George Marshall calls for a European Recovery Program funded by the USA (Marshall Aid).

July: 20th, in Indonesia, Dutch troops launch 'police action' against independence movement and succeed in establishing rule over Dutch estates.

Aug: 1st, Security Council of the UN calls for ceasefire in Indonesia (leads to truce 17th Jan 1948).

15th, Independence of India proclaimed, partitioning India; Nehru becomes prime minister of India, Muhammad Ali Jinnah (leader of the Muslim League) becomes viceroy of Pakistan with Liaquat Ali Khan prime minister; British authority in remaining states ends.

31st, Communist successes in Hungarian elections.

Oct: 5th, Warsaw Communist conference establishes the Cominform (Communist Information Bureau) to coordinate activities of European Communist Parties.

29th, Belgium, Netherlands, and Luxembourg ratify customs union (Benelux) (effective from 1st Nov).

Dec: 22nd, new constitution in Italy centralizes government and provides for popularly elected senate.

30th, under Communist pressure, King Michael of Romania abdicates.

Politics, Government, Law, and Economy

R McCallum and A Readman, *The British General Election of 1945*, the first work of psephological analysis.

In Britain, the coal industry is nationalized (from 1st Jan); acts of parliament (Aug) nationalize railways and road transport (from 1948).

(3rd May) New constitution introduced in Japan, with approval of the Diet, the emperor, and the people by means of a referendum (in which women vote for the first time); the emperor's powers are limited and the country renounces the use of war.

(23rd June) US Congress passes Taft–Hartley act over President Truman's veto, prohibiting use of union funds for political purposes, outlawing the 'closed shop' and strengthening the government's hands in strikes and lockouts.

Society, Education, and Religion

Partition of India into India and Muslim Pakistan leads to massacres and killings, especially in divided Bengal and Punjab; within a year of independence over 6 million people move from each state to the other.

Michael Polanyi, *Science, Faith and Society*.

Science, Technology, and Discovery

ENIAC (acronym for '*E*lectronic, *N*umerator, *I*ntegrator, *A*nalyser, and *C*omputer'), the first general purpose, fully electronic digital computer is completed at the University of Pennsylvania, USA.

First supersonic air flight by US plane.

Hungarian-British physicist Dennis Gabor invents holography, the production of three-dimensional images.

(Aug) Britain's first atomic pile at Harwell comes into operation.

Humanities and Scholarship

In Palestine, discovery of main series of Dead Sea Scrolls at Qumran on the shores of the Dead Sea.

Art, Sculpture, Fine Arts, and Architecture

Architecture Le Corbusier, Unité d'habitation, Marseilles, France (–1952).

Music

In Scotland, foundation of the Edinburgh Festival of Music and Drama.

Literature

Albert Camus, *The Plague*.

Anne Frank, *The Diary of Anne Frank*.

Compton Mackenzie, *Whisky Galore*.

Drama Tennessee Williams, *A Streetcar Named Desire*.

Sport and Recreation

(10th May) In football, Britain beats the Rest of Europe 6–1 in a match at Hampden Park to mark the British Associations' readmission to FIFA.

Media

Film *Quai des Orfèvres* (director, Henri Clouzot).

Le Silence est d'or (director, René Clair).

1948

Jan: 4th, Union of Burma (now Myanmar) proclaimed as an independent republic.

20th, in Delhi, India, Mahatma Gandhi is assassinated by an extremist Hindu, Nathuram Godse.

Feb: 4th, Ceylon (now Sri Lanka) becomes a self-governing dominion.

20th, in Czechoslovakia, 11 anti-Communist government ministers resign in protest at increasing Communist strength in police force; popular protests against the government are crushed.

25th, President Beneš of Czechoslovakia accepts an all-Communist cabinet, though Jan Masaryk remains foreign minister.

March: 17th, France, Belgium, Netherlands, Luxembourg, and Britain sign Brussels Treaty, for 50-year alliance against armed attack in Europe and providing for economic, social, and military cooperation.

20th, in response to developments in the US and British bizone in Germany, Soviet delegates walk out of Allied Control Commission for Germany.

31st, US Congress passes Marshall Aid Act, contributing $5.3 billion for European recovery.

April: 16th, meeting in Paris, France, of countries participating in the European Recovery Programme; sets up the Organization for European Economic Co-operation (OEEC).

18th, Christian Democrats win absolute majority in Italian elections (winning 305 out of 574 seats).

May: 14th, as British mandate in Palestine ends, the Jewish National Council and General Zionist

Council in Tel Aviv proclaim the establishment of a Jewish state, Israel, and assume the role of Provisional Government; David Ben-Gurion becomes prime minister (16th May, Chaim Weizmann is elected president); the USA recognizes the new state (as does the USSR on 17th).

26th, in South African election, J C Smuts's coalition of United and Labour Parties is defeated by the Nationalists and the Afrikaner Party, who advocate 'apartheid'; 3rd June, D F Malan becomes prime minister and forms government of Afrikaners.

June: 28th, Yugoslavia is expelled from Cominform for hostility to USSR.

July: 24th, USSR stops road and rail traffic between Berlin and the West forcing Western powers to organize massive airlift (–30th Sept 1949).

Nov: 2nd, in US presidential election, Harry Truman, Democrat, wins 304 electoral votes against Thomas E Dewey, Republican, 189, confounding public opinion polls; popular vote: Truman, 24,105,695; Dewey, 21,969,170; J Strom Thurmond, State-Rights Democrat, 1,169,021; Henry A Wallace, Progressive, 1,156,103. In Congressional elections, Democrats gain majority in both Houses.

7th, in France, Charles de Gaulle's RPF gains large number of seats in elections for the Council of the Republic.

Dec: 28th, USA, Britain, France, and Benelux countries establish an International Ruhr Authority.

Politics, Government, Law, and Economy

Electoral reform in Britain abolishes plural voting, including the business vote and university seats.

The Military and Political Consequences of Atomic Energy by P M S Blackett argues that an independent nuclear deterrent is beyond Britain's means; Blackett is excluded from government advisory circles for over a decade.

In Britain, railways (from 1st Jan), the electricity industry (from 1st April), and gas are nationalized.

End of bread-rationing in Britain.

Society, Education, and Religion

The General Assembly of the United Nations adopts the Universal Declaration of Human Rights.

Belgian women enfranchised.

World Health Organization (WHO) founded, as United Nations agency, in Geneva, Switzerland.

Foundation of the British National Health Service (effective from 5th July).

World Jewish Congress held at Montreux, Switzerland.

P Tillich, *The Shaking of the Foundations.*

(30th July) British Citizenship Act confers status of British subjects on all Commonwealth citizens.

(22nd Aug) (–4th Sept) Representatives of 147 churches from 44 countries meet in Amsterdam, Netherlands, to inaugurate the World Council of Churches (WCC).

(2nd Nov) In USA, Margaret Chase Smith is the first elected woman senator.

Science, Technology, and Discovery

Wilfred Thesiger crosses Arabian desert and penetrates Oman Steppes.

Humanities and Scholarship

T S Eliot, *Notes Towards the Definition of Culture.*

Art, Sculpture, Fine Arts, and Architecture

Painting Bill Brandt, *Camera in London* (photographs).

Jackson Pollock, *Composition No. 1* (tachisma).

Music

Columbia Record Company releases the first long-playing record (LP), invented by Peter Goldmark; by 1950 the playing speed of 33.3 revolutions per minute is established.

Literature

Graham Greene, *The Heart of the Matter.*

Alan Paton, *Cry, the Beloved Country.*

Drama Christopher Fry, *The Lady's Not for Burning.*

Terence Rattigan, *The Browning Version.*

Sport and Recreation

(29th July) (–14th Aug) The 14th Olympic Games are held in London. The USA wins 38 gold medals; Sweden, 16; France and Hungary, 10 each; Italy and Finland, 8 each; Turkey and Czechoslovakia, 6 each; Switzerland, Denmark, and Holland, 5 each. Mrs Fanny Blankers-Koen of the Netherlands wins 4 golds, for the 100-m, the 200-m, the 80-m hurdles, and the 4 × 100-m relay.

Media

Film *Abbot and Costello Meet Frankenstein.*

Bicycle Thieves (director, Vittorio de Sica).

The Fallen Idol (director, Carol Reed; starring Ralph Richardson).

Hamlet (director and star, Laurence Olivier).
The State of the Union (director, Frank Capra; starring Spencer Tracy and Katherine Hepburn).

Statistics

Pig-iron production (in thousand tons): US, 55,085; USSR, 14,000; Great Britain, 9,425; France, 6,625; West Germany, 4,670 (with Saar, 1,125): Belgium, 3,943.

Steel production (in thousand tons): US, 80, 285; USSR, 16,500; Great Britain, 15,116; France, 7,255; West Germany, 5,278 (with Saar, 1,212); Belgium, 3,917.

1949 **Jan: 21st**, Chiang Kai-shek resigns presidency of China, following successive reversals for Nationalist Armies.

March: 4th, in USSR, Andrei Vyshinsky replaces Vyacheslav Molotov as foreign minister.

April: 4th, foundation of the North Atlantic Treaty Organization ('NATO'): the North Atlantic Treaty is signed in Washington, DC, USA, by foreign ministers of USA, Canada, Britain, France, Luxembourg, Belgium, Netherlands, Italy, Portugal, Denmark, Iceland, and Norway, providing for mutual assistance against aggression.

18th, Republic of Ireland is formally proclaimed in Dublin; Ireland leaves the Commonwealth.

19th, US Foreign Assistance bill authorizes $5.43 billion for European Recovery Programme.

May: 5th, Statute of Council of Europe is signed in London by Belgium, Denmark, France, Britain, Ireland, Italy, Luxembourg, Netherlands, Norway, and Sweden (and subsequently by Greece, Iceland, and Turkey); members commit themselves to support freedom and the rule of law; Strasbourg is chosen as seat of the Council; the Council's institutions include a Consultative Assembly, a Committee of Ministers, and the European Court of Human Rights.

12th, Berlin blockade is officially lifted.

12th, to aid Japan's recovery, the Far Eastern Commission terminates Japan's reparation payments.

23rd, Federal Republic of Germany (West Germany) comes into being, with capital at Bonn (West Berlin is excluded from the new state but associated with it).

June: 14th, Vietnam State is established by French, with capital at Saigon, but conflict with Vietminh continues.

July: 16th, Chinese Nationalists organize Supreme Council under Chiang Kai-shek, which begins to remove forces to the island of Formosa (now Taiwan; evacuation completed, 8th Dec).

Oct: 1st, in China, Communist leader Mao Zedong proclaims the establishment of the People's Republic, with its government based in Beijing (Zhou Enlai is prime minister and foreign minister).

16th, defeat of rebels ends Greek Civil War (since May 1946).

Nov: 24th, Allied High Commission makes further economic concessions to West Germany on its accession to the International Ruhr Authority.

26th, India adopts constitution as a federal republic, remaining within the Commonwealth (to come into force on 26th Jan 1950).

Dec: 15th, West Germany becomes full member of Marshall Plan for European recovery.

27th, Netherlands transfers sovereignty to United States of Indonesia (comprising all the former Dutch East Indies except western New Guinea).

30th, France transfers sovereignty to Vietnam.

Politics, Government, Law, and Economy

In the new state of Israel, a single-chamber parliament, the Knesset, is established, which (in place of a constitution) passes an interim organic law defining legislative, executive, and judicial powers; religious tribunals are to operate alongside the civil courts.

In Britain, Iron and Steel Act passed to nationalize that industry, but its operation is suspended until the 1950 election.

Saudi Arabia grants a 60-year concession to Getty Oil of the USA, controlled by J P Getty (the deal makes Getty a billionaire).

Society, Education, and Religion

In South Africa, social legislation begins the implementation of 'apartheid'; the South African Citizenship Act suspends automatic granting of citizenship to Commonwealth immigrants after five years; the Prohibition of Mixed Marriages Act outlaws marriage between Europeans and non-Europeans; an amendment to the Immorality Act of 1927 bans sexual intercourse between Europeans and Coloureds; the Population Registration Act starts the process of defining people as White, Coloured, or African.

Simone de Beauvoir, *The Second Sex*.

Science, Technology, and Discovery

First atomic bomb tests in USSR.

US physician Philip Hench discovers that Cortisone can be used as a cure for rheumatoid arthritis.

Humanities and Scholarship
Gilbert Ryle, *The Concept of Mind.*

Art, Sculpture, Fine Arts, and Architecture
Sculpture Jacob Epstein, *Lazarus.*

Music
South Pacific (musical), lyrics by Oscar Hammerstein, music by Richard Rodgers (first performed at the Majestic Theatre, New York, 7th April).

Literature
George Orwell, *Nineteen Eighty-four.*

Drama Arthur Miller, *Death of a Salesman.*

Sport and Recreation
In Britain, the Badminton Olympic Three-Day Event (horse-riding) is held for the first time on the Duke of Beaufort's estate.

The National Parks and Access to Countryside Act is passed, creating National Parks and long-distance footpaths in England and Wales.

Media
Publication of *Paris-match*, an illustrated French news magazine.

Film *The Third Man* (director, Carol Reed; starring Orson Welles).

Television RCA in the USA produces a colour television system.

1950

Jan: 27th, bilateral agreements for aid in defence signed in Washington, DC, USA, between USA and (separately) Britain, France, Belgium, Netherlands, Luxembourg, Norway, Denmark, and Italy.

31st, in USA, President Truman instructs Atomic Energy Commission to proceed with development of the hydrogen bomb (a far more powerful kind of atomic weapon).

Feb: 14th, in Moscow, USSR, the USSR and Communist China sign a 30-year Treaty of Friendship, Alliance, and Mutual Assistance (in the event of attack) and other agreements.

23rd, general election in Britain results in a reduced Labour majority (315 seats; Conservatives, 298; Liberals, 9; others 3).

March: 1st, Chiang Kai-shek resumes presidency of Nationalist China (Formosa, now Taiwan).

May: 9th, announcement in Paris of the Schuman Plan, for placing the French and German coal industries and iron and steel production under a single authority which could then be joined by other countries.

June: 15th, West Germany admitted to Council of Europe.

25th, North Korean forces invade South Korea with several armies advancing southwards; UN Security Council passes resolution demanding withdrawal of North Korean forces (26th in US).

Sept: 26th, in Korea, UN forces recapture Seoul, the capital of South Korea.

Nov: 7th, in US elections, Republicans gain 30 seats in House of Representatives.

24th, in Korea, UN troops launch offensive into NE Korea.

26th, Chinese troops enter Korean War, forcing UN forces to retreat southwards.

28th, Poland and East Germany proclaim the Oder–Neisse line as the frontier between the two countries.

Dec: 16th, state of emergency proclaimed in USA following reversals of UN forces in Korea.

19th, conference of North Atlantic Conference (established under the North Atlantic Treaty of April 1949) agrees to create an integrated defence force, under the supreme command of General Dwight Eisenhower.

Politics, Government, Law, and Economy
(25th Jan) In USA, Alger Hiss is found guilty of perjury in concealing membership of Communist Party.

(1st March) In Britain, the atomic scientist Klaus Fuchs is sentenced to 14 years' imprisonment for betraying atomic secrets to Soviet agents; his evidence in confession to MI5 is used to incriminate his contact in the USA, Harry Gold, and the spies Julius and Ethel Rosenberg.

Society, Education, and Religion
Pope Pius XII issues encyclical *Humani Generis*, against Existentialism and 'erroneous' scientific theories.

Science, Technology, and Discovery
Jet-propelled, pilotless aircraft constructed in Australia.

Existence of 'V'-particles is confirmed in Pasadena, California, USA, and on the Pic du Midi d'Ossau.

Art, Sculpture, Fine Arts, and Architecture

Architecture Mario Pani and Enrique del Moral, University City, Mexico.

Literature

Pablo Neruda, *General Song.*
Ezra Pound, *Seventy Cantos.*

Sport and Recreation

The fourth football World Cup is held in Brazil, when Uruguay beats Brazil 2–1 in the final, witnessed by 199,854 spectators (July 16th); British sides compete for the first time, England losing 1–0 to the USA (June 29th).

Media

Film *Orphée* (director, Jean Cocteau).
Rashomon (director, Akira Kurosawa).
Sunset Boulevard (director, Billy Wilder; starring Gloria Swanson and William Holder).
Radio (May) In Britain, start of *The Archers* in the Midland region of the BBC; broadcast nationally from 1st Jan 1951 (–).

Statistics

Populations of cities (in millions): London, 8.3; New York, 7.8; Tokyo, 5.3; Moscow, 4.1; Chicago, 3.6; Shanghai, 3.6; Calcutta, 3.5; Berlin, 3.3.
Religious denominations in Britain (in thousands): Roman Catholics, 3,884; Church of England, 1,867; Presbyterian Church of Scotland, 1,273; Methodists, 776; Congregationalists, 387; Baptists, 338; Presbyterians, 82; Episcopal Church of Scotland, 57; Jews, 450.

1951

Jan: 1st, in Korea, North Korean and Chinese forces break United Nations lines on 38th parallel and, 4th take Seoul, the capital of South Korea.

April: 22nd, in Britain, Aneurin Bevan (minister for labour) and Harold Wilson (president of the board of trade) resign from Labour cabinet in protest at imposition of health service charges to meet increasing defence spending.
22nd, (–25th) in Korea, Battle of Imjin River: defensive action by UN troops against Chinese and North Koreans.

May: 25th, in Britain, diplomats Guy Burgess and Donald Maclean are warned by art historian and Soviet spy Anthony Blunt that they are under suspicion for espionage; they leave Britain (their presence in Moscow, USSR, is revealed on 11th Feb 1956).

June: 17th, in elections for French National Assembly Gaullists win 107 seats; Communists, 97; Socialists, 94; Conservatives, 87; Popular Republicans, 82; Radical Socialists, 77.

July: 5th, in dispute between Iran and Britain over oil nationalization, the International Court issues interim order, which is rejected by Iran (15th, President Truman sends Averell Harriman to Iran to urge a compromise settlement).

Aug: 11th, French ministerial crisis (since elections on 17th June) ends with René Pleven forming a coalition of the Centre.

Sept: 8th, peace treaty with Japan signed at San Francisco by representatives of 49 powers, though USSR and satellites boycott final session of peace conference.

Oct: 25th, in British general election Conservatives win 321 seats (net gain 23) over Labour with 295 (net loss 20) and Liberals with 6 (net loss 3), United Ireland, 3.
27th, in Britain, Winston Churchill forms ministry, with Anthony Eden as foreign secretary and R A ('Rab') Butler as chancellor of exchequer.

Nov: 11th, Juan Perón is re-elected president of Argentina.
29th, in Syria, army mounts *coup d'état*, instigated by the chief of staff, Colonel Chichekli.

Dec: 13th, French National Assembly ratifies the Schuman Plan (placing French and German coal, iron, and steel industries under common authority to which other European nations might accede) by 377 to 233 votes.
20th, Greece is elected to the UN Security Council after 19 ballots, in preference to Belarus, which had been nominated by Russia (USSR).
24th, Libya (an Italian colony from 1911 to 1942, and under British military administration since then) becomes an independent federation under King Idris I, previously emir of Cyrenaica.
30th, public announcement made in Paris at meeting of foreign, finance, and defence ministers of France, Italy, Luxembourg, Belgium, Netherlands, and West Germany that the proposed European defence force is to be called the European Defence Community; and that they envisage that one day the Community will be replaced by a federal body.

Society, Education, and Religion
Fraudulent Medium Act in Britain repeals provisions of the Witchcraft Act of 1735.
Talcott Parsons, *The Social System.*
In England and Wales, the General Certificate of Education 'Ordinary' and 'Advanced' examinations (popularly known as O and A levels) replace the 'School Certificate'.
(3rd May) (–30th Sept) Festival of Britain held in London.

Science, Technology, and Discovery
(Dec) Electric power is satisfactorily produced from atomic energy at Arcon, Idaho, USA.

Art, Sculpture, Fine Arts, and Architecture
Sculpture Henry Moore, *Reclining Figure.*

Music
Benjamin Britten, *Billy Budd* (opera).
Igor Stravinsky, *The Rake's Progress* (opera).

Literature
Isaac Asimov, *Foundation.*
Robert Frost, *Complete Poems.*
Nicholas Monsarrat, *The Cruel Sea.*
J D Salinger, *The Catcher in the Rye.*
Herman Wouk, *The Caine Mutiny.*
Drama Jean Anouilh, *Colombe.*
Jean-Paul Sartre, *Le Diable et le Bon Dieu.*

Media
Film *Othello* (director, Orson Welles).

Statistics
Populations (in millions): China, 490; India, 357; USSR, 190; US, 153 (of whom 136 whites, 16 African-American and 0.7 other races); Japan, 85; Pakistan, 76; Great Britain, 50; West Germany, 48; Italy, 47; France, 42. S. Africa has 2.4 Europeans and 9.3 non-Europeans.

1952

Jan: **24th**, Vincent Massey is first Canadian to be appointed governor general of Canada (–Sept 1959).

March: **1st**, in India's first national elections Pandit Nehru's Congress Party wins 364 of 489 seats in the National Assembly.

June: **18th**, British scheme for Central African Federation published.

July: **25th**, European Coal and Steel Community in force.

Aug: **4th**, (–25th Sept) conference in Honolulu of Pacific Council (Australia, New Zealand, and USA; held under Pacific Security Treaty of Sept 1951).
5th, Japan resumes diplomatic relations with Nationalist China (Formosa, now Taiwan).
23rd, Arab League Security Pact of 1950 comes into force following ratification by member states.

Oct: **5th**, opening of 19th Congress of the USSR Communist Party, the first Congress since 1939.
20th, state of emergency proclaimed in Kenya because of Mau Mau (nationalist) disturbances; about 200 leading members of the Kenya African Union are arrested.
22nd, Iran breaks diplomatic relations with Britain over oil dispute.

Nov: **—**, Bill introduced in British Parliament to denationalize iron and steel.
4th, Republican landslide in US presidential election with Dwight D Eisenhower winning 442 electoral votes over Adlai Stevenson, Democrat, with 89; popular vote: Eisenhower, 33,936,252; Stevenson, 27,314,992.

Politics, Government, Law, and Economy
(11th Dec) In Britain, the Bentley case: Derek Bentley is convicted of murdering a policeman and sentenced to death, even though the fatal shots were fired by accomplice Christopher Craig who, at age 16, is too young to suffer capital punishment (Bentley is hanged 28th Jan 1953); the case remains controversial because of Bentley's ambiguous instruction to Craig, 'Let him have it Chris', which could refer to either the gun itself or to firing the gun.

Society, Education, and Religion
Reinhold Niebuhr, *Christ and Culture.*

Science, Technology, and Discovery
G D Searle laboratories in the USA make a contraceptive tablet of phosphorated hesperidin.
(6th Nov) USA explodes the first hydrogen bomb, at Eniwetok island in the Pacific.

Humanities and Scholarship

Archaeologists use radioactive carbon (C14) tests for dating finds.
Kathleen Kenyon begins her excavation at Jericho, Jordan.
F R Leavis, *The Common Pursuit.*

Art, Sculpture, Fine Arts, and Architecture

Architecture Skidmore, Owings, and Merrill, Lever House, New York; Manufacturers Trust Bank, New York (–1954).

Sculpture Henry Moore, *King and Queen.*

Music

John Cage, *4'33".*
Michael Tippett, *The Midsummer Marriage* (opera).
White US disc jockey Alan Freed plays African-American music on his programme *Moondog's Rock 'n' Roll Party* (popularizing the term Rock 'n' Roll).
(14th Nov) *New Musical Express* publishes Britain's first pop singles chart.

Literature

Dylan Thomas, *Collected Poems.*
Evelyn Waugh, *Men at Arms.*
Drama Agatha Christie, *The Mousetrap.*

Everyday Life

(Dec) 'Smog' hits London.

Sport and Recreation

(19th July) (–3rd Aug) The 15th Olympic Games are held in Helsinki. The USA wins 40 gold medals; USSR, 22; Hungary, 16; Sweden, 12; Italy, 8; Czechoslovakia, 7; France, Finland, and Australia, 6 each. In the course of one week, the Czech athlete, Emil Zatopek wins the 5,000 m, the 10,000 m, and the marathon (20th–27th July).

(23rd Sept) Rocky Marciano defeats Jersey Joe Walcott (both of USA), to win the World Heavyweight Boxing title.

Media

Film *High Noon* (director, Fred Zinnemann; starring Gary Cooper and Grace Kelly).
Limelight (director and star, Charlie Chaplin; with Claire Bloom).
The Quiet Man (director, John Ford; starring John Wayne and Maureen O'Hara).
Singin' in the Rain (director and star, Gene Kelly).

Television The BBC's *Watch With Mother* programmes introduce Bill and Ben, *The Flowerpot Men.*

1953

Jan: 1st, conference held in London of representatives of British government and those of Northern Rhodesia, Southern Rhodesia, and Nyasaland (respectively modern Zambia, Zimbabwe, and Malawi), regarding proposed creation of federation of those countries to handle external affairs, defence, and currency (scheme to establish Central African Federation published 5th Feb; created by Federation (Constitution) Order in Council 1st Aug).

12th, Yugoslav National Assembly adopts new constitution (14th, Marshal Tito is elected first president of Yugoslav Republic).

14th, Consultative Assembly of Council of Europe meets in Strasbourg to draft constitution for European Political Community (adopted 10th Feb).

Feb: 28th, treaty of friendship between Greece, Turkey, and Yugoslavia.

March: 5th, Joseph Stalin dies (6th, Georgi Malenkov, designated by Stalin, succeeds as chairman of council of ministers).

31st, Dag Hammarskjöld of Sweden is elected secretary general of the United Nations by the Security Council in succession to Trygve Lie (7th April, ratified by General Assembly).

April: 8th, in Kenya, following a massacre at Lari in the Rift Valley, Jomo Kenyatta and five other Kikuyu convicted of organizing Mau Mau terrorism.

15th, National Party under D F Malan secures clear majority in South African elections.

June: 2nd, in Britain, coronation of Queen Elizabeth II at Westminster Abbey, London.

7th, in Italian elections, Christian Democrats and their allies win seats from Socialists and Communists.

July: 5th, in Hungary, Mátyás Rákosi is removed as prime minister and replaced by Imre Nagy, leading to more relaxed regime.

9th, in USSR, Lavrenti Beria, minister of internal affairs, is arrested, dismissed from the Communist Party, and accused of attempting to seize power (he is shot as a traitor on 23rd Dec).

Sept: 6th, Christian Democratic Union wins West German general election, winning 243 seats; Social Democrats win 151; Free Democrats, 48; others, 45.

12th, in USSR, Nikita Khrushchev is appointed first secretary of central committee of Communist Party.

Oct: 9th, Arab Liberation movement wins Syrian elections.

20th, Konrad Adenauer forms new government in West Germany.

23rd, federal constitution of Central African Federation (North and South Rhodesias and Nyasaland, now Zambia, Zimbabwe, and Malawi) comes into force.

Politics, Government, Law, and Economy

In Britain, steel is denationalized (March), followed by road transport (May).

(30th March) Denmark adopts new constitution; the Upper House is abolished and the voting age reduced to 23.

Science, Technology, and Discovery

Astronomers in Australia, South Africa, and USA discover a new scale of space outside the solar system. Cosmic ray observatory is established on Mt Wrangell, Alaska, USA.

(29th May) Edmund Hillary and Norkey Tenzing, from John Hunt's expedition climbing Mt Everest, reach the summit.

Humanities and Scholarship

British architect and archaeologist Michael Ventris publishes his decipherment of the Minoan writing called 'Linear B'.

Ludwig Wittgenstein, *Philosophical Investigations.*

(21st Sept) W Le Gros Clark and others prove that the skull of 'Piltdown Man', found in S England in 1912, is a fraud.

Art, Sculpture, Fine Arts, and Architecture

'Mexican Art' exhibition (from Pre-Columbian art to the mid-20th century), Royal Academy, London.

Architecture Pier Luigi Nervi and others, UNESCO Conference Hall, Paris (–1957).

Music

Benjamin Britten, *Gloriana* (opera).

Dmitri Shostakovich, Symphony No. 10.

Literature

Drama Arthur Miller, *The Crucible.*

Media

(Dec) In USA, publication of 'girlie' magazine *Playboy*, founded by Hugh Hefner.

Film *The Big Heat* (director, Fritz Lang; starring Glenn Ford).

From Here to Eternity (director, Fred Zinnemann; starring Burt Lancaster and Frank Sinatra).

Gentlemen Prefer Blondes (director, Howard Hawks; starring Jane Russell and Marilyn Monroe).

Roman Holiday (director, William Wyler; starring Gregory Peck and Audrey Hepburn).

I Vitelloni (director, Federico Fellini).

1954

Jan: 8th, (–15th) Commonwealth finance ministers meet at Sydney, Australia, under Australian Prime Minister Robert Menzies, to consolidate economic progress of the sterling area and Commonwealth.

17th, expulsion from Yugoslav Communist Party of Chairman Milovan Djilas, who had pleaded for greater freedom of expression.

25th, (–18th Feb) foreign ministers of USA, USSR, Britain, and France meet in Berlin to reduce world tension, but USSR rejects the West's proposal for the reunification of Germany through free elections (conference ends with proposal for a further conference in April at Geneva with Chinese and Korean representatives).

Feb: 25th, in Egypt, Colonel Gamal Abdel Nasser usurps power as prime minister (but, on 27th, General Muhammad Neguib is again in control).

April: 5th, in USA, President Eisenhower makes broadcast about the H-bomb and the Communist threat.

18th, General Nasser becomes prime minister and military governor of Egypt.

May: 7th, in N Vietnam, Vietminh siege of French forces at Dien Bien Phu ends with surrender of French.

18th, European Convention on Human Rights in force.

June: 15th, in Gold Coast (now Ghana), Convention People's Party wins elections (21st, Dr Kwame Nkrumah forms government).

July: 20th, armistice for Indochina signed in Geneva by which France evacuates N Vietnam; the Communists evacuate S Vietnam, Cambodia, and Laos; and France undertakes to respect the independence of Cambodia, Laos, and Vietnam; Ho Chi Minh forms government in N Vietnam.

Sept: 8th, South-East Asian Defence treaty (for mutual defence) and Pacific Charter signed in Manila, Philippines by USA, Australia, New Zealand, Pakistan, Thailand, Philippines, Britain, and France (the Defence treaty establishes SEATO, the South-East Asia Treaty Organization, based in Bangkok, Thailand).

Oct: 3rd, nine-power conference in London on European unity agrees that West Germany should enter NATO.

23rd, USA, Britain, France, and USSR agree to end occupation of Germany; nine-power agreement on Western European Union signed, permitting Italy and Germany to accede to the Brussels treaty of 1948.

30th, (–1st Nov) insurrection in Algeria, with over 60 attacks on French police and troops; the rebels call themselves the Front for National Liberation (FLN) and call for the establishment of an independent Algeria.

Nov: 14th, in Egypt, President Neguib is deposed (18th, General Nasser becomes head of state).

Dec: —, France sends 20,000 troops to Algeria.

2nd, US Senate censures Joseph McCarthy.

Politics, Government, Law, and Economy

International convention on the prevention of oil pollution at sea.

(3rd July) In Britain, rationing ends.

Society, Education, and Religion

US evangelist Billy Graham holds massive meetings in London, Berlin, and New York.

Paul Tillich, *Love, Power and Justice.*

Science, Technology, and Discovery

First 'flying bedstead' aircraft, with vertical take-off, developed.

National Cancer Institute in the USA suggests link between smoking and lung cancer.

John Charnley starts research that leads to effective hip replacement operations (from 1961).

Polio vaccine prepared by US physician Jonas E Salk is released for general use.

Humanities and Scholarship

W G Grimes discovers remains of a Roman Temple of Mithras in the City of London.

Arthur Koestler, *The Invisible Writing.*

Art, Sculpture, Fine Arts, and Architecture

(3rd Nov) Death of Henri Matisse.

Sculpture Barbara Hepworth, *Two figures, Menhirs.*

Music

Benjamin Britten, *The Turn of the Screw* (opera).

Arnold Schoenberg, *Moses and Aaron* (posthumous opera).

Salad Days (musical), by Julian Slade (first performed at the Vaudeville Theatre, London, 5th Aug).

Bill Haley and the Comets, 'Rock Around the Clock'.

Literature

Kingsley Amis, *Lucky Jim.*

William Golding, *Lord of the Flies.*

François Sagan, *Bonjour Tristesse.*

J R R Tolkien, *The Lord of the Rings*, Vols. 1 and 2 (Vol. 3, 1955).

Drama Tennessee Williams, *Cat on a Hot Tin Roof.*

(25th Jan) Dylan Thomas's dramatic poem, *Under Milk Wood* (a 'play for voices', written for radio), broadcast on BBC Third Programme.

Sport and Recreation

The fifth football World Cup is held in Switzerland; West Germany beats Hungary 3–2 in the final in Berne.

(6th May) Roger Bannister is the first man to run a mile in under 4 minutes, at the Iffley Road Sports Ground, Oxford, England.

(30th May) D Leather of Birmingham University, England, is the first woman to run a mile in under 5 minutes.

Media

Film *On the Waterfront* (director, Elia Kazan; starring Marlon Brando, Rod Steiger, and Lee J Cobb).

Rear Window (director, Alfred Hitchcock; starring James Stewart and Grace Kelly).

The Seven Samurai (director, Akira Kurosawa).

La Strada (director, Federico Fellini; starring Giulietta Masina).

Television In Britain, the Television Act establishes the Independent Television Authority to manage the introduction of commercial television (from 1955).

1955 Border raids between Israel and Jordan increase in intensity.

Feb: **23rd**, foreign ministers of SEATO countries (established in Sept 1954) confer at Bangkok, Thailand.

24th, Turkey and Iraq sign treaty of alliance, the Baghdad Pact, which provides for mutual support against Communist militants.

March: **11th**, Italy, West Germany (on 18th), and France (on 27th) ratify Paris agreement of Oct 1954 for establishing Western European Union.

31st, purge of Chinese Communist Party.

April: **4th**, Britain signs treaty with Iraq, and Parliament decides to adhere to the Baghdad Pact (of 24th Feb).

5th, in Britain, Winston Churchill resigns as prime minister because of age and ill health (succeeded on 6th by Anthony Eden who, 7th, reforms Conservative ministry, with Harold Macmillan as foreign secretary and R A Butler chancellor of the exchequer).

May: **5th**, end of occupation régime in West Germany.

6th, Britain submits dispute with Argentina and Chile over ownership of Falkland Islands to International Court; but those countries refuse to present counterclaims.

7th, USSR annuls treaties with Britain and France in retaliation for the ratification of the Paris agreement on European Union.

9th, West Germany is admitted as a member of NATO.

14th, Warsaw Treaty (of Friendship, Co-operation, and Mutual Assistance) signed by USSR, Albania, Bulgaria, Czechoslovakia, East Germany, Hungary, Poland, and Romania, establishing the 'Warsaw Pact'; provides for unified military command (with headquarters in Moscow) and stationing of Soviet military units in member countries.

26th, in British general election Conservatives win 345 seats over Labour with 277, Liberals with 6, and United Ireland with 2.

July: **5th**, Assembly of Western European Union holds first meeting at Strasbourg, France.

Aug: **30th**, (–7th Sept) conference in London of foreign ministers of Greece, Turkey, and Britain to discuss Cyprus and E Mediterranean; Britain's proposals for government of Cyprus are rejected.

Sept: **19th**, Juan Perón resigns as president of Argentina, going into exile (23rd, General Lonardi assumes presidency).

Oct: **23rd**, referendum in South Vietnam advocates deposition of Emperor Bao Dai (26th, republic is proclaimed under Ngo Dinh Diem).

Nov: **2nd**, in Israel, David Ben-Gurion, the former prime minister, now back from retirement, forms coalition ministry.

3rd, Iran joins the (Iraq–Turkey) Baghdad Pact.

9th, South Africa withdraws from UN General Assembly, because UN decides to continue consideration of Cruz Report of 1952 on 'apartheid'.

Dec: **13th**, in Britain, following retirement of Clement Attlee as leader of the Labour Party, Hugh Gaitskell is elected leader by Labour MPs and peers with 157 votes, against 70 for Aneurin Bevan and 40 for Herbert Morrison.

19th, Sudan's parliament passes resolution calling on Egypt and Britain to recognize Sudan as an independent state (recognition granted 1st Jan 1956; Sudan joins Arab League on 19th Jan).

Politics, Government, Law, and Economy

(13th July) In Britain, Ruth Ellis is hanged for murdering her lover; she is the last woman to be hanged in Britain.

(14th Dec) Albania, Austria, Bulgaria, Cambodia, Ceylon (now Sri Lanka), Finland, Hungary, Republic of Ireland, Italy, Jordan, Laos, Libya, Nepal, Portugal, Romania, and Spain are admitted to United Nations.

Science, Technology, and Discovery

In Britain, chemist Dorothy Hodgkin discovers composition of Vitamin B_{12} (a liver extract for treating pernicious anaemia).

Detection of the 'neutrino' (a particle of no electric charge) at Los Alamos Laboratory, USA, by Clyde Cowan and Fred Reines.

In Britain, Christopher Cockerell develops the first hovercraft.

Art, Sculpture, Fine Arts, and Architecture

Architecture Le Corbusier, La Torette, Eveaux-sur-l'Arbresle, Lyons, France.

Eero Saarinen, General Motors Technical Center, Michigan, USA.

Literature
James Baldwin, *Notes of a Native Son.*
Graham Greene, *The Quiet American.*
Vladimir Nabokov, *Lolita.*
Drama Samuel Beckett, *Waiting for Godot.*

Everyday Life
(18th July) 'Disneyland' theme park opens in Anaheim, California, USA.

Media
Film *The Blackboard Jungle* (director, Richard Brooks; starring Glenn Ford).
The Ladykillers (the last of the Ealing Comedies).
Pather Panchali (director, Satyajit Ray).
Rebel Without A Cause (director, Nicholas Ray; starring James Dean).
The Seven Year Itch (director, Billy Wilder; starring Marilyn Monroe).
(30th Sept) US heartthrob cinema actor James Dean dies in car crash, near Los Angeles, at age of 24.
Radio Sony of Japan launch the first mass-produced transistor radio.
Television (22nd Sept) In Britain, commercial television is introduced, supervised by the Independent Television Authority (ITA); the BBC spoils ITA's first evening by killing Grace Archer, a leading character in the popular radio series *The Archers*, in a fire.

1956 **Feb: 25th**, in USSR, at closed session of the 20th Conference of the Communist Party, general secretary Nikita Khrushchev denounces policies of Stalin (speech made public on 18th March).
29th, Pakistan parliament passes bill containing constitution for independent Islamic Republic of Pakistan (2nd March, decides to stay in Commonwealth; 23rd March becomes independent, with Iskander Mirza, the governor general, as provisional president).

March: 2nd, France recognizes independence of Morocco (Spain grants recognition 7th April).
20th, France recognizes independence of Tunisia; the Bey of Tunis is head of state with Habib ben Ali Bourguiba as prime minister.

April: 10th, general election in Ceylon (now Sri Lanka) is won by the Sri Lanka Freedom Party; Solomon Bandaranaike replaces Sir John Kotalawala as prime minister.
17th, USSR abolishes the Cominform (Communist Information Bureau, established in 1947), in move to help rapprochement with Yugoslavia and the West.
21st, military alliance signed by Egypt, Saudi Arabia, and Yemen at Jiddah, Saudi Arabia.
29th, Dag Hammarskjöld, UN secretary general, obtains agreement of Israel and Jordan to respect ceasefire undertakings (similar agreement obtained 1st May from Lebanon and 2nd May from Syria).

May: 1st, in Argentina, Peronist constitution is revoked and replaced by liberal constitution of 1853.
9th, plebiscite in British Togoland votes for integration with Gold Coast.

June: 4th, Egypt declares that it will not extend the Suez Canal Company's concession after expiry in 1968.
24th, Colonel Nasser (unopposed) is elected president of Egypt by popular vote, which also approves new constitution.

July: 26th, in Egypt, President Nasser announces nationalization of the Suez Canal (owned partly by France and Britain), under decree outlawing the company (–31st, Britain, France, and USA retaliate with financial measures).

Aug: 2nd, Britain rejects request of Federation of Rhodesia and Nyasaland for status as separate state within Commonwealth.
3rd, Gold Coast League Assembly adopts Kwame Nkrumah's resolution demanding independence (granted by Britain, 18th Sept).
16th, (–23rd) international conference on Suez Canal held in London by British and French governments, attended by representatives of 22 countries (but not Egypt); 18 countries support the Dulles Plan for an international Suez Canal Board associated with the UN to manage the Canal.
22nd, John Harding, British governor of Cyprus, offers surrender terms to EOKA guerrillas, which they reject.

Sept: 9th, President Nasser of Egypt rejects Dulles Plan for international control of the Suez Canal.
23rd, Britain and France refer Suez dispute to UN Security Council.

Oct: 8th, Israel withdraws from Israeli–Jordan Mixed Armistice Commission.
13th, UN Security Council adopts first part of British–French resolution on Suez Canal, but USSR vetoes second part requiring Egypt to comply with set of principles.

23rd, demonstrations in Hungary, starting with university students in Budapest, call for democratic government, return of Imre Nagy to power, withdrawal of Soviet troops, and release of Cardinal Mindszenty; the prime minister, Ernö Gerö (appointed 18th July) calls in Soviet troops.

24th, Imre Nagy is appointed prime minister of Hungary and promises reforms.

30th, Britain and France present ultimatum to Egypt and Israel, calling for ceasefire and withdrawal of forces 16 km/10 mi from Suez Canal; Israel accepts but not Egypt.

31st, British and French planes bomb Egyptian airfields; public outcry in Britain over the Suez War.

Nov: 1st, in Hungary, Prime Minister Imre Nagy forms new government, including non-Communists.

2nd, Hungarian government renounces Warsaw Treaty (of 1955) and appeals to UN and Western powers for assistance against Soviet invasion.

4th, Soviet forces attack Budapest; Imre Nagy takes refuge in Yugoslav Embassy; defection of János Kádár who forms a 'revolutionary peasant-worker' government.

5th, in Egypt, British paratroops land at Port Said, at the north end of the Suez Canal.

6th, in US presidential election, Dwight D Eisenhower, Republican, is re-elected with 457 electoral votes over Adlai Stevenson, Democrat, with 73; popular vote: Eisenhower, 35,575,420; Stevenson, 26,033,066; Republicans fare badly in state elections.

7th, Britain and France accept ceasefire in Egypt, but Britain declares it will evacuate troops only on arrival of UN force.

Dec: 2nd, Fidel Castro and followers land in Cuba; after an initial setback they begin a campaign of guerrilla war, aiming to overthrow Batista's government.

5th, in South Africa, 150 Europeans, Asians, and Natives are in arrested in dawn raids and charged with treason (preliminary hearing held 19th Dec–9th Jan, though defendants are released on bail for Christmas).

5th, British and French forces begin withdrawal from Egypt (completed, 22nd Dec).

Politics, Government, Law, and Economy

(16th Aug) CND members and sympathizers march from Aldermaston in protest against nuclear arms and the dangers of radiation; such dangers are discussed in a World Health Organization report.

Society, Education, and Religion

W H Whyte, *The Organization Man.*

Buddhist Council held in Rangoon, Burma (now Yangon in Myanmar) ending in May; the sixth such council since 483 BC.

Rudolf Bultmann, *Essays Philosophical and Theological.*

Karl Mannheim, *Essays on the Sociology of Culture.*

Science, Technology, and Discovery

In USA, Bell Telephone Company develops 'visual telephone', transmitting pictures simultaneously with sound.

Jack Backus at IBM in USA invents FORTRAN, the first computer-programming language.

Humanities and Scholarship

Winston S Churchill, *History of the English-Speaking Peoples* (–1958).

A J Ayer, *The Problem of Knowledge.*

Music

Benjamin Britten, *The Prince of the Pagodas* (ballet; first performed 1957).

My Fair Lady (musical), text by Alan Jay Lerner, music by Frederick Loewe (first performed at the Mark Hellinger Theatre, New York, 15th March).

Fats Domino, 'Blueberry Hill'.

Elvis Presley, 'Heartbreak Hotel', 'Don't Be Cruel', 'Love Me Tender'.

'Rock 'n' Roll' dominates dance floors.

In Britain, Member of Parliament Robert Boothby calls for banning of the film *Rock Around the Clock*, following disturbances around the country.

The BBC starts the Eurovision Song Contest.

Literature

Drama John Osborne, *Look Back in Anger* (opens 8th May; the first major success of the English Stage Company, at the Royal Court Theatre).

Everyday Life

(19th April) US film star Grace Kelly marries Prince Rainier of Monaco.

(25th Sept) Transatlantic telephone service inaugurated.

Sport and Recreation

(22nd Nov) (–8th Dec) The 16th Olympic Games, held in Melbourne, Australia, are affected by political boycotts: Egypt, Lebanon, Netherlands, Spain, and Switzerland refuse to take part following the French–British–Israeli action in Egypt, and the Soviet invasion of Hungary. China also withdraws in protest at the participation of Formosa (Taiwan). The USSR wins 37 gold medals; the USA, 32; Australia, 13; Hungary, 9; Italy and Sweden, 8 each; Britain, 6; West Germany, 5.

Media

Film *Aparajito* (director, Satyajit Ray).

Baby Doll (director, Elia Kazan; script by Tennessee Williams; starring Karl Malden and Carroll Baker).

The King and I (starring Yul Brynner and Deborah Kerr).

A Town Like Alice (director, Jack Lee).

1957 **Jan: 9th**, Anthony Eden resigns as prime minister of Britain.

10th, in Britain, Queen Elizabeth, after consulting former prime minister Winston Churchill and senior Conservative peer the Marquess of Salisbury, appoints Harold Macmillan prime minister; 13th, he forms ministry with R A Butler as home secretary, Selwyn Lloyd foreign secretary, and Peter Thorneycroft chancellor of the exchequer.

Feb: 6th, the Gold Coast (comprising the former colonies of the Gold Coast, Ashanti, the Northern Territories, and Trans-Volta–Togoland) becomes an independent state, within the Commonwealth, as Ghana (8th, is admitted to UN); Kwame Nkrumah is prime minister.

11th, (–11th April) Singapore Constitutional Conference held in London; agrees on internal self-government during 1958.

March: 21st, (–24th) Bermuda Conference, of President Eisenhower of USA and Harold Macmillan prime minister of Britain; re-establishes the 'special relationship' which had been strained by Suez Crisis; USA undertakes to make certain guided missiles available to Britain, with warheads remaining under US control.

25th, Belgium, France, West Germany, Italy, Luxembourg, and Netherlands (the 'Six') sign the Treaty of Rome establishing the European Economic Community (EEC) or 'Common Market' and a second Rome treaty establishing the European Atomic Energy Authority or 'Euratom' (to take effect from 1st Jan 1958).

April: 25th, King Hussein proclaims martial law in Jordan; USA dispatches 6th Fleet to E Mediterranean (29th, provokes protest from USSR).

28th, King Hussein of Jordan visits King Saud of Saudi Arabia; 29th, they state the crisis in Jordan is an internal affair; Saudi Arabia pays first instalment of subsidy to Jordan.

June: 6th, in Britain, royal assent is given to the Rent Act, removing many rent controls; in protest against the Act, Labour MPs boycott the procession to the House of Lords for announcement of the assent.

10th, Progressive Conservatives win Canadian elections, with 112 seats; Liberals win 105, Cooperative Commonwealth Federation wins 25; others, 23 seats (17th, Louis St Laurent, Liberal, resigns; 21st, John Diefenbaker forms Conservative ministry, ending 22 years of Liberal rule).

July: 29th, USA, Britain, France, and West Germany issue declaration on principles for German reunification and call for free elections.

Aug: 31st, independence of Malayan Federation in force.

Sept: 15th, sweeping victory for Konrad Adenauer's Christian Democratic Union in West German elections.

Oct: 2nd, Poland, with support of Czechoslovakia and East Germany, outlines Rapacki Plan, for a denuclearized zone in Central Europe, to UN General Assembly.

16th, following incidents on frontier with Turkey, Syria declares state of emergency.

29th, Fulgencio Batistá suspends Cuban constitution.

Nov: 11th, full internal self-government in force in Jamaica.

Dec: 15th, at UN General Assembly, Greek resolution that Cyprus is entitled to self-determination fails to gain two-thirds majority required for adoption.

Politics, Government, Law, and Economy

(25th March) Under the Treaty of Rome (in force from 1st Jan 1958), the European Steel and Coal Community Court becomes the European Court of Justice (also covering the European Economic Community and Euratom).

(29th July) International Atomic Energy Agency comes into being.

Society, Education, and Religion

(4th Sept) In Britain, the Wolfenden Report (by the Home Office Committee on Homosexual Offences and Prostitution, established in 1954) recommends the decriminalization of private homosexual acts between consenting adult males and measures to prevent street prostitution (recommendations rejected by government, 4th Dec).

(5th Sept) In USA, Governor Orval Faubus of Arkansas attempts to prevent the admission of African-American pupils to a school in Little Rock; President Eisenhower sends federal troops to enforce integration and protect the children.

Science, Technology, and Discovery

US expedition is flown in to South Pole.
A B Sabin in USA produces an oral polio vaccine.
(4th Oct) USSR launches the artificial satellite *Sputnik 1* to study the cosmosphere; weighing 83.4 kg/184 lb, it circles the Earth in 95 minutes. *Sputnik 2* is placed in orbit a month later (3rd Nov) carrying the dog Laika, to study living conditions in space.

Humanities and Scholarship

New Cambridge Modern History (–1979).
Kenneth Clark, *The Nude*.

Art, Sculpture, Fine Arts, and Architecture

Architecture Le Corbusier, Tokyo Museum (–1960).
Oscar Niemeyer is named chief architect of Brasilia, Brazil.
Jørn Utzon wins competition for design of the Opera House, Sydney, Australia.
Painting Francis Bacon, *Screaming Nurse*.
Sculpture Alexander Calder, *Mobile*, at J F Kennedy Airport New York.
Jacob Epstein, *Christ in Majesty* (for Llandaff Cathedral, S Wales).
Henry Moore, *Reclining Figure*, at UNESCO building, Paris, France.

Music

Francis Poulenc, *Les Dialogues des Carmélites* (opera).
West Side Story (musical), lyrics by Stephen Sondheim, music by Leonard Bernstein (first performed at the Winter Garden Theatre, New York, 26th Sept).

Literature

John Braine, *Room at the Top*.
Ted Hughes, *The Hawk in the Rain* (poems).
Jack Kerouac, *On the Road*.
Patrick White, *Voss*.
In USA, Kerouac's novel *On the Road*, describing a journey across the USA by drop-outs, inspires the 'Beatniks', who scorn materialism and seek ways of avoiding the 'rat race'.
Drama Samuel Beckett, *Endgame*.

Everyday Life

(13th Sept) *The Mousetrap* by Agatha Christie becomes Britain's longest-running play, with its 1,998th performance, in London.

Media

Film *Bonjour Tristesse* (director, Otto Preminger).
The Cranes are Flying (director, Mikhail Kalatozov).
The Prince and the Showgirl (director, Laurence Olivier; starring Marilyn Monroe).
Television New programmes in Britain include: *Emergency – Ward 10* (ITV), a 'soap opera' set in a hospital; *The Sky at Night* (BBC), presented by Patrick Moore (–).

1958

Jan: 1st, European Economic Community (EEC) and European Atomic Energy Commission (Euratom) in force.

Feb: 1st, presidents of Egypt and Syria sign documents creating union as the United Arab Republic, intended as the first step in creation of a larger Arab State (21st, plebiscite approves President Nasser of Egypt as head of state).
3rd, treaty signed at The Hague, Netherlands, by Belgium, Luxembourg, and Netherlands, establishing 'Benelux' Economic Union (for 50 years).
5th, North Korea proposes withdrawal of all foreign troops from North and South Korea (7th, China agrees to remove its troops from North Korea, but UN refuses to withdraw troops unless free elections are held throughout Korea; withdrawal of Chinese troops completed 28th Oct).
11th, Tunisia informs France that French warships will no longer be allowed to use the port at Bizerta.
14th, Rapacki Plan, proposed by Polish foreign minister Adam Rapacki, for denuclearized zone in Central Europe, delivered to foreign envoys in Warsaw (rejected by USA on 3rd May, by Britain on 18th May).
14th, kingdoms of Iraq and Jordan unite in Arab Federation, with King Faisal II of Iraq as head of state.

March: 27th, in USSR, Nikita Khrushchev ousts and replaces Nikolai Bulganin as prime minister (chairman of Council of Ministers; 6th Sept, Bulganin is dismissed from Communist Party Presidium; becomes Chairman of Soviet State Bank).

April: 16th, French Assembly defeat's government's proposals for restoring relations with Tunisia; Felix Gaillard's government resigns.

May: 2nd, following attacks by Yemeni tribesmen, state of emergency declared by Governor Sir William Luce in Britain's Aden colony.

15th, in France, General Charles de Gaulle states readiness to assume the powers of the republic; 19th, praises achievements of the French army in Algeria.

June: 1st, in France, following the resignation of Pierre Pflimlin 28th May, Charles de Gaulle forms government (2nd, de Gaulle is granted emergency powers for six months; 3rd, is granted authorization to draw up new constitution and submit it to a popular referendum).

1st, Iceland extends limit reserved for its own fishing vessels to 19 km/12 mi.

17th, execution in Hungary of Imre Nagy, former prime minister, after secret trial.

19th, Britain announces new plan for Cyprus, involving representatives of the Greek and Turkish governments in the island's administration (rejected by Archbishop Makarios and the Greek government; plan is implemented on 1st Oct, with participation by Turkey).

July: 14th, in Baghdad, Iraq, Brigadier Abdul Karim Kassem mounts *coup d'état*: King Faisal II, his heir, and prime minister Nuri-es-Said are murdered; and King Hussein of Jordan assumes power as head of Arab Federation.

17th, following coup in Iraq, British paratroops land in Jordan at request of King Hussein (remain until 2nd Nov).

19th, United Arab Republic (Egypt and Syria) and Iraq sign treaty of mutual defence (20th, the UAR severs relations with Jordan).

Aug: 1st, King Hussein dissolves the Federation of Jordan with Iraq.

5th, Nikita Khrushchev withdraws previous support for UN Security Council meeting on Middle East (given on 28th July) and proposes meeting of UN General Assembly, which is accepted by USA and Britain.

14th, Britain, France, and other NATO countries announce relaxation of prohibitions on trade with Soviet bloc and Communist China; but USA maintains embargo on trade with China, North Korea, and North Vietnam.

24th, death of J G Strijdom, prime minister of South Africa; succeeded 3rd Sept by Hendrik Verwoerd.

Sept: 28th, referendum held in France, Algeria, and territories overseas approves constitution for Fifth French Republic (promulgated 5th Oct followed by electoral law 13th); gives president greater powers and strengthens position of the government in the Assembly.

Oct: 23rd, USSR makes loan to United Arab Republic for building Aswan Dam on River Nile.

Nov: 4th, in USA, Democratic victory in mid-term Congressional elections, leaving Democrats with 62 seats in Senate (Republicans, 34) and 281 seats in House of Representatives (Republicans, 153).

30th, in France, Neo-Gaullist Union for a New Republic (UNR) wins largest number of seats in general election (198 out of 465).

Dec: 3rd, Indonesia nationalizes Dutch businesses.

8th, (–13th) All-Africa People's Conference held in Accra, Ghana, with representatives from most countries; establishes permanent secretariat and resolves to work for freedom of Africa.

21st, Charles de Gaulle elected president of French Republic by electoral college, with 78.5% of votes (Communist candidate wins 13.1%, the candidate of the Union of Democrat Forces, 8.4%).

30th, French West African states (Chad, Congo, Gabon, Mali, Mauritania, and Senegal) decide to form a federation within the French Community.

Politics, Government, Law, and Economy

In Britain, the Life Peerages Act dilutes the hereditary content of the House of Lords (first life peerages created 24th July).

Public Records Act provides for most British government documents to be available for inspection after 50 years.

(17th Feb) Foundation in Britain of the Campaign for Nuclear Disarmament, at public meeting in London; speakers include philosopher Bertrand Russell, author J B Priestley, politician Michael Foot, historian A J P Taylor, and the chairman Canon John Collins (holds first official 'Aldermaston March', from London to nuclear research centre at Aldermaston, on 7th April following success of event in 1956).

(5th Dec) First section of motorway is opened in Britain, the Preston bypass in NW England (closed because of frost damage, 29th Jan 1959).

Society, Education, and Religion

In USA, new crisis at Little Rock, Arkansas, over racial integration of education: 21st June, district court permits two-year suspension of integration, which is overturned by the Supreme Court on 12th Sept; Governor Faubus then orders the town's High Schools to close from 15th Sept.

J K Galbraith, *The Affluent Society.*

C N Parkinson, *Parkinson's Law.*

In USA, the Church of the Brethren, at its 250th meeting at Des Moines, Iowa, approves ordination of women.

Evangelical Church of the Palatinate, West Germany, decides to admit women to ordination.

Legislation to admit women to Swedish Lutheran pastorate is passed by convocation and parliament.

(May) Formation in USA of the United Presbyterian Church, the country's fourth largest denomination with 3 million members.

(June) US Congregationalists and Evangelicals form United Church of Christ with 2 million members.

(8th Sept) (–9th) Serious race riots in Notting Hill Gate, London.

(25th Oct) Following the death of Pius XII (9th Oct), Cardinal Angelo Roncalli is elected Pope at the age of 81 and takes the name John XXIII.

Science, Technology, and Discovery

(15th May) USSR places *Sputnik 3* in orbit for aerodynamic studies, and also fires a rocket carrying two dogs to a height of 450 km/279 mi (27th Aug) and brings it safely back to Earth.

Humanities and Scholarship

Ludwig Wittgenstein, *The Blue Book* and *The Brown Book* (posthumous).

Art, Sculpture, Fine Arts, and Architecture

Architecture Ludwig Mies van der Rohe and Philip Johnson, Seagram Building, New York.

Pier Luigi Nervi and Gio Ponti, Palazzo dello Sport, Rome (–1960); Pirelli Building, Milan.

Painting Mark Rothko, commissioned to paint Seagram murals (eventually donated to Tate Gallery, London, by the artist in 1964).

Music

Benjamin Britten, *Noye's Fludde.*

Jean Françaix, *Divertimento.*

Perry Como, 'Magic Moments' (written 1957 by Burt Bacharach).

In USA, first stereophonic ('stereo') records sold.

Literature

Iris Murdoch, *The Bell.*

Boris Pasternak, *Dr Zhivago.*

T H White, *The Sword in the Stone.*

The 'Beatnik' movement, originating among young poets of California, spreads to Britain; devotees are unkempt, penurious, and take drugs.

Drama Harold Pinter, *The Birthday Party.*

Everyday Life

(10th July) Parking meters introduced in Mayfair, London.

Sport and Recreation

The sixth football World Cup tournament is held in Sweden. All four British teams qualify for the finals for the first time. Brazil wins, beating the host nation 5–2 in the final in Stockholm.

Water-skiing becomes popular.

(6th Feb) Eight members of the Manchester United football side from England are killed in an air crash at Munich, Germany, while returning from a European Cup tie in Belgrade.

Media

Film *Ashes and Diamonds* (director, Andrzej Wajda).

Mon Oncle (director and star, Jacques Tati).

Vertigo (director, Alfred Hitchcock; starring James Stewart and Kim Novak).

Statistics

Electronic computers: 1,000 in use in US; 160 in use in Europe.

1959

Jan: 1st, in Cuba, the guerrilla campaign of the 26 July movement forces President Fulgencio Batista to resign and flee to Dominica; military junta appoints Carlos Piedra as provisional president.

2nd, in Cuba, the 26 July Movement ignores the military junta and proclaims Dr Manuel Urratía provisional president; announces cabinet on 3rd, with Fidel Castro as prime minister (takes oath on 16th Feb).

3rd, in USA, Alaska is admitted to the union as the 49th state.

19th, in South Africa, re-opening of treason trial of those arrested in Dec 1956.

Feb: 19th, agreement signed in London by prime ministers of Greece, Turkey, and Britain for independence of Cyprus; Cyprus to be republic with presidential regime; president to be Greek, vice-president Turkish; the two communities are to be allowed considerable autonomy. Britain will retain two military bases on the island, and Enosis (union with Greece), for which EOKA has been fighting, is ruled out.

20th, disturbances in the British territory of Nyasaland (now Malawi) where, 3rd March, state of emergency is declared and Hastings Banda and other leaders of Nyasaland African Congress are arrested.

March: 3rd, in Kenya, the 'Hola incident': incident at Hola Camp causes death of 11 Mau Mau prisoners; news of the deaths, on 7th, is followed by protests in Kenya and Britain.

12th, in Northern Rhodesia, the Zambia African National Congress is banned for intimidating Africans planning to vote in election on 20th.

20th, United Federal Party wins Northern Rhodesian elections.

April: 4th, (–30th May) Ivory Coast signs series of agreements with Niger, Upper Volta (now Burkina Faso), and Dahomey (now Benin) to form Sahel–Benin Union.

26th, detachment of Cubans invades Panama (arrested and flown to Havana, Cuba, where imprisoned).

27th, Liu Shaoqi elected chairman of Chinese Republic in succession to Mao Zedong, who remains head of Communist Party.

June: 3rd, Singapore becomes self-governing.

17th, Éamon de Valera resigns as prime minister of Ireland to become third president (in succession to Sean O'Kelly); 23rd, Sean Lemass becomes prime minister.

July: 4th, Jamaica is granted internal self-government within the West Indies Federation.

Aug: 16th, United Arab Republic (Egypt and Syria) restores diplomatic relations with Jordan (severed 20th July 1958).

21st, following withdrawal of Iraq from Baghdad Pact (24th March), the Pact changes name to Central Treaty Organization, known as CENTO (moves headquarters to Ankara, Turkey).

21st, in USA, Hawaii is admitted to the union as the 50th state.

Sept: 22nd, UN votes against admission of People's Republic of China.

25th, Solomon Bandaranaike, prime minister of Ceylon (Sri Lanka), is assassinated by a Buddhist monk; succeeded by Wijayananda Dahanayake.

Oct: 8th, in British general election, Conservatives under Harold Macmillan win 365 seats; Labour, 258; Liberals, 6; other, 1.

Nov: 10th, UN General Assembly condemns apartheid in South Africa and racial discrimination in any part of the world.

10th, announcement of ending of emergency in Kenya after ten years (proclamation signed by governor on 12th Jan 1960).

20th, (–29th) conference at Stockholm, Sweden, at which the finance ministers of Austria, Denmark, Great Britain, Norway, Portugal, Sweden, and Switzerland (the 'Seven') initial convention establishing the European Free Trade Association or EFTA.

Dec: 9th, Britain and United Arab Republic (Egypt and Syria) resume diplomatic relations (severed in Nov 1956).

Politics, Government, Law, and Economy

(23rd Feb) (–28th) First meeting of European Court of Human Rights at Strasbourg.

(1st Nov) Opening in Britain of the first section of the M1 (London–Leeds motorway).

Society, Education, and Religion

In Britain, novelist and educationalist C P Snow delivers the Richmond Lecture *The Two Cultures and the Sciences.*

Pope John XXIII announces the calling of the first Vatican Council since 1870.

Karl Barth, *Dogmatics in Outline.*

Pierre Teilhard de Chardin, *The Phenomenon of Man.*

(1st Feb) Swiss referendum rejects female suffrage in federal elections.

(1st June) World Refugee Year begins.

Science, Technology, and Discovery

The USA places 11 artificial satellites in orbit around the Earth; *Explorer 6* (launched 7th Aug) investigates the Van Allen radiation belt around the Earth (discovered in 1958 by *Explorer 1*); the Moon probe *Pioneer 4* (launched 3rd March) passes within 59,000 km/37,000 mi of the Moon.

The USSR places *Lunik 3* in orbit round the Earth (launched 4th Oct); it also launches three Moon probes. *Lunik 1* passes within 6,400 km/4,000 mi of the Moon; *Lunik 2* (launched 12th Sept) hits the Moon; *Lunik 3* (launched 4th Oct) passes behind the Moon and goes into orbit around the Earth, having taken photographs of the Moon's surface (including the hidden side).

(25th July) British hovercraft crosses the Channel in two hours.

Humanities and Scholarship

Mary Leakey discovers a human skull thought to be 1.75 million years old at Olduvai Gorge, Tanganyika (now Tanzania); Louis B Leakey finds the skull of an early hominid, 'the Nutcracker Man', thought to be 600,000 years old.

Remains of Nonsuch Palace are excavated successfully during Britain's driest summer for 200 years.

Iona and Peter Opie, *The Lore and Language of Schoolchildren.*

Art, Sculpture, Fine Arts, and Architecture

Architecture Frank Lloyd Wright, Beth Sholom Synagogue, Elkin Park, Pennsylvania, USA.

Music

Francis Poulenc, *La voix humaine* (opera).

The Sound of Music (musical), lyrics by Oscar Hammerstein, music by Richard Rodgers (first performed at the Lunt-Fontanne Theatre, New York, 16th Nov).

In Detroit, USA, Berry Gordy founds Motown Records (a major African-American-owned record company) and launches the Tamla record label.

US jazz pianist and composer Thelonius Monk forms his own big band.

(3rd Feb) Buddy Holly dies in plane crash.

Literature

Saul Bellow, *Henderson the Rain King.*

William Burroughs, *The Naked Lunch.*

Günther Grass, *The Tin Drum.*

Drama Brendan Behan, *The Hostage.*

Shelagh Delaney, *A Taste of Honey.*

Harold Pinter, *The Caretaker.*

Arnold Wesker, *Roots.*

Media

Film *Ben Hur* (director, William Wyler; starring Charlton Heston).

Hiroshima, mon Amour (director, Alain Resnais).

Look Back in Anger (director, Tony Richardson; starring Richard Burton and Mary Ure).

Some Like it Hot (director, Billy Wilder; starring Marilyn Monroe, Jack Lemmon, and Tony Curtis).

Le Testament d'Orphée (director, Jean Cocteau).

Television Sony of Japan produces a transistorized television receiver.

In USA, the 'Quiz Show Scandal' when participants in the quiz show *Twenty-One* confess that they had been supplied with answers before the show.

(Oct) In Britain, first coverage of general election.

Statistics

Television sets: US, 36 million; Great Britain, 10 million; France, 1.5 million.

1960

Jan: 1st, French Cameroon becomes the independent Republic of Cameroon.

6th, (–5th Feb) Harold Macmillan, prime minister of Britain, visits Ghana, Nigeria, Rhodesia (now Zimbabwe), and South Africa; on 3rd Feb, speaking in Cape Town to South Africa's Parliament, he declares: 'The wind of change is blowing through this continent ... and our national policies must take account of it.'

12th, in Indonesia, President Sukarno forms National Front.

16th, (–18th) London conference on independence terms for Cyprus; ends without agreement.

March: 5th, President Sukarno suspends Indonesian parliament; 27th, announces formation of 'Mutual Co-operation' legislature, to comprise members nominated by himself (meets on 25th June).

21st, in South Africa, the 'Sharpeville massacre': at Sharpeville township near Vereeniging (S of Johannesburg) members of the Pan-Africanist Congress demonstrate against pass laws; the police panic and shoot into the crowd, killing 69 Africans and wounding 186.

30th, following demonstrations, strikes, and marches by Africans, the South African government proclaims a state of emergency (–31st Aug) and passes the Unlawful Organizations Act; April 8th, the African National Congress and Pan-African Congress are banned (Nelson Mandela and others form Umkonto we Sizwe, 'Spear of the Nation', as the guerrilla wing of the ANC).

April: 27th, the French-governed part of Togoland becomes the independent Republic of Togo, Africa's smallest independent country.

May: 1st, In USSR, Soviet military forces shoot down a US high-altitude U-2 spy aircraft over the Ural Mountains, flown by Gary Powers (19th Aug, Powers is sentenced to 10 years' imprisonment for espionage).

3rd, European Free Trade Association (EFTA) comes into force, with 20% tariff cuts between members from July.

7th, Leonid Brezhnev replaces Marshal Klement Voroshilov as president of the USSR.

16th, (–19th) summit meeting in Paris, France, of Nikita Khrushchev (USSR), Harold Macmillan (Britain), President Eisenhower (USA), and Charles de Gaulle (France); Khrushchev uses the U-2 incident to break up the summit, when President Eisenhower refuses to give a public apology for the incident and to pledge that there would be no further intrusions into Soviet air space.

23rd, Israel announces arrest (after abduction in Argentina) of Adolf Eichmann, who had been responsible for organizing the Germans' mass extermination of Jews in World War II.

June: 24th, Greece, Yugoslavia, and Turkey dissolve Balkan alliance of Aug 1954.

26th, Madagascar proclaimed independent as the Malagasy Republic (remains within the French Community; 20th Sept, admitted to UN).

26th, British Somaliland becomes independent and, 27th, joins Somalia.

30th, Belgian Congo becomes independent as the Congo Republic (now Zaire), with Joseph Kasavubu as president and Patrice Lumumba prime minister.

July: 5th, (–6th) in Congo Republic (now Zaire), the army mutinies; Europeans flee from Léopoldville (now Kinshasa) area to Brazzaville (French Congo).

8th, Belgium sends troops to Congo Republic; Patrice Lumumba appeals to the UN for military assistance.

11th, in Congo Republic, Moïse Tshombe, prime minister of Katanga province, proclaims independence.

11th, (–12th), France agrees to independence from Aug of the Republics of Dahomey (now Benin), Niger, Upper Volta (now Burkina Faso), Ivory Coast, Chad, Central Africa (now the Central African Republic), and Congo.

14th, government of the Congo Republic (now Zaire) severs relations with Belgium.

15th, UN emergency force arrives in Congo Republic.

20th, end of general election in Ceylon (now Sri Lanka), which is won by the Sri Lanka Freedom Party; 21st, Mrs Sirimavo Bandaranaike, widow of the prime minister assassinated the previous Sept, is appointed prime minister (the first woman prime minister of the Commonwealth).

Aug: 8th, UN demands evacuation of Belgian troops from Congo Republic (last leave, 2nd Sept).

8th, (–9th) *coup d'état* in Laos, by parachute battalion; leads to appointment of General Souvanna Phoumi 17th Aug.

16th, Cyprus becomes an independent republic with Archbishop Makarios as president and Turkish Cypriot Dr Fazil Kütchük as vice-president.

25th, manifesto of the Soviet Communist Party condemns dogmatism of Chinese leader Mao Zedong.

Oct: 1st, Nigerian Federation becomes independent, with Nnamdi Azikiwe as governor general.

5th, in Britain, the Labour Party Conference votes in favour of unilateral nuclear disarmament against the policy of the Leader, Hugh Gaitskell.

Nov: 8th, in US presidential election, John F Kennedy, Democrat, wins 303 electoral votes over Richard Nixon, Republican, with 219; popular vote: Kennedy, 34,227,096; Nixon, 34,108,546; 502,773 for minor candidates. Democrats lose 21 seats in House of Representatives.

Dec: 14th, convention of Organization for Economic Co-operation and Development (OECD) signed in Paris, France, by USA, Canada, and 18 member countries of the Organization for European Economic Co-operation (OEEC), replacing the OEEC and providing an Atlantic economic community.

31st, Cuba requests UN Security Council to consider its complaint about US aggression.

Politics, Government, Law, and Economy

Capital of Brazil moved to Brasilia.

In Cuba, land expropriation continues; in July the government seizes the Shell and Esso oil refineries; also in July the USA suspends purchases of sugar.

(3rd March) In Britain, the Guillebaud Committee's report on railwaymen's pay embodies principle of fair comparison with other employment.

(14th April) Collectivization of East Germany's agriculture completed.

(30th June) In South Africa, the Promotion of Bantu Self-Government Act comes into force.

Society, Education, and Religion

Neo-Nazi groups are banned in West Germany after antisemitic incidents.

Churchill College, Cambridge, founded.

Kneel-in campaign by African-Americans in segregated churches in US Southern States.

(2nd Feb) In USA, sit-ins begin in Greensboro, North Carolina, to protest against segregated lunch counters; Martin Luther King is arrested in Georgia; the Student Nonviolent Co-ordinating Committee (SNCC) is founded to organize civil rights campaigning.

(10th April) Civil Rights bill for safeguarding African-Americans' voting rights passes US Senate.

Science, Technology, and Discovery

Surgeons at Birmingham, England, develop a pacemaker for the heart.

British chemist G N Robinson discovers methicillin, an antibiotic drug.

Chlorophyll is synthesized simultaneously by Martin Strell of Munich, Germany, and by R B Woodward of Harvard University, USA.

Humanities and Scholarship

Archaeologists begin to save treasures in Aswan High Dam region of Nubia before flooding begins.

Excavations at Stonehenge, S England, by officials of Ministry of Works.

Further Biblical texts are discovered in Dead Sea region.

A J Ayer, *Logical Positivism.*

William L Shirer, *The Rise and Fall of the Third Reich.*

Art, Sculpture, Fine Arts, and Architecture

Architecture Brasilia, the new capital of Brazil, is officially opened.

Frank Lloyd Wright, Guggenheim Museum, New York, completed.

Music

Benjamin Britten, *A Midsummer Night's Dream* (opera).

Oliver! (musical), text and music by Lionel Bart (first performed at the Wimbledon Theatre, London, 10th June).

First public performance by John Lennon, Paul McCartney, George Harrison, and Pete Best as The Beatles (in Hamburg, West Germany).

Literature

Alain Robbe-Grillet, *Dans la labyrinthe.*

John Updike, *Rabbit Run.*

Drama Robert Bolt, *A Man For All Seasons.*

Eugène Ionesco, *The Rhinoceros.*

Sport and Recreation

(25th Aug) (–11th Sept) Eighty-four nations compete in the 17th Olympic Games, held in Rome. The USSR wins 43 gold medals; the USA, 34; Italy, 13; West Germany, 10; Australia, 8; Turkey, 7, Hungary, 6. Cassius Clay of the USA wins the light-heavyweight boxing gold.

Media

In Britain, the *Manchester Guardian* is renamed the *Guardian.*

Film *La Dolce Vita* (director, Federico Fellini).

The Magnificent Seven (director, John Sturges).

Psycho (director, Alfred Hitchcock).

Saturday Night and Sunday Morning (director, Karel Reisz).

Statistics

Ownership of private cars (in millions): US, 75; France, 7.3; Great Britain, 6.5; Canada, 5; W. Germany, 4.5; USSR, 3.8.

Population of cities (in millions): Tokyo, 9.6; London, 8.1; New York, 7.7; Shanghai, 6.2; Moscow, 5; Mexico City, 4.8; Buenos Aires, 4.5; Bombay, 4.1.

1961

Jan: 3rd, USA severs diplomatic relations with Cuba.

7th, Casablanca Conference of heads of state in Africa; adopts African Charter, which provides for the establishment of four permanent committees to coordinate policies.

Feb: 27th, Britain and Iceland settle fisheries dispute: after three years, British ships will not fish within 19.2 km/12 mi of Iceland's coast.

March: 8th, (–17th) meeting of Commonwealth prime ministers in London; Hendrik Verwoerd announces that South Africa will leave the Commonwealth on 31st May.

8th, (–12th) conference of political leaders from Congo Republic (now Zaire) in Tananarive (now Antananarivo) in Madagascar; agrees on formation of confederation of 18 states.

9th, Dalai Lama appeals to UN to restore independence of Tibet.

26th, in Belgian elections, Christian Socialists lose overall majority and form coalition government with Socialists; Théodore Lefèvre succeeds Gaston Eyskens (both Christian Socialists) as prime minister.

29th, 28 people (including Nelson Mandela) tried for treason in South Africa are all acquitted.

April: 13th, UN General Assembly condemns apartheid in South Africa.

17th, 1,500 Cuban exiles, trained by US military instructors, invade Cuba; an expected sympathetic rising fails to occur and the invaders are killed or captured.

21st, in Algeria, revolt by army rebels under General Maurice Challe, members of the OAS (Secret Army Organization); President de Gaulle declares a state of emergency in France on 23rd; the coup collapses on 26th; rebel leaders are tried on 11th July, and eight are sentenced to death (including General Raoul Salan, who was tried in absentia).

27th, British territory of Sierra Leone becomes independent within the Commonwealth.

May: 1st, UN Trust Territory of Tanganyika (now Tanzania) achieves internal self-government with Julius Nyerere as prime minister.

31st, South Africa becomes an independent republic outside the Commonwealth, with C R Swart as president.

June: 4th, Nikita Khrushchev of USSR proposes to President Kennedy of USA a German peace conference to conclude a treaty and establish Berlin as a free city; also proposes that disarmament discussions should proceed simultaneously with talks about ban on nuclear tests (rejected by West, 17th July).

19th, by arrangement, Kuwait abrogates its agreement with Britain of 1899 (Britain declares itself ready to assist Kuwait if necessary).

19th, US and USSR representatives begin disarmament talks in Washington, DC, USA.

Aug: 10th, Britain applies for membership of the European Economic Community.

13th, East Germany seals off border between East and West Berlin, closing the Brandenburg Gate.

17th, (–18th) East German building workers construct the Berlin Wall, a near-impregnable physical barrier sealing off West Berlin and preventing the escape of East Germans to the West.

Sept: 17th, Christian Democratic Union and allies lose overall majority in West German elections.

17th, (–18th), Dag Hammarskjöld, UN secretary general (aged 56), is killed in air crash in Congo Republic while travelling to see President Tshombe of Katanga province (U Thant of Burma is acting secretary general from 3rd Nov).

18th, (–9th Oct) Uganda constitutional conference held in London; ends with agreement for internal self-government in Oct 1962.

28th, army *coup* in Damascus, Syria; 29th, Syria secedes from United Arab Republic and forms Syrian Arab Republic.

Nov: 8th, start of negotiations for Britain's entry into the European Economic Community; Britain's chief negotiator is Edward Heath.

24th, UN General Assembly resolves to treat Africa as a denuclearized zone.

Politics, Government, Law, and Economy

In Israel, Adolf Eichmann is tried and found guilty of crimes against the Jewish people during the Holocaust (executed 31st May 1962).

(5th June) US Supreme Court rules that Communist Party should register as a foreign-dominated organization (Party refuses, 17th Nov).

(17th Sept) (–18th) Sit-down demonstrations by CND members in Trafalgar Square, where police make 1,314 arrests.

(30th Sept) Organization for Economic Co-operation and Development (OECD) founded, as successor to the Organization for European Economic Co-operation (OEEC); the OECD includes the USA and Canada among its founder members.

Society, Education, and Religion

In USA, the Campaign for Racial Equality (CORE) organizes the Freedom Rides; a group of people travel around the South to check that bus services introduced desegregation; the riders face violent opposition.

Oral contraceptive pill licensed for use in Britain (on sale from 30th Jan).

In England, foundation of the University of Sussex, at Falmer near Brighton (buildings designed by Basil Spence).

Papal Encyclicals issued on Catholic Social Doctrine (*Mater at Magistra*) and on Christian reconciliation under Roman Primacy (*Aeterna Dei*).

Closure of Synagogues in Moscow.

The New English Bible, New Testament (complete Bible published in 1970).

Science, Technology, and Discovery

British astronomer Martin Ryle concludes from radio-astronomical observations that the universe changes with time; his burial of 'the steady state' theory is challenged by Fred Hoyle.

British chemist Francis Crick and South African chemist Sydney Brenner claim to determine the structure of deoxyribonucleic acid (DNA), thus breaking the genetic code.

(12th April) USSR puts first person in space, Yuri Gagarin, who orbits the Earth and returns after flight lasting 108 minutes (5th May, US astronaut Alan Shepard makes 15-minute suborbital flight).

Art, Sculpture, Fine Arts, and Architecture

Architecture In London, Hardwick's neo-classical arch at Euston Station is demolished, despite protests.

Music

British cellist Jacqueline du Pré makes her debut as a soloist in London, aged 16.
'Moon River' by Henry Mancini.
Elvis Presley, 'Are You Lonesome Tonight?'
In Britain, formation of the Rolling Stones.
(21st March) Debut of The Beatles at the Cavern Club, Liverpool, NW England.
(16th June) Soviet ballet star Rudolf Nureyev defects to the West while at Le Bourget airport, Paris.
(6th Sept) Debut of Bob Dylan at the Gaslight Cafe in Greenwich Village, New York.

Literature

Drama Jean Anouilh, *Becket.*
John Osborne, *Luther.*
Beyond the Fringe (revue).

Media

Film *L'Année dernière à Marienbad* (director, Alain Resnais).
Breakfast at Tiffany's (starring Audrey Hepburn).
Jules et Jim (director, François Truffaut; director, Jeanne Moreau).
One Hundred and One Dalmatians (producer, Walt Disney).
A Taste of Honey (director, Tony Richardson).

Statistics

Populations (in millions): China, 660; India, 435; USSR, 209; US, 179 (of which 159 white, 19 black and 1 other race); Japan, 95; Pakistan, 94; Brazil, 66; West Germany, 54; Great Britain, 53; Italy, 50; France, 47.

1962

Jan: 1st, Western Samoa becomes first sovereign independent Polynesian State.
9th, trade pact between Cuba and USSR.

March: 1st, Uganda attains full internal self-government, with Benedicto Kiwanuka as prime minister.
2nd, Britain applies to join European Coal and Steel Community (and, 5th, to join Euratom).
2nd, military *coup* in Burma (now Myanmar), when Ne Win overthrows U Nu.
18th, following secret discussions (completed at Évian-les-Bains, France), the French government and the Provisional Government of Algeria make the 'Évian agreements'; a Provisional Muslim-French government is to be installed in Algeria and a referendum held on self-determination.
23rd, Scandinavian States of Nordic Council sign Helsinki Convention on Nordic Co-operation.

July: 3rd, France proclaims independence of Algeria, following referendum (on 1st) of 91% in favour; the Provisional Government in exile returns.

Aug: 6th, Jamaica becomes independent within the Commonwealth.
31st, Trinidad and Tobago (previously members of the West Indies Federation) become an independent nation within the Commonwealth.

Sept: 2nd, USSR agrees to send arms to Cuba.

Oct: 5th, French National Assembly censures proposed referendum to sanction future president's election by popular mandate; Georges Pompidou, prime minister, resigns, but President de Gaulle asks him to continue in office.
9th, Uganda becomes independent within the Commonwealth.
10th, *Der Spiegel* publishes article on NATO exercise criticizing weakness of West German army (the offices of the paper are occupied by the police, 16th).
22nd, start of the 'Cuba missile crisis': in USA, President Kennedy announces in broadcast that the USSR has installed a missile base in Cuba; he declares a naval blockade to prevent the delivery of missiles and calls on Nikita Khrushchev of the USSR to eliminate the threat to world peace.
26th, Nikita Khrushchev sends letter to President Kennedy of the USA; 27th, publishes message saying that he is prepared to remove weapons 'regarded as offensive' if the USA removes its missiles from Turkey; Kennedy rejects the condition and states that work on the missile bases in Cuba must stop.
28th, Nikita Khrushchev of USSR announces that he has ordered the withdrawal of the 'offensive weapons' from Cuba.
28th, referendum in France favours election of president by universal suffrage.
31st, UN General Assembly requests Britain to suspend enforcement of new constitution in Southern Rhodesia (now Zimbabwe), but constitution comes into effect on 1st Nov.

Nov: **2nd**, President Kennedy announces that USSR has been dismantling bases in Cuba.

5th, Franz Joseph Strauss, West German defence minister, is relieved of his duties over the *Spiegel* affair because it is alleged that he was involved in police action against the magazine (19th, five Free Democrat ministers resign in protest at government involvement).

5th, Saudi Arabia breaks off diplomatic relations with United Arab Republic (Egypt), following a period of unrest partly caused by the defection of several Saudi princes to Egypt.

20th, USSR agrees to withdraw Ilyushin bombers from Cuba and USA announces end of blockade.

29th, British–French agreement signed to develop the *Concorde* supersonic airliner.

30th, U Thant of Burma (now Myanmar) is elected UN secretary general.

Dec: **9th**, Tanganyika (now Tanzania) becomes a republic within the Commonwealth, with Julius Nyerere as president.

11th, formation in West Germany of coalition government of Christian Democrats, Christian Socialists, and Free Democrats.

19th, Britain acknowledges the right of Nyasaland (now Malawi) to secede from the Central African Federation.

Politics, Government, Law, and Economy

Second stage of integration of the European Economic Community, following agreement on the establishment of the Common Agricultural Policy (agreement reached 14th Jan, but backdated to 1st Jan).

Wal-Mart store opened in Rogers, Arkansas, USA; the chain expands rapidly and makes the Waltons extremely rich by the late 1980s.

Milton Friedman, *Capitalism and Freedom.*

(12th Feb) In Britain, six members of the Committee of 100 of the Campaign for Nuclear Disarmament (CND) are found guilty of a breach of the Official Secrets Act in conspiring to enter an air force base; sentenced to imprisonment.

(14th May) Milovan Djilas, former vice-president of Yugoslavia, is given further sentence for publishing *Conversations with Stalin.*

(25th June) In USA, the Supreme Court rules in Engel v. Vitale that prayers in public schools are unconstitutional.

Society, Education, and Religion

In USA, James Meredith gains admission to the University of Mississippi under federal guard against racist violence.

In Britain, the Commonwealth Immigrants Act, aiming to reduce immigration from the 'New Commonwealth', comes into force.

The Thalidomide drug is withdrawn in Britain and France after evidence that it causes birth defects.

Anthony Sampson, *The Anatomy of Britain.*

Pope John XXIII insists on retention of Latin as the language of the Roman Catholic Church.

Second Vatican Council opens in Rome, with observer delegates from other Christian Churches; Pope John XXIII orders the controversial document on Sources of Revelation to be revised.

Science, Technology, and Discovery

The German drug thalidomide, used as a sedative by pregnant women, is established as the cause of an increase in babies born with congenital malformations; the drug is banned in many countries.

Report of Royal College of Physicians on Smoking and Health.

(10th July) (–11th) The Satellite *Telstar* is launched from Cape Canaveral, USA, circles the earth every 157.8 minutes, enabling live television pictures transmitted from Andover, Maine, to be received at Goonhilly Down, Cornwall, SW England, and in Brittany, France.

Art, Sculpture, Fine Arts, and Architecture

Architecture Coventry Cathedral is consecrated; architect, Basil Spence; engraved windows, John Hutton; sculpture, Jacob Epstein; baptiztery window, John Piper; ten nave windows, Lawrence Lee; tapestry, Graham Sutherland.

Pan-American Airways Building, New York, provides world's largest office accommodation.

Music

Benjamin Britten, *War Requiem.*

Michael Tippett, *King Priam* (opera).

A Funny Thing Happened on the Way to the Forum (musical), music and lyrics by Stephen Sondheim (first performed at the Alvin Theatre, New York, 8th May).

Bob Dylan, 'Blowin' in The Wind'.

The Four Seasons, 'Sherry'.

Neil Sedaka, 'Breaking Up Is Hard To Do'.

The Beatles sign a management contract with Brian Epstein (24th Jan) and a recording contract with the Parlophone record label (9th May).

Literature

Alexander Solzhenitsyn, *One day in the Life of Ivan Denisovich.*

Drama Edward Albee, *Who's Afraid of Virginia Woolf?*

Sport and Recreation

The seventh football World Cup is held in Chile. Brazil retains the trophy, beating Czechoslovakia 3–1 in the final in Santiago.

Graham Hill, driving a BRM, wins the world Grand Prix championship. He is only the second Briton to do so.

Media

The weekly sociology magazine *New Society* is published in Britain.

(Feb) Publication in Britain of satirical magazine *Private Eye* (saved from financial difficulties by comedian Peter Cook in April).

Film *The Birds* (director, Alfred Hitchcock).

How the West Was Won (director, John Ford).

A Kind of Loving (director, John Schlesinger, starring Alan Bates).

Lawrence of Arabia (director, David Lean).

Lolita (director, Stanley Kubrick).

A Taste of Honey (director, Tony Richardson).

Television In USA, Johnny Carson takes over *The Tonight Show.*

New programmes in Britain include: *Animal Magic* (BBC), presented by Johnny Morris (–1984); *Dr Finlay's Casebook* (–1971); *Oliver Twist* (BBC); *The Saint,* starring Roger Moore (–1969); *Steptoe and Son* (BBC; –1965); *That Was The Week That Was* ('TW3'), presented by David Frost; *Z Cars* (BBC; –1978).

Statistics

African Religion: (in millions; total population 230 million) Roman Catholics 29 million; Protestant, 19 million; Coptic and Orthodox Churches, 5 million. The religions of Africa total 2,000 sects.

1963

Jan: 14th, President de Gaulle of France states objections to Britain's entry into the European Economic Community (EEC) and rejects US offer of Polaris missiles.

23rd, 'Kim' Philby, a former British diplomat working in Beirut, Lebanon, disappears.

29th, Britain is refused entry into the EEC.

Feb: 1st, Nyasaland (now Malawi) becomes self-governing with Hastings Banda as prime minister.

April: 6th, Britain and USA sign Polaris missile agreement.

15th, in Britain, disorder breaks out during last stages of the Aldermaston March (a protest march from London to the nuclear research centre at Aldermaston, organized by the Campaign for Nuclear Disarmament).

17th, United Arab Republic (Egypt), Syria, and Iraq agree to federate.

May: 16th, Geneva Conference on General Agreement on Tariffs and Trade (GATT) begins 'Kennedy round' of negotiations for tariff cuts.

June: 5th, In Britain, John Profumo resigns from the government, admitting that he misled the House of Commons on 22nd March (9th, the *News of the World* publishes Christine Keeler's account).

19th, in USA, President Kennedy gives address to Congress on civil rights.

20th, agreement between USA and USSR to establish a 'hot line' from the White House, Washington, DC, to the Kremlin, Moscow.

26th, during tour of West Germany (23rd–27th), President Kennedy visits West Berlin; he tells a crowd of 150,000 Berliners: 'All free men ... are citizens of Berlin. And therefore, as a free man, I take pride in the words, "Ich bin ein Berliner".'

July: 1st, In Britain, it is revealed that 'Kim' Philby was the 'third man' involved in espionage for the USSR with Guy Burgess and Donald Maclean.

20th, end of USSR–Chinese ideological talks in Moscow.

30th, Soviet newspaper *Izvestia* announces that British spy 'Kim' Philby, who disappeared from Beirut in Jan, has been granted asylum in USSR.

Aug: 5th, USA, USSR, and Britain sign nuclear test ban treaty (subsequently signed by 96 states, but not France, before coming into force, 1st Oct).

8th, in Britain, the 'Great Train Robbery', the work of a 15-man gang, who fake a red light to stop the London–Glasgow mail train (near Cheddington in Buckinghamshire) and steal £2½ million in bank notes.

28th, in USA, 200,000 African-Americans take part in a peaceful demonstration for civil rights in Washington, DC; they are addressed by the Reverend Martin Luther King, who proclaims: 'I have a dream that one day this nation will one day rise up and live out the true meaning of its creed: "We hold these truths to be self-evident, that all men are created equal".'

Sept: 4th, Riots over school desegregation in Birmingham, Alabama, USA (15th, bomb kills African-Americans in Birmingham).

16th, Malaya, North Borneo, Sarawak, and Singapore form Federation of Malaysia which, 17th, breaks off relations with Indonesia, following Sukarno's increased hostility.

Oct: 1st, Nigeria becomes a republic within the Commonwealth, with Nnamdi Azikiwe as president.

18th, in Britain, Harold Macmillan resigns as prime minister for reasons of health, and 19th, is succeeded by the Scottish peer, the 14th Earl of Home (who later disclaims peerage, is made a Knight of the Thistle, and becomes Sir Alec Douglas-Home; 8th Nov he is elected a member of the Commons, for Kinross).

Nov: 1st, Army *coup* in South Vietnam; President Ngo Dinh Diem is assassinated and succeeded by General Duong Van Minh.

22nd, in USA, President Kennedy is assassinated is Dallas, Texas, by Lee Harvey Oswald; Vice-President Lyndon Baines Johnson is sworn in as president.

24th, Lee Harvey Oswald, arrested in Dallas, USA, for the murder of President Kennedy, is shot by Jack Ruby.

Dec: 10th, Zanzibar becomes independent within the Commonwealth (now part of Tanzania).

12th, Kenya becomes independent within the Commonwealth.

22nd, clashes in Cyprus between Greeks and Turks lead to a major breakdown in relations between the two communities; 30th, following visit by Duncan Sandys, a neutral zone is agreed upon.

31st, dissolution of Central African Federation of Rhodesia and Nyasaland (now Zambia, Zimbabwe, and Malawi).

Politics, Government, Law, and Economy

The Peerage Act in Britain allows members of the House of Lords to disclaim their titles (and thus be eligible for membership of the House of Commons; existing peers can disclaim within six months, new peers within one month of succession to title); the 2nd Viscount Stansgate, formerly Mr A N Wedgwood Benn, renounces his peerage (31st July) and decrees that he is to be known henceforth as 'Tony Benn'.

London Government Act reshapes local government in London, creating a Greater London Council (GLC) and 32 London Boroughs covering most of the metropolitan area (first elections for the GLC are held 9th April 1964).

(27th March) In Britain, the Beeching Report recommends the closure of many passenger rail lines and stations.

(May) Organization of African Unity (OAU) founded by conference of African leaders in Addis Ababa, Ethiopia; it aims to maintain solidarity between African leaders and remove colonialism from the Continent.

Society, Education, and Religion

In USA, Timothy Leary is dismissed from the Harvard faculty after running a popular series of experiments into the effects of psychedelic drugs such as psilocybin.

In Britain, the Newsom Report, about the education of less academic children, argues that schools must relate 'more directly to adult life, and especially by taking a proper account of vocational interests'.

The Robbins Report marked the beginning of a 10-year period of expansion in higher education; the Universities of East Anglia, Newcastle-upon-Tyne (formerly part of the University of Durham), and York are founded.

Pope John XXIII issues encyclical *Pacem in Terris*, which deals with the peaceful settlement of disputes and with relations with non-Catholics and with Communists.

Vatican Council approves the use of vernacular liturgies.

(March) Publication of *Honest to God* by John Robinson, Bishop of Woolwich in London, arouses widespread controversy; a newspaper article about the book is headed 'Our Image of God Must Go' and helps to sell almost a million copies within three years; Archbishop Michael Ramsey later responds with *Images Old and New*.

(21st June) Following the death of Pope John XXIII (3rd June), Cardinal Giovanni Battista Montini is elected Pope and takes the name Paul VI.

(July) In Britain, the Labour Member of Parliament Ben Parkin raises the problem of 'slum landlords' in the House of Commons by exploiting the fact that Mandy Rice-Davies (involved in the Profumo affair) had once cohabited with the notorious landlord Peter Rachman; an independent inquiry is established to investigate housing in London (22nd).

Science, Technology, and Discovery

Vaccine for measles is perfected.

Rachel Carson in her book *The Silent Spring* draws attention to the dangers of chemical pesticides.

Art, Sculpture, Fine Arts, and Architecture

Architecture G Bunshaft, Beinecke Library (a windowless building), Yale University, New Haven, USA.

Le Corbusier, Carpenter Center for the Visual Arts, Harvard University, Cambridge, USA.

Music

Gerry and the Pacemakers, 'You'll Never Walk Alone'.

The Beatles, 'Please Please Me' (album of same title recorded in 12 hours at EMI's Abbey Road studios, London), 'She Loves You', 'I Want to Hold Your Hand'.

Gene Pitney, '24 Hours from Tulsa'.

Cliff Richard, 'Bachelor Boy', 'Summer Holiday'.

Literature

Drama Eugène Ionesco, *Exit the King*.

(22nd Oct) In Britain, first performance of the new National Theatre, London; the architect Denys Lasdun is commissioned to design a permanent home for the company.

Everyday Life

Britain endures coldest Jan and Feb since 1740.

Sport and Recreation

(1st May) Alf Ramsey is appointed England's football manager.

Media

Film *Billy Liar* (director, John Schlesinger).

Cleopatra (director, Joseph L Mankiewicz; starring Elizabeth Taylor and Richard Burton; costing a record £12 million).

The Great Escape (director, John Sturges).

The Leopard (director, Luchino Visconti).

The Silence (director, Ingmar Bergman).

Statistics

Indian religious denominations (in millions): Hindu, 366; Moslem, 47; Christian, 10; Buddhist, 3.

1964

Jan: 9th, anti-US riots in Panama which, 10th, breaks off diplomatic relations with USA.

20th, (–24th) in Tanzania, mutiny of Tanganyika Rifles, followed by troop mutinies in Uganda and Kenya; quelled by British military forces.

22nd, Kenneth Kaunda, president of the United National Independence Party, becomes first prime minister of Northern Rhodesia (now Zambia).

24th, (–31st) referendum in Ghana, which supports giving the president the power to remove judges from the supreme and high court and establishing the Convention People's Party as the sole party (results announced 3rd Feb).

28th, riots in Salisbury (now Harare), Southern Rhodesia (now Zimbabwe).

Feb: 11th, fighting between Greeks and Turks at Limassol, Cyprus.

April: 4th, Archbishop Makarios abrogates 1960 treaty between Greece, Turkey, and Cyprus; heavy fighting occurs in the NW of the island.

13th, Winston Field resigns as prime minister of Southern Rhodesia (now Zimbabwe) on policy grounds; Ian Smith forms ministry.

27th, Tanganyika and Zanzibar are united, with Julius Nyerere as president (29th Oct, the state is named the United Republic of Tanzania).

May: 27th, death (aged 74) of Jawaharlal Nehru, prime minister of India; succeeded on 2nd June by Lal Bahadur Shastri.

June: 11th, Greece rejects direct talks with Turkey over Cyprus.

11th, in South Africa, at the end of the 'Rivonia trial', Nelson Mandela is sentenced to life imprisonment; eight defendants receive lesser sentences, and one is discharged.

July: 6th, Nyasaland Protectorate, renamed Malawi, becomes independent within the Commonwealth.

18th, race riots in Harlem, New York.

Aug: 5th, in Congo Republic (now Zaire), rebels capture Stanleyville (now Kisangani); 7th, declare foundation of a People's Republic of the Congo.

8th, Turkish planes attack Cyprus; 9th, UN orders ceasefire.

Sept: 2nd, Indonesian army lands in Malaya; 4th, Commonwealth troops move in.

21st, Malta becomes an independent state within the Commonwealth.

Oct: 14th, Martin Luther King, US African-American leader, is awarded the Nobel Peace Prize.

15th, in British general election Labour win 317 seats, Conservatives, 304, with Liberals, 9; (Labour receives 44.1% of votes cast, Conservatives, 43.4, and Liberals, 11.2; overall national swing to Labour 3.2%).

15th, Nikita Khrushchev is replaced as first secretary of Soviet Communist Party by Leonid Brezhnev and as prime minister by Alexei Kosygin.
16th, China explodes an atomic bomb.
16th, in Britain, Alec Douglas-Home resigns as prime minister and Harold Wilson forms Labour ministry, with Patrick Gordon Walker, defeated at Smethwick, as foreign secretary, George Brown secretary of state for economic affairs, James Callaghan chancellor of the exchequer, and Lord Gardiner as lord chancellor.
24th, Northern Rhodesia, renamed Zambia, becomes an independent republic within the Commonwealth, with Kenneth Kaunda as president (Southern Rhodesia is now known as just Rhodesia).

Nov: 3rd, in US elections President Lyndon Baines Johnson, Democrat, with 486 electoral votes, has sweeping victory over Barry Goldwater, Republican, with 52; popular vote: Johnson, 43,126,506; Goldwater, 27,176,799; the Democrat gains in the House of Representatives leave them with 295 seats against the Republicans with 140.
5th, in referendum in Rhodesia (now Zimbabwe), 90% (of a 61% poll) favour independence.
10th, Kenya becomes a single-party state, after members of parliament belonging to the Kenya African Democratic Union join the Kenya African National Union.
26th, Britain borrows $3,000 million from foreign bankers to save pound.

Dec: 12th, Kenya becomes a republic within the Commonwealth with Jomo Kenyatta as president; ministers include Tom Mboya.
16th, the British government, Trades Union Congress, and employers sign a statement on productivity, prices, and incomes, intended as the first stage in development of an incomes policy.

Politics, Government, Law, and Economy

In USA, the Warren Report into the assassination of President John F Kennedy (Nov 1963) concludes that Lee Harvey Oswald acted alone; its findings were later challenged and contradicted by a House committee investigation in 1978.
In USA, the Free Speech Movement in Berkeley marks the start of a period of campus protest.
The new Labour government in Britain establishes a ministry of technology.
United Nations establishes the Conference on Trade and Development (UNCTAD), to promote trade and negotiate trade agreements between countries.
British government grants licences to drill for oil and gas in the North Sea.
(5th March) British White Paper on *Monopolies, Mergers and Restrictive Practices*.

Society, Education, and Religion

Marshall McLuhan, *Understanding Media*.
Creation of the Department of Education and Science for England and Wales, which assumes the responsibilities of the previous Ministry of Education and also for universities.
Oxford University appoints Franks Commission to examine the University's role in higher education.
Roman Catholic hierarchy in England and Wales rules against the use of the contraceptive pill (7th May), but authorizes joint prayers with other churches (6th Dec).
(22nd March) Outbreaks of anti-Muslim violence in India.
(3rd July) In USA, the Civil Rights Act 1964 prohibits racial discrimination in employment, unions, public accommodation, and restaurants.
(1st Dec) Howick Committee, appointed by Archbishop of Canterbury, favours retaining system of Crown appointments to bishoprics and deaneries.

Science, Technology, and Discovery

Fred Hoyle and J V Narlikar of Cambridge University, England, propound new theory of gravitation, which solves the problem of inertia.
British chemist Dorothy Hodgkin wins the Nobel Prize for Chemistry for her work on X-ray crystallography (she is the third woman to win the prize).
US surgeon general's report *Smoking and Health* confirm the links between cigarette smoking and lung cancer and heart disease.
(31st July) *Ranger 7*, launched from Cape Kennedy, succeeds in obtaining close-up photographs of the Moon's surface before crashing.

Humanities and Scholarship

Robert Fogel, *Railroads and American Growth*.

Art, Sculpture, Fine Arts, and Architecture

Architecture Arne Jacobsen, St Catherine's College, Oxford, England.
Painting 'OP' art – geometric designs which give illusion of movement.

Music

Fiddler on the Roof (musical), lyrics by Sheldon Harnick, music by Jerry Bock (first performed at the Imperial Theater, New York, 22nd Sept).

Literature

Saul Bellow, *Herzog*.
Philip Larkin, *The Whitsun Weddings*.
Robert Lowell, *For the Union Dead*.
Jean-Paul Sartre, *Les Mots*.
Hubert Selby, *Last Exit to Brooklyn*.
Drama Peter Shaffer, *The Royal Hunt of the Sun*.

Everyday Life

(30th March) In Britain, outbreaks during the Easter weekend of Mods v. Rockers disturbances in Clacton and other seaside resorts.

Sport and Recreation

(25th Feb) Cassius Clay beats Sonny Liston after six rounds of their fight in Miami, USA, to win the World Heavyweight title; Clay then announces his conversion to Islam, changing his name to Muhammad Ali.

(10th Oct) (–24th) The 18th Olympic Games are held in Tokyo. The USA wins 36 gold medals; the USSR, 30; Japan, 16; Italy and Hungary, 10; West Germany and Poland, 7; Australia, 6; Czechoslovakia, 5.

Media

Film *Doctor Strangelove* (director, Stanley Kubrick).
A Hard Day's Night (starring The Beatles).
Mary Poppins (starring Julie Andrews).
Zorba the Greek (starring Anthony Quinn).
Radio (29th March) First offshore 'pirate' radio station broadcasting to Britain, Radio Caroline, starts transmission.

1965

Jan: 2nd, In Pakistan, President Ayub Khan gains clear victory over Fátima Jinnah in presidential elections.

2nd, Indonesia withdraws from the United Nations (the first member to do so); and on 8th, more Indonesian landings in Malaya.

Feb: 7th, US aircraft bomb North Vietnam, following attacks on US areas in South Vietnam; attack leads to regular US bombing of North Vietnam.

18th, Gambia becomes independent within the Commonwealth.

21st, in USA, Malcolm X, Muslim African-American leader, is shot dead in Manhattan, New York.

24th, British government rejects Robbins Committee's recommendations for creating new universities.

25th, Regional Economic Planning Councils are set up in Britain.

March: 21st, in USA, Martin Luther King heads procession of 4,000 civil rights demonstrators from Selma to Montgomery, Alabama, to deliver petition on grievances of African-Americans.

April: 4th, North Vietnamese Mig aircraft shoot down US jets.

6th, British Budget introduces 30% capital gains tax and disallows expenses incurred in business entertainment; James Callaghan, Chancellor of the Exchequer, also announces the cancellation of the TSR-2 aircraft.

9th, clashes between Indian and Pakistani forces on Kutch–Sind border (between India and W Pakistan).

21st, 114-nation Disarmament Commission resumes talks in New York after five-year interval.

23rd, large-scale US raid over North Vietnam.

29th, Australia decides to send troops to South Vietnam.

May: 7th, In general election in Rhodesia (now Zimbabwe), Ian Smith's Rhodesian Front Party wins sweeping victory.

12th, West Germany establishes diplomatic relations with Israel; Arab states break off relations with West Germany.

June: 8th, US forces in South Vietnam are authorized to engage in offensive operations against the Vietcong.

30th, India–Pakistan ceasefire signed.

July: 2nd, France announces boycott of all European Economic Community meetings apart from those concerned with day-to-day management of existing problems.

Aug: 8th, Singapore secedes from Malaysia; Yusof Bin Ishaq becomes president (with Lee Kuan Yew remaining prime minister).

11th, (–16th) race riots in the Watts District of Los Angeles, California, USA, which break out after an African-American is arrested for drunken driving.

Sept: 1st, Pakistani troops cross Kashmir ceasefire line.

6th, India invades West Pakistan and bombs Lahore.

22nd, ceasefire in war between India and Pakistan, which is subsequently violated by both sides.

29th, USSR admits to supplying arms to North Vietnam.

Oct: 4th, (–11th) Ian Smith, prime minister of Rhodesia (now Zimbabwe), attends talks in London on Rhodesia.

19th, in USA, the Un-American Activities Committee of the House of Representatives begins public hearings on Ku Klux Klan.

Nov: 9th, in Britain, the Murder (Abolition of Death Penalty) Act comes into force.

11th, Ian Smith, prime minister of Rhodesia (now Zimbabwe) makes Unilateral Declaration of Independence; Britain declares the régime illegal and introduces exchange and trade restrictions.

Dec: 17th, Britain imposes oil embargo on Rhodesia (now Zimbabwe); 19th, begins airlift of oil to Zambia.

19th, Charles de Gaulle defeats François Mitterrand in second round of presidential election.

31st, the executives of the European Economic Community, the European Coal and Steel Community, and Euratom are merged into one executive authority.

Politics, Government, Law, and Economy

US poet Allen Ginsburg coins term 'Flower Power' at an anti-war rally.

Britain accepts the jurisdiction of the European Court of Human Rights.

Queen's Awards for Industry established in Britain.

(1st Jan) Amalgamation of the British Foreign and Commonwealth Services as the Diplomatic Service.

(1st April) The Greater London Council (chairman, Harold Shearman) and 32 London Borough Councils come into being.

Society, Education, and Religion

In England, Judge Elizabeth Lane is the first woman to be appointed a High Court Judge.

Race Discrimination Act bans discrimination in public places in Britain.

Hindi becomes an official language of India.

First 'teach-in' against the Vietnam War held at University of Michigan, USA.

In Britain, the Labour government publishes Circular 10/65, requesting all local authorities to submit plans for secondary school reorganization along comprehensive lines.

Universities of Kent and Warwick are found in England and the University of Ulster in Northern Ireland.

Pope Paul VI visits New York to address the United Nations General Assembly; before the Vatican Council closes, promulgates a document exonerating the Jews of responsibility for the death of Christ.

The Orthodox Church annuls its excommunication of the Church of Rome in 1054.

(4th Jan) In USA, in his State of the Union address, President Johnson proclaims the building of the 'Great Society', to comprise extensive federal programmes to support education (Head Start), medicine for the poor and elderly (Medicaid and Medicare), urban development schemes (Model Cities), and welfare benefits (AFDC).

(8th Jan) In USA, Lorna Elizabeth Lockwood is the first woman to be appointed chief justice of a state supreme court (Arizona).

(2nd Aug) In Britain, White Paper on Commonwealth immigration proposes annual limit of 8,500 on work permits.

Science, Technology, and Discovery

Edward White walks for 20 minutes in space from US *Gemini 4* (3rd June), and *Gemini 5* makes 120 orbits (21st–29th Aug).

The *Early Bird* communication satellite put into synchronous orbit by the USA.

(18th March) Soviet cosmonaut Alexei Leonov leaves spacecraft *Voskhod 2* and floats in space for 20 minutes.

(Dec) *Gemini 7* (launched 4th), meets *Gemini 6* in orbit and returns (on 18th) after flight of record length.

Art, Sculpture, Fine Arts, and Architecture

Architecture Lord Snowdon, new Aviary, London Zoo.

Music

The Beach Boys, 'California Girls'.

Tom Jones, 'It's Not Unusual'.

The Rolling Stones, 'Satisfaction'.

Literature

Norman Mailer, *An American Dream.*

Drama Frank Marcus, *The Killing of Sister George.*

Neil Simon, *The Odd Couple.*

Everyday Life

The first miniskirts appear in Mary Quant's boutique in King's Road, Chelsea, London, and rapidly become fashionable across the western world.

Britain decides to adopt metric measurements.

(7th Oct) In Britain, opening in London of the Post Office Tower (now the Telecom Tower), the tallest building in Britain.

Sport and Recreation

Mme Vaucher, the first woman to climb the Matterhorn, climbs the north wall of the mountain on the centenary of the first ascent.

Media

Film *Doctor Who and the Daleks* (director Gordon Fleming; starring Peter Cushing and Roy Castle).

Doctor Zhivago (director, David Lean).

The Sound of Music (starring Julie Andrews).

Television The BBC programme *The War Game*, about the possible effects of a nuclear attack on Britain, is considered too disturbing to be shown.

In Britain, Mrs Mary Whitehouse founds the National Viewers' and Listeners' Association to campaign against offensive and immoral broadcasting.

(2nd May) *Early Bird*, US commercial communications satellite, is first used by television.

Statistics

British households owning electrical goods (1955 percentages in brackets):

TV set 88 (40)	Vacuum cleaner 82 (45)	Washing-machine 56 (20)
Refrigerator 29 (10)	Telephone 22 (21)	

1966

Jan: 1st, Pope Paul VI appeals for peace in Vietnam.

10th, Tashkent peace agreement between India and Pakistan.

11th, death of Lal Bahandra Shastri, Prime Minister of India; succeeded by Indira Gandhi (19th).

30th, France ends boycott of EEC meetings.

31st, US resumes bombing of North Vietnam after 37-day pause.

Feb: 21st, President de Gaulle calls for dismantling of NATO.

24th, overthrow of President Nkrumah of Ghana by military coup while away on tour of Asia.

March: 11th, after anti-Communist demonstrations, President Sukarno of Indonesia transfers all political powers to General Raden Suharto.

30th, National Party wins sweeping victory in South African general election.

31st, in British general election Labour win 363 seats, Conservatives, 253, with Liberals, 12 (Labour receives 47.9% of votes cast, Conservatives, 41.9%, and Liberals, 8.5%).

April: 2nd, Unrest breaks out in Saigon, as protesters demand end of military rule in South Vietnam; (14th, government promises elections within 3–5 months).

9th, UN authorizes Britain to prevent oil shipments to Rhodesia by force.

May: 3rd, British Budget introduces selective employment tax and corporation tax at 40%.

26th, British Guiana becomes independent as Guyana.

June: 2nd, Éamon de Valera re-elected President of Ireland.

3rd, purge of 'rightists' in Chinese leadership begins.

29th, USA bombs Hanoi and Haiphong. Britain dissociates itself from bombing of populated areas.

July: 1st, France withdraws its forces from NATO.

11th, USSR announces further aid to North Vietnam.

12th, (–23rd) race riots in Chicago, Cleveland, and Brooklyn.

24th, EEC reaches agreement on Common Agricultural Policy.

Aug: 13th, Central Committee of Chinese Communist Party, in first plenary session since 1962, endorses the 'Great Proletarian Cultural Revolution', the movement to 'purify' Chinese Communism through young Red Guards violently removing members of the intelligentsia.

15th, Israeli and Syrian forces clash around Sea of Galilee.

Sept: 6th, H F Verwoerd, Prime Minister of South Africa, is stabbed to death in Parliament in Cape Town. succeeded by B J Vorster (13th).

6th, (–14th) Commonwealth conference in London commits Britain to seeking UN mandatory sanctions against Rhodesia.

27th, race riots in San Francisco after shooting of African-American boy.

30th, Bechuanaland becomes independent as Botswana, with Sir Seretse Khama as President.

Oct: 1st, Chinese Defence Minister, Lin Biao, accuses USSR of plotting with USA over Vietnam.

4th, Basutoland becomes independent as Lesotho under King Moshoeshoe II.

24th, (–25th) Manila Conference of Vietnam war allies: South Vietnam, USA, Australia, New Zealand, Philippines, South Korea, Thailand.

Nov: 22nd, Spanish Cortes passes new constitution proposed by General Franco (95% approval in referendum, 14th Dec).

30th, Barbados becomes independent within Commonwealth.

Dec: 2nd, (–4th) Harold Wilson and Ian Smith meet aboard HMS *Tiger* and prepare plan for settlement of Rhodesian dispute (5th, Rhodesia rejects the plan).

20th, Britain rules out legal independence for Rhodesia except under black majority rule.

22nd, Smith declares Rhodesia a republic.

Politics, Government, Law, and Economy

(4th April) (–6th May) In London, trial of the 'Moors murderers': Ian Brady and Myra Hindley are both convicted of the murder of a child and a youth, and Brady for the murder of another child, and receive life imprisonment. One child was buried on Saddleworth Moor in the Pennines; Brady and Hindley are thought to be responsible for the deaths of two other missing children.

(13th June) In Miranda v. Arizona, the US Supreme Court rules that evidence obtained by confession is only valid when the police can show that the suspect's right to silence was observed and the suspect was aware of the rights given in the constitution.

(31st Dec) Members of the European Free Trade Association (EFTA) abolish tariffs on industrial goods, creating a customs union.

Society, Education, and Religion

British government introduces Supplementary Benefit for the sick, disabled, unemployed, and widows.

In Britain, foundation of the Universities of Aston (in Birmingham), Bath, and Surrey (at Guildford), Brunel University (Uxbridge), City University (London), Heriot-Watt University (Edinburgh), and Loughborough University of Technology; 30 polytechnics are created.

In England, establishment of Wolfson College, Oxford; foundation of Clare Hall and Fitzwilliam College, Cambridge.

In Britain, the US evangelist Billy Graham mounts the Greater London Crusade.

Office of Inquisitor abolished at the Vatican.

Index of books prohibited to Roman Catholics is abolished.

Publication of *The Jerusalem Bible.*

Science, Technology, and Discovery

US scientists Harry M Meyer and Paul D Parman develop a live virus vaccine for rubella (German measles), which reduces the incidence of the disease.

(3rd Feb) Soviet spacecraft *Luna 9* makes the first soft landing on the Moon, followed by US *Surveyor 1* (2nd June).

Humanities and Scholarship

K V Flannery and associates begin detailed survey of the Valley of Oaxaca, Mexico.

Michael Coe and associates from Yale University, USA, begin detailed study of Olmec culture, Mexico.

E A Wrigley, *An introduction to English Historical Demography.*

Theodor Adorno, *Negative Dialectics.*

Jacques Lacan, *Ecrits.*

Art, Sculpture, Fine Arts, and Architecture

(4th Nov) Severe floods in Florence leave the Renaissance centre under 2 m/6 ft of water.

Architecture John Andrews and Page and Steele, Scarborough College, University of Toronto, Canada.

Painting Term 'Arte Povera' coined by Germano Celant, Italy.

Sculpture Carl André, *Equivalent 8.*

Music

Hans Werner Henze, *The Bassarids* (opera).

György Ligeti, *Aventures et Nouvelles Aventures.*

Opening of new Metropolitan Opera House in New York.

Cabaret (musical) by John Kander and Fred Ebb (first performed at the Broadhurst Theater, New York, 20th Nov).

The Beach Boys, 'Good Vibrations'.

The Four Tops, 'Reach Out, I'll Be There'.

Avant-garde rock band the Velvet Underground does multi-media shows with Pop artist Andy Warhol.

(4th March) John Lennon speculates that The Beatles are more popular than Jesus Christ; in response, Beatles records are burnt in the US 'Bible belt'. The Beatles give their last concert, at Candlestick Park. San Francisco, USA (29th Aug).

Literature

John Fowles, *The Magus.*
Graham Greene, *The Comedians.*
Yukio Mishima, *The Sailor who fell from Grace with the Sea.*
Sylvia Plath, *Ariel* (poems).
Jean Rhys, *The Wide Sargasso Sea.*
Drama Joe Orton, *Loot.*

Everyday Life

In Britain, the soccer world cup (the Jules Rimet Trophy) is stolen while on show at a stamp exhibition in London (found a week later, on 27th March, wrapped in newspaper).

Sport and Recreation

Following a court case, the British Jockey Club allows women to hold licences for training race horses.
Alan Ball is the first British soccer player to be transferred for £100,000 (from Blackpool to Everton).
(17th March) Arkle, ridden by Pat Taaffe, wins the Cheltenham Gold Cup in Britain for the third successive year.
(30th July) Host nation England wins soccer's World Cup, beating West Germany in the final 4–2 after extra time.
(4th Sept) Australian Jack Brabham wins the World Formula One motor racing championship in a car manufactured by his own company.

Media

Film *Alfie* (director, Lewis Gilbert; starring Michael Caine).
Andrei Rublev (director, Andrei Tarkovsky).
(1st Dec) Walt Disney dies (65).
Television New programmes in USA include: *Batman*; *The Monkees*; *Star Trek.*
New programmes in Britain include: *Cathy Come Home* (BBC), *Softly Softly* (BBC; –1970), *Thunderbirds*, *Till Death Us Do Part* (BBC), written by Johnny Speight and starring Warren Mitchell.

1967 **Jan: 6th**, US and South Vietnamese forces launch major offensive in Mekong Delta.
Feb: 2nd, President Johnson offers to halt US bombing of North Vietnam, if North Vietnamese cease infiltration of South Vietnam (Ho Chi Minh rejects proposals, 5th March).
10th, curfew imposed in Aden after nationalist riots.
15th, (–21st) ruling Congress Party sustains heavy losses in Indian general election.
March: 28th, U Thant discloses his Vietnam peace plan, accepted by USA, but rejected by North Vietnam.
29th, US Court of Appeals in New Orleans orders complete desegregation of schools in Alabama, Florida, Georgia, Louisiana, Texas, and Mississippi.
31st, supreme headquarters of NATO moves from France to Casteau in Belgium.
April: 7th, border clashes between Syria and Israel around Lake Tiberias.
8th, fighting resumes between Greek and Turkish Cypriots near Limassol.
13th, heavy Labour losses in county council elections. In Greater London, Conservatives have 82 seats and Labour 18.
21st, military coup in Athens establishes the regime of the 'Greek Colonels'.
27th, (–29th Oct) 'Expo 67' exhibition in Montreal marks centenary of Canadian confederation.
May: 10th, Greek military junta takes control of Greek Orthodox Church.
11th, Britain, Denmark and Ireland formally apply to join EEC.
11th, Conservatives make net gain of 535 seats in borough elections.
16th, President de Gaulle, in press conference, virtually vetoes British entry into EEC.
22nd, President Nasser of UAR closes Gulf of Aqaba to Israeli shipping. Israel and UAR call up reserves.
28th, secession of Biafra under Colonel Chukwuemeka Odumegwu-Ojukwu provokes civil war in Nigeria.
June: 5th, War breaks out between Israel and Arab States (UAR, Syria, Jordan, Lebanon and Iraq); Arab states declare oil embargo on Britain and USA; Israel destroys over 300 enemy aircraft.
6th, President Nasser closes Suez Canal and alleges that US and British forces are aiding Israel.
8th, Israel wins control of Sinai Peninsula, Gaza strip and Old Jerusalem. UAR and allies agree to ceasefire.

9th, Israel attacks Syria after breach of ceasefire.
10th, end of Six-Day War. USSR breaks off diplomatic relations with Israel.
30th, 46 nations sign Final Acts of 'Kennedy Round' of General Agreement on Tariffs and Trade.

July: 1st, Commissions of EEC, European Coal and Steel Community and Euratom merge into a Commission of the European Communities (EC).
18th, British Defence White Paper announces drastic reduction in commitments in Far East.
27th, outbreak of race riots in Detroit. President Johnson appoints commission to investigate causes.

Aug: 15th, Martin Luther King urges US African-Americans to launch a campaign of massive civil disobedience.
25th, British troops start withdrawal from Aden.

Sept: 20th, mid-west Nigeria proclaims itself independent as Benin.
20th, Queen Elizabeth launches Cunard liner *Queen Elizabeth II*.

Oct: 21st, UAR navy sinks Israeli destroyer off Sinai (24th, Israeli artillery destroys Suez oil refineries).

Nov: 18th, devaluation of sterling from $2.80 to $2.40.
25th, Cyprus asks UN Security Council to prevent Turkish invasion (Turkey, Greece and Cyprus agree peace formula, 3rd Dec).
26th, proclamation of People's Republic of South Yemen (29th, last British troops leave Aden).

Dec: 19th, at EC Council, France vetoes negotiations for British entry; Britain states application will not be withdrawn.

Politics, Government, Law, and Economy

In USA, the 'Boston strangler', Albert de Salvo, is sentenced to life imprisonment for sex offences and robbery.

Criminal Justice Act introduces majority verdicts, suspended sentences, and parole in England and Wales.

Indonesia, Malaysia, Singapore, Thailand, and the Philippines form the Association of South-East Asian Nations (ASEAN), to promote regional growth and western security interests in SE Asia; they establish a secretariat in Jakarta, Indonesia.

(27th Jan) Treaty banning nuclear weapons from outer space signed by 60 countries, including USA and USSR.

(7th March) First landing of North Sea gas in Britain.

Society, Education, and Religion

Colorado is the first state in the USA to permit abortion.

In Tanzania, President Julius Nyerere makes the Arusha Declaration, outlining a version of 'African socialism'; his programme for the development of his country includes nationalization of major enterprises and the creation of ujamaa ('familyhood') villages, rural centres where basic services and education are provided.

Occupation of Old City of Jerusalem by Jews for the first time since CE 135.

(10th Jan) In Britain, the Plowden Report, *Children and their Primary Schools*, generally favours child-centred learning in the classroom and also backs the establishment of 'Educational Priority Areas' to combat inequality.

(July) In USA, extremely destructive race riots take place in Detroit, Michigan, Newark, New Jersey, and about 70 other cities; they accelerate the trend of the 'white flight' to the suburbs.

(27th July) In Britain, the Sexual Offences Act decriminalizes homosexual acts between consenting males over 21.

Science, Technology, and Discovery

S Manabe and R T Wetherald warn that the increase in carbon dioxide in the atmosphere, produced by human activities, is causing a 'greenhouse effect', which will raise atmospheric temperatures and cause a rise in sea levels.

Rene Favaloro in Cleveland, USA, develops the coronary bypass operation.

Introduction of mammography (an X-ray technique) for the detection of breast cancer.

Desmond Morris, *The Naked Ape*.

(4th Jan) In Britain, Donald Campbell is killed on Coniston Water while trying to break the world water-speed record in his jet-powered *Bluebird*.

(3rd Dec) Dr Christiaan Barnard performs the first heart transplant operation, in South Africa; the patient, Louis Washkansky, survives for 18 days.

Humanities and Scholarship

Start of excavation of Mycenaean palace (and frescoes) at Akrotiri on the Aegean island of Thera.

The Agrarian History of the Middle Ages.

Art, Sculpture, Fine Arts, and Architecture

Architecture Frederick Gibberd, Metropolitan Cathedral Church of Christ the King, Liverpool.

Painting David Hockney, *A Neat Lawn.*

Andy Warhol, *Marilyn Monroe.*

Sculpture Richard Long, *A Line Made by Walking* (sculpture).

Music

Witold Lutoslawski, Symphony No. 2.

Toru Takemitsu, *November Steps.*

Hair (musical), lyrics by Gerome Ragni, music by Galt MacDermot (first performed at the Public Theatre, East Greenwich Village, New York, 29th Oct).

The Beatles, *Sergeant Pepper's Lonely Hearts Club Band.*

The Doors, *The Doors.*

The Jimi Hendrix Experience, *Are You Experienced?, Axis: Bold As Love.*

The Monkees, 'I'm A Believer', 'Last Train to Clarksville', 'Daydream Believer'.

Velvet Underground, *The Velvet Underground and Nico.*

(30th Sept) In Britain, start of the BBC's national pop station, Radio One.

Literature

Gabriel García Márquez, *One Hundred Years of Solitude.*

Naguib Mahfouz, *Miramar.*

Drama Peter Nichols, *A Day in the Death of Joe Egg.*

Harold Pinter, *The Homecoming.*

Tom Stoppard, *Rosencrantz and Guildenstern are Dead.*

Derek Walcott, *Dream on Monkey Mountain.*

Sport and Recreation

(14th March) Queen's Park Rangers becomes the first English Third Division side to win a Wembley soccer cup final, beating West Bromwich Albion 3–2 in the League Cup.

(25th May) Glasgow Celtic is first Scottish team to win soccer's European Cup, beating Inter Milan 2–1 in Lisbon.

(5th Oct) The British Lawn Tennis Association abolishes the distinction between amateurs and professionals – as does the International Lawn Tennis Federation in 1968.

(12th Dec) After 226 days (starting 27th Aug 1966), Francis Chichester, in his yacht *Gipsy Moth IV*, completes the first solo round-the-world voyage.

Media

Closure of the British cooperative movement's paper *The Sunday Citizen.*

Film *Accident* (director, Joseph Losey).

Far from the Madding Crowd (director, John Schlesinger).

Radio In Britain, the BBC replaces its Light, Home, and Third Services with four numbered stations.

In Britain, the BBC starts local radio.

Television New programmes in Britain include: *The Forsyte Saga* (BBC); *Callan*, with Edward Woodward; *The World About Us* (BBC; –1986), presented by David Attenborough.

Statistics

Religious denominations in US (in millions): Roman Catholics,47.9. Baptists, 24.7. Methodists, 13.2. Lutherans, 8.7. Presbyterians, 4.1. Protestant Episcopal, 3.4. Mormons, 2.1. Greek Orthodox, 1.8. Jews, 5.7.

1968

Jan: 16th, British government re-introduces prescription charges, cuts capital spending, and proposes complete military withdrawal from east of Suez (except Hong Kong) by 1971.

30th, Vietcong launches Tet offensive against South Vietnamese cities.

Feb: 7th, Flemish campaign against French-speakers at University of Louvain brings down Belgian government.

March: 11th, major US and South Vietnamese offensive in Saigon area.

31st, President Johnson announces decision not to seek re-election and restricts US bombing of North Vietnam.

April: 4th, assassination of Martin Luther King in Memphis, Tennessee.

9th, British Race Relations Bill published.

10th, President Johnson signs Civil Rights Bill prohibiting racial discrimination in housing.

20th, Enoch Powell attacks coloured immigration: 'like the Roman, I seem to see the River Tiber foaming with much blood' (21st, dismissed from Shadow Cabinet).

May: 2nd, Violent clashes between students and police begin in Latin Quarter of Paris.

10th, 'Night of the Barricades' in Paris (11th, French government makes concessions to student demands).

13th, US and North Vietnamese negotiators begin peace talks in Paris.
14th, Czechoslovak government announces wide range of liberalizing reforms.
17th, students and strikers occupy factories and hold protest marches in French cities.
24th, rioters set fire to Paris Bourse; President de Gaulle asks for vote of confidence in referendum.
30th, President de Gaulle postpones referendum and calls general election, as riots continue.

June: 5th, Senator Robert Kennedy shot in Los Angeles after winning California primary election (6th, dies).
12th, French government bans demonstrations and dissolves 11 student organizations.
24th, (–25th July) negotiations between Greek and Turkish Cypriots in Nicosia (second round, 29th Aug–9th Dec).
30th, Gaullists win landslide victory in second round of French general election.

July: 2nd, Britain offers famine relief to Nigeria and Biafra (4th, Biafra refuses it while Britain sells arms to Nigeria).
14th, USSR halts withdrawal of troops from Czechoslovakia after Warsaw Pact exercises.
16th, Soviet, East German, Hungarian, Polish, and Bulgarian leaders declare Czechoslovak reforms unacceptable.
29th, (–1st Aug) Czechoslovak and Soviet leaders hold talks at Cierna-nad-Tisou.

Aug: 20th, Soviet and allied forces invade Czechoslovakia and arrest reform leaders.
21st, Congress of Czechoslovak Communist Party, meeting in secret, rejects collaboration and re-elects Dubček.
23rd, President Svoboda of Czechoslovakia flies to Moscow for talks (25th, secures release of Dubček).

Sept: 6th, Swaziland becomes independent under King Sobhuza II.

Oct: 31st, President Johnson halts bombing of North Vietnam and announces agreement on Vietnamese delegations for peace talks.

Nov: 5th, in US elections Richard Nixon, Republican, with 302 electoral votes, wins narrow victory over Hubert Humphrey, Democrat, with 191, and George Wallace, Independent, with 45; popular vote: Nixon, 31,770,237; Humphrey, 31,270,533; Wallace, 9,906,141. Democrats keep control of Congress.
30th, violence erupts between Catholic and Protestant demonstrators in Armagh.

Dec: 2nd, Iraqi artillery in Jordan shells Israeli villages (4th, Israel bombs Iraqi bases).

Politics, Government, Law, and Economy

The first decimal coins are introduced in Britain.
(26th June) Fulton report criticizes the British civil service for class stratification, amateurism, and insularity.
(16th Oct) British Commonwealth merges with the Foreign Office, to form the Foreign and Commonwealth Office.

Society, Education, and Religion

The Race Relations Act outlaws discrimination in Britain.
All laws dealing with Church–State relations in Albania are abrogated, implying that religious bodies have been eliminated and that Albania has therefore become the world's first complete atheist state.
The South African Council of Churches declares the doctrine of racial separation to be 'truly hostile' to Christianity.
(27th April) Abortion is made lawful in Britain, when pregnancy endangers the physical or mental health of a woman or child.
(29th July) Publication of the Papal Encyclical *Humanae Vitae*, prohibiting use of artificial contraception by Roman Catholics.

Science, Technology, and Discovery

Inauguration of the Aswan High Dam on the River Nile in Egypt.
First crewed US Apollo space mission, *Apollo 7*, tests *Apollo* spacecraft (11th–22nd Oct); *Apollo 8* makes the first crewed mission to the Moon; it completes 10 orbits and returns to Earth (21st–27th Dec).

Humanities and Scholarship

M R D Foot and H C G Matthew (eds.), *The Gladstone Diaries* (–1994).
Michel Foucault, *The Archaeology of Knowledge.*
Jürgen Habermas, *Knowledge and Human Interests.*

Art, Sculpture, Fine Arts, and Architecture

Architecture Hubert Bennett and architects of Greater London Council, Hayward Gallery, London.

Ludwig Mies van der Rohe, National Gallery, West Berlin.
James Stirling, History Faculty Building, Cambridge University, Cambridge, England.
Painting Richard Hamilton, *Swinging London.*
Sculpture Sol Lewitt, *Untitled Cube (6).*

Music

Luciano Berio, *Sinfonia.*
Luigi Dallapiccola, *Ulisse* (opera).
Joseph and the Amazing Technicolour Dreamcoat (musical), first performed at Colet Court School, London (1st March; first commercial theatre performance of longer version, 16th Oct 1972).
James Brown, 'Say It Loud, I'm Black and I'm Proud'.
Marvin Gaye, 'I Heard It Through the Grapevine'.
The Rolling Stones, *Beggar's Banquet.*
Simon and Garfunkel, 'Mrs Robinson'.
(29th Aug) (–31st) In Britain, second Isle of Wight pop festival, starring Bob Dylan.

Literature

Yasunari Kawabata awarded Japan's first Nobel Prize for Literature.
Drama Alan Bennett, *Forty Years On.*
(26th Sept) The Theatres Act in Britain abolishes theatre censorship, previously exercised by the Lord Chamberlain.

Sport and Recreation

In London, at the first 'open' Wimbledon tennis championship, the Singles titles are won by Rod Laver of Australia and Billie Jean King of the USA.
(29th May) Manchester United becomes the first English soccer team to win the European Cup, beating Benfica of Potugal 4–1 in the final in London.
(31st Aug) In Britain, Gary Sobers, batting for Nottinghamshire against Glamorgan at Swansea, hits six sixes in one over off Malcolm Nash.
(24th Sept) The South African prime minister, B J Vorster, cancels the tour of South Africa by the MCC team from Britain after the MCC includes the Cape Coloured player Basil D'Oliveira in the MCC team.
(12th Oct) (–27th) The 19th Olympic Games are held in Mexico City. The USA wins 45 gold medals; USSR, 29; Japan, 11; East Germany, 9; France and Czechoslovakia, 7 each; West Germany, Britain, and Poland, 5 each; Romania, 4; Bob Beamon of the USA establishes a new Long Jump world record of 8.89 m/29 ft 2.5 in.

Media

Sir William ('Pissing Billy') Carr sells a 51% stake in the British paper the *News of the World* to Rupert Murdoch of Australia, having rejected an offer from British businessman Robert Maxwell.
Film *Butch Cassidy and the Sundance Kid* (director, George Roy Hill; starring Paul Newman and Robert Redford).
The Good, The Bad and the Ugly (director, Sergio Leone).
The Graduate (director, Mike Nichols).
If.. (director, Lindsay Anderson).
Night of the Living Dead (director, George Romero).
2001, A Space Odyssey (director, Stanley Kubrick).

1969

Jan: 3rd, Roman Catholic and Protestant demonstrators clash in Londonderry (11th, in Newry).
17th, British government issues *In Place of Strife: A Policy for Industrial Relations.*
20th, Richard Nixon takes oath as 37th US president.

Feb: 3rd, Palestine Liberation Organization elects Yassir Arafat as chairman.
7th, Anguilla votes to break all ties with Britain.

March: 12th, in Anguilla, British emissary forced to leave at gun-point (19th, 250 British troops land and re-establish control).
25th, military government takes over in Pakistan amid escalating violence; President Ayub Khan is replaced by General Yahya Khan.

April: 17th, in Northern Ireland 21-year-old civil rights activist Bernadette Devlin wins Mid-Ulster by-election.
20th, British troops guard public utilities in Northern Ireland after post offices bombed.
28th, resignation of President de Gaulle; Alain Poher becomes interim President.

May: 10th, local elections leave Labour in control of only 28 out of 342 borough councils in England and Wales.
11th, Vietcong launch rocket and ground attacks throughout South Vietnam.

14th, President Nixon suggests mutual withdrawal of US, Allied, and North Vietnamese troops from South Vietnam.
15th, violence in Kuala Lumpur between Malays and Chinese.
30th, Gibraltar's constitution comes into effect (30th July, general election).

June: 8th, President Nixon announces withdrawal of 25,000 US troops from Vietnam (further 35,000, 16th Sept).
8th, Spain completely closes land frontier with Gibraltar (27th, suspends ferry service from Algeciras).
9th, in Britain Enoch Powell calls for repatriation of black immigrants.
15th, Georges Pompidou becomes President of France (20th, appoints Jacques Chaban-Delmas as Prime Minister).
20th, Rhodesia votes to become a republic (24th, Britain cuts last official links).
25th, US Senate passes resolution calling on President not to commit troops to foreign countries without Congressional approval.

July: 4th, General Franco offers Spanish citizenship to all Gibraltarians.
19th, car driven by US Senator Edward Kennedy plunges into river at Chappaquiddick Island; his passenger, Mary Jo Kopechne, drowns.
19th, Indira Gandhi issues ordinance for nationalization of 14 major Indian banks.
20th, Neil Armstrong becomes first man to walk on the Moon.
24th, heaviest fighting between UAR and Israel since Six-Day War.

Aug: 11th, in Zambia President Kenneth Kaunda announces nationalization of copper mines.
12th, arson and street-fighting in Belfast and Londonderry (14th, British troops intervene to separate rioters).
13th, USSR forces cross Chinese border in Sinkiang.
17th, Ulster Unionists rule out coalition government at Stormont.
19th, British army assumes full responsibility for security in Northern Ireland.

Oct: 10th, Lord Hunt's committee recommends disarming Royal Ulster Constabulary and disbanding part-time police, the 'B' specials (11th, intense rioting in Belfast).
14th, 50 new pence coin replaces 10-shilling note as prelude to decimalization.
15th, millions demonstrate across USA in peaceful 'moratorium' against Vietnam War.
21st, Social Democrat Willy Brandt becomes Chancellor of West Germany.
26th, Portuguese government holds every seat in first significantly contested elections since 1926 (8th Nov, opposition parties dissolved).

Nov: 3rd, President Nixon promises complete withdrawal of US ground forces from Vietnam on secret timetable (50,000 more troops withdrawn, 15th Dec).
11th, UN General Assembly rejects admission of Communist China for 20th time.
17th, US–Soviet talks on strategic arms limitation (SALT) open in Helsinki.
19th, details emerge of shooting of over 100 Vietnamese civilians by US troops at My Lai on 16th March 1968.

Dec: 27th, UAR, Libya, and Sudan form alliance.

Politics, Government, Law, and Economy

Isaiah Berlin, *Four Essays on Liberty*.
Warren Burger appointed to the US Supreme Court, serving until 1986 (President Johnson first proposed Abe Fortas but the nomination was withdrawn).
Capital punishment is permanently abolished in Britain and is replaced by a mandatory life sentence for murder.
Dow Jones share index in USA crosses the 1,000 mark for the first time.
(March) Japan's Gross National Product exceeds that of West Germany for the first time.
(12th May) Representation of the People Act 1969 reduces voting age in Britain from 21 to 18.
(11th June) In Britain, the Redcliffe-Maud Report (report of the Royal Commission on Local Government) recommends a radical simplification of the structure.
(10th Aug) In Los Angeles, USA, cult gang directed by Charles Manson invades the home of actress Sharon Tate, killing her and her unborn child, three guests, and a passer-by.

Society, Education, and Religion

Riots follow a police raid at the Stonewall Tavern in New York, leading to the gay rights movement.
A scheme for Anglican–Methodist union in England fails to reach the necessary 75% majority in the Convocations of Canterbury and York of the Church of England.
Catherine McConnochie is ordained at the Presbytery of Aberdeen, Scotland, as the first woman minister in the Church of Scotland.
(17th Oct) In Britain, the Divorce Reform Act, known as the 'Casanova's Charter', permits divorce by consent of both parties after two years' separation and at the wish of one party after five years.

Science, Technology, and Discovery

Internet established by the US Department of Defense.

In USA, Jonathan Beckwith and associates at the Harvard Medical School isolate a single gene for the first time.

Development and implant of the first effective artificial human heart, used as a temporary device for patients requiring transplants.

(15th Feb) R G Edwards of the Cambridge Physiological Laboratory, Cambridge, England, makes the first in vitro fertilization of human egg cells.

(July) US *Apollo 11* space mission (16th–24th) leads to the first crewed landing on the Moon and first walk on the Moon (20th) by Neil Armstrong and Buzz Aldrin.

(Aug) British scientist Dorothy Hodgkin announces the structure of insulin.

Humanities and Scholarship

Kenneth Clark, *Civilization.*

M Wilson and L Thompson (eds.), *The Oxford History of South Africa*, Volume 1 (Volume 2, 1971).

J R Searle, *Speech Acts.*

Art, Sculpture, Fine Arts, and Architecture

'When Attitude Becomes Form' exhibition, Institute of Contemporary Art, London.

Architecture Denys Lasdun and Partners, First Phase of University of East Anglia, Norwich, England.

Sculpture Donald Judd, *Untitled* (minimal sculpture, vertically arranged metal and glass boxes).

Music

Peter Maxwell Davies, *Eight Songs for a Mad King.*

(21st Aug) (–24th) In the USA, half a million people attend the three-day Woodstock Music and Arts Fair.

Literature

John Fowles, *The French Lieutenant's Woman.*

Mario Puzo, *The Godfather.*

Philip Roth, *Portnoy's Complaint.*

Kurt Vonnegut, *Slaughterhouse Five.*

Drama Joe Orton, *What the Butler Saw.*

Everyday Life

The mini dress is followed by the ankle-length 'maxi'.

Sport and Recreation

US professional football is reorganized into two 'conferences', the National Football Conference (NFC) and the American Football Conference (AFC), each with 13 teams.

(22nd April) Robin Knox-Johnston wins the first single-handed round-the-world yacht race.

(18th May) British driver Graham Hill wins the Monaco Grand Prix for a record fifth time.

(8th Sept) Rod Laver of Australia achieves his second Grand Slam, winning all four major tennis championships (the Australian Open, the French Open, Wimbledon, and the US Open) in the same calendar year.

Media

Australian Rupert Murdoch buys the British paper the *Sun*, which is relaunched as a tabloid.

Film *Easy Rider* (director, Dennis Hopper).

Oh! What a Lovely War (director, Richard Attenborough).

The Prime of Miss Jean Brodie (starring Maggie Smith).

Satyricon (director, Federico Fellini).

The Wild Bunch (director, Sam Peckinpah).

Television New programmes in USA include: *The Bill Cosby Show*; *Sesame Street*, first shown on almost 200 non-commercial stations.

New programmes in Britain include: *Civilization*, presented by Kenneth Clark (BBC); *Monty Python's Flying Circus (BBC)*; *On The Buses* (LWT); *Pot Black* (BBC), which starts a craze for snooker.

Statistics

Immigrant workers in western European countries (with immigrants as percentage of total population in brackets): Austria, 68,000 (0.9). Belgium, 679,000 (7.1). France, 3,177,000 (6.4). West Germany, 2,977,000 (4.8). Great Britain, 2,603,000 (5.0). Holland, 72,000 (0.6). Luxembourg, 28,000 (8.3). Sweden, 173,000 (2.2). Switzerland, 972,000 (16.0).

1970 **Jan: 30th**, severe fighting between Israel and Syria on Golan Heights.

Feb: 4th, British government proposes making introduction of comprehensive schools compulsory.

23rd, Guyana becomes a republic within the Commonwealth.

March: 1st, Socialists win unexpected victory in Austrian general election.

2nd, Rhodesia formally declares itself a republic (Clifford Dupont becomes President, 14th April).
11th, Iraq recognizes Kurdish autonomy, thus ending nine-year war.
18th, overthrow of Prince Norodom Sihanouk of Cambodia.
19th, first-ever meeting of East and West German heads of government takes place at Erfurt (21st May, Willi Stoph and Willy Brandt meet again at Kassel).

April: 1st, Vietcong launch major assaults throughout South Vietnam after six-month lull.
3rd, 500 British troops fly to Northern Ireland to reinforce 6,000 already there.
19th, Pathet Lao advances on Phnom Penh (20th, Cambodian government appeals for US assistance).
24th, Gambia becomes a republic within the Commonwealth.

May: 2nd, USA bombs North Vietnam for first time since Nov 1968.
4th, US National Guardsmen shoot dead four anti-war demonstrators at Kent State University, Ohio.

June: 18th, in British general election, Conservatives win 330 seats, Labour, 287, and Liberals, 6 (Conservatives win 46.4% of votes cast, Labour, 43, and Liberals, 7.4).
19th, Harold Wilson resigns and Edward Heath forms Conservative ministry, with Sir Alec Douglas-Home as Foreign Secretary, Iain Macleod as Chancellor of the Exchequer and Reginald Maudling as Home Secretary.
28th, US ground troops withdraw from Cambodia.
30th, Britain, Denmark, Norway, and Eire open negotiations in Luxembourg for EC membership.

July: 3rd, Security forces begin search for arms in Falls Road area of Belfast.
16th, (–29th) British national dock strike over pay; government declares State of Emergency.

Sept: 5th, Marxist candidate, Salvador Allende, wins Chilean Presidential election (24th Oct, Chilean Congress ratifies his election).
6th, Palestinian terrorists hijack four aircraft, one to Cairo, two to Dawson's Field, Jordan, and one to Heathrow, where hijacker Leila Khaled is arrested.
16th, King Hussein orders Jordanian army to disband Palestinian militia (17th, house-to-house fighting begins in Amman).
19th, Syrian tanks invade Jordan in support of Palestinians.
27th, King Hussein, Yassir Arafat and other Arab leaders sign agreement in Cairo to end civil war in Jordan.
28th, President Nasser of Egypt dies (29th, succeeded by Anwar Sadat).

Oct: 5th, Quebec separatists kidnap Jasper Cross, British Trade Commissioner in Canada (3rd Dec, released).
7th, President Nixon proposes five-point peace plan for Indo–China (14th, North Vietnam rejects plan).
9th, Cambodia declares itself the Khmer Republic.
10th, Fiji becomes independent within the Commonwealth.
11th, Quebec separatists kidnap Pierre Laporte, Minister of Labour (17th, body found).
15th, British governmental re-organization creates Department of Trade and Industry and Department of the Environment.

Nov: 8th, UAR, Libya, and Sudan agree to federate (27th, joined by Syria).

Dec: 3rd, British government publishes Industrial Relations Bill to make collective agreements enforceable at law.
7th, West Germany and Poland sign treaty recognizing Oder–Neisse Line as frontier.

Politics, Government, Law, and Economy

The 26th Amendment to the US Constitution gives 18 year-olds the vote from 1971.
In England and Wales, the Administration of Justice Act constitutes a commercial court as part of the Queen's Bench division of the High Court; it also leads to the creation of the Family Division and abolishes imprisonment for debt.
(19th Oct) The British Petroleum company makes major oil discovery in the North Sea.

Society, Education, and Religion

The Equal Pay Act in Britain makes discrimination in wages and conditions of employment on the basis of sex illegal from 1975.
Germaine Greer, *The Female Eunuch.*
Kate Millett, *Sexual Politics.*
The World Council of Churches holds its first consultation on 'Dialogue with Men of Living Faiths'.
Publication of the complete *New English Bible* (in Britain, a million copies are sold within a week).
The General Synod of the Church of England is inaugurated.

(1st Jan) Family Law Reform Act reduces the age of majority in Britain from 21 to 18.
(June) The British Methodist Church votes to allow women to become ministers.
(31st Aug) In USA, the first desegregated classes are held in over 200 school districts in the South.
(1st Dec) Divorce becomes legal in certain cases in Italy.

Science, Technology, and Discovery

In USA, the IBM company develops the 'floppy disc' for storing computer data.

Humanities and Scholarship

The Cambridge History of Islam.
R C Latham and W Matthews (eds.), *The Diary of Samuel Pepys* (–1983).
T S Kuhn, *The Structure of Scientific Revolution.*
Willard Quine, *Philosophy of Logic.*

Art, Sculpture, Fine Arts, and Architecture

Record price paid for a *Campbell's Soup Tin* by Andy Warhol – £25,000.
Architecture Yamasaki, World Trade Center, first tower topped out, New York.
Painting David Hockney, *Mr and Mrs Ossie Clark and Percy.*

Music

Luciano Berio, *Opera.*
Michael Tippett, *The Knot Garden* (opera).
The Beatles, *Let It Be* (single and album).
The Grateful Dead, *Workingman's Dead* and *American Beauty.*
Sacha Distel, 'Raindrops Keep Falling on my Head'.
Led Zeppelin, *Led Zeppelin II, III.*
Joni Mitchell, *Ladies of the Canyon.*
Simon and Garfunkel, 'Bridge Over Troubled Water' (single and album).
The Beatles officially split up, all four of them releasing solo albums.
Death from drug overdose of superstar guitarist Jimi Hendrix.

Literature

Richard Bach, *Jonathan Livingston Seagull.*
Ted Hughes, *Crow* (poems).
Japanese author Yukio Mishima commits ritual suicide.
Drama Dario Fo, *Accidental Death of an Anarchist.*

Sport and Recreation

(4th June) Nijinsky, ridden by Lester Piggott, wins the Derby in the fastest time since 1936. In the same season Piggott also wins the 2,000 Guineas, the King George VI and Queen Elizabeth Diamond Stakes and the St Leger, completing the first Triple Crown of major British races since 1935.
(21st June) Brazil is victorious in the soccer World Cup, held in Mexico, for the third time (beating Italy by 4–1 in the final); it wins the Rimet Trophy outright.
(21st June) Tony Jacklin wins the US Open at Hazeltine Golf Club, Minnesota; he is the first Briton to win since Ted Ray in 1920.
(13th Sept) Margaret Court of Australia becomes only the second woman, after Maureen Connolly in 1953, to win the Grand Slam of all four major tennis tournaments.

Media

Film *Kes* (director, Ken Loach).
Love Story (director, Arthur Hiller; starring Ali MacGraw and Ryan O'Neal).
Television New programmes in Britain include: *Play for Today* (BBC), which includes John Osborne's *The Right Prospectus; The Six Wives of Henry VIII* (BBC); *Up Pompeii* (BBC), starring Frankie Howerd.

Statistics

European populations working in agriculture (percentages): Belgium, 4.5; Bulgaria, 23.6; Czechoslovakia, 10.6; Denmark, 10.6; Eire, 25.1; France, 15.1; East Germany, 11.7; West Germany, 7.5; Great Britain, 2.7; Greece, 40.6; Holland, 6.1; Hungary 24.5; Italy, 16.4; Poland, 38.6; Romania, 36.8; Spain, 24.8; Sweden, 7.9; Yugoslavia, 44.6.
TV sets (per thousand of population): US, 412; France, 201; West Germany, 272; Great Britain, 293; Italy, 181; Japan, 215.
Social and educational composition of British Conservative Cabinet: aristocrats, 4, middle class, 14, working class, 0; attendance at public school, 15 (inc. 4 at Eton); attendance at University 15 (all Oxford or Cambridge).

1971 **Jan: 20th,** (–8th March) nationwide strike by British postal workers.
25th, in Uganda, General Idi Amin deposes President Obote and seizes power.
31st, telephone service between East and West Berlin re-established after 19 years.

Feb: **1st**, (–31st March) strike halts Ford car production in Britain.
5th, Robert Curtis is first British soldier to be killed on duty in Northern Ireland.
14th, international oil companies accept higher prices demanded by Gulf States.
14th, USSR announces ninth Five-Year Plan, with high priority for consumer goods.
15th, Britain introduces decimal currency.
24th, British government publishes Immigration Bill to restrict rights of abode of Commonwealth citizens.
March: **10th**, Indira Gandhi's Congress Party wins landslide victory in Indian general election.
26th, Awami League declares independence of East Pakistan as Bangladesh; troops from West Pakistan fight separatists.
April: **15th**, Britain restores telephone link with China (cut in 1949).
17th, Egypt, Syria, and Libya sign Benghazi Agreement to establish Federation of Arab Republics.
19th, Sierra Leone becomes a republic within the Commonwealth.
19th, British unemployment, at 3.4%, reaches highest level since 1940.
29th, US combat deaths in Vietnam exceed 45,000.
May: **11th**, 120 Labour MPs declare opposition to British entry into EC.
20th, Leningrad court sentences nine Jews to hard labour for anti-Soviet activities.
20th, (–21st) Edward Heath and President Pompidou, meeting in Paris, reach general agreement on terms for British membership of EC.
27th, Egypt signs 15-year treaty of friendship with USSR.
June: **7th**, Deals between Britain and EC on Commonwealth sugar and status of sterling (23rd, final agreement on British entry).
10th, USA ends embargo on trade with China.
13th, The *New York Times* begins publication of secret Pentagon Papers detailing US government deception in handling of Vietnam War (30th, US Supreme Court upholds right to publish).
22nd, Dom Mintoff, Prime Minister of Malta, demands resignation of Governor-General and re-negotiation of British-Maltese defence agreement.
25th, British Education Secretary, Margaret Thatcher, announces end of free milk for primary school children.
30th, Yugoslav Federal Assembly passes 23 amendments to 1963 constitution, devolving power to constituent republics.
July: **7th**, White Paper, entitled *The United Kingdom and the European Communities*, outlines terms for British entry.
Aug: **5th**, in Britain, Industrial Relations Bill receives Royal Assent.
9th, Northern Ireland government introduces internment and forbids processions.
9th, (–11th) in Northern Ireland, over 22 people die in fighting between troops and IRA in Belfast, Newry and Londonderry; Eire opens refugee camps for Catholics.
14th, Bahrain declares independence from Britain (Qatar becomes independent, Sept 6th).
15th, President Nixon suspends conversion of dollars into gold and imposes 90-day price freeze and 10% import surcharge in response to first US trade deficit since 1894.
18th, Australia and New Zealand announce withdrawal of their forces from Vietnam.
Oct: **25th**, UN General Assembly votes to admit Communist China and expel Taiwan (15th Nov, China takes its seat).
28th, House of Commons votes 356 to 244 in favour of EC entry; 69 Labour MPs vote with Government, 39 Conservative MPs vote with Opposition.
Nov: **12th**, President Nixon proclaims end of US offensive role in Vietnam War and withdraws 45,000 more troops.
16th, Compton Report rejects allegations of brutality in internment camps in Northern Ireland.
Dec: **1st**, Abu Dhabi, Sharjah, Dubai, Umm al Qaiwain, Ajman, and Fujairah form United Arab Emirates.
3rd, Pakistan bombs Indian air-fields.
4th, explosion in Belfast public house kills 15 (subsequent reprisals bring annual death-toll to 173, including 43 troops).
6th, India recognizes independence of Bangladesh; war breaks out along border between India and West Pakistan.
16th, East Pakistan forces surrender to India; India orders ceasefire on West Pakistan front.
17th, end of Indo-Pakistan War; East Pakistan becomes independent as Bangladesh.

Politics, Government, Law, and Economy

Greenpeace international environmental campaign organization founded.
The British Industrial Relations Act establishes a completely new system of labour law, with a National Industrial Relations Court and legally binding contracts.
John Rawls, *A Theory of Justice*.

In USA, President Nixon introduces a 'New Economic Policy', in which the Bretton Woods system (founded in 1944) of agreed exchange rates is effectively ended despite an attempt to patch matters up at the Smithsonian conference; domestically wages and prices are subjected to direct controls.

Decimalization of British currency.

(30th June) The 26th Amendment to the US Constitution extends full voting rights to 18-year-olds.

Society, Education, and Religion

Joyce Bennett and Jane Hwang Hsien Yuen are ordained priests by the Anglican Bishop of Hong Kong.

General Synod of the Church of England allows baptized members of other Christian denominations to receive communion in Anglican churches.

(7th Feb) Referendum in Switzerland approves the introduction of female suffrage.

Science, Technology, and Discovery

Introduction of quadraphonic sound reproduction system.

Intel in the USA introduces the microprocessor, a minute device on a single 'chip' for processing information within a computer.

Surgeons develop the fibre-optic endoscope for looking inside the human body.

(19th April) USSR launches *Salyut 1* space station which is visited by a three-person crew in June (7th–29th); the cosmonauts die during their descent to Earth when a faulty valve causes their capsule to lose pressure.

Humanities and Scholarship

C W Ferguson of the University of Arizona, USA, establishes a tree-ring chronology dating back to *c.* 6000 BC.

Cambridge Ancient History, Volumes 1, 2, 3rd edition (–1977).

Art, Sculpture, Fine Arts, and Architecture

Conceptual art dominates Paris Biennale, Prospect 71, Düsseldorf, West Germany, and 6th Guggenheim International, New York.

Architecture Destruction of Pruitt Igoe public housing blocks in St Louis, Missouri, USA (architect Minoru Yamasaki), heralds end of modern architecture.

Sculpture Gilbert and George, *Underneath the Arches*.

Music

Benjamin Britten, *Owen Wingrave* (opera).

Dmitri Shostakovich, Symphony No. 15.

Godspell (rock musical), lyrics and music by Stephen Schwartz.

Jesus Christ Superstar (rock musical), lyrics by Tim Rice, music by Andrew Lloyd Webber (first performed at the Mark Hellinger Theatre, New York, 12th Oct).

Led Zeppelin, *Led Zeppelin IV*.

T Rex, *Electric Warrior* – glitter rock starts in Britain.

Literature

Alexander Solzhenitsyn, *August 1914*.

Drama Wole Soyinka, *Madmen and Specialists*.

Sport and Recreation

The British Lions win a rugby Test series in New Zealand for the first time.

(5th Jan) First limited-overs one-day cricket international; Australia beats England in Melbourne.

Media

(May) In Britain, the *Daily Sketch* is merged into the *Daily Mail*, which is then relaunched as a tabloid.

Film *A Clockwork Orange* (director, Stanley Kubrick).

Death in Venice (director, Luchino Visconti).

Fiddler on the Roof (director, Norman Jewison; starring Topol).

The Garden of the Finzi-Continis (director, Vittorio de Sica).

The Go-Between (director, Joseph Losey).

Sunday Bloody Sunday (director, John Schlesinger).

Television New programmes in Britain include: *Edna the Inebriate Woman* (BBC), starring Patricia Hayes; *Elizabeth R* (BBC), starring Glenda Jackson; *The Old Grey Whistle Test* (BBC); *The Onedin Line* (BBC; – 1980); *The Two Ronnies* (BBC; –1986), with Ronnie Barker and Ronnie Corbett; *Upstairs Downstairs* (LWT; –1975).

1972

Jan: 9th, British national coal strike begins (9th Feb, state of emergency proclaimed).

20th, number of unemployed in Britain exceeds 1 million.

22nd, Britain, Denmark, Ireland and Norway sign Treaty of Accession to EC in Brussels.

30th, 'Bloody Sunday' in Northern Ireland: British troops shoot dead 13 civilians when violence erupts at anti-internment march in Bogside, Londonderry.

30th, Pakistan leaves the Commonwealth in anticipation of British recognition of Bangladesh (on Feb 4th).

Feb: 2nd, demonstrators burn down the British Embassy in Dublin.

21st, (–27th) President Nixon visits China.

March: 30th, Britain assumes direct rule over Northern Ireland, with William Whitelaw as Secretary of State.

April: 19th, North Vietnamese aircraft attack US 7th Fleet in Gulf of Tonkin.

23rd, in French referendum, 67.7% vote in favour of enlargement of EC.

May: 8th, President Nixon orders blockade and mining of North Vietnamese ports.

14th, Ulster Defence Association sets up first Protestant 'no go' areas in Belfast.

17th, West German Bundestag ratifies 1970 treaties with USSR and Poland with Christian Democrats abstaining.

22nd, (–29th) Richard Nixon becomes first US President to visit USSR (26th, signs treaty limiting anti-ballistic missile sites).

22nd, Ceylon ceases to be a British dominion and becomes a republic within the Commonwealth as Sri Lanka.

June: 1st, (–15th) West German police round up Baader–Meinhof urban guerrilla group.

17th, US police arrest five intruders planting electronic 'bugs' at the Democratic Party headquarters in the Watergate apartment complex, Washington.

27th, French Socialist and Communist Parties agree on a common programme.

July: 2nd, India and Pakistan agree to renounce force in settlement of disputes.

7th, William Whitelaw holds secret talks with IRA in London.

8th, President Nixon announces that USSR will purchase $750 million worth of US grain over three years.

18th, President Sadat of Egypt expels 20,000 Soviet advisers after accusing USSR of failing to supply promised armaments.

28th, (–16th Aug) nationwide dock strike, after union rejects Jones–Aldington proposals to ease unemployment resulting from 'containerization'.

31st, army destroys Catholic and Protestant barricades to end 'no go' areas in Belfast and Londonderry.

Aug: 1st, TUC and CBI agree to set up independent conciliation service.

1st, Egypt and Sudan announce plans for full union by Sept 1973.

4th, President Amin asserts that Ugandan Asians are frustrating the involvement of Africans in Uganda's business and commercial life; he gives them 90 days to leave the country.

Sept: 1st, Iceland unilaterally extends its fishing limit from 12 to 50 miles (5th, Icelandic gunboat cuts fishing gear of British trawler).

5th, Arab terrorists murder 11 members of Israeli Olympic team at Munich. West German police kill five terrorists in gun battle.

7th, South Korea withdraws its 37,000 troops remaining in Vietnam.

18th, first plane-load of expelled Ugandan Asians arrives in Britain (22nd, President Amin orders 8,000 Asians to leave within 48 hours).

21st, William Whitelaw ends internment without trial in Northern Ireland.

24th, 53.5% vote against EC membership in Norwegian referendum.

Oct: 3rd, US and USSR sign final SALT accords limiting submarine-carried and land-based missiles (SALT II talks begin in Geneva, 21st Nov).

26th, North Vietnam publishes ceasefire agreement with USA; Henry Kissinger says peace is at hand in Indo-China.

Nov: 1st, President Thieu of South Vietnam rejects US ceasefire plan.

6th, British government imposes 90-day freeze on price, pay, rent, and dividend increases as Phase One of anti-inflation programme.

7th, in US elections Richard Nixon, Republican, with 520 electoral votes, wins landslide victory over George McGovern, Democrat, with 17; popular vote: Nixon, 47,168,963. McGovern, 29,169,615. Republicans lose 2 Senators and gain 12 Representatives. Democrats keep control of both Houses.

8th, deadline for Asians to leave Uganda (25,000 come to Britain by end of year).

21st, eight-hour battle between Israel and Syria on Golan Heights.

25th, Norman Kirk becomes Prime Minister of New Zealand after Labour Party wins sweeping electoral victory.

Dec: 2nd, Australian Labour Party wins general election (5th, Gough Whitlam becomes Prime Minister).

20th, Diplock Commission recommends wider powers of arrest in Northern Ireland and suspension of trial by jury in certain cases.

21st, West and East Germany sign Basic Treaty to establish 'neighbourly relations on the basis of equality'.

Politics, Government, Law, and Economy

European Communities Act gives European institutions power to override British law.

(29th June) In USA, in Furman v Georgia, the Supreme Court rules that the death penalty is unconstitutional.

(13th Oct) The Bank of England replaces fixed bank rate with fluctuating minimum lending rate (MLR) tied to discount rate of Treasury bills.

Society, Education, and Religion

Native Americans march on Washington, DC, and occupy the Bureau of Indian Affairs.

Formation of United Reformed Church by union of Congregational Church in England and Wales and Presbyterian Church in England.

John V Taylor, *The Go-Between God.*

(9th Nov) Andrew Young is the first African-American to be elected from the South to the US Congress since the mid-19th century.

Science, Technology, and Discovery

First home video-cassette recorders introduced.

Humanities and Scholarship

'Treasures of Tutankhamun' exhibition at the British Museum, London, to celebrate the 50th anniversary of the discovery of Tutankhamun's tomb.

Discovery of tomb of Han dynasty prince south of Beijing, China, including jade suits.

Michael Baxandall, *Painting and Experience in Fifteenth-Century Italy.*

Karl Popper, *Objective Knowledge.*

Art, Sculpture, Fine Arts, and Architecture

Architecture Alvar Aalto, North Jutland Museum at Aalborg, Denmark.

Louis Kahn, Kimbell Art Museum, Fort Worth, Texas, USA.

Sculpture Michelangelo's Pietà in St Peter's Basilica, Vatican, is attacked with a hammer by lunatic.

Tate Gallery, London, makes controversial purchase of Carl André's 'bricks' (*Equivalent 8*, 1966).

Christo, *Valley Curtain, Colorado.*

Music

Harrison Birtwistle, *The Triumph of Time.*

Grease (musical), lyrics and music by Jim Jacobs and Warren Casey (first performed at the Eden Theatre, New York, 14th Feb).

David Bowie, *The Rise and Fall of Ziggy Stardust and the Spiders from Mars.*

Roxy Music, *Roxy Music.*

The Wailers, *Catch a Fire.*

Era of 'Teenybop', with prominence of singers appealing to teenagers (The Bay City Rollers, The Jackson Five, The Osmonds, and David Cassidy).

Literature

Anthony Burgess, *A Clockwork Orange.*

Frederick Forsyth, *The Day of the Jackal.*

V S Naipaul, *In a Free State.*

Sir John Betjeman is appointed Britain's Poet Laureate.

Drama Athol Fugard, *Sizwe Banzi is Dead.*

Tom Stoppard, *Jumpers.*

Everyday Life

'Pong' is the first known computer game.

Sport and Recreation

Eddie Merckx of Belgium wins his fourth consecutive Tour de France cycling race.

The British Jockey Club allows women jockeys to compete in horse-racing.

(22nd June) (–26th) Bob Massie of Australia takes 16 England wickets in the second cricket Test at Lord's – a record for an Australian bowler.

(26th Aug) (–11th Sept) The 20th Olympic Games are held in Munich, West Germany. USSR wins 50 gold medals; USA, 33; East Germany, 20; West Germany and Japan, 13 each; Australia, 8; Poland, 7; Hungary and Bulgaria, 6 each; Italy, 5; Sweden and Britain, 4 each; Mark Spitz of the USA wins 7 gold medals in swimming, all in world record times.

(1st Sept) Bobby Fischer of the USA beats Boris Spassky of the USSR in World Chess Championship in Reykjavik, Iceland.

Media

(June) In Australia, Rupert Murdoch purchases the *Sydney Daily Telegraph* and *Sunday Telegraph*.

Film *The Decameron* (director, Pier Paolo Pasolini).

The Discreet Charm of the Bourgeoisie (director, Luis Buñuel).

The Godfather (director, Francis Ford Coppola).

Radio In Britain, broadcast of the last *Goon Show*.

Television In Britain, the BBC launches CEEFAX, a television information system.

1973 **Jan:** **1st**, Britain, Ireland, and Denmark become members of the EC.

4th, Australia abandons colour bar in admission of new settlers.

8th, trial opens in Washington of seven men accused of bugging Democratic Party headquarters in the Watergate apartment complex.

27th, USA, North and South Vietnam, and Vietcong sign ceasefire agreement in Paris.

Feb: **7th**, Protest strikes, arson, and gun battles in Northern Ireland, following first detention of Protestant terrorist suspects.

27th, first-ever full strike by British civil servants.

March: **1st**, In Eire, Fine Gael coalition wins general election (14th, Liam Cosgrave becomes prime minister).

2nd, (–19th) closure of European exchange markets in face of new currency crisis.

8th, in Northern Ireland referendum, 591,820 (59% turn-out) vote to remain in United Kingdom, and 6,463 to join Eire.

11th, Perónist candidate, Hector Campora, wins Argentinian general election (13th July, resigns to make way for General Perón).

16th, finance ministers from 14 countries, meeting in Paris, agree to establish floating exchange rate system.

20th, White Paper on Northern Ireland proposes new assembly, power-sharing executive, and talks on an all-Ireland council.

29th, last US troops leave Vietnam and last US prisoners of war are released.

April: **1st**, Phase Two of British government's anti-inflation programme limits pay rises to £1 per week plus 4%.

12th, Labour wins control of Greater London Council and six new metropolitan councils.

17th, President Nixon drops ban on White House staff appearing before Senate Committee on Watergate affair (hearings begin, 17th May).

27th, Andrei Gromyko and Yuri Andropov enter Soviet Politburo in first major reshuffle since 1964.

30th, President Nixon accepts responsibility for bugging of Watergate building but denies any personal involvement.

May: **1st**, TUC calls one-day protest strike against pay policies.

30th, Erskine Childers succeeds Éamon de Valera as President of Eire.

June: **1st**, British Honduras changes name to Belize.

7th, Icelandic coastguard vessel rams British warship in escalation of 'Cod War'.

24th, Leonid Brezhnev, during visit to USA, declares that the Cold War is over.

28th, election by proportional representation of new Northern Ireland Assembly leaves official Unionists dependent on SDLP and Alliance support.

July: **10th**, the Bahamas become independent within the Commonwealth.

19th, British government announces weekly cash payments to mothers of £2 per child.

21st, France resumes nuclear tests at Mururoa Atoll despite protests from Australia and New Zealand.

26th, in Cyprus, EOKA terrorists blow up Limassol police station in continuing campaign for Enosis (union with Greece).

31st, militant Protestants, led by Rev Ian Paisley, disrupt first sitting of Northern Ireland Assembly.

Aug: **14th**, new Pakistani constitution takes effect, with Zulfikar Ali Bhutto as President.

19th, formal abolition of Greek monarchy; George Papadopoulos becomes President.

29th, Presidents Sadat and Khaddafi proclaim unification of Egypt and Libya, including plan for a joint Constituent Assembly (3rd Oct, first meeting held).

30th, Kenya bans hunting of elephants and trade in ivory.

Sept: **11th**, (–12th) military junta, headed by General Augusto Pinochet, seizes power in Chile; over 2,500 die in fighting; President Allende reportedly commits suicide.

18th, UN admits East and West Germany.

23rd, Juan Perón and wife Isabel are elected President and Vice-President of Argentina (inaugurated 12th Oct).

Oct: 6th, Full-scale war in Middle East, as Egypt and Syria attack Israel while Jews are observing Yom Kippur.

10th, USSR starts airlift of military supplies to Arab states. Iraq joins war against Israel (as do Saudi Arabia and Jordan on 13th).

11th, counterattacking Israelis break through on Golan Heights and invade Syria.

15th, Britain and Iceland end 'Cod War' with agreement on fishing rights.

16th, Israelis cross Suez Canal and invade Egypt (19th, President Nixon asks Congress to approve $2,000 million worth of military aid for Israel).

17th, 11 Arab states agree to cut oil production by 5% each month until US changes its Middle Eastern policy.

21st, Henry Kissinger and Leonid Brezhnev, meeting in Moscow, agree plan to stop war in Middle East (22nd, Egypt and Israel accept UN ceasefire, but fighting continues).

23rd, US House of Representatives orders judiciary committee to assess evidence for impeachment of President Nixon.

24th, Syria accepts ceasefire and fighting halts on both fronts.

Nov: 1st, Phase Three of British government's anti-inflation programme limits pay rises to 7% or £2.25 per week.

13th, energy crisis prompts British government to declare state of emergency (19th, 10% cut in fuel and petrol supplies).

21st, in Britain, National Union of Mineworkers (NUM) rejects any pay deal under Phase Three.

Dec: 9th, talks at Sunningdale, England, between Irish and British governments reach agreement on formation of a Council of Ireland with representatives from both governments. It is also agreed that the status of Northern Ireland will not be changed without majority support in the province.

13th, Edward Heath orders industry to work three-day week from 31st Dec to save energy.

18th, IRA launches Christmas bombing campaign in London.

20th, assassination of Spanish Premier, Carrero Blanco, in Madrid (29th, succeeded by Carlos Arias Navarro).

23rd, Shah of Iran announces that Gulf states will increase oil price from $5.10 to $11.65 a barrel from 1st Jan 1974.

Politics, Government, Law, and Economy

Opening of the first market for share options, in Chicago, USA.

E F Schumacher, *Small is Beautiful: A Study of Economics as if People Mattered.*

(Feb) European Trade Union Confederation, with 29 million members, is formed in the 14 countries belonging to the European Community and the European Free Trade Association.

(10th April) The British lord chief justice rules that physical obstruction on picket lines is unlawful.

(31st Oct) Kilbrandon Commission on the Constitution recommends devolved parliaments for Scotland and Wales.

Society, Education, and Religion

In Britain, the school leaving age is raised to 16.

Mother Teresa of Calcutta receives the first Templeton Prize for Progress in Religion.

(22nd Jan) In USA, the Supreme Court, in Roe v. Wade, legalizes abortion (in the first six months of pregnancy) in all states.

Science, Technology, and Discovery

The first calf is produced from a frozen embryo.

In Britain, Paul Lauterbur obtains the first NMR (nuclear magnetic resonance) image.

Humanities and Scholarship

The Cambridge History of China.

L A Marchand (ed.), *Byron's Letters and Journals* (–1982).

Allardyce Nicoll, *English Drama 1900–1930: The Beginnings of the Modern Period* (a companion to Nicoll's six-volume *History of the English Drama, 1660–1900*).

Saul Kripke, *Naming and Necessity.*

Art, Sculpture, Fine Arts, and Architecture

Architecture Jorn Utzon, Hall, Todd and Littlemore, Sydney Opera House, Sydney, Australia.

Minoru Yamasaki and Associates, World Trade Centre, New York.

Music

Benjamin Britten, *Death in Venice* (opera).

György Ligeti, *Clocks and Clouds.*

Elton John, 'Goodbye Yellow Brick Road' (single and album), *Don't Shoot Me, I'm Only the Piano Player.*

Mike Oldfield, *Tubular Bells.*

Pink Floyd, *The Dark Side of the Moon.*

Literature
Richard Adams, *Watership Down.*
Graham Greene, *The Honorary Consul.*
Patrick White, *The Eye of the Storm.*
Drama Alan Ayckbourn, *The Norman Conquests.*
Peter Shaffer, *Equus.*

Sport and Recreation
The first women's cricket World Cup (final 28th July).
(5th May) In soccer, Sunderland becomes the first second-division side to win the English Football Association Cup Final since 1931, beating Leeds United 1–0.

Media
Film *Day for Night* (director, François Truffaut).
Don't Look Now (director, Nicholas Roeg).
The Exorcist (director, William Friedkin).
Last Tango in Paris (director, Bernardo Bertolucci).
Mean Streets (director, Martin Scorsese).
O Lucky Man (director, Lindsay Anderson).
Radio (8th Oct) In Britain, launch of the first legal commercial radio station, the London Broadcasting Company (LBC), specializing in news and current affairs, followed by Capital Radio (9th), specializing in entertainment and music.

1974

Jan: 14th, in Britain, talks between Edward Heath and TUC on miners' dispute break down (28th, Heath accuses Mick McGahey of NUM of aiming to bring down government).

Feb: 7th, Grenada becomes independent within the Commonwealth.
10th, British mineworkers begins all-out strike in support of pay claim of 30–40%.
11th, John Poulson, a British architect who undertook numerous contracts for local authorities and other public bodies, is sentenced to five years' imprisonment for corruption (15th March, sentenced to another seven years on further charges).
13th, USSR deports dissident author Alexander Solzhenitsyn.
17th, Harold Wilson announces 'social contract' between Labour Party and TUC, whereby a Labour government will sponsor social legislation in return for wage restraint.
27th, new constitution strips Swedish monarchy of all remaining powers.
28th, British general election produces no overall majority, as Labour win 301 seats, Conservatives, 297, Liberals, 14, Scottish Nationalists, 7, Plaid Cymru, 2 (Conservatives win 37.9% of votes cast, Labour, 37.1%, and Liberals, 19.3%).

March: 4th, Edward Heath resigns after Liberals refuse to enter coalition.
5th, Harold Wilson forms minority Labour government, with James Callaghan as Foreign Secretary, Denis Healey as Chancellor of the Exchequer, Roy Jenkins as Home Secretary, and Michael Foot as Secretary for Employment.
9th, British industry returns to five-day working week.
11th, state of emergency ends in Britain after miners' union accepts £103 million pay deal.

April: 1st, re-organization of local government in England and Wales re-draws county boundaries.
19th, Israeli-Syrian air battle over Golan Heights.
25th, General Antonio de Spinola effects military coup in Portugal (26th, junta vows to dismantle authoritarian state and end wars in Angola, Mozambique and Guinea).

May: 8th, Willy Brandt resigns as West German Chancellor after aide, Gunther Guillaume, admits to spying.
18th, atomic bomb test makes India the world's sixth nuclear power.
19th, Valery Giscard d'Estaing wins second round of French Presidential election with 50.8% of votes to François Mitterrand's 49.2%.
19th, Protestant general strike begins in Northern Ireland against Sunningdale agreement and power-sharing (22nd, Executive postpones Council of Ireland till after 1977).
28th, Northern Ireland Executive collapses when all Unionist members resign (29th, Britain re-imposes direct rule and general strike ends).
31st, Henry Kissinger secures agreement between Syria and Israel to disengage forces on Golan Heights.

July: 1st, Isabel Perón becomes President of Argentina on the death of her husband.
14th, left-wing government takes office in Portugal under Colonel Vasco Goncalves.
15th, Cypriot National Guard, with Greek support, overthrows President Makarios and installs former EOKA terrorist Nicos Sampson in his place.

20th, Turkey invades Cyprus, claiming right of intervention under 1960 treaty (22nd, ceasefire).

23rd, Greek military government resigns (24th, Constantine Karamanlis returns from exile to form civilian administration).

24th, US Supreme Court orders President Nixon to surrender all Watergate tapes to Special Prosecutor.

26th, US House Judiciary Committee recommends impeachment of President Nixon.

31st, in Britain, repeal of Industrial Relations Act and abolition of NIRC.

Aug: 1st, restoration of 1952 constitution in Greece.

5th, President Nixon admits complicity in the Watergate cover-up.

9th, President Nixon resigns; Gerald Ford becomes 38th US President.

12th, Turkey issues 24-hour ultimatum demanding creation of autonomous ultimatum demanding creation of autonomous Turkish cantons in Cyprus (14th, Turkish forces resume offensive).

16th, second ceasefire leaves 40% of Cyprus under Turkish control.

Sept: 12th, military coup deposes Emperor Haile Selassie of Ethiopia.

Oct: 5th, IRA bombs kill 5 and injure 65 in two public houses in Guildford, Surrey, England.

10th, British general election gives Labour an overall majority of 3, with 319 seats to Conservatives, 277, Liberals, 13, Scottish Nationalists, 11, Plaid Cymru 3 (Labour take 39.2% of votes, Conservatives, 35.8%, and Liberals, 18.3%).

Nov: 20th, British Labour MP John Stonehouse disappears in Miami (24th Dec, arrested with false passport in Australia).

21st, IRA bombs two public houses in Birmingham, killing 21 people and injuring 120.

26th, Kakuei Tanaka resigns as Japanese premier amid allegations of corruption (9th Dec, succeeded by Takeo Miki).

28th, following spate of IRA outrages in Britain, the Prevention of Terrorism Bill is passed through Parliament in 24 hours. Police are given power to hold terrorist suspects for five days without charge and suspects can be banned from the British mainland or deported to Northern Ireland.

Dec: 7th, President Makarios returns to Cyprus after five months in exile.

31st, during 1974 British retail prices have risen by 19%, wage rates by 29%, while total industrial production fell by 3% (each sum a post-war record).

Politics, Government, Law, and Economy

Bob Woodward and Carl Bernstein, *All the President's Men.*

In US v. Richard M Nixon, the US Supreme Court rules that executive privilege does not cover evidence of criminal conduct, forcing Nixon to surrender subpoenaed Watergate tapes; the judgement confirms that the Supreme Court and not the president is the final arbiter of the Constitution.

In USA, Congress passes several bills designed to deal with abuses that came to light during the Watergate scandal; the Federal Election Campaign Amendments Act limits the scale of individual and corporate campaign contributions and provides for the Treasury to match funds if they have been raised in at least 20 states; the Budget and Impoundment Control Act which establishes the Congressional Budget Office to provide independent advice on government finance.

Prevention of Terrorism (Temporary Provisions) Act is passed in response to IRA bombings in England; it allows the home secretary to restrict individuals' movements between Northern Ireland and Britain and gives the police wider powers to detain suspects.

Rent Act in Britain extends indefinite security of tenure to tenants in furnished accommodation without a resident landlord.

(12th Nov) 'Lucky' Lord Lucan disappears from London after the murder of his children's nanny (tried in absentia and convicted of murder on 19th June 1975).

Society, Education, and Religion

(11th March) The new British secretary of state for education, Reg Prentice, proposes abolition of the 11-plus examination and the establishment of a fully comprehensive school system.

(28th March) In Britain, inauguration of National Health Service family planning service.

Science, Technology, and Discovery

M Molina and F S Rowland warn that chlorofluorocarbons (used in fridges and as propellants in sprays) may be damaging the atmosphere's ozone layer (which filters out much of the ultraviolet radiation from the Sun).

H M Georgi and S L Glashow propose the first Grand Unified Theory which envisages the strong, weak, and electromagnetic forces as variants of a single superforce.

Humanities and Scholarship

Discovery of the 'terracotta army' – over 6,000 life-size model soldiers – guarding the tomb of China's first Emperor, Qin Shihuangdi, near Xi'an in central China.

Colin Renfrew, *Before Civilization: The Radiocarbon Revolution and Prehistoric Europe.*

Jennifer Sherwood and Niklaus Pevsner, *Oxfordshire*, the final volume in Pevsner's 'Buildings of England' series.

Encyclopaedia Britannica, 15th edition, in three sections: Propaedia, Micropaedia, Macropaedia.

P F Strawson, *Freedom and Resentment*.

Art, Sculpture, Fine Arts, and Architecture

Architecture John Andrews and Webb Zerata, Canadian National Tower, Toronto, is topped out, world's tallest freestanding structure.

Music

Swedish pop group Abba win the Eurovision Song Contest with 'Waterloo' and shoot to international stardom.

Bob Dylan and The Band undertake a classic US tour, giving 39 shows.

The film *The Sting* revives ragtime.

Literature

Erica Jong, *Fear of Flying*.

John Le Carré, *Tinker, Tailor, Soldier, Spy*.

Alexander Solzhenitsyn is expelled from the USSR after publication of *The Gulag Archipelago, 1918–56*.

Drama Dario Fo, *Can't Pay? Won't Pay!*

Tom Stoppard, *Travesties*.

Everyday Life

In USA and Britain, 'Streaking' (running nude in public places) enjoys a burst of popularity at sports fixtures.

First observance of New Year's Day as a public holiday in England and Wales.

Sport and Recreation

Gary Sobers retires from Test cricket, holding the record for the number of runs: 8,032, from 93 Tests.

(7th July) Host nation West Germany wins the World Cup, defeating Holland by 2–1 in the Final in Munich, West Germany.

Media

Film *Amarcord* (director, Federico Fellini).

Céline and Julie Go Boating (director, Jacques Rivette).

Lacombe Lucien (director, Louis Malle).

Radio In USA, *The Prairie Home Companion* with Garrison Keillor.

Television New programmes in Britain include: *Arena* (BBC), an arts programme; *The Family*, the BBC's 'fly on the wall' documentary about living with the Wilkins family; *Happy Days*; *Porridge* (BBC), a comedy series set in a prison, starring Ronnie Barker; *Rising Damp* (Yorkshire TV).

Statistics

Social and educational composition of British Labour Cabinet: aristocrats, 1, middle class, 16, working class, 4; attendance at public school, 7 (none at Eton); attendance at University 16 (inc. 11 at Oxford or Cambridge).

1975

Jan: 15th, Portugal agrees to grant independence to Angola.

Feb: 11th, Margaret Thatcher elected leader of the Conservative Party, with 146 votes (William Whitelaw wins 79 votes, with 49 for three other challengers).

13th, Northern Cyprus declares separate existence as the Turkish Federated State of Cyprus.

24th, Bangladesh becomes a one-party state.

March: 2nd, Iran becomes a one-party state.

April: 9th, House of Commons vote confirms EC membership, by 396 to 170.

13th, civil war starts in Lebanon when clashes between Palestinians and Christian Falangists outside a Beirut church leave 30 dead.

17th, in Cambodia Khmer Rouge revolutionaries capture Phnom Penh; there is considerable brutality as people flee the city.

25th, the first free elections in Portugal since the 1920s produce no overall majority, the Socialists under Mario Soares emerge as the largest party.

29th, last US personnel flee Saigon by helicopter from the US Embassy compound.

30th, President Minh of South Vietnam surrenders Saigon to Communist forces.

June: 5th, consultative referendum approves Britain's membership of EC; turn-out is 64.5%, of whom 67.2% vote in favour.

12th, Indira Gandhi found guilty of electoral corruption but remains Indian Prime Minister pending appeals.

18th, first North Sea Oil pumped ashore in Britain.
25th, Mozambique becomes independent with Samora Machel as president.
26th, Indira Gandhi declares a state of emergency in India; censorship is imposed and opposition leaders, including Morarji Desai, are imprisoned.

July: 11th, White Paper *The Attack on Inflation* is published, proposing an incomes policy for 1975–76 which would allow only a flat-rate £6 per week increase.

Aug: 1st, Helsinki Conference on Security and Co-operation in Europe issues 'Final Act', signed by 30 states: states are to respect each other's equality and individuality, avoid use of force in disputes, and respect human rights.
12th, British inflation peaks at 26.9%.

Sept: 16th, Papua New Guinea becomes independent from Australia.

Oct: 15th, start of the 'Cod War', when Iceland increases its territorial waters from 50 to 200 miles and confronts German trawlers with gunboats.
21st, British unemployment breaches 1 million for first time since 1940s.
22nd, the 'Guildford Four' are sentenced to life imprisonment after being found guilty of planting IRA bombs in pubs in Guildford and Woolwich.
26th, Transkei becomes the first nominally independent South African black 'homeland'.
27th, House of Commons votes to abolish grants to 'direct grant' schools.

Nov: 11th, Sir John Kerr, the Governor-General of Australia, dismisses Prime Minister Whitlam and appoints the Opposition leader, Malcolm Fraser.
20th, General Franco dies (22nd, the monarchy is restored and Juan Carlos becomes King of Spain).
25th, Surinam (former Dutch Guyana) becomes independent.
27th, White Paper *Our Changing Democracy* proposes devolution for Scotland and Wales.
29th, New Zealand National Party defeats the Labour government. Robert Muldoon becomes prime minister.

Dec: 3rd, Communist forces take control of Laos; the King abdicates.
6th, (–12th) IRA gang is besieged at Balcombe Street in London and eventually surrenders.
13th, general election in Australia gives large majority to the newly installed Fraser government.

Politics, Government, Law, and Economy

Richard Crossman, *Diaries of a Cabinet Minister.*
New York City suffers shortage of funds; bailed out by New York state and federal government aid (bill for federal loan signed on 9th Dec, two days before the city would have defaulted on debts).
Microsoft founded by Bill Gates, aged 19, and a friend.
(31st Aug) The International Monetary Fund (IMF) abandons the remaining role of gold in world monetary affairs.

Society, Education, and Religion

Sex Discrimination Act in Britain outlaws discrimination in employment or education on grounds of sex or marital status and establishes the Equal Opportunities Commission.
Michel Foucault, *Discipline and Punish.*
In England, the new Archbishop of Canterbury, Donald Coggan issues a 'call to the nation' for moral and spiritual renewal.

Science, Technology, and Discovery

The first 'personal computer', the Aetair 8800, is marketed in the USA.
US astronomer Charles T Kowal discovers the 14th moon of Jupiter.

Humanities and Scholarship

20,000 clay tablets with cuneiform texts found at Tell Mardikh (ancient Ebla) in Syria.
The Cambridge History of Africa (–1986).
Paul Fussell, *The Great War and Modern Memory.*
Michel Foucault, *Discipline and Punish.*
H-G Gadamer, *Truth and Method.*

Art, Sculpture, Fine Arts, and Architecture

Architecture I M Pei, John Hancock Tower, Boston, Massachusetts, USA.

Music

Pierre Boulez, *Rituel in memoriam Bruno Maderna.*
Witold Lutoslawski, *Les Espaces du sommeil.*
Queen, 'Bohemian Rhapsody' (single and the first major rock video).
Patti Smith, *Horses.*
Bruce Springsteen, 'Born to Run' (single and album).

Literature

Saul Bellow, *Humboldt's Gift.*
Jorge Luis Borges, *The Book of Sand.*
Primo Levi, *The Periodic Table.*
In Britain, P G Wodehouse is knighted, just before his death.
Drama Athol Fugard, *Statements.*
Wole Soyinka, *Death and the King's Horseman.*

Sport and Recreation

Junko Tabei of Japan is the first woman to climb Mt Everest.
(3rd April) Anatoly Karpov of the USSR becomes world chess champion when Bobby Fischer fails to meet the deadline for their match in Manila, Philippines.
(5th July) Arthur Ashe of the USA becomes the first African-American Men's singles champion at the Wimbledon tennis tournament, London.

Media

Film *Dog Day Afternoon* (director, Sidney Lumet).
Jaws (director, Steven Spielberg).
One Flew Over the Cuckoo's Nest (director, Milos Forman).
The Rocky Horror Picture Show (director, Jim Sharman).
Television New programmes in Britain include: *Fawlty Towers* (BBC), starring John Cleese; *The Naked Civil Servant* (Thames TV), with John Hurt as Quentin Crisp; *Rumpole of the Bailey*; *The Sweeney*; *The World at War.*

Statistics

Average annual increase in per capita gross national budget 1970–80: Japan, 3.5; France, 3.1; Belgium, 2.8; Canada, 2.7; Germany, 2.7; Italy, 2.4; U.S, 2.3; Holland, 2.0; Great Britain, 1.8; Sweden, 1.7.

1976

Jan: 13th, Argentina suspends diplomatic ties with Britain over Falkland Islands.
18th, British Labour MPs Jim Sillars and John Robertson launch the Scottish Labour Party (SLP) to campaign for greater devolution for Scotland.
23rd, following an anti-Communist speech delivered by Margaret Thatcher, a report in the USSR newspaper *Red Star* brands her the 'Iron Lady'.
28th, Spanish Prime Minister proposes lifting ban on political parties (enacted 14th July).
29th, a male model, Norman Scott, alleges in court that he was the homosexual lover of Liberal Party leader Jeremy Thorpe in the 1960s; a Department of Trade report criticises Thorpe's judgement in becoming involved with a crashed 'secondary bank'.
31st, population of the world reaches 4 billion.

Feb: 19th, Iceland breaks off diplomatic relations with Britain over the 'Cod War'.
24th, (–5th March) 25th Congress of the Communist Party of the Soviet Union (27th, Italian Communist leader Enrico Berlinguer announces to the conference that a communist Italy would stay in NATO and remain pluralist).

March: 5th, The pound falls below $2 for the first time ever.
15th, the French franc is forced out of the European currency 'snake'.
16th, in Britain, Harold Wilson announces that he is to resign as prime minister.
24th, military coup deposes President Isabel Perón of Argentina; all political parties and unions are 'suspended'.
25th, in Britain, Michael Foot wins the first ballot for the Labour Party leadership with 90 votes. James Callaghan wins 84, Roy Jenkins 56, Tony Benn 37, Denis Healey 30, Anthony Crosland 17. A second ballot follows (30th) with three contestants only, giving Callaghan 141, Foot 133, and Healey 38.

April: 2nd, A new Portuguese constitution with a commitment to socialism is promulgated.
3rd, James Callaghan wins final ballot of Labour leadership election with 176 votes to 137 for Foot (5th, Callaghan becomes prime minister).
16th, India and Pakistan normalise diplomatic relations, for the first time since the war of 1971.
26th, (–5th Aug) trial of John Stonehouse, resulting in seven years' imprisonment for fraud, theft, and forgery.

May: 12th, in Britain, Jeremy Thorpe resigns as Liberal leader and is replaced by Jo Grimond as interim leader.

June: 1st, Cod War ends with agreement between Iceland and Britain about fishing.
16th, (–25th) South African police kill 76 students in Soweto and other townships during protests and riots about teaching in Afrikaans (6th July, Afrikaans education plan dropped).
20th, Italian general election produces a major advance for the Communist Party.
29th, Seychelles gains independence.

July: 2nd, North and South Vietnam are formally unified.

7th, in Britain, David Steel wins the Liberal leadership election, defeating John Pardoe.

Aug: 1st, Trinidad and Tobago becomes independent.

Sept: 9th, Mao Zedong, Chairman of the Chinese Communist Party, dies.

19th, Swedish general election ends 40 years of government by Social Democrats (7th Oct, Thorbjorn Falldin becomes Conservative prime minister).

19th, Ian Smith accepts the principle of majority rule in Rhodesia.

28th, British Chancellor of the Exchequer Denis Healey, at Heathrow Airport en route to a conference, turns back to deal with a steep fall in the value of the pound.

Nov: 2nd, In US presidential election Jimmy Carter, Democrat, defeats Republican President Gerald Ford, with 297 electoral college votes to 241. Popular vote: Carter, 40,828,587l; Ford, 39,147,613. Congress retains large Democratic majorities in both Houses of Congress.

15th, Parti Québecois wins large victory in Quebec provincial elections and new Premier René Levesque promises a vote on independence by 1980.

26th, Catholicism ceases to be the state religion of Italy.

30th, British government publishes bill for devolution in Scotland and Wales.

Dec: 5th, Jacques Chirac re-founds the Gaullist party as the RPR (Rassemblement pour la République).

5th, Jean-Bedel Bokassa proclaims the Central African Republic an Empire.

15th, mini-Budget in Britain cuts £2.5 billion from public spending in accordance with terms for the IMF loan.

Politics, Government, Law, and Economy

(2nd July) The US Supreme Court rules that capital punishment is not unconstitutional.

Society, Education, and Religion

Race Relations Act in Britain makes inciting racial hatred an offence and establishes the Commission for Racial Equality.

The Education Act in England and Wales requires local education authorities who have not introduced comprehensive education to plan for comprehensivization.

(16th Sept) Episcopalian Church in USA approves ordination of women to the priesthood.

Science, Technology, and Discovery

British–French supersonic airliner Concorde begins regular passenger service across the Atlantic.

In USA, a mystery disease afflicts people who attended the meeting of the American Legion in Philadelphia; 29 die within a month and the disease becomes known as Legionnaire's disease.

(26th July) A massive release of poisonous dioxin gas from a pesticide plant near Seveso in Italy kills domestic and farm animals in the surrounding region.

Humanities and Scholarship

J M Roberts, *The Hutchinson History of the World.*

E S de Beer (ed.), *The Correspondence of John Locke* (–1989).

Louis Althusser, Essays in Self-Criticism.

Noam Chomsky, *Reflections on Language.*

Art, Sculpture, Fine Arts, and Architecture

'Sand Circles', exhibition at Hayward Gallery, London.

Architecture Denys Lasdun, National Theatre, South Bank Centre, London.

Roche and Dinkeloo, One UN Plaza, New York.

Music

Henryk Górecki, Symphony No. 3 ('Symphony of Sorrowful Songs').

Pop group Abba become Sweden's biggest export earner after Volvo.

Literature

Alex Haley, *Roots.*

Drama Britain's National Theatre opens in its new building on the South Bank, London.

Everyday Life

Drought in Britain necessitates water standpipes in the streets of many cities; Denis Howell is appointed minister for drought – heavy rain begins within days.

Sport and Recreation

(31st July) The 21st Olympic Games open in Montreal, Canada, boycotted by 20 African nations, Iraq, and Guyana following New Zealand's rugby tour of South Africa; Taiwan withdraws after the Canadian government refuses to recognize it as the Republic of China. The USSR wins 49 gold medals; East Germany, 40; USA, 34; West Germany, 10; Japan, 9; Poland, 7; Bulgaria and Cuba, 6 each; Romania, Hungary, Finland, and Sweden, 4 each. Nadia Comaneci of Romania achieves 7 'perfect' scores of 10 in the gymnastics events.

(4th Aug) First women's cricket match is played at Lord's, London.

Media

Film *Kings of the Road* (director, Wim Wenders).
Marathon Man (director, John Schlesinger; starring Laurence Olivier and Dustin Hoffman).
Rocky (director, John G Avildsen; starring Sylvester Stallone).
Sebastiane (director, Derek Jarman).
Television Broadcast in USA of *The Muppet Show*.

Statistics

Main components of British government spending (million pounds with percentages in brackets): social security, 16.2 (19.9); education, science, arts, libraries, 11.3 (14.0); health and personal social services, 10.6 (13.1); defence, 9.4 (11.6); housing, 7.4 (9.1); industry, energy, trade, employment, 5.1 (6.3); transport, 4.8 (5.9); environmental services, 4.7 (5.9); miscellaneous, 3.1 (3.8); law and order, 3.0 (3.8); agriculture, fisheries, food, 2.4 (3.0); government lending to nationalized industries, 1.7 (2.1); overseas aid, 1.1 (1.4).

1977

Jan: 1st, US Episcopal Church ordains its first women priests.
3rd, IMF lends Britain $3.9 billion.
7th, advocates of human rights in Czechoslovakia publish 'Charter 77' manifesto, pressing for implementation of human rights guarantees given at Helsinki conference in 1975.

Feb: 22nd, in Britain, guillotine motion on the Devolution Bill fails after 22 Labour No votes and 21 abstentions and the Bill is dropped.

March: 7th, Zulfikar Ali Bhutto claims massive victory in Pakistan's general election.
11th, (–23rd) widespread violent protests in Pakistan allege that Bhutto's election victory is fraudulent.
15th, British government nationalizes aircraft and shipbuilding industries.
20th, Congress Party defeated in Indian election and Indira Gandhi loses her seat (24th, Morarji Desai becomes Prime Minister of a Janata Party government).
20th, large gains for the Left in French local elections, but conservative Jacques Chirac becomes the first elected Mayor of Paris since the 1870s.
23rd, British Prime Minister James Callaghan and Liberal leader David Steel agree a pact between Labour and Liberals (the 'Lib–Lab Pact') to avoid defeat in a confidence motion.

April: 9th, Spanish Communist Party is legalized.
20th, US President Jimmy Carter proposes a radical energy conservation plan.

May: 17th, Likud bloc wins Israeli elections for the first time (21st June, Menachem Begin becomes prime minister).

June: 4th, Fourth constitution of the USSR published, making explicit the leading role of the Communist Party (adopted 7th Oct).
14th, (–11th July) violence outside Grunwick photographic processing plant in London in bitter industrial dispute.
15th, Adolfo Suarez wins small majority in Spain's first elections since 1936.
16th, Leonid Brezhnev combines post of head of state with that of Communist Party secretary.
30th, SEATO dissolved.

July: 5th, General Zia ul-Haq takes power in coup in Pakistan.
22nd, 'Gang of Four' expelled from the Chinese Communist Party and Deng Xiao-ping reinstated as deputy premier.

Aug: 18th, 11th Chinese Communist Party Congress indicates a swing away from hard-line Maoism towards economic improvement.
25th, in Britain Scarman Report recommends reinstatement of Grunwick strikers but is ignored by the management.

Sept: 1st, Cyrus Vance and David Owen propose peace plan for Rhodesia, recommending a large role for Nkomo and Mugabe's Patriotic Front.
7th, US and Panama sign the Panama Canal Treaty which returns the canal zone to Panama.

Nov: 11th, Anti-Nazi League set up to combat the growth of the National Front in Britain.
19th, (–21st) Egyptian President Sadat visits Israel and addresses the Knesset.
24th, Ian Smith proposes a new Rhodesian constitution with equal votes.
30th, ruling National Party wins record majority in South African elections.

Dec: 4th, Bophuthatswana, a black homeland in South Africa, becomes nominally independent.

Politics, Government, Law, and Economy

Adam Smith Institute founded in London to research and promote free market policies.
Ronald Dworkin, *Taking Rights Seriously*.
(17th Jan) Gary Gilmore is executed in Utah, the first execution in the USA since 1967.
(26th Jan) Publication of Bullock Report on industrial democracy, recommending that British

companies with over 2,000 employees should be run by boards comprising equal numbers of employee representatives, ownership representatives and co-opted directors.

(20th June) Inauguration of 1,300-km/800-mi trans-Alaska oil pipeline.

(1st July) The European Community (EC) and the European Free Trade Association (EFTA) agree to free trade in industrial goods.

Society, Education, and Religion

In Italy, Latin is abolished as a compulsory subject in middle schools.

Foundation of Robinson College, Cambridge, England.

10,000 copies of the *Torah* are shipped from the USA to the Moscow Synagogue, USSR, for the first time since 1917.

John Hick (ed.), *The Myth of God Incarnate.*

Science, Technology, and Discovery

Production of images of human tissues using NMR (nuclear magnetic resonance) scanning.

In New York two homosexual men are diagnosed as having the rare cancer Karposi's sarcoma; they are thought to have been the first victims of AIDS (Acquired Immune Deficiency Syndrome) in New York.

A baby mammoth, 40,000 years old, is found frozen in ice in the USSR.

Humanities and Scholarship

J K Galbraith, *The Age of Anxiety.*

H Orton, S Sanderson, J Widdowson (eds.), *The Linguistic Atlas of England.*

Art, Sculpture, Fine Arts, and Architecture

In Italy, extra Venice Biennale held, devoted to art of dissent and dissidents, especially in Eastern Europe and USSR.

Exhibition of unofficial Soviet art at Institute of Contemporary Art, London.

Architecture Renzo Piano, Richard Rogers, and Gio Franco Franchini, Centre National d'Art et de Culture Georges Pompidou ('Pompidou Centre'), Paris.

Music

Michael Tippett, *The Ice Break* (opera).

Annie (musical), by Martin Charnin and Charles Strouse (first performance in New York at the Alvin Theatre, 21st April).

The Clash, *The Clash.*

The Sex Pistols, 'God Save the Queen'.

Wings, 'Mull of Kintyre'.

'Punk' rock music prominent.

(16th Aug) Death of Elvis Presley from drug overdose at his home, Graceland in Memphis, Tennessee, USA.

Literature

Patrick Leigh Fermor, *A Time of Gifts.*

Leonardo Sciascia, *Candido.*

Drama Steven Berkoff, *East.*

Sport and Recreation

(2nd April) In Britain Red Rum, ridden by Tommy Stack, wins its third Grand National horse race.

(1st July) Virginia Wade is first British woman since 1969 to win a Singles title at the Wimbledon tennis tournament, London.

Media

In Britain, circulation of the *Sun* overtakes that of the *Daily Mirror.*

(Nov) Australian newspaper-owner Rupert Murdoch acquires *The New York Post.*

Film *Annie Hall* (director, Woody Allen).

Close Encounters of the Third Kind (director, Steven Spielberg).

Padre Padrone (directors, Paolo and Vittorio Taviani).

Saturday Night Fever (starring John Travolta).

Star Wars (director, George Lucas).

That Obscure Object of Desire (director, Luis Buñuel).

Statistics

Oil production (in thousand barrels per day): USSR, 10,995; US, 9,797; Saudi Arabia, 9,017; Iran, 5,663; Iraq, 2,348; Venezuela, 2,238; Nigeria, 2,085; Libya, 2,063; Algeria, 1,152; Mexico, 1,050; Great Britain, 776; Kuwait, 368; Norway, 279.

1978

Jan: 3rd, Indian Congress Party splits (from 25th Feb the rump led by Indira Gandhi is called the Congress (I) Party).

18th, European Court of Human Rights clears British government of torture but finds it guilty of inhuman and degrading treatment of prisoners in Northern Ireland.

23rd, Sweden bans aerosol sprays because of damage to environment, the first country to do so.

Feb: 16th, House of Commons passes Bill establishing direct elections to European Assembly.

March: 11th, in Italy, in the 'Historic Compromise', a new government led by Giulio Andreotti is installed with the support of the Communist Party.

16th, Red Brigade terrorists kidnap former Italian Prime Minister Aldo Moro.

18th, death sentence passed on former Pakistani Prime Minister Zulfikar Ali Bhutto.

April: 7th, German Chancellor Schmidt proposes European currency stabilization plan; later enacted as the European Monetary System (EMS).

25th, European Court of Human Rights condemns judicial birching in Isle of Man as degrading.

27th, Communist and Islamic forces take power in Afghanistan.

May: 9th, Aldo Moro found dead in Rome after Italian government refuses to make concessions to his captors.

25th, David Steel announces end of the Lib–Lab Pact.

June: 13th, Israelis pull out of south Lebanon but fighting erupts in the north.

July: 7th, Solomon Islands gain independence.

Aug: 6th, death of Pope Paul VI.

26th, Albino Luciani, Patriarch of Venice, is elected Pope; he takes the name John Paul I.

Sept: 5th, (–17th) summit between Carter, Sadat, and Begin at Camp David, Maryland; concludes with a 'framework' peace treaty ending 30 years of hostility between Israel and Egypt.

20th, B J Vorster resigns as prime minister of South Africa, on grounds of ill health (29th, P W Botha replaces him; 10th Oct, Vorster becomes president).

28th, sudden death of Pope John Paul I.

30th, Tuvalu, formerly the Ellice Islands, gains independence.

Oct: 10th, British unions and government fail to resolve their differences on pay during talks at 10 Downing Street.

16th, Karol Wojtyla, Archbishop of Cracow, is elected Pope; he takes the name John Paul II.

26th, World Health Organization announces that smallpox has been eradicated except for laboratory stocks.

Nov: 3rd, Dominica gains independence.

8th, Indira Gandhi returns to the Lok Sabha in a by-election.

22nd, Ford workers in Britain accept 17% pay offer, a flagrant breach of the 5% pay policy.

30th, Times Newspapers suspend publication of their papers indefinitely because of industrial dispute.

Dec: 6th, James Callaghan announces that Britain will not join the new European Monetary System.

17th, OPEC decides to raise oil prices by 14.5% by the end of 1979.

19th, (–26th) Indira Gandhi is expelled from the Lok Sabha for contempt and imprisoned.

25th, Vietnam begins full-scale invasion of Cambodia.

Politics, Government, Law, and Economy

The European Court affirms the superiority of Community law over the national law of member states.

First meeting held, in Bonn, West Germany, of the 'Group of Seven' largest capitalist economic powers (USA, Canada, Japan, West Germany, France, Italy, Britain).

(3rd April) Radio broadcasts of the British Parliament begin.

Society, Education, and Religion

In China, after the fall of the 'Gang of Four', a new constitution declares that education should be developed to raise the cultural and scientific level of the whole nation; a new standardized curriculum and textbooks are produced, marking a return to a more academic curriculum.

In Britain, publication of the Warnock Report on children with special educational needs.

Deaths of Pope Paul Vl (6th Aug) and his successor John Paul I (26th Sept); John Paul's successor, John Paul II (Karol Wojtyla, Archbishop of Kraków), is the first non-Italian Pope since 1522.

General Synod of the Church of England rejects the ordination of women to the priesthood and episcopate.

Science, Technology, and Discovery

(15th June) (–2nd Nov) Two Soviet cosmonauts spend a record 139 days and 14 hours in space.

(25th July) In Britain, birth of the first 'test tube' baby, Louise Brown.

Humanities and Scholarship

Footprints of a hominid, made 3.6 million years ago, found near Laetoli, Tanzania.

Excavation of tomb of Philip of Macedon (died 336 BC) at Vergina in northern Greece.

Discovery of the foundations of the Aztec great temple under the centre of Mexico City.

Art, Sculpture, Fine Arts, and Architecture

'The State of British Art', Institute of Contemporary Art, London.

Architecture I M Pei, extension to the National Gallery, Washington, DC, USA.

Painting Sandro Chia, *Perpetual Motion.*

Music

György Ligeti, *Le Grand Macabre* (opera).

Andrzej Panufnik, *Metasinfonia.*

Evita (musical), text by Tim Rice, music by Andrew Lloyd Webber (first performed at the Prince Edward Theatre, London, 21st June).

Blondie, *Parallel Lines.*

Disco music popular: the Bee Gees' *Saturday Night Fever* becomes the biggest-selling soundtrack album yet.

The film of *Grease* (starring John Travolta and Olivia Newton-John) produces the best-selling singles 'You're The One That I Want' and 'Summer Nights'.

Literature

Graham Greene, *The Human Factor.*

John Irving, *The World According to Garp.*

Armistead Maupin, *Tales of the City.*

Drama Brian Clark, *Whose Life is it Anyway.*

David Hare, *Plenty.*

Harold Pinter, *Betrayal.*

Sport and Recreation

(15th Feb) In cricket, New Zealand beats England in a Test match for the first time, after 48 years of matches.

(25th March) The Cambridge boat sinks in the English University Boat Race.

(8th June) Naomi James completes her solo round-the-world voyage, taking two days fewer than Sir Francis Chichester in 1967.

(25th June) Host nation Argentina wins the soccer World Cup, beating the Netherlands in the Final 3–1.

Media

(30th Nov) In Britain, suspension of *The Times, The Sunday Times,* and *Times* supplements as a result of an industrial dispute.

Film *The Deer Hunter* (director, Michael Cimino; starring Robert de Niro).

Midnight Express (director, Alan Parker).

Superman (director, Richard Donner; starring Christopher Reeve).

Television Broadcast in USA of *Dallas.*

New programmes in Britain include: *All Creatures Great and Small* (BBC); *The BBC Television Shakespeare* (–1985); *Lillie* (LWT), starring Francesca Annis as Lillie Langtry; *The Mayor of Casterbridge* (BBC), adapted by Dennis Potter and starring Alan Bates; *Pennies from Heaven* (BBC), by Dennis Potter; *The South Bank Show* (LWT), an arts programme presented by Melvyn Bragg.

In Britain, the BBC broadcasts the 667th and final episode of *Z Cars,* and the final edition of *The Black and White Minstrel Show.*

1979

Jan: 1st, USA and China open diplomatic relations.

7th, Vietnamese troops and Cambodian rebels capture Phnom Penh and oust the Khmer Rouge regime.

16th, the Shah of Iran and his family flee Iran for Egypt.

22nd, in Britain one-day strike of public sector workers closes schools and hospitals (–6th March, continuing industrial action by local authority workers such as dustmen and grave-diggers; –20th March, health service workers take industrial action; the *Sun* labels the surge of strikes 'the winter of discontent', an allusion to Shakespeare's 'Now is the winter of our discontent... ').

26th, (–29th) Islamic revolutionary violence in Tehran.

31st, in Italy the Andreotti government resigns, ending the 'Historic Compromise' between Christian Democrats and Communists.

Feb: 1st, Ayatollah Khomeini returns to Iran from exile in Paris (since 1964).

12th, Dr Bakhtiar flees Iran; a Revolutionary Council loyal to Ayatollah Khomeini is created, with Mehdi Bazargan as Premier-designate.

14th, British government and TUC sign a Concordat to end the 'winter of discontent' strikes.

20th, 11 members of a loyalist gang known as the 'Shankill butchers' are sentenced for 19 sectarian murders in Belfast following a sensational trial.

22nd, St Lucia becomes independent.

23rd, (–16th March) war between North and South Yemen.

March: **1st**, Referenda on devolution in Scotland and Wales; devolution is approved in Scotland by 51.6% of voters but those approving fall short of the required 40% of the electorate (32.9% of electorate voted Yes, 30.8% No, 36.3% did not vote); 79.8% of voters in Wales reject devolution (11.9% voted Yes, 46.9% No, 41.2% did not vote).
13th, European Monetary System (EMS) becomes operational.
26th, Egypt and Israel sign peace treaty in Washington, DC.
28th, British Labour government loses a motion of no confidence by 310–311 in the House of Commons. Prime Minister Callaghan calls a general election.

April: **1st**, Following a referendum Iran is declared an Islamic Republic by Ayatollah Khomeini.
4th, Zulfikar Ali Bhutto is executed in Pakistan for conspiracy to murder.
10th, (–20th) multi-racial elections held in Rhodesia.
11th, Kampala falls to Tanzanian and rebel forces; Idi Amin flees (13th, Yusufu Lule is inaugurated as President of Uganda).

May: **28th**, Greece signs Treaty of Accession to EC, for entry in 1981.

June: **1st**, Bishop Abel Muzorewa, a black leader, is appointed Prime Minister of the renamed Zimbabwe Rhodesia.
3rd, Conservatives win British general election with 339 seats. Labour wins 269, Liberals, 11, Unionists, 12, Scottish Nationalists, 2, Plaid Cymru 2 (Conservatives win 43.9% of votes cast, Labour, 36.9%, Liberals, 13.8%).
4th, Margaret Thatcher becomes Britain's first woman prime minister.
7th, (and 10th) first direct elections for the European Parliament; low turnout and results influenced by popularity of national governments; in Britain the Conservatives win 60 seats, Labour, 17, Liberals, 0 (Conservatives win 48.4% of votes cast, Labour, 31.6%, and Liberals, 12.6%); the Scottish Nationalists win 1 seat, the Ulster Unionists, 3.
14th, (–26th) in Nicaragua, Sandinista rebels close in on the capital, Managua.
15th, (–18th) summit meeting in Vienna of Carter and Brezhnev ends with the signing of the SALT II treaty limiting nuclear weapons.

July: **11th**, Kiribati (formerly the Gilbert Islands) becomes independent.
17th, Anastasio Somoza, dictator of Nicaragua, flees to the USA.
19th, in Nicaragua, Sandinista rebels take Managua and set up a new government.

Aug: **10th**, workers in the British engineering industry impose a four-day week.
27th, British engineering workers step up industrial action by imposing a three-day week.

Sept: **6th**, 30,000 'boat people' who have fled from Vietnam are allowed to settle in the USA.
10th, (–21st Dec) Lancaster House conference held in London to seek settlement of the Rhodesia problem.
10th, British Leyland motor manufacturing company announces 25,000 redundancies.

Oct: **16th**, President Zia of Pakistan cancels elections and bans political activity.
16th, British government announces plans to sell 5% of its holding in British Petroleum, in order to raise £290 million, leaving the government with just over 25% of BP.
25th, referenda in Spain approve devolution of power to Catalonia and Euzkadi (the Basque provinces).
27th, St Vincent and Grenadines gains independence.

Nov: **1st**, British government announces spending cuts for 1980–81 financial year of £3.5 billion.
4th, Iranian students seize the US embassy in Tehran, taking 63 US citizens and 40 others hostage; they demand the return of the Shah for trial.
6th, Ayatollah Khomeini's Islamic Revolutionary Council takes power in Iran from the provisional government.
12th, in response to the seizure of US hostages in Iran, Carter imposes an embargo on Iranian oil (14th, Iranian assets in the USA are frozen).
30th, British Steel announces loss of 50,000 jobs.

Dec: **5th**, Jack Lynch resigns as Prime Minister of Eire (7th, replaced by Charles Haughey).
10th, the rebel parliament in Zimbabwe Rhodesia winds itself up, ending UDI.
21st, Lancaster House agreement signed in London, providing for an end to Rhodesian civil war and introduction of majority rule (28th, ceasefire in Rhodesia).
25th, USSR invasion of Afghanistan, in bid to halt civil war and protect USSR interests.
31st, at year end oil prices are 88% higher than at the start of 1979.
31st, publication of British New Year's Honours List in which Prime Minister Thatcher bestows political honours for the first time since 1974.

Politics, Government, Law, and Economy

France imposes a prohibitive tariff on British lamb exports in defiance of the European Court.

European Monetary System (EMS) and its Exchange Rate Mechanism (ERM) are established to regulate European currency fluctuations.

Successful completion of the Tokyo Round of negotiations of the General Agreement on Tariffs and Trade (GATT).

Society, Education, and Religion

Abortion is legalized in France.

In England and Wales, the Education Act repeals the comprehensive school legislation of 1976, freeing local authorities from compulsion to introduce comprehensive education.

Mother Teresa awarded the Nobel Peace Prize.

(7th Sept) Robert Runcie appointed to replace Donald Coggan as Archbishop of Canterbury (Runcie enthroned 25th March 1980).

Science, Technology, and Discovery

First spreadsheet programme for personal computers – expands business use of PCs.

The US space station *Skylab 1* falls back to Earth after travelling 87 million miles in orbit since 1973.

The satellite *HEAO2* (*High Energy Astronomy Observatory* – later renamed the Einstein Observatory) discovers a possible 'black hole' in the constellation Cygnus X-1.

Physicists in Hamburg at DESY (Deutsches Elektron Synchroton) observe gluons – particles that carry the strong nuclear force which holds quarks together.

(29th March) Major accident at the Three Mile Island nuclear power station in Pennsylvania, USA; some radioactive material escapes.

Humanities and Scholarship

M T Clanchy, *From Memory to Written Record: England 1066–1307.*

E H Gombrich, *The Sense of Order: A Study in the Psychology of Decorative Art.*

Jean-François Lyotard, *The Post-modern Condition.*

Art, Sculpture, Fine Arts, and Architecture

French government accepts large gift of works from the Picasso estate (museum to be established in Paris).

Velázquez, portrait of *Juan de Pareja* sold at Christie's for $5.5 million, the most expensive painting bought at auction.

Sculpture Judy Chicago, *The Dinner Party.*

Music

Alban Berg, *Lulu* (opera), first complete performance (with the score of Act 3 orchestrated by Friedrich Cerha).

Sweeney Todd (musical), lyrics and music by Stephen Sondheim (first performed at the Uris Theatre, New York, 1st March).

Boomtown Rats, 'I Don't Like Mondays'.

The Clash, *London Calling.*

Elvis Costello, 'Oliver's Army'.

Pink Floyd, 'Another Brick In The Wall'.

Literature

Italo Calvino, *If on a Winter's Night a Traveller.*

Nadine Gordimer, *Burger's Daughter.*

Milan Kundera, *The Book of Laughter and Forgetting.*

Alain Robbe-Grillet, *Le Rendez-vous.*

Drama Bernard Pomerance, *The Elephant Man.*

Peter Shaffer, *Amadeus.*

Martin Sherman, *Bent.*

Sport and Recreation

(14th Feb) Trevor Francis moves from Birmingham City to Nottingham Forest in the first £1 million transfer deal in English football; the record is broken again when Steve Daley of Wolverhampton Wanderers moves to Manchester United for £1.45 million and Andy Gray from Aston Villa to Wolverhampton for £1.47 million.

(15th Aug) British athlete Sebastian Coe is the first man to hold three indoor world records simultaneously, for the 800 m, the mile and the 1,500 m.

(26th Nov) International Olympic Committee decides (by 62 votes to 17) to admit athletes from the People's Republic of China to the next Olympic Games.

Media

(25th Sept) One of Canada's most important newspapers, the 111-year-old *Montreal Star*, ceases publication eight months after a lengthy strike over the introduction of new technology and manning practices.

(13th Nov) In Britain, resumption of publication of *The Times*, *The Sunday Times*, and supplements.

Film *Alien* (director, Ridley Scott).

Mad Max (director, George Miller; starring Mel Gibson).

Manhattan (director and star, Woody Allen).

Monty Python's Life of Brian (director, Terry Jones; starring the Monty Python team).

Statistics

Social and educational composition of British Conservative Cabinet: aristocrats, 3; middle class, 19; working class, 0; attendance at public school, 20 (inc. 6 at Eton); attendance at University, 18 (inc. 17 at Oxford or Cambridge).

1980 **Jan: 8th**, US President Carter describes Soviet invasion of Afghanistan as greatest threat to peace since World War II (23rd, warns USSR against interference in Persian Gulf).

Feb: 19th, publication of Employment Bill outlawing secondary picketing and requiring unions to hold secret ballots before strikes.

22nd, proclamation of martial law in Kabul as resistance to USSR invaders continues.

26th, Israel and Egypt exchange ambassadors for first time.

March: 4th, ZANU wins Rhodesian general election (11th, Robert Mugabe forms coalition government with Joshua Nkomo as Minister of Home Affairs).

11th, President Zia crushes attempted military coup in Pakistan.

16th, proclamation of martial law in Aleppo as political violence sweeps Syria.

20th, Lord Underhill, the former national agent of the Labour Party, publishes documents detailing methods by which the Party had been infiltrated by the Trotskyite Revolutionary League under the name of 'Militant Tendency'.

24th, Archbishop Oscar Romero shot dead while celebrating mass in San Salvador (30th, violence at his funeral kills 40).

26th, British Budget increases spending on defence, police and pensions, and raises duties and prescription charges.

April: 2nd, In Britain, riots in St Paul's district of Bristol after police raid on a club used by the black community.

7th, USA bans trade with Iran, breaks off relations, and expels Iranian diplomats.

10th, Spain agrees to re-open border with Gibraltar (closed 1969).

18th, Rhodesia gains legal independence as Zimbabwe under President Canaan Banana.

25th, US commando mission to rescue hostages in Iran fails with loss of eight lives (29th, Cyrus Vance resigns as US Secretary of State; succeeded by Edmund Muskie).

30th, terrorists seize Iranian embassy in London, demanding release of political prisoners in Iran (Special Air Service storms embassy, 5th May).

May: 1st, Sweden is practically at a standstill as pay negotiations crumble amidst strikes and lock-outs.

4th, death of President Tito of Yugoslavia; replaced by eight-man collective presidency.

18th, EC imposes trade sanctions against Iran.

20th, referendum in Quebec on possible separation from Canada produces a 59.9% vote against.

June: 17th, British Ministry of Defence announces plan to deploy US Cruise missiles at Greenham Common and Molesworth military bases.

July: 30th, New Hebrides becomes independent as Vanuatu.

Aug: 5th, Belgian parliament passes Bill dividing country into three autonomous linguistic regions.

14th, Polish strikers occupy Lenin shipyard in Gdansk.

26th, leadership changes in China consolidate power of pragmatic reformers led by Deng Xiao-ping.

27th, British unemployment total exceeds 2 million.

31st, Lech Walesa, leader of Gdansk strikers, signs agreement with Polish government allowing formation of independent trade unions and granting release of political prisoners.

Sept: 9th, closure of British Embassy in Tehran.

10th, Libya and Syria proclaim themselves a single state.

22nd, Iraq invades Iran in attempt to gain control of Shatt al-Arab waterway.

Oct: 10th, Margaret Thatcher tells Conservative Party conference of her determination to persist with monetarist policies: 'U-turn if you want to; the Lady's not for turning'.

15th, James Callaghan resigns as leader of the Labour Party.

24th, Polish authorities register a new independent trade union, named 'Solidarity'.
26th, London protest march by Campaign for Nuclear Disarmament attracts 50,000.
27th, (–18th Dec) seven IRA prisoners in the Maze prison on hunger strike, demanding 'political status'.

Nov: 4th, In US presidential election, Republican Ronald Reagan wins a sweeping victory over President Carter. Reagan wins 489 electoral votes, Carter, 49. Popular vote: Reagan, 43,899,248; Carter, 35,481,435; John Anderson (Independent), 5,719,437. Republicans win control of the Senate and gain 33 seats in the House of Representatives.
10th, in Britain, Michael Foot defeats Denis Healey to become leader of Labour Party, winning 139 votes to Healey's 129 in the second ballot.
24th, Sir Geoffrey Howe announces £1.06 billion reduction in public spending and £3 billion increase in taxation.

Dec: 16th, OPEC increases crude oil prices by 10%.

Politics, Government, Law, and Economy
Companies Act in Britain makes 'insider dealing' in shares a criminal offence.
(June) Britain becomes a net exporter of oil.

Society, Education, and Religion
Housing Act gives council tenants in Britain the right to buy their homes at cheap rates.
The British television film *Death of a Princess*, about the enforcement of Islamic law in Saudi Arabia, causes widespread controversy in the Islamic world.
The Alternative Service Book 1980 is published as the first authorized prayer book of the Church of England since 1662.

Science, Technology, and Discovery
Japanese Company Sony launches the 'Walkman', a small portable, personal tape recorder/player.
Intelpost, the first public international electronic facsimile service.
A new vaccine for prevention of hepatitis B is tested in the USA; it has a success rate of 92%.

Humanities and Scholarship
John Baines and Jaromír Málek, *Atlas of Ancient Egypt.*
Jerome J McGann (ed.), *Lord Byron: The Complete Poetical Works* (–1993).
Stanley Sadie (ed.), *The New Grove Dictionary of Music and Musicians.*
Richard Rorty, *Philosophy and the Mirror of Nature.*

Art, Sculpture, Fine Arts, and Architecture
Painting Cindy Sherman, *Untitled* no 66.
Sculpture Tony Cragg, *Plastic Palette I.*

Music
Elliott Carter, *Night Fantasies.*
Philip Glass, *Satyagraha* (opera).
Oliver Knussen, *Where the Wild Things Are* (opera).
Krzysztof Penderecki, Symphony No. 2.
Barnum (musical), lyrics by Michael Stewart, music by Cy Coleman (first performance at the St James Theatre, New York, 30th April).
Les Misérables (musical), lyrics by Herbert Kretzmer, music by Claude-Michel Schönberg (first performed at the Palais de Sports, Paris, 17th Sept).
Joy Division, *Closer*, 'Love Will Tear Us Apart'.
Pink Floyd, *The Wall.*
Ska revival by British bands, e.g. Madness and The Specials.

Literature
Joseph Brodsky, *A Part of Speech.*
Anthony Burgess, *Earthly Powers.*
Umberto Eco, *The Name of the Rose.*
John Le Carré, *Smiley's People.*
Drama Brian Friel, *Translations.*
Mark Medoff, *Children of a Lesser God.*
Howard Brenton, *The Romans in Britain*, at the National Theatre, London, causes controversy on account of scenes involving nudity and sexual violence; prosecution for obscenity is threatened (all tickets are sold).

Sport and Recreation
The European Football Association (UEFA) fines the English Football Association £8,000 because of the 'violent and dangerous conduct of English supporters' who rioted during England's opening match against Belgium in Turin (12th June); police had used tear gas to break up the rioting and the match was stopped for five minutes when players became affected by gas.

(11th Jan) Nigel Short, age 14, from Bolton in Britain, becomes youngest International Master in the history of chess.

(3rd May) Liverpool Football Club win the English League Championship for the second year running, the fourth time in five years, and the 12th time in all – a record.

(5th May) Cliff Thorburn of Canada is first non-British player to win the world snooker championship.

(19th July) (–3rd Aug) The 22nd Olympic Games are held in Moscow, USSR. Following the Soviet invasion of Afghanistan, the Games are boycotted by 65 countries, most notably the USA, West Germany, Japan, and Kenya. The USSR wins 80 gold medals; East Germany, 47; Bulgaria, Cuba, and Italy, 8 each; Hungary, 7; Romania and France, 6 each; Great Britain, 5; Poland, Sweden, and Finland, 3 each.

(28th Aug) (–2nd Sept) The centenary Test match between England and Australia is held at Lord's; the match is drawn after 10 hours are lost to rain – on the Saturday MCC members assault the umpires.

Media

(24th Sept) Japan's leading newspaper, *Asahi Shimbun*, is produced by use of new technology – 'untouched by human hands'.

(31st Oct) London's *Evening News* is merged into *The Evening Standard.*

Film *Elephant Man* (director, David Lynch).

The Empire Strikes Back (director, Irvin Kershner).

Kagemusha (Akira Kurosawa).

Raging Bull (director, Martin Scorsese).

The Shining (director, Stanley Kubrick; starring Jack Nicholson).

1981

Jan: 1st, Greece becomes 10th member of EC.

20th, Iran releases all 52 US hostages (held since 4th Nov 1979) after agreement is signed in Algiers releasing Iranian financial assets in USA.

25th, former British Labour ministers Roy Jenkins, Dr David Owen, William Rodgers and Shirley Williams issue the 'Limehouse Declaration', advocating a new central political position to pursue radical change, and form the 'Council for Social Democracy'.

25th, show trial in Beijing convicts 'Gang of Four' of treason. Chiang Ch'ing, widow of Chairman Mao, receives suspended death sentence.

Feb: 3rd, Gro Harlem Brundtland becomes first woman Prime Minister of Norway.

23rd, 200 civil guards storm Spanish Parliament and hold MPs at gun-point in coup attempt (24th, guards surrender after denunciation by King Juan Carlos).

March: 2nd, 12 British MPs and nine Peers resign Labour whip to sit as Social Democrats (16th, one Conservative MP joins them).

26th, in Britain, official launch of Social Democratic Party (SDP), with programme of incomes policy, proportional representation, and support for EC and NATO.

April: 10th, (–12th) severe riots in inner London area of Brixton.

30th, Central Committee of Polish Communist Party approves programme of moderate reforms.

May: 5th, riots in Northern Ireland, following death of IRA hunger striker Bobby Sands in the Maze prison.

6th, USA expels all Libyan diplomats because of Libyan support for international terrorism.

10th, François Mitterrand becomes first Socialist President of France with 51.7% of vote to Valéry Giscard d'Estaing's 48.3%.

13th, gunman seriously wounds Pope John Paul II in assassination attempt in St Peter's Square (22nd July, Mehmet Ali Agca jailed for life in Italy).

26th, Italian government falls after revelations of infiltration by Masonic Lodge 'Propaganda 2' (24th July, Italy bans secret societies).

30th, assassination of President Zia ur-Rahman of Bangladesh (succeeded by Vice-President Abdus Sattar).

June: 8th, Israeli air force bombs Osirak nuclear reactor under construction near Baghdad (19th, UN Security Council condemns attack after Iraq denies military use).

16th, in Britain, Liberals and SDP issue joint statement of principles, *A Fresh Start for Britain.*

21st, Socialists win landslide victory in second round of elections to French National Assembly (23rd, new government includes three Communists).

30th, British government announces that the armed survey ship HMS *Endurance*, on patrol in the South Atlantic, will be withdrawn and not replaced.

July: 3rd, clashes between National Front supporters and Asian immigrants in Southall.

4th, (–6th) arson and riots in Toxteth district of Liverpool, England; disturbances follow in Manchester, Brixton, Reading, Hull, and elsewhere.

Aug: 3rd, (–5th) in Poland, 'Solidarity' blockades Warsaw city centre in protest at food shortages.

3rd, strike by US air traffic controllers; (6th) they are dismissed for not complying with Presidential order to return to work.

19th, US air force shoots down two Libyan fighters during naval exercises off the coast of Libya in the Gulf of Sirte.

30th, bomb in Tehran kills President Rajai and Prime Minister Bahonar of Iran.

Sept: 5th, (–10th) first national congress of 'Solidarity' union in Gdansk, Poland.

9th, French government announces nationalization of 36 banks and 11 industrial groups.

16th, British Liberal Party conference in Llandudno votes for electoral alliance with SDP.

20th, Belize becomes independent within the Commonwealth.

Oct: 3rd, IRA hunger-strike at Maze prison ends after 10 deaths.

6th, assassination of President Sadat of Egypt (14th, succeeded by Hosni Mubarak).

18th, Panhellenic Socialist Movement wins Greek general election (21st, Andreas Papandreou forms first Socialist government in Greek history).

Nov: 1st, Antigua and Barbuda become independent within the Commonwealth.

Dec: 13th, imposition of martial law in Poland: mass detention and curbs on civil liberties and trade unions.

14th, Israel formally annexes the Golan Heights, occupied in 1967.

29th, President Reagan introduces economic sanctions against USSR for compelling Poland to adopt martial law.

Politics, Government, Law, and Economy

Milton Friedman, *Monetary Trends in the United States and the United Kingdom.*

(22nd May) In Britain, Peter Sutcliffe, the 'Yorkshire Ripper', is found guilty of the murder of 13 women and sentenced to life imprisonment.

(30th Sept) French National Assembly abolishes the death penalty and thereby use of the guillotine.

(22nd Oct) (–23rd) International Meeting on Cooperation and Development held by representatives of 22 countries at Cancún, Mexico, to discuss economic problems facing developing countries.

Society, Education, and Religion

British Nationality Act replaces universal British subjecthood with three status categories (British citizenship with right of abode, citizenship of dependent territory, overseas citizenship).

(13th March) British government reduces grant to universities by 3%.

(12th Nov) The General Synod of the Church of England votes overwhelmingly to recognize the sacraments of the Free Churches and their women ministers and to allow women to be ordained to the Anglican diaconate.

Science, Technology, and Discovery

French railways introduce their high-speed train, the *Train à Grande Vitesse* (TGV).

The IBM company launches its personal computer, using the Microsoft disc-operating system (MS-DOS) which becomes a standard programme throughout the computer industry.

Astronomers at the University of Wisconsin, USA, discover the most massive star yet known, R136a, which is 100 times brighter than the Sun and 2,500 times larger.

US Center for Disease Control recognizes AIDS (Acquired Immune Deficiency Syndrome), thought to be caused by the HIV virus.

The US Food and Drug Administration grants permission to Eli Lilley and Co to market insulin produced by bacteria, the first genetic engineering product to go on sale.

Humanities and Scholarship

UNESCO, *General History of Africa.*

E A Wrigley and R S Schofield, *The Population History of England, 1541–1871: A Reconstruction.*

Jürgen Habermas, *The Theory of Communicative Action.*

Alisdair MacIntyre, *After Virtue.*

Art, Sculpture, Fine Arts, and Architecture

Following the restoration of democracy in Spain, Picasso's *Guernica* is taken from the Museum of Modern Art, New York, to the Prado in Madrid, Spain.

Figuration Libre movement, France, based on comic strips and graffiti.

Music

Arvo Pärt, *Passio domini nostri Jesu Christi secundum Joannem.*

Cats (musical), by Andrew Lloyd Webber, based on poems by T S Eliot (first performed at the New London Theatre, 11th May).

Grandmaster Flash and the Furious Five, *The Message* (a seminal hip-hop album).

The Human League, *Dare*, 'Don't You Want Me?'

Soft Cell, 'Tainted Love'.
The Specials, 'Ghost Town'.
Ultravox, 'Vienna'.

Literature

William Golding, *Rights of Passage.*
Salman Rushdie, *Midnight's Children.*
Martin Cruz Smith, *Gorky Park.*
Mario Vargas Llosa, *The War of the End of the World.*
Publication of Terence Kilmartin's reworking of Scott Moncrieff's translation of Proust's *Remembrance of Things Past.*

Drama Harvey Fierstein, *Torch Song Trilogy.*

Sport and Recreation

(29th March) First London Marathon held, with 7,055 competitors.
(21st July) In cricket, in the Third Test at Headingley, Leeds, home team England beat Australia by 18 runs after being forced to follow on, only the second time this has happened in 104 years of Test cricket.
(Aug) In nine days, British athletes Steve Ovett and Sebastian Coe establish three new world records for the mile; the record is cut by over 1 second to 3 minutes 47.53 seconds.

Media

Rupert Murdoch buys *The Times* and other *Times* newspapers in Britain.
Roland 'Tiny' Rowland's Lonrho company purchases the *Observer* in Britain (effective from July).

Film *Chariots of Fire* (director, Hugh Hudson).
The French Lieutenant's Woman (director, Karel Reisz).
Man of Iron (director, Andrzej Wajda).

Television New programmes in USA include *Dynasty.*
New programmes in Britain include: *Brideshead Revisited* (BBC), based on the novel by Evelyn Waugh; *Cagney and Lacey*; *Country* (BBC), by Trevor Griffiths; *Only Fools and Horses*; *Postman Pat* (BBC).

Statistics

Populations (in millions): China, 991.3; India, 690.2; USSR, 268.0; US, 229.8; Indonesia, 149.5; Brazil 120.5; Japan, 117.6; Bangladesh, 90.7; Nigeria, 87.6; Pakistan, 84.5; Mexico, 71.2; West Germany, 61.7; Italy, 56.2; Great Britain and Northern Ireland, 56.0; France, 54.0.

1982 **Jan: 8th**, Spain agrees to end blockade of Gibraltar (Dec, frontier opened).
24th, Egypt's President Mubarak announces policy of non-alignment and seeks assistance from USSR on industrial projects.
26th, according to government statistics, unemployment in Britain passes 3 million.
March: 19th, Argentine scrap-metal dealer lands on island of South Georgia and raises Argentine flag.
23rd, military coup in Guatemala.
24th, military coup in Bangladesh.
25th, Roy Jenkins of SDP wins Glasgow Hillhead in by-election from Conservatives.
April: 2nd, Argentine troops invade Falkland Islands; Britain breaks diplomatic relations with Argentina.
3rd, UN Security Council Resolution 502 demands withdrawal of Argentine forces from Falklands.
16th, Queen Elizabeth proclaims new Canadian constitution, severing Canada's last colonial links with Britain.
25th, British forces recapture South Georgia.
May: 1st, 50,000 Solidarity supporters demonstrate against martial law (4th, military controls tightened).
1st, RAF bombs Port Stanley airport on Falkland Islands.
2nd, British submarine HMS *Conqueror* sinks Argentine cruiser *General Belgrano*, killing 368.
3rd, Israeli Prime Minister Begin announces that Israel will assert sovereignty over occupied West Bank.
4th, Argentine missiles sink British destroyer HMS *Sheffield*; 20 killed.
6th, Conservatives make large gains in British local elections.
21st, British troops land on East Falkland Island and establish bridgehead at Port San Carlos.
28th, British troops recapture Port Darwin and Goose Green, taking 1,400 Argentines prisoner.
28th, (–2nd June) first-ever Papal visit to Britain.
June: 3rd, Israel's Ambassador to Britain, Shlomo Argov, is shot and wounded in London street.
4th, Israeli jets bomb guerrilla targets in Lebanon in retaliation for Argov shooting.
5th, Israeli armed forces invade Lebanon (6th, Israeli and Syrian forces clash in southern Lebanon; UN Security Council calls for halt to fighting).

14th, Argentine forces surrender at Port Stanley, ending Falklands War; 255 Britons and 652 Argentines died in Falklands conflict.

27th, Israel demands surrender of PLO guerrillas in West Beirut (29th, offers to allow them to leave Beirut with arms).

July: 2nd, In Britain, Roy Jenkins elected leader of SDP.

17th, Israeli Prime Minister Begin gives PLO guerrillas in West Beirut 30 days to leave the city.

20th, PLO offers acceptance of UN Security Council Resolution 242 (recognizing Israel's right to exist) in return for US recognition of PLO (25th, Palestinian leader Arafat signs document accepting Resolution 242; 26th, USA refuses to recognize PLO).

23rd, International Whaling Commission votes for complete ban on commercial whaling by 1985.

Aug: 19th, Israeli Cabinet accepts US plan to evacuate PLO guerrillas and Syrian troops from Beirut (21st, first convoys of guerrillas leave for Cyprus; 30th, Yassir Arafat leaves for Tunisia).

Sept: 1st, US announces new Middle East peace proposals (2nd, rejected by Israel).

18th, over 800 Palestinians killed after Christian Phalangist militiamen enter West Beirut refugee camps (25th, protests in Israel over Beirut massacre; 28th; Prime Minister Begin agrees to independent three-man board of inquiry into massacre).

26th, Israeli troops withdraw from West Beirut; replaced by peace-keeping force of French, Italian and US troops.

Oct: 8th, new law in Poland bans Solidarity and forbids setting up of new trade unions.

11th, Sikhs besiege Indian Parliament in New Delhi following murders of Sikhs in Punjab state.

Nov: 10th, President Brezhnev dies (12th, Yuri Andropov elected First Secretary of Soviet Communist Party).

11th, bomb destroys Israeli military HQ in Tyre, Lebanon; 100 killed.

11th, SDLP and Sinn Fein boycott opening of new Northern Ireland Assembly.

12th, Solidarity leader Lech Walesa released from detention.

Dec: 12th, in Britain, 20,000 women encircle Greenham Common air base in protest against proposed siting of US Cruise missiles there.

19th, Poland's Council of State announces suspension of martial law (from 31st).

Politics, Government, Law, and Economy

Local Government Finance Act increases British central government's control over local authority spending.

Mexico defaults on a loan payment, leading to general concern about the ability of Third World countries to meet their international debts and about consequences of defaults for lending nations; the International Monetary Fund intervenes with debt rescheduling and imposes austerity measures on debtor countries.

(4th April) The British government proposes new political institutions in Northern Ireland in the White Paper *A framework for Devolution*; it envisages a new elected Northern Ireland Assembly.

Society, Education, and Religion

In USA, a federal court in Little Rock, Arkansas, declares it unconstitutional to teach creationism on a par with evolutionary theory.

Publication of *The Final Report* of the Anglican–Roman Catholic International Commission (ARCIC).

General Synod of the Church of England fails to gain necessary majority for a proposed covenant of unity with the Methodists, the United Reformed Church, and the Moravians.

(16th Jan) Britain and the Vatican resume full diplomatic relations after break of over 400 years.

(25th Feb) Ruling by European Court of Human Rights allows British parents to refuse use of corporal punishment on children at school.

(30th June) In USA, the Equal Rights Amendment (passed by Congress in 1972), prohibiting discrimination on the basis of sex, fails to secure ratification of a sufficient number of states to ensure inclusion in the Constitution; opponents to the Amendment include Phyllis Schlafly.

Science, Technology, and Discovery

Compact disc (CD) players go on sale.

Humanities and Scholarship

The Cambridge Ancient History, Volume 3, 2nd edition (–).

Richard Rorty, *The Consequences of Pragmatism*.

Art, Sculpture, Fine Arts, and Architecture

Young British sculptors gain notoriety – Tony Cragg, Richard Deacon, Bill Woodrow, Barry Flanagan.

Sculpture Jenny Holzer, *Times Square*.

Music

Luciano Berio, *La vera storia* (opera).
Culture Club, 'Do You Really Want To Hurt Me?'
Dexy's Midnight Runners, 'Come On Eileen'.
Dire Straits, *Love Over Gold.*
Michael Jackson, *Thriller.*
Simon and Garfunkel's reunion concert in Central Park.

Literature

Isabel Allende, *The House of the Spirits.*
Carlos Fuentes, *Distant Relations.*
Thomas Keneally, *Schindler's Ark.*
Primo Levi, *If Not Now, When?*
Drama Tadeusz Cantor, *The Dead Class.*
Julian Mitchell, *Another Country.*
Britain's Royal Shakespeare Company moves into its new London home, the Barbican Theatre.

Everyday Life

Time magazine's 'Man of the Year' is 'Pac-Man', a character from a computer game that sweeps the USA in 1982.

(7th July) In Britain, Michael Fagan, a burglar, breaks into Buckingham Palace in London, steals a bottle of wine from a cellar, and enters the Queen's bedroom; the Queen awakes to find him drinking and only manages to obtain help when Fagan asks for a cigarette.

Sport and Recreation

The soccer World Cup is held in Spain; Italy beats West Germany 3–1 in the Final.

Daley Thompson of Britain wins the European decathlon title in Athens, setting a new world record of 8,743 points; he simultaneously holds the Olympic, Commonwealth, and European decathlon titles.

Media

Film *ET* (director, Steven Spielberg).
Fitzcarraldo (director, Werner Herzog).
Gandhi (director, Richard Attenborough; sets world record for the number of extras).
An Officer and a Gentleman (director, Taylor Hackford; starring Richard Gere).

Television Start of broadcasts by Britain's Channel 4 television station; also of S4C, a station transmitting some programmes in Welsh.

New programmes in Britain include: *Boys from the Blackstuff*, a play by Alan Bleasdale; *Cheers*; *The Flight of the Condor* (BBC); *A Kind of Loving* (Granada); *St Elsewhere*; *Smiley's People*, starring Alec Guinness; *Wogan*, chat show with Terry Wogan.

Statistics

Unemployment rates (percentage of working population): Australia, 7.2; Belgium, 13.8; Canada, 11.0; Denmark, 10.0; Eire, 16.5; Finland, 5.9; France, 8.0; West Germany, 7.5; Great Britain and Northern Ireland, 13.1; Greece, 3.2; Holland, 12.6; Italy, 9.1; Japan, 2.4; Spain, 16.3; Sweden, 3.2; Yugoslavia, 12.4; US, 9.7.

1983

Jan: 18th, Franks Report published; it exonerates Margaret Thatcher's government of blame for Argentine junta's decision to invade Falklands Islands 2nd April 1982.

19th, South Africa re-imposes direct rule on South-West Africa (Namibia).

24th, 32 Italian Red Brigade terrorists jailed for kidnap and murder of Aldo Moro in 1978.

27th, US–Soviet talks resume in Geneva with USSR proposing nuclear-free zone for central Europe.

Feb: 24th, in India, 1,500 reported dead in violence during local elections in Assam.

28th, Yorkshire and South Wales miners called out on strike to protest against planned pit closures.

March: 5th, Labour Party wins Australian general election.

6th, Christian Democrats win general election in West Germany; Green Party wins 24 seats in Bundestag.

14th, OPEC agrees to cut oil prices for first time since formation in 1961; price of Saudi light crude reduced from $34 a barrel to $29.

23rd, President Reagan proposes 'Star Wars' defence system for USA, using satellites to detect enemy missiles and effect destruction.

April: 10th, US Middle East peace plan collapses when Jordan withdraws from talks.

May: 4th, President Reagan declares support for aim of Nicaraguan Contras to overthrow Sandinista government.

June: 9th, Conservatives win overall majority of 144 seats in British general election, taking 397 seats, against Labour, 209, Liberal–SDP Alliance, 23, others 21 (Conservatives win 42.4% of votes cast, Labour, 27.6%, Liberal–SDP Alliance, 25.4%).

12th, Michael Foot announces intention to resign as leader of Labour Party.
14th, Roy Jenkins resigns leadership of SDP (21st, Dr David Owen named as successor).

July: 7th, British Chancellor announces cuts of £500 million in public expenditure.
12th, China and Britain hold talks in Peking on future of Hong Kong.
21st, Polish government announces end to martial law and amnesty for political prisoners.

Aug: 21st, Philippines opposition leader Benigno Aquino assassinated at Manila airport.
28th, Israeli Prime Minister Menachim Begin announces intention to resign (15th Sept, succeeded by Yitzhak Shamir).

Sept: 1st, 269 killed when South Korean Boeing 747 airliner is shot down by Soviet fighter after straying into Soviet air space near Sakhalin Island (5th, West European nations impose 14-day ban on Aeroflot flights).
4th, civil war breaks out in Lebanon's Chouf mountains following withdrawal of Israeli troops.
6th, final document of European Conference on Security and Co-operation adopted in Madrid, pledging governments to continue 'Helsinki process' of peaceful settlement of disputes and increased respect for human rights.
19th, Caribbean islands of St Kitts-Nevis achieve independence from Britain.
26th, ceasefire agreed in Lebanon; government agrees to conference of national reconciliation.

Oct: 2nd, Neil Kinnock elected leader of British Labour Party.
5th, Nobel Peace Prize awarded to Lech Walesa.
6th, Indian government takes over direct control of Punjab state in response to growing violence.
12th, Chinese Communist Party commences biggest purge of membership since Cultural Revolution; qualifications of 40 million party members to be reviewed.
14th, British Trade and Industry Secretary Cecil Parkinson resigns following revelations of adultery with his secretary, Sarah Keays (16th, succeeded by Norman Tebbit).
19th, left-wing military coup in Grenada, in which Prime Minister Maurice Bishop is killed.
22nd, anti-nuclear protests held across Europe against deployment of US Pershing II and Cruise missiles.
25th, US Marines invade Grenada to depose military government (28th, USA vetoes UN resolution deploring invasion).

Nov: 14th, Defence Secretary Heseltine announces arrival of first Cruise missiles at Greenham Common (15th, 141 people arrested at demonstration outside Greenham Common airbase).
14th, Turkish Cypriot Legislative Council issues unilateral proclamation of independence of Turkish part of island (18th, UN Security Council Resolution 541 declares action illegal).
23rd, USSR walks out of arms limitation talks in Geneva following deployment of US missiles in Europe (24th, President Andropov announces USSR to increase number of submarine missiles targeted at USA).

Politics, Government, Law, and Economy

The number of Members of Parliament in Britain is increased to 650; the pay of MPs is linked to civil service rates.
(8th Sept) NHS hospitals in Britain are obliged to allow private contractors to tender for cleaning, catering, and laundry services.
(7th Oct) British government White Paper proposes abolition of Greater London Council and metropolitan counties.
(2nd Nov) The government of South Africa holds referendum of white voters on Constitution Act, providing for parliament to be reconstituted as three chambers (one each for whites, coloureds, and Indians) and for parliament to elect the state president; two-thirds of voters support the plan.

Society, Education, and Religion

Wearing of seat belts by front-seat car passengers made compulsory in Britain.
United Reformed Church becomes the first church in Britain officially to support unilateral nuclear disarmament.
(13th April) In USA, Harold Washington is elected the first African-American mayor of Chicago.

Science, Technology, and Discovery

IBM in the USA produces the first personal computer with a built-in hard disc.
Apple Computers in USA devise a computer programme featuring 'pull-down' menus with instructions given by means of a 'mouse' control box.
In USA, a research team at the University of California at Los Angeles led by John Buster and Maria Bustillo performs the first successful transfer of a human embryo.
Andrew W Murray and Jack W Szostak create the first artificial chromosome.
Researchers at the US National Cancer Institute and at the Pasteur Institute in Paris, France, isolate the virus thought to cause AIDS; it becomes known as the HIV virus.

(18th–24th June) A mission by space shuttle *Challenger* includes the first US woman to go into space, Sally Ride.

Humanities and Scholarship

Final (48th) volume of W S Lewis (ed.), *Horace Walpole's Correspondence.*

Karl Popper, *Realism and the Aim of Science.*

Art, Sculpture, Fine Arts, and Architecture

Painting Cindy Sherman, *Untitled* No. 131.

Sculpture Niki de Saint Phalle, Jean Tinguely, Fountain, Pompidou Centre, Paris.

Music

Harrison Birtwistle, *The Mask of Orpheus* (opera).

Olivier Messiaen, *Saint François d'Assise* (opera).

David Bowie, 'Let's Dance' (single and album).

Duran Duran, 'Is There Something I Should Know?'

Michael Jackson, 'Beat It', 'Billy Jean'.

Literature

Gabriel García Márquez, *Chronicle of a Death Foretold.*

Alice Walker, *The Color Purple.*

Drama Howard Brenton, *The Genius.*

Sam Shepard, *Fool for Love.*

Sport and Recreation

The first World Athletics Championships are held in Helsinki, free of boycotts, with 157 nations competing; the USA leads the gold medal table with 8.

(1st June) In Britain, Lester Piggott, riding Teenoso, wins a record ninth Derby.

Media

In Britain, Eddie Shah launches the Messenger group of free newspapers in Warrington, produced by non-union workers; 29th Nov, police used to break union picket.

(May) *Stern* magazine in Germany publishes extracts from *The Hitler Diaries*, which are considered authentic by historian Hugh Trevor-Roper but later exposed as a fake produced by a dealer in Nazi memorabilia.

Film *Danton* (director, Andrzej Wajda).

Local Hero (director, Bill Forsyth).

Television Launch in Britain of 'TV AM', breakfast-time television station.

Statistics

Illiteracy in selected countries (percentage of adult population): Afghanistan, 81.8; Angola, 59.0; Argentina, 6.1; Bangladesh, 70.8; Brazil, 22.2; China, 34.5; Egypt, 61.8; Ethiopia, 37.6; India, 59.2; Indonesia, 32.7; Iran, 45.2; Israel, 8.2; Malaysia, 30.4; Mexico, 17.0; Pakistan, 73.8; Peru, 18.1; Saudia Arabia, 48.9; Sri Lanka, 13.2; Sudan, 68.6; Tunisia, 49.3.

1984

Jan: 1st, Brunei becomes independent after 95 years as British Protectorate.

19th, Islamic Conference Organization votes to invite Egypt back to membership (suspended since Camp David accord).

Feb: 9th, President Andropov of USSR dies (13th, Konstantin Chernenko named First Secretary of Soviet Communist Party).

11th, Iraq commences bombing of non-military targets in Iran.

March: 7th, Polish students stage sit-in at Stanislaw Staszic College in Mietne to demand restoration of crucifixes in classrooms.

8th, leaders of British NUM support planned strikes in Yorkshire and Scotland over proposed pit closures.

12th, in Britain, miners' strike spreads to 100 pits (15th, only 21 pits working, most of these in Nottinghamshire).

31st, Indian government agrees to amend Punjabi constitution to acknowledge Sikhism as religion distinct from Hinduism.

April: 5th, Nottinghamshire miners reject NUM Executive Committee's recommendation not to cross picket lines.

May: 2nd, Publication of report of New Ireland Forum, formed by three main parties in Eire and the SDLP in Northern Ireland. It advocates creation of united Ireland by federation of Eire and Northern Ireland or by government of Northern Ireland under joint authority of Britain and Eire.

24th, US House of Representatives votes to continue military aid to El Salvador, but against further aid to Nicaraguan Contras.

June: 6th, 250 Sikh extremists killed when Indian troops storm Golden Temple at Amritsar (11th, Sikh soldiers mutiny at eight army bases in protest at attack).

Aug: 4th, violent clashes between Tamils and Sinhalese in Sri Lanka.

Sept: 3rd, 14 die in rioting in Sharpeville and other black townships around Johannesburg.
14th, South African Prime Minister Botha sworn in as country's first Executive President (17th, first 19-member multi-racial Cabinet sworn in).
26th, draft agreement for return of Hong Kong to China in 1997 signed by British and Chinese representatives at ceremony in Beijing.

Oct: 12th, IRA bomb explodes at Grand Hotel, Brighton, during Conservative Party Conference, killing 4, injuring 32, and nearly killing Margaret Thatcher (13th Nov, fifth person dies).
31st, Indian Prime Minister Indira Gandhi assassinated by Sikh bodyguards; her son Rajiv sworn in as Prime Minister. Communal violence follows.

Nov: 4th, Sandinista Front wins Nicaraguan elections; Daniel Ortega elected President with 63% of popular vote.
6th, in US presidential election Republican President Ronald Reagan, with 525 electoral college votes, wins landslide victory over Democrat Walter Mondale, with 13 college votes. Reagan wins all states bar Minnesota and District of Columbia. Republicans retain majority in Senate and increase representation in House of Representatives. Popular vote: Reagan, 54,455,075 (58.8%); Mondale, 37,577,185 (40.6%).
20th, shares in British Telecom offered to public; issue is four times oversubscribed (3rd Dec, trading opens with premium of 45p above offer price of £1.30p).
26th, US restores full diplomatic relations with Iraq (severed in 1967).

Dec: 3rd, leak of toxic gas from Union Carbide pesticide plant near Bhopal, India, kills 2,500 and injures 200,000.
7th, front page article in China's *People's Daily* argues that Marxist theory is not solution to all country's economic problems (10th, 'correction' criticizes article for failure to emphasize continued importance of Marxist principles).

Politics, Government, Law, and Economy

British Police and Criminal Evidence Act ('PACE') reforms police powers of entry, search, and arrest, and revises rules on treatment and interrogation of suspects.
The Data Protection Act regulates the use of computer data in Britain and establishes the office of the Data Protection Registrar to oversee the requirements of the Act.

Society, Education, and Religion

British Parliament approves the new GCSE (General Certificate of Secondary Education) examination, to replace 'O' level and CSE from 1988.
The Concordat of 1929 between the Vatican City State and Italy is revised, with Roman Catholicism losing its status as official state religion of Italy.
(March) In Britain, Brenda Dean is the first woman to lead major British union; elected leader of print union SOGAT '82.
(July) The appointment of Rev Professor David Jenkins as Bishop of Durham in England arouses controversy because of the Bishop-elect's views on Christian doctrine; after the Bishop's consecration in York Minster (6th) lightning strikes the Minster (9th), prompting discussion about a possible act of God.
(18th July) In Britain, report of Committee of Inquiry into Human Fertilization and Embryology, chaired by Dame Mary Warnock, recommends control of research into 'test-tube' babies and ban on surrogate motherhood agencies.
(3rd Sept) The Roman Catholic Sacred Congregation for the Doctrine of the Faith publishes *An Instruction on Certain Aspects of the Theology of Liberation*, warning against acceptance of Marxist ideology.

Science, Technology, and Discovery

In Britain, Dr Alec Jeffreys of the University of Leicester discovers that a core sequence of DNA is unique to each person; this examination of DNA, known as 'genetic fingerprinting', can be used to establish family relationships and in criminal investigations.
(Jan) An Australian woman gives birth to a child created by in vitro fertilization of her husband's sperm with another woman's egg.

Humanities and Scholarship

Leslie Bethell (ed.), *The Cambridge History of Latin America* (–1991).

Art, Sculpture, Fine Arts, and Architecture

Neo-Geo movement in the USA.
Architecture (30th May) The Prince of Wales, in an address to the Royal Institute of British Architects at Hampton Court, London, attacks Modern Architecture (describing the proposed extension to the National Gallery as 'a carbuncle on the face of an old friend').

Music
Einsturtzende Neubauten, 'Strategien gegen Architekturen'.
Frankie Goes to Hollywood, 'Relax', 'Two Tribes', 'Welcome To The Pleasure Dome'.
Madonna, 'Like a Virgin'.
Prince, *Purple Rain.*
The Smiths, *The Smiths.*
Bruce Springsteen, *Born in the USA.*
The Band Aid single 'Do They Know It's Christmas?' raises £8 million for famine relief in Africa.

Literature
Martin Amis, *Money.*
Milan Kundera, *The Unbearable Lightness of Being.*
New edition of James Joyce's *Ulysses*, correcting 5,000 errors.

Everyday Life
Publication of *The Yuppie Handbook* draws attention to the 'young upwardly mobile professional', one of the defining icons of the mid 1980s.

Sport and Recreation
Sweden wins Lawn Tennis's Davis Cup for the first time, beating the USA 4–1 in the Final.
In three competitions (European Championships, Winter Olympics, World Championships), the British ice dancers Jayne Torvill and Christopher Dean are awarded 59 'perfect' scores of 6.
(28th July) (–12th Aug) The 23rd Olympic Games are held in Los Angeles, USA, and are boycotted by the Soviet bloc, with the exception of Romania, and by Iran and Libya, in retaliation for the US boycott of the Moscow Olympics in 1980. The USA wins 83 gold medals; Romania, 20; West Germany, 17; China, 15; Italy, 14; Canada and Japan, 10 each; New Zealand, 8; Yugoslavia, 7; South Korea, 6; Britain, France, and the Netherlands, 5 each. In the athletics, Carl Lewis of the USA wins four gold medals.

Media
(13th July) In Britain, Robert Maxwell buys the Mirror group of newspapers.
Film *A Nightmare on Elm Street* (director, Wes Craven).
Nostalgia (director, Andrei Tarkovsky).
Paris, Texas (director, Wim Wenders).
Terminator (director, James Cameron).
End of capital allowances on films in Britain – producers announce they will leave the country.
Television New programmes in Britain include: *The Jewel in the Crown*; *The Living Planet*; *Rainy Day Women* (BBC), by David Pirie; *Spitting Image* (Central), satire of contemporary politics using puppets; *Threads*, which dramatizes the presumed effects of a nuclear explosion over the city of Sheffield in N England.
In Britain, Edgar Reitz's *Heimat*, an epic lasting almost 16 hours, is shown on BBC television.

1985

Jan: 7th, (–8th) US Secretary of State Shultz and USSR Foreign Minister Gromyko hold talks in Geneva over resumption of arms control negotiations.
17th, (–20th) summit conference at UN between President Kyprianu of Cyprus and Turkish Cypriot leader Rauf Denktaş fails to resolve differences.
18th, FT 100 Share Index exceeds 1,000 points for first time.
25th, President Botha opens South Africa's new three-chamber Parliament for Whites, Indians, and Coloureds.

Feb: 4th, Reagan administration's defence budget calls for tripling of expenditure on 'Star Wars' research programme.
5th, Gibraltar's frontier gates with Spain re-opened after 16 years.

March: 3rd, in Britain, NUM delegates conference votes to return to work without settlement of strike.
10th, President Chernenko of USSR dies.
11th, Mikhail Gorbachev is named First Secretary of Soviet Communist Party; he calls for more *glasnost* ('openness') in Soviet life and later pursues policy of *perestroika* ('reconstruction').
15th, military rule ends in Brazil.

April: 11th, Enver Hoxha, First Secretary of Albanian Communist Party and national leader for more than 40 years, dies. Ramiz Alia named new First Secretary.

May: 1st, USA imposes financial and trade sanctions on Nicaragua.
1st, 10,000 Solidarity supporters clash with police during May Day demonstrations in Gdansk.

June: 12th, Spain and Portugal sign treaty of accession to EC.
14th, two Shi'ite Muslim gunmen hijack TWA jet with 145 passengers and crew of eight, demanding release of 700 prisoners held by Israel. One passenger, a US Navy diver, is shot dead (17th, hostages removed from jet and held in south Beirut).

15th, South Africa names multi-racial administration for Namibia but retains control of foreign policy and defence.

30th, 39 US hostages from TWA jet taken to Damascus, released following Syrian intervention.

July: 2nd, Andrei Gromyko named President of USSR; Edvard Shevardnadze becomes Foreign Minister.

11th, explosion sinks Greenpeace ship *Rainbow Warrior* in Auckland harbour, New Zealand, killing one man – ship was in South Pacific to disrupt French nuclear tests (two people later charged with explosion and discovered to be French agents).

18th, (–20th) Organization of African Unity Conference in Addis Ababa declares that most African countries on verge of economic collapse.

Aug: 15th, President Botha of South Africa re-states commitment to apartheid and rules out Parliamentary representation for coloured population.

23rd, West German counterespionage official Hans Joachim Tiedge seeks asylum in East Germany (28th, head of West German Secret Service sacked).

26th, report exonerates French government of involvement in sinking of *Rainbow Warrior*; findings rejected by New Zealand government (27th, French Prime Minister Laurent Fabius orders further investigations).

Sept: 2nd, Pol Pot resigns as Commander in Chief of Khmer Rouge Army; replaced by Sol Senn.

9th, USA announces selective economic sanctions against South Africa.

9th, riots in Handsworth area of Birmingham.

10th, EC Foreign Ministers approve sanctions against South Africa (Britain delays decision until 25th).

22nd, French Prime Minister Fabius admits that *Rainbow Warrior* was sunk by French secret service agents.

26th, elections held for Hong Kong's Legislative Council; first in 100 years of colonial rule.

28th, (–29th) riots in Brixton, London, following police wounding of black woman, Cherry Groce.

Oct: 6th, riots in Tottenham, London, during which PC Keith Blakelock is murdered.

7th, four Palestinian guerrillas hijack Italian cruise liner *Achille Lauro* with 450 people on board in Mediterranean (9th, hijackers surrender to Egyptian authorities after killing one US passenger, Leon Klinghoffer, a crippled elderly Jew).

18th, British miners in Nottinghamshire and South Derbyshire vote to disaffiliate from the NUM and form the Union of Democratic Mineworkers (UDM).

Nov: 15th, Anglo-Irish Agreement signed at Hillsborough Castle, giving Eire a consultative role in the affairs of Northern Ireland; British Treasury Minister Ian Gow resigns in protest.

Dec: 3rd, Church of England publishes report *Faith in the City*, critical of government policies on inner cities; government spokesmen denounce it as 'Marxist'.

17th, Ulster Unionist MPs all resign from House of Commons over Anglo-Irish Agreement.

30th, General Zia ends martial law in Pakistan.

Politics, Government, Law, and Economy

Crown Prosecution Service established in England and Wales, taking over responsibility for criminal prosecutions from the police.

World Bank sets up fund for Africa.

Japanese company Nissan negotiates single-union deal with Amalgamated Union of Engineering Workers for employees at new car construction plant at Washington in NE England.

International Whaling Commission bans commercial whaling, in order to prevent extinction of whales.

Society, Education, and Religion

Major famine in Ethiopia.

Bernie Grant elected leader of Haringey Council, Britain's first black council leader; Venerable Wilfred Wood consecrated Bishop of Croydon, Britain's first black bishop.

General Synod of the Church of England approves ordination of women to the diaconate by large majority.

(20th Feb) In Republic of Ireland, the Dáil legalizes shop sales of contraceptives.

(28th May) European Court of Human Rights finds Britain guilty of sex discrimination in immigration policy.

(4th July) Ruth Lawrence achieves the best first-class mathematics degree at the University of Oxford, England, at age 13.

(17th Oct) The House of Lords in Britain, in the Gillick case, permits doctors to prescribe oral contraceptives to girls aged under 16 without parental consent.

(2nd Oct) US film star Rock Hudson is the first celebrity to die of AIDS; on 16th Dec it is reported that 8,000 Americans have died from the disease.

Science, Technology, and Discovery

The British Antarctic Survey detects a hole in the ozone layer over Antarctica.

Humanities and Scholarship

Jürgen Habermas, *The Philosophical Discourse of Modernity.*

P F Strawson, *Scepticism and Naturalism: Some Varieties.*

Bernard Williams, *Ethics and the Limits of Philosophy.*

Art, Sculpture, Fine Arts, and Architecture

Saatchi Collection opens in London.

Architecture Richard Meier, Museum für Kunsthandwerk, Frankfurt-am-Main, West Germany.

Norman Foster, Hong Kong and Shanghai Bank Headquarters, Hong Kong.

Richard Rogers, Lloyds Building, City of London.

Sculpture Christo wraps Pont Neuf, Paris.

Music

Andrew Lloyd Webber, *Requiem.*

Toru Takemitsu, *Riverrun.*

Les Miserables (musical).

Dire Straits, *Brothers in Arms.*

The Smiths, *Meat is Murder.*

Sonic Youth, *Bad Moon Rising.*

Live-Aid – televised concerts in USA and Britain to raise funds for famine relief; USA for Africa produces the single 'We Are The World'.

Literature

Julian Barnes, *Flaubert's Parrot.*

Ivan Klima, *My First Loves.*

Patrick Suskind, *Perfume.*

Ted Hughes is appointed Britain's Poet Laureate.

Drama Howard Brenton and David Hare, *Pravda.*

Jean-Claude Carrière and Peter Brook, *The Mahabharata.*

Everyday Life

In USA, the Coca-Cola company introduces a sweeter formula for its drink, but has to reinstate the old formula under the Classic name following protests.

Sport and Recreation

(29th May) In Belgium, 39 people are killed at the Heysel Stadium in Brussels following a riot by Liverpool fans before the European Cup Final between Liverpool and Juventus of Italy; as a consequence, English football clubs are banned from all European competitions.

(7th July) In tennis, Boris Becker, at 17 years and 227 days, wins the Men's Singles title in the Wimbledon tournament, London: he becomes the youngest winner, the first West German winner, and the first unseeded player to win the title.

(15th Sept) Europe's golfers, captained by Tony Jacklin, win the Ryder Cup at the Belfry, England, the first European team to defeat the US team since 1957.

Media

(Dec) Canadian Conrad Black takes control of Telegraph newspapers.

Film *Back to the Future* (director, Robert Zemeckis).

Kiss of the Spider Woman (director, Hector Babenco).

Ran (director, Akira Kurosawa).

Television In Britain, the BBC bans *At the Edge of the Union* on account of its interviews of IRA members – TV journalists strike.

New programmes in Britain include: *EastEnders* (BBC), a 'soap opera' set in the East End of London; Troy Kennedy, *Edge of Darkness* by Troy Kennedy Martin; *The Golden Girls*; *Taggart*; *The Triumph of the West* (BBC), an interpretation of world history presented by J M Roberts.

1986

Jan: 1st, Spain and Portugal become 11th and 12th members of EC.

7th, USA imposes sanctions on Libya for involvement in international terrorism.

28th, US space shuttle *Challenger* explodes shortly after take-off, killing crew of seven.

Feb: 7th, President Jean-Claude Duvalier of Haiti flees to France following anti-government demonstrations. General Henri Namphy forms new government.

24th, President Marcos flees Philippines; Corazon Aquino sworn in as President.

28th, Sweden's Prime Minister Olof Palme assassinated in Stockholm street.

March: 2nd, Queen Elizabeth signs Australia Bill in Canberra, severing remaining legal ties with Britain.

6th, USSR Communist Party Congress agrees sweeping changes in membership of Central Committee and Politburo.

31st, Greater London Council and six metropolitan counties cease to exist.

April: 14th, House of Commons rejects bill to deregulate Sunday trading in England and Wales.

15th, bombers from US warships and bases in Britain attack targets in Libya; 100 killed, 1 plane shot down.

17th, bodies of two kidnapped Britons and one American found near Beirut; they had been murdered after the US raid on Libya.

17th, John McCarthy, acting bureau chief for Worldwide Television in Beirut, is taken hostage.

18th, President Botha of South Africa announces end to country's pass laws, restricting movement within the country.

26th, major accident at Chernobyl nuclear power station near Kiev announced after abnormally high levels of radiation reported in Sweden, Denmark, and Finland.

June: 12th, President Botha announces state of emergency throughout South Africa in response to deteriorating security situation; 1,000 black activists arrested.

12th, Northern Ireland Secretary announces dissolution of Northern Ireland Assembly set up in 1982.

20th, conference of 120 nations in Paris organized by UN Special Committee against Apartheid, OAU, and Non-Aligned Movement, calls for sanctions against South Africa.

July: 7th, French agents jailed for sinking of *Rainbow Warrior* released into French custody.

11th, inflation in Britain falls to 2.5%, lowest since Dec 1967.

Sept: 7th, Rt Rev Desmond Tutu enthroned as first black Archbishop of Cape Town, South Africa.

Oct: 2nd, Indian Prime Minister Rajiv Gandhi survives assassination attempt in New Delhi.

2nd, US Senate votes to impose economic sanctions on South Africa, overturning presidential veto.

Nov: 25th, President Reagan's National Security Adviser, Vice-Admiral John Poindexter, resigns and aide, Lieutenant-Colonel Oliver North, is dismissed from National Security Council after revelation that money from arms sales was channelled to Contra rebels in Central America (26th, Reagan appoints former Senator John Tower to head inquiry into role of National Security Council in 'Iran–Contra scandal').

Politics, Government, Law, and Economy

British Government Green Paper proposes introduction of the Community Charge (popularly known as the 'poll tax') in place of domestic rates.

The Public Order Act increases police powers over gatherings and processions in Britain.

US national debt reaches $2 trillion.

Comprehensive Anti-Apartheid Act in USA imposes strict sanctions on South Africa and causes many multinational firms to disinvest (General Motors ceases operations in South Africa on 22nd Oct).

(8th Sept) Nissan of Japan opens car assembly plant in Sunderland, NE England.

(27th Oct) 'Big Bang' deregulation of the London stock exchange abolishes distinctions between various types of trader.

Society, Education, and Religion

Liechtenstein allows women to vote for first time in elections to National Diet.

In South Africa, repeal of the Urban Areas Act (including removal of the pass laws).

A major Vatican document, *Instruction on Christian Freedom and Liberation*, recommends passive resistance against injustice and countenances armed struggle as 'a last resort to put an end to obvious and prolonged tyranny.' The Vatican declares Father Charles Curran of the USA unfit to teach Catholic theology because of his writings on divorce, contraception, abortion, and homosexuality.

The Dutch Reformed Church in South Africa declares that racism is a sin.

Science, Technology, and Discovery

Return of Halley's Comet; it is photographed by five space probes, including the European probe *Giotto*, which flies into the comet's tail (14th March).

British surgeons perform the first heart, lung, and liver transplant.

(28th Jan) Explosion of US space shuttle *Challenger* leads to suspension of shuttle flights.

Humanities and Scholarship

Final volume of *The Collected Works of Walter Bagehot*, edited by Norman St John-Stevas.

Arthur M Schlesinger, Jr, *The Cycles of American History*.

Stanley Wells and Gary Taylor (eds.), *William Shakespeare: The Complete Works*.

Final volume of the *Supplement to the Oxford English Dictionary*.

Art, Sculpture, Fine Arts, and Architecture

Architecture Gae Aulenti and international team of architects, Musée d'Orsay, Paris, France.

Painting Frank Auerbach, *Head of Catherine Lampert.*

Lucien Freud, *Painter and Model.*

Music

Chess (musical), lyrics by Tim Rice, music by Bjorn Ulvaeus and Benny Anderson (first performed at Prince Edward Theatre, London, 14th May).

Phantom of the Opera (musical), lyrics by Charles Hart, music by Andrew Lloyd Webber (first performed at Her Majesty's Theatre, London, 9th Oct).

Paul Simon, *Graceland.*

Literature

Garrison Keillor, *Lake Wobegon Days.*

Vikram Seth, *The Golden Gate.*

Endu Shusaku, *Scandal.*

Everyday Life

(21st Sept) Prince of Wales admits he talks to plants.

Sport and Recreation

(25th May) An estimated 30 million people take part in Sportaid's 'Race Against Time', a series of fun runs held around the world to raise money for the starving of Africa.

(29th June) In the soccer World Cup, held in Mexico, Argentina beats West Germany 3–2 in the final.

Media

(24th Jan) (–25th) In Britain, production of *The Times*, *Sunday Times*, the *Sun*, and the *News of the World* is moved overnight from premises in central London to a new plant in Wapping, E London.

(7th Oct) In Britain, Andreas Whittam-Smith and associates launch the *Independent.*

Film *Betty Blue* (director, Jean-Jacques Beneix).

Blue Velvet (director, David Lynch).

Jean de Florette (director, Claude Berri).

My Beautiful Laundrette (director, Stephen Frears).

Platoon (director, Oliver Stone).

Sacrifice (director, Andrei Tarkovsky).

Top Gun (director, Tony Scott).

Television New programmes in Britain include: *Bread* (BBC), a comedy based in Liverpool, by Carla Lane; *Casualty*, a hospital drama; *Inspector Morse* (Central), based on the novels of Colin Dexter; *The Singing Detective* (BBC), a controversial television play by Dennis Potter.

1987

Jan: 20th, Archbishop of Canterbury's envoy Terry Waite disappears in Beirut (Feb 2nd, reported to be 'under arrest' in Beirut).

24th, 162 police and 33 demonstrators injured in clashes outside Rupert Murdoch's News International plant at Wapping, London.

Feb: 5th, SOGAT ends picket of Wapping plant.

5th, Iran launches missile attack on Baghdad (19th, truce agreed in 'war of cities').

22nd, 4,000 Syrian troops enter West Beirut in effort to end fighting between Shi'ite Muslim and Druze forces.

26th, report of Tower Commission, which investigated the management of the White House during the period of the 'Iran–Contra affair', is critical of White House Chief of Staff, Donald Regan (27th, Regan replaced by former Senator Howard Baker).

March: 4th, President Reagan accepts full responsibility for Iran–Contra scandal.

6th, Townsend Thoresen cross-channel ferry, *Herald of Free Enterprise*, capsizes off Zeebrugge, killing 187.

17th, British Budget reduces basic rate of income tax to 27%, introduces new personal pension scheme, announces borrowing requirement of £7 billion.

19th, Czechoslovak leader Gustáv Husák announces political and economic reforms.

25th, 6th National People's Congress opens in Beijing; Premier Chao Tzu-yang confirms new liberal economic policies.

April: 27th, US Justice Department bars President Waldheim of Austria from entering USA for alleged involvement in Nazi atrocities.

May: 1st, Quebec agrees to sign amended Canadian constitution recognizing it as a 'distinct society'.

14th, Egypt breaks off diplomatic relations with Iran over financing of Islamic fundamentalism.

June: 11th, Conservatives win British general election with overall majority of 101, winning 375 seats, against Labour, 229, Liberal–SDP Alliance, 22. (Conservatives win 42.3% of votes cast, Labour, 30.8%, Liberal–SDP Alliance, 22.6%).

14th, large gains for Socialists in Italian general election.

18th, unemployment in Britain falls below 3 million.

25th, Karoly Grosz, a reactionary, becomes Hungary's Prime Minister and later introduces an austerity programme to deal with economic problems.

July: 7th, in USA, in evidence before Iran–Contra hearings, Colonel Oliver North claims his actions were sanctioned by superiors.

17th, Vice-Admiral John Poindexter states that he authorized diversion of funds to Contra rebels.

Aug: 4th, Tamil rebels in Sri Lanka agree to surrender arms to Indian peacekeeping force.

6th, Dr David Owen resigns leadership of SDP, following vote in favour of merger negotiations with Liberals (28th, succeeded by Robert Maclennan).

12th, President Reagan insists he was not told of diversion of funds from arms sales to Nicaraguan Contras.

19th, gunman Michael Ryan kills 16 in English town of Hungerford, before shooting himself (22nd Sept, government bans automatic weapons of kind used by Ryan).

Oct: 6th, Colonel Rabuka declares Fiji a republic.

19th, US destroyers and commandos attack Iranian oil installations in Gulf.

Nov: 2nd, USSR leader Gorbachev, in speech to mark 70th anniversary of Russian Revolution, criticizes Stalin for political errors.

18th, report of joint Senate/House of Representatives Iran–Contra Committee blames President Reagan for abuse of law; eight Republicans refuse to sign report.

23rd, (–24th) Secretary of State Shultz and USSR Foreign Minister Shevardnadze agree treaty to eliminate all intermediate-range nuclear (INF) weapons.

Dec: 7th, (–10th) US–USSR Summit in Washington; Reagan and Gorbachev agree to eliminate intermediate nuclear forces.

Politics, Government, Law, and Economy

Peter Wright, *Spycatcher* (published first in Australia, against the wishes of the British government).

Members of the European Community complete ratification of the Single European Act; it comes into force on 1st July, starting the creation of a single market in Europe by 1993.

First suspect is convicted in Britain of two murders by evidence derived from genetic fingerprinting.

Society, Education, and Religion

Allan Bloom, *The Closing of the American Mind.*

General Synod of the Church of England debates homosexuality; published report states that sexual intercourse belongs properly within marriage, and that homosexuals should be met with compassion and a call to repentance.

(10th March) Vatican document, *Instruction on Respect for Human Life in its Origin and on the Dignity of Procreation: Replies to Certain Questions of the Day*, condemns artificial methods of fertilization and calls for ban on experiments on living embryos.

(11th July) Formal announcement that world population has reached 5,000,000,000, double the level of 1950.

Science, Technology, and Discovery

First glass-fibre optic cable laid across the Atlantic Ocean.

International protocol to limit use of damaging CFCs.

Discovery of ceramics with superconducting properties.

(24th Feb) The first supernova (explosion of a star) visible to the naked eye to be observed since 1604.

(Nov) Start of construction of Channel Tunnel between England and France.

Humanities and Scholarship

Jacques Derrida, *Of Spirit: Heidegger and the Question.*

Art, Sculpture, Fine Arts, and Architecture

Christie's sells Vincent van Gogh's *Irises* for £30 million, a world record sale price for art of any kind.

Architecture Renzo Piano, de Menil Museum, Houston, Texas, USA.

Sculpture Richard Deacon, *The Back of my Hand.*

Music

Nigel Osborne, *The Electrification of the Soviet Union* (opera).

Judith Weir, *A Night at the Chinese Opera* (opera).

Iannis Xenakis, *Horos.*

Whitney Houston 'I Wanna Dance With Somebody', *Whitney Houston* (the first record album by a woman singer to go straight to number one in the album charts).

New Order, *Substance.*
U2, *The Joshua Tree.*

Literature

Margaret Atwood, *The Handmaid's Tale.*
Kazuo Ishiguro, *An Artist of the Floating World.*
Michael Ondaatje, *In the Skin of a Lion.*
Tom Wolfe, *Bonfire of the Vanities.*

Sport and Recreation

(7th March) In cricket, Sunil Gavaskar of India, playing in his 124th Test match, becomes the first batsman to score 10,000 Test runs.

(28th July) Laura Davies is the first British golfer to win the US Women's Open Championship.

Media

Film *Fatal Attraction* (director, Adrian Lyne; starring Michael Douglas and Glenn Close).
The Last Emperor (director, Bernardo Bertolucci).
Robocop (director, Paul Verhoeven).
Wings of Desire (director, Wim Wenders).

Statistics

Divorces (as percentage of marriages contracted): Australia, 34; Belgium, 31; Canada, 43; Czechoslovakia, 32; Denmark, 44; Finland, 38; France, 31; West Germany, 30; Great Britain and Northern Ireland, 41; Greece, 13; Holland, 28; Italy, 8; Japan, 22; Norway, 40; Sweden, 44; US, 48.

1988 **Jan: 2nd**, Canada and USA sign free-trade agreement.

3rd, Margaret Thatcher becomes longest-serving British Prime Minister in 20th century.

8th, New York stock market registers third largest one-day fall in history, with Dow Jones average closing 140.58 points down on the day.

March: 6th, three suspected IRA terrorists are shot dead by SAS team in Gibraltar.

April: 2nd, Indian forces seal border with Pakistan against infiltration of Sikh extremists after 120 deaths in week of violence in the Punjab.

3rd, peace agreement between Ethiopia and Somalia ends 11 years of border conflict.

May: 8th, President Mitterrand (Socialist) defeats Jacques Chirac (Gaullist) in French Presidential elections, with over 54% of poll.

10th, Chirac resigns as French Prime Minister and is replaced by Michel Rocard (Socialist).

15th, USSR troops begin withdrawal from Afghanistan after eight and a half years.

23rd, in Britain, the second largest turn-out of peers in the 20th century secures majority of 134 for the Government's Poll Tax Bill in the House of Lords.

June: 1st, Reagan and Gorbachev sign Intermediate-range Nuclear Forces (INF) treaty at Moscow Summit (29th May–2nd June).

28th, (–1st July) at 19th Communist Party conference in Moscow, President Gorbachev outlines plans for changes in the administrative structure of the USSR, intended to make the Party more democratic and businesses more autonomous.

July: 3rd, US warship *Vincennes* shoots down Iranian civilian airliner in the Gulf, with loss of 290 lives.

Aug: 8th, Iraq and Iran announce ceasefire.

17th, President Zia ul-Haq and the US ambassador to Pakistan are killed when plane carrying them explodes in mid-air; state of emergency is declared.

31st, Lech Walesa holds first talks with Polish authorities since the banning of Solidarity in 1981.

Sept: 20th, in speech to Council of Europe at Bruges, Margaret Thatcher warns against the 'folly' of moves toward political and economic union of Europe.

30th, major changes are made in USSR Politburo, including retirement of President Andrei Gromyko and dismissal of leading figures.

Oct: 1st, Mikhail Gorbachev is elected President of USSR by Supreme Soviet.

Nov: 8th, in US Presidential elections Republican George Bush, with 426 electoral college votes, defeats Democrat Michael Dukakis, with 112 votes, but the Democratic Party increases its majority in the Senate and House of Representatives. Popular vote: Bush, 48,886,097; Dukakis, 41,809,074.

16th, Benazir Bhutto's Pakistan People's Party win 94 seats in general election (2nd Dec, she is sworn in as Prime Minister of Pakistan).

21st, general election in Canada won by Progressive Conservative Party led by Prime Minister Brian Mulroney.

22nd, Queen's Speech at State Opening of Parliament announces Bills for Privatization of Water and Electricity services.

Dec: 21st, terrorist bomb explodes on Pan Am Boeing 747 airliner flying over Lockerbie in Scotland, killing all on board and 11 on the ground.

22nd, agreement reached at UN for Namibian independence, with phased withdrawal of Cuban forces.

Politics, Government, Law, and Economy

USA and Canada sign a free-trade agreement.

In bid to reduce over-production of foodstuffs, the European Community agrees the 'Setaside' agriculture policy, whereby farmers are subsidized for taking land out of production.

(Jan) In Britain, the Liberal Party (23rd Jan) and the Social Democratic Party (31st Jan) vote to form a new party (from 3rd March), the Social and Liberal Democrats (known as the Liberal Democrats from 16th Oct 1989).

Society, Education, and Religion

The 'Baker' Education Reform Act in Britain introduces a ten-subject national curriculum, testing at four 'key stages', envisages further City Technology Colleges and permits schools to 'opt out' of local education authority control.

The Holy Shroud of Turin, claimed by some to be Christ's mortuary cloth, is shown by carbon dating to date from the 14th century.

In the Apostolic Letter *Mulieris Dignitatem* Pope John Paul II reiterates his opposition to women priests.

The film *The Last Temptation of Christ*, directed by US director Martin Scorsese, is widely regarded as blasphemous.

(25th Sept) In USA, Barbara Harris, a divorcee, is elected as first woman bishop in the Anglican communion, to serve as suffragan Bishop of Massachusetts (consecrated 11th Feb 1989).

Science, Technology, and Discovery

Serious damage is done to computer systems world-wide by 'viruses' implanted by 'hackers' breaking into computer networks.

Stephen Hawking, *A Brief History of Time.*

A French company markets the abortion-inducing drug RV486; anti-abortion groups protest.

(April) US Patent and Trademark Office grants Harvard University a patent for a mouse developed by genetic engineering.

Humanities and Scholarship

A rich tomb of *c.* AD 300 is found near Sipan in Peru.

Eighth and final volume of the official biography of Winston Churchill by Martin Gilbert.

Alisdair MacIntyre, *Whose Justice? Which Rationality?*

Art, Sculpture, Fine Arts, and Architecture

Jasper Johns's *False Start* sold for $17,050,000, a world record for contemporary art and for a work by a living artist.

Sculpture Anish Kapoor, *Mother as Void.*

Music

György Ligeti, Concerto for Piano and Orchestra.

Witold Lutoslawski, Piano Concerto.

Karlheinz Stockhausen, *Montag aus Licht* (opera).

Bros, 'I Owe You Nothing'.

k d lang, *Shadowland.*

Kylie Minogue, 'I Should Be So Lucky'.

Public Enemy, *It Takes A Nation Of Millions To Hold Us Back.*

Concert held at Wembley Stadium, London, to celebrate the 70th birthday of Nelson Mandela.

Literature

Kobo Abe, *The Ark Sakura.*

Peter Carey, *Oscar and Lucinda.*

Gabriel García Márquez, *Love in the Time of Cholera.*

Eduardo Mendoza, *The City of Marvels.*

Milorad Pavic, *Dictionary of the Khazars.*

Salman Rushdie, *The Satanic Verses.*

Anatoli Rybakov, *Children of the Arbat* (published after a 20-year ban in the USSR).

Drama David Henry Hwang, *M Butterfly.*

Sport and Recreation

Steffi Graf of West Germany becomes only the third woman to win the 'Grand Slam' of all four major tennis tournaments; she also wins an Olympic gold, following the restoration of tennis to the Olympic Games at Seoul.

(17th Sept) (–2nd Oct) The 24th Olympic Games are held in Seoul, South Korea, and are free of boycotts. The USSR wins 55 gold medals; East Germany, 37; USA, 36; South Korea, 12; West

Germany and Hungary, 11 each; Bulgaria, 10; Romania, 7; France and Italy, 6 each; China, Great Britain, and Kenya, 5 each. In the Athletics, Ben Johnson of Canada wins the 100 m in a world record time of 9.79 seconds; he is then stripped of the title when drug tests reveal traces of an anabolic steroid, stanozol.

Media

(Feb) British weekly *New Society* is merged into *New Statesman.*

Film *The Last Temptation of Christ* (director, Martin Scorsese).

Dekalog (director, Kryzystof Kieslowski).

Rain Man (director, Barry Levinson).

Women on the Verge of a Nervous Breakdown (director, Pedro Almodovar).

1989 **Jan: 6th**, USSR announces mass rehabilitation of thousands of citizens who were victims of Stalin's purges 1930–50.

7th, Emperor Hirohito of Japan dies after a 62-year reign; his son, Crown Prince Akihito, succeeds him.

10th, Cuban troops begin withdrawal from Angola.

11th, Hungarian Parliament passes law allowing formation of political parties.

Feb: 14th, Ayatollah Khomeini issues *fatwa* against Salman Rushdie, calling for his death for blasphemy in his book *The Satanic Verses*; Rushdie goes into hiding.

March: 7th, China imposes martial law in Lhasa, Tibet.

26th, voters have a choice of candidates for first time in elections for Congress of People's Deputies in USSR. Boris Yeltsin, dismissed from the Politburo 17 months before, gains 89% of vote in his Moscow constituency, while many senior Party officials fail to get elected.

April: 5th, Lech Walesa and Polish Government sign agreement for political and economic reforms.

17th, students march on Beijing's Tiananmen Square to call for democracy.

20th, first multi-party elections in Czechoslovakia since 1946.

May: 3rd, centre-right coalition under Ruud Lubbers in Holland becomes first European government to resign over an environmental issue, when Liberal Democrats refuse support for proposals for financing of anti-pollution measures.

June: 3rd, In China, People's Army tanks move into Tiananmen Square in Beijing, killing 2,000 pro-democracy protesters.

4th, Solidarity achieves landslide victory in elections to Polish Parliament.

12th, President Gorbachev and Chancellor Kohl of West Germany sign Bonn Document affirming right of European states to determine their own political systems.

23rd, President Jose Eduardo dos Santos of Angola and Dr Jonas Savimbi, leader of UNITA rebels, sign declaration ending 14-year civil war in Angola.

Sept: 12th, Solidarity-dominated government takes office in Poland, the first government in Eastern Europe since 1940s not under Communist control.

27th, national parliament of Slovenia approves constitutional amendments giving right to secede from Federation of Yugoslavia.

Oct: 4th, Mass demonstration in Leipzig demands political reform in East Germany.

7th, Hungarian Socialist Workers' Party votes for its own dissolution.

8th, Latvian Popular Front announces intention to seek independence from USSR.

23rd, new Hungarian Republic is declared, with a constitution allowing multi-party democracy.

Nov: 9th, East Germany announces opening of its border with West Germany. The authorities begin demolishing sections of the Berlin Wall the following day.

Dec: 17th, army fires on demonstration in Timişoara, Romania, killing about 100 people, but rumours report far higher figure (20th, President Ceauşescu declares state of emergency as protests spread).

19th, US troops invade Panama to overthrow regime of General Noriega.

22nd, army joins forces with anti-government demonstrators in Romania and overthrows President Ceauşescu (25th, Nicolae and Elena Ceauşescu are captured, given summary trial and executed by the army).

29th, Vaclav Havel is elected Czechoslovakia's first non-Communist President for 41 years.

Politics, Government, Law, and Economy

Members of the Association of South-East Asian Nations (ASEAN) join Canada, Australia, New Zealand, Japan, and South Korea in forming the Council for Asia–Pacific Economic Co-operation.

(17th Feb) Leaders of Morocco, Libya, Algeria, Tunisia and Mauritania form new economic bloc called Arab Maghreb Union.

(17th Oct) In Britain, the 'Guildford Four' are cleared on appeal of bombing convictions (passed in Oct 1975) after serving 14 years of their life sentences.

Society, Education, and Religion

In Britain, several National Curriculum subject working-party reports and final orders are published.

Mikhail Gorbachev is the first leader of the USSR to visit the Vatican; he and John Paul II agree to reestablish diplomatic relations between the USSR and the Vatican.

(11th March) South African law commission publishes working paper calling for the abolition of apartheid and introduction of universal franchise.

Science, Technology, and Discovery

M Harrison and colleagues remove a foetus from its mother's womb, operate on its lungs, and return it to the womb.

(14th July) Inauguration of LEP (Large Electron Positron Collider) at the CERN research centre in Switzerland; the new accelerator has a circumference of 27 km/16.8 mi.

(16th Oct) Convention on International Trade in Endangered Species agrees total ban on trading in ivory.

Humanities and Scholarship

Remains of the Rose and Globe Theatres uncovered in London, where Shakespeare's plays were originally performed.

J A Simpson and E S C Weiner (eds.), *The Oxford English Dictionary* , 2nd edition.

Art, Sculpture, Fine Arts, and Architecture

Architecture I M Pei, Pyramid, Musée du Louvre, Paris, France.

Johann Otto von Spreckelsen and Paul Andreu, La Grande Arche, La Défense, Paris, France.

Music

John Cage, *Europera III/IV.*

John Tavener, *The Protecting Veil.*

Aspects of Love (musical), lyrics by Don Black and Charles Hart, music by Andrew Lloyd Webber (first performed at the Prince of Wales Theatre, London, April).

Guns 'n' Roses, *G 'N' R Lies.*

Lou Reed, *New York.*

Simple Minds, *Street Fighting Years.*

Literature

Breyten Breytenbach, *Memory of Snow and Dust.*

Kazuo Ishiguro, *Remains of the Day.*

Everyday Life

In Britain, acid-house rave parties attract tens of thousands of young people, despite a clampdown by police.

Sport and Recreation

During the 1988–89 English horse-racing season, Peter Scudamore becomes the first National Hunt jockey to saddle 200 winners in one season; on 18th Nov he sets a new record of 1,139 wins over jumps.

(15th April) In England, 96 Liverpool fans die in a crush during the Football Association Cup semi-final against Nottingham Forest at Hillsborough, Sheffield.

Media

Film *Batman* (director Tim Burton).

Do the Right Thing (director, Spike Lee).

My Left Foot (director, Jim Sheridan).

When Harry Met Sally (director, Rob Reiner).

Television (5th Feb) Launch of satellite station Sky TV in Britain.

1990

Jan: 3rd, In Panama, General Noriega surrenders to US authorities and is taken to Florida to face charges of drug-smuggling.

Feb: 2nd, President de Klerk ends 30-year ban on ANC.

7th, Central Committee of Communist Party in USSR votes to end Party's monopoly on political power.

11th, Nelson Mandela is released after 27 years in prison in South Africa.

16th, SWAPO leader, Sam Nujoma, is elected first president of independent Namibia (21st, Republic of Namibia becomes an independent sovereign state).

25th, in elections in Nicaragua, US-backed coalition under Violeta Chamorro defeats Ortega's Sandinista government.

March: 11th, Lithuania declares independence from USSR.

15th, Gorbachev sworn in as first executive president of USSR.

18th, in East Germany's first free elections since 1933, 'Alliance for Germany' wins 48% of vote.
24th, ruling Labour Party is returned for fourth term in Australian general election.
31st, huge anti-poll tax demonstration in Trafalgar Square, London, ends in confrontations with the police, and rioting and looting in the West End.

April: 1st, In Britain, 1,000 inmates riot in Strangeways Prison, Manchester, and take over large parts of the prison (25th, last prisoners surrender after storming of the prison by specially trained officers).
1st, Robert Mugabe gains decisive victory in presidential elections in Zimbabwe, and ruling ZANU–PF wins 117 of the 120 seats.

May: 1st, Opposition demonstrations disrupt May Day parade in Red Square, Moscow.
4th, Latvia declares itself an independent sovereign state.
8th, Estonia declares independence from USSR.
20th, Romania holds first free elections since 1937; National Salvation Front wins two-thirds of seats and Ion Iliescu wins landslide victory in presidential elections.
22nd, North and South Yemen merge to form Yemen Republic.
29th, Boris Yeltsin elected President of Russian Federation, defeating Gorbachev's candidate.

June: 8th, Russian Parliament votes that its laws should take precedence over those of USSR (12th, Russian Federation formally declares itself a sovereign state).
12th, in Algerian local elections, fundamentalist Islamic Salvation Front wins control of most municipal and provincial assemblies
20th, Uzbekistan declares independent sovereignty.
22nd, Manitoba and Newfoundland refuse to ratify Meech Lake Accord recognizing Quebec as a 'distinct society'.

July: 1st, East Germany cedes sovereignty over economic, monetary, and social policy to West German government and Bundesbank; Deutschmark becomes official currency.
8th, Indian army takes direct control of Kashmir after separatist violence.
12th, Boris Yeltsin and other reformers resign from Communist Party in USSR.
16th, Ukrainian Parliament votes for sovereignty and to become a neutral state.

Aug: 2nd, Iraqi forces invade Kuwait; deposed Emir flees to Saudi Arabia.
6th, UN Security Council imposes sanctions against Iraq, including oil embargo.
7th, President Bush sends US forces to Saudi Arabia to prevent Iraqi invasion.
9th, Iraq announces annexation of Kuwait.
31st, East and West Germany sign reunifiçation treaty.

Oct: 2nd, German Democratic Republic ceases to exist at midnight; 3rd, East and West Germany are reunited.
27th, National Party led by James Bolgar defeats ruling Labour Party in New Zealand elections.
28th, non-Communist parties triumph in elections in Georgia, USSR, with calls for independence and a market economy.

Nov: 7th, Mary Robinson wins Irish elections to become first woman president of Republic of Ireland.
20th, election held for leadership of British Conservative Party, with Michael Heseltine as challenger to Mrs. Thatcher; Thatcher fails to secure the margin needed for re-election, with 204 M.P.s' votes against Heseltine's 152 (22nd, Mrs Thatcher stands down from second ballot).
25th, Christian militias withdraw from East Beirut in agreement to create reunified city policed by government troops and Syrian soldiers.
26th, Lee Kuan Yew resigns as Singapore's leader after 31 years as Prime Minister.
27th, John Major wins second ballot for leadership of Conservative Party with 185 votes to 131 for Heseltine and 56 for Hurd; Heseltine and Hurd withdraw from third ballot; John Major becomes Conservative leader.
28th, Mrs. Thatcher resigns, and John Major takes over as British Prime Minister.

Dec: 9th, Lech Walesa achieves landslide victory in Polish presidential election.
9th, Slobodan Milosovic (Serbian Socialist Party) is elected president in Serbia's first free elections for 50 years.
16th, Fr Jean-Bertrand Aristide wins first-ever presidential election in Haiti.
23rd, Slovenia votes for independence in plebiscite.

Politics, Government, Law, and Economy

The British government announces the banning of broadcasting of speakers from unconstitutional parties in Northern Ireland; the ban principally affects Sinn Féin).
In Britain, Dr David Owen's 'continuing' Social Democratic Party is wound up.
In USA, budget crisis leads to the temporary closure of federal government facilities while an emergency package is agreed.
National Health Service and Community Care Act introduces self-managing trust hospitals and

fund-holding general practitioners into British National Health Service, creating the so-called 'internal market'.
Clean Air Act in USA raises standards for emissions made by utilities and industrial concerns.
(27th Oct) EC Summit opens in Rome; with exception of Britain, members vote to begin second stage of economic and monetary union by 1994 and to achieve single currency by 2000.

Society, Education, and Religion
The world's largest cathedral is consecrated by Pope John Paul II in Yamoussoukro, Ivory Coast.
A new Council of Churches for Britain and Ireland replaces the British Council of Churches; Roman Catholics and Black-led churches participate for the first time.
John MacQuarrie, *Jesus Christ in Modern Thought.*
(15th May) Home-produced beef is banned in UK schools and hospitals as result of concern over 'mad-cow disease' (bovine spongiform encephalopathy, or BSE).

Science, Technology, and Discovery
First human gene experiment: defective white blood cells are taken from a four-year-old girl, given a gene that controls an enzyme in the immune system, and reinserted.
Canadian scientists discover fossils of the oldest known multi-cellular animals, dating from 600 million years ago.
(24th Jan) Japan launches the first probe to be sent to the Moon since 1976; it places a small satellite in lunar orbit (March).

Humanities and Scholarship
F M L Thompson (ed.), *The Cambridge Social History of Britain 1750–1950.*
Karl Popper, *A World of Propensities.*

Art, Sculpture, Fine Arts, and Architecture
Sculpture Damian Hirst, *My Way.*
Jeff Koons, *Jeff and Ilona (Made in Heaven).*

Music
Brian Ferneyhough, String Quartet No. 4.
György Ligeti, Concerto for Violin and Orchestra.
Happy Mondays, *Pills 'n' Thrills and Bellyaches.*
Jane's Addiction, *Ritual De Lo Habitual.*
Sinead O'Connor, 'Nothing Compares To You'.
Pink Floyd perform *The Wall* in Berlin, Germany.
Concert held at Wembley Stadium, London, to celebrate the release of Nelson Mandela.

Literature
Martin Amis, *London Fields.*
A S Byatt, *Possession.*
Ian McEwan, *The Innocent.*
V S Naipaul, *India.*
Alexander Solzhenitsyn is awarded the Russia State Literature Prize for *The Gulag Archipelago.*
Drama Derek Walcott, *Remembrance.*

Sport and Recreation
(4th Feb) In cricket, Richard Hadlee of New Zealand becomes the first bowler to take 400 Test wickets.
(7th July) Martina Navratilova of the USA wins her ninth Women's Singles title in the Wimbledon tennis tournament, London, beating the record of Helen Wills Moody, set between 1927 and 1938.
(8th July) In the soccer World Cup, held in Italy, West Germany beats Argentina 1–0 in the Final.

Media
(May) Robert Maxwell publishes *The European,* a weekly English-language newspaper for circulation throughout Europe.
Film *Cinema Paradiso* (director, Giuseppe Tornatore).
Dances With Wolves (director and star, Kevin Costner).

1991 **Jan: 16th,** US-led coalition commences air offensive 'Operation Desert Storm' to liberate Kuwait from Iraqi occupation.
18th, Iraq launches Scud missiles against Israel.
Feb: 24th, US-led coalition in Gulf launches ground offensive against Iraqi forces.
27th, coalition forces enter Kuwait City and declare Kuwait liberated.
March: 1st, In Iraq popular revolt against government begins in Basra and spreads to other Shi'ite cities; separate Kurdish revolt starts in the north.
26th, Iraqi government forces bomb Kirkuk, held by Kurdish rebels; by 30th, Iraqi government has recovered most of the country.
31st, military structure of Warsaw Pact is dissolved.

April: 9th, Parliament of Georgia votes to assert independence from USSR.
23rd, British government announces proposals for a new 'council tax' to replace the community charge ('poll tax') in 1993.
30th, Kurdish refugees begin to move into Western-protected havens.

May: 9th, Yugoslavia's Collective State Presidency grants special powers to Yugoslav National Army for operations in Croatia, freeing it from effective government control.
21st, former Indian prime minister, Rajiv Gandhi, is assassinated by a Tamil suicide bomber during India's general elections campaign.
31st, President Dos Santos and Jonas Savimbi, leader of UNITA, sign peace agreement in Lisbon to end civil war in Angola.

June: 12th, Boris Yeltsin becomes first ever directly elected leader of the Russian Federation.
25th, republics of Croatia and Slovenia declare independence from Yugoslavia.

July: 31st, Bush and Gorbachev sign Strategic Arms Reduction Treaty (START) to reduce arsenals of long-range nuclear weapons by a third.

Aug: 8th, John McCarthy, British journalist held hostage in Lebanon, is released after 1,943 days in captivity.
19th, Communist hardliners, led by Gennady Yanayev, stage coup in USSR against President Gorbachev, who is placed under house arrest in the Crimea; radio and television stations are shut down and military rule imposed in many cities.
20th, Estonia declares independence.
21st, coup in USSR collapses following widespread popular resistance led by Boris Yeltsin (22nd, Gorbachev returns to Moscow).
21st, Latvia declares independence.
24th, Mikhail Gorbachev resigns as First Secretary of USSR Communist Party (29th, Parliament suspends Communist Party and seizes its assets).
27th, Croatian town of Vukovar falls to Serb-dominated army after 86-day siege.
30th, Azerbaijan declares independence.

Sept: 6th, Soviet authorities make formal grant of independence to Latvia, Lithuania, and Estonia.
22nd, Armenia declares independence.
25th, peace accord is signed in El Salvador to end 11-year civil war.

Nov: 1st, the Quorn Hunt is banned from National Trust land in Derbyshire and Leicestershire after revelations of cruelty by the hunt's masters.
24th, general election in Belgium produces gains to Flemish extremists and Green Party.

Dec: 5th, Robert Maxwell's business empire collapses with huge debts and revelations about misappropriation of money in pension funds.
8th, leaders of Russia, Belarus, and Ukraine agree to formation of Commonwealth of Independent States (CIS) (21st, eight of the nine other USSR republics sign the agreement).
9th, (–10th) summit of EC heads of government at Maastricht in Holland agree treaty on closer economic and political union.
20th, Ante Markovic resigns as federal Prime Minister of Yugoslavia.
25th, Mikhail Gorbachev resigns as President of USSR; the USSR officially ceases to exist.

Politics, Government, Law, and Economy

(14th March) In Britain the 'Birmingham Six' are released after Appeal Court finds their conviction in 1974 for IRA pub bombings in Birmingham 'unsafe and unsatisfactory'.
(5th April) European Bank of Reconstruction and Development, to assist economic development in East European and the former USSR, is opened in London; its splendid offices feature specially purchased marble.
(July) Collapse of the Bank of Credit and Commerce International in western countries, after discovery of massive fraud and involvement in organized crime, arms dealing, and the drug trade.
(4th Dec) Pan Am airline (founded 1927), burdened with massive debts, is closed down.

Society, Education, and Religion

First compulsory tests for seven year-olds are held in Britain, but few head teachers agree to declare the results, fearing the implications of 'league tables'.
Rabbi Dr Jonathan Sacks is invested as British chief rabbi.
Pope John Paul II awards the title 'Venerable' to 19th-century British Cardinal John Henry Newman.
(19th April) Dr George Carey succeeds Dr Robert Runcie as Archbishop of Canterbury; his enthronement service includes modern informal music, reflecting the new archbishop's more evangelical vision of the Church of England.
(15th May) Edith Cresson becomes first woman prime minister of France.

(June) Legal framework for apartheid in South Africa is destroyed with repeal of Land Acts, Group Areas Act (4th), and 1950 Population Registration Act (17th).

Science, Technology, and Discovery

Astronomers at Mt Palomar, California, USA, announce the discovery of the most distant object yet seen, a quasar.

In Britain, first production of a significant amount of power by atomic fusion by JET (Joint European Torus) at Culham near Oxford.

Researchers announce the discovery of a gene responsible for mental handicap.

(18th May) (–26th) Chemist Helen Sharman is the first Briton to go into space, as a participant in a Soviet space mission.

Humanities and Scholarship

Discovery in the Italian Alps of the preserved body of a man from *c.* 3,300 BC, with clothes, bow, arrows, axe, and other implements.

Alexander P Kazhdan et al. (eds.), *The Oxford Dictionary of Byzantium.*

Frank A J L James (ed.), *The Correspondence of Michael Faraday.*

Michael Dummett, *The Logical Basis of Metaphysics.*

Art, Sculpture, Fine Arts, and Architecture

Thyssen Collection of paintings opened in Madrid, Spain.

Architecture Sir Norman Foster, Sackler Galleries, Royal Academy, London; Stansted Airport, Essex, SE England.

Robert Venturi and Denise Scott Brown, Sainsbury Wing, National Gallery, London.

Music

Harrison Birtwistle, *Sir Gawain and the Green Knight* (opera).

Bryan Adams, 'Everything I Do, I Do For You'.

Nirvana, *Nevermind* – emergence of grunge music from Seattle, USA.

Literature

Angela Carter, *Wise Children.*

Bret Easton Ellis, *American Psycho.*

Ben Okri, *The Famished Road.*

John Updike, *Rabbit at Rest* (concluding volume of *Rabbit* quartet).

Drama Alan Bennett, *The Madness of George III.*

Ariel Dorfman, *Death and the Maiden.*

Everyday Life

Sonic the Hedgehog leads Sega's computer-game war against Nintendo's *Mario Bros.*

Sport and Recreation

Twenty-two soccer clubs break away from the English Football League, under the auspices of the Football Association, to form a 'premier league'; it commences in Aug 1992.

Media

Closure of *The Listener* magazine in Britain (first published 1929).

A consortium led by Canadian businessman Conrad Black takes over the Fairfax Group of newspapers in Australia.

(13th March) Robert Maxwell purchases *The New York Daily News.*

(5th Nov) Following the death of British businessman Robert Maxwell, the *Mirror* group is taken over and run by receivers; *The European* ceases publication (revived in 1992).

Film *Beauty and the Beast* (director, Walt Disney).

The Double Life of Véronique (director, Krzysztof Kieślowski).

JFK (director, Oliver Stone).

Silence of the Lambs (director, Jonathan Demme; starring Jodie Foster and Anthony Hopkins).

Thelma and Louise (director, Ridley Scott).

Television New programmes in Britain include: *GBH*, by Alan Bleasdale; *Noel's House Party* (BBC); *Prime Suspect*, starring Linda La Plante.

Statistics

Populations (in millions): China, 1,149.7; India, 871.2; USSR, 291.0; US, 252.0; Indonesia, 181.5; Brazil 153.3; Pakistan, 126.4; Japan, 123.9; Nigeria, 123.8; Bangladesh, 115.6; Mexico, 82.2; Germany, 79.0; Vietnam, 67.6; Philippines, 62.4; Italy, 57.6; Great Britain and Northern Ireland, 57.6; Turkey, 57.3; Iran, 57.0; France, 56.9.

1992

Jan: 1st, Boutros Boutros Ghali becomes UN Secretary-General on retirement of Javier Perez de Cuellar.

15th, EC recognizes Croatia and Slovenia as independent republics.

March: 1st, Referendum in Bosnia-Herzegovina, boycotted by Bosnian Serbs, decides in favour of becoming an independent sovereign state.

2nd, violent clashes take place in Sarajevo between militant Serbs, Croats, and Muslims.

April: 6th, in Italy's general election, established parties suffer losses to the Lombard League, the Greens, and the anti-Mafia La Rete Party.
7th, EC formally recognizes independence of Bosnia-Herzegovina; fighting escalates as federal air force aids Serb forces.
8th, Serb and federal army forces begin bombardment of Sarajevo.
9th, British General Election confounds predictions of opinion pollsters by returning the Conservatives for a fourth term, though with a reduced majority of 21. Conservatives win 336 seats, Labour, 271, Liberal Democrats, 20. (Conservatives receive 41.9% of votes cast, Labour, 34.4%, and Liberal Democrats, 17.8%).
9th, Neil Kinnock and Roy Hattersley resign as leader and deputy leader of British Labour Party.
29th, four white policemen in Los Angeles are acquitted of beating a black motorist, despite video-tape evidence; 30th–3rd May, 58 people die in riots and looting which break out in protest at the acquittals.

June: 2nd, Danish referendum votes against ratification of the Maastricht Treaty.
18th, referendum in Eire endorses ratification of Maastricht.

July: 18th, in Britain, John Smith is elected leader of the Labour Party and Margaret Beckett deputy leader.

Aug: 3rd, ANC begins 'mass action' protest campaign in South Africa.
13th, UN condemns the Serbs' 'ethnic cleansing' (forced removal) programme as a war crime.
22nd, (–26th) five nights of serious rioting at a reception centre for asylum seekers in Rostock marks resurgence of anti-foreigner violence in eastern Germany.

Sept: 16th, sterling crisis: British Chancellor of Exchequer, Norman Lamont, increases base rate from 10% to 12%, then to 15% in attempt to defend the pound against speculative selling; sterling is withdrawn from the ERM and allowed to 'float'; base rate returns to 12% (22nd, cut to 9%).
20th, French referendum produces vote narrowly in favour of ratification of Maastricht Treaty.

Oct: 13th, in Britain, announcements are made that coal production will cease at 31 of the country's 50 pits (19th, government postpones some of the closures after huge outcry and public support for the miners).
26th, Canadian referendum rejects Charlottetown reform agreement which would grant concessions to French-speaking Quebec.

Nov: 3rd, Democrat William Jefferson ('Bill') Clinton, Governor of Arkansas, wins the US presidential election with 370 electoral college votes. President Bush (Republican) gains 168 electoral votes and H Ross Perot (Independent) fails to win any, although he took 19% of the popular vote. In the Congressional elections, Democrats retain control of both chambers. popular vote: Clinton, 43,728,375; Bush, 38,167,416; Perot, 19,237,247.
16th, Goldstone Commission in South Africa exposes evidence of state 'dirty tricks' campaign against the ANC.

Dec: 6th, Hindu extremists demolish 16th-century mosque at Ayodhya, provoking sectarian violence throughout India which claims over 1,200 lives.
9th, US troops arrive in Mogadishu, Somalia, to oversee delivery of international food aid, in operation 'Restore Hope'.
9th, separation is announced of Prince and Princess of Wales (married 1981).
11th, (–12th) Edinburgh summit of EC heads of state meets Danish objections to Maastricht treaty.
16th, Czech National Council adopts Constitution for the new, separate, Czech Republic to come into being on 1st Jan 1993.
29th, Fernando Collor de Mello resigns as President of Brazil as impeachment proceedings begin against him in the Senate (30th, found guilty of corruption and official misconduct, and banned from public office for eight years).

Politics, Government, Law, and Economy

The Lloyds insurance market in London reveal losses of £2bn, the first in a series of severe losses.
(2nd Jan) Price controls are lifted in Russia, Ukraine, and many other CIS republics.
(13th Feb) Carl Bildt announces end of Sweden's policy of neutrality.
(5th March) Establishment of Council of Baltic Sea States, to aid economic development and strengthen links with the European Community.
(2nd April) John Gotti, head of largest Mafia family in New York, is convicted of murder and racketeering.

Society, Education, and Religion

J K Galbraith, *The Culture of Contentment.*

Polytechnics and several colleges of higher education in Britain are granted university status.

Ten women are ordained to the Anglican priesthood in Australia, despite a ruling against by the New South Wales Court of Appeal.

Senior Church of England bishops devise a two-tier system of episcopal oversight to enable opponents of women priests to stay within the Church in the event of the General Synod voting in favour of women's ordination.

In Britain, a Methodist Church report supports inclusive language in publications and condemns patriarchy as deep sin.

(6th Feb) Barbara Mills, QC, is appointed first woman Director of Public Prosecutions in England and Wales.

(27th April) In Britain, Betty Boothroyd is elected the first woman speaker of the House of Commons.

(12th Oct) Demonstrations held in many Latin American countries against celebrations of 500th anniversary of arrival of Columbus in the Americas.

(31st Oct) Vatican formally rehabilitates Galileo Galilei, forced by the Inquisition in 1633 to recant his assertion that the Earth orbits the Sun.

(11th Nov) The Church of England General Synod votes to allow women to be ordained to the priesthood.

Science, Technology, and Discovery

(11th Feb) President Bush announces that the USA will phase out CFCs by 1995, five years earlier than planned; Michael Heseltine makes a similar announcement for Britain (14th).

(3rd June) (–14th) The United Nations holds a Conference on Environment and Development in Rio de Janeiro, Brazil, attended by delegates from 178 countries; most countries sign binding conventions on prevention of climate change and preservation of biodiversity.

Humanities and Scholarship

Bruce Redford (ed.), *The Letters of Samuel Johnson.*

The Cambridge History of the English Language.

Art, Sculpture, Fine Arts, and Architecture

Sculpture Damian Hirst, *The Physical Impossibility of Death in the Mind of Someone Living.*

Music

Whitney Houston, 'I Will Always Love You'.

The Orb, *U F Orb* – ambient house music.

Shamen, 'Ebeneezer Goode'.

Literature

Jung Chang, *Wild Swans.*

Ian McEwan, *Black Dogs.*

Michael Ondaatje, *The English Patient.*

Drama Tony Kushner, *Angels in America.*

Everyday Life

(19th March) Buckingham Palace announces the separation of Duke and Duchess of York (married 1986).

(23rd April) In Britain, Princess Royal is granted divorce from Captain Mark Phillips.

(20th Aug) The *Daily Mirror* publishes compromising photographs of the Duchess of York on holiday in France with a so-called 'financial adviser' (24th, newspapers carry transcript of a telephone conversation allegedly between Princess of Wales and an intimate male friend).

Sport and Recreation

(25th July) (–9th Aug) The 25th Olympic Games are held in Barcelona, Spain. The Unified Team (comprising the 11 nations of the Commonwealth of Independent States and Georgia) wins 45 gold medals; USA, 37; Germany, 33; China, 16; Cuba, 14; Spain, 13; South Korea, 12; Hungary, 11; France, 8; Australia, 7; Italy and Canada, 6 each. Chris Boardman, in the 4,000 m individual pursuit, becomes the first Briton to win an Olympic cycling gold since 1908.

Media

(8th April) Closure of *Punch* in Britain (first published 1841; relaunched Sept 1996).

Film *Howard's End* (director, James Ivory; starring Anthony Hopkins and Emma Thompson).

Orlando (director, Sally Potter).

The Player (director, Robert Altman).

Tous les Matins du Monde (director, Alain Corneau).

1993

Jan: 1st, European Community's single market comes into force.

1st, Czech and Slovak republics become separate sovereign countries.

14th, in USA, President Clinton's choice for post of Attorney General, Zoë Baird, is revealed to be under FBI investigation for employing illegal immigrants (5th Feb, second choice Kimba Wood withdraws on the same grounds).

Feb: 10th, In Italy, first of a series of ministerial resignations as corruption scandal shakes government.

22nd, UN Security Council decides to create war crimes tribunal relating to former Yugoslavia – the first such tribunal since Nuremberg (1945–46).

March: 10th, in USA, gynaecologist Dr David Gunn is shot dead by an anti-abortion activist in Pensacola, Florida, in wave of violent attacks on abortion clinics by 'Rescue America'.

12th, emergency session of Russian Congress votes to restrict powers of president and defeats Yeltsin's constitutional amendments (20th, Yeltsin announces 'special rule' and sets date for referendum on constitution; 28th, attempt to dismiss Yeltsin are defeated in Congress).

12th, North Korea withdraws from Treaty on Nuclear Non-Proliferation of Nuclear Weapons.

16th, in Britain, Chancellor Norman Lamont announces imposition of Value Added Tax on domestic fuel.

27th, Jiang Zemin becomes state president of China.

29th, Edouard Balladur becomes prime minister of France after victory for right-wing RPR–UDF alliance in elections; ruling Socialist Party retain only 54 of their 252 seats.

May: 4th, opening of Scott inquiry into British Government's involvement in export of arms to Iraq.

6th, UN Security Council declares 'safe areas' in Sarajevo, Tuzla, Zepa, Goradze, Bihać, and Srebrenica in Bosnia-Herzegovina (30th, Bosnian Serbs attack Goradze and Srebrenica).

18th, in second referendum, Denmark approves the Maastricht Treaty by a narrow majority.

27th, US House of Representatives narrowly votes to approve Clinton's programme of tax increases and spending cuts.

29th, five Turkish women are killed in a neo-Nazi arson attack in Solingen, Germany (Turkish demonstrations and rioting throughout Germany over following days).

June: 13th, Kim Campbell, Progressive Conservative, becomes first woman prime minister of Canada.

23rd, international sanctions are imposed on Haiti.

July: 18th, after governing Japan since 1955, the Liberal Democrats lose their overall majority in general election (6th Aug, replaced by seven-party coalition).

22nd, in Britain, government fails to win vote on the Maastricht Treaty in House of Commons; 23rd, government policy is confirmed by vote of confidence, proposed by Prime Minister John Major with threat of dissolution if the government loses.

Aug: 2nd, Following speculative pressure on currencies in the European Exchange Rate Mechanism, the Mechanism collapses and currencies are allowed to fluctuate within broad band of 15% on either side of central rates.

Sept: 13th, in Washington, DC, USA, peace agreement (the 'Declaration of Principles') is signed between Israel and the Palestine Liberation Organization, providing for Israeli withdrawal from Gaza Strip and Jericho; Yassir Arafat and Yitzhak Rabin shake hands.

21st, Yeltsin suspends Russian parliament and calls elections; Supreme Soviet defies this action and swears in Alexandr Rutskoi as President.

27th, White House in Moscow, seat of Russian parliament, is sealed off by troops (telephone links, water and electricity supplies had been cut off in preceding days).

Oct: 4th, Rebels holding out in Moscow parliament building surrender after fire breaks out; state of emergency in force until 18th Oct.

25th, Liberal Party wins decisive victory in Canadian general election; Progressive Conservative Party, in office since 1984, retains only two seats, while Bloc Québecois becomes second-largest party (4th Nov, Liberal leader Jean Chrétien is sworn in as prime minister).

Nov: 1st, Maastricht Treaty (the Treaty on European Union) comes into force; the European Community becomes the European Union (EU).

Dec: 12th, in legislative elections in Russia, largest share of vote (22.8%) goes to nationalist Liberal Democratic Party of Russia, led by Vladimir Zhirinovsky; voters approve Yeltsin's draft constitution in simultaneous referendum.

14th, Downing Street declaration sets out principles for peace talks on Northern Ireland.

Politics, Government, Law, and Economy

Margaret Thatcher, *The Downing Street Years*.

In Italy, end of the 'First Republic' as referendum supports change to the electoral system, replacing proportional representation by one-member constituencies.

In Britain, two 11-year-old boys, Robert Thompson and Jon Venables, are convicted of the murder of two-year-old James Bulger in Liverpool, NW England, in Feb.

(11th Feb) Queen Elizabeth II of Britain and the Prince of Wales both volunteer to pay income tax

and capital gains tax on their private income; the Queen also takes over civil list payments to junior members of the royal family.
(25th Feb) First direct elections to national assembly held in Cuba, with official turn-out of 99.6%.
(17th May) In Britain, nurse Beverley Allitt is convicted of murdering four babies under her care at the Grantham and Kesteven hospital.
(30th Nov) In USA, the Brady Act (named after former White House press secretary James Brady, who was wounded during attempted assassination of President Reagan in 1981) introduces some controls on acquisition of firearms.
(15th Dec) The prime ministers of Britain and the Republic of Ireland (John Major and Albert Reynolds) make the 'Downing Street Declaration', stating basis for trying to achieve peace in Northern Ireland.
(15th Dec) Conclusion in Geneva, Switzerland, of the 'Uruguay Round' of negotiations for a revised General Agreement on Tariffs and Trade (started Sept 1986); 117 nations agree the GATT Final Act.

Society, Education, and Religion

Community Care Act in Britain changes the way in which health and social services deal with the elderly, disabled, and mentally ill (in theory providing for care at a more local level rather than in institutions).
The Education Act makes it easier for schools in England and Wales to 'opt out' of local authority control; permits the establishment of specialist Technology Colleges; and provides for the establishment of a Funding Agency for Schools and for 'Educational Associations' to run schools judged to be 'failing'.
E P Sandars, *The Historical Figure of Jesus.*
(12th March) Janet Reno becomes the first woman to be appointed attorney general of the USA.
(19th April) In USA, FBI siege of headquarters of Branch Davidian cult in Waco, Texas, ends after 51 days, with the compound consumed by fire; cult leader David Koresh is amongst the dead.
(5th Oct) Papal encyclical *Veritatis splendor* (The Splendour of Truth) is published; it condemns relative moral judgements and affirms Catholic moral teaching.

Science, Technology, and Discovery

In Princeton, USA, the most successful nuclear fusion experiment yet, when hydrogen isotopes are heated to 300 million degrees, creating 3 million watts of power.
British mathematician Andrew Wiles solves 'Fermat's Last Theorem', a mathematical problem posed by the French mathematician Pierre de Fermat, 1601–65.
Dean Hammer and colleagues at the US National Cancer Institute publish the approximate location of a gene that could predispose male humans to homosexuality.
(15th Sept) Publication in USA of *The National Information Infrastructure: Agenda for Action*, proposing framework for the creation of a national 'information highway'.

Humanities and Scholarship

Andrew Motion, *Philip Larkin: A Writer's Life.*
Michael Dummett, *Origins of Analytical Philosophy.*

Art, Sculpture, Fine Arts, and Architecture

It is revealed that Russia possesses the 'Schliemann Gold' – objects found by Heinrich Schliemann at Troy in 1873 which disappeared from Berlin at the end of World War II.
Architecture Alex Schultes wins competition to build new administrative district around the Reichstag, Berlin, Germany.
Sculpture In Britain, Rachel Whiteread is awarded the Turner Prize for *House*, the plaster cast of the inside of a house in the East End of London; she also receives a spoof prize from the 'K Foundation' for the 'worst artist of the year'.

Music

Rise of Ragga.
Suede, *Suede.*
Take That, *Everything Changes*, 'Pray', *Take That And Party.*
U2, *Zoorupa.*

Literature

Isabel Allende, *The Infinite Plain.*
Roddy Doyle, *Paddy Clarke Ha Ha Ha.*
Vikram Seth, *A Suitable Boy.*
Drama Harold Pinter, *Moonlight.*

Everyday Life

Genetic material from the Duke of Edinburgh and other relatives of the Romanov royal family in Russia are compared, using techniques of 'genetic fingerprinting', with the supposed remains of Nicholas II and his family, proving that the remains are genuine.

(22nd May) In USA, the runways at Los Angeles airport are closed for about 40 minutes while Christophe, a fashionable Beverly Hills hairdresser, cuts President Bill Clinton's hair on board his official plane, Air Force One; in addition to the cost of disrupting air traffic, the cut costs $200 and the incident becomes known as 'Hairgate'.

(6th Aug) Buckingham Palace, London, is opened to the general public.

Sport and Recreation

(3rd April) In horse racing, the Grand National (held at the Aintree course in NW England) is declared void after two false starts. Over half the runners fail to respond to the second red (cancellation) flag and complete the course. The void race is won by Esha Ness, ridden by John White.

Media

Film *In the Name of the Father* (director, Jim Sheridan; starring Daniel Day Lewis).

Jurassic Park (director, Steven Spielberg).

Philadelphia (director, Jonathan Demme).

The Remains of the Day (director, James Ivory).

Schindler's List (director, Steven Spielberg).

Radio Following a public campaign against the BBC's plan to stop broadcasting Radio 4 on long wave, the proposal is withdrawn, enabling listeners in Europe to continue to hear *The Archers* and other popular programmes.

Television US businessman Rupert Murdoch purchases Star TV, a five-channel satellite station based in Hong Kong and broadcasting to an estimate 40 million viewers in Asia.

In Britain, following competition for franchises, four commercial stations lose their licences and are replaced by new companies.

1994 **Jan: 1st**, Zapatista National Liberation Army leads rebellion of Indian groups in state of Chiapas, Mexico.

31st, Gerry Adams, president of Irish republican party Sinn Féin, is granted a visa to visit the USA.

Feb: 21st, former head of CIA Soviet counterintelligence, Aldrich Hazen Ames, is arrested with his wife on charges of having spied for the USSR.

March: 1st, Negotiations are concluded on enlargement of European Union to include Sweden, Finland, and Austria; on 16th, Norway is also included.

18th, Bosnia-Herzegovina and Croatia sign accord on creation of a federation of Bosnian Muslims and Croats.

24th, allegations are made in the US Congress that President and Mrs Clinton may have used their part-ownership of the Whitewater Development Corporation in Arkansas for improper purposes, especially in connection with the failed Madison Guaranty Savings bank (the affair becomes known as 'Whitewatergate').

24th, factions in Somalia sign peace agreement (25th, US troops withdraw).

26th, (–27th) in Italy, Freedom Alliance led by businessman Silvio Berlusconi wins parliamentary election.

April: —, The presidents of Rwanda and Burundi, respectively Juvénal Habyarimana and Cyprien Ntaryamira, are killed in an air crash; violence erupts on huge scale, with hundreds killed in Rwanda's capital Kigali.

26th, (–29th) first non-racial general election in South Africa, which results in an overwhelming victory for the African National Congress.

May: 10th, in South Africa, Nelson Mandela is sworn in as president; 11th, new cabinet includes representatives from all four racial groups into which the population had been divided under apartheid.

12th, in Britain, sudden death of John Smith, leader of the Labour Party (21st July, Tony Blair is elected leader).

13th, Israel withdraws military forces from the Jericho area of the occupied West Bank to make way for self-rule by Palestinian National Authority; 18th, withdraws from Gaza Strip.

June: 1st, South Africa rejoins the Commonwealth.

15th, Jimmy Carter, former president of the USA, visits North Korea and helps diffuse crisis over nuclear inspections.

24th, (–25th) summit of EU heads of government at which, on 25th, Prime Minister John Major of Britain vetoes nomination of Jean-Luc Dehaene, prime minister of Belgium, as president of the European Commission (15th July, Jacques Santer, prime minister of Luxembourg, is chosen as president).

July: 1st, Yassir Arafat, chairman of the Palestine Liberation Organization, enters Gaza, setting foot on Palestinian territory for the first time for 25 years; 5th, visits Jericho.

8th, leader of North Korea, Kim Il Sung, dies at age of 82.

16th, (–22nd) fragments of the comet Shoemaker-Levy 9 collide with Jupiter.

18th, Rwandan Patriotic Front claims victory in Rwandan civil war; Pasteur Bizimungu assumes presidency; 24th, over 2 million Rwandans are reported to have left the country; international relief effort airlifts supplies to vast refugee camps on the borders as cholera spreads and many refugees remain afraid to return home (1st Aug, UN establishes commission to investigate human rights violations in Rwanda).

25th, King Hussein of Jordan and Yitzhak Rabin, prime minister of Israel, sign joint declaration in Washington, DC, USA, formally ending their conflict (26th Oct, peace treaty is signed in a desert ceremony on border between Jordan and Israel).

31st, UN Security Council authorizes 'all necessary means' to remove military regime in Haiti.

Aug: 14th, 'Carlos the Jackal', wanted for numerous terrorist attacks, is arrested in Khartoum, Sudan.

31st, in Northern Ireland, Irish Republican Army announces complete cessation of violence (16th Sept, British government lifts broadcasting ban on representatives of Sinn Féin).

Sept: 19th, US troops invade Haiti, encountering no resistance; 26th, USA lifts sanctions.

26th, in USA, President Clinton's attempts to introduce health-care reforms collapse in face of opposition from legislature.

28th, car ferry *Estonia* sinks in the Baltic off Finland, with loss of estimated 900 lives.

Oct: 15th, President Aristide returns to Haiti after three years in exile; 17th, Aristide agrees to leave the Roman Catholic priesthood in attempt to mend relationship with the Vatican, which opposed his liberation theology and had been the only sovereign state to recognize Cédras's military regime.

Nov: 8th, Democrats suffer defeat in US mid-term elections; Republicans gain control of House of Representatives and achieve majority in Senate for first time in 40 years.

22nd, Italian Prime Minister Silvio Berlusconi is revealed to be under investigation for bribery.

25th, (–26th) in breakaway Russian republic of Chechnya, opposition forces with Russian backing launch unsuccessful attack on the capital Grozny; 29th, Yeltsin issues an ultimatum, requiring both sides in Chechnya to lay down their arms.

27th, (–28th) Norwegian referendum rejects EU membership.

Dec: 11th, Russian forces invade the breakaway republic of Chechnya.

15th, in Republic of Ireland, following the resignation of Albert Reynolds as prime minister, John Bruton of Fine Gael forms a new coalition and becomes prime minister.

22nd, Silvio Berlusconi, the new prime minister of Italy, resigns to avoid probable defeat in no-confidence vote in parliament.

31st, Russian forces launch offensive against Grozny, the capital of the breakaway republic of Chechnya.

Politics, Government, Law, and Economy

The Criminal Justice and Public Order Act in Britain criminalizes squatting and trespass by protesters, restricts the right to silence, and introduces a new police caution.

(1st Jan) North American Free Trade Agreement (NAFTA), between Mexico, the USA, and Canada comes into effect.

(1st Jan) Second stage of economic and monetary union in Europe comes into force with establishment of European Economic Area.

(21st Jan) In Virginia, USA, Lorena Bobbitt is cleared of maliciously wounding her husband after she cut off his penis (June 1993); it was accepted that she had become temporarily insane.

(12th July) Federal Constitutional Court in Germany approves principle that Germany's armed forces can be deployed outside the NATO area in collective security operations.

(9th July) Government of the People's Republic of China announces that Hong Kong's legislative council will be terminated on China's resumption of sovereignty in 1997; it rejects the reform package approved in the colony on 30th June.

(17th Dec) In Ouro Preto, Brazil, the presidents of Argentina, Brazil, Paraguay, and Uruguay sign pact creating the Southern Common Market (Mercosur), the world's second-largest customs union (in force from 1st Jan 1995).

Society, Education, and Religion

Homosexual age of consent lowered to 18 in Britain.

(12th March) In England, first women priests in Church of England are ordained in a service at Bristol Cathedral.

(26th May) In USA, Freedom of Access Act declares that the obstruction of abortion clinics and places of worship is a federal offence.

(8th Nov) In Oregon, USA, voters support Measure 16, permitting euthanasia in regulated circumstances for the terminally ill.

Science, Technology, and Discovery

The Hubble Space Telescope takes clear pictures of galaxies in their infancy (published 6th Dec).

(6th May) Inauguration of Channel Tunnel between Britain and France, with ceremony attended by Queen Elizabeth II and President Mitterrand.

Humanities and Scholarship

Eric Hobsbawm, *Age of Extremes: The Short Twentieth Century, 1914–1991.*

Gerhard L Weinberg, *A World at Arms: A Global History of World War II.*

William Child, *Causality, Interpretation, and the Mind.*

Art, Sculpture, Fine Arts, and Architecture

Painting Completion of the controversial cleaning of Michelangelo's paintings in the Sistine Chapel in the Vatican.

Sculpture Damian Hirst, *Away from the Flock.*

Music

Peter Maxwell Davies, Symphony No. 5.

Blur, *Parklife.*

M People, *Elegant Slumming.*

Snoop Doggy Dogg, *Doggy Style.*

Wet Wet Wet, 'Love Is All Around'.

(8th April) Kurt Cobain of Nirvana commits suicide.

Literature

Joseph Heller, *Closing Time.*

V S Naipaul, *A Way in the World.*

Barbara Trapido, *Juggling.*

(27th May) Russian writer Alexander Solzhenitsyn returns to Russia after 20 years in exile.

Drama Terry Johnson, *Dead Funny.*

Arthur Miller, *Broken Glass.*

Everyday Life

(30th Sept) Russian presidential plane lands at Shannon airport in Republic of Ireland, but President Yeltsin remains on board, failing to meet the prime minister of Ireland who was waiting for him on the runway.

Sport and Recreation

West Indian cricketer Brian Lara sets four records: he makes highest individual Test scores of 375 runs (18th April, playing against England in Antigua) and 501 runs (6th June, playing in England for Warwickshire against Durham at Edgbaston); during the June match he also achieves a record seven centuries in eight innings and scores a record 390 runs in one day (3rd and 6th June respectively).

(30th Jan) In chess, Peter Leko becomes the world's youngest-ever grand master.

(30th March) The West Indies cricket team dismisses England for 46, the lowest total reached by an English side since 1887.

(2nd July) Andrés Escobar, the Colombian soccer player who scored an own goal in the match that eliminated Colombia from the World Cup, is murdered on his return to Medellín.

Media

Newspaper price war in Britain: the *Telegraph* cuts its sale price (22nd June) in response to price cut by *The Times* in 1993; the *Independent* follows (31st July).

Film *Forrest Gump* (director, David Zemeckis; starring Tom Hanks).

Four Weddings and a Funeral (director, Mike Newell).

Natural Born Killers (director, Oliver Stone).

Pulp Fiction (director and writer, Quentin Tarantino).

Radio (28th March) In Britain, the BBC launches Radio Five Live, a channel dedicated to news and sport.

1995

Jan: 1st, Austria, Finland, and Sweden join the European Union.

2nd, Chechen fighters repel the Russian offensive against Grozny, the capital of the breakaway republic of Chechnya (started 31st Dec 1994); 3rd, the Russian army resumes its offensive (19th, Russian troops capture the presidential palace, the main centre of Chechen resistance; 8th Feb, Chechens withdraw from Grozny while fighting continues elsewhere).

6th, the Sri Lankan government and the Tamil Tigers independence fighters sign a cease-fire (April, fighting resumes).

Feb: 22nd, the British and Irish governments present a framework document for Northern Ireland peace negotiations.

28th, unable to end its civil war, UN troops withdraw from Somalia.

March: 5th, all members of the British colony of Hong Kong's regional and urban councils are elected for the first time; 'pro-democracy' parties do well.

20th, the cease-fire in Bosnia-Herzegovina (agreed Dec 1994) is broken when the Bosnian army attacks Serb positions (-30th, Serbs respond with attacks on government forces and Muslim towns).

April: 19th, in USA, a bomb explodes underneath a federal building in Oklahoma City, killing 166 people, the worst terrorist attack in American history.

30th, cease-fire in Bosnia-Herzegovina expires (May, violence escalates).

May: 7th, in France, Jacques Chirac (Gaullist) defeats Lionel Jospin (Socialist) for the presidency.

10th, British minister Michael Ancram meets Sínn Fein representatives, the first official meeting of a government minister and Sínn Fein since 1973.

16th, Serbs resume shelling of the besieged Bosnian capital, Sarajevo.

25th, NATO launches airstrikes against the Serbs after their refusal to surrender artillery.

26th, Bosnian Serbs hold UN troops hostage in response to the threat of NATO airstrikes (released 2nd-18th June).

June: 14th, Bosnian government forces launch a major offensive against Bosnian Serb forces; Bosnian Serbs renew bombardment of Sarajevo.

22nd, British Prime Minister John Major announces his resignation as Conservative Party leader in a bid to restore his authority in a leadership contest (4th July, Major defeats his challenger, John Redwood).

July: 11th, Serbs capture the UN-designated safe area of Srebrenica in E Bosnia-Herzegovina; Muslim women and children and moved to Tuzla while men are held back and massacred (25th, UN safe haven of Zepa falls to Serbs).

20th, Serbs and allies attack UN safe haven of Bihać in NW Bosnia-Herzegovina (27th, Croat troops enter Bosnia to relieve pressure on Bihać).

30th, a Chechen-Russian peace agreement is signed in Grozny.

Aug: 4th, (-9th) Croat armed forces invade and occupy the Serb-inhabited region of Krajina in Croatia; Serb refugees pour into Serb areas of Bosnia-Herzegovina and Serbia.

10th, several close relatives of Iraqi President Saddam Hussein who hold government positions defect to Jordan in protest at his despotic rule (23rd Feb 1996, they return and are executed).

28th, Serb troops in Bosnia-Herzegovina bombard Sarajevo market place, killing 37 people.

30th, NATO aircraft begin large-scale attacks on Serb positions in Bosnia.

Sept: 8th, in Geneva, representatives of the 'Contact Group' (Britain, France, Germany, Russia, and the USA) and the foreign ministers of Bosnia-Herzegovina, Croatia, and Yugoslavia agree basic principles between the warring parties in Bosnia.

11th, Bosnian government forces launch an offensive in W and central Bosnia-Herzegovina, reducing Serb-controlled territory from 70 to 50%.

Oct: 5th, the agreement of a 60-day cease-fire in Bosnia-Herzegovina is announced (12th, comes into effect).

20th, Willy Claes, NATO Secretary-General, resigns after the Belgian parliament lifts his immunity from prosecution so that he can be tried for alleged corruption.

30th, in Quebec, voters in a referendum narrowly defeat the proposal that the province should leave the Canadian federation (50.56% against).

Nov: 1st, in USA, peace talks between the warring parties in Bosnia-Herzegovina are held near Dayton.

4th, Israeli prime minister Yitzhak Rabin is assassinated in Tel Aviv, Israel.

Dec: 14th, in Paris, a peace plan for Bosnia-Herzegovina is signed, creating a Muslim-Croat federation and a Serb republic within Bosnia-Herzegovina, and replacing a UN peacekeeping force with a NATO implementation force.

Politics, Government, Law, and Economy

Will Hutton, *The State We're In*.

(1st Jan) The World Trade Organization is inaugurated, the successor organization to the General Agreement on Tariffs and Trade (GATT), to regulate commercial relations between signatory nations.

(26th Jan) Britain's oldest merchant bank, Barings, is placed in administration after Nicholas Leeson, a Singapore-based futures trader, accumulates massive losses. It is bought by the Internationale Nederlande Groep NV of the Netherlands.

(29th April) A special conference of the British Labour Party confirms the replacement of its 1918 constitution's socialistic Clause IV with a new statement of aims and values.

(3rd Oct) The former American football star O J Simpson is acquitted of the murders of his former wife Nicole Brown Simpson and her friend Ronald Goldman (on 12th June 1994) after claims of racial bias in the investigating police force.

(Nov) The former French colony of Cameroon (1st) and the former Portuguese colony of Mozambique (13th) are admitted to the Commonwealth.

Society, Education, and Religion

(20th March) A release of the nerve gas sarin on the Tokyo underground by a Japanese religious sect, Aum Shinrikyo, kills 12 people and injures about 5,000.

(27th Nov) A referendum in Ireland votes in favour of maintaining the illegality of divorce.

Science, Technology, and Discovery

The Prince Gustav Ice Shelf and the northern Larsen Ice Shelf in Antarctica begin to disintegrate – a result of global warming.

(4th Jan) The first atoms of antimatter are created at the CERN research centre in Switzerland.

(April) The British police establish the world's first national DNA (deoxyribonucleic acid) database.

(Aug) Microsoft launches Windows 95, a new computer operating system.

Humanities and Scholarship

Christopher Lasch, *The Revolt of the Elites and the Betrayal of Democracy.*

(6th Aug) Scholars meet at the University of Mississippi, Oxford, Mississippi, for the first annual International Conference on Elvis Presley.

(28th Sept) The net book agreement (setting minimum prices for books) is abolished in Britain.

Art, Sculpture, Fine Arts, and Architecture

Architecture Moshe Safdie, Library Square, Vancouver, Canada.

Painting Delmas Howe, *Liberty, Equality, and Fraternity.*

Music

The Beatles, *Anthology 1*, 'Free As A Bird' (their first new single for 25 years).

Alanis Morissette, 'You Oughta Know', *Jagged Little Pill.*

In Britain, 'Britpop' comes to the fore – song-based pop, inspired by 1960s British bands.

Blur, 'Country House', *The Great Escape.*

Oasis, 'Some Might Say', 'Roll With It', *(What's the Story?) Morning Glory.*

Pulp, *Different Class.*

Literature

Martin Amis, *The Information.*

Kate Atkinson, *Behind the Scenes at the Museum.*

Pat Barker, *The Ghost Road* (the final part of her 'Regeneration' Trilogy).

Drama Timberlake Wertenbaker, *Break of Day.*

Sport and Recreation

(31st March) After 232 days, the major-league baseball strike in the US over the proposed capping of players' salaries is called off. The strike had caused the first-ever cancellation of the World Series.

(18th Sept) The International Association of Professional Footballers is founded by Eric Cantona and Diego Maradona.

Media

(17th Nov) The last edition of the British newspaper *Today* is published (launched 1986).

Film *Babe* (director, Chris Noonan).

Goldeneye (director, Martin Campbell; starring Pierce Brosnan as James Bond).

Il Postino/The Postman (director, Michael Radford).

Sense and Sensibility (director, Ang Lee; starring Emma Thompson and Kate Winslet).

In USA, Steven Spielberg, Jeffrey Katzenberg and David Geffen found Dreamworks SKG, the first major Hollywood studio to be founded since 1935.

Television (15th Feb) The Iranian parliament passes a law banning the import, distribution and private use of satellite reception dishes.

Statistics

Population of cities (in millions): Tokyo (21.9); São Paulo (16.4); New York (16.3); Mexico City (15.6); Bombay (15.1); Shanghai (15.1); Los Angeles (12.4); Beijing (12.4).

1996

Jan: 21st, in the first Palestinian general elections, the PLO leader Yassir Arafat is chosen as president.

Feb: 9th, the IRA breaks its cease-fire (in force since Aug 1994) with a bomb in E London.

19th, in Madrid, Spain, one million people demonstrate against the violence of the Basque separatist group ETA.

24th, Cuban forces shoot down two light aircraft from the organization 'Brothers to the Rescue', formed by expatriate Cubans to assist those attempting to escape to the USA.

March: 8th, (-25th) China stages military exercises in the Taiwan Strait in an attempt to intimidate voters in Taiwan's first free presidential elections.

25th, the EU bans the export of British beef after fears over the potential transmission of the cattle disease BSE to humans as CJD (Creutzfeld-Jakob disease) (1st April, Britain proposes a programme to eradicate the disease, involving the mass culling of older cattle).

April: 6th, fighting resumes in the Liberian civil war (10th, the USA deploys warships off the Liberian coast to evacuate its citizens and other foreign nationals).

23rd, the Commonwealth votes to impose sanctions on Nigeria in protest of human-rights abuses.

May: 10th, in Hong Kong, 3000 Vietnamese boat people riot in protest at plans to repatriate them.

21st, Britain begins a policy of non-cooperation with its European partners to protest the EU ban on British beef exports (21st June, the policy ends when a deal is made for the lifting of the ban).

June: 10th, multi-party talks on the future of Northern Ireland begin in Belfast; Sínn Fein, the IRA's political wing, is not admitted because of the IRA's cease-fire violations.

July: 7th, (-13th) violence follows the ban of a controversial Loyalist apprentice boys' march in Londonderry, Northern Ireland (11th, the ban is lifted so that the march can take place).

9th, Boris Yeltsin is inaugurated as Russian president, having been successful in his bid for re-election.

Aug: 6th, (-8th) Chechen rebels launch a major offensive on Grozny, capturing key points there.

11th, (-14th) fierce inter-ethnic fighting flares up in Cyprus between the Greek and Turkish communities.

16th, a peace agreement to end the Liberian civil war is signed in Ajuba, Nigeria.

22nd, a cease-fire is negotiated between Russia and Chechnya for the breakaway Russian republic (29th, a peace deal postpones a decision on sovereignty until 2001).

31st, Iraqi aircraft violated the UN no-fly zone in N Iraq to attack Kurdish targets (3rd Sept, the USA launches cruise missiles against S Iraq).

Sept: 27th, in Afghanistan, the Taliban Islamic fundamentalist movement takes over the capital, Kabul, and imposes Islamic law.

Oct: 21st, the UN High Commission for Refugees reports that 250,000 Hutu refugees have fled NE Zaire after fighting between ethnic Tutsi Banyamulenge and Zairean armed forces (15th Nov, the refugee crisis in Zaire and Rwanda is defused when Tutsi armed rebels defeat extremist Hutu militiamen, and allow 700,000 Hutus under their control to return to Rwanda).

Nov: 5th, in USA, Bill Clinton is re-elected president, defeating Republican Bob Dole, with 379 electoral college votes to 159. Popular vote: Clinton, 45,590,703; Dole, 37,816,307; Reform candidate Ross Perot, 7,866,284. Republicans retain control of both houses of Congress.

11th, a Saudi Arabian airliner and a Kazakh plane collide near Delhi, India, killing 351 people, the worst midair collision ever.

Dec: 21st, loyalist terrorists break their cease-fire (in force since August 1994) with a car-bomb attack in Belfast.

29th: the Guatemalan government signs an agreement ending its civil war (waged since 1961) with the Guatemalan National Revolutionary Unity Movement.

Politics, Government, Law, and Economy

(29th April) A UN war crimes tribunal opens in The Hague, the Netherlands, to investigate alleged crimes against humanity committed during the Yugoslavian civil war. (19th July) Radovan Karadžić, president of the Serb region of Bosnia-Herzegovina, resigns after his indictment on war crimes charges.

(1st July) The first legislation in the world permitting euthansia takes effect in the Northern Territory, Australia. (24th March 1997, the federal Senate overturns the law.)

(15th Nov) The petroleum giant Texaco makes an out-of-court settlement in the USA of $175 million with former employees claiming racial discrimination.

Society, Education, and Religion

In Britain, the Orange Prize for the best novel in English written by a woman is inaugurated. The first winner is Helen Dunmore for *A Spell of Winter*.

(5th Dec) Madeleine Albright becomes the first female US secretary of state.

Science, Technology, and Discovery

US geophysicists discover that the Earth's core spins slightly faster than the rest of the planet.

A new human muscle is discovered. Running from the jaw to just behind the eye socket, it helps to support and raise the jaw.

The World Health Organization (WHO) launches an obesity task force in Barcelona, Spain, to combat a worldwide epidemic of obesity.

(5th Dec) General Motors launches the Saturn EV1, the first mass-market electric car, in California and Arizona, USA. Sales are slow due to a lack of recharging centres.

Humanities and Scholarship

Daniel Jonah Goldhagen, *Hitler's Willing Executioners: Ordinary Germans and the Holocaust.*
Robert Fagles publishes his new English translation of Homer's *Odyssey.*

Art, Sculpture, Fine Arts, and Architecture

Architecture Poundbury, England, a new town sponsored by Prince Charles and designed by Luxembourg architect Leon Krier, opens its first 250 homes.
(9th March) The Petronas Towers (designed by Cesar Pelli), under construction in Kuala Lumpur, Malaysia, become the tallest buildings in the world at 452m/1,483 ft tall.

Music

Luciano Berio, *Outis* (opera).
Jonathan Larson, *Rent* (rock musical, based on Giacomo Puccini's *La Bohème*).
Robert Miles, 'Children'.
Prodigy, 'Firestarter'.
Spice Girls, 'Wannabe', *Spice.*

Literature

Margaret Atwood, *Alias Grace.*
Seamus Deane, *Reading in the Dark.*
Junot Díaz, *Drown.*
T S Eliot, *Inventions of the March Hare: Poems, 1909-1917* (published posthumously).
Graham Swift, *Last Orders.*
Drama Yasmina Reza (translated by Christopher Hampton), *Art.*
(Aug) The restored Globe Theatre opens on the South Bank of London with a production of William Shakespeare's *The Two Gentlemen of Verona.*

Everyday Life

Attack dogs become the most popular pets in Russia, as increased security measures become necessary after the collapse of communism. In Moscow, attacks by dogs increase by more than 50% during the year. Owners are the most frequent victims.
(28th Aug) The marriage of Charles and Diana, Prince and Princess of Wales, is formally ended.

Sport and Recreation

(14th April) The English golfer Nick Faldo becomes the first European to win the US Masters three times, and is the first British golfer to win six major tournaments since 1914.
(19th July) (-4th Aug) The 26th Olympic Games are held in Atlanta, USA. The USA wins 44 gold medals; Russia, 26; Germany, 20; China, 16; France, 15; Italy, 13; and Australia, Cuba, and Ukraine, 9 each. (27th July) A bomb explodes in Centennial Olympic Park, Atlanta, killing 2 people.

Media

Film *Breaking the Waves* (director, Lars von Trier).
The English Patient (director, Anthony Minghella; starring Ralph Fiennes, Kristin Scott Thomas).
Fargo (director, Joel Coen).
Independence Day (director, Roland Emmerich; starring Will Smith).
Trainspotting (director, Danny Boyle; starring Ewan McGregor).
Television New programmes in Britain include: *Cold Lazarus* and *Karaoke* (BBC and C4), by Dennis Potter; *Our Friends in the North* (BBC).

1997

Jan: 1st, Kofi Annan of Ghana replaces Boutros Boutros Ghali as UN Secretary-General.
15th, agreement signed between Israel and the PLO reaffirming Israeli withdrawal from the West Bank town of Hebron (17th, troops are withdrawn).
26th, serious violence breaks out in Albania protesting the collapse of pyramid savings schemes (1st March, state of emergency is declared).

Feb: 23rd, Deng Xiao-ping, China's 'paramount leader' since 1978, dies aged 92.

March: 6th, in Poland, protests follow an announcement that the Gdansk shipyard, birthplace of the trade union Solidarity, is to close.

April: 11th, the first troops of an EU 'advisory force' arrive in Albania; the force remains in the relatively stable north of the country.
22nd, in Peru, troops storm the Japanese ambassador's residence in Lima, killing all 14 Tupac Amarú guerillas, and ending the hostage crisis that began Dec 1996.

May: 1st, the Labour Party under Tony Blair wins the British general election with 418 seats. Conservatives win 165, Liberal Democrats 46 (2nd, John Major resigns as Conservative leader).
26th: in Zaire, antigovernment Tutsi rebels take the capital, Kinshasha, and rename the country the Democratic Republic of Congo (29th, rebel leader Laurent Kabila is sworn in as president).

June: 1st, in France, the Socialist Party wins a general election (3rd June, Lionel Jospin becomes prime minister).

2nd, in Canada, ruling Prime Minister Jean Chrétien's Liberal Party is re-elected with a majority of four.

5th, Algerian elections return the ruling National Democratic Rally party of President Liamine Zeroual, but widespread vote-rigging is alleged.

6th, Sínn Fein wins its first Daíl seat in inconclusive Irish elections; 26th Bertie Ahern of Fianna Fáil forms a minority coalition government.

10th, in Cambodia, notorious Khmer Rouge leader Son Sen and his family are killed by a supporter of his rival, Pol Pot (25th Aug, Pol Pot is found guilty of ordering the murder and given a life sentence).

19th, William Hague, aged 36, is elected leader of the British Conservative Party.

25th, in the British dependency of Montserrat, a volcanic eruption kills 23 (-Dec, further eruptions follow as much of the island is devastated; controversy surrounds the question of British aid).

July: 1st, the British crown colony of Hong Kong reverts to Chinese control.

5th, in Cambodia, Second Prime Minister Hun Sen (Cambodia People's Party) overthrows First Prime Minister Norodom Ranariddh of the royalist Funcinpec party in a *coup d'etat.*

20th, the IRA restores its cease-fire (broken Feb 1996) (29th Aug, Northern Ireland Secretary Mo Mowlam invites Sínn Fein, the political arm of the IRA, to multi-party talks on Northern Ireland).

23rd: Sadi Berisha resigns as president of Albania following months of unrest over the collapse of pyramid investment schemes.

Aug: 31st, Diana, Princess of Wales, is killed in a car crash in Paris. There is an unprecedented massive outpouring of public grief (7th Sept, an estimated 2 billion people worldwide watch the funeral service on television).

Oct: 1st, Fiji rejoins the Commonwealth after repealing legislation discriminating against Fijian Indians.

23rd, in Congo, rebel 'Cobra' militiamen leader Denis Sassou-Nguesso arrives in the capital, Brazzaville, after victory in his war with President Pascal Lissouba.

Dec: 29th, Hong Kong begins killing its entire population of 1.25 million chickens for fear of a pandemic of 'bird flu' following the deaths of 12 people.

Politics, Government, Law, and Economy

(23rd Jan) Switzerland establishes a fund to compensate Holocaust victims and their families following the discovery of Nazi gold in Swiss banks.

(4th Feb) In a civil trial in Santa Monica, USA, former American footballer O J Simpson is found guilty of causing the death of his wife Nicole Brown Simpson and her friend Ronald Goldman.

(31st March) In USA, the trial of Timothy McVeigh, charged with the Oklahoma City bombing of April 1995, opens (2nd June, McVeigh is found guilty and, 13th, sentenced to death).

(28th April) Russian President Boris Yeltsin decrees far-reaching economic reforms designed to combat price-fixing and corruption in the state-owned monopolies.

(3rd June) Germany abandons plans to use its gold reserves to meet the financial criteria set by the EU for joining a single currency, following domestic and international criticism.

(11th June) The British House of Commons votes for a total ban on handguns.

(20th June) In USA, tobacco companies agree to settle claims against them by former smokers by paying $368.5 billion into a compensation fund over the next 25 years.

(2nd July) A SE Asia economic crisis begins when the Bank of Thailand abandons its attempts to support the baht, which loses 17% of its value. (20th-24th Oct) Hong Kong's Hang Seng share index falls 20% because of hostile currency speculation before recovering.

(Sept) In referenda, Scottish voters support the creation of their own parliament (11th), and Welsh voters narrowly approve an assembly for Wales (18th).

Society, Education, and Religion

One third of Europeans speak English in addition to their mother tongue, making English the lingua franca of Europe.

(Feb) Harpist Anna Lelkes becomes the first female member of the Vienna Philharmonic in Austria.

(26th March) In USA, 39 members of Heaven's Gate religious cult are found dead in Rancho Santa Fe, California. They committed suicide, believing that they would board a spaceship following the comet Hale-Bopp.

(15th April) At least 217 Muslim pilgrims are killed and 1300 injured as fire sweeps through a tent city near Mecca.

Science, Technology, and Discovery

(Jan) The World Health Organization (WHO) estimates that 22.6 million people have to date been infected by HIV, the virus that causes AIDS. About 42% of adult sufferers are female, with the proportion of women infected steadily increasing.

(27th Feb) Scottish researcher Ian Wilmut announces that British geneticists have cloned an adult sheep, the first time cloning is successfully achieved using non-reproductive cells. DNA (deoxyribonucleic acid) from an adult cell was combined with an unfertilized egg that had had its DNA removed. The resulting lamb is called 'Dolly'.

(June) (-Nov) The worst forest fires in SE Asian history causes smoke to blanket the region, including Malaysia, Singapore, Brunei, and Indonesia, closing airports, offices, and schools, and affecting the health of millions of people.

(26th June) In New York, delegates at the second Earth Summit fail to agree a deal to address the world's escalating environmental crisis. The breakdown is caused by dramatic falls in aid to developing countries that the 1992 Rio summit promised to increase.

(7th Aug) The US spacecraft Mars Global Surveyor reports the discovery of bacteria on Mars.

(15th Oct) In USA, at Black Rock Desert, Nevada, UK driver Andy Green, driving *Thrust SSC*, sets a new land speed record and breaks the sound barrier with two runs of 759mph (Mach 1.015) and 767mph (Mach 1.020).

(25th Nov) In USA, the Federal Energy Regulatory Commission orders the demolition of the Edwards Dam in Maine, so that salmon and sturgeon can reach their spawning grounds. It is the first time a working hydroelectric dam has been ordered to be so removed.

Humanities and Scholarship

Orlando Figes, *A People's Tragedy*.

Art, Sculpture, Fine Arts, and Architecture

Architecture Building begins on the Millenium Dome, a temporary exhibition hall, designed by Richard Rogers, in Greenwich, London.

Frank Gehry, the futuristic branch of New York's Guggenheim Museum, Bilbao, Spain.

Painting (Sept) An earthquake in Assisi, Italy, seriously damages some frescoes in the St Francis Basilica.

Music

Elton John, 'Candle in the Wind '97', a tribute to Diana, Princess of Wales.

Radiohead, 'Paranoid Android', *OK Computer*.

Reprazent featuring Roni Size, *New Forms* – 'drum 'n' bass'.

The Verve, 'Bitter Sweet Symphony', *Urban Hymns*.

Literature

Jim Crace, *Quarantine*.

Ted Hughes, *Tales from Ovid*, a loose translation of Ovid's *Metamorphoses*.

Bernard MacLaverty, *Grace Notes*.

Philip Roth, *American Pastoral*.

Everyday Life

Tamagotchis, beeping electronic key-chain creatures that need constant care or they die, become a hit with children.

Sport and Recreation

(5th April) In horse racing, the Grand National at Aintree in NW England is postponed less than an hour before it is due to start after an IRA bomb warning is received.

(11th May) In chess, the IBM computer Deep Blue defeats the world champion Garry Kasparov.

Media

Film *The Full Monty* (director, Peter Cattaneo; starring Robert Carlyle)

LA Confidential (director, Curtis Hanson)

Men in Black (director, Barry Sonnenfeld; starring Tommy Lee Jones and Will Smith)

Television (30th March) Britain's final terrestrial station, Channel 5, is launched.

Index

Books, publications, films, musicals, television series, and ships appear in italic.
Numbers preceded by a minus sign indicate BC dates. The abbreviation (b of) means "battle of".

A

B

C

D

F

G

H

I

J

K

L

M

N

O

P

Q

R

S

T

U

V

W

X

Y

Z